The SHAH

Abbas Milani

palgrave
macmillan

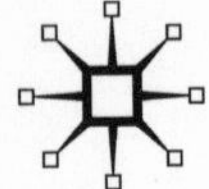

THE SHAH

First published in 2011 by
PALGRAVE MACMILLAN®
in the United States—a division of St. Martin's Press LLC,
175 Fifth Avenue, New York, NY 10010.

Where this book is distributed in the UK, Europe and the rest of the world, this is by Palgrave Macmillan, a division of Macmillan Publishers Limited, registered in England, company number 785998, of Houndmills, Basingstoke, Hampshire RG21 6XS.

Palgrave Macmillan is the global academic imprint of the above companies and has companies and representatives throughout the world.

Palgrave® and Macmillan® are registered trademarks in the United States, the United Kingdom, Europe and other countries.

ISBN: 978–1–4039–7193–7

Library of Congress Cataloging-in-Publication Data is available from the Library of Congress.

A catalogue record of the book is available from the British Library.

Design by Newgen Imaging Systems (P) Ltd., Chennai, India.

First edition: January 2011

10 9 8 7 6 5 4

Printed in the United States of America.

Contents

For Hamid Moghadam

A humanist, a visionary, and a friend who best embodies Iran's quest for democracy and dignity

Introduction

You would pluck out the heart of my mystery.
Shakespeare, Hamlet, *3.2.358*

Why a biography of the Shah now?

There have been at least a dozen books on his life. Most have been "commissioned," written to lionize or demonize him. Even those that were dedicated to finding and reporting the truths of his life were stymied by the fact that much remained hidden in still-classified documents, mired in adulating or acrimonious whispers, or marred by conspiracy theories concocted by his friends and his foes, or by himself.

He was one of the pivotal figures of the second half of the twentieth century, and certainly one of the most tragic. The passion and pathos of his thirty-seven-year tenure on the Peacock Throne first turned Iran into one of the fastest-industrializing authoritarian countries in the world, comparable to Taiwan, South Korea, and Turkey. But the pathologies of his rule ultimately begot a revolution that turned the country into a center of Islamic radicalism.

The Cold War began in Iran when the Shah was but a novice king, and his fall more than three decades later heralded the beginning of its end. The failure to predict his fall must be considered one of the great intelligence failures of the twentieth century. The aftershocks of his fall in 1979 continue to be felt not just in Iran but in the Middle East and the rest of the world. Understanding his life, and mapping out the contours of his fall, are possible only now, when thousands of pages of hitherto classified documents in British, American, and Iranian archives have been made public.

In fact, a new look at the Shah's life, free from the excesses of his overzealous defenders and detractors, is now not only possible but more than ever necessary.

The revolution that overthrew him in 1979 was democratic in its nature and demands. Sadly, it begot a regime more despotic than the Shah's own modernizing authoritarianism. The continuous tumult in Iranian politics over the last three decades is rooted in the fact that the democratic dreams and aspirations of that revolution were aborted and remain unrealized. Understanding the forces that overthrew the Shah, then, helps us understand the dynamics of Iran's current democratic movement. Like all histories, this one is as much about the future as it is about the past.

The book has been ten years in the making. My work on the Shah's life began as soon as I finished *The Persian Sphinx*—an account of the life of Amir Abbas Hoveyda, the prime minister who served the Shah for thirteen years. The new study was partially delayed when I accepted the invitation to lead a research project about the lives of eminent men and women who shaped Iran during the postwar period. The two-volume *Eminent Persians* was the result of that project. All through my work on these two books, and on virtually everything else I wrote in the last decade, the Shah cast a shadow.

Though books often have the name of one person as their author, they are invariably a collective effort—every conversation, every question, every book or essay we read, every criticism, fair or unfair, that we encounter, combine to shape our vision and words and leave indelible marks on any narrative we form. I have made every effort to reduce the affects of these influences to a minimum and allow the facts, reflected first and foremost in primary documents, to speak for themselves. I have conducted more than 500 interviews with people who knew the Shah, or whose lives were touched by him and his policies. Members of the royal family refused my repeated requests for interviews. More than once they agreed to meet, and every time, for reasons never explained to me, they changed their minds at the last moment.

It is easy to sensationalize the Shah's public and private lives and infuse them with "enticing" stories of sex, power, backstabbings, and financial corruption. I have steered clear of sensationalist stories and have covered only those aspects of his private life that had serious public repercussions. My silence on some issues, and my decision to discuss others, may anger the ideological readers of the book. But my responsibilities are fulfilled only if impartial readers find some answers to the enigmas of his remarkable rise and fall.

There is an element of hubris to biography as a genre. It claims to illuminate the dark corners and the infinite complexities in the life of an individual, a life invariably shaped by concentric influences, dreads, dreams, and pressures. James Joyce used all his mastery of language and narrative to try and capture one day in the life of a man, yet after some 900 masterful pages of *Ulysses*, he could offer but a glimpse of that life. Any narrative of a life entails a constant process of cutting, encapsulating, eliminating, glossing, and sometimes surmising. A good biography is not one that forgoes these choices, but one that makes them without any a priori assumptions and in the humble recognition that the search for the truth of a life is ever-elusive, yet never bereft of interest. The Shah's sixty-plus-year life, more than half of it on the throne of a country at the vortex of history, is exponentially more difficult to capture.

For the sake of brevity, I have not listed all archivists, librarians, and friends who in different ways helped me in the process of writing or researching this book. But some debts are too great not to mention. When I began working on the book ten years ago, my brother Hassan Milani and his friends Farhad Tale and Ahmad Tabrizi spared no effort in facilitating my early research. They believed in the value of the project and went out of their way to make it possible for me to conduct my preliminary research. To them, I owe a debt of infinite gratitude.

For the last twelve years, one of the pleasures and privileges of my life has been the friendship of Ebrahim Golestan. With his legendary attention to detail, his unsparing honesty, his penchant for perfectionism, and the infinite generosity known best to his friends, he read the entire manuscript and offered extensive marginal notes on everything from substance and style to the use of language and the precision of translations. He has been a mentor, critic, model, and, most important of all, a treasured friend.

Ardeshir Zahedi is one of the most remarkable statesmen of the ancien régime. I met him in the early phase of this research, and his subsequent endless hospitality, his generosity with his time, his memories, and his archive have been indispensable to this project. The complex reality of his character and his passionate nationalism stand in sharp contrast to the caricature drawn of him by his opponents.

Hamid Moghadam kindly read the entire manuscript and, with his remarkable attention to detail and editorial acumen, offered invaluable comments, criticism, and suggestions.

My sister Farzaneh read a few chapters, and my brother Mohsen heard parts of a few others. More than once, Farzaneh's words of encouragement were just the necessary balm to my exhausted anxieties.

My dear friend of four decades, Parviz Shokat, read the book in its early iteration and offered much useful advice. My debt to him is more than words can convey.

At Stanford, Farbod Faraji and Chuck Stern have been sterling student assistants. Their brilliance in locating even the most obscure passages and essays has been a great source of support. The perceptive questions of my students in the classes I have taught in the last eight years have helped hone the arguments of this book. My esteemed colleagues Larry Diamond and Mike McFaul have also helped formulate some of the arguments about U.S. foreign policy in this crucial period.

Airié Stuart at Palgrave Macmillan has been more than a great editor. Without her passionate interest in stewarding the manuscript to its conclusion, without her resolute dedication to navigating the many obstacles in our path, *The Shah* might never have seen the light of publication. In her office, the work of Isobel Scott, Victoria Wallis, and Alan Bradshaw, who oversaw the process of copyediting and proofreading, have made my unwieldy typewritten manuscript into the book you have in your hands.

My son, Hamid, and his avid and increasing curiosity about the history of the land of his childhood have been not just a source of encouragement and of many delightful discussions, but have convinced me that a whole generation of young men and women like him, around the world and in Iran, are deeply interested in the history that begot Khomeini and his followers. Their curiosity and their relentless fight for democracy, particularly over the last year, made understanding the rise and fall of the Shah doubly urgent and relevant.

My wife, Jean, has been the first and last relentlessly careful critic and heroically patient reader of the entire manuscript. It is hard to avoid hyperbole when describing her patience and magnanimity in allowing not just my life but ours to be consumed with the exigencies of finishing the book. Oftentimes, when I concluded in desperation that the book might finish me before I could finish it, only her calming words and her optimism and her offer to help even more had the needed soothing effect on my intermittent feelings of frustration and exhaustion.

ABBAS MILANI
Stanford University

Chapter 1

THE FLYING DUTCHMAN

The pale-faced moon looks bloody on the earth,
And lean-looked prophets whisper fearful change;
Rich men look sad, and ruffians dance and leap...
These signs forerun the death or fall of kings.
Shakespeare, King Richard II, *2.4.10–12, 15*

As the Shah sat on the vast veranda of the Al Janan-e Kabir—"The Great Garden of Eden Palace"—overlooking the city of Marrakesh, he saw not a paradise but a purgatory. The once-powerful King of Kings, the Light of the Aryans, Mohammad Reza Shah Pahlavi, was alone and did not know where he would go next. Oblivious to the vast sun-drenched sky shimmering on the horizon, he had the dour disposition of a jilted lover, "Of one that loved not wisely but too well."[1] Above his head hung a massive chandelier made of dozens of handcrafted colorful bulbs. In the light breeze, the Shah felt a chill.

For the past two years now, he had been besieged by increasingly ominous news. In the beginning, his response to the surge of protest in Iran had been defiant disbelief. For a quarter of a century, he had been met with what looked like jubilant throngs of grateful subjects. Economic indicators often registered leaps of development, sometimes placing Iran on top of the list of countries marching toward rapid industrialization. A constant chorus of sycophants, both domestic and foreign, sang songs of his singular greatness. In 1975 his Court minister and closest confidante, Assadollah Alam, had assured him that he was as wise as a prophet, as politically astute as General De Gaulle—the Shah's great "ego-ideal."[2] During the same period, Nelson Rockefeller had compared the Shah to Alexander the Great, adding, "We must take His Majesty to the US for a couple of years so that he can teach us how to run a country."[3] This praise gave the Shah a false sense of security, and he developed a haughty disposition toward many Western leaders. On one occasion, Alam told the Shah, "these miserable Americans needed some words of encouragement from Your Majesty, and Your Majesty surely gave them what they needed." The Shah, Alam wrote, was particularly pleased by this comment.[4]

The ubiquity of the adulation, along with Iran's impressive economic improvements in the sixties and early seventies, had created in the Shah a strong sense of imperial grandiosity, even political imperviousness. As late as 1964, his country had been in desperate need of a $5 million loan.[5] Eleven years later, the Shah went on what the CIA called his "lending binge,"[6] giving away, to a variety of countries, almost $2 billion. Even England, once the imperial overlord of Iran, was now the recipient of royal largesse. With this radical change of fortune in the back of his mind, it is not hard to understand why the Shah found it difficult to fathom the idea that Iranians—those he often called "my people"—were now in revolt. Less than five years after that lending binge, he had, in desperation, become a guest of the Moroccan king, unable to find a country willing to grant him asylum. And so there he sat on the great veranda, beneath the chandelier.

By the mid-seventies, his many "eyes and ears" had been either unwilling to tell him the truth, or unwelcome in his entourage. In the forties, when the Shah had just ascended the throne, he traveled freely amongst the people. He loved driving, and in those early years he would often take one of his many fast and fancy cars and drive around the city.

During some of these drives, the people converged on his car, showering him with words of support and notes of supplication. But after failed assassination attempts against him, first in 1949 and then again in 1965, security around the Court and the Shah changed. The idea of the Shah's driving around Tehran became unthinkable, and in the seventies he could only fly over the city in a helicopter.

In the early years, what the Shah might not see or learn in his drives he was likely to hear from a variety of elder statesmen who had easy and regular access to the throne and were usually not afraid to tell him the truth. These men were often as old as his father and had served with distinction in many key positions. But beginning in the early 1960s, these advisors were increasingly unwelcome at the Court. The Shah surrounded himself with young and docile technocrats—men like Amir Abbas Hoveyda, who was for thirteen years Iran's prime minister and had an unimpeachable trust in the wisdom of the Shah's absolutist power. Only late in 1978, when the country was already engulfed in a serious and systemic crisis, did the Shah call the wise elder statesmen he had shunned back into his inner circle. But it was too little too late.

By then the secret police (known by its acronym of SAVAK) was one of the Shah's main pillars of power. According to a blueprint provided by the United States, SAVAK was meant to undertake functions performed by both the CIA and the FBI in the United States. In the sixties, as a leftist urban guerrilla threat appeared on the scene in Iran, SAVAK developed a notorious international reputation for using torture. At the same time, some in SAVAK had come to consider financial corruption a matter of national security and monitored the activities of not just the political and economic elite, but also members of the royal family. The Shah was often angered by their reports—as much by their content as by the temerity of the security agents to pry into matters he considered beyond their purview.

When the Shah was at the height of his power, a journalist asked about his knowledge of what was happening in the country. He boasted that he received intelligence from at least thirteen different sources. But in retrospect, it is clear that these sources of intelligence were badly compromised. In one case, the Shah threatened to court-martial Parviz Sabeti, the powerful head of internal security in SAVAK, simply because he had dared write a report critical of one of the Shah's close friends.[7]

In 1971, when the Shah seemed most secure on his throne, the CIA noticed his growing estrangement from reality and warned of its consequences. As the Shah's power grew, according to the agency's analysis, so did his isolation. This combination, the CIA suggested, was likely to ensure that he would "fail to comprehend the intensity of, say, a political protest movement." This failure, in turn, would inevitably increase "the chances for miscalculation in dealing with" such a movement.[8] The price for the Shah's miscalculation would turn out to be the end of the short-lived Pahlavi dynasty and an end to the almost 2,500-year-old tradition of monarchy in Iran.

By early 1978 massive demonstrations had begun across the country's urban centers. The Shah's initial defiance turned into disbelief and then disdain for his subjects; finally, it collapsed into paralyzing despair. More than once during the days of revolution, and later in exile, he asked, with unmistakable hints of contempt in his tone, "What kind of people are these Persians? After all *We* have done for them, they still chose to opt for this disastrous revolution."[9]

Some of the Shah's supporters today praise his demeanor in the heady days of revolutionary upheaval as consistent with his stoic devotion to nonviolence and his respect for human life; he could have easily retained his power, they argue, had he been willing to shed blood and use the full force of his mighty military. The Shah championed this argument himself when, in his last book, *Answer to History,* he wrote, "A sovereign may not save his throne by shedding his countryman's blood."[10] But this was, at best, only one of the many reasons for his stoic behavior. With the onset of the crisis, the Shah lost his resolve. The man who only months earlier had taunted the West as lazy and dismissed democracy as only befitting the blue-eyed world; the King who had previously stood up to pressures from U.S. presidents—including Richard Nixon, with whom he had a particularly close relationship—to reduce the price of oil was suddenly unable to make any decisions without prior consultation with the British and American ambassadors. Adding to the Shah's distress was the fact that these ambassadors had made it clear that their governments would not support a military crackdown against the opposition.

Some of the Shah's supporters conceded that, in his last months of rule, he suffered from inaction, even vacillation, but they attribute it all to the debilitating side effects of the drugs he had been taking for his lymphoma. They conveniently overlook a long history that underscored, long before the beginning of the new wave of protests, the Shah's inability to withstand pressure and his storied indecisiveness in times of crisis. For the Shah, character was destiny, and many of his weaknesses as a leader were his virtues as a human being. In 1978 the cancer that ate away at his body and the side effects of the drugs he took to battle it only reinforced behavior patterns that were in fact rooted more in his personality than in any of his physician's prescriptions.

Now, overlooking the Moroccan city of Marrakesh, it seemed to the Shah that God had forsaken him. He arrived in Morocco on January 22, 1979, with his entourage. Though King Hassan II greeted him at the airport, the pomp and ceremony that Anwar al-Sadat, the president of Egypt, had organized when the disheartened Shah arrived in Cairo a few days earlier was glaringly absent. As the plane had landed in Egypt, a disheveled Shah was languishing in his chair. The moment he saw the honor guards and realized he was being afforded a welcome worthy of a king, he perked up, dressed up, and with an upright gait walked off the plane. But in Morocco there was no similar welcome. The Shah can't have been but deeply disappointed by the lack of a royal reception. Of all the countries in the world, if there was one where the Shah could have reasonably expected that his past favors would now beget him a warm welcome, it was Morocco. But this would be the first of his many surprises.

All his adult life, the Shah had demonstrated a solid sense of loyalty to the royalty of the world. With the sudden surge of petrodollars in the early seventies, he became the veritable patron saint of deposed kings, widowed queens, and unemployed princes and princesses, past and present. Tehran was in those days a virtual mecca for the likes of the deposed King of Greece, the ever-needy King of Jordan, the daughter of the last Italian King, or members of Holland's royal family. In one notable instance, for example, Jordan's King Hussein left Tehran with the "gift" of twenty-five free F-5 fighter jets.[11] Even the long-deposed King of Albania came to Tehran for his share of Persian hospitality.

Among the kings who had benefited from the Shah's generous financial and military aid, King Hassan II of Morocco occupied a unique place. Iran, in apparent collusion with the United States, had begun helping King Hassan militarily as early as 1967. Iranian army officers trained Moroccan soldiers then fighting separatist militants, and Iran sent hundreds of millions of dollars to Morocco over the next decade.[12] In one case alone, Iran gave Morocco an almost interest-free loan of a $110 million for the construction of a dam.[13] But, as the Shah soon learned, there was no guarantee that those who had benefited from his past patronage and extravagance—a royal largesse, the final costs of which were shouldered by the people of Iran—would, in his hour of need, return the favor. Some, like King Hussein of Jordan, never allowed him to visit their country during his exile. Others, like King Hassan, were willing to help but only so long as the help did not threaten their own power.

As the Shah's stay in Morocco grew longer, King Hassan's hospitality became increasingly cold. According to Richard Parker, the American ambassador to Morocco at the time, "Moroccans believed that the Shah was worth about two billion dollars, and they wanted to take their share of the loot."[14] Ardeshir Zahedi, who was one of the lead negotiators in the attempt to find the royal family a place to stay, rejects this claim, adding emphatically that "King Hassan and the entire royal family acted with absolute nobility with the Shah. Not an extra penny, other than the expenses was taken from the Shah while they were in Morocco."[15] Regardless of what happened in Morocco, wherever else the Shah and his family landed in their exilic ordeal, gouging the royal family became a favorite sport of the local elites, with Egypt being the only exception.

Despite all this, in his first days in Morocco, there was a bit of gaiety in the air. On his arrival, the Shah and the Moroccan King, both airplane aficionados, bragged about the skills of their special pilots, and there was even a "soft landing" contest between the two.[16] The Shah's pilot, a young man named Captain Moezzi, won the contest.

But a few days after arriving in Morocco, the Shah gathered his entourage for a meeting, with an air of foreboding and resignation hanging in the air. He informed them that he had decided to trim the number of guards and aides that had hitherto served him and the royal family. He was teary-eyed, and others in the room wept silently. The Shah's decision was as much political as financial. On leaving Iran, he had declared that he was going on a vacation and would return to the country when he felt rested. By the second week after his arrival in Morocco, the vacation myth was no longer tenable.

The decision was also yet another sign of the royal family's storied fiscal restraint, or miserliness, according to some. The news from Ja'far Behbahaniyan, the man who had managed nearly all of the Shah's foreign assets for more than two decades, had been less than satisfying. A day after arriving in Egypt, the Shah had summoned his moneyman and asked him for a full accounting of his assets. The meeting had ended in acrimony. What Behbahaniyan claimed the Shah possessed was less than the figure the Shah had expected. The two men met again in Morocco—and the acrimony soon turned into open animosity. Not long after this meeting, Behbahaniyan disappeared into a world his detractors claim is one of incognito living and assumed aliases. He has maintained silence about these matters and has, in the process, become the subject of endless gossip and innuendo. Many of the Shah's friends and family still claim that Behbahaniyan walked away with a substantial portion of the Shah's assets. The truth may never be known. But one definite result was that the Shah told his assembled entourage that since the journey was turning out to be longer than he had anticipated, he could no longer afford to pay all their wages. Those who had family and obligations at home, the Shah said, should feel free to leave or to go back to Iran.

He had come to Egypt in two jets—one filled with four crates carrying the royal belongings, as well as some of the people who were leaving Iran with the Shah. Dozens of courtiers and high-ranking officials of the regime were desperately trying to get on those jets, but only a handful succeeded. It was a measure of the Shah's state of mind that he had relegated the authority to decide who could travel in the royal entourage to one of his valets.[17] The second jet was set aside for the Shah, the Queen, their guards, the chef, a physician, the dogs, and their groomer. In Morocco, around the time of his meeting with his entourage, the Shah ordered that both planes be sent back to Iran. One of his aides suggested that at least one of the planes be kept and sold—for around $20 million—to defray some of the immediate expenses; the Shah demurred.[18]

A few days after his unceremonious arrival in Morocco—local media and even international television crews were barred from the airport—the American ambassador, Richard Parker, paid a courtesy call on the Shah. He wanted to reassure him—after receiving inquiries from the Iranian Embassy—that the royal family would be welcome in the United States, if they decided to settle there. William Sullivan, the American ambassador in Tehran, had also told the Shah before he left the country that he would be welcome to settle in America. While the Shah was in Egypt, President Carter had declared in a press conference,

"The Shah is now in Egypt, and will come to our country."[19] As it turned out, Sullivan's promises might well have been part of an effort to "sweeten" the deal to convince the Shah to leave Iran as soon as possible. The Shah should have remembered the fact that his father too was "persuaded" to leave Iran in 1941 with the promise of asylum somewhere in the Americas. As soon as his father, Reza Shah, was out of the country, he was told, rather unceremoniously, that his planned visit to the Americas was no longer possible.

In Mohammad Reza Shah's case, the decision to delay his arrival in America would have far-reaching implications not just for him, but also for the United States and for Iran. The hostage crisis was only the first of the many cataclysmic dominos that ultimately fell as the result of this delay.

In his exile, the Shah still followed events in Iran closely.[20] In his own words, "even in the first months in exile, I was convinced that the Western governments had some plan in mind, some grand conception or overview to stop Communist expansion and xenophobic frenzy in places like Iran."[21]

Many of the Shah's friends and supporters had the same illusion. They reassured themselves that "America must have a plan. They can't let a place like Iran fall into the wrong hands." This assumption accounts for the fact that so many of the Shah's generals and ministers stayed in Iran and did not flee in the face of the rising tide of revolution. The Shah's enemies were no less concerned about this fact. Only weeks before the fall of the Shah, Ayatollah Mottaheri, the closest confidante of Ayatollah Khomeini, said, "America will not allow the revolution to win. Iranian oil is for America like water is for human life. America will not give up Iranian oil. Imam [Khomeini] should behave in a way that America does not see its interests jeopardized in Iran."[22]

But soon after arriving in Morocco, the bleak reality gradually dawned on the Shah that there was little hope of return. All such hope was irrevocably dashed when, on February 11, he heard the media announce that the armed forces—hitherto the most reliable pillar of his power—had declared their neutrality and would be returning to their barracks. "The revolution has won," Radio Tehran announced, "the bastion of dictatorship has collapsed."[23] The Shah's already somber mood darkened drastically after hearing of these developments. Afterwards, Iranian radio, calling itself the "Voice of Revolution"—and soon enough, the "Voice of the Islamic Revolution"—was regularly filled with harangues against the Shah and his family. To the consternation of the Queen and his entourage, the Shah sometimes listened to the diatribes, and with every passing day, he grew more despondent.

In Morocco the Shah gradually grew resigned to the fact that, for the rest of his life, he would eat the "bitter bread of banishment." The bond between the Shah and the people, a bond he often praised as "eternal" and unbreakable, was broken, and "ruinous disorder" was spreading everywhere.[24] In a rare interview, he confided to a British journalist that "he would die in exile."[25]

Now, on that mid-March morning in the Moroccan palace, the Shah asked Farhad Sepahbodi, Iran's ambassador to Morocco, to help move his table and chair away from the breeze. It was nine in the morning and the Shah was having breakfast and the breeze was making him uncomfortable. The sun was bright and the heavy chandelier hanging above his head was turned off.

All his life, the Shah ate a very light breakfast, usually nothing more than a couple of pieces of toast, some feta cheese, a small glass of orange juice, and some coffee. He had an affinity for exotic homemade jams, and in Tehran, courtiers used to compete in finding ever more exotic fruits or flowers for the royal palate to savor.[26]

Meager as his daily breakfast was, he still never finished it himself. Invariably, he shared a piece of his buttered toast with Beno, his great black German shepherd. Even during regular meals, the Shah, to the Queen's consternation, fed Beno from his own dish. Many Persians, still under the emotional, if not doctrinal, sway of Islam, are phobic about dogs and consider them, as their religion mandates, the epitome of *najes,* or "unclean." All the waters in the oceans, Shiites believe, cannot wash off the filth of a dog's saliva.

Now, to alleviate the problem of the breeze, Farhad Sepahbodi moved the table and chairs to a sheltered corner. By then, most Iranian embassies around the world had been taken over by "diplomats," sometimes students who claimed to represent the unfolding Islamic Revolution. By the time of this March breakfast, Sepahbodi had received a threatening letter from the Foreign Ministry, recalling him to Tehran. But at great risk to himself and his family, he chose to remain loyal to the Shah. His loyalty was particularly interesting in light of the fact that, a few years before his appointment to Morocco, he had been banished by the Shah.[27] But on that breezy March morning, his mind was occupied with the situation in Iran. Only seconds after Sepahbodi moved the tables and chairs, the large wrought-iron chandelier, with its handcrafted glass tulips, came crashing down. The heavy impact cracked the marble floor and sent shards of glass flying everywhere. The Shah was jolted first by the sound, and then by the recognition that the chill he had felt had saved him. Had he not moved, he might have been killed under the weight of the wrought-iron chandelier. His first instinct, honed after almost four decades on a throne coveted by others, was to think of a conspiracy. In the world according to conspiracy theory adherents, there are no accidents or serendipity, and natural deaths are unnaturally rare.

"Do you think they are trying to get rid of us?" the Shah asked in a shaken voice. Sepahbodi tried to calm the Shah's jittery nerves, facilely assuring him that he was most welcome in Morocco. While the Shah might have still been in denial about the reality of his status in King Hassan's court, Sepahbodi by then knew all too well that the Shah's days in the Garden of Eden Palace were numbered.

Soon, the Shah too was forced to acknowledge the fact that a tortured odyssey in search of a safe haven was about to begin. His wanderings would earn him the nickname "The Flying Dutchman." Ultimately, after almost a year-long desperate search for safety, he would find his final sanctuary back in Egypt, where the journey had begun. President Sadat, who, on the gloomy January day when the royal family first left Iran, greeted the Shah with the full pomp and ceremony accorded a head of state, was at that time the only leader willing to offer the Shah a place to die in peace.

But perhaps the most fitting name for the benighted Shah was the one used by the Israelis even before the wanderings began; in their confidential documents they called him Saul—the first anointed ancient king of the Jews. But eventually God abandoned this moody king. And the Philistines, according to the Bible, defeated Saul.

Chapter 2

A COMPROMISED CONSTITUTION

Wrath-kindled gentlemen, be ruled by me
. . . Deep malice makes too deep incision
Shakespeare, King Richard II, *1.1.152, 155*

The Shah was born in Tehran, a city that lives in the shadow of mountains and myth. More than any other city in Iran, its real and mythopoeic history captures the tormented soul of Iran.

To the north stands the towering, sometimes snowcapped, often eulogized Mount Damavand, haloed by clouds that emanate from the coast of the Caspian Sea. According to *Shahnameh,* the grand epic poem of pre-Islamic Persian history, Zahak, the dreaded demon of Iranian mythology, lurks in some dark recess of the 18,600-foot mountain. The story goes that Jamshid, a reformist king who "rendered iron pliable," made from the mountain helmets, breastplates, and other arms and "laid up stores of weapons." He built houses and baths, castles and palaces, and his service to his people was commemorated on a day they called No-Ruz, which is still, many millennia later, celebrated as the Persian New Year. But Jamshid, legend has it, fell prey to hubris. He told "the elders and army commanders and priests . . . that there is no leader or king in all the world" greater than him. The gods punished him by taking away his charisma—*farrah-e izadi*—and before long, the people rose up against him. After a long period of chaos and confusion, people sought "Zahhak the Arab"[1] to come and rule over them. His thousand-year reign then became, in the collective memory of Iranian history, the epitome of oppression and cruelty.*

From the south come the desert winds, howling from the flatlands that cover the geographic heart of the country. Less than a hundred miles south of Tehran, in the midst of that desolate landscape, there is Chamkaran—a mosque built atop a well that has long been dry of water but is effervescent of messianic hope. Shiites, the majority in Iran, believe that their twelfth Imam, the Mahdi, went into hiding some thousand years ago, and some of these millenarian Shiites believe that once he decides to reappear, as he certainly will, he will ascend from the pit of that well.

Caught between the mythic mountain and the magic well, constrained by the inexorable force of its geography and history, sits the city of Tehran, where on October 26, 1919, in "a small and modest house" in one of the city's "older residential districts"[2] a boy was born. They called him Mohammad Reza. His mother, Taj ol Muluk, was a self-assertive woman of strong views; his father, Reza Khan, was a charismatic officer of the Cossack Brigade, initially established by the Russian Tsar and by the time of Mohammad Reza's birth already under the command of Iranian officers. In fact, Reza Khan was one of the first Iranians to take such a command.

The house was a typical example of traditional urban Persian architecture—an insular, inward-looking building with high walls to keep away the intrusive gaze of strangers. Like the Persian language, in which the surface and substantive meanings of words—their *zaher* and *batan*—are often in discordant contrast, in traditional Persian architecture, houses are sharply divided between the *andarun* and *birun*—the private and public domains. The façades of these houses are humble and bereft of ostentation. In contrast to the feigned simplicity of the façades, the interiors are, usually, rich with lavish appointments. Mohammad Reza's house of birth was no exception. Protected by high brick walls, on two sides of the yard stood interconnected rooms, five steep stone steps above the ground; underneath the building were rooms, often used for storage in winter and as a cool haven in the sometimes-sizzling days of summer. In the middle of the yard stood a small, round pond.

---

* In recent years, some cultural critics have tried to deduce, from Iranian mythology, the predestined path of the country's history. The long night of despotism, they argue, has been the result of the murder of Sohrab by his father Rostum, the hero of *Shahnameh*. Filicide, they say, is a precursor for stasis and patriarchic despotism. If Iran is ever to transcend its cursed cycle of replacing one despot with another, or one father with another, in the words of Fereydoon Hoveyda, it must jettison its attachment to Rostum and embrace instead the story of Kaykavous—a benevolent and democratic king who shared power with others and descended from the throne when he could no longer be of service to his people. See Fereydoon Hoveyda, *The Shah and the Ayatollah: Iranian Mythology and Islamic Revolution* (New York, 2003), pp. 102–105.

As Reza Khan's fortunes grew, the family moved into bigger houses and better neighborhoods. Of those early years, and the houses he lived in, Mohammad Reza remembers only "the beauty of the mountains . . . that loomed over the city."[3]

Not far from where he was born, there were a dry moat and a mud wall that encircled the capital. The wall, with its twelve[†] (mostly) ornate gates, conjuring the twelve Imams of Shiism, and its 114 crenellations, celebrating the 114 chapters of the Qu'ran, was a relic of Nasir al-Din Shah's late-nineteenth-century "journey of discovery" to Europe.[4] At night, the city gates were closed, while during the day, the moat, ever dry and a bleak reminder of Tehran's aridity and its distance from water, became a hangout for dope fiends, pederasts, the musicians disparagingly called *motrebs*, and stray dogs—the tormented ghosts that often prowled Iran's urban landscape. Tehran was in 1919 a city of dirt roads and mud houses, of small streams that acted as open sewage; and at night it was a dark, dread domain dominated by hooligans and bandits, as well as *daroogeh*—or the police—whose cruelty and corruption made them even more dangerous and more predatory than the thieves they supposedly kept at bay.

Mohammad Reza was barely six years old when his father became king and ordered the encircling mud wall razed and the moat filled. In his ambitious effort to modernize the capital, Reza Shah re-drew the map of the city, willing into existence two tree-lined boulevards that cut through the labyrinthine maze of the old capital. In forcing his linear, rational grid on the old village that now masqueraded as a city and the capital of the country, Reza Shah also ordered the destruction of all but one of the twelve gates. In this razing frenzy, he was participating in an age-old pattern of Iranian history, in which memories of the past, and relics of the ancien régime, are deemed counter-revolutionary and subversive.

Five hours after Mohammed Reza was born, in the early afternoon, his twin sister, Ashraf, joined him in the world. Compared with the jubilant celebration that had followed his birth, Ashraf's belated arrival, in her own wounded words, begot "none of the excitement that greeted my brother's birth. To say that I was unwanted might be harsh, but not altogether far from the truth."[5]

An iconic picture, taken when she and her twin brother were about three years old, captures both Mohammad Reza's privileged position and his twin sister's sense of alienation and anguish. The father, mustachioed, stern, impatient, with piercing eyes, sits on a bench in the backyard of their house—surrounded by pots of flourishing flowers. He is clothed in the dashing white tunic worn by commanders of the Cossack Brigade, tight black trousers tucked neatly into his

---

[†] Some sources have the city with thirteen gates, but as thirteen is a number of ill omens, most historians talk of twelve gates. Jafar Shahri, in his *Tehran Gadim* [Old Tehran] talks of thirteen doors. (Tehran, 1355/1977).

shiny knee-high black boots, the quintessential Cossack fur cap on his head. On his lap sits Mohammad Reza. The father's oversized hands are wrapped around his son's diminutive body. The boy looks at once blissful and anxious. He is biting his lips (lip-biting and twirling a strand of his hair around one of his fingers, were, all his life, signs of his anger and anxiety). But in spite of the nervous bite, the boy also has the contented look of a mariner who has, at long last, safely arrived in harbor.

Standing between Reza Khan's legs, possessively clutching her father's hand, is Shams, Reza Khan's older and favorite daughter. Even as a girl, she wears the petulant and spoiled expression that would define her life. A few steps away, Ashraf stands alone, looking almost disheveled, gazing at the camera in dismay. While the two daughters are attired in similar drab cotton dresses and long dark stockings, the young future Shah wears what looks to be an expensive sailor suit. In his short pants and knee-high socks, the boyish Mohammad Reza looks like a European schoolboy.

Reza Khan, the father, was a soldier by temperament, fearless in war, towering in physique, and commanding in comportment. He was relentless in pursuit of his goals and willing to use any means necessary—including bullying and brute force—to achieve his ends. Not long after Mohammad Reza's birth, Reza Khan became the power behind the Iranian throne—and soon enough, its occupant.

The Shah had an intense and paradoxical relationship with both the person and the legacy of his father. In his first book, the 336-page *Mission for My Country*, there are no fewer than 784 distinct references to his father, or in other words, an average of more than two per page.[6] In comparison, he mentions his mother only 12 times. He writes of his father as a man "of strength . . . determination . . . a towering figure . . . a dominant personality . . . no man ever believed more in his country . . . selfless . . . one of the greatest mind readers."[7]

At the same time, in the part of the narrative ostensibly set aside for celebrating his father, he insists that his father influenced him both "positively and negatively." He calls one chapter "My Unconventional Childhood," and refers to Reza Shah as "one of the pleasantest men in the world" but also "one of the most frightening."[8]

This ambivalence was evident not just in the Shah's writings but in his life as well. He was highly sensitive to too much praise of his father. It was something of a rule amongst seasoned courtiers that Reza Shah must not be praised too profusely in front of his son. Mohammad Reza Shah often complained that he had accomplished infinitely more than his father, but that people failed to adequately appreciate his efforts and continued to harp on his father's feats. In 1961, long before accomplishing any serious reforms of his own, he wrote that although his father "carried out so many ambitious and progressive projects, he never promulgated any comprehensive development program such as our present second seven years plan."[9]

In a later book, written in the mid-seventies, the Shah offers a summary of fifty years of Pahlavi rule in Iran and is even more openly critical of his father, concluding that "in the first twenty years"—or in other words, during the reign of his father—"the country's efforts were focused on neutralizing the negative effects of the past.... There was in practice little time left for constructive work.... Our country's real effort towards progress and prosperity began only after August 19, 1953."[10] More incredibly still, in the fifteen-page introduction to the book, the Shah never mentions, even once, his father's name. Even when referring to his own ascent to the throne, he praises "a will superior to all human wills" for putting the fate of the nation in his hands, making no reference to his father's role in establishing the dynasty. While his failure to praise his father is subtle in these public pronouncements, in private he sometimes went further. In 1972, for example, just at the time when he had squared off against big oil companies, his confidant, Alam, asked about Reza Shah's valor. "Of course I had never seen him in war," the Shah responded, "but when he was sick, he didn't have much valor."[11]

❧

It is not clear where his father was on that chilly October day, around noon, when Mohammad Reza was born. Some have him fighting in jungles in the province of Guilan. His daughter Ashraf offers a different version, claiming that the father was at home, pacing the yard—pacing was a constant habit of both Reza Shah and his son, Mohammad Reza Shah—anxiously awaiting word from the midwife. In those days, Iran had nine hospitals, forty-one clinics, and four trained nurses. There was not a single gynecologist in the country. It was therefore not just customary, but necessary, for women to deliver their children at home. Lucky and prosperous were those like Mohammad Reza's mother, the willful Taj ol Muluk, who could also afford to have a midwife present. The high infant mortality rate in Iran at the time was one consequence of these medical deficiencies.

The paucity of modern public health amenities made life precarious for the infant Mohammad Reza. It soon became apparent that he was a sickly infant, particularly vulnerable to the numerous diseases that wreaked havoc on the country—a country that had, according to one astute medical historian, a compromised constitution at the time.[12]

The year Mohammad Reza was born, 1919, saw the height of a worldwide influenza epidemic that had its origins in the heartland of America, but came to be known as the "Spanish flu." In sheer number of people killed—estimated to be nearly 100 million worldwide—it is considered the most deadly plague of all time.[13] While the number of people killed in Iran is a matter of considerable controversy, the country was devastated by the disease. Experts suggest that famine, malaria, anemia, and, finally, opium, were responsible for Iran's unusually high mortality rate.

The problem of addiction was itself something of a plague. It is estimated that around the time of Mohammad Reza's birth, in Tehran, of the city's 250,000 inhabitants, no fewer than 25,000 people, or 10 percent, were addicted to opium.[14] In cities outside the capital, the problem was at times even more serious. Kerman, for example was notorious, with 25,000 addicts out of a population of 60,000.[15]

The advent of World War I only exacerbated conditions in Iran. Russian, Turkish, German, and British forces occupied parts of the country. Tribal disorder made an already-enfeebled central government weaker and more vulnerable. Famine took many lives.[16] Predatory and parasitic gangs roamed the countryside and made travel hazardous; even many of the important urban centers, like Yazd and Kashan, were in the parasitic grip of hoodlums and gangs. In Kashan, Seyyed Hussein Kashi had established his own veritable dukedom, milking the rich and menacing the poor.

It was in the midst of these tumults that Reza Khan contacted the German Embassy in Tehran to solicit their help. The idea of using Germany as a "third force" to countervail against Russia and Britain—the two poles of colonial power in Iran—was beginning to take serious root in Iran at the time. Before long, a group of Iranian nationalists who had settled in Berlin also solicited German assistance in the fight against British and Russian colonialism. In the case of Reza Khan, however, Germany showed no willingness to offer help. But the story of his relationship with Germany, particularly after the rise of Nazism, proved singularly important not only in his life, but in the fate of his son, Mohammad Reza.

Next to the war, the Bolshevik Revolution, leading to the removal of Tsarist forces from Iran, had the most profound impact on the country's political dynamics. In 1918, with Russia temporarily out of the picture, Britain, in a policy championed by Lord Curzon, opted to make Iran a virtual protectorate. By bribing the monarch, Ahmad Shah (the last king of the Qajar dynasty), his Prime Minister, and two other key members of the cabinet, the British government tried to pass what came to be known as the 1919 Agreement. It would place British "advisors" at the helm of the most important ministries, as well as of the army.

A strong nationalist movement developed in opposition to the Agreement. On the international scene, the United States, the new Soviet government, and France were also actively campaigning against the agreement.[17] Amongst the few

Persian advocates of the Agreement was a journalist called Seyyed Zia. His support marked him irrevocably with the infamy of being a "British stooge," and thus 1919, the year Mohammad Reza was born, marked a turning point in Seyyed's long and eventful life.

1919 was also the year of the Treaty of Versailles. Iran tried desperately to take part in the negotiations and to make its case about the damages the country had suffered as a result of the war. Britain was adamantly opposed to Iran's participation, while the United States intervened on Iran's behalf.

Seyyed Zia openly ridiculed Iran's effort to participate in the conference. The British Foreign Office describes Seyyed as "a man of outstanding singleness of purpose and courage. Personally attractive, religious without being fanatical or obscurantist.... He is both honest and energetic—a very rare combination in Persia.... Has something of a mystic in him."[18] Iranian sources have called Seyyed Zia the most notorious Anglophile politician in modern Iranian history.[19] Seyyed never denied having close ties with the British. "I was a friend of the British," he declared, "because being their friend, you only pay a price...but being their enemy guarantees your destruction. All my life I have paid the price for this friendship, but as a rational man, I was never ready to be destroyed."[20] Seyyed would soon play a huge role in the establishment of Reza Khan's dynasty and his installation on the throne.

By 1921, when the young Mohammad Reza was only two years old, Iran was on the verge of disintegration. In each corner of the country, a warlord or a revolutionary leader had staked a claim to parts of the territory. In the northern provinces, an alliance between Iranian Communists, Soviet forces that had landed on the Iranian side of the Caspian coast, and a nationalist figure called Mirza Kouchik Khan led to the creation of the first Soviet Socialist Republic in Iran.[21] In Khorasan, there were increasing signs of Bolshevik influence. There were even indications that the province's governor, Ahmad Qavam, often simply called Qavam al-Saltaneh, was contemplating a declaration of independence. Qavam went on to become a lifelong nemesis of the young Mohammad Reza Shah. Another nationalist colonel, named Pessiyan, led a rebellion against the central government. Finally, Sheikh Khaz'al, an unabashed agent of the British government, declared the oil-rich province of Khuzestan a veritable British protectorate.

The Sheikh acted as a virtual head of state and went so far as to publish a book titled *Agreements and Treaties between the British Government and His Honor, Sheikh-e Mahamareh.*[22] So crucial was Khuzestan to British geostrategic plans that when it became clear that the 1919 Agreement was heading for defeat, Britain began contemplating plans to help the region break away from Iran. In all of their plans in Iran, the British could invariably count on the complicity of some mendacious Iranians. In this case, Mohammad Ali Mirza, Iran's Crown Prince at the time, contacted the British government and suggested that "he was prepared to head new government in Southern Persia, separate from Northern Persia."[23] If installed as the king, he would, he promised, protect British oil interests.

The British had become concerned about the rise of Bolshevism in Iran and closely monitored the activities of every known Communist and worked with Reza Khan who took particular pride in his record as an anti-Communist.[24] In 1925, for example, according to a report of the British Embassy in Tehran, there were "about 300 suspects under close surveillance, as Bolshevik agents ... mostly Russian."[25] The embassy kept a close watch on their vulnerability and movement.

Hitherto, the British, still hoping for the ratification of the 1919 Agreement, had worked hard to prevent the emergence of a powerful central government. Now they were in favor of the creation of just such a government—one that could withstand the Bolshevik onslaught. It was in this context that the idea of the 1921 coup took shape, and with it, the life of the two-year-old Mohammad Reza was forever changed.

The British were not alone in hoping for a strong central government in Iran at the time. Some of Iran's leading democrats, like the poet Malek-Shoara Bahar and his circle of friends around the journal *Daneshkadeh*, had also begun advocating the virtues, indeed the necessity of a "strong," enlightened, but law-abiding leader. It is an often-repeated pattern of history that when societies experience prolonged periods of instability and conflict, particularly when opposing poles of power prove incapable of asserting hegemony and maintaining order, that the masses, as well as many in the elite, begin to crave a leader like Julius Caesar or Napoleon. Iran was no exception. By 1921, segments of the middle class and the bazaar merchants began advocating the necessity for a strongman, someone who could establish, after fifteen years of chaos and civil strife, some semblance of order. The British were by then in full agreement with this idea.

British General Edmund Ironside's famous phrase goes, "What we need now is a military dictatorship." While the military muscle of this dictatorship was to be provided by Reza Khan, the charismatic leader of the Cossack Brigade, the political savvy and connections would come from Seyyed Zia, the journalist who had ridiculed Iran's efforts at participating in the Versailles treaty.

In the early hours of the morning of Esfand 3, 1299/February 21, 1921, the famous Cossack Brigade, led by Reza Khan, moved to take control of the capital, Tehran. They met virtually no resistance. Of the existing state machinery, only the weak, vacillating, and corrupt King was left in power. Hearing of the movement of troops towards the capital, Ahmad Shah became "very agitated ... and talked of immediate flight, but Mr. Smart [of the British Legation] was able to calm him sufficiently to make him abandon his intention."[26] While the British supported the coup, they hoped to maintain a "figurehead" monarchy.

As soon as the Cossacks entered the city, the pusillanimous Ahmad Shah sent for the British Ambassador and asked his opinion "regarding the line which he should follow. He was nervous." The Ambassador was, in his words, "able to reassure [the King] regarding the intentions of the leaders of the movement...and advised him to put himself in communication with them, ascertain their wishes, and grant whatever they might ask."[27] His Majesty of course followed the "advice" of the British, and the next day called Seyyed Zia to the Court and "entrusted him with the task of forming a government....Seyyed at first proposed to the king that the title of dictator should be given to him, but His Majesty demurred on the ground that this would constitute a humiliation to the person and dignity of the Sovereign."[28] Seyyed was named prime minister.

From their first encounter, it was clear that Seyyed Zia, with his "revolutionary" disregard for the courtesies of the Court, and Ahmad Shah, the timid king, who had nothing other than these courtesies left of his power, despised one another. The brewing tension between the weak monarch and the taunting Seyyed created just enough space for Reza Khan to establish an increasingly prominent place in the complicated but crumbling labyrinth of Qajar power.

Within hours of taking power, Seyyed Zia and his ally, Reza Khan, arrested some 400 of the country's "grandees." For the British Embassy this was one of the "embarrassing features" of the coup. Many of those imprisoned were, according to the embassy, "prominent Persians universally known as friends of [the British]."[29]

The purpose of the arrests was, according to Seyyed Zia, simply to fill the empty state coffers. "In spite of the emptiness of the treasury," Seyyed told the British Embassy, "there is plenty of money in the country," and he knew "where to look for it."[30] Those arrested, he said, owed thousands of *tooman* to the government in back taxes and levies. The British Embassy agreed with Seyyed and confessed that, in its opinion, "the arrested princes owe large sums to the Government on various accounts."[31]

But beneath the revolutionary rhetoric and aggressive actions of the new cabinet, there was a more sinister purpose, and it had to do with the infamous 1919 Agreement. The cabinet, according to its master architects, Seyyed Zia and Reza Khan, came not to bury the 1919 Agreement but to revive it. Seyyed's proposed strategy was cold and calculating in its goals and cunningly Machiavellian in its proposed method for manipulating public opinion. He advised the British Embassy that he would verbally and publicly denounce the infamous 1919 Agreement, since, again in his words, "Without such denunciation new government can not get to work." At the same time, the cabinet took steps, quietly and without public notice, to introduce, as the Agreement had stipulated, British advisors in key positions in the government and the military.[32] In order to camouflage the role of British "advisors," Seyyed Zia confided to Herman Norman, the British ambassador, "public announcements will be made that Persian Government proposes to bring in advisers from 'different' European states . . . the idea is to . . . throw dust in the eyes of Bolsheviks and native malcontents, while placing two essential administrations in British hands."[33] In short, as the Foreign Office succinctly declared, the new cabinet wanted "to scrap the Agreement but to carry out its vital provisions."[34] Despite these realities, in his memoir *Mission for My Country,* the Shah claimed that his "father and his government at the same time denounced the Anglo-Iranian treaty of 1919."[35]

While there is no record of Reza Khan's views on some of these crucial discussions, there are clear indications that he was at least in agreement with the overall contour of Seyyed's deals with the British. Furthermore, once Seyyed Zia fell, Reza Khan reassured the British Embassy that he would continue the policies of his fallen ally.[36] A report from the embassy indicates that Reza Khan gave "oral assurances of his readiness to co-operate with [them], to accept British control of the Ministry of Finance and Ministry of War and to retain British officers in the north as instructors."[37] At the same time, in discussions with the Ambassador, Reza Khan "expressed goodwill towards Great Britain and said that no foreigners had any reason to fear the presence of his men at Tehran." In fact, in the course of this discussion Reza Khan made it clear that his Cossacks, as well as the "leaders of the movement," were, more than anything, worried about Bolshevik advances in Iran. They feared that in the absence of a strong government, the expected departure of British forces would bring about a victory for the Bolsheviks.[38]

The new cabinet of Seyyed Zia and Reza Khan—often referred to by its opponents as "The Black Cabinet"—set out to change the fabric of social life in Iran. Soon after his forces took control of Tehran, Reza Khan issued two important declarations. The first made it clear that his Cossacks were loyal to Ahmad Shah and had come to establish law and order. The second began with his now famous self-assertive phrase, "I order." He went on to set out the nine principles of the new government. They included, "all the residents of the city of Tehran must keep quiet. . . . The state of siege is established . . . all newspapers and prints will be stopped . . . public meetings in the houses and in different places are stopped . . . all shops where wines and spirits are sold, as well as theaters, cinemas and clubs, where gambling goes on, must be closed."[39]

In all of this, Reza Khan acted as a pragmatist, while Seyyed Zia never tired of reminding anyone who cared to listen that he considered himself a revolutionary; his two political heroes were, he often said, Lenin and Mussolini.[40] His program included such far-reaching measures as "formation of an army . . . eventual abolition of the capitulations [granting foreigners immunity from prosecution]. . . . Legislation for the readjustment of relations between landlords and peasants." At the same time, he tried to implement a truly impressive number of changes in the capital itself—from ordering new rules of hygiene for stores that dealt with foodstuffs to an attempt to bring light to city streets. He talked of land reform, making him one of the early champions of the idea in modern Iran. He talked of making education available to every Iranian.[41] Many of these measures would, in later years, become pillars of Mohammad Reza Shah's reform programs.

Seyyed and his ally Reza Khan often declared that fighting Communism and aborting a Bolshevik revolution in Iran was their chief purpose and the foundation of their ideology. At the same time, Seyyed became a relentless advocate of the necessity of a rapprochement between Iran and its new Soviet neighbor, leading to the 1921 agreement between Iran and the Soviet Union. The agreement ended open hostilities between the two countries, but its infamous article five stipulated that if Iran were ever used as a staging area for anti-Soviet aggression, the Soviets would have the right to enter Iran and address the threat.

From the outset, there was something amiss in Seyyed Zia's attempt to don the mantle of a dictator. It soon became clear that nearly all actual power was in the hands of Reza Khan, and every new sign of Seyyed's weakness further emboldened the increasing ranks of his enemies. One of his most embittered foes was the King himself. Seyyed's attitude, defiant, filled with self-importance, and unabashed in the use of the rhetorical devices of revolution, was evident in his treatment of the King, as well as in his first pronouncement as the head of the coup cabinet. In a long, meandering text, he wrote of how "fate has designed me to take in hand the destinies of my people in this dangerous crisis and to save it from the abyss, to the edge of which will-less and unworthy governments have brought it." He attacked the "few hundred nobles, who hold the reins of power by inheritance . . . [and who] sucked, leechlike, the blood of the people."[42]

Seyyed had always been defiantly oblivious to the Court's solemnities and the rules of etiquette for a royal audience. More than once, he had walked into an audience with the King casually dressed, with a cigarette dangling from his lips. He had flouted protocol by sitting down before he was granted permission by His Majesty. In reprisal, Ahmad Shah had ordered all chairs removed from his office. In their next meeting, Seyyed found an even better way to insult the King he despised. He sat on the windowsill throughout the audience. Ahmad Shah was incensed and practically threw the Prime Minister out of the office; before long he joined forces with Seyyed's many enemies and arranged for his dismissal.

Reza Khan was only too happy to abide by the King's wishes.[43] The British did everything in their power to keep Seyyed in power and, in the words of the

Ambassador, tried unsuccessfully to "dissuade the conspirators from this disastrous intrigue."[44] But their efforts failed. They failed, they said, because Reza Khan, "since the withdrawal of our troops . . . no longer fears us" and had convinced Ahmad Shah that Seyyed might try to kill him.

With the help and complicity of Reza Khan, Seyyed was dismissed; only as the result of the British efforts on his behalf was he allowed to leave Iran safely. In fact, as Seyyed was making his way out of the country, his enemies still tried to have him arrested and returned for trial. Once again the British Embassy came to rescue their "friend," and received guarantees that he would be allowed safe passage through Iran. Reza Khan, happy to be rid of his ambitious partner, told him to take any sum he wanted from the treasury. Seyyed took 25,000 *tooman*—by no measure a large sum—and left Iran in May 1921.[45]

The British, however, were not happy with Reza Khan. They described him as "an ignorant, but astute peasant" who had promised to cooperate with the embassy, but who was "not to be trusted and is anyhow so politically inexperienced that his regime offers little prospect of stability."[46] The British, in their own way, mourned Seyyed's departure. They wrote of him as a "paragon of all the virtues," as a man "having been born altogether a century too soon."[47] For the next four decades, every time Iran faced a political crisis, the British sought the solution by pushing for the return of Seyyed Zia as prime minister. More than once, the only obstacle to Seyyed's return to the center of power was Mohammad Reza Shah's obdurate opposition.

❦

As the country was undergoing these radical changes, and as Reza Khan's political power was increasing almost daily, his son Mohammad Reza's life began to change as well. His early family life was anything but peaceful. His parents had been, for all practical purposes, separated at the time of his birth and were on the verge of divorce. He lived with his domineering and deeply devout mother and his sisters. The mother's religion was one of amulets and sacrificial lambs, of evil eyes and ominous dreams, of prayers and offerings of penance to the Lord. Mohammad Reza's own religiosity—his firm belief that he was in communion with the divine, that the heavens protected him, that omnipotent God had entrusted him with the arduous task of leading the ship of state, his firm conviction that "a supernatural force" guided him in his kingship—can, in no small measure, be attributed to his mother's habits of heart and mind.

His father, on the other hand, was decidedly averse to all such beliefs. He dismissed them as superstitions and "womanly" preoccupation. But he was an absentee father, too often away in those early years of his son's life. He was, furthermore, a soldier and a peasant by temperament, disinclined towards demonstrative shows of affection toward his children, even to his favorite son, Mohammad Reza. Such signs of affection, he thought, were effeminate and begot irresolution and an effeminate disposition in those who received them. When the young Mohammad Reza most needed his father, the man was busy with wars and with politics.

ꝏ

Mohammad Reza's early years were also important for his later life from a different perspective. He was born a soldier's son, but he grew up to become a king. His formative experiences as a boy did not ready him for the kind of life that was "thrust upon him" by history. Kings are born not "to sue, but to command."[48] Mohammad Reza was born to sue, and his temperament, as well as his early boyhood, ill-prepared him to command.

Furthermore, many of his father's friends first met Mohammad Reza as a shy young boy, exhibiting due deference to his elders; when, two decades later, he became king, the same politicians were expected to show him the reverence due to a king. Some in this group found the transition hard, if not impossible, to manage. Acquired or "borrowed" majesty, as Shakespeare wisely wrote, is a hard thing to achieve. Moreover, the mundane details of everyday life can have a corrosive power on the supposed haloed majesty of monarchs. Traditional monarchies spare sovereigns and their subjects these agonies by suffusing the life of royalty from birth in a mist of majesty and mystery. Future kings often live in the lush isolation of "forbidden cities," and while such estrangement and isolation might well dampen their abilities to cope with reality, it affords them the requisite aura of mystery. Modernity is, as Machiavelli was the first to note, the age when inherited legitimacy is no longer viable, and princes must engineer and maintain their own legitimacy. While traditional monarchies thrived on the idea of divine legitimacy, and thus required pious and docile subjects, modernity begets and demands instead a knowledgeable citizenry. Monarchies thus seem incompatible with modernity and the age of paparazzi; they find it hard to survive in the world of investigative journalists, inquisitive scholars, archives, and cameras that capture the life of royalty in its every mundane detail and leave little to the imagination. Monarchies require a certain degree of opacity, and modernity is an age of transparency.

Some of those who had seen the young Mohammad Reza as a small boy of three or four, and thus had seen him when he was altogether bereft of the aura of majesty and of the pomp and ceremony that power later afforded him, found it hard to take him seriously as a king. One of these men was amongst the handful of politicians who openly challenged Reza Khan's claim to the throne in 1925 and later defied his son when he ascended the throne.

His name was Qavam, and he was a cabinet minister a good ten years before Mohammad Reza was even born. By blood, Qavam was connected to the

Qajars, and by temperament, he was insatiably ambitious. In 1921 he was the governor of Khorasan province, but his appetite for power seemed to have no limit. Seyyed ordered him arrested and brought to Tehran. But before he arrived in the capital, Seyyed had fallen, and Qavam was appointed prime minister. Mohammad Reza was but three years old when his father became the war minister in Qavam's cabinet. Early in his tenure as prime minister, on the occasion of the Persian New Year, Qavam paid a courtesy visit to Reza Khan's house. As is customary in such visits, the older Qavam sat the three-year-old Mohammad Reza on his lap, whispered sweet nothings in his ears, and gave him a gold coin—an *ashrafi*—as *aydee,* or New Year's gift. Giving cash and coins on such occasions was in those days, when toys and other commodities were a rarity in Iran, nothing usual. Almost exactly twenty years later, the two met again—by this time, that boy had grown into a king and Qavam was granted an audience to be appointed, again, as prime minister. He had spent many of the years in between these two meetings in exile. He had allegedly hired two assassins to kill Reza Khan. No sooner had he walked into the Shah's office than the wily and ironic Qavam is reported to have said, "*Masha-allah* [Praise God], Your Majesty has surely grown since I last saw you."

But in 1921, Qavam's rapid fall and rise were the direct result of Seyyed's hubris. Though real power was in the hands of Reza Khan, Seyyed behaved more and more like a dictator. The ranks of his enemies swelled and his days in office were now numbered. Exactly one hundred days after his appointment as prime minister, Seyyed Zia was, to the relief of his detractors, dismissed from his post. His last meeting with Ahmad Shah, a dedicated foe of Seyyed, took place only days before Seyyed's dismissal. Not long after leaving Iran in 1921, Seyyed was peddling Persian carpets in the bustling street corners of Weimar Berlin. He then settled in the aristocratic quiet of Montreux in Switzerland. As he later confessed in an interview, in the days and months after leaving Iran, grief and anger sometimes tore asunder his façade of calm. "I would take cold showers," he said, "and scream in anger at my fate."

Back in Tehran, his ex-partner, Reza Khan, was methodically climbing the political ladder. Not long after Seyyed's dismissal, Reza Khan issued an unusually long declaration, setting out the reasons why he had undertaken the coup, and declaring that henceforth, if any paper or magazine suggested that anyone other than him was the coup's mastermind, that paper would be banned and the journalist punished.[49] At the same time, he began amassing an illicit fortune, a habit that proved to be his Achilles' heel as a ruler. The British Embassy reported that, on more than one occasion, Reza Khan used the coercive power of his office to purchase land and property in Tehran and other places around the country at a fraction of their real price. In March 1925, for example, the embassy reported that Reza Khan "added to his already extensive estates in Mazandaran by purchasing more land to the value of 800,000 tooman,"[50] in those days a considerable fortune.

Changes in Reza Khan's fortune meant changes in his son's life. More money brought more opulence, while more power brought a more constricted life for Mohammad Reza. As the family moved to a bigger house in a more prosperous section of the city, his father insisted on choosing his son's friends. His closest friend, aside from his twin sister—who, in a desperate attempt to endear herself to her brother, became more and more of a tomboy—was Majid A'lam. He was chosen because his father was a Court physician, and Reza Khan wanted his son mingling only with the children of the elite. But the games they played were those enjoyed by any normal children of the time—hide and seek, cops and robbers, and soccer. More than once, A'lam remembered wistfully, "I had, while playing, pushed or shouted at the future king, or his twin sister."

Reza Khan was still the prime minister when he asked the parliament to pass the "Law of Identity and Personal Status." All titles, military or civilian, inherited or purchased, were to be abolished. Every Iranian male was now asked to choose and register a family name for himself and his family. Hitherto, people had been known by their first names, followed by a nickname reflecting their infirmity, their profession, or their town or village of birth. For his own family name Reza Khan picked Pahlavi[51]—the name of the pre-Islamic language of Persia.

For Reza Khan, being a rich and powerful prime minister was no longer enough. With the help of other charismatic officers, he had successfully put down all the rebellious forces around the country and forged a unified Iran. Of these rebels, the most sensitive case was surely that of Sheikh Khaz'al. The British were, in the words of their Ambassador, "placed in a most embarrassing position: on the one hand stood our definite assurances to the Sheikh . . . on the other our . . . desire to see and help a strong and stable central government in Persia."[52] Reza Khan assured the Ambassador that in arresting the Sheikh, and dismantling his fiefdoms, he was in fact doing the Sheikh "a good turn."[53]

Reza Khan toyed with the idea of turning Iran into a republic, with himself as the first president. By then he was already a fan of Atatürk in Turkey and was interested in emulating his success in changing the Islamic Ottoman Sultanate into the militantly secular Republic of Turkey. But a combination of forces, including his political enemies and his critics in the political establishment, as well as some in the ranks of the Iranian clergy, ever watchful of the dangers of creeping secularism, opposed the idea.[54] It was not that difficult to convince Reza Khan to change his mind. Even more than the presidency, he now coveted the throne. In December 1924, the British Embassy, which closely monitored events in Tehran, offered this succinct summary of the changes that were taking place: "A movement has been worked up during the last few days for a crowd to stop PM

[Reza Khan] carriage on his imminent return here and insist on taking him to palace to be crowned Shah.... I do not think the Persian government is privy to this.... It is significant that Persian divisional commanders in the provinces have been secretly warned of probable impending changes.... Their previous instructions were to pave the way for a republic. These are now suspended."[55]

From early 1925, Reza Khan began to make it increasingly clear that "he cannot continue to work effectively in the present conditions and that the country must now choose between him and the Shah."[56] By then Ahmad Shah, the sitting king, who had been spending his time gambling and investing, often with disastrous results, in the European stock market, was itching to come home again but had grown frightened of Reza Khan. The British had lost all hope and respect for Ahmad Shah. One of their diplomats railed against his "contemptible cowardice, avarice and treachery."[57] And when the embarrassingly weak and vacillating king approached the British Embassy in Paris "with a request for British advice whether he should return to Persia or not, the same reply had been returned to His Majesty as was given to him last year, viz, that the question of his return to Persia was a purely internal one... that the British government was... unwilling to be involved in any way in the issue."[58]

About the same time, Ahmad Shah sent his Crown Prince—who despised his father and used every opportunity to take his place[59]—to visit the British Legation in Tehran and "ask the personal views" of the Ambassador about the possibility of Ahmad Shah's return. But the answer in Tehran was no different than that in Paris. The Ambassador declared that he was shocked to be asked for such advice, and "declined to be involved in this purely internal question."[60]

During these weeks of turmoil and tension in Tehran, and in most other major cities, Reza Khan apparently instigated mass demonstrations against the return of the Shah.[61] Both Ahmad Shah and Reza Khan clearly understood this to be the deathknell of the Qajar dynasty.

In the mind of Reza Khan, the last hurdle between him and the throne was the support of the British government. He knew well that Qajar kings and princes had for a long time enjoyed the support and sometimes the "largesse" of the British government. By late 1925, he had set the stage to get rid of the Qajars, but in the words of the British Embassy, he still "fears disapproval of His Majesty's Government." Britain had maintained a studied silence on his activities, and Reza Khan had interpreted this as a sign of their discontent and their continued support for the Qajar dynasty. The British Ambassador arranged a meeting with a close confidante of Reza Khan and sent him a message. Reza Khan should not, the message said, "hope for more than loyal and friendly attitude of strict noninterference" by the British.[62] This message of "neutrality" was music to Reza Khan's anxious ears. He could now make his final move.

In his march to power and to the throne, his most important move was to convince the parliament to pass a law, on February 12, 1925, that made him the "Supreme Commander of all Defensive and Security Forces of the Country." Hitherto, that title had been the monopoly of the king, and it did not take Reza Khan long to use his position as the commander in chief to become king himself. This experience had a profound impact on his son, Mohammad Reza, and helped shape one of the central tenets of his own later political vision. In Iran, the Shah believed, the military is the key to power, and if a king wants to have any political relevance or even remain in power, he must keep not just the titular role of commander in chief, but the actual and practical command of the armed forces. By October 31, 1925, Reza Khan was ready to make his last move. He set the stage for the Majlis (parliament) to pass a resolution abolishing the Qajar dynasty, making him the head of a provisional government, and ordering elections for a Constituent Assembly. Only four deputies, each fulsome in their praise of Reza Khan as prime minister, voted against the abolition of the Qajar dynasty—and all four went on to play crucial roles in the life of the future king, Mohammad Reza Shah.

On December 12, 1925, the Constituent Assembly voted to name Reza Khan the new king, and make his male descendents heirs to the throne. When news of the change was sent to the Foreign Office, the Minister wrote on the margin of the report, "The new dynasty, if it survives the first generation, will be purely Persian, whereas the Qajar were Turkish and remained Turkish."[63] In fact, it had been hundreds of years since a Persian family ruled Iran. Both the Qajar and the Safavid dynasties, who together ruled Iran for over four centuries, were Turkish.

On January 14, 1926, the day after his coronation, Reza Shah signed a decree conferring the title of Vali Ahd (Crown Prince) on his oldest son, Mohammad Reza Pahlavi. He was six years old.[64]

Chapter 3

THE PEACOCK THRONE

Landlord of England art thou, not King
Shakespeare, King Richard II, *2.1.113*

The Peacock Throne, that "superb and barbarous divan of enamel and precious stones,"[1] with its Arabesque designs, was wrought of 26,000 gems brought back from India as spoils of war. It uses bright red rubies, deep blue sapphires, and verdant green emeralds, and it is flanked by two golden snakes each peering from one side.* In the beginning the Peacock Throne was called Takht-e Khorshid—the Sun Throne. It was built for Fath-Ali Shah, the "super-procreant"[2] Qajar king infamous for his ignorance and incompetence, and for signing the 1828 Turkemanchai Treaty that ceded a good third of Iran to Tsarist Russia—the treaty recognized in Iranian history as the beginning of the country's decline. Fath-Ali Shah was also notorious for his lechery and for the "close to 1000 wives of diverse origins"[3] he kept. One of his favorite concubines was named Tavous, Persian for "peacock." And as the Throne was used on the night of the King's marriage to his beloved Tavous, it was, the next morning, renamed the Peacock Throne.[4] In January 1926, the Peacock Throne, and the room and the palace where it was kept, indeed the whole city of Tehran,

* The snakes are particularly eerie in light of the fact that in Iranian mythology, Zahak, the dread despot, had two snakes on his two shoulders, put there by the devil, and every day they each required a diet of two brains from two Iranian youths.

were undergoing a facelift. The Throne was about to have a new occupant, and the country a new King.

By fortuitous coincidence, Vita Sackville-West, the renowned Victorian writer and intimate of Virginia Woolf, was visiting Tehran at the time of Reza Shah's coronation. At that time, her husband, Harold Nicolson, served as a diplomat in the British Embassy. Before long, she was involved in planning a few aspects of the coronation. Her masterful narrative of her Persian journey describes not only the official coronation ceremonies, but the backdrop to the unfolding drama. The Crown Prince, a boy of six and the future Shah, played a fascinating role in the ceremonies.

Though enamored of Persia and its past grandeur, Sackville-West found Tehran bereft of any charm. She found it a "squalid city of bad roads," of "rubbish-heaps" and "few pretentious buildings and mean houses on the verge of collapse." At the same, she found the city's air "as pure as the note of a violin."[5]

On the eve of the coronation, there was "an air of excitement hanging about" the city. In the public squares "flags were out; festoons of electric light bulbs swooped along the face of the municipal buildings. Wild romantic horsemen paraded the streets in little bunches. Triumphal arches were in the process of erection." At the same time, according to Sackville-West, the government authorities had "with characteristic lack of foresight . . . left everything to the last." Nevertheless, no one seemed nervous; they acted "like people preparing for amateur theatricals . . . sustained by the conviction that it would be all right on the day."[6]

Tehran still had no electricity, yet the entire city seemed lit up by everything from the official lanterns and fireworks to oil lamps, night-light glasses, and candlesticks.[7] Streets and even some buildings were covered with Persian carpets. The city was no longer of "bricks and plaster" but "a great and sumptuous tent open to the sky."[8] With the colorful representatives of different tribes and ethnicities parading through the city—from the Baluchies with embossed bucklers to the Turkmans and their tunics of rose-red silk, and the Kurds with turbans of fringed silk—Tehran had a new face.[9] On the morning of Coronation Day, the people of the capital "woke to a Tehran spruce and furnished beyond recognition."[10] At Golestan Palace, the changes were no less far-reaching. The throne room was "repainted, the garden paved, such breaches in the walls as revealed the presence of rubbish-heaps were to be filled up." The unmistakable Persian flavor of Reza Shah's coronation stands in sharp contrast to his son's later celebrations marking 2,500 years of Persian monarchy, when even the food was flown in from Maxim's of Paris.

There was, however, according to Sackville-West, an endearing anxiety amongst the new members of Reza Shah's Court to impress the Europeans who attended the celebration. There was "no point, however humble, on which they would not consult their British friends."[11] In fact they asked for a copy of the "proceedings at Westminster Abbey for the Coronation of His Majesty George V. The copy was procured, but was stiff with ceremonial language and created consternation; one of the ministers who prided himself on his English came to ask [Sackville-West] what a Rougedragon Poursuivant was, evidently under the impression that it was some kind of animal."[12]

In the days leading to the celebrations, the British government was worrying about the gift they should give the new Shah. They certainly did not want to give him a gift cheaper than the one given his predecessor, Ahmad Shah—"a pair of silver gilt urns... cost 210 pound sterling."[13] They first considered "a highly caparisoned horse cloth, saddle, etc in the possession of the Foreign Office, prepared for the Sultan of Turkey" but never presented to him. That idea was rejected as inadequate. At last, "two large silver gilt cups at a cost of 200 pound sterling" were ordered for the occasion from Mssr. Collingwood.[14] They were barely ready at the time of the coronation.

The ceremonies were set to begin at three in the afternoon. At two o'clock, Reza Shah was to leave his home, head for the Majlis (parliament), take the oath of office, and then go to Golestan Palace for a reception and the actual coronation. Every detail of the ceremonies had been meticulously planned—from the number of soldiers guarding the royal cavalcade (one hundred and seventy) to the number of cannon salutes during the taking of the oath (fourteen).[15] The event's program stipulated that twenty-two of the country's top political dignitaries, led by the Prime Minister, would follow the Crown Prince when he entered the coronation hall.[16] But nothing went as planned.

Punctuality had always been one of Reza Khan's most celebrated characteristics. With capitalism, time itself became a commodity, and was thus in need of ever more precise measurement. In Europe, clocks began to become part of the city landscape after the rise of the Renaissance; in Iran, the first, and for decades the only, public clock was put up late in the nineteenth century—and it never kept time properly. Before long, the clock became a perch for a pair of owls, and the birds became, for the superstitious population of Tehran, omens of good or evil.

Of his father's famed punctuality, Mohammad Reza remarked, "Father was a strict disciplinarian. His sense of timing was simply amazing... before he became emperor [*sic*], we Iranians never really bothered about time."[17] Meetings he chaired began at the exact announced time. If cabinet ministers were even a few minutes late, they would be barred from entering. Moreover, he had placed a clock on his desk and set it ten minutes ahead of time; all top officials of the government also fixed their watches to match the royal clock.[18]

Despite all this, on the day of Reza Shah's coronation, at half past three, there was still no sign of him. He was already more than half an hour late. The hall set aside for the actual coronation was by then filled with Iranian and foreign dignitaries. Near the steps of the Throne, to one side, "shuffled and squatted and pressed a crowd of mullahs." To Sackville-West, this bevy of "bearded old men in long robes and huge turbans" seemed like a "baleful chorus in a Greek play"; they seemed arrogant and churlish, and she noted looks of dread and hatred cast upon the clerics by those guests. The Shiite clergy had played an important role in Reza Shah's masterfully orchestrated rise to power. In a clear and successful ploy to garner their support, before his ascent to the throne, Reza Khan had exhibited fervent signs of piety. He participated in religious mourning processions and, like the most pious of the mourners, he beat his chest and brushed his forehead and the top of his head with ashes of sorrow and grief. Not long after he was crowned, Reza Shah would change course and begin a carefully planned policy of limiting the power and role of the clergy in Iran.

At the coronation, a rumor spread throughout the room that the new King was about to arrive. Even Vita Sackville-West, who found the idea of a coronation "absurd," and dismissed its pageantry as fallacious and childish, found something gripping in the expectant atmosphere of the glittering hall. Like everybody else in the room, something made her crane to see the enthronement.[19]

At last there was a stir; the doors were opened and the six-year-old Mohammad Reza appeared in the hall. Behind him walked the procession of the twenty-two political dignitaries, led by the Prime Minister. They were carrying the many royal accoutrements necessary for the coronation—three different crowns, a scepter, three swords belonging to past kings, and even a diamond-studded royal bow and arrow.[20] One of the swords belonged to Nadir Shah, a powerful king who united Iran and was reported to have been planning limits on the powers of the clergy; Nadir Shah was also alleged to have attempted a reconciliation between Shiites and Sunnis, and he was Reza Shah's "great hero."[21]

Before entering the hall, the young Mohammad Reza had been waiting in the adjacent room, playing with some of the jewels and medals that were to be taken to the coronation hall by the procession that he would lead. He particularly liked the medals made to commemorate the coronation, and he tried to give one of them to Suleiman Behboudi, Reza Shah's chief of staff and one of the Crown Prince's favorite personalities working at the Court.[22] But by the time the young boy, now known as His Imperial Highness Shahpur Mohammad Reza, Crown Prince of Persia, walked into the coronation hall, he looked somber and serious, dressed in an exact miniature replica of the uniform his father wore. The young boy marched down the length of the room, saluting the generals who stood at attention, and finally took his place on the lowest step of the Peacock Throne.

Finally, Reza Shah entered and, escorted by generals, moved toward the Throne, slowly but with resolution. There was a strange quiet in the room. As a gesture of reconciliation to the mullahs, all musical gaiety except the new royal anthem played by the military band had been left out of the ceremonies. The Crown Prince seemed "frightened, possessed himself of a corner of his father's cloak."[23]

After the long delay, and after the heavy silence, broken only by the low murmur of hushed voices, suddenly the only sound in the room was that of the new King, reading in his low voice the oath of office. Like everything he said or read, there was a terse economy to his declaration. He was, all his life, a man of few words. When he participated in the ceremonies commemorating the construction of the first modern university in Iran, he said, we should have had a university long ago and I am happy we finally have one. His coronation was no different. He read the oath of office—just over a hundred words. He swore by God, and by the Qu'ran, and by all that is "sacred to the people of Iran" to do all in his power to safeguard the independence of the country, maintain its territorial integrity, abide by the constitution, and work to promote Shiism. Then, taking his cue from past monarchs like Napoleon, Nadir, and Shah Abbas (the powerful Safavid king who ruled Iran about the same time as Queen Elizabeth I ruled England in the sixteenth century), he took the crown into his own hands and placed it on his head. He would allow no mullah or, for that matter, no other mortal to presume to bestow upon him his crown. He had willed himself onto the throne, and now he insisted on reserving for himself the privilege of anointing himself king. All through these rituals, a subdued Mohammad Reza watched in silence. He would all but exactly replicate the ceremony when it became his turn to have a coronation.

With the newly designed red-velvet-lined crown on his head, Reza Shah sat on the Throne looking stern, content, and older than his age. He had a bejeweled sword in one hand, the scepter of power in the other, and a pearl-studded cloak over his shoulders beneath which he wore a military uniform. The cloak was blue, and blue is, in Persian mythology, the color of royal thrones, and in the Old Testament, the color of God's throne. In Babylonian mythology and European lore, blue is the color of royal blood.[24]

The blue cloak was covered with a paisley design; paisley, it is said, is the quintessential visual metaphor of Iran's bifurcated and tormented identity—riven between Arabic Islam and pre-Islamic Persian creeds. The paisley, they say, is a bent cedar, and the cedar is the tree Zarathustra planted in heaven. The heavenly tree was "bent" under the weight of the Arab invasion. The paisley's appearance on the cloak was an early omen of what was to come. Soon after his coronation, Reza Shah adopted a policy of glorifying the pre-Islamic part of the Iranian identity and weakening the Islamic component. His son, Mohammad Reza, also continued this policy, but under different circumstances and with drastically different results.

After the salvo of guns celebrating the advent of a new dynasty, the new King left the palace and rode through the city in a glass coach drawn by six horses, followed by the Crown Prince in another coach, both shining in the sun. The streets were lined with people. Pictures of the young boy sitting in the royal carriage betray a sense of dread and boredom. Until then, he had lived a more or less normal life, not jaded by the unseasonable demands of decorum. He was now forced to live through more than two hours of ceremonies, under the gaze not only of the public, but of his stern father. Hard as the ordeal must have been, the real challenge of living a ritualized life was only about to begin.

A week of celebration followed the coronation, but the King refused to attend most of the events, "sending his son instead, who seated in an immense scarlet tent, guarded by two soldiers with fixed bayonets, spent his time solemnly eating through the sweets piled on a table before him."[25] Years later, in the course of an interview, the Shah confided to a journalist that during that first coronation, he had "tried to behave like a young soldier, according to my father's wishes, just as my son behaved when I was crowned."[26]

On the day Reza Shah ascended the throne, the leisurely pace of the life of Mohammad Reza, who had hitherto been raised by his doting mother, suddenly and drastically came to an end. The first traumatic change came when the six-year-old boy was abruptly taken away from his mother and his home. He had spent much of his time at his mother's, in his own words, "fighting all the time" with his older sister, Shams, and his twin sister, Ashraf.[27] But now his father was the king, and Reza Shah wanted to make sure that his son was not, in his own words, "in a woman's skirt."[28] It was important that the Crown Prince receive a manly education, so Reza Shah took this education into his own hands. The young boy was settled in a palace of his own, located in Reza Shah's large compound, and put in the care of a distant relative, Amir Akram Pahlavan, who was to "combine the functions of royal mentor with those of proxy governor of the province of Mazandaran."[29]

But beneath the starched formalities of his new official life and title, there beat a curious child's heart. For Mohammad Reza and at least one of his siblings, Ashraf, the "first few days of royalty were spent exploring the lush gardens of cypress and pine, the great halls with their huge wall frescoes, and ceilings of mosaic mirrors that glittered like diamonds."[30]

A special "elementary military school" was set up at the Court for the Crown Prince and some of his brothers and half-brothers from Reza Shah's other marriages. The Shah later described how he was placed "in a carefully selected class of twenty students, mostly sons of government officials and army officers."[31] As with every other detail of the Crown Prince's life, it was Reza Shah who decided the composition of the class. Amongst the select group he chose there was a boy named Hussein Fardust, whose father was an army lieutenant.[32] Before long, Hussein became the Crown Prince's "special friend" and would retain that special status for nearly all the rest of the Shah's life.

The elementary school was, in every sense, a miniature military academy. The boys wore uniforms; their curriculum was a mixture of military matters and traditional reading and writing lessons. The Shah later said, "the whole set up was so rigid... [it was an] atmosphere of absolute discipline and almost rigidness [*sic*]."[33]

The same military discipline was enforced throughout the country's rapidly multiplying schools.[34] Girls were, for the first time in the history of the country, required to go to school, and both girls and boys wore uniforms—gray cloth with peaked caps for boys and gray overalls for girls.[35] All schools began their day with calisthenics; before classes began, teachers and principals inspected each student for cleanliness and hygiene—short clean nails, short hair, and a tidy uniform.

At the Court, Reza Shah had ordered his son's teachers to make no special allowance for the Crown Prince. But neither the teachers, nor the young Mohammad Reza, were able or willing to heed the King's command. By then a subtle change had, not unexpectedly, occurred in the young boy's general demeanor. According to his father's trusted Chief of Staff, the Crown Prince became "extremely sensitive. For example, when buying toys, before he was the Crown Prince, he paid little attention to how good or bad, how big or small a toy was, but no sooner had he become Crown Prince than he would criticize everything and become disgruntled. I remember him often... trying to convey to me that I am now the Crown Prince, and those days I was not the crown prince."[36]

While a child's demand for such deference from adults would be surprising under any circumstances, it was particularly startling in the case of the hitherto shy and timid Mohammad Reza. It demonstrated both the elasticity of his character and the corrosive power of his position as crown prince to an authoritarian potentate. His character was no doubt malleable; it was often said that he was easily influenced by those around him. The deferential treatment afforded him easily overpowered whatever resistance his native modesty might have provided to the perks of potentate power.

There was in the Shah a sharp and even jarring disharmony between his public and private behavior. His public persona was cold, aloof, and somewhat pompous. At the same time, the few who knew him as a friend or confidante speak of him as a man shy and diffident in demeanor, polite and kind in disposition, and very willing to overlook the solemnities of royal protocol. At least one aspect of this stark behavioral dualism he seems to have learned from his father. Reza Shah believed that familiarity begot, first, a laxity of discipline, and ultimately, contempt for those in power. Father and son both kept their distance, allowing only a handful of people entry into their inner sanctum.

There was yet another dichotomy in the Shah's behavior. His treatment of Iranians was different from the way he treated Westerners. With Europeans and Americans, he was more comfortable, less starchy, and less pompous. In audiences, only a handful of Iranians were ever allowed to sit down, while every Westerner, regardless of rank and riches, was allowed to sit. Anecdotes throughout the span of his life, from the time he was a boy of five, to the days when he was at the height of his power, illustrate again and again these complex, and often contradictory, facets of his public and private personae.

A few days after Mohammad Reza was anointed by his father as the crown prince, his closest friend, Majid A'lam, came to play, as he had done so often in the past. But unbeknownst to the young boy, things had changed drastically in the life of his friend. Before he could enter the room where his old playmate awaited him, a liveried attendant—Reza Shah had himself helped design the uniform to be worn by all staff at the Court—instructed him, in a stern, uncompromising tone, "You are no longer to call His Highness anything other than His Highness." Even his siblings were "ordered by the Shah to call their brother, Vala Hazrat, 'Your Highness.'" His mother, too, began addressing him as "Your Highness." She stood up every time her Crown Prince son entered a room. Even Reza Shah started to call his son "Sir." He would never use the familiar pronoun, *tow* (the singular "you" in Persian), to address his son, insisting instead on the formal *shoma*.[37] Everyone was expected to follow the King in the use of this more formal language. In the beginning, however, the young Mohammad Reza was clearly ill at ease with these formalities. And his first meeting with his friend exhibited this discomfort.

With the pomp and ceremony befitting an audience with a crown prince, Majid A'lam was led into the room. But no sooner had the handlers and valets left the room than the young Mohammad Reza warmly greeted his friend as he had in earlier, less complicated days. "When they're around," the Crown Prince told his young friend, "call me Your Highness, but when we are alone together, you can call me the same name you always used."[38] But before long, the young A'lam too joined the chorus of those who called the Crown Prince only by his title and with the kind of deference owed his title, not his age. In fact, for the young Mohammad Reza, the circle of intimacies was rapidly and forever closing.

He was in elementary school when he had his first brush with death. In the course of his eventful life, he would have several more such close encounters. At the Court, in the courtyard of his school, a murder of crows flocked every day. They not only soiled the grounds, but in Persian culture they are considered omens of evil and bad fortune. In lieu of a scarecrow, a soldier was given the task of spending every night in the yard keeping the crows away with a pellet gun. One day, the gun was inadvertently left in the classroom, and when the young Mohammad Reza walked in, he saw it, and as was his wont as a young boy, began playing with it in the yard. A classmate tried to grab it, and in the tussle, the gun went off. A pellet hit the rim of the Crown Prince's hat and ended up in the opposite wall. Alarmed guards and teachers ran into the room and seized the gun; then their first concern was how to hide the episode from Reza Shah.[39]

A second, more serious brush with death came about the same time, but the Crown Prince was altogether unaware of the threat. In October 1926, about twenty-five Iranian officers and civilians were arrested on the "grounds of a plot against" Reza Shah and the Crown Prince. While the Soviet papers claimed that many of those arrested—including one of the leaders named Haim, hitherto the head of the Zionist organization in Iran—were British agents, the British Legation, fearing what it called the King's "insane and vindictive suspicions," refused to intervene. The conspirators had allegedly planned to kill the Shah, the Crown Prince, and a number of other leading members of the government.[40] Instead of telling his son about these threats, Reza Shah concentrated on teaching him the disciplined life of a soldier.

Military training was not, of course, all that Reza Shah had in mind for his Vali Ahd (Crown Prince). He also hired a tutor—the wife of a general—to take charge of the young Mohammad Reza's non-military and non-traditional training. She was a Russian-born, French-speaking woman, who had been a ballerina of considerable beauty and grace, and the Crown Prince mastered the French language under her tutelage. He attributed to her "the advantage [I acquired] of being able to read, speak and write French as if it was my own language."[41] In later years, he also learned English. All his life, his command of French and English was a crucial part of his political capital and an important element of his persona as a modernizing monarch. The Shah claimed that it was also because of his tutor that his mind was opened to the spirit of Western culture and his palate to the mysteries of French food.[42]

Before long, this combination of "manly education" and cosmopolitan training came to include horseback riding and hunting. He also played soccer, dabbled in wrestling and boxing, and played a game they called "bicycle polo." While his favorite early childhood game was "cops and robbers," he also had an affinity for building. "I would spend long hours," he says, "making mechanical models with my Meccano."[43]

In becoming the crown prince, perhaps the single most important change in the life of the young boy was that his formerly distant and often absent father began to meet with him regularly. Even more importantly, the father began to show his young son tenderness. With everyone else, Reza Shah was stern and serious, formal and forbidding; with the young Mohammad Reza, he indulged in "informal and easy-going humor." He would joke with his son "in the most informal and affectionate manner" and even sing lullabies to him—but all in private.[44] Reza Shah also made his son, at least in title and appearance, a precocious military man. The Crown Prince was eleven years old when he was named colonel in chief of the crack Pahlavi Regiment.[45]

A picture commemorating his appointment captures the jarring incongruence of an eleven-year-old colonel. He stands in the middle of a crowd of older colonels and generals. He wears a heavy coat and is in full royal regalia. The other officers all stand at full attention, frozen in the solemnity of the moment, while the eleven-year-old colonel stands casually, his right hand royally, even "Napoleonically," tucked into his pocket.

In their meetings, Reza Shah wanted to make sure that his son "was well acquainted with everything that was going on"[46] in the country. In the son's words, his father did not "discuss politics with [him] but he would talk about general aspects of life."[47] If Reza Shah hoped to use these meetings to mold his son in his own image, he, like any other father, succeeded in some areas and failed in others.

The most glaring difference of attitude between father and son was on the question of religion. As a child, in the span of three years, Mohammad Reza claimed to have had three mystical experiences. In each case, he said he had communed with saintly apparitions. To his devout and doting mother, these were blissful signs of heavenly favor. To Reza Shah they were inane fantasies, unbecoming a modern monarch. His father "scoffed at"[48] these stories. Others claim that Reza Shah did much more than scoff at the alleged saintly encounters and actually forbade his son to repeat them in his presence. As a young boy, Mohammad Reza had no choice but to abide by his father's commandment. But thirty years later, when he was king and was writing his memoirs—and at least momentarily free of his father's disbelieving ghost—he wrote about the three experiences at some length and with relish. In his rendition,

> Soon after my investiture as Crown Prince, I had fallen ill with typhoid fever, and for weeks, I had hovered between life and death. This had been a dreadful ordeal for my devoted parents.... I then had a dream about Ali who in our faith was the chief lieutenant of Mohammed.... In my dream, Ali had with him his famous two-pronged sword, which is often seen in paintings of him. He was sitting on his heels on the floor, and in his hands he held a bowl containing a liquid. He told me to drink, which I did. The next day, the crisis of my fever was over, and I was on the road to rapid recovery.... I was only seven.... This experience was within the same year followed by two other events which were also significantly to influence my life. Almost every summer my family and I made an excursion to Emam-Zadeh-Dawood, a lovely spot in the mountains above Tehran.... since I was so young, a relative who was an army officer placed me in front of him on the saddle of his

> horse. Some way up the trail, the horse slipped, and I was plunged head first on to a jagged rock. I fainted. When I regained consciousness, the members of the party were expressing astonishment that I had not even a scratch. I told them that as I fell, I had clearly seen one of our saints, named Abbas, and that I had felt him holding me and preventing me from crashing my head against the rock.... The third event occurred while I was walking with my guardian near the royal palace.... Suddenly I clearly saw before me a man with a halo around his head—much as in some of the great paintings, by Western masters, of Jesus. As we passed one another, I knew him at once. He was the Imam, a descendent of Mohammed who, according to our faith, disappeared but is expected to come again to save the world.[49]

He never had a vision again. His proclivity towards illness, however, continued unabated—in the span of three years, he contacted whooping cough, diphtheria, malaria, and "several other ailments."[50] And while his mother encouraged his affinity for miracles and divine interventions, his father made every effort to convince his son that while he was indeed the anointed one, nothing other than his own disciplined dedication would determine his fortune.

Chapter 4

JOCUND JUVENILIA

Thus play I in one person many people,
And none contented. Sometimes am I king,
Then treasons make me wish myself a beggar.
Shakespeare, King Richard II, *5.5.32–34*

Tragic is a young life whose happiest moments are spent in exile. In September 1931, the Crown Prince, Mohammad Reza, was sent abroad for his European education. He was almost twelve years old.

From the late nineteenth century, when Iran's encounter with a now-dominant West intensified, sending children to Europe became for the country's elite the ultimate sign of power, prestige, and prosperity. Reza Shah was sometimes handicapped in his dealings with Iran's Eurocentric elite by what the British called his "sublime ignorance"[1] of foreign cultures and his inability to speak a foreign language—other than his smattering of Russian. He wanted to make sure his son did not suffer the same cultural deficit.

For the young Mohammad Reza, being shipped off to Europe must have placed him in a genuine double bind. He craved his father's affection and approval, yet felt intimidated by his tough disciplinarian approach. He certainly wanted to leave the many ritualistic demands of life at the upstart Court, but in the months before his departure, his distant father had initiated regular lunches and meetings with his Crown Prince. For Reza Shah, these meetings were part of his son's royal tutelage.[2] He wanted to familiarize the young boy with the complexities of power and politics in Iran. But, for the young Mohammad Reza, the lunches were in his own admission more than anything a chance to spend time with his father.

The decision to send away his Crown Prince had also been wrenching for Reza Shah. As he told a trusted confidante, it had been very hard for him to see his son go. Ultimately, he said, he knew he must "think of the country. Iran needs educated and enlightened rulers; we the old and ignorant must go."[3]

It is a measure of the institutionalized misogyny of the time that despite Reza Shah's own enlightened views on women—evident, for example, in his edict requiring all parents to send their daughters to school—he did not allow his own daughters to go to Europe for their education. Princess Ashraf, the Crown Prince's twin sister, was at the time just as intelligent, inquisitive, ambitious, and independent as any of her brothers. Actually, early plans had called for her to accompany young Mohammad Reza and his brothers to Switzerland. But at the last minute, just before departure, Reza Shah changed his mind, allowing only the boys to go. Princess Ashraf was relegated to the role of an auxiliary to her twin brother's life. Though this was on a par with what most Iranian fathers at the time would have done, in Reza Shah's case it stands in sharp contrast to his otherwise ambitiously progressive views on women. Two years after being left behind, Ashraf was dispatched—along with her mother—to visit the Crown Prince, lest he be homesick. Enthralled with Europe and "What life was like in Switzerland," Princess Ashraf sent a telegram to her father, asking Reza Shah's permission to "remain and study in a European school." Her father's response was as curt as it was cruel. "Stop this nonsense," he wrote back, "and come home at once." There was no explanation, but this too, according to his daughter, was typical of Reza Shah.[4]

Switzerland was chosen as the Crown Prince's destination for a variety of reasons. It was, first of all, a neutral country, and sending the future king there would disengage his education from the complex labyrinth of "Big Game" politics and rivalries. Furthermore, a Swiss education guaranteed mastery of the French language, and French was in those days still one of the coveted signs of distinction for the country's status-obsessed elite. In the years before the Second World War, French was for the Persian elite still the lingua franca of power and culture. Moreover, Swiss boarding schools were known for instilling in their students the etiquette, if not the affectations, of European aristocratic affluence. Finally, in the Shah's words, Switzerland was chosen because it had "a salubrious climate."[5]

On September 5, 1931, the Crown Prince, his father, and a small entourage left Tehran for the Caspian coast. In those days there were no direct air or railroad links connecting Iran to the heart of Europe. Circuitous routes, either through Russia and eastern Europe, or through Lebanon and the Mediterranean, were the two most common ways Iranians used to reach Europe. What is today a five-hour plane ride was, in 1931, at least a seven-day journey even for royalty. On September 7, after bidding farewell to his misty-eyed father, Mohammad Reza boarded a special steamer headed for Baku in the Soviet Union.

A debonair and dashing man named Abdol-Hussein Teymourtash headed the Crown Prince's entourage. He was the Court minister, and along with Ali-Akbar Davar, then minister of justice, he was considered one of the most powerful men in Iran.[6] A man called Moadeb Naficy was to act as the Crown Prince's guardian and physician, while another man, Mostashar-al Mulk, was to teach the future king the Persian language. Reza Shah wanted his son not only to learn how to speak Persian well, but to write it with elegance and eloquence. He was more than anything a nationalist, and for at least a thousand years, since the Arab invasion of Iran, the Persian language had become a bastion of nationalism for Persians. Like so much else in his vision of a modern Iran, Reza Shah seemed to have known, more by intuition than learning, that in the transition to modernity, language was the cement of the new nationalism—the cohesive element of what political scientist Benedict Anderson called the "Imagined Communities" of modernity.[7] All through his tenure in Switzerland, the Crown Prince was expected to write home on a weekly basis "one letter, in the form of a composition, one lesson in Persian dictation and one lesson in penmanship directly."[8] Reza Shah not only read his son's letters carefully, but also occasionally asked trusted scholars in Tehran, and of course the Crown Prince's tutors in Switzerland, about his son's progress in learning and mastering the Persian language.

In the public imagination, the Shah went to a boarding school named Le Rosey, where he was a good student but a better athlete and returned to Iran with some modicum of modern liberal values indelibly etched in his mind. The British, who were clearly following the Crown Prince's footsteps in Europe, were the first to make such an observation. On the margins of a report from British officials in Berne, prepared not long after the Crown Prince arrived in Switzerland, the receiving official at the Foreign Office wrote, "a most encouraging report. It may be that the Crown Prince having been sent to Europe sufficiently young, may have really absorbed a European outlook."[9]

But in fact, Mohammad Reza's educational experience in Switzerland did not begin at Le Rosey. On October 17, 1931, after a long journey through Russia and eastern Europe, the Crown Prince and his entourage arrived in Lausanne.

For his part, Mohammad Reza seemed happy to be leaving home. From Lausanne, he moved in with a law professor named André Mercier in the small town of Vennes. To accommodate the princely presence, the professor had undertaken major construction around his house. After settling in, the Crown Prince began a course of studies at the École Nouvelle in Chailly.[10]

What happened at the small, exclusive boarding school is a matter of some controversy. Most sources, relying on the account of the Shah himself, simply suggest that he went to the school to learn French, and once he had a fair command of the language, went on to Le Rosey. A report from the British Consulate in Tehran at the time offers another story. It claims that the "1) *Valihad* (sic) [Crown Prince] has been at two schools in Switzerland, and was requested to leave the first. 2) That he was guilty of a heinous foul on the football ground, and that the other boys sent him to Coventry* or something of the kind. Hence his removal. 3) That he gave himself airs such as his schoolmates could not endure and they set on him and gave him a bad time. The headmaster requested his removal."[11] The consulate was unable to confirm these stories, but the prison memoirs of Mohammad Reza's friend Hussein Fardust confirm much of the story. According to Fardust, Mohammad Reza got into regular fights with an Egyptian student. When the boy was forced to go to hospital at the end of one such fight, the school asked the Crown Prince to leave.[12] Either way, less than a year after arriving in Switzerland, he moved to a new boarding school called Le Rosey.

Le Rosey was established in 1880 by a Belgian named Paul Carnal. The fact that he was married to an American woman allowed the school to combine the pragmatism of the New World and the tradition and culture of old Europe. The Shah's days at the school were easily the happiest of his life. Though he was still under the constant gaze of his many handlers and minders, nannies and teachers, he was nevertheless free from the militarist discipline and the obsessively punctual daily routines of his father. His schoolmates remember him arriving at Le Rosey much in the manner of an Oriental potentate; at the same time, they praise him for his ability to quickly learn how to live with the reality of his new status—an equal among equals, who can neither expect nor dispense any royal rights or favors.

Le Rosey was, in those days, a haven for the sons of affluent diplomats and businessmen, or "tourists who wanted to travel without their noisy sons."[13] One of the Shah's classmates was, for example, the older brother of Richard Helms, the director of the CIA during the Watergate break-in, and later the U.S. ambassador to Iran.† Le Rosey had more than its fair share of royalty and children of the aristocracy—from the children of the Metternichs and the Radziwills to young princes from Egypt. With an enrollment of one hundred boys, there were roughly two Americans for each non-American at Le Rosey,[14] and "the sixty-odd Americans were not at all impressed by the thirty-odd non-Americans. In fact, the Americans seemed to make an indelible impression on the little rajahs, shahs, and princes."[15]

---

* A British idiom, used to damn someone to the equivalent of an inferno.

† Many biographers have mistakenly claimed that the Helms at Le Rosey was the future head of the CIA.

On the first day of the Crown Prince's arrival in the new school, the "affair Pahlavi" took place. He had arrived at the school in a canary-yellow Hispano-Suiza. He was not alone; his entourage included a chauffeur, a footman, a valet, and "a spectacularly handsome, silver-haired old gentleman who . . . was a Persian diplomat of high rank."[16]

As the young boy descended from the Hispano-Suiza, he looked at his peers "with a stare that he must have intended to be regal."[17] If that was his intent, he certainly failed; his peers, like him devotees of fancy cars, were oblivious to his royalty, but were instead "busy examining the snake-like chrome tubes that coiled out of the hood of this car."[18] The Hispano-Suiza, used in those days only to drive him to school, was only the first in a long litany of the Shah's fascination with such cars. By the time he left Iran in 1979, he had a vast collection worth millions of dollars.

School officials greeted the Iranian Crown Prince with due deference, bowed and beamed with joy, and led the young boy to his quarters—one of the two biggest rooms in the school dormitory, made even more special by the Persian rugs that lay on the floor. The one special privilege afforded the Iranian Crown Prince was that, unlike all the other students, he had the room to himself.

The Crown Prince spent the next few moments overseeing "the unpacking of his impedimenta (such a collection of baskets, coffers, hampers, trunks, boxes, and suitcases can hardly be called baggage)."[19] By the time he finished and returned to the yard, it was early afternoon.[20] One can only imagine the anxieties and trepidations in Mohammad Reza's young mind as he was about to enter the yard. He would, at that moment, leave behind the insulated safety and solemnities that define royal status. If the story of his expulsion from the first school is indeed correct, he had already learned, the hard way, that when bereft of the protections and privileges of rank, he did not have the "technologies of the self" to cope with the real world. The moment his newly kinged father named him the crown prince, the young Mohammad Reza forfeited the fun, freedom, and frivolity of a normal childhood.

There is a common Persian expression that says, "Kill the cat on the first night of the wedding." Authority and power must, according to the proverb, be established early in any relationship. Maybe that principle explains the young Mohammad Reza's strange behavior when he first entered the Le Rosey courtyard. A small bevy of boys had huddled around a bench "that ringed the dignified old tree" whose majestic silhouette had become part of the school's logo. Immersed in their conversation about baseball and Babe Ruth, they failed to notice the arrival of their new peer—the boy they eventually came to call Pahlavi. By the time the two boys finally noticed him, he was "stalking up and down like an angry tiger," about three feet away from the tree and the bench.

Pahlavi had apparently been pacing angrily for some moments. Suddenly, he stopped, made an angry sweep of his right arm and using what sounded to the boys like a "mixture of French and Hollywood-gangster English,"[21] made it clear that the students who were sitting should stand up. Assuming he wanted to sit down, the boys, engrossed in their baseball talk, moved to clear a small corner of the bench for the angry newcomer.

But a mere place on the bench was not what Pahlavi wanted. What he wanted them to know, the boys soon learned, was that people usually stood in the presence of the Crown Prince of Iran.[22] Imbued by his father's nationalistic pride, pampered by a doting mother and dutifully supplicant servants, the young Mohammad Reza had developed not just a fierce sense of nationalism, but an exaggerated set of expectations of what being a Persian crown prince could or should beget him in the world. He was about to discover the harsh realities of the world outside the Court cocoon.

By then other boys had gathered around the tree. Some snickered, while others made derogatory comments. "Pahlavi's royal dignity was shattered. He flew at the nearest boy, who happened to be [an American boy named] Charlie Childs, and seized him by the throat."[23] Before long, Charlie had the better of the Crown Prince, who was "panting on the ground and Charlie was straddling the royal chest, pummeling the royal face."[24]

After a couple of minutes, the boyish melee came to an end, and the young Pahlavi was grunting for mercy. "His black hair dank and falling over his eyes, his face scratched and bleeding, his shirt torn, he slowly got to his feet." His next move, like his initial attack, surprised the students. He smiled, "shook Charlie's hand a couple of times, and patted him on the back."[25] Pahlavi had, in one sense, certainly failed to kill the cat. What he achieved, however, was peace of mind. From then on, he lived amicably with the other students. They accepted him as equal.[26]

The young Mohammad Reza soon learned to enjoy his new life at school and even began writing for the school paper. A year before his return home, at Christmas of 1935, he wrote a long article for *L'Echo du Rosey*, indicating that what he loved most about his life at the school was its "*esprit collectif*" (collective spirit) and the "pure, amicable, and sincere solidarity" that existed amongst the students.[27]

In an apparent reference to his own experience, and in an almost confessional tone, he wrote about the joys and challenges of fashioning a new, more egalitarian, less hierarchic persona for himself. "Every student who comes to Rosey," he wrote, "brings his own baggage, his own way of seeing things." But at the new school, students face new realities, "different from what they knew," and the "new is always a bit disconcerting."[28]

Except for a note of condolence at the death of His Majesty, King of the Belgians, and a small joke at the expense of the British,[29] the rest of his article is filled with gossip about student life at Le Rosey, as well as news of school sports—clearly the passion of his youth. There is, in his narrative, a carefree, light spirit that shines through nearly all the juvenilia written in this period.

The future Shah soon settled into a happy routine, dominated by his participation in almost every sport activity he could find at Le Rosey. In 1933, for example, he participated in soccer and was named captain of the team. He played tennis and lost a match to a young man named Baxter.[30] He competed in track and field events, where he came in third in the 200-meter- and fourth in the 400-meter dash. He took part in the long-jump competition, where he came in last. In his first year of school, his academic performance was less than sterling and did not win him any prizes, or a mention in the list of the top three students of his class.[31]

His performance in soccer was clearly his forte, but that too was not always, according to the school paper, singular or outstanding. In an article analyzing the 1933 season, while his team is praised for its overall performance, Pahlavi is criticized for "a bit of timidity" in his playing.[32] Timidity was one of the Shah's characteristics. In others, it could well be construed as a sign of reason and intelligence. It is, after all, according to Hamlet, conscience that makes cowards of us all. But in the Shah, particularly when he took on the persona of an authoritarian king, timidity could only lead to disaster. In his Le Rosey days, such timidity only begot him a bad notice in the school paper.

By the next academic year, the student called Pahlavi had clearly emerged as one of the better players on the soccer team.[33] His performance in other sports was uneven and sometimes less than spectacular. In tennis, for example, as a member of the doubles team for the class in 1934, he was for a while "not able to bring off a victory." In the first set of singles matches, too, he was "trounced" by a boy named Symington.[34] In his third year, the Crown Prince improved his tennis and was praised for his "perfect style" and convincing victories over his competitors.[35] For the rest of his life, tennis remained one of his favorite pastimes. He sometimes played friendly matches with some of Iran's top players.

It seems that the same release he found in sports, he found as well in writing for the school paper. Aside from the handful of his personal letters, the articles he wrote there are easily the most important pieces of writing of his early years, as there is no hint of the entrenched honorifics found in his letters to his father or the stiff style of his notes to his teachers. Instead, the articles exude an air of comfort, with an informal style, and their content is no less carefree.

In the first issue to which he made a contribution, Pahlavi had two long articles—one was the lead editorial, called "Chronique Roseene," and the other,

"Croquis Roseene" (Silhouettes from Rosey). The first is a report of the mundane details of life on campus—who is in, who is out, who has a new desk light, and, of course, who has done well in sports. The tone is light and jovial, often tinged with a touch of youthful romance about the "Rosey honor." He writes of the beauty of the Rosey chateau and praises the grandeur of the snowcapped mountains surrounding the school's winter campus at Gstaad.[36] The article called the "Silhouettes from Rosey" also covers student life but has a more sober and literary style. It shows his reading in the classics of Western culture—a central point of Le Rosey's curriculum. He again speaks of Rosey honor, but also refers to concepts such as "the malady of our century," and alludes to mythical figures such as Orpheus.[37]

Both academically and athletically, 1934 was a better year for the Crown Prince. He was ranked second in his class academically, scoring in the eighty-fourth percentile of his class. In athletic excellence, he was ranked third.[38] The same pattern, combining his newfound love of journalism with his avid love of sport, and his efforts to make sure he passed his academic exams, defined his next year at Le Rosey. In a lengthy essay at Easter 1935, he writes of the heroic effort of the school administration to make sure that students like him who did not go home to their families during holidays did not feel lonely. He waxes eloquent about the "profound impression" that one of his teachers, Monsieur Henri, had on his life. He talks of his teacher's respect for tradition and for the law, and of his ability to harmoniously connect the past to the present and the future.[39] These articles provide us a rare glimpse of the naked soul of Mohammad Reza, a portrait of the king as a young man.

But as he indulged in his passion for sports and tried to live the normal life of a Le Rosey student, the outside world was still watching him carefully. In 1935 the British Vice-Consul to Berne traveled to Le Rosey to find out just how the young Crown Prince was doing. The Vice-Consul wrote, "I lunched yesterday with M. Carnal, headmaster of Le Rosey School, and saw the Crown Prince of Persia ('saw' because I was not introduced and did not like to press the matter on the first occasion)." He describes the young Mohammad Reza as "tall and well-built (lacking the usual miniature-like Persian finesse)" and says that he "is an excellent all round athlete, being specially prominent in the football field. He is in fact one of Le Rosey's crack players." He writes of him as "extremely intelligent" and a hard worker who won the Prix d'Excellence for academic work. He confirms other reports that "the Crown Prince is treated just like other boys, who even 'tutoyer' him [address him with the informal 'you']; the only difference lying in certain privileges such as not filing in and out of meals with the other boys, a room to himself."[40] According to the British Consulate report, the "Crown Prince appears to be popular with other boys, who in no way resent his small privileges, as they are themselves in many cases the sons of princes or diplomats (Lignes, Radziwills, Thurn, and Taxis, Metternichs, etc)."[41]

The 1935 consulate report is important for another reason beyond establishing the Crown Prince's popularity or athletic prowess. It includes the first official reference to the enigma that was Ernest Perron. Perron became easily one of the most controversial characters in the life of the Shah. Described by his friends and foes as everything from "diabolic to mysterious and from most odd to pure, ingenuous and innocent,"[42] Perron played a crucial role in the Shah's life and became a religious soulmate of Princess Shams, the Shah's sister. He was a man of many paradoxes—both devoutly Catholic and decidedly homosexual.

They met at Le Rosey, and for the next two decades, Perron was the Shah's closest, and near-constant, companion. Though, in the lore of Iranian politics, Perron was branded a British spy, the British Consulate describes him, in an almost alarmed tone, as "the oddest young man, a Swiss . . . who appears to be the Prince's chief guide, philosopher, and friend. He was apparently engaged as a sort of Super-Servant for the prince in Switzerland."[43]

Perron was in fact the son of a gardener or handyman at Le Rosey. He was born on June 29, 1909, making him ten years older than the Crown Prince. He was also something of a poet who eventually became the self-declared master of mirth for the Shah and the chief of protocol for the Pahlavi Court. He was "short and thin, almost fragile." He limped, and he lived in "the servant quarter of Le Rosey."[44] In another report, the British Legation describes him as "a curious fellow . . . dressed like a musical-comedy Bohemian who also reads characters from hand-writing and the palms of your hand, and makes the most surprising statements on the strength of it about your 'vie sexuelle'! . . . It is rather alarming that such an odd specimen should have such a hold over the young Prince. The Belgian Charge here, a most sensible fellow, has said that he would not entrust any young man to Monsieur Perron, let alone a future monarch, and his description of him as 'un exalté, un illuminé, un mystique' is just about right."[45] It is not hard to imagine that in the context of Le Rosey's international congregation of pampered and status-conscious boys, life was not easy for a young man like Perron—in social rank, inferior as the son of a gardener, and in social demeanor, saddled with what was then the double stigma of effeminacy and the physical handicap of a limp. He was subject to constant taunts and even physical abuse. On one such occasion, Mohammad Reza apparently took pity on the gardener's son and decided to offer him what protection he could.[46] This turned out to be the commencement of a close and increasingly controversial relationship. In the beginning, it was not clear whether the Crown Prince would dare take his new friend back to Iran with him. It was not hard to surmise that Reza Shah, obsessively concerned with giving his son a "manly education" and on constant watch for any hint of effeminate behavior, would not be happy with the idea of his son's returning from his "Grand Tour" of Europe with a gay man ten years his senior. The wrath of Reza Shah was something even his favorite son, the Crown Prince, would not risk easily. Yet Perron did go back to Iran with his friend, and as they anticipated, Reza Shah proved hard to convince, or to circumvent.

But in the meantime, in Switzerland, Perron became the Crown Prince's constant companion. At Perron's behest, Mohammad Reza began reading French poetry; he read Chateaubriand and Rabelais and before long, he thought of them as "my favorite French authors."[47] During weekends, the two often visited the house of Anoushirvan Sepahbodi—Iran's ambassador to Switzerland at the time. For the Crown Prince in his youthful exile, the Sepahbodi house was a piece of Persia where he was treated like royalty. In a strange twist of fate, that same ambassador's son was Iran's envoy to Morocco when the Shah, more than four decades later, was in exile. But in the carefree days of Switzerland, the Ambassador's house was where he had Persian food—*chelo kebab* was one of the Crown Prince's favorite dishes—and listened to both Persian and classical Western music. For a while Liszt and Mozart were his favorites.

Before Perron, every relationship in Mohammad Reza's life had been chosen for him by his father. Now he was making a choice of his own, and it was, by all accounts, a strange one. What role Perron played in the Shah's life has never been clear. The Shah's foes were particularly keen on turning this friendship into a serious liability for him.[48] Others have used theories of modern psychology to explain the enigma. Perron, they say, was the Shah's "selfobject"—a term coined by Heinz Kohut to refer to a particular form of psychic identification.[49] A selfobject—as the concocted morphology of the word betrays—refers to a person who has been chosen by another, usually suffering from some variety of psychic disorder, to act as an extension of their Self. For fragile souls, the selfobject is used to bolster self-esteem, to provide much-needed support and succor.[50] What this theory fails to explain is why, of all the people in the world, the Crown Prince would choose Perron as his primary selfobject. But in 1935 Switzerland, all such concern was for the future king still in the state of blissful "suspended animation."

At the same time, the normal problems of youth—his desire to buy a fancy new car, rumors of his illicit liaison with one of the school's maids[51]—interfered with his Persian lessons and the mandatory letters and reports he had to write to his father every week. Reza Shah would begin his normal routine only after he received and read his son's letter. So central were these letters to Reza Shah's mood, that on the rare occasions when one was late in arriving, the work of the Court would come to a screeching halt, and sometimes the Minister of Post and the Court Minister were sent to scour the city's postal pipeline to locate it.

Knowing full well how attentive his father would be to every detail of its style and content, preparing the letter had become something of a major challenge for the Crown Prince. He referred to the time he spent writing the reports and learning the language as his "hour of purgatory."[52] Nevertheless, the Shah developed a legible, at times even beautiful, handwriting style and prose that was succinct and polished.

Perhaps because of comments like this, a consensus has developed amongst his biographers that the Shah was particularly unhappy during his days in Switzerland. The Shah himself helped the spread of this idea. In talks he gave, as well as in his memoirs, he complained about his isolation in Le Rosey, how he was forced to spend time alone while his friends were at parties and balls. He wrote that "when I was at school in Switzerland, yes, yes, terrible . . . feeling, as you said, in a straitjacket, like a prisoner,"[53] and finally, he complained that his guardians were unusually harsh and stern with him.[54] The complaints have led compliant biographers to the conclusion that Le Rosey was "an extraordinarily unhappy period for the Crown Prince."[55]

In reality, however, the Shah's own writings of the period, the testimony of others, a closer reading of his memoirs, as well as photos from the period, tell an entirely different story. As a king, entrapped in the requisite rhetoric of love for his father and for the fatherland, it was politically untenable for him to admit to the fact that he loved life away from the Court, the country, and cares of the state. But beneath this thin, politically expedient façade was the reality of his youthful exile. Happy years of exile away from his country might be hard to reconcile with the divine dedication to save that country. In his memoirs, when he is not describing the politically exigent image of his unhappy days in a foreign country, he makes it clear that his health had improved in Switzerland because his mood had improved. The improvement, he writes, had nothing to do with better food or with the weather.

His doting sister Princess Ashraf writes of seeing him at Le Rosey and finding that he looked "healthy, and happy too, stronger and more fit than he had been in Tehran. I saw at once how much he had been influenced by Europe." When she goes on to describe the nature of these changes, she exhibits a surprising sense of Eurocentrism—a belief in the superiority of the European culture. "Before he left Tehran," she writes, "he had been, in spite of his quiet nature, a little rough around the edges. . . . In moments of excitement, he might . . . ride his horse into the house . . . but now his manners had been refined and Europeanized."[56] In the long hours of discussion Mohammad Reza had with his sister, there is no evidence of his complaining about the "straitjacket," but conversely, much to indicate how happy he was and how impressed he was with all he had learned in his new environment. If anything, in the course of these discussions, the young Mohammad Reza complained not about his life in Switzerland, but of Iran.

"My brother told me," she writes, "how impressed he had been by the democratic attitudes he had seen at school. . . . He talked about how he had come to realize for the first time how much economic and social disparity there was among the people of Iran."[57] The unhappy exile story was an invention, intended to support the Shah's assumed political persona of a man on a divine and historic mission to save his country.

Chapter 5

HAPPY HOMECOMING

A thousand flatterers sit within thy crown
Shakespeare, King Richard II, *2.1.100*

He left a chaperoned boy and returned a dashing debonair man, dressed in a trim and tailored suit, his dark curly hair perfectly coiffed. He went in docility with an entourage handpicked by his father; he returned in quiet defiance in the company of a friend he had chosen himself, and who he knew would not meet with the approval of his father.

No less dramatic were the changes that had taken place in Iran in the five years of his absence. Reza Shah's far-reaching reforms touched nearly every facet of Iranian life. From disparate parts of a country on the verge of collapse—what in today's social science terminology would be called a "failed state"—Reza Shah had created a modern nation, with a strong central government, a small and budding industrial sector, and a modern but brittle army and bureaucracy.

About the time of the Crown Prince's return, Iran was set to finish a transnational railroad. Reza Shah had ordered it built in spite of domestic and international opposition. Britain initially tried to dissuade him from the idea altogether; when it found that he would not be deterred, the British government tried to convince him to build it along an east–west axis, connecting Turkey and Europe to Pakistan and India.[1] Reza Shah opted instead for a plan that connected the Persian Gulf to the Caspian Sea.

Although the Crown Prince was out of Iran when work on the railroad began, he was, unbeknownst to himself, entangled in some of the controversies surrounding the project. Reza Shah was unhappy that the trestles used in building the tracks were all imported from the Soviet Union. In response to his concern, a small group of politicians and businessmen created a company called Sherkate-e Jangalat (Forests Company) that used Iranian lumber to make the trestles. To "facilitate" their work, they named the Crown Prince as a partner in the company.

Soon, Reza Shah learned that the company had been greedily razing some of the beautiful forests and ancient trees of his beloved province of Mazandaran. He angrily ordered the company closed and its properties confiscated. There is no evidence that Prince Mohammad Reza, in Switzerland at the time, knew anything about his own ghost partnership in the company. But during his own reign, the practice of giving partnerships to members of the royal family to "facilitate" work became a common practice and occasionally a major headache for him and his regime.[2]

Reza Shah had also opened Iran's historic sites, including religious centers and schools, for inspection and study by American and European scholars and anthropologists. Arthur Pope and André Goddard were two of the most important such experts. Many of the mosques discussed and displayed in books on Iranian art history were, for the first time, opened to non-Muslims under the direct order of Reza Shah. The future Shah would continue his father's fervent patronage of both Goddard and Pope, as well as other Western archeologists and art historians. Pope's monumental study of Persian art was one of the fruits of this patronage.

On May 13, 1928, Reza Shah unilaterally declared null and void all existing capitulary rights—a despised vestige of colonialism by which citizens of the colonial country were granted immunity from prosecution in Iranian courts.[3] The decision was, rightly, celebrated with much fanfare as a sign of Iran's newfound independence. But the end of capitulary rights also signaled a change in the nature of Iran's relationship with the outside world, increasing tension with Britain.

Reza Shah's first major confrontation with the British came soon after his 1926 coronation. The Iranian Foreign Ministry had written a "categorical note" to the British Embassy "demanding the removal of Indian *Savars* [mounted guards] from Persia." The British had been using such guards in some of their consular offices. In those days, Harold Nicolson—husband to Vita Sackville-West and the man who, in his own words, had a "Kipling inside him, and something of an 'empire builder'"[4]—was Britain's chargé d'affaires in Iran. He rushed to the Iranian Foreign Ministry to object. Only the armed forces of the Imperial Army of Iran, the Iranian note said, are now permitted to carry arms in Iran. The note was, in the opinion of Nicolson, "so categorical as to be almost offensive." He wanted Iran to take back or change the note. Much to his displeasure, the Foreign Ministry informed Nicolson that the disputed note had been imposed upon the ministry by none other than Reza Shah and thus could, under no circumstances, be taken back or amended.[5] Eventually, a solution was found by adding an annex to the text, softening the tone of the initial note. But at the end, the British were forced to abide by the content of what diplomats would call the "frank and honest" letter.

A number of other issues, large and small, continued to come up between Reza Shah and the British government, causing an almost chronic rift between the two. There was, for example, the time when representatives from the British Embassy tried to visit Sheikh Khaz'al in Tehran, where he was under house arrest, but were told they must go through normal channels required for visiting prisoners.[6] In the "Bas'idu incident" the British decided to fly their own flag over the small settlement on one of the Iranian islands in the Persian Gulf that they had been using as a coaling station for their ships. The Iranian government ordered and the British government agreed to take down their flag and instead fly the Persian flag. By then the British were already becoming increasingly agitated by Reza Shah's recalcitrance.[7] In fact, on the day of the Crown Prince's return to Iran, there was another minor altercation between Iran and Britain when British sailors tried to land on Iranian soil without receiving the requisite permission or answering the normal queries of Iranian customs officials.

The most controversial confrontation between Reza Shah and Britain took place, as expected, over oil. In April 1933, after prolonged and contentious negotiations—in one instance, Reza Shah angrily tore to pieces the text of the D'Arcy Concession initially signed in 1900 that had given Britain a monopoly on Persian oil—and after the issue was taken up by the League of Nations, a new agreement was eventually signed, known as the 1933 Agreement. Reza Shah and his supporters declared it a great victory for Iran. Many years later, one aspect of these negotiations would become the subject of some debate. In the language of article ten of the agreement, it was clearly stipulated that Iran should have 20 percent of the profits not only of the Anglo-Iranian Oil Company in Iran, but of all its subsidiaries around the world. After a few years, the company had in fact spawned dozens of extremely profitable subsidiaries, and Iran's share amounted to millions of dollars.[8] The British fought hard not to pay any such royalties, and when Iran's oil industry was nationalized in 1951, article ten, along with everything else in the 1933 agreement, was declared null and void. There were at the time experts who argued that, in the long run, Iran's revenues from these subsidiary rights would be greater than new revenues resulting from the nationalization of the country's oil industry.

But of Reza Shah's reforms, the one that most directly affected his son's political future was the plan to secularize the Iranian polity and limit the influence of the Shiite clergy. The clergy's main source of economic power and social status had until then been their control over the judiciary and the education system. A third source of their income had been their role as executors of vast religious endowments *(vagf)*. Reza Shah disenfranchised the clergy by depriving them of the revenues they historically received from the *vagf* and from running both the judiciary and the education system. The start of a modern university and the establishment of a secular law school were serious blows to the power of the clergy. Limiting their roles in these areas meant a radical curtailment of the clergy's ideological, economic, and political power. The policy left a lingering sense of betrayal in at least some of the clergy. Ironically, while the Shah changed this aspect of his father's policy and attempted a rapprochement with the clergy, he ended up paying the price for the clergy's seething anger.

Reza Shah's confrontation with the clergy reached its zenith in mid July 1935, in the city of Meshed, where the shrine of Shiism's eighth Imam, Reza,* is located. A few weeks before the confrontation, Reza Shah had ordered a ban on traditional forms of Shiite mourning—particularly self-flagellation and self-mutilation, in which mourners beat their backs with chains, or their foreheads with machetes. Also banned were *t'aziye,* a traditional form of Shiite passion play that mourns the martyrdom of Shiism's third Imam, Hussein, in the Battle of Karbala. To Reza Shah and his cultural advisors, *t'aziye* was nothing but an emblem of reactionary tradition.

The 1935 ban did not take place in a social vacuum: this was an era when similar ideas were being advocated by many Iranian thinkers and secular intellectuals. Even a large number of Shiite writers and theologians had also begun promoting a new form of Shiism—rational in vision; bereft of superstitions, tokens, amulets, and self-mutilation; and free from the grim cult of grief as a sign of piety and guarantor of salvation. Moreover, in a pattern that echoed one of the demands of the Protestant Reformation in Europe, these Shiite reformers also wanted a faith free from the domination of the traditional clergy.

One young reformist named Ali Akbar Hakamizadeh launched a journal called *Homayoun* in January 1935 and published ten issues. Each one had exactly

* Of the twelve Imams revered by the version of Shiism dominant in Iran—Esna Asha'ri, or Twelvers—only one, Reza, is buried in Iran. His sister is buried in the city of Qom. But the Iranian landscape is also strewn with an estimated hundred thousand *imamzadeh*, big and small shrines, all claiming to be the burial site of some descendent of an Imam. Though it is all but impossible to substantiate these claims of divinity, the shrines invariably satisfy the devotional needs of the truly devout.

thirty-two pages and, aside from iconoclastic articles on Shiism, contained articles on hygiene and at least one "entertainment" piece. Hakamizadeh also published a book in 1934 called *Asrare Hezar-Saleh,* or *Thousand-Year-Old Mysteries,* in which he advocated a Shiism without the obscurantism of the clergy, and a polity guided by the rule of law and reason.[9]

It was a measure of the power of these reformist ideas, and of Hakamizadeh's book, that Ayatollah Khomeini's first published book was an angry polemic against them. He called the proponents of these ideas "infidels" and "corrupters of the earth"—a concept that came back into bloody vogue in the days and months after the Islamic Revolution of 1979—and asked for their execution.[10] Ayatollah Khomeini not only defended the rituals of mourning, but argued that the rituals and the tears of the pious and, most important of all, the presence and power of Shiite clergy, are in fact the true pillars of Shiism and the key to its survival.[11] In the sixties and seventies, when ideas critical of the clergy were once again in vogue, it was Ayatollah Khomeini more than anyone else who rose to suppress these ideas and defend the role of the clergy in preserving his "beloved Islam."

But Reza Shah's most contentious orders had to do with how men and women appeared in public. In Iran, as in other countries, sartorial changes are often one of the earliest signs and most sensitive barometers of social change and of the transition from tradition to modernity. The first controversial order banned the traditional headgear worn by most Persian men, requiring everyone to wear instead a new "modern" hat, invariably called a Pahlavi hat. The clergy, pining for a confrontation with Reza Shah, and anticipating more pressure from him in the future, challenged the order. Some ayatollahs issued *fatwas* (religious decrees) against the new hats, and against the emerging fashion of neckties, arguing that these represented surrogate crosses.[12] On July 17, 1935, protestors in the city of Meshed took to the streets and then, chased by the police, took refuge in Imam Reza's shrine. For many centuries, mosques and shrines had been considered sanctuaries, safe havens free from the reach of the government. Reza Shah defied the tradition, ordering the army to attack the demonstrators. Scores of protesters were killed. Casualty figures ranged from sixty to several thousand.[†]

Ayatollah Hussein Gomi, then one of Iran's top Shiite clerics, left Meshed in protest. He had been, to that point, a supporter of Reza Shah, publicly declaring that Iran's glories were all due to Reza Shah.[13] He came to Tehran, hoping to visit with Reza Shah and register his strong protest over the shrine episode, but to his dismay, Reza Shah refused a meeting. As a gesture of protest, the Ayatollah left

† A common error of many historical narratives of the period is the assumption that the big Meshed confrontation was over the issue of women's headgear.

the country, but his voluntary exile lasted only six years. No sooner had Reza Shah abdicated than his son, in a major reversal of policy and attitude, invited the Ayatollah back to Iran in 1941. His return was to have far-reaching ramifications for Iran and for the new Shah.

On January 7, 1936 Reza Shah issued another order, this one even more controversial, decreeing that Iranian women would henceforth only be allowed in public shorn of their traditional veils. From the time of the Constitutional Revolution (1905–1907), a number of autonomous women's group had appeared throughout the country. The Bolshevik Revolution, too, had a profound influence on Iranian women. Beginning in 1926, a number of women, many of them living in Tehran, had begun to test the limits of their freedom by appearing in public wearing only a hat rather than the traditional veil.[14] The government and the police implicitly protected these women from the wrath of the more pious citizens. In 1934, a conference was held to celebrate the life and work of the poet Ferdowsi in the city of Tous, not far from the city of Meshed, long a Shiite stronghold. In the course of the conference, a few women appeared without a veil, and the clergy, though angry, chose to do nothing.[15]

Despite these early hints of change, Reza Shah's order created something of a shock amongst the more traditional sectors of Iranian society. Even today, more than half a century after that decision, many secular Iranians, as well as advocates of women's rights, have rejected Reza Shah's order as an act of brazen despotism. He dictated by royal fiat, they say, and overlooked the fact that social transformations can only come through a gradual, endogenous process of change. The clergy once again spared no effort to fight the new decree. By then, Reza Shah had such a strong grip on power that religious forces could do little but accept defeat. They would bide their time, and only when Reza Shah was off the throne would they resume their effort to turn back the clock and bring back the veil, or at least the right of Muslim women to wear it in public.

Reza Shah believed that his strong-arm tactics were the indispensable tools for fostering modernity and fighting stubborn forces of tradition. But this tempting dialectic of despotism and development turned out to be a vicious circle—self-generating and self-fulfilling in the short run, and self-negating and self-destructive in the long run. He needed an iron hand, Reza Shah claimed, if he was to make changes in an otherwise ossified social structure. The more changes he made in that structure, the more convinced he became that his iron hand had been the panacea.

In 1936, when the teenage Mohammad Reza returned from his European sojourn, he remained simply a passive and docile observer of his father's iron hand and the changes it forced not just on the body politic, but on his life and that of other members of the royal family. Less than a month after his return home, his twin sister, Princess Ashraf, asked him, in desperation, to intercede on her behalf and convince Reza Shah to change his mind about the marriages he had planned for her and for her older sister, Princess Shams. Among the royal family, the only person who dared challenge the decisions of Reza Shah was the Queen Mother. It was a source of great amusement in the royal family that the man whose gaze brought terror to the hearts of ministers and military men went into hiding when he saw the Queen Mother coming. All through her life, her relationship with her estranged husband, Reza Shah, and his fear of her, as well as his mode and manner of intimacy with her, was a favorite subject of joking banter between her and Mohammad Reza Shah.[16] "How did you fall in love?" the Shah asked his octogenarian mother at a Court dinner in April 1976. "How often did you sleep together?" A giggling Queen Mother answered that "most of the time we spent together, we were not on speaking terms," but she clearly enjoyed the light banter. In 1936, however, she was not willing to come to her daughters' aid. Neither was the Crown Prince.

Princess Ashraf was nearly seventeen years old when Reza Shah decided that she and her eighteen-year-old sister, Princess Shams, must get married. Unbeknownst to them both, he had asked Prime Minister Mahmoud Jam to prepare a list, accompanied by photos, of young men from prominent Iranian families in the country who were eligible to marry the Shah's two daughters. In compiling the list Jam also decided to include the name and a picture of his own son, Fereydoon, in those days a lieutenant registered in France's storied Saint Cyr military academy. In the elaborately embroidered uniform of a French Saint Cyr officer, he cut a dashing figure, and Reza Shah was immediately impressed. He chose him for Princess Ashraf and picked Ali Qavam, the scion of the famous Anglophile family from the city of Shiraz, for Princess Shams. While engaged in this matchmaking frenzy, he also decided that Qavam's daughter, Taj, should marry Assadollah Alam, the son of the Alam family that had been prominent in the Khorasan province of Iran for several hundred years. The engagements were announced on October 1, 1936. No sooner had Princess Shams laid eyes on Jam than she decided she preferred him over Ali—the man her father had picked as her designated husband. The ever-petulant and spoiled "favorite daughter" who invariably got what she wanted prevailed yet again, and when the official announcement was made, she was set to wed Jam.[17] Princess Ashraf had no choice but to resign herself to a forced marriage to Ali Qavam. Before long, Reza Shah decided that the Crown Prince, too, needed to find a wife and future queen.

All of these changes in the Court took place in the context of a world that was also radically changing. The specter of Nazism haunted not just Europe but Asia, Africa, and America. Iran was not spared. Hitler had his eyes on the oil fields of Iran and the Persian Gulf, and he spared no effort in trying to appeal to the people and governments of the area. The fact that his harangues were often targeted against the British and Soviet menace, the two colonial foes of Persia, made the Nazis' sinister work easier. The appeal of Germany as the supporter of a "Third Way"—neither British nor Russian—preceded the rise of Nazism and first appeared in Iran during the time of the First World War. In the thirties, the Nazi propaganda machine in Iran was well oiled. One of the earliest signs of this Nazi intellectual onslaught was the publication of a magazine called *Iran-e Bastan* (Ancient Iran).

On January 14, 1933, the first issue of *Iran-e Bastan,* printed on noticeably expensive glossy paper, appeared in Tehran. There can be no doubt that the launch of the magazine was done with the consent of the Iranian government as, in those days, no paper or magazine could be published in the country without the government's permission; according to its editors, one of their main sources of revenue was government-sponsored advertisements. In its first issue, *Iran-e Bastan* declared itself "partisans of the present policy of the Persian empire to uplift Persia to the grandeur of ancient Iran."[18]

The first issue featured Reza Shah on its front page, and the second carried a similarly large picture of the Crown Prince—both in full royal regalia. While the first issue gave no overt hint of the magazine's Nazi sentiments, beginning with the second issue, *Iran-e Bastan* became increasingly aggressive and unabashed in its defense of Hitler and the Third Reich. In the second issue, for example, there is a picture of Hitler, who is described as "a strong man, of firm ideas" and a leader whose "ideas are followed by millions of people."[19]

In later issues, the magazine became even more open in its advocacy of Nazi ideology. It often wrote to glorify the Aryan race and spoke of Iran's shared common legacy with Germany's Aryan Reich. After a few months, *Iran-e Bastan* claimed it had a readership of more than 20,000, and its advocacy of Nazism became more pronounced. In its fourteenth issue, there were four pictures of Hitler: as an infant, "with his father looking at his son in admiration," Hitler when he is a few months old, Hitler and his dog, and finally Hitler showing affection to German laborers.[20] A few weeks later, the front page of the magazine carried an image of the swastika, describing it as "the symbol of Aryans and a banner of their liberation and happiness."[21]

Iran-e Bastan regularly discussed National Socialism and its goal of "cleansing the country" of "the material and spiritual influence of foreigners and Jews."[22] The magazine continued to appear well into its second year, when it suddenly folded. The discourse developed by the magazine helped shape the ideology of the Iranian Nazis who became active again in the forties and, in the guise of new parties, advocated proto-Nazi ideologies like extreme nationalism, anti-Semitism, Aryan supremacy, and the cult of a fuehrer *(rahbar).*

In 1936, at the time of his son's return from Europe, Reza Shah seemed intractably entrenched in power. The Crown Prince's return, on May 11, 1936, even more than his departure, was greeted with much fanfare in the state-dominated media. Once again, Reza Shah and the royal family were on hand to greet the returning prince.

While the Shah claimed in his 1961 memoir, *Mission for My Country*, that he had finished his course of studies at Le Rosey and was awarded his diploma before returning to Iran in 1936, Le Rosey school records dispute his claims. The records state that the Shah did not "graduate in the school, his father took him back to Iran for politic[al] conveniences, where he finished his studies."[23] They describe the Shah as "a very good student, and a great sport-man (football, swimming)."[24] Not long after returning to Tehran, the Crown Prince was placed in a class in the Officer's Academy, where he continued his education. But the real contentious issue between father and son was not whether he had finished high school.

To Reza Shah's great dismay, the Crown Prince had come back with his newfound friend, Ernest Perron. Aside from their experience in Switzerland, there was much that connected the unlikely friends. Perron was an incorrigible gossipmonger, and he rejoiced in gathering all the gossip and sharing it with his powerful friend.[25]

Another quality that possibly further endeared Perron to the Shah was his devout Catholicism. The Crown Prince must have felt particularly pressured by Reza Shah's determined irreligious disposition, and Perron offered him the solace and company of a man of religious fervor. In fact, the Shah claims that during his Switzerland journey, after a short respite, he returned to his faith and religion, and "started to recite the Moslem daily prayers . . . and I said them with real fervor and conviction."[26] These revelations, made public in 1961, when he was on the verge of a major confrontation with the mullahs who opposed him, are as important for what they portend of his policies on religion as they are for the glimpses they offer into his habits and beliefs as a young man in Switzerland, away from the sway of his father and from the demands of his status as a crown prince.

But their shared past and common proclivities could not convince Reza Shah that Perron should be allowed to stay near the Crown Prince. He banished him from the Court, but not from the country. There are reports that on one occasion, when Reza Shah accidentally ran into Perron, he went after him with the military staff he invariably carried.[27] To keep Perron in Iran and away from Reza Shah's sight, he was given a job attending to the gardens of one of the hotels owned by Reza Shah. While Perron bided his time for an occasion to return to the center of power near his friend, Reza Shah chose a wife for his son.

The task of finding the right future queen was, once again, delegated to Prime Minister Mahmoud Jam. The Crown Prince himself was not involved in, or even informed of, the process. No stone was to be left unturned, Jam was told, in finding the most suitable candidate. Many Iranian families considered their daughters eligible and worked hard behind the scenes to influence the selection process. Ultimately, royal families of other countries, particularly in the Muslim world, were also scouted. The most eligible candidates were the two sisters of King Farouk of Egypt—Faeze and Fawzia. A new Iranian Ambassador to Egypt was named, and his special mandate was to further inquire into the "character of the bride-to-be" and ascertain the wisdom of a marriage.[28]

Once in Egypt, the new Ambassador clumsily broached the idea with the Egyptian Prime Minister, who summarily dismissed it. "The marriage of a Sunni Princess to a Shiite Prince," he declared, "is a recipe for disaster."[29] When told about this rejection, Reza Shah was incensed. He felt the Ambassador had mishandled the situation and he recalled him. A new Ambassador was dispatched to Cairo with the mandate of arranging the betrothal of an Egyptian Princess to the Crown Prince. One of the main qualifications the wife-to-be had to have was being "well-versed in the ways of royalty."[30]

In Egypt the new Ambassador found a way of endearing himself and his wife to members of the Egyptian royal family. Once assured of King Farouk's friendship, he finally raised the idea of a wedding that would join the royal families of Iran and Egypt. By then, Reza Shah had settled on Fawzia as the more suitable of the two Egyptian princesses. In the meantime, as Reza Shah and his Prime Minister were fast at work in finding a suitable wife for the future king, the Crown Prince was himself, by his own admission, altogether unaware of these efforts. He learned about them only when they bore fruit.

Once apprised of the good news that King Farouk had agreed to at least begin talks on an Egypto-Iranian union, Reza Shah was overjoyed. He picked a committee that was to go to Egypt and, following a long tradition in Islamic societies, ask for the hand of Princess Fawzia for Iran's Crown Prince.

Fawzia was the oldest of King Farouk's four sisters; she was seventeen at the time the marriage was first proposed. She had lived "her young life within the walled palaces and gardens of Cairo and Alexandria, Abdin, Kubbeh and Montaza." In 1938 these palaces were the playgrounds of her family. Four decades later, some of the same palaces would be the last refuge for the pariah Shah. Fawzia was once described as a "supremely naïve, over-protected, cellophane-wrapped, gift packaged little girl" living in "bucolic surroundings, mobbed by adoring servants, aunts, ladies in waiting."[31]

Before long, Jam received a telegram from Egypt. Though bedridden and burning with a high fever, he immediately set out for the Court, where he told Reza

Shah that Farouk had agreed to the royal matrimony, predicated on his sister's approval. At the same time, he had consulted with religious authorities to ensure that the marriage did not represent any insurmountable theological obstacle. She was, after all, a Sunni princess set to marry a prince of a Shiite nation. Assured of approval of the clerics, the only remaining obstacle was the approval of the princess and, before long, she too consented.

The committee left for Egypt, taking with them a letter from Reza Shah to King Farouk and a large collection of fine gifts—"diamond necklace, diamond broach, diamond earrings"[32]—but the Egyptians were far from impressed. In fact, they made a point of taking the Iranian delegation to the royal family's many palaces and "their Thousand and One Night splendor, their hundreds of bedrooms, with golden fawcets and golden beds,"[33] to show their wealth to the Iranian delegation. Still, before long, agreements were reached for a wedding, and on May 26, 1938, the Iranian and Egyptian courts simultaneously issued a communiqué announcing the engagement of Iran's Crown Prince to Princess Fawzia. A tutor was assigned to teach the future queen of Iran the Persian language. When she finally settled in Iran, she was something of a polyglot—speaking Arabic and French fluently and Persian competently, but with a hint of an accent. To bypass the constitutional requirement that only an Iranian citizen could be queen, a parliamentary bill was hurriedly passed declaring her Iranian-born. In describing why his father had chosen Fawzia, the Shah felt that his father had two goals: he wanted someone from "a good family," and he wanted "to connect the [Pahlavi] family to another royal family."[34]

An understandable undertone of bitterness is evident in the Shah's description of the process leading to his marriage. "I don't think anyone will criticize me," he wrote, "if I say that a king must have as much freedom about his private life as a simple peasant."[35] He suggested that in every civilized society, "family relations are considered part of the private domain, and free from outside interference, and all I wanted was the same right for myself."[36] He makes these critical comments a few paragraphs away from the lines where he describes, with prescribed joy, his first marriage. Before being told that he must go to Egypt and meet his future wife, he had never even seen a picture of her.

The Crown Prince learned of his engagement to Princess Fawzia on the same day that his nation was informed. In March 1939, the Crown Prince set out for Egypt to meet and marry his future wife and officially celebrate their wedding. From Tehran, he flew to Beirut, where he arrived on March 1, 1939, and immediately boarded the royal yacht *Mahroussa*—one of Khediv Ismail's extravagant mementos of modernity, "finished in late Victorian splendor." In 1939, the *Mahroussa* carried the Iranian Crown Prince to Egypt; less than a quarter century later, King Farouk would use the same yacht to leave his country after a coup toppled his increasingly corrupt and sclerotic regime.

The storied boat carried the groom-to-be to Alexandria with two Egyptian cruisers escorting and Egyptian planes flying over as it neared its destination. There the Iranian wedding party boarded the royal train for Cairo, where there was a gala to celebrate the engagement at the Abdin Palace. At eleven o'clock on the morning of March 15, the official wedding ceremonies were conducted. While the Crown Prince was in Egypt, the semi-official daily paper *Al-Ahram* carried a picture of him and his bride on the front page virtually every day. Those were also the days when the Second World War was beginning, and every happy piece of news about the wedding was invariably accompanied, on the same page, with a report of some ominous development in Europe. In the meantime, the Crown Prince visited a number of historic places—some like Al-Azhar University, considered the oldest university in the world, and some like the pyramids, considered one of the wonders of the world. The contrast between the splendor of the Egyptian royal family with their corpulent but melancholy king, their fez-hatted ministers, their liveried servants, and a forlorn Iranian Crown Prince, often in a simple military uniform, heralded a marriage marred from its inception by widely differing sensibilities and aesthetic values.

On November 2, 1939, the royal couple returned to Iran, where they were afforded a welcome befitting the grandeur they had seen in Egypt. Many parties celebrated the wedding, this time in Iranian style. The streets of Tehran were dotted with elaborately decorated arches and banners, welcoming the royal couple back to Iran. The Crown Prince and his bride settled in a palace that was surely, in comparison with the princess's Egyptian places of abode, meager. But their biggest problems were not rooted in magnitudes of architectural grandeur. The constant intrusions of some of the Shah's siblings and his domineering mother, stories of the newly married groom's philandering, and finally the ever-nearer menace of war combined to make the newlyweds' life increasingly fraught with tension.

That season, in Tehran's otherwise anemic social scene, the most coveted sign of power and "connection" was an invitation to the Iranian wedding ceremony. There was a big celebration arranged in the Amjadiye stadium, with a capacity of 25,000; tickets to the event were reserved for those in the highest echelons of power. Tehran was abuzz with talk of the European glamour of the future queen and the petty jealousies already evident among the Crown Prince's siblings. Fawzia was the new maven of fashion.

The stadium wedding was long on manly sports and short on arts and dances. It began with the playing of the two countries' national anthems, followed by synchronized acrobatics by students—always a favorite of authoritarian societies who use this synchronicity as a metaphor for social efficiency and harmony. It was followed by traditional Iranian calisthenics *(bastani)* with half-naked men of heavy muscular build playing with dumbbells, followed by fencing, football, a bevy of Boy Scouts exhibiting tropes and tricks they had mastered, and finally a recessional, singing the national anthems of the two countries.

Dinner was a more formal affair—in everything from the attire to the menu. "Caviar from the Caspian sea," followed by "Consommé Royal" and a variety of fish, fowl, and lamb. Fruit and jelly were served for dessert. Princess Fawzia's large entourage were all present, and by all accounts, she looked as glamorous as her elegant reputation demanded.

Not long after his marriage, the Crown Prince had his adenoids successfully removed. Just before the operation, Tehran was ripe with rumors of the arrest of about twelve officers, charged with espionage on behalf of the Soviet Union.[37] Others talked of a plot to kill the King. So worried was the government about regicide that "no films [were] ever passed by the censors which contain[ed] scenes of an assassination plot against a crowned head."[38] In this atmosphere of intrigue the Crown Prince insisted on the surgeons removing their face masks, lest there be someone with mischief on his mind.

A few weeks after the wedding, in 1940, Tehran had its first "scientifically conducted" census. At the beginning of the 1940s, the population of the city was 531,246—more than double the estimated population at the time of the foundation of the Pahlavi dynasty.

But while Reza Shah and his Crown Prince were busy with wedding plans, Nazi Germany was expanding its European war into global mayhem. The government of Iran declared its neutrality, something Iran had underscored many times before. But threatening clouds were clearly on the horizon, and Reza Shah and his son both knew it. Though some embassies reported at the time that after his marriage "the Crown Prince appears to have somewhat lost the full confidence" of his father,[39] every indication is, in fact, that with every passing day, Reza Shah involved his designated successor more and more in matters of state. At the same time, in a meeting with members of the parliament, Reza Shah ominously stated that, though they were relying on the "correct policy of neutrality... this is not enough. We must prepare for harder days. This meeting is primarily for me to register my dismay at the work of the government. They keep telling us, 'Your Majesty's mind can rest assured,' but when we look at how things actually are, we realize that we can be anything but assured."[40]

Chapter 6

CROWN OF THORNS

Or that I could forget what I have been,
Or not remember what I must be now!
Shakespeare, Richard II, *3.3.139–140*

As the dogs of war were unleashed in Europe, the West became increasingly concerned about Iran. Hitler had his eye on the land of the Aryans. In the words of the American Ambassador to Tehran at the time, Reza Shah began to feel like "a helpless pawn upon the slippery chess board of power politics."[1] And anything that changed Reza Shah's fate affected the political fortunes of the Crown Prince.

For both the Nazis and the Allies, Iran held the key to wartime victory. Long before hostilities actually reached Iran, both camps launched a new charm offensive to endear themselves to Reza Shah. Germany began ingratiating itself with Reza Shah by offering him, amongst other things, the steel mill he obsessively coveted. In 1936, the Hitler cabinet decreed that "Iranians were exempted from the restrictions of the Nuremberg Racial laws as pure-blooded Aryans."[2] This cynical propaganda ploy in 1936 became in 1941 a helpful tool for the government of Reza Shah and his son, Mohammad Reza Shah, to save Iranian Jews from the murderous Nazi machine. When the "Final Solution" began to turn the anti-Semitic Nuremberg Laws into a license for genocide, Iran used, amongst other things, the 1936 decree to save Iranian Jews from the ovens of Auschwitz. Thousands of European Jews who received Persian passports were also saved.[3]

It was in conjunction with this appeasing law that Reza Shah decided to change the way the countries of the West referred to Iran. For over 2,500 years, those who have lived in Iran have called themselves Irani, or Iranian. But when Greeks and Iranians were entangled in a long bloody war more than 2,000 years ago, the Greek historian Herodotus chose to call the foes not Irani, but Persians—after Pers (or Pars), a province of Iran where Persepolis, the imposing capital of the Iranian empire, was located at the time. From that time on, Westerners continued to use "Persian" to refer to Iranians, and by the early twentieth century, the name conjured everything the Romantics loved about the country—from the poetry of Omar Khayam and the beauty of Persian carpets to the delicacies of caviar and the beauty of the Persian feline.

Nevertheless, Reza Shah chose to forfeit the name Persia for Iran—evoking not the grandeur of the Persian past but consanguinity with the Aryan myth. It had obviously not reached Reza Shah that the Nazi concept of "Aryan" had little to do with the historic race of Aryans who lived on the Persian plateau.[4]

While the British and American governments worried about these apparently pro-Nazi gestures, as well as other signs of increased German influence in Iran, they also began mending fences with Reza Shah. When the Pahlavi Court announced the engagement of the Crown Prince to his Egyptian bride, the U.S. Ambassador in Iran wrote a letter to President Franklin Roosevelt suggesting that "in view of the state of our relations with Iran, I believe that the absence of a message from you [will] create an unfavorable impression in Tehran. Inasmuch as it is understood that the relations between the Shah and the Crown Prince are particularly close I believe that the Shah would be especially appreciative of a message on this occasion."[5] Several heads of state, including the President of Poland and the Emperor of Japan, had earlier sent such notes of congratulations. On April 19, 1939, the King and Queen of England had sent the Princess of Albania and the Earl of Athlone as their personal representatives to the wedding. Franklin Roosevelt not only sent the suggested note, but followed it with another letter, this time congratulating Reza Shah "for the important and far-reaching reforms that have been introduced in Iran under Your Majesty's inspiration and guidance," and in particular for the completion of the Trans-Iranian Railway.[6] The warmth of the two notes was particularly striking in light of the fact that only a couple of years earlier, Reza Shah had suspended Iran's diplomatic ties to the United States over a minor incident in Washington.

The British were concerned not only about Nazi Germany and its plans for Iran, but also about Soviet designs on the entire region. They anticipated that the inevitable "Soviet expansion would, in the first instance, be directed against Iran and Afghanistan."[7] These anxieties only increased when Stalin and Hitler signed their infamous 1939 Non-Aggression Pact. After the surprising agreement, "the Soviet and German Legations began to work"[8] in close collaboration in Iran. In November 1939, a coup attempt masterminded by the Soviets was discovered in Tehran and, according to Soviet archives, "three hundred officers were arrested."[9] Toward the end of the same year, the British Embassy in Tehran learned that seven to twelve officers of the Iranian army had been arrested and accused of espionage on behalf of the USSR.[10] In late 1939, Russia coerced Iran into a new "commercial agreement" that forced Iran to use "exclusively Russian oil in the North" of the country and to guarantee Germany transit rights through Iran. Some 300 new "alleged German commercial" travelers came to Iran through the Soviet Union. In this period, the Germans went so far as to promise Iran that, should they win the war, they would return Bahrain—the oil-rich island in the Persian Gulf, claimed by Iran at the time (and for the next quarter of a century) as one of its provinces and controlled by Britain—to Iranian control.

In May 1941, the British Embassy in Iran began developing strategies that it would implement in the case of a "German or Russian occupation of Northern Iran."[11] In August 1941, the British Embassy reported that Germans had been "planning a coup" in Iran.[12] Nazis had also found willing allies in leaders of the Qashgai tribes who not only helped hide two of Nazi Germany's spymasters—Berthold Schulze-Holthus and Franz Mayer—in their midst, but declared themselves ready to help a massive uprising in favor of Germany.[13]

Another reliable source told the British Embassy about a planned "attempt on the life of [Reza] Shah and the declaration of a republic in August 1941."[14] Documents from Nazi archives confirm some of these reports and show, in detail, the German government's effort to bring about a coup to end the Pahlavi era. One of the Pahlavi dynasty's nemeses, Ahmad Qavam, was an accomplice and the designated leader of one such failed coup attempt.[15] Other sources suggest General Ayrom as the coup leader.

As a countermeasure to these Nazi and Soviet conspiracies, the British government began to develop two contingency plans. They took steps to create a network of "organizations capable of operating in territory threatened with invasion." Their job would be to stiffen "the resistance of the national forces and population against Soviet encroachment."[16] According to the British and American embassies, during this period the Nazis too were busy trying to build a pro-Nazi militia network. It was believed that the German Embassy could, through its secret network, place "500 tough and well-armed men in the streets of Tehran within a few hours."[17]

The second contingency plan called for the occupation of the oil-rich southern regions of Iran. From the time oil was discovered in Khuzestan and the British landed a contract affording them monopoly rights over it, they had considered Iran's southern regions as their "sphere of interest."[18] They were interested in the rest of the country only to the extent that it allowed them to keep control of the oil fields. More than once, including the days when Reza Khan organized his coup in 1921, they had entertained plans to simply separate the oil-rich province of Khuzestan from Iran altogether if that was the only way they could keep their hands on the oil fields.

Reza Shah took false comfort in the belief that Iran's often-declared neutrality would suffice to keep him and the country safe from the engulfing flames of the coming war. He might have been banking on a Nazi victory in the war. He was more interested in training his Crown Prince to assume power, and preparing the army and the nation to take orders from a new king. In fact, in his memoirs, the Shah claims that a few years before the advent of the war, his father had even contemplated resigning from the throne, to "stay around as an elder statesman, and avail me of his advice."[19] It is impossible to confirm this claim. Even for the Shah, the story was nothing but hearsay. As the Shah himself admits, his father never discussed the resignation idea even with him. Only long after Reza Shah's death did a close aide reveal the alleged plan to the Shah. There is, however, no doubt that from 1939, Reza Shah was beginning to groom his Crown Prince more actively for his future responsibilities. He took the Crown Prince to more official functions and inspections and ordered every new ambassador to Tehran to call on the Crown Prince after they had presented their credentials to Reza Shah—as diplomatic protocol required.

Reza Shah also began to use his Crown Prince as an interpreter in some of the most sensitive negotiations with foreign officials. On June 17, 1939, when Lord Cadman, the storied British oilman, met with Reza Shah, "HIM, the Crown Prince was also present and acted as interpreter." The conversations were reportedly useful, and as a result, "it is openly stated in the capital" that the Anglo-Iranian oil company would pay 2 million pounds "as advance on royalties, or as a gift to the Shah."[20]

Amongst those making courtesy calls on the Crown Prince was Sir Reader Bullard, the British ambassador, who made just such a visit in January 1940. He found the "manner of the Prince... more engaging than that of [Reza] Shah, but the cynical gloom of the father" had become "in the son a pessimistic petulance which he does not attempt to restrain." According to the same report, the Crown Prince "[took] a keen interest in public affairs" and followed events in Europe rather carefully. He considered the war "a nuisance" and thought it could have been prevented. He criticized Western strategies on both the diplomatic and military plains. It was, he believed, "a great pity" that "Germany had been driven into the arms of Russia."[21] And foreshadowing his future love of military matters, and his tendency to think himself a great military strategist, he even offered strong opinions about the conduct of the war, and the military decisions of generals. Bullard reported this part of his conversation with the equivalent of a smirk on his prose. By then, he had developed this prosaic smirk into an art.

Another sign of the changing times came on October 27, 1940. The Crown Prince's twenty-first birthday was celebrated throughout the country with greater-than-usual fanfare. In the morning there was a ceremony at the Court where government officials and commanding officers of the armed forces offered their congratulations and paid allegiance to the future king.

As in previous years, the centerpiece of the celebration had been a grand exhibit by Iran's Boy Scouts. Participation in paramilitary exercise had become part of the curriculum for every school in the country, and the Boy Scouts were one of the ways of inculcating Spartan ways and values in the impressionable minds of the youth. Boys often practiced up to six weeks preparing for the Crown Prince's birthday celebration, rehearsing their march and other feats of wondrous discipline and coordination. That year the Crown Prince attended the event with a special guest. His name was Baldur von Schirach, the storied leader of Hitler's infamous youth movement, the Hitlerjugend. Von Schirach participated in the celebrations standing next to the Crown Prince.[22] He later became a poster boy for Nazi propaganda and an infamous convict at the Nuremburg Trials.

Part of that year's program called for the Boy Scouts to exhibit their dexterity and prowess in putting out a fire. The script called for them to set up tents in a makeshift camp, and then, when one of the tents caught fire, the Scouts would work in tandem, quickly creating a queue and passing buckets of water to put it out. But instead of a controlled fire, as the script stipulated, the tent was suddenly engulfed in flames. Instead of a choreographed show of discipline and creativity, hundreds of frightened boys, forgetting any semblance of order, panicked and fled the scene in utter chaos, embarrassing the grown-ups.[23] In retrospect, the Boy Scout spectacle, the failure of the organizers to practice even once with an actual fire, and the poor planning in setting a tent on fire, all foreshadowed what would be the surprisingly quick collapse of the Iranian military.

In spite of the joyous mood of official celebrations in 1940, "The Annual Political Report" prepared by the British Embassy in Tehran for that year offers a grim image of realities in Iran. The 1940 report describes Reza Shah as "the mainspring of all activities" in the country. He appeared to many in the diplomatic corps "more greedy, more arrogant, and more unpopular" than before. By 1940, there was a palpable perception amongst the populace that every mailbox in the country was under police surveillance, and that anyone seen putting a suspicious envelope, particularly one critical of the King, into a mailbox would be arrested.[24]

Reza Shah did not even see foreign diplomats except at "formal visits." The British Ambassador, for example, had not met Reza Shah in private for more than three years. Reports from the American Embassy in Iran confirm that the same was true about other ambassadors. There is "ample evidence that Ministers habitually give the Shah hasty and optimistic reports." A shortage of bread causing long lines had created new waves of public resentment. Nobody in the royal family, according to the British Embassy, including the Crown Prince, enjoyed the support and goodwill of the people.[25]

Reza Shah, according to the "Annual Report," continued to be "morbidly sensitive" to any reference in the foreign press that is not adulatory, and thus within a year, this led to diplomatic rows with "the American, Swedish, and Swiss legations." In 1939 Iran broke diplomatic ties with France over a magazine's use of two homophonic words—the Persian word Shah, and the French *chat*, meaning cat—for a comical pun. Two years later, another article in the French press led to another suspension of diplomatic ties. The Crown Prince was intimately involved in the way Iran responded to what it considered the insulting pun, telling his father of a new law in France prohibiting attacks on heads of state.[26] In fact, in the heat of negotiations between Iran and France over this controversy, the Iranian ministers of Foreign Affairs and Culture met directly with the Crown Prince instead of with Reza Shah and took orders from him about how to proceed.[27] The experience seemed to have had a formative influence on the Crown Prince: all his life, he too remained obsessively sensitive to every imagined slight in the Western media, and he invariably saw an elaborate conspiracy behind each such criticism.

The "Annual Report" went on to say that Reza Shah "entertains for economic development a feverish passion which in many cases is heightened by a personal and financial interest."[28] In spite of the economic gains in the country, according to the British Embassy, dissatisfaction was widespread, and the government's only "remedy . . . is a vigilant police, a controlled press and now a controlled wireless broadcast service. Tehran radio was opened in April."[29] The Crown Prince took part in the official launch of the studio.

Fear of public incitements to riots and regicide were great enough that the Iranian press remained silent on the subject of the failed attempt on the life of King Farouk, the Crown Prince's brother-in-law, and even on the Munich assassination attempt against Hitler.[30] The accumulated result of the discontent and political dysfunction was the British Embassy's conclusion that there is little chance "that the Pahlavi dynasty will maintain itself."[31] What makes this prediction less an indication of British prescience but more of rancor between them and Reza Shah is the fact that the British had made the same dire predictions as early as 1926. In October of that year, for example, the British *chargé* in Tehran wrote that, "I do not think there are too many intelligent men in Persia who imagine that [Reza] Shah can for long maintain his throne."[32]

For the royal family, maybe the only good news of that year came on October 27, when the Crown Prince and his wife, Princess Fawzia, had their first child, a girl named Shahnaz.[33]

While Reza Shah was preoccupied with domestic developments, the European war inched closer to Iran every day. He made every effort to maintain an air of normalcy in the country, but try as he might, the European war was never as remote as he liked to pretend. Even his attempt to assuage British anxieties by appointing, in July 1941, the notoriously Anglophile Ali Mansur as prime minister and dismissing the no less Germanophile prime minister, Ahmad Matin-Daftary, was of no avail. Only four days after the Nazi invasion of the Soviet Union, Britain and the Soviet Union delivered a threatening note to Iran about what they perceived was the danger of Nazi presence in the country. In the note they claimed that there were more than 5,000 German nationals in Iran. In the parlance of World War II, such a large population was the perfect embryo for a Nazi "fifth column." By then, Hitler had reneged on his 1939 Non-Aggression Pact with the Soviet Union—a disingenuous pact both sides signed only to buy themselves time for what they knew was the inevitable war between them. When the pact was broken, the Soviet Union and Britain became allies and worried about the German presence in Iran—a presence made even more dangerous by the fact that many Germans worked in the Iranian state-run railroad system. By then it was clear that this railroad was a key to supplying the badly beleaguered Soviet army. The rapidly advancing Nazi forces inside the Soviet Union were moving toward the oil fields of Baku, and thus the Iranian border. The fact that eight Axis ships were also anchored off the Iranian port of Bandar Shapur made the Russo-British fears about a German threat more plausible.[34]

In retrospect, however, it seems clear that for the Allies, talk of the German "fifth column" was as much a tactical tool of propaganda as it was a genuine military concern. While the American Embassy in Tehran put the number of German nationals in Iran at about 2,500, about half the figure claimed by the British, even the British Embassy in Iran considered its own government's claims exaggerated. As late as July 1941, Sir Reader Bullard had indicated that, in his view, the "number of Germans in Iran is not more than 2000 including dependents."[35] When the Ambassador finally wrote a memo to the Foreign Office, indicating his belief about the exaggerated nature of the British government's claim, Winston Churchill was angry enough to write a terse note to the Foreign Secretary himself, saying, "Your Minister in Tehran does not seem to be at all at the level of events. . . . I feel this business requires your personal grip."[36] Churchill had declared earlier that "we mean to get the Germans [in Iran] in our hands, if we have to come to Tehran and invite the Russians there too.... Undoubtedly, we must acquire complete military control of Persia during the war."[37]

Reza Shah all but ignored these increasingly threatening notes and other hints of British and Soviet anxiety. Clearly, the Crown Prince, who accompanied his father constantly in those days, made no effort to change Reza Shah's views. Father and son both believed, and reiterated often to foreign or domestic visitors, that Iran, and only Iran, could decide which foreigners worked in the country.

While spending his days with his father, the Crown Prince's nights were spent at Court with a small group of friends, nearly all foreign-trained technocrats or married to a foreigner, gambling, playing parlor games, or watching movies. One night early in 1941, when he and his friends were enjoying a few drinks and playing a card game, Reza Shah suddenly walked in. He had never come to any of these events unannounced, and his appearance shocked everyone into silence. The Crown Prince was a serious smoker in those days and had a cigarette in his hand. He too got up, standing at military attention, and, lest his father see him smoking, he hid the cigarette in his hand behind his back.

Reza Shah had come to inquire about progress on a building project. The visit, to the Crown Prince's relief, lasted only a few minutes. While Reza Shah's nocturnal visit showed his desire to attend to all affairs of state, he nevertheless ignored threatening notes from Britain and the Soviet Union. Was his failure to take them seriously the result of his arrogance, his ignorance of international realities, his calculation, or even the hope that Hitler's early victories on the Eastern Front would translate into Axis victory in the war? Some have argued that Anglophile politicians, particularly Ali Mansur, Iran's prime minister at the time, intentionally kept Reza Shah in the dark about the seriousness of the threats. Theirs, it is claimed, was a premeditated act of treason intended to pave the way for the British invasion of Iran. After the British Ambassador met with Reza Shah to deliver the first serious note of threat, he came away convinced that Reza Shah "had been kept badly informed by his ministers as to the state of negotiations."[38] When reminiscing about his life while he was in exile, Reza Shah offered a different reason for his inaction. He told Fereydoon Jam, his favorite son-in-law, that in his view, "Iran had no reason to help the Allies, and besides the war did not indicate who would emerge as the victor."[39] The Shah, on the other hand, suggests that the cabinet did not tell his father the truth because they were "too afraid... to tell him that the Allies were intent on forcefully carrying out their threats."[40] Even after twenty years, when the Shah looked at the letters exchanged between Iran and the Allies, he still categorically rejected the idea that the Germans' presence presented any threat to the Allies. Furthermore, Mohammad Reza Shah rejected the claim that his father harbored Nazi sympathies. With surprising candor and naiveté, he declared, "because my father had himself dictatorial tendencies, he could not have tolerated another dictator like Hitler."[41]

After the receipt of the initial note of protest from the Anglo-Soviet allies in 1941, the Iranian government had initially declared, in a defiant tone of wounded nationalist pride, that the work of Germans in Iran was a matter concerning the sovereign Iranian government and no one else. Two days after the receipt of the initial threat, Reza Shah gave one of his characteristically short speeches—this one to a class of graduating officers—and though he made no direct reference to the threat, he declared that all leaves of absence for officers had been cancelled. He ended by suggesting that "the army and its officers must take an active interest in the present situation and if need be, must be prepared to sacrifice their lives."[42]

The next day, the semi-official daily paper, *Etela'at*, published an editorial calling on the people to "action and sacrifice to save the nation's honor."[43] In meeting with diplomats, Reza Shah insisted that "the war was no business of his" and when a cash-strapped British government asked for a respite in the annual payment of oil revenues to Iran—increased substantially after a new round of negotiations in 1940—Reza Shah demurred, insisting instead "on a guaranteed minimum four million pounds a year, for two years, and a payment down of arrears."[44] Iran's urgent need to industrialize, Reza Shah told the British Ambassador, was far more important than the war in distant Europe. After the meeting, Bullard poignantly captured his government's frustrations with Reza Shah when he wrote that "Reza Shah has twisted the lion's tail often enough over the oil concessions to get the erroneous idea that our patience is almost unlimited."[45] The angry notes Britain delivered to Iran on those August days signaled the end of the "lion's patience."

But Iran gradually changed its defiant tune and took, particularly in private, a far more conciliatory attitude. Iranian officials began to declare repeatedly that the actual number of German officials in the country was less than a thousand, and that all of them were under the tight control of the Iranian police. To assuage Britain's concern about Nazi sabotage in Iran's oil-rich regions, Iran "ordered all German nationals to leave those provinces."[46] The day after receiving the first threatening note, Iranian officials informed the British Embassy that they had already arrested three of the top Nazi operatives in Iran, and that they had launched "a program . . . of expelling about thirty Germans a month."[47] Yet, it was far too little and far too late.

Reza Shah and the Crown Prince both failed to recognize how serious the British and Soviet governments were about the Nazi threat, and this failure provided the British and Soviet governments with the excuse they so desperately needed for their planned invasion of Iran. Finally, around four o'clock in the morning on August 25, 1941, in an operation code-named Countenance, the British and Soviet forces invaded Iran from the south and the north.

On the day of the invasion, Reza Shah came to lunch with his family looking so tense that none of his children, including the Crown Prince, dared to speak. The Allies have invaded Iran, Reza Shah told his family, and that "will be the end for me—the English will see to it."[48] Earlier that day, immediately upon hearing of the invasion, Reza Shah had asked for an emergency meeting with the ambassadors of both countries. His anxiety at lunch was at least partially the result of what had transpired during this dread meeting.

When the two ambassadors arrived at the Court around ten in the morning, Reza Shah tried to reassure them by suggesting, "if [your countries'] only objection was about the Germans...I am ready to send away all Germans within one week, with few exceptions."[49] But by then armies of both countries had already entered Iranian territory.

Before the end of that day, Reza Shah also wrote an urgent plea to President Roosevelt, declaring that "Russian and British forces have crossed brusquely and without prior notice" into Iran and had begun bombing open cities "without defense." Reza Shah went on to "beg Your Excellency to take efficacious and urgent humanitarian steps to put an end to these acts of aggression."[50] In those days, and well into the next decade, the United States enjoyed a special position in the minds of many in the Iranian political class. From the nationalist Dr. Mohammad Mossadeq—as subsequent events showed—to Reza Shah, as his telegram to President Roosevelt exhibited, many in Iran's elite saw the United States as a potential ally in the country's fight against the two chief colonial foes—Russia and Britain. Indeed Iran's relationship with the United States had begun in 1850, during the tenure of Amir Kabir, the reformist prime minister who wanted to use the Americans as a countervailing force against his colonial enemies. In the same spirit, even before sending his urgent plea to Roosevelt, Reza Shah had tried to get the United States interested in Iran's security by offering to buy eighty American warplanes for Iran's fledgling air force.[51] Iran also asked an American company to undertake the construction "and equipment of an airline factory in Iran."[52] Even more enticing was the fact that representatives of Standard Oil were invited to Iran, and a major new trade agreement was put on the table by Iran.[53]

In these efforts, Reza Shah and soon afterwards his son were making the same mistake as other Iranian politicians before and after them. They all overlooked the vast and complicated web of U.S. relations with an ally like the British; Iranian leaders wrongly assumed that America would jeopardize these relations simply for the promise, or even the reality, of a bigger piece of the Iranian market. Not only did the United States decide against the sale of American bombers to

Iran, but after pressure from the British, who feared the "planes might be utilized against the British forces"—arguments incidentally that the U.S. officials found cynical and self-serving—[54] the proposal for the construction of a plant was also rejected. Reza Shah probably did not know when he wrote his urgent plea that Roosevelt had been consulted on every stage of the planned Soviet–British invasion of Iran. A full week before Reza Shah learned of the Soviet–British occupation of Iran, Roosevelt had received a copy of the letter and had been fully briefed about the exact timetable for the invasion. The British did not want Reza Shah to find comfort in the hope that the United States would come to his aid. After successfully blocking the sale of American airplanes to Iran, Churchill suggested that the U.S. government ask its representative in Iran to accompany the Russian and British ambassadors when they delivered their declaration of war, or at least find ways to inform the Iranian government that America supported "the British and Russian point of view" and considered the steps they were taking right and necessary and, finally, believed that "Iran should meet"[55] the demands made by these two countries.

Roosevelt rejected both ideas, and his decision in this case, and on a number of other issues, was a blow to British plans. There was considerable tension between Sir Reader Bullard, with his haughty colonial manners, and the humane disposition of the American ambassador, Louis Dreyfus, a preacher turned diplomat who despised some of the bare-knuckle tactics of his British counterpart. Bullard concluded that the United States and Britain did not share the same goals in Iran.[56] These were only the first hints of the reality that, behind the rhetoric of the Atlantic Charter and the amity between the United States and Britain, there were, from 1940, serious tensions and at times intense rivalries for power and influence between the two countries over Iran. The British frustration with the United States was poignantly captured by Sir Alexander Cadogan, Britain's permanent under-secretary at the Foreign Ministry during the war, when he wrote, "Americans becoming impossible at all points. Americans are lecturing us now on Persian [affairs], about which they know nothing. I urge that we should put our foot down. It will only be more difficult and dangerous later."[57]

In spite of any misgiving Roosevelt might have had about the British policy, he decided to take a long time to answer Reza Shah's urgent plea. He clearly did not want to give him any false hopes. The meaningful delay dismayed many of Iran's pro-American liberals who had hoped to use American goodwill to rid Iran of British and Russian influence.[58]

In his belated response, FDR assured Reza Shah that he had "been following the course of events in Iran with close attention." In an obvious but biting reference to the allegations of Reza Shah's pro-Nazi sympathies, Roosevelt suggested that the situation in Iran must be viewed "in full perspectives of the world event," and in light of "considerations arising from Hitler's ambition for world conquest." The last few lines of FDR's otherwise vapid reply turned out to have historic significance, particularly in the months after the end of hostilities in the Second World War. Roosevelt informed Reza Shah that he had received assurances from the British and Soviet governments that "they have no designs on the independence and territorial integrity of Iran."[59]

But on the day of the Soviet-British invasion, when Reza Shah wrote his urgent plea, the question of postwar Soviet plans was eclipsed by the grim realities of the hour. As news of the Allied invasion reached the Court, Reza Shah panicked, and the entire edifice of power in Iran began to crumble into near anarchy. The microcosm of the royal family mirrored developments in the social macrocosm. The institutions Reza Shah had willed into existence in Iran, no less than the marriages he had forcefully arranged for his children, all began to collapse.

By then, the marriages of his two daughters were already nothing but a charade. Each princess was involved with secret paramours. The Crown Prince's own marriage was made rocky by his continuous and increasingly open philandering. Stories of his affairs were the favorite gossip of high society and a tool of subversion in the hands of the opposition. Often, the Crown Prince was seen driving around the city in one of his favorite convertible cars. Whispers about his love for a beautiful young girl named Firuzeh were common knowledge.* His wife, Princess Fawzia, also suffered from the adversarial relationships that had developed between her and the Crown Prince's aggressively domineering and possessive mother and at least one of his sisters. Fawzia herself was timid and shy and felt lonely and under siege. All the "Egyptian servants" who had come with her to Iran were dismissed and even the "Egyptian ambassador and his family," who were her relatives and had been assigned to Tehran primarily to keep her happy, "were seldom permitted to see HIM, the Crown Princess Fawzia."[60]

By the second day of the invasion, British and Soviet planes, with the latter's unmistakable red star shining on some of their wings, continued to attack the capital and other big cities. Though the casualties were minimal—in Tehran, for example, only two people were reported killed by the attacks—the continued bombardment of open cities brought fear and terror to the defenseless citizens of the country. Soviet planes appeared on Tehran's horizon, then flew overhead to drop leaflets, warning the citizens of an impending attack. The much-vaunted, much-feared Iranian military collapsed in panic around the country. So much of Reza Shah's time and energy and so much of the country's budget had been spent on building this army that the embarrassing rapidity of the collapse left a

* In deference to the privacy of the lady, I have chosen not to divulge her last name. As it happened, I saw her once when she was a septuagenarian. Even the ravages of time could not hide all hints of her beauty.

permanent mark on the mind of the young Crown Prince. Never again, he would often vow later, would the Iranian army be so defenseless in the face of adversity. During his own reign, he used this argument to legitimize his increasingly ambitious plans to expand and modernize the Iranian army.

In 1941, however, before the end of the second day, the army's top brass met to discuss surrender. When Reza Shah learned of his generals' temerity in convening such a meeting in his absence, and of their decision to decree the summary surrender of the military, he beckoned General Ahmad Nakhjavan, the top army commander and the ostensible minister of war, to the Court. In a now famous confrontation, Reza Shah used profanity-laced language to belittle the petrified general, beat the man with a stick, tore off his stars, and finally grabbed the hapless general's pistol and seemed bent on executing him on the spot. The Crown Prince was a silent observer of the spectacle. As his father's now-constant companion, the two men consulted on virtually every decision.[61] In fact, according to Nakhjavan, he and the other generals made their decision to surrender only after they called the Crown Prince and received his blessing.[62] On the day the General was pistol-whipped, the Crown Prince finally convinced his father that the General's life should be spared and that, instead of instant execution, he should be sent to prison to face court-martial. He did not volunteer the fact that the frightened general apparently had consulted him before the meeting.

The Crown Prince also played a crucial role in other key decisions in the first forty-eight hours after the invasion. By the time Fereydoon Jam, Reza Shah's son-in-law, arrived at the palace, the scene was, even to him, unfathomable. As he drove through the city, he had seen disbanded army units aimlessly wandering about and soldiers and officers, sometimes in civilian clothes, sometimes wearing portions of their discarded uniforms, roaming nervously through the streets. Many of the solders were barefoot. Soon the city was abuzz with rumors of generals fleeing covered under women's veils. In the macho culture of the time, fleeing the scene of a fight, let alone doing so dressed as women, was as debilitating as any allegation. Another rumor reported an imminent attack on Reza Shah's palace by disgruntled officers of Iran's fledgling air force. Jam had witnessed the utter chaos at the army headquarters, and he had been an eyewitness to the anxious and frightened looks on people's faces as they scrambled through the half-closed shops for the last supplies of food and water. Tehran had no running water in those days and, depending on their social rank, people had to find water to drink, water to irrigate their yards, water to fill their pools or ponds, and water to take baths. A rumor had spread throughout the city that the Red Army was about to enter and occupy Tehran, and that once there, they would go door to door, executing any member of the Iranian military.

In anxious anticipation, many in the military made bonfires in their homes and burned any uniforms, insignias, or other indications of their military connection.[63] Even after witnessing these apocalyptic images of the collapse of a once-disciplined army, and the chaos in a once-regimented city, the young Jam was ill-prepared for what he saw at the Court—which had been, only a few hours earlier, the intimidating seat of power and majesty in the capital.

Reza Shah was in the palace, pacing alone in the abandoned gardens. Even the military guards of the Court had abandoned their posts. Members of the royal family, including the Crown Prince, had taken refuge in the Sa'ad Abad Palace compound. The Queen Mother was inconsolable over the disappearance of Najmeh Naneh, her favorite servant and companion. The arrival of Jam, armed with a pistol and a rifle, brought a semblance of comfort to the frightened royal family.[64]

By late that evening, it was decided that most of the royal family—particularly the women and children—should leave the capital under the cover of night and head for Isfahan, a city still not occupied by either the British or Russian forces. Reza Shah and the Crown Prince would remain in Tehran and attend to the business of the beleaguered state. Jam, with his pistol and rifle, was asked to drive the lead car, with Princess Ashraf and Crown Princess Fawzia sitting in the front seat of Jam's Buick. The Queen Mother, her daughter Shams, and a servant were in the back. A second car carried Shahnaz and her nurse as well as Shahram—Ashraf's new-born son—and his attendant. Before long, the Crown Prince's friend Hussein Fardust joined the royal sojourners. He spent the first night awake, holding guard. After a couple of days he was recalled to Tehran, where he would be the Crown Prince's most trusted lieutenant. There was, according to Jam, no guarantee that the traveling members of the royal family would come to no harm should they run into one of the gangs roaming the city streets and country roads.[65] Lucky for them, their nocturnal journey ended without incident. By the next day, they were in the relative safety of Isfahan.

For Reza Shah and the Crown Prince, the invasion and the departure of their families from Tehran was not the only bad news of the day. On the night after the invasion, the BBC began a series of programs attacking Reza Shah for his despotism, his breach of the constitution, and the millions and millions of dollars he had allegedly stashed away in banks, domestic and foreign. It was a "seven days weekly Persian Program" to expedite "the recommendations of the Embassy in Tehran," particularly in criticizing Reza Shah.[66]

The country was mesmerized by these nightly programs. In Tehran, streets emptied as the hour of the nightly broadcast neared. They were a potent brew of gossip and politics, facts and fictions, and real news and fantastic rumors. The Persians, who had long believed in the omnipotence of the "British hand," and had always assumed the BBC to be nothing but a handmaiden of British power and the voice of empire, construed the broadcasts as a clear indication that Reza Shah's days were now numbered. By then German radio, launched in conjunction with the Nazis' vast propaganda in Iran, had suddenly changed its tune. Until then the radio had been full of profuse praise for Reza Shah for standing up to British and Bolshevik bullying tactics. But now, as Iran began to throw out German citizens, Nazi radio began to attack Reza Shah. In their programs, the towering voice of Bahram Shahrokh had come to embody the Nazis' aggressive foreign policy.

A few days after the commencement of the BBC attacks, Reza Shah tried to save his throne by sacking Mansur, the incompetent Anglophile prime minister, and replacing him with Zoka al-Mulk Foroughi, an esteemed elder statesman, assumed by Reza Shah to be close to the British. The British Embassy clearly understood the meaning of the new gesture and reported to the Foreign Office that the Foroughi appointment was "intended to conciliate us." To Bullard, it was clear that with the appointment Reza Shah also hoped to enlist "British support against the Russians," and warned that these developments must be most carefully watched.[67]

Changing the prime minister was not Reza Shah's only conciliatory move. On September 7, he summoned the American ambassador, Dreyfus, to the Court, ostensibly to thank President Roosevelt for the belated response to his urgent message. In reality, Reza Shah wanted to solicit the assistance of the American government in his effort to retain his throne. He told the Ambassador "that he has no sympathy for the Germans," and that "he wanted the British to know his views, and had no objection to bringing the above to the British Minister's attention."[68]

As requested, the American Ambassador conveyed the message to the British representatives in Tehran. The initial response was not unfavorable. "If [Reza] Shah is willing to cooperate fully with the British and correct some of his more serious shortcomings," the British Ambassador said, "I believe he may still be able to save his throne."[69] As late as September 3, Churchill declared that "at the present time we have not turned against the Shah," but unless he can give "loyal and fateful help and show all proper alacrity" his "misgovernment of his people will be brought into account."[70] Churchill's note, as well as numerous other documents from the British archives, shows that when the British attacked Iran, they still did not have a clear and definitive plan to end Reza Shah's rule, or a clear idea about what or who should succeed him. The Persian habit of affording the British hand omnipotence begot the assumption that the BBC attacks were but a first step in an already clearly laid out plan of action, including ending Reza Shah's rule.

A few days after meeting with the American Ambassador, Reza Shah sent Zoka al-Mulk Foroughi, the new prime minister, and Mohammad Saed, the foreign minister, to the British Embassy to ask "what the broadcasts in Persian meant, and whether they could not be stopped." Clearly Reza Shah had sent the emissaries to try and convince the British to stop the incendiary broadcasts. But instead of pleading Reza Shah's case, his emissaries seemed bent on encouraging the British to get rid of him. Foroughi, who had been forced into early retirement by Reza Shah and had seen his son-in-law sent to the firing squad by Reza Shah, now had the King's fate in his hands. It is hard to know his motive, but from the outset, he and Saed made it clear to the British Ambassador that "they had been merely acting as a mouthpiece." More crucially, Foroughi added that "the Shah can be persuaded to abdicate." He also made it clear that Persians like him would not "take any action" to force the abdication of Reza Shah unless they knew "it will not be contrary to the wishes" of Britain. The word within the word of Foroughi's response was clear: people want to be rid of Reza Shah but they won't dare to move unless the British government moves. The Ambassador assured Foroughi that "if they concluded that the Shah must go, His Majesty's government would not interfere." Could Reza Shah have remained on the throne if Foroughi and Saed had simply conveyed in earnest the message they were sent to deliver? Would the British government have acted differently if it had not heard the complaints of two key Iranian politicians? Surely these are the kinds of historical questions that make for good parlor games but are indeed impossible to answer. But one thing does seem certain: without the cooperation and advice of Iranians like Foroughi, the British and the Soviets could never have carried out their plans.

Once Foroughi and Saed were assured that forcing Reza Shah to abdicate was not contrary to Britain's plans, the question of succession was discussed. Both emissaries made it clear that in their view, "the Crown Prince was the best candidate." The British Ambassador was not easily convinced, venturing to say that the Crown Prince had become "obnoxious to His Majesty's government" and that the Soviet government was also "unfavorably inclined" toward him.[71] To their credit, Foroughi and Saed stood their ground and insisted on the wisdom of the Crown Prince's replacing his father.

As to the issue of the BBC attacks on Reza Shah, the embassy of course repeated, as was its wont, that the BBC was altogether independent from the British government. In fact, during those months, directions for the programs critical of Reza Shah and suggestions on their content were sent from the embassy in Iran. Even before these attacks began, the British government had decided to retool its propaganda in Iran. The embassy had criticized the fact that "the Persian news broadcasts contain occasional complimentary references to the [Reza] Shah and his modernizing policy." Such references, it declared, "should easily be omitted."[72]

One of the most incendiary parts of the new programs attacking Reza Shah were allegations about his massive fortune, much of it allegedly ill-gotten and stashed away in foreign accounts. Sometimes exact and, by the standards of the time, astronomical estimates of Reza Shah's fortune were given by the BBC. Based on these reports, it was hard not to assume that the British government and the BBC must have had detailed knowledge about Reza Shah's wealth. Thus these stories about Reza Shah's fantastic fortunes became accepted as gospel truth. The question of this fortune, its size and source, the tactics used to accumulate it, and finally, what should be done with it became not only the first crisis faced by the Crown Prince when he became Shah, but continued to haunt him for the rest of his political life. Documents from the British and American Embassies on the eve of the 1979 Islamic Revolution make it clear that the question of the Shah's fortune, and the alleged corruption of his family, was, as in 1941, easily one of the most potent issues raised by the opposition. Even in exile, in his famous interview with David Frost, the Shah was repeatedly asked about the extent of his wealth, and he was more coy than angry about it.

The woman who in 1941 drafted "the material for the BBC Persian broadcasts"[73] against Reza Shah went on to become a nemesis of Mohammad Reza Shah and one of the most influential scholars and advisors to the British government. Her name was Ann Lambton. During the war years, she was the cultural attaché at the British Embassy. In later years, she returned to the abstract world of British Oriental Studies and wrote seminal works on such topics as the medieval history of Iran and the history of Iranian agriculture and land reform. Nevertheless, she played a crucial role in determining the British policy toward Dr. Mossadeq in 1951. It was clear that British officials believed that "she knows as much about Persia as anyone," and thus when Lambton talked, Whitehall listened.[74] Her influence over British policy continued well into the 1960s.

In 1941, her directive to BBC, titled "Some of the Acts of Reza Shah," included fourteen items, ranging from making the Majlis "his rubber stamp," beating his ministers" with a kick or "the flat of his sword," neglecting agriculture, forbidding "cultivation of rice in Isfahan . . . to protect his own rice from the Caspian from competition," and even using water to irrigate the flowers of the palace instead of sharing it with the people.[75]

Incredible as these attacks were, they were still not enough to force Reza Shah to abdicate. What truly sealed Reza Shah's fate—aside from the belief of those like Foroughi who were convinced he could no longer stay in power—was the decision of the Soviet army to move toward Tehran and occupy it. More accurately, simply the rumor of an imminent Soviet incursion morally crushed the city, and Reza Shah, who had built his reputation partially on his anti-Communism, decided that he must not only leave the city but also abdicate. Hundreds of the city's richest families also fled upon hearing the news of the Red Army's anticipated arrival.[76]

If Reza Shah's abdication was intended to ensure the continuation of the Pahlavi dynasty, there was, in the early hours and days after the announcement, no guarantee that the gesture would have the intended consequence. Britain and the Soviet Union, as the two occupying forces, were at first reluctant to approve the ascent of the Crown Prince. When the soon-to-be-Shah went to the parliament to take the oath of office, only the Soviet and British Legations were pointedly absent from the gallery set aside for the diplomatic corps. They had earlier informed the Iranian Foreign Ministry, which had invited the entire diplomatic corps for the occasion, that they had "no instructions regarding the succession of the Crown Prince."[77]

In fact, the British were seriously considering either ending the Pahlavi dynasty and restoring the Qajars to the throne or changing the nature of the regime and creating a republic. Neither alternative worked. Foroughi and Saed were the first two candidates considered for the post of president, and they both flatly refused the offer, suggesting instead that in their view Iran still needed a monarchy headed by the Crown Prince.[78] While the two men had betrayed Reza Shah and had advocated his abdication instead of carrying his message of reconciliation to the British, they were also instrumental in preserving the Pahlavi dynasty itself. The search for a viable candidate for the Qajar "restoration" turned out to be even more problematic than finding a willing and capable president.

That search led the British authorities to the "natural" successor, Prince Hamid, the son of the last Qajar Crown Prince, Mohammad Hassan Mirza. In a strange twist of fate, in the early thirties the same Prince Hamid had caught the attention of Reza Shah. What had seemed at the time like a perfect example of Reza Shah's pathological paranoia became in 1941 the absurd truth. In 1934, the British paper the *Evening Standard* printed a picture of Prince Hamid, showing him saluting the British flag. He had just joined the Royal Navy, having become a British citizen even earlier. But that was not why his picture had appeared in the paper in 1934. It was there because he was playing the role of Caliban in a local production of Shakespeare's *The Tempest.* Caliban was a "native" who was enslaved by Prospero, the Duke of Milan. The Duke had lost his power due to his brother's treachery. Prospero was put on a boat, set to roam the open seas. He ended up on an island where he enslaved the natives, and one of them, Caliban, became his servant—he served the master and in return learned how to curse in the new language of Prospero. Trying to decode the dizzying parallels between Shakespeare and the Iranian reality in those years is at best a Sisyphean task, the similarities becoming more sobering the more we ponder the two stories. In 1934, upon seeing the translation of the article—and the fact that such a translation would be shown to him was itself material for fantastic conspiracy theories—Reza Shah grew angry, and saw it as a first step in a British conspiracy to return the Qajars to power. Ironically, even at the time of the paper's publication, the King's anger was not just paranoia.

As it happened, four months after the article appeared, the Foreign Office did indeed began to contemplate "the question of the Qajars" and their possible return to power. The British concluded that there was "no chance now . . . at the same time, the dynasty might find itself brought once more into the limelight through fortuitous circumstances."[79] The abdication of Reza Shah was clearly one such "fortuitous circumstance."

In fact, Prince Hamid recounts witnessing "many meetings in London" between his father and the British officials, all long before Reza Shah's abdication. Eventually, on September 13, 1941, Harold Nicolson, who had served in the Tehran Legation from 1925 to 1927, talked to Mohammad Hassan Mirza about the idea of restoring the Qajar dynasty to the throne. In the course of these discussions, Mirza was asked "whether his son spoke Persian. 'Pas un seul mot.' "[80] But the British, though desperate to find a replacement for the Pahlavi regime, could not fathom the idea of putting on the Peacock Throne a British citizen who spoke no Persian and who was serving in the Royal Navy.

Even Rudyard Kipling might have found the scenario too strange for reality. Nevertheless, when, a few days later, at 4:30 in the afternoon on September 17, 1941, a visibly nervous Mohammad Reza Shah took the oath of office, the Foreign Office had still not given up on the idea of a Qajar restoration. On September 19, the Foreign Office wrote to Bullard, the British ambassador, that "the Crown Prince must be ruled out on account of his well-known pro-German sympathies and we cannot regard [Reza] Shah's abdication in his favor as anything but a ruse to prolong anti-Allied policy. Alternatives one of the younger Pahlavis, or a Qajar restoration."[81]

The reasons for Britain's ultimate failure to find an alternative to the Pahlavi family can be found in a telegram sent from their embassy in Tehran the day after the Shah took the oath of office. First there was the pragmatic consideration that, in Bullard's words, they "could always get rid of [the new Shah] quickly if he proved unsuitable." Accepting the Crown Prince as the new king had the advantage that it was sanctioned by the constitution and was the "solution least disturbing to the country." Finally, the Qajar dynasty, in the embassy's assessment, enjoyed little support. In fact, "PM [Foroughi] is against that dynasty." Another problem with the Qajar dynasty, according to Bullard, was the fact that there "are hundreds of (repeat hundreds of) Qajars in the country, and they are all waiting hungrily, many of them on my doorsteps for return of the days when the country was bled not by one leach but by hundreds."[82]

While these deliberations were going on in London and at the British Embassy in Tehran, at the Court, Foroughi, who had authored Reza Shah's first speech as a king, now drafted Reza Shah's brief note of abdication "using the king's own gold-laced and hand-carved [monnabat kari] pen."[83] The Crown Prince was busy preparing his oath of office.

In spite of all the planning and thinking about what to do in Iran after occupation, the British were surprised not so much by Reza Shah's abdication itself, but by its timing. They grew concerned that once he left Tehran, he might reach "some area not in Allied occupation" and that he might there be tempted to create trouble. The War Cabinet sent an urgent message to the embassy and to military commanders in Tehran saying, "military authorities have been informed that it is important to prevent [Reza Shah], if possible, from leaving Tehran," and that if necessary they should "use force to detain him."[84]

The British were not the only ones surprised by Reza Shah's sudden decision to abdicate. As he was leaving the Court in an unmarked car, the Crown Prince was inclined to leave with his father. He too, according to ministers present at the Court, was worried about what the Russian army might do to him. In fact, when Foroughi first broached the topic of abdication, Reza Shah is reported to have said, "who will replace me; this Crown Prince is sure not up to the job." But now, at the gates of the palace, ministers and the abdicated King finally prevailed over the reluctant Mohammad Reza, convincing him to stay and take over the reins of the state. The Shah alluded to this episode, albeit cryptically, when he wrote that his father "could not stand the infamy of remaining in his capital city when it was occupied by foreign troops. I had of course to obey my father who commanded me to take over the job."[85]

In 1925 Reza Shah had begun his oath of office by declaring, "now that with God's help, I am ascending the throne entrusted to me by the people of Iran, I must declare my plans so that everyone knows that I will, like the past, focus all my efforts towards putting our beloved nation on the path of excellence and progress." Clearly, for Reza Shah, at least at the abstract intellectual level, his legitimacy as the king lay with the support of the people, and the throne was a trust placed in his care by the people. In reality, he had grabbed the throne, but even then, his first instinct had been to create a republic, where ballots, not blood, determined the line of succession. In his oath of office, God played only an auxiliary, enabling role. Reza Shah went on to say, "I hope the Lord will make us victorious in this endeavor."

Mohammad Reza Shah's oath of office, on the other hand, was longer and suffused with the language of faith and of the divine right of anointed kings. Of its ninety-three words, forty-nine were directly related to some religious idea or concept. In the case of Reza Shah, only ten of the total seventy-two words had any relationship to divine rights. Even more revealing are the fundamental philosophical differences between the two oaths. While Reza Shah's oath was that of a modern monarch, his son's trafficked in medieval ideas about the divine right of kings.

Mohammad Reza Shah began his oath by saying in a trembling voice, "I hereby take the Good Omnipotent Lord as witness, and I swear to the Sacred words of Allah, and to whatever is sacred in the eyes of God that I will focus all of my efforts towards safeguarding the borders of the nation, and the rights of the people." He further promised to rule in strict accordance to the constitution, but immediately added that he would "make every effort to promote the Twelver Shiism," and "in everything I do I will take the Good Lord as my witness." He ended the oath by beseeching the good grace of God and of the lofty saints of Islam. Contrary to his father's oath, the Shah never acknowledged the proposition that monarchy is a gift given by the people. Moreover, in his oath, Reza Shah did not accept the promotion of Islam as one of the main responsibilities of the king. For the Shah, on the other hand, such promotion was not only one of his key responsibilities, but Allah and the Islamic saints—not the people—were the judges and witnesses, and the source of anointment for all he did.

As the young, reluctant new Shah watched all of this and saw how easily British and Russian power had forced the abdication of his once-omnipotent father, he seemed to have internalized the idea that big powers, particularly Britain, Russia, and America, could do anything in Iran, and that in fact nothing would happen in the country without their overt approval or their covert intrigue. His own thirty-seven-year reign was haunted, even deformed, by this conviction. As Iran's oil revenues increased, and as there was enough money for the Shah to buy all the arms he wished, one of the recurring arguments he made to legitimize the expenditure of such vast sums on the military budget was that he would never again allow another surprise defeat like the one that had befallen his father in August 1941.[86] He could, of course, have learned an entirely different lesson from that experience, concluding that armies, regardless of their majesty and power, cannot save a regime in the face of sustained popular resentment, or that, faced with big powers, little nations can survive not by the sheer power of their military but by the sustained support of their people.

Lest the new Shah had missed the message implicit in his father's abdication, in September 1941, the British Ambassador to Egypt called on the Egyptian Prime Minister. The Ambassador wanted the Egyptians to take a message to the new Shah. They wanted him to pay close attention to his father's fate—to "read, mark, learn and inwardly digest what happened to his father."[87] A copy of the memorandum of this conversation was sent to the British Embassy in Iran, and Egypt was chosen as the conduit for the important message because the King of

Egypt was then the Shah's brother-in-law. The Egyptian Prime Minister immediately began to look for "some genuine Anglophile of sufficient caliber to lead a mission"[88] to Iran. The Shah, it seems, learned the lesson only too well.

His reluctance to take the throne and his belief that his rise to power was part of a divine design for his life and for his country, mixed with the grandiosity that characterized his pronouncements in the petro-crazed seventies, led him to tell a journalist in 1976, "Yes, Karanjia, uneasy is the head that wears the crown and I in particular had inherited a crown of thorns."[89] Mixed metaphors and Shakespearean paraphrase notwithstanding,[90] the words, seen in the context of his early behavior, capture his transformation from a reluctant monarch to a messianic monarch.

Chapter 7

HURLEY'S DREAMS

With mine own tears I wash away my balm,
With mine own hands I give away my crown,
With mine own tongue deny my sacred state,
With mine own breath release all duteous oaths;
All pomp and mystery I do forswear.
Shakespeare, King Richard II, *4.1.201–205*

In politics, the Shah had a baptism by fire. He was a reluctant young king on a shaky throne in the turbulent years of the Second World War amid a hotbed of fierce competition between the war's competing forces. Before the first decade of his tenure ended, he would witness the creation of breakaway republics in two of Iran's biggest provinces, the dawn of the Cold War, an assassination attempt on his life, and open challenges to his power from some of the prime ministers he had reluctantly appointed. During this first decade, the Shah also convened the Constituent Assembly to increase his own constitutional powers. Contrary to the common perception that during his first years in power the Shah happily resigned himself to his limited constitutional role, he was in fact trying to regain as much of his father's power as possible. In the meantime, many in the Western media, enamored with the romance of royalty, were busy turning the new young Shah into an exotic Oriental monarch.

On September 21, 1942, the cover of *Life* magazine was dedicated to a Cecil Beaton portrait of a woman of exotic beauty—she had sad and mournful eyes, pitch-black hair, a perfectly sculpted face, and soft, graceful hands, bereft of the wrinkles of labor, holding a small sprig of blue bells, and she wore an elegantly cut dark dress, strewn with designs of light pansies. A diamond-studded necklace and a cloisonné fish pendant hung from her neck. The caption read: "The Queen of Iran."

The Beaton portrait was a metaphor for an important change in the cultural sensibilities of the Pahlavi Court. Reza Shah had been unmistakably local in his desires and dispositions. The glitterati, the international "jet set," celebrity photography, and haute couture were altogether alien to his tastes. But his oldest son, the new Shah, had been educated in Europe. His wife, Fawzia, was steeped in the modes and manners of European royalty and high fashion. In portraits of her while she was still in Egypt, she wore the hats and the bags, the dresses and the gloves of a Hollywood glamour girl.

Also included in the same issue of *Life* was a picture of a dapper Shah. By the time Beaton came to Tehran, the Shah, too, had already started having his shirts made by the exclusive House of Sulka, in Paris. He was a true creature of habits—the same shirt maker for almost three decades, the same Italian tailor, even the same dentist in Switzerland (where he traveled for regular checkups). Every morning his valet set out for him what he was to wear that morning. Late each night, the valet received a copy of the Shah's engagements for the next day and, based on the exigencies of these meetings, the valet would choose and lay out that day's clothes. Still, the valet's choice was limited to the wardrobe accumulated by the Shah himself. By the mid-seventies, the Shah's strangely large, dark-rimmed glasses, his big-lapelled suits, and his "daring" ties were a radical departure from the staid, somber, trim, and fit contoured suits he was wearing when *Life* magazine published a photo gallery of him and his family in 1942.

Page ninety-six of a war-consumed *Life* showed the Beaton pictures of the Iranian royal family. In spite of the clear attempt by *Life*'s editors to show a happy family, the pictures inadvertently revealed fissures and tensions that would soon break out into the open.

There was a photo of a debonair Shah, sitting on a bench in the palace garden, his daughter on his lap and Queen Fawzia sitting a few noticeable inches away. Their dour expressions betrayed what was by then an open secret in Tehran. The Queen was unhappy. Compared with her family's almost two-centuries-old history of kingship, the Pahlavi royal pedigree was thin, and thus many in the Shah's family construed Fawzia's natural reserve and shyness as a haughty and dismissive demeanor.

The article described Iran as "the threatened supply link between Russia and the Allies." Of the royal marriage, it ventured the guess that "Few marriages have weathered as much. . . . Fawzia's dynasty is a hundred years old and rich. The Shah's only 17 years and poor. The two are different sects of Islam." And finally, alluding to some of the machinations in the Court, it said, "Iranians come to say she had a bad foot (bad luck) as she produced only a daughter."[1] Many years later, in 1961, when the Shah published his memoirs, he claimed for the first time that her failure to produce a male heir was the factor in the breakup of their marriage.[2]

The *Life* article ended by referring to the Shah as a king "on probation." While the Soviet and British governments may have viewed him this way, in reality the Shah was surprisingly active and assertive. In 1941, around the time he took the oath of office, he was busy at the Court, remaking it in his own image. One of his first steps was to dismiss his chief of staff, Moadeb Naficy, who had earlier accompanied him on his Le Rosey journey and was, according to the British Embassy, "a useless yes-man."[3] The new Court minister was Hussein Ala, a seasoned politician who was also the preferred British candidate for the job.[4] According to Ann Lambton, it was "more than anyone else Ala who convinced" the British "that the Crown Prince should be given a chance."[5] Ala was considerably older than the Shah and soon developed a kind of avuncular disposition toward the young monarch. He tried to educate the Shah by giving him useful books to read, including the works of Bernard Shaw. Ala was not the only person trying to educate the young Shah. The British ambassador, Sir Reader Bullard, was also active in this pedagogical effort and, in his own words, "managed to excite the interest of the Shah in Thucydides."[6] In return, the Shah sent Bullard a painted Persian box full of Persian nuts, and the Ambassador lamented that, financially, he was the loser in the deal.[7]

Of the educators, the earliest, of course, was Ernest Perron, who was after Reza Shah's abdication a constant presence at the Court and continued the practice of sharing books and poems with the Shah. The Shah also used him in some of the most sensitive missions, from deciding Court protocol and insisting on courtiers emulating the ways of European courts to acting as the Shah's emissary in contacting foreign embassies, or resolving some of the tensions in the quarrelsome royal family.

⁂

By the time a nervous Shah[8] entered the Majlis around 4:30 in the afternoon on September 17, 1941, and took the oath of office, his father was already on his way out of the country. Another request of the Allies, particularly the British, was that the new Shah expel from Iran Reza Shah's many sons from his four marriages.[9] Most would leave the country with Reza Shah, but the Shah reassured the British that he would also "send away the two remaining members of the royal family, viz his mother and his sister [Princess Ashraf who] is said to hanker after a career in Hollywood."[10] Though the biting tone of the rest of the report is indicative of the embassy's troubled relationship with the Princess, hobnobbing with Hollywood celebrity remained, all her life, something of a passion.[11] Within five years of the Shah's making that promise, every member of the royal family was back in Iran, and before long, Princess Ashraf and the Queen Mother once again took on increasingly powerful and controversial roles in Iran's domestic politics and in the Shah's private life. Within thirty years, Princess Ashraf even found her way to a career in Hollywood, not as an actress but as a producer. But in 1941, the Shah was in no position to "defend" his family's desire to live in Iran.

A photo of the Shah entering the parliament building to take the oath of office captures the frailties of his personality and position. Though dressed in a full military uniform and knee-high boots, with the ornate sword of power dangling from his waist—much like his father in official ceremonies—the young Shah looked tentative, almost sunken and shrunken in his uniform. He had more the defensive pose of an anxious officer than the joyful defiance of a prince bent on putting his seal of authority on a shaky Peacock Throne. A large crowd had gathered outside the parliament to show their support for the King. Why and how they had come there remains the subject of some controversy. The Shah says it was all the spontaneous exhibition of love by his people. In his memoirs, he writes of being "confirmed on the throne by popular support."[12] Some embassies, however, believed the people gathered on the few streets between the Court and the parliament were part of a "rented crowd" gathered by royalists to breathe a whiff of confidence into the Shah's badly shaken resolve. No sooner had the Shah taken the oath of office than he was faced with a plethora of problems. His first challenge was the fate of his father.

The young Shah's first speech after taking the oath of office reflected the precarious position in which his father had left him. He promised to pay "full attention to the principles of a constitutional government" and to the separation of the three branches mandated by law. Every citizen in the country, he said, must be vigilant about our responsibilities and must never lose sight of the limits of governmental power. "I have ordered all government employees," he went on to say, "to make sure that they follow the letter of the law."[13] These promises to abide by the constitution in the future were a clear, albeit tacit, confirmation that his father had acted in breach of those very laws.

As the Shah was making his speech, his father was on his way to Isfahan, his first stop on the way to an uncertain destination. The sight of the "plume-plucked"

Reza Shah carrying a suitcase was, for his family, unfathomable. It has never been clear what was in the suitcase. Three decades later, in his *Daily Journals,* Assadollah Alam referred to "certain documents" inherited from Reza Shah, kept in those days by the Shah in a safe, and "so sensitive" that Alam felt he could still not talk about them. Are these documents the same material Reza Shah so carefully guarded while on his journey of banishment?

When he got out of an old, unmarked car to meet his family, having already been ensconced in Isfahan for some time, Reza Shah looked old and pale. During his days as a king or a Cossack commander, he was never seen carrying anything other than his staff; now he carried around a suitcase from which he never parted. To his family, he seemed a tragically broken man. "After leaving Tehran," Fereydoon Jam, Reza Shah's son-in-law, remembered, "there was never any life in his eyes. The joy of life seemed to slip away from him with every passing day."[14] Reza Shah's mantra in those days was "I would rather die in Iran than go abroad."[15] His once-intimidating gravitas and charisma turned rapidly to grief and despair.

A bitter reminder of his fallen state was the fact that it was not even clear whether he stopped at Isfahan of his own volition, or, as suggested by the American Embassy, "the British held him for negotiations as to the disposition of his properties." Newspapers in the country were by then filled with rumors and stories about his allegedly fantastic and illicit fortune. A few members of the parliament and many opposition papers even alleged that on his way out of Iran, Reza Shah had taken some of the Crown Jewels—a vast collection of thousands of rare jewels, and some other gems brought back by Nadir Shah after he invaded India.

Early in his tenure, Reza Shah established the Iranian National Bank (Melli) and by 1931 ordered the bank to take over the power of mintage for the Iranian currency, until then in the hands of the British. The jewels were at the time used as the main backing for this currency. But as the Iranian currency was rapidly losing its value, the new Shah was busy trying to convince the people and the parliament that his father had not pilfered the royal jewels. In Isfahan, Reza Shah, at the apparent urging of the British, was begrudgingly transferring all of his assets to his oldest son, the Shah.

To assuage public fears about the allegedly missing Crown Jewels, a committee of trusted public servants and twelve members of the Majlis were chosen to take a reliable inventory of the jewels and to establish whether any were actually missing. After several visits to the National Bank depository, where the jewels were held, the committee concluded that none of the jewels were missing and cleared Reza Shah of any wrongdoing.[16]

While it has been something of a favorite national pastime in Iran to see the "British hand" behind every political turn of event, and while the Shah and his father both attributed much of what happened to them at least partially to the British hand, the decision to raise the issue of the Crown Jewels against Reza Shah was one of the cases where the British were indeed involved. When the British Embassy learned of the committee's findings, and of the planned appearance by Iran's Acting Minister of Finance before a session of the Majlis to "swear that Crown Jewels are still in the bank," Sir Reader Bullard sent an urgent telegram to the Foreign Office, saying "it is probably true that such jewels as were deposited were still there, but I believe that many of the most valuable had been taken by the Shah and made up into tiaras etc. and that these were in fact sent away when ladies of the royal family left." The Ambassador then offered the draft of what should be broadcast over the BBC. The broadcast, Bullard suggested, should declare, "It is alleged that Crown Jewels are still in the banks of Tehran. What public want to know is whether all the Crown Jewels were ever deposited in the bank? Were some kept back? Was it these that were taken away from Tehran recently by the chief of Police who made a mysterious journey? There must be a list of the Crown Jewels. Public enquiry is essential."[17]

Even in recent years, critics of Reza Shah have continued to insist that "the best parts" of the jewels "had already been taken by Reza Shah" before a full inventory was even taken. The evidence for these later allegations, as well as for those made by the British Embassy, is little more than guesswork and innuendo.[18]

The British had two apparent motives for their unusual "interest" in Iran's Crown Jewels. The British wanted a free hand in running Iran, and a self-assured Shah was the last thing they wanted. Moreover, in those days, the British government was engaged in a tug of war with Iranian officials over the rate of exchange between the two countries' currencies. Hoping to lessen the cost of keeping their soldiers in Iran, the British pressured Iranian officials to devalue the Iranian currency. Surely if the Crown Jewels, as the Iranian currency's main backing, were pilfered, then the value of the Iranian currency would fall.

In Isfahan, one of Reza Shah's biggest concerns was obviously the fate of his fortune. Not long after his arrival, lawyers and notaries carrying files and forms began arriving at his residence—the house of the Kazeruni family, successful Iranian textile manufacturers who had greatly benefited from Reza Shah's policy of support for domestic industries. Moreover, a tailor was called to make Reza Shah a civilian suit. Ever since joining the Cossack Brigade as a boy, and all through his days as a king, he had usually never worn anything other than his military uniforms, most of them made from fabric manufactured by the Kazeruni industries. Even the socks he wore were those made of coarse wool and used by soldiers. When in exile, he needed new socks, and Fereydoon Jam bought him some from the local store. Reza Shah, shocked at the price paid for them, rejected the whole package, asking instead for the rough-woven wool socks of his past.[19] Knowing his taste, Jam said, "I had not even bought him fancy socks. Nevertheless he refused to wear them."[20] Reza Shah was also uncomfortable in the new suits that were hurriedly tailored for him. His shrunken power, maybe the weight of his grief, seemed to have shrunken his body. In every picture after he was "un-kinged," his body seems barely able to hold up his drooping suits.

Having surrendered his power, he was now forced to surrender his wealth. In a terse note, he transferred the ownership of all his properties, whether in cash or in real estate, stocks, or bonds, to his oldest son, the new Shah. A key "facilitator" of this transfer was Ebrahim Qavam—nominally his daughter's father-in-law and the same man who had "negotiated" on his behalf in Tehran on the eve of the country's occupation. By then all semblance of a relationship between Gavam's son, Ali, and Reza Shah's daughter, Ashraf, had ended. Even in signing the "deed of donation" that transferred his wealth, Reza Shah tried to justify his virtual confiscation of about 2,000 of the country's most fertile and beautiful villages at a nominal price throughout his tenure. He wrote that since ascending the throne, he aimed only at the development, prosperity, and growth of the country, and he took over the properties "as an example, and model for the landlords."

By the time the Crown Prince returned home from Switzerland, his father, the once-poor soldier who had lived in a rented house when his first son was born, had become the richest man in Iran. The U.S. Ambassador in Tehran at the time, reporting on Reza Shah's economic activities, wrote, "There was little of value in the country, in fact, in which he was not interested. His greed knew no bounds and in addition to acquiring a large part of Mazandaran, he bought city properties, built hotels and operated factories.... [He] took any and all lands he wanted to his avaricious bosom under formal or implied threat of some kind of harm to the owners. He paid whatever pleased him to pay, usually a tenth or twentieth part of the value." After Reza Shah's abdication, when the issue of his wealth became the subject of a heated national debate, the Iranian Prime Minister told the parliament that Reza Shah had cash deposits in Iranian banks amounting to "the unbelievable sum of 68 million rials (4.25 million dollars)."[21] This amounted to 46 percent of the entire liquidity of the Iranian government. Other scholars have offered even larger figures for the total amount of money amassed by Reza Shah in his accounts in Iran. One source, for example, claims that the $4.25 million figure referred only to Reza Shah's savings account, and that there was another 85 million rials ($5.3 million) in his checking account.[22] This fantastic but contested fortune now belonged to the young Shah.

In the "deed of donation" prepared in the "office of the public Notary no. 17" in the city of Isfahan, with Mahmoud Jam acting as a witness, Reza Shah offered as "gift and present" to his eldest son all his "properties and chattels, whether moveable, immovable, factories, etc. whatsoever," in return for "10 grams of sugar" that he may apply them "in charitable, national education etc. in such manner as he may deem it expedient."[23] In the parlance of Shiite legalese, this practice, common in Iran, was called *habe kardan*—making a coerced transfer of property legitimate by making it appear as a voluntary sale in exchange for the payment of a cube of sugar.

In monarchies, political primogeniture is the norm; but this was a case of economic primogeniture, in which millions of dollars were bequeathed to one son, and everyone else in the large, sometimes bickering family of his three living wives, was left virtually penniless. At the time the transfer took place, the Shah's siblings did not complain about their father's decision. After a few months, when the political dust of succession had settled, Reza Shah's other sons and daughters as well as his other living wives began to grumble about the arrangement, demanding their share of the inheritance. Reza Shah retracted, and ordered the young Shah to transfer to each sibling a million *tooman* (about $500,000) and the deed to their individual palace within the Sa'ad Abad compound.[24] The rest of Reza Shah's vast fortunes remained in the Shah's hands and, as he learned the hard way, the specter of the fortune continued to haunt him for the rest of his political life.

By the time of Reza Shah's abdication, the issue of this fortune had become so controversial that the Shah ascended the throne only after promising, first to the British and Soviet governments and then to the people of Iran, that he would return all properties illegally confiscated by his father back to their lawful owners. The political landscape of Iran had in those days been changed by the plethora of newly formed opposition groups and papers that had burst onto the political scene. The British Embassy estimated the number of new parties to be more than a hundred. The most powerful of these parties was as much the creation of the Soviet occupying forces as the result of the newfound freedoms. It was called the Tudeh Party—the Party of the Masses. It was, in every aspect, Iran's de facto new Communist party.

Stalin was now an ally of the West and did not want to disturb the sensitive alliance between the socialist Soviet Union and its capitalist allies. As a result, he ordered the new Communist parties, as well as those already established, to pursue the policy of forging a united anti-Fascist front with all forces willing to resist Hitler and his allies. In Iran, one manifestation of this strategy was the new party's decision to eschew any overt affiliation with the Communist name, lest it frighten away religious and moderate forces who could come together in the coveted united front. The fact that Reza Shah had passed a law banning any organization that espoused "a collective creed" added to the urgency of avoiding an overtly Communist collectivist ideology.

In order to fight the Left's sudden power and influence—a fear soon augmented by the gradual dawning of the Cold War—and to improve his own image in the country, the Shah launched a three-pronged policy. He began donating large sums of money to different public causes. This was, essentially, in lieu of his promise to return the ill-gotten gains he inherited from his father to their rightful owners. In the same spirit, he also undertook a kind of unilateral, individual land reform and sold at discount prices some of the farmlands formerly called "Royal Properties." The land was distributed amongst the peasants who had long toiled on it, not the land owners from whom the property was initially "purchased."

The Shah also tried to give some of his controversial fortune back through publicized acts of philanthropy. The donations varied in their size and intended use. On September 27, 1941, he announced fifteen different donations, ranging from money to build three new medical schools around the country, a homeless shelter in Tehran, and a nursery to funds set aside to support research in science and medicine.[25] It has never been clear how many of these promised charitable institutions were in fact ever launched.

There was also the question of the funds Reza Shah had allegedly stashed away in foreign banks. Relying on the Shah's repeated declarations, and upon hearing from the British government that they had no specific information on the whereabouts of Reza Shah's foreign fortune, the Foroughi cabinet eventually issued a terse statement declaring that "we have so far found no evidence that [Reza Shah] had any accounts in foreign banks."[26] In spite of its declaration of ignorance, the British government continued to monitor the new Shah's financial activities. Their efforts soon bore surprising fruit.

Only months after the new Shah had come to power, the British government intercepted a telegram from a European bank to an American financial institution and learned that "the shah has one million (repeat one million) dollars in America and that he is now looking for safe investment for this money."[27] Two years later, the Shah opened another private account for himself in Guarantee Trust Company in the United States. Only this time, the sum was being transferred from one of the Shah's bank accounts in Iran. According to a March 10, 1943, telegram from the U.S. Ambassador to the State Department, "the rials with which the dollars were purchased were part of the more than six hundred millions left by the Shah Reza to present Shah. It would appear that Shah desires to have money abroad for two reasons: . . . to take care of himself and family should he ever have to leave Iran, and because he is being mulcted out of his money through contributions under pressure from charitable and other purposes."[28]

An interesting aspect of this second transfer is the way the Shah went about doing it. Realizing that he must try and keep all such foreign account transactions and transfers away from the public and the media, the Shah successfully convinced the American Embassy to allow him to use their diplomatic pouch for all correspondence about his bank accounts.[29] On another occasion, the British Embassy in Tehran reported from what it called a reliable source, "The Shah was buying large quantities of foreign exchange."[30] According to the British Embassy, the Shah's concern for his foreign assets was "because he foresees popular opposition to his attempt to secure complete control of the army."[31] In later years, as the issue of his wealth in foreign banks continued to remain a sensitive political issue, the question of using America's diplomatic pouch remained a viable option and a temptation for the Shah.

Making donations was the first element of the Shah's three-pronged strategy for consolidating the monarchy. The second was his decision to fight fire with fire. Responding to the sudden creation of hundreds of newspapers around the country, most of them critical of him and his father, he began paying a subsidy to a number of journalists, hoping they would defend him. The British government tried to dissuade the Shah from these efforts, but their advice seems to have had little practical effect. Amongst the most enduring such ties was that with Ali Asghar Amirani, the editor of *Khandaniha*—Iran's homegrown version of *Reader's Digest*. For the next three decades, Amirani played a complicated role in Iranian journalism—often critical of politicians, always faithful to the Shah.

In the arena of cultivating ties with journalists, the Shah's boldest step was his eventual decision to launch a paper whose job would be to present the point of view of the monarchy. As the publisher, he chose a young, talented, French-trained law professor by the name of Mostafa Mesbahzadeh. Before long, the daily paper *Keyhan* was launched, with the Shah providing a check from his personal account for 200,000 *tooman* as seed money. Abdolrahman Faramarzi, one of the country's most esteemed journalists of the time, became the paper's editor in chief.

A few weeks after the check for the seed money was paid, the Shah was given the equivalent of 200,000 *tooman* worth of stock in the company set up to publish *Keyhan*. The Shah did not keep the stock for himself but made a gift of them to Hussein Fardust—who claims he never cashed the shares but instead kept them in his basement as a relic.[32]

The Shah also felt that some of the attacks in the Iranian media were instigated by foreign powers. In some cases, he tried to solve the problem by directly negotiating with representatives of the country allegedly responsible for the attack. For example, after Seyyed Zia returned home from twenty-two years of exile and launched a paper that immediately began to criticize the Shah for the breach of the constitution and attacked Reza Shah for stashing away millions in his bank accounts, the Shah sent his Court minister, Hussein Ala, to meet with British

Embassy officials. The Shah, Ala told the British Embassy, "should be immune from attacks." The embassy's response was as interesting as the Shah's gesture. Instead of repeating the standard line about not interfering in Iran's domestic affairs, this time they told Ala that the attacks were payback for the fact that the "Shah had breached" his truce with Seyyed Zia. In fact, the embassy had come to believe that Mossadeq (at the time a member of Majlis and, in a few years, prime minister) was "one of [the Shah's] men," and thus implied that attacks by Seyyed Zia on the Shah were "payback" for his alleged alliance with Mossadeq.[33]

The third and most important component of the Shah's three-pronged strategy for consolidating power, and the one that marked the sharpest departure from the policies of Reza Shah, was his attempt to reconcile with the clergy. The Shah and his father shared nearly every element of their respective paradigms of authoritarian modernization. They both believed in the indispensable necessity of an authoritarian monarch (in place of a king who reigned—not ruled—according to the letter of the Iranian constitution). They both afforded a key, if not decisive, role to the state in not only jump-starting the economy on its march to progress, but making investments in key industries and controlling the economy (in place of free markets and the force of market mechanism). They were both willing to use the coercive power of the state to replace market mechanisms, even control prices, and fight inflation. The Shah and his father both believed that key sectors of the economy must remain a monopoly of the state. Neither was averse to the idea of expropriating trailblazing investors in the interest of achieving such monopoly—or of eliminating the possibility of the emergence of an entrepreneurial class rich and powerful enough to challenge the king's claims to absolute power. They both valued industrialization and believed that having a steel mill was the ultimate economic and symbolic measure of modernity. They both believed in using agriculture to facilitate industrial development. They both wanted a more educated working class, a larger and better trained technocratic class, a larger middle class. They both believed women should be fully enfranchised members of Iranian society. They both saw Iran's future tied to the West and were committed to fighting Communism. They both saw urbanization as a key to progress, and they believed in the urgency of a modernized infrastructure. They were both fierce advocates of cultural and aesthetic modernity, so long as it did not tread in political waters. For both, Iran's imperial grandeur in its pre-Islamic days was the essential ingredient of a new national cultural identity for the country. And they both considered a strong military, under their own direct control, a necessary element for the success of their modernization project and for the maintenance of the country's security and of their own hold on power. In this sense, the Shah's desire for a large military was even stronger than his father's. The craving is particularly remarkable when we remember that the young Shah had seen, with great sadness and surprise, how quickly his father's much-vaunted military all but disappeared overnight.

But father and son differed—and differed drastically—in their views on the role and place of religion and of the clergy in their paradigms. Reza Shah, acting in a spirit much like that of Atatürk in Turkey, moved aggressively to limit the role and number of the clergy in Iran. From the time he took over in 1925 to the time he left the country in 1941, though the population had more than doubled, the number of mosques had been reduced by half—turning some to schools, cinemas, and, in one case, an opera house. Before then, the idea of converting a mosque, even one in a state of derelict disrepair, to some other use had been nothing short of sacrilege. An expression in the Persian vernacular captures the essence of this convention: to compare someone to the door of a mosque is to imply sardonically that, in spite of their uselessness, they are irremovable from the position they hold. Reza Shah changed all of that and put many old mosques to modern use. The reduction in the total number of the clergy in the country was even greater. He also moved to deprive the clergy not just of their revenues from running the judicial system, but of their lucrative guardianship of *vagf*—religious endowments that covered such institutions as mosques, seminaries, and hospitals and that had been considered a crucial element in the backwardness of traditional Islamic economies.

The Shah, on the other hand, saw the clergy—the inconvenience of their radical minority notwithstanding—as an indispensable ally against Communists, and his new paradigm was evident from his first days on the Peacock Throne. His faith, and his belief that he was indeed God's "anointed," added a sense of personal poignancy to this political paradigm. A few years after ascending the throne, he claimed that "Islamic tenets are humanity's source of salvation. Following these rules in my time, and in any other will bring common welfare and comfort."[34] To realize his dream of using the clergy against his enemies, the Shah took two important steps. He helped to drastically increase the number of mosques in the country, and he made peace with the mullahs. During his tenure, the number of mosques increased to more than 55,000 (some say 75,000). The number of religious schools also witnessed a sharp rise, going from 154 to 214 in 1960. The rise in the second half of the Shah's rule was even greater.[35]

On June 3, 1943, Ayatollah Hussein Gomi, virtually exiled by Reza Shah eight years earlier, returned home to a hero's welcome. Even before returning, he had let it be known amongst religious circles that he was returning home at the direct invitation of the Shah. He was not lying. The Shah had sent a special envoy—Zeyanl-Abedin Rahnama, a writer of renown and a critic of Reza Shah who was known for his extensive contacts amongst the clergy—to Iraq and entrusted him with the task of bringing back Ayatollah Gomi. Ironically, the British Embassy was one of the few voices warning the Shah against bringing back the powerful ayatollah. But the Shah was undeterred. By then, he had come to conclude that mullahs are "all royalists at heart."[36] They knew that Islam could not survive in Iran without the monarchy. The monarchy, the Shah often said, is the only reliable bulwark standing in the way of Iran's becoming a secular or a Communist society, and the mullahs, he believed, knew this. What the Shah failed to realize is that some mullahs might well have believed all of this, but might also have had dreams of power themselves.

Ayatollah Gomi was afforded a hero's welcome by both the government and the people. The police in Tehran reported that some hundred thousand people had gathered near Gomi's temporary residence to welcome him.[37] The only public protest against the treatment afforded the returning Ayatollah came from Ahmad Kasravi, the eminent historian, social critic, and a sometime prophet of his own new "Behdini" doctrine—the Good Faith Religion. Kasravi had also written a daring critique of Shiism.[38]

In those days, in the seminary in the city of Qom, a new, young rabble-rousing cleric named Navvab Safavi had emerged, talking the fiery language of revolution and espousing the view that Muslims must take up arms in defense of their faith, in silencing heretics, and in creating an Islamic state. The more traditional ayatollahs, particularly Ayatollah Boroujerdi, who was rapidly emerging as the preeminent leader of Shiites in the world, disdained Safavi and ordered other mullahs to stay clear of him and his brand of radical Islam. Ayatollah Khomeini took exception to this command and began to cultivate close ties with Safavi, who went on to create the Feda'yan-e Islam (Martyrs of Islam)—easily the most successful terrorist organization in modern Iran.

The group's first target would be Kasravi, who was brutally mutilated in March 1946 as he was being deposed on a pending lawsuit in the Ministry of Justice. Safavi had himself earlier tried but failed to assassinate Kasravi. The Shah would hear of this group's existence only after they had committed their first murder. There was no independent intelligence organization at the time. Special units in the military and police performed the functions of an intelligence agency, but their work was focused on fighting Communism. Before long, the Feda'yan-e Islam would focus its wrath on the Shah and his ministers. It was in this context that Ayatollah Gomi returned home in triumph.

A few days after settling back into his native city of Meshed, Ayatollah Gomi wrote a note to the Governor of the province, demanding action on the issues he claimed he had raised with the Shah. Before long, he sent another note, this time to Prime Minister Ali Soheili, and surprisingly haughty in tone, raising the same issues. Finally, on August 20, 1943, the Ayatollah received a letter from the Prime Minister, informing him that all of his demands would be met. Ayatollah Gomi had demanded the abolition of the law banning women from appearing in public wearing scarves and veils. As the Prime Minister's letter makes clear, women would henceforth be allowed to appear in public anyway they chose.

The Ayatollah's second demand was a reversal of Reza Shah's policy of putting religious endowments *(vagf)* under government control. The management of these properties, according to the Prime Minister's letter, was to be returned to those stipulated in the endowment letter—in most cases the clergy. In agreeing to the Ayatollah's third demand, the government decided to make classes on Islamic theology and ethics a mandatory part of the curriculum in Iranian schools. The clergy were put in charge of determining the content of these classes. Ayatollah Gomi also demanded the closing of coeducational schools around the country that had arisen toward the end of the Reza Shah period.[39] Every one of the Ayatollah's major demands was, on the order of the Shah, accepted by the government and became policy.

The clergy, always in tune with the political pulse of society, realized that a new era had begun and that Reza Shah's policy of weakening them had ended. When in 1945 Ayatollah Boroujerdi was hospitalized in Tehran, the Shah made a point of making a much-publicized visit to his bedside. The visit symbolized the Shah's new policy. Caught in a fierce battle for control with powerful prime ministers and a rising tide of Communist activism, the Shah in those days went so far as to advocate the clergy's active participation in politics. The clergy, he said, shoulder a great responsibility in ensuring that the state does not at any time veer off the path of tending to the needs of the people. He lived to rue the day he uttered those words. But in those days, ambitious prime ministers like Qavam-al Saltaneh (Ahmad Qavam) were a more pressing threat.

The Shah first encountered the problem in 1942, when, much to his surprise and in spite of his resistance, he was forced to name Qavam prime minister. Only a few months earlier, the British and Soviet governments had both been adamantly opposed to a Qavam appointment; now they were both his chief proponents. Both had considered Qavam a Nazi sympathizer. British support for Qavam was particularly startling in that, according to their own sources, he had not only participated in planning a coup attempt with Nazi Germany but had later met with Ali Akbari, a special Nazi envoy sent to Iran, to coordinate further pro-Nazi activities, including seizing power when Nazi troops arrived near Iran's borders.[40] But somehow, in 1942, Qavam had overcome British and Soviet objections and became their favorite candidate for the post of prime minister.

The fact that the United States was also in favor of Qavam's appointment at the time was not surprising. After all, it was Qavam who, during his first tenure as prime minister in the early 1920s, had tried to get American oil companies, particularly Standard and Sinclair, interested in Iranian oil. Now, somehow, Qavam had also convinced the Soviets and the British that he was the man of the hour. All three governments afforded his cabinet their full support.

Qavam had first become prime minister in 1922, when the Shah was three years old, and his ambitions clearly went far beyond ensuring that the office of the prime minister was afforded all the power the constitution mandated. The Shah believed that Qavam wanted to replace him as the head of state and, in retrospect, there is considerable archival evidence to suggest that his fears were not altogether baseless. In fact, Qavam's grandiosity and ambitions had been evident as early as 1918, when he was just a governor in the province of Khorasan. In those days, during official national ceremonies, unless the King was himself present, units of the army and police were expected to march past a portrait of the monarch. However, Qavam often put his own picture in place of the monarch's. As prime minister, too, he used every occasion to show his preeminence over the King and embarrass the young Shah. He would sometimes mischievously ignore protocol and show up "late" to ceremonies, thus arriving after the Shah. On other occasions, when he and the Shah walked side by side, Qavam would, again contrary to protocol, walk a step or two ahead of the Shah. During much of his first decade on the throne, the young Shah used all of his power to block Qavam's appointment as prime minister. When he failed, as he did on three occasions, he worked behind the scenes to cripple Qavam's cabinets and bring about their demise.

Some of these efforts were contrary to the pledge the Shah had made to the nation and to the Allies. He had promised to forgo the authoritarian political habits of his father and become instead a constitutional monarch. During those early years, the Shah would often repeat the idea that democracy and the rule of law were the best form of government for Iran. The "most suitable form of government," the Shah said on more than one occasion, "is democracy," where "the spiritually rejuvenating winds of freedom blow."[41] In his first speech after taking the oath of office, he declared, "I find it necessary to strictly adhere to the principles of the constitution and the separation of power."[42]

In spite of these pledges, about four weeks after taking the oath of office, the Shah sent a secret message to the British Ambassador, "saying that he would like to see [him] fairly often, alone, and without the knowledge of politicians.... He wished he said to have the support of the British empire and to work in close agreement with His Majesty's Legation with greatest discretion."[43] The ambassador, Sir Reader Bullard, rejected the offer, saying "it would not be possible for him to be received without the knowledge of the Persian cabinet, and of my Soviet colleagues."[44] A few days earlier, on October 9, the Shah had tried to form a de facto alliance with the British against the Soviet Union. In both of these meetings, another aspect of the Shah's mature political style began to manifest itself, as in both discussions, the young Shah "showed a preoccupation with army matters." The conversations, according to Bullard, were "far too much about the army."[45]

The Shah's attempt to form a discreet alliance with the British must be understood in the context of his mental state in those days. The British reminded him, more than once, that the humiliating fate of his father could easily happen to him, and many of his advisors whispered into his ears that "the British [had] already brought about the abdication of three Shahs: Muhammad Ali, Ahmad Shah and Reza Shah."[46] The British government's continued humiliation of Reza Shah, a man who cast a giant shadow on the mind of the Shah, was in those days another reminder of Britain's intimidating power.

The Shah next tried the same tactic with the American Ambassador, offering to establish discreet ties with his embassy, against the Soviet and British influence, and without the knowledge of the Iranian cabinet. Once again, he was politely brushed off, and reminded that he must stay within the confines of the constitution. These early efforts, and many more in the course of the 1940s, strongly contradict the common perception that the Shah was, in the first twelve years of his rule, simply a shy and timid constitutional monarch, happy with his ceremonial role. In fact, from the moment he ascended the throne, though he was obviously in a weakened position with the occupying governments of Britain and the Soviet Union considering him to be on probation, and though both governments had often let him know that they expected him to abide by the constitution, the Shah made every effort to increase his power and regain as much of his father's lost authority as he could. Even in those early days, he would often declare in private that, in Iran, progress is possible only when there is a powerful king. His skirmishes with Qavam, which began as soon as Qavam was named prime minister in August 1942, were a clear example of these early efforts.

The British Embassy, aware of the Shah's fear and dislike of Qavam, tried to ensure that he survived as prime minister.[47] On December 9, 1942, however, Qavam's tenure all but ended in blood and defeat. On that day, food shortages in Tehran led to "bread riots"—an intermittent feature of Iranian politics since the time of the Constitutional Revolution. Moreover, since the advent of World War II, when food shortages had become a fact of life in Iran, Britain often used delivery of grain—much of it actually gifts to Iran from the United States—as a bargaining chip against the Iranian government. Now that very issue of grain and bread was undermining the British plan to keep Qavam in power.

The bread riots were accompanied by fairly serious looting; Qavam's house was "denuded and set on fire." The army and the police were conspicuous by their absence and by their failure to make any attempt to restore order.[48] Considering the Shah's domination of the military and security forces, the British Embassy concluded that the Shah was complicit in the bread riot and its violent turn against Qavam. "I cannot acquit the Shah of a share in the responsibility," Bullard concluded.[49]

In the midst of the riots, the Shah summoned to the Court a number of the Majlis deputies and told them, "unless something drastic was done there could be a revolution from below," and suggested "that a revolution from above would be better."[50] What the Shah meant by this "revolution" was made clear when, in the course of a subsequent meeting with the British Ambassador, he said that "a change of government" would be needed "to satisfy public opinion" and abort the revolution. In future years, the Shah would often refer to these words as his first call to revolution—a call that he claimed he could finally put into action in 1962.

The day after the bread riots, the British Ambassador was instructed to meet with the Shah urgently and tell him that his "attitude [was] most disappointing," and that the Allies were dismayed at having "learned of the attitude taken by His Majesty during the recent disturbances." The British had also learned that the Shah had been conspiring with members of the Majlis to bring about a vote of no confidence against Qavam. The Shah was to be told that should he try to use the Majlis and its "most irresponsible elements" against Qavam, the Allies would have no choice but to bring about the parliament's "enforced dissolution." Bullard was instructed to end with a not-too-subtle threat, telling the Shah, "it is now for him to assert himself in support of the Prime Minister who has the confidence of the Allies."[51]

To the utter surprise of the British and Soviet Embassies, and contrary to the image of the young Shah as a mere malleable tool of the British, only an hour after meeting with Bullard and receiving the threatening message that virtually ordered him to support Qavam, the Shah called the Prime Minister to the Court and "pressed [him] to resign."[52] But Qavam was nothing if not ambitious, and, aware that he had the support of the Allies, he ignored the Shah's pressures.

Faced with Qavam's intransigence and with the British support for Qavam, the Shah tried another approach. He "sounded out Soviet ambassador about the possibility of forming cabinet with considerable military elements," but without Qavam; there too he received what he considered a deeply discouraging response.[53] What the Shah failed to realize in those days was that the Soviet Union, Britain, and America were unwilling to endanger their strategic alliance against Hitler simply for some tactical gain in Iran.

When the British heard about the Shah's surprising moves against Qavam, even after he had been warned, they sent him a more threatening second message. He was told in so many words that Qavam was the choice of the Allies and must stay in power. This time the Shah saw the writing on the wall, and a few days later, in his next meeting with Bullard, he "admitted that he had committed an error of judgment" in "trying to remove Qavam after promising [the British] to keep" him. The reason, the Shah said, was that the riots had been "rapidly getting worse," and "in the stress of the moment [Qavam] had failed to understand the situation as clearly as he should have."[54]

But Qavam was not the Shah's only problem. The Allies' decision to arrest some 200 prominent Iranians on the charge of having pro-Nazi sympathies put the Shah in a quandary. Many of these figures were his staunch allies and supporters, and the Allies did not inform the Shah and the Iranian government of their arrest until after the fact. In Isfahan, when the Allied forces entered the house where the German spy Franz Mayer was hiding, they discovered documents showing "the existence in Persia of a wide organization" that was preparing a coup against the Allies by "seizing aerodromes, blocking roads." Many prominent Persians were amongst those arrested for their alleged roles in the conspiracy. The wording of the British Embassy's conclusion that the Shah himself did "not seem to be directly involved" in the German conspiracy was hardly a sign of their strong trust or confidence in the Shah.[55] Nevertheless, he registered his dismay at the arrests.

In his attempt to navigate between increasingly brazen Soviet and British pressures on him, the Shah found assistance from an unexpected source. In 1942, Franklin D. Roosevelt sent General Patrick Hurley as his personal emissary to Iran. Hurley was an odd and eccentric character. He had made a fortune as an attorney and joined the army in World War I. By the time he was sent to Iran on his mission, he was a general. His cowboy hats and his aversion to the circumlocutions that are part and parcel of diplomatic discourse made him an oddity in Tehran and put him on a collision course with the British Ambassador.

In Tehran, Hurley was horrified by what he found: abject poverty amongst the people and arrogant disdain for the populations by the British and Soviet ambassadors. Even before Hurley's arrival, officials in the U.S. Embassy had clashed with Britain over the American idea of replacing the corrupt political personalities that dominated the Iranian scene with younger, Westernized technocrats. The British dismissed these suggestions as absurdly utopian, a sign of America's dangerous naiveté about Iran. Most of the personalities thus criticized by the American Embassy had long reputations of being "friendly" with the British.

As he attended to his sensitive role of managing the logistics of the 1943 Tehran Conference—with Churchill, Stalin, and Roosevelt all attending—Hurley began a series of meetings with Iranian officials, particularly the Shah. When Roosevelt came to Iran, Hurley briefed him on the situation. In fact, on his way out of Tehran, at the airport, Roosevelt had a long conversation with Hurley and then asked him to turn the gist of their conversation into a report about the future of

U.S. policy in Iran. The often maligned and ignored Hurley Report became the first blueprint for American efforts to promote democracy in Iran and then the rest of the Muslim Middle East.

Hurley began his report by suggesting that Iran, as "a country rich in natural resources," stood a good chance of becoming a free and independent nation with a government "based upon the consent of the governed." Aside from the domestic scourge of illiteracy, the other obstacle to democracy in Iran was, according to Hurley, the machinations of the twin colonial powers of Great Britain and the Soviet Union. The General railed against the idea that noble American blood was being shed in the ignoble effort to maintain what he considered the moribund British Empire and the expansionist Soviet Union.

Roosevelt found the report interesting and along the lines of his own thoughts. He sent a copy to Churchill, maybe more in mischief than in earnest consultation, writing in an accompanying note, "This is for your eyes only. I rather like his general approach." Churchill took umbrage at this clear snub. He waited almost three months before he chose to respond. Using his legendary wit, he wrote, "I make bold, however, to suggest that British imperialism has spread and is spreading democracy more widely than any other system of government since the beginning of time." He ended his chiding note by insisting that Britain is certainly "no less interested than the US in encouraging Persian independence, political efficiency and native reform."[56]

During these months, as the Shah fought on many fronts, he also had to contend with the issue of his father's fate. The British seemed bent on doing everything they could to humiliate the once-proud Reza Shah. From the moment he had left Tehran, the British had controlled his every move, reminding him more than once that he was in fact no more than a prisoner of war. More than once, when Reza Shah asked about his destination, the young British officer who was "accompanying" him refused to answer, claiming ignorance. In reality, even as early as the time the entourage was in the city of Kerman, about seven hundred miles south of Tehran, the British had already decided that Reza Shah would be sent to Mauritius. A few days later, when Reza Shah and his family boarded the ship that was to take them away from Iran, they were not told their destination. When the ship—a cargo ship used for carrying mail—finally anchored off the waters of India, Reza Shah and his entourage wanted to disembark for a visit. In Tehran they had received visas for India. But now they were told that, in spite of their visas, they could not disembark, nor would "their destination . . . necessarily be India."[57] Distraught and angry, Reza Shah sent a tartly worded telegram to the British Viceroy of India, complaining about the treatment he had been receiving.

"Before leaving Tehran," he wrote, "I was informed through British Minister [in] Tehran that British Government agreed my going to America with my family, and it was on this understanding that I left Iran. Now I have been arrested at Bombay and have been told that I can not go to America."[58] Back in Tehran, the Shah made every effort to ensure his father's physical safety, emotional sanity, and human dignity. The boat anchored off Bombay for five days, and Reza Shah spent most of the hot, humid days walking along the deck.

Eventually, Reza Shah learned that he was being sent to the island of Mauritius. Again he wrote to British authorities, asking whether the decision to send him there was "taken after I had left Iran . . . or whether it was in accordance with deliberate policy of British government?"[59] He further reminded them that in Tehran, he had been promised safe passage to the Americas. In their internal deliberations, the British agreed that Bullard might have given Reza Shah the impression that he would be allowed a temporary stay in India, followed by permanent refuge in South America. But now they decided to tell the un-kinged Reza Shah that the British government had "never agreed that he should go to America." While they were pondering his fate, the Secretary of State for Colonies informed the Governor of Mauritius that he had full discretion to restrict Reza Shah and his family's freedom and that their correspondence must be fully censored and if "necessary, Persian speaking clerk should probably be sent from India."[60] For much of his seven-month stay on the island (September 1941 to April 1942), Reza Shah and his entourage received no communications from Tehran.

By then, the British found themselves in something of a quandary about Reza Shah. On the one hand, they worried that he was becoming part of another "Napoleon legend." Persians, the British Embassy opined in its inimitable tone, "are not a logical race";[61] in another note during the same week, they called Persians "base people" who might now be inclined to create a Pahlavi legend.[62] The British were in fact worried that Reza Shah is "now becoming popular again as the alleged victim of the British cruelty. The myth is being created that we got rid of the Shah because he defended the independence of Persia and wanted to modernize the country."[63]

Bullard, as usual, favored the most brutal answer to the fallen Reza Shah's request. He wrote, "We are not under any obligation, moral or contractual, expressed or implied, in this matter. The Shah may say that 'when he abdicated to facilitate our plans, he put his trust in the British government to let him retire to any neutral country which he might select.' But if the prisoner at the bar pleads guilty, that does not put the judge under any obligation to let him off hard labor, even if he may thereby have saved the Crown the trouble of a prolonged case."[64]

However, after some time, the British attitude toward Reza Shah changed a bit. He was eventually allowed to receive letters and packages from Iran. In the first handwritten note he sent to his father, the new Shah wrote that "the grandeur and dignity Your Imperial Majesty's presence had afforded Iran has now dissipated with your departure."[65] In the meantime, Reza Shah and his son both pressured the British government to move the fallen king and his entourage to a new location. Eventually, the British succumbed to the wishes of the father and son and arranged for Reza Shah's transfer to South Africa on April 10, 1942. South America and Canada were both ruled out, and South Africa was the only place, the British felt, safely far from Iran where they could keep close watch on the fallen Reza Shah.

The trip took eight days. Reza Shah was told there was German submarine activity in the area, causing considerable delay. They landed in Durban on April 18, 1942, and Reza Shah was immediately taken by the gaiety and urban vivacity of his new place of exile. The house set aside for him was too small for his entourage, and a new house was hard to find in the city. Ultimately, they moved to Johannesburg, where he and his family first stayed in a hotel and then rented two adjoining half-completed houses.

Even in Johannesburg, Reza Shah was depressed and despondent. In a letter from exile, written only seventeen days before his death, he wrote to his son about his fears of the future and offered some advice. He wrote of his own despondency, confessing that the only thing that kept him alive was the slim hope of one day seeing his son and the rest of the family again. Those who saw Reza Shah in South Africa describe a broken man, bereft of any desire to live. "Without a hope of seeing you," he wrote to the Shah, "I would no longer have any attachment to life."[66] While heaping praise on his son for his love of country and his youth, he also warned against the danger of listening to sycophants. He asked his son to fortify his courage, fight his anxieties, and remain strong. "Be firm and steadfast," he told his son, "fear nothing, as a single mistake by you might well destroy our efforts of twenty years and sully our family name; never succumb to anxiety; remain so resolute that no force can change your determined will."[67] But in trying to heed his father's last wishes and maintain the throne and preserve the dynasty, the Shah was fighting against not just a destiny determined by his character but also a strong current of Iranian history that underscored the crisis of monarchy as an institution.

In the early morning of July 26, 1944, Reza Shah died of what doctors described as a heart attack and his family believed was heartbreak. He died a broken man. Days before his death, a local paper published a scathing attack on Reza Shah—"an article full of insults and accusations" according to his Chief of Staff—and Reza Shah was not only saddened by the article, but believed it to be the work of "secret hands" pursuing him even as far away as Johannesburg. Now he was dead, and he had requested to be buried back in Iran. But bringing the body back to the country at the time was, for political reasons, untenable. Leaving it in South Africa, a non-Muslim land, was also a political liability. The embalmed body was laid to temporary rest at the royal Al-Rifa'i mosque in Cairo. Some £5,000 were spent moving Reza Shah's coffin from South Africa to Egypt.[68]

After many months, the Shah finally decided to re-inter the body of his father. Even the Iranian cabinet was opposed to this relocation, worried about the public reaction to such a move. The Shah sent the cabinet an angry message, saying their attitude was "an insult to his father which he would not brook."[69] The Shah went on to show unusual determination to bring the body back and overcame the cabinet's resistance. He still had two other obstacles to overcome. The Egyptian government, by then indignant at the Shah's relations with Fawzia, had said it would refuse to "stage any ceremonies in Cairo to mark the re-interment."[70]

Finally, when the body was on its way to Iran, the Shah declared his intention to inter the body in the grounds of the Sa'ad Abad Palace, a place he knew his father loved. But the clergy opposed the idea, producing a "ruling to the effect that a body which had been temporarily interred in non-Shia ground must, if re-interred in Persia, lie in the proximity of a Shrine of an Imam."[71] Obviously, the most important shrine in Iran was in Meshed, where Imam Reza was buried, and the Shah decided he wanted his father buried there. The choice was dictated more by the Shah's own desires and beliefs than by those of his father, who had, in his prime, used heavy artillery against rabble-rousing clerics who had taken refuge in the Meshed shrine. The clergy had not forgotten this transgression and, helped by the more-religious members of the bazaar, they successfully opposed the idea of Reza Shah's burial in the city.

The Shah's second choice was Qom, but the clergy in that city also successfully blocked the move. After all, a few years earlier, Reza Shah had defied tradition and transgressed against that shrine too, walking into the most sacred parts of the monument in his military boots. Ultimately, a new mausoleum, inspired by Napoleon's burial place at Les Invalides in Paris, was built for Reza Shah in the city of Rey, not far from Tehran.[72]

Chapter 8

DAWN OF THE COLD WAR

Well, well, I see the issue of these arms.
I cannot mend it, I must needs confess,
Because my power is weak and all ill left.
Shakespeare, King Richard II, *2.3.151–153*

As the Big War was ending in Europe, the Cold War was beginning in Iran, and the Shah was faced with increasingly serious challenges to his rule. He was a virtual single parent, as his Queen continued her long stay in Egypt—officially described by the Court as a holiday. Two of his most tenacious adversaries were becoming the indispensable poles of Iranian politics, while the power and relevance of his allies were waning. A burgeoning nationalist movement threatened the status quo, while cells belonging to the rapidly spreading Communist Party continued to penetrate every part of the Iranian body politic, including the military.

The Shah's precarious position and his tenuous hold on power in the early part of the forties became most evident during the Tehran Conference of 1943. The meeting brought together leaders of the United States, the Soviet Union, and Great Britain. It was, in his words, his "first brush with international diplomacy."[1] He wrote, "although I was technically the host of the conference, the Big Three paid me little notice . . . we were after all what the French called a quantité négligeable, . . . I was a king barely 24 years old."[2]

The three big powers had decided to adopt the severest measure of secrecy and chose to tell the Shah about the meeting only at the last moment. Still more insulting for the Shah was the fact that "neither Churchill nor Roosevelt bothered with international protocol that required they call on [him], their host." Instead, they both summoned the Shah to their embassies. The Shah's recollections of what transpired in these meetings changed as his sense of his self and his place in the world changed. In his 1980 *Answer to History*, written in exile when he felt betrayed and rejected, he called the meetings "perfunctory" and "without real significance."[3] In 1976, when he basked in the glory of his own accomplishments, and when he was constantly reminded by those he met of his genius for leadership and for matters military, his iteration of the meeting with Churchill was far from perfunctory. In 1976, the Shah claimed, with what he called "justifiable pride," that he had essentially changed the course of the war by telling Churchill "that the Allies should open the second front through the soft underbelly of Italy." According to the Shah, Churchill "sat in thought and a strange light came into his eyes."[4]

Of the three Allied leaders meeting in Tehran, only Stalin decided to bother with protocol and call on the Shah. It was an indication of the Shah's beleaguered state in 1943 that even this visit did not take place without embarrassing preconditions. The Soviets did not trust the guards around the Shah's palace and insisted on using Red Army soldiers to guard the building in the hours leading to the meeting. The Shah accepted the condition. On the day of the visit, he was nervous and excited; he anxiously moved about the Court, making sure every detail was taken care of. "This is my most important meeting," he told his confidante, Hussein Fardust.[5]

Stalin began the meeting by reassuring the Shah that he should "have no worry about the next fifty years" and advised him "to keep a strong hold over his people."[6] In recounting the conversation to the British Ambassador, the Shah wondered whether this was Stalin's way of offering him a guarantee of power. The Shah was "burning to talk to [Stalin] about [Iran's] need for planes and tanks." No sooner had the Shah raised his concern than Stalin offered "a tank regiment and a squadron of planes, with troop training and method of delivery to be discussed later." Was the gift too good to be true?

"Thirty tanks, and thirty airplanes, some fighters and some bombers," were to be offered, along with a bevy of 250 Soviet experts whose salaries the Soviet government offered to pay.[7] The tank regiment would remain under the command of Russian officers and would be based in Qazvin, a two-hour drive west of Tehran. It was, after all, rumors of movement by the Soviet army based in Qazvin that had led to Reza Shah's abdication and speedy departure from Tehran. The tanks and the rest of the gift were, in short, Stalin's Trojan Horse, and the Shah had no desire to accept it. The British and American Embassies encouraged him to reject the Soviet offer. He was also reminded by his advisors that the actual price of the Soviet "gift" was less than the economic loss Iran suffered every year it was forced "to sell rice to [the Red Army] at an uneconomic price."[8]

Aside from his lifelong distrust of the Soviet intentions in Iran, there was an added reason for the Shah's refusal of the Russian offer. The Shah had come to believe that Stalin was the real victor in the Second World War—a view shared by some in the West who either believed Roosevelt was duped by "Uncle Joe," or accused him of betraying the fate of East and Central European nations by relegating them to the Soviet Union's "sphere of influence."[9] It was, the Shah believed, "Stalin who pulled the strings at Tehran, Yalta and Potsdam and he imposed a Soviet peace on the world that has now lasted for thirty-five years."[10] Allowing a couple hundred Soviet advisors to roam around the country was, for the Shah, a recipe for disaster. In the months after the offer was made, the Shah's distrust of the Soviets only increased, putting him on the certain path of confrontation with Stalin.

To some Western diplomats, the Shah's views on the Soviet Union around the time the Second World War ended seemed "unrealistic and alarmist." The views became particularly disturbing when the Shah "held forth... about the atom bomb" and appeared to be immensely impressed with its military potential.[11] Aware of America's post-Hiroshima nuclear monopoly, he advocated that the West should have used that monopoly to wage "a preventive war" against the Soviets.[12]

Once the Shah decided to reject Stalin's disingenuous gift, he tried to parlay it into some benefits for Iran. He told Sir Reader Bullard, the British ambassador, that "Stalin's call [on him] had made a very good impression" on the Iranian public. They construed it "as a sign of respect for Persian sovereignty." He then suggested that "His Majesty's Government must not allow themselves to be left behind but should come forward with something equally striking."[13]

Bullard was both surprised and angered by the Shah's words and what they implied. He told the Shah that his was a preposterous suggestion and warned against the idea of trying to pit the Soviet Union against Britain. In another of his long litany of racist disparagements of the Persian character, Bullard concluded his report to the Foreign Office by saying, "throughout the interview, the Shah showed how thoroughly Persian he is in character and how thin the veneer is which he acquired in Switzerland."[14] For Bullard, being Persian was synonymous with cowardice, duplicity, and depravity of character. Bullard's demeanor and disposition were so soundly insulting that on numerous occasions, American envoys to Iran clashed with him. Eventually, the Shah informally requested that someone else replace Bullard as ambassador—something well within Iran's rights as a sovereign nation. The British government ignored the request.[15]

Even something as innocuous as giving a gift to the three visiting heads of state became a quandary for the Shah, a potential political minefield. The three leaders were allies at the time, but they were also competitors and were destined to soon become adversaries. It was crucial that none feel slighted. The Persian habit of hospitality and the culture's knack for survival, for bending with prevailing winds and waiting for the occasion to rise again, was handy in solving the gift quandary.

The best living Iranian miniaturist was given the commission. He prepared three paintings that were exactly alike, save in one minor detail. Inspired by miniatures depicting scenes from the *Shahnameh*, Iran's epic mytho-history, the gift paintings show two battling armies on horseback, swords and spears in hand. On one side are the Allies, obviously victorious and poised to deal the final blow to the retreating Axis forces. Emperor Hirohito, Mussolini, and Hitler are shown fleeing or fallen, pursued by the victorious Allied forces led by Churchill, Roosevelt, and Stalin. Behind a small hill, in the far corner, stand the people of Iran, watching but unmistakably disengaged from the raging battle. The only difference between the three paintings is that each head of state received a painting that showed him riding the white horse of victory and leading the other two Allied leaders in the charge against the defeated and retreating Nazis and their hapless Italian and Japanese allies.

The miniature ploy solved the gift quandary, but the end of the war created for the Shah a far bigger challenge. The very idea of Iran as a multiethnic quilt faced an existential challenge. Such ethnic pluralism had hitherto been a source of richness for Iranian history; now it threatened to become the country's Achilles' heel. At the end of hostilities in Europe, the United States and Britain swiftly abided by their earlier pledges and withdrew their forces from Iran. Stalin had other plans, and the first hints of them came during the Potsdam Conference in July–August 1945. At that time, the Soviet Union announced its intention to keep its troops in Iran past the agreed date.

Two years earlier, in June 1943, unbeknownst to the Shah and the Iranian government, the Soviet Union had dispatched to Iran's northern provinces geologists disguised as military engineers. Their mission was to explore for gas and oil. They concluded that oil and gas reserves in Iran's northern provinces "were not less than those controlled by the British" in the South.[16] Ever since the early years of the century, when Stalin was a sometime gangster, sometime revolutionary in the city of Baku in Azerbaijan, he had known that the Caspian region was rich in oil. In fact, Baku was called at that time "the greatest oil city in the world."[17] It was in Baku that Stalin became, in the words of his brilliant biographer, Simon Sebag Montefiore, the "godfather of a small but useful fund-raising operation that really resembled a moderately successful Mafia family, conducting shakedowns, currency counterfeiting."[18] Half a century later, it was Iran's turn for a "shakedown."

But the riches of Iran's northern provinces surprised even Stalin. Soon after the receipt of the geologists' report, on August 16, 1944, Stalin's infamous last chief of police, Lavrenty Beria, sent him a telegram suggesting that the Soviet Union must "set out vigorously to negotiate with Iran with the goal of obtaining a [Soviet] concession in Northern Iran."[19] In this effort, Beria could count on the support of the Soviet leaders running Soviet Azerbaijan who had long been advocating plans to force Iran's northern provinces to join the Soviet Union and create what they imagined was "the Greater Azerbaijan." With the war's end in sight and the Soviet Union's power and status increasingly recognized and feared around the world, the vast oil riches of Iran's northern provinces finally convinced Stalin to make his move.

In a memorandum dated July 6, 1945, and signed by the Communist Party's Politburo but believed to have been written by Stalin himself, the Communist Party of Soviet Azerbaijan was ordered to take all measures necessary to "organize a Separatist movement in Southern Azerbaijan and other provinces of Northern Iran." Stalin ordered the creation of a "national autonomous Azerbaijan with broad powers within the Iranian state" as well as "work among the Kurds of Northern Iran to draw them into the separatist movement to form a national autonomous Kurdish district." The leader of the Tudeh Party, Samad Kambaksh, was summoned to Baku, where he was ordered to dissolve the Tudeh Party apparatus in Azerbaijan and meld its members into the new organization. The Tudeh branch in the city of Tabriz, the capital of Azerbaijan, had only been created in 1942, and four of its five founding members had spent some time in the Soviet Union in the decade before the war.[20]

Some Tudeh leaders, driven more by their genuine nationalist sentiments than by the servile "internationalist spirit" favored by Stalin, objected to this Soviet policy. They wrote a surprisingly harshly worded letter to Soviet leaders, but their effort was of no consequence. It was, after all, an article of faith and part of the bylaws of the Third International of Communist Parties (Comintern), created by Lenin and Stalin after October 1917, that the interests of the Soviet Union, as the "bastion of the Proletarian Revolution" always took precedence over the parochial interests of any Communist Party that joined the organization.[21]

Stalin's directive even offered detailed guidance on the number of publications the separatist movement in Iran should have ("an illustrated magazine [published] in Baku for distribution in Iran and also three new newspapers on Southern Azerbaijan") as well as the policies it should follow (land reform and "radical improvement in Soviet–Iran relations," amongst others). Stalin ended by allocating "a special fund of one million foreign-currency rubles (for conversion into toomans)" to defray some of the movement's costs.[22] Less than two months after the Moscow directive, in August 1945, sympathizers of the newly launched movement took over government buildings in the city of Tabriz and issued a manifesto. The continued Soviet occupation of Iran and the creation of a separatist movement in Azerbaijan (and, before long, also in the Iranian region of Kurdistan) led to the first major political crisis in the Shah's reign.

In December 1944, Dr. Mossadeq, who had easily won a seat in the Majlis, shepherded through the parliament a bill prohibiting the Iranian government from negotiating about or granting any new oil concessions during the war. In arguing for the virtues of his proposed new bill, Mossadeq articulated the essential elements of his philosophy for Iran's foreign policy. It came to be known as *movazeneye manfi* (negative balance). He criticized the idea of "positive balance," propagated at the time by both the Soviet Union and Britain. It "advocated a concession for the Soviets to balance the British concession. If Iran does so," Mossadeq said, "her action would resemble that of a person with one hand amputated who, in pursuance of balance, would consent to have his right hand amputated."[23]

By the time Mossadeq introduced his bill, the Soviet Union had already begun pressuring Iran for oil concessions in the North. Their first mission demanding such a deal had arrived in Tehran in September 1944. Their demand was based not just on what they had found in Iran, and what Iran had given to the British, but also on the incredible idea that without concessions in Iran's northern provinces, the "Baku oil fields" would be threatened. Stalin told an American diplomat that "saboteurs, even a person with only one box of matches . . . could risk our oil resource."[24]

The Russians were not the only ones seeking a new concession in Iran. By then, American-owned companies like Standard-Vacuum and Sinclair Oil and European concerns like the Shell Oil Company were also asking for oil concessions in Iran. The Shah had also let it be known that he favored "more American oil concessions" at the time.[25] As these companies competed for a deal with Iran, the Tudeh Party also began to unabashedly defend Russia's "legitimate interests" in Iran's northern provinces.[26]

Worried that the Tudeh Party members in the Majlis—not incidentally, nearly all elected in the Soviet-occupied territories—would filibuster his bill, Mossadeq maintained complete secrecy about his intentions, and the Tudeh deputies were apparently taken completely by surprise when the bill was introduced.[27]

The Shah called Mossadeq to the Court in 1944, around the time of the bill's passage, and offered the surprised deputy the job of prime minister. Much to the Shah's surprise—and to his perpetual derision afterwards—Mossadeq predicated his acceptance of the prime minister's job on the prior approval of the British government. For the Shah, the condition was a sign of Mossadeq's cowardice or political chicanery, or even an indication that he was working in collusion with the British government.

According to Mossadeq, he refused the offer first because he did not think the Shah had the constitutional authority to appoint a prime minister. The job of the King, Mossadeq wrote, was "more of a figure-head." The argument, made while Mossadeq was in jail and long after the time the offer was made, seems inconsistent and concocted after the fact. In reality, in his meeting, Mossadeq told the same "figure-head" Shah that should the British agree with the appointment, he would accept the offer. Mossadeq further added that he knew full well the power of the British in Iran—at the time, they were occupying half of the country. Moreover, Mossadeq wrote that he knew of the British opposition to his politics and personality, and thus knew the appointment would never materialize.[28]

As it turned out, Mossadeq was right on this point. When the Shah raised with Bullard the issue of the offer he had made to Mossadeq, the ambassador was incensed, and tried, in his own words, to "deprecate" the idea by telling the Shah that such an appointment would be a "departure from the constitution."[29] Of course, at other times, this same Bullard had no compunction asking, even demanding, that the Shah fire one prime minister or appoint another. So concerned was the British government about the possibility of a Mossadeq appointment that Bullard was instructed to meet with the Shah again and draw "his attention to the effect such unconstitutional action might be expected to have on public opinion abroad (to which he is sensitive)." In case even this warning did not work, Bullard was instructed to remind the Shah "about the danger of following in his father's footsteps."[30] In 1944, the "father's footsteps" had led him to a lonely house in Johannesburg where he was a virtual prisoner of the British. A couple of days after the meeting, the Shah called Mossadeq to tell him about British opposition to the idea.

In the meantime, as the Azerbaijan crisis continued, the Soviet Union made it clear that they would not negotiate with any prime minister other than Qavam. They particularly ruled out the then-sitting prime minister, Ebrahim Hakimi. By the end of the war, the Soviets had up to 60,000 soldiers in Iran, and the vast territories they occupied included Qazvin, a mere two-hour drive from Tehran.[31] About this time, Qavam decided to try his hand in politics yet again. On June 4, 1945, he sent Javad Ameri to the British Embassy, "to sound [the Ambassador out] about Qavam as a candidate for the Prime Minister." The embassy was less than enthusiastic. While "it would be difficult to work with Qavam,"[32] they said, they were also no longer opposed to such an appointment. The British knew that the Shah would be opposed to Qavam's premiership. Two years earlier, the same embassy had all but concluded that the Shah had conspired with the military to topple Qavam during his earlier turn at the helm. Moreover, as late as January 24, 1944, the British Ambassador had "informed the Shah that HM Legation no longer considers Qavam . . . a suitable candidate for the post of Prime Minister." At that time, Bullard had shown the Shah a "note drawn up by British Security authority and based on good evidence showing that Qavam had at least connived at fifth column activities [with the Nazis] when he was Prime Minister."[33] But much to the Shah's surprise, the British were now in favor of Qavam's premiership. The British wanted Iran's problems with the Soviet Union resolved, lest the issue jeopardize their own monopoly of the southern region's oil, and Qavam was, in their view, the only man capable of bringing about such a resolution. The American Embassy, too, had all along shown a favorable disposition toward Qavam while the Soviets were all but demanding Qavam's appointment as prime minister.

During those months, the Shah had two things on his mind: an overambitious prime minister like Qavam and what Great Britain might have in store for Iran. He was worried that Qavam might be planning to appease Stalin as a first step toward overthrowing the monarchy. He was also anxious that the continued impasse between the Soviet Union and the West would tempt the British to make a secret deal with the Soviets and bargain away Iran's independence or territorial integrity. So worried was the Shah about this possibility, that on January 28, 1945, in a two-and-a-half-hour meeting with the British ambassador, he threw his customary caution to the wind and asked Bullard point-blank, "Do you think there is any possibility that the British government . . . might give Persia up . . . and fall back on a division of the country, for example on the 1907 model [when Tsarist Russia and Britain divided Iran in half, each claiming a part as their virtual protectorate]." Bullard's response was less than reassuring. On the one hand, he said "absolutely no" to the possibility of Britain's participating in a new partition of Iran. But then he went on to say that "the only situation which could conceivably bring about the physical partition of Persia . . . would be one which necessitates our armed intervention to protect our oil interests."[34]

The Shah's fears were initially the result of some unusual moves the British had been making those days. These fears were confirmed during the Yalta Conference in February 1945, for example, when the British Foreign Secretary told his Soviet counterpart that "it was not part of the British policy to prevent Soviet Union obtaining oil in Northern Iran," adding that in Britain's view, Russians were "a natural consumer for Iranian oil."[35] Once the Soviets made their push for just such a concession, the Shah realized that the British were toying with what was initially called the "Bevin Plan," giving the North to the Soviets and keeping the South and its oil-rich Khuzestan province for themselves. According to the Shah, in anticipating such a prospect, the British had gone so far as to "unite the varieties of tribes of the South into a federation"[36] and resume their ties to the Khaz'al family, which had once run that region as a virtual British protectorate; in addition, "British troops in the Iraqi city of Basra [had been] reinforced and two warships were sent to Abadan."[37] Britain's expressed hope that Russia would obtain the petroleum rights in the North was based on the calculation that such a concession would make British rights in the South safer. They assumed that no future Iranian government would dare take on both the Russian and British governments and nationalize the country's oil.[38]

Another key component of the British policy had been to dissuade Iran from filing a complaint against the Soviet Union in the UN Security Council—the first complaint ever filed with the newly created international body. For his part, the Shah made every effort to keep and push forward Iran's complaint on the Security Council agenda. British policy paralleled the Soviet point of view and insisted on the idea that the "Azerbaijan question" was a domestic Iranian issue, and therefore no concern of the United Nations.[39] At one time, the British Ambassador marched into the offices of Ebrahim Hakimi, Iran's prime minister, with British tanks standing outside, and dictated a letter to Iran's representatives to the UN, demanding that they withdraw Iran's complaint against the Soviet Union. Lest Hakimi get cold feet, Bullard insisted on using the British military's secure lines to send the coerced telegram. As it happened, Hussein Ala, Iran's ambassador to the UN and the United States at the time, buoyed by words of support from American officials and from some of his colleagues, decided to ignore the telegram or, more accurately, he decided to pretend it had arrived too late and he proceeded with the complaint.

So worried was the Shah about these British machinations that, as a gesture of displeasure, he refused to meet with the British Ambassador for a short while in 1946.[40] A few months earlier, in an attempt to force Britain's hand and abort the possibility of an Anglo-Soviet collusion, the Shah had toyed with the idea of ordering Iran's military forces into Soviet-occupied Kurdistan without seeking "Russian permission." This would, he hoped, "create an incident" and pit the British and American forces against the Soviet Union.[41] The United States defused the situation by convincing the Shah to seek Soviet permission, but the sense of distrust continued to fester.

The Shah's anxieties about Qavam were also not baseless. Fully aware of Qavam's past ambitions, the Shah was now faced with the reality that the three big powers, which had once either reviled or at least distrusted Qavam, were suddenly all enamored of him. Eventually, the Shah had no choice but to succumb to these pressures, and he appointed Qavam prime minister on January 26, 1946. For decades after the end of the war, Qavam and his supporters cultivated the myth that only his cunning, nationalism, and political acumen had saved Iran's territorial integrity and fooled Stalin into pulling Soviet troops out of Iran. Archival evidence does not support this claim.

The Soviets' sudden affection for Qavam was no accident, but had been carefully solicited by Qavam himself. Even "before coming to power, [Qavam] had met in secret with members of the Russian Commission visiting Iran" and assured them that, had he been the prime minister, "he would have complied with all the suggestions of the Soviet Union."[42] He knew that the Soviet threats, and their intentionally provocative act of occasionally moving their forces near the Iranian border, had cowed and frightened many members of the Majlis, and he publicized his intention to appease the Soviet Union if he became prime minister.[43]

To lessen America's objection to a Russian concession, Qavam promised American officials that if any arrangements were made with the Soviet Union, he would see that America was given some "rights for exploration of oil in Baluchestan."[44] In other words, Qavam's plans were in reality to give the "Russians all they wanted";[45] he would balance the Russian concession by giving American companies a stake in Iran's oil. The American Ambassador ended his report by concluding that it was now up to the Shah to dissuade Qavam from making the ominous deal with the Soviet Union.

But the Shah was never in favor of appeasing the Soviets and by the time of Qavam's new tenure as prime minister had become unflinchingly opposed to any deal with them. He had long been concerned about the American Embassy's close relations with Qavam, and he wanted to make sure that, if ever forced to choose, the Truman administration would not hesitate to pick the Shah over Qavam. Standing up to the Soviets was, he knew, a sure way to ensure American support. The Shah declared that he considered it "unthinkable to allow Soviet technicians to wander freely over Northern provinces during 50 year life of the proposed agreement."[46]

Qavam quickly realized the seriousness of the Shah's opposition to the Soviet deal and first tried to convince him that Iran should at least "prepare a counterproposal." The Shah objected, suggesting that the Soviets were so eager to get a toe in the door that they would in fact agree to any deal, "no matter how favorable to Iran." Qavam then tried to frighten the Shah into submission by telling him that failure to grant some kind of a concession to the Soviets might well beget their full attack on Iran, and that Americans have been unwilling "to give . . . any categorical assurances of prompt and effective"[47] support in case such an attack took place. But this too failed to change the Shah's mind. The Shah had ties of his own to the American Embassy and figured, rightly as it turned out, that the Truman administration would not abide "losing" Iran to the Communists.

The question of a possible Soviet attack was, of course, not just a Qavam ploy. With the Shah and members of the parliament increasingly hardening their position against Qavam's proposed concessions, the Soviet Union began to move its troops on the Iranian border, intimating the possibility of an attack on at least parts of Iran. Instead of withdrawing their forces from Azerbaijan, the Soviets began reinforcing them, particularly by pouring offensive mechanized units into Iran. The Soviets even made an "official" threat by declaring that it would be "very dangerous" for Iran if Russia did not get the concession she sought.

The Shah and the U.S. Embassy in Iran grew concerned that these Soviet threats might not be a mere bluff or bluster. On March 4, 1946, the American Consul in Tabriz sent an "urgent cable . . . reporting ominous Russian troop movements: Some 500 trucks, leaded with ammunitions and supplies and twenty tanks were being deployed in the direction of Tehran."[48] A few days later, the American Ambassador warned the Shah and Qavam that "Russians might occupy Tehran."[49] An authority no less informed about the Soviet intentions than George Kennan—the chief architect of America's containment policy—concluded that it was "a foregone conclusion that Soviets must make some effort in immediate future to bring into power in Iran a regime prepared to accede to major Soviet demands."[50] While in Moscow as America's chargé d'affaires, he had followed developments in Iran closely. According to Kennan, the future success of the containment policy and the West's ability to manage the Soviet threat were predicated on "the cohesion and rigor it could muster" against the USSR in Iran.[51]

Based on these warnings, the American Embassy in Tehran began to prepare several contingency plans for just such an attack. In the midst of this dire planning, in June 1946, the Shah received a surprising communication from the Russian Embassy inviting him to a special dinner party. The Soviet ambassador, Ivan Sadchikov, insisted that "it would create a very favorable impression on Soviet circle if HM would accept the invitation." Lest the Shah had somehow missed the full implication of the invitation, the Ambassador added that accepting such an invitation "would be a serious blow for the Tudeh Party." The target of the invitation was as much the Tudeh Party as Qavam. The Soviets were willing to make a deal with anyone to get the concession they so coveted, and if Qavam was unable to seal the deal, they were ready to sacrifice him, or even their comrades in the Tudeh Party, to make the deal with the Shah. The Shah demurred, suggesting that it would be more proper if the King invited the Ambassador to the Court for tea.[52]

While the Shah refused to conspire with the Soviets against Qavam, he had no qualms about meeting secretly with politicians opposed to Qavam and encouraging them to act against him. At the same time, the Shah began offering covert financial help to some royalist political parties. Of these, the most unusual was the Sumka Party, led by a scholar named Davud Monshizadeh who modeled his looks and ideology, as well as his title of "rahbar," on Hitler. The Shah, according to one source, even helped buy a house as the party's headquarters.[53]

By then, the Shah was also taking an active role in monitoring the activities of opposition parties, particularly the Tudeh Party. Probably unbeknownst to the Shah, in late 1945, leaders of the party had contemplated the idea of seizing power in Iran and "inviting" the Soviet Union to join in their plans, which would have made Iran the first instance of the kind of "People's Republics" that soon came to dot the map of Eastern Europe. Tudeh Party leaders had at the time prepared a document called "Political Conditions in Iran and Measures on the Development of a Democratic Movement." It referred to the "frequent change of governments" in Iran as a sign that the "ruling classes" were incapable of solving Iran's problems. The party leaders recommended a "democratic coup" against the Shah and his family, who, in their words, were "at the center of intrigues." The party claimed to have 1,000 members in Meshed, the capital of the province of Khorasan, and 6,000 in Tehran, all ready to participate in the coup. In an early reference to their clandestine network of military officers that was discovered some years later, the document added that "Tudeh-supporter pilots would bomb the buildings of Majlis and army."[54] By then the Truman administration had made it abundantly clear to Stalin that Iran was in the West's "sphere of influence" and that Soviet adventurism there would not be tolerated. At Yalta and at Potsdam, the two big powers' "spheres of influence" had been discussed. Stalin even walked into one meeting with a small note on which he had jotted down the countries he considered in his "sphere of influence." He allowed Churchill to keep the note as a souvenir while keeping the countries written on the note himself. The Tudeh Party plan for a "democratic coup" ran counter to these "spheres of influence" and was rejected by the Soviet "Big Brother."

The Shah was, of course, never oblivious to the danger posed by the Tudeh Party. During this period, Colonel Hassan Pakravan was in charge of the section of the army intelligence unit—Rokne do—entrusted with the task of fighting Communists. Pakravan reported directly to the Shah, who, one day, ordered him to find a reliable officer for a highly sensitive job. By then tensions over turf had already developed between the police and army intelligence, particularly on the question of who should have the lead role in fighting Communists. More than once, these battles allowed the Tudeh Party to escape detection.

Pakravan chose his close friend and colleague, Lieutenant Hassanali Alavi-Kia. Both Pakravan and Alavi-Kia would go on to play important roles in the life of the Shah and his security organization, SAVAK. The Shah ordered Alavi-Kia to meet once a week, at an already set time and place—"Tuesdays, at two, in the corner of Seyyed Ali avenue"—with a man[55] who would report on the activities of the Tudeh Party leadership. It was a sign of the treacherous nature of Iranian politics in those years that the "mole" was allegedly introduced to the Shah by Mozzafar Baghai—a man of myriad talents and as many mysteries who was considered in those years a fierce foe of the Shah and who continued to play a peripheral role in the Shah's political life for the next quarter century. According to Alavi-Kia, the "mole" often provided firsthand knowledge of the most sensitive decisions of the party.[56] His reports would be directly conveyed to the Shah.

In fact, the Tudeh Party machinations, their alliance with Qavam—evident most clearly in the fact that at one time, three of their leaders were given ministerial portfolios in Qavam's cabinet—the continued crisis in Azerbaijan, Qavam's increasing power and arrogance, and finally, signs that he harbored plans for "overthrowing the monarchy," and establishing "a republic (Russian model perhaps) in its place,"[57] all combined to make the Shah particularly despondent in those months. His trepidation only increased when, in February 1946, Qavam and an entourage of advisors, translators, and ministers left Tehran for Moscow, where they met with Soviet officials. The night before the group's departure, Qavam took them to the Court and introduced them to the Shah, but in reality he made every effort to keep the Shah marginal to his negotiations not just with the Soviets, but with the American and British Embassies. More than once, he confided in the American or British Embassy and asked them to keep the Shah in the dark about it.

In Moscow, Qavam met twice with Stalin. Tehran was rife with rumors that Qavam had made a "secret deal" with the Russians to overthrow the Shah. The British Embassy at the time reported that "Qavam might yield to Soviet pressure and become the president for a democratic front."[58] Shortly after arriving back in Tehran, Qavam went to the Court to report on his trip to the Shah. If the intent of the meeting was to dispel any anxieties the Shah might have had about what "deal" Qavam had made with Stalin, it failed. The Shah tried to fend off Qavam's plans in several ways.

Eventually, the Shah decided to warn Qavam directly about his ambitions. It was a measure of the two men's estrangement that when the Shah decided to warn his prime minister about the dangers of flirting with the Soviet Union, he needed the help of the American Ambassador. Through the Ambassador, the Shah told Qavam that if the Soviets had promised to "install him in high office" they would do so, but that once they had squeezed him dry, they would toss him aside. In fact, the day before the Shah's plea, the American Ambassador had, on his own, warned Qavam about rumors from Moscow "to the effect that he might be tempted toward disloyalty." Qavam denied the charges, but the Ambassador remained convinced that Qavam had not "told full story of Moscow plans."[59]

So worried was the Shah about the Soviet threat and about Qavam's conspiracies that for a while he reduced the number of his public appearances. His mood grew increasingly despondent. In a June 1946 meeting with the British Embassy, the Shah was "obviously weary about his future" and articulated "defeatist ideas about the end of all regimes of constitutional monarchy." He predicted that neither the King of Greece, nor Juan Carlos of Spain have "an outside sporting chance of staging a comeback."[60] On another occasion, he complained that Qavam had hired goons to physically assault him and the royal family. The British warned the Shah about "his failure to appear in public," suggesting that people were beginning to think that "he may be afraid." The Shah looked "unhappy, discouraged, and very frightened, even less sure of himself than usual." He often repeated what was becoming a mantra. It was, he said, "impossible to be a constitutional ruler" in Iran. The answer he received was less than satisfactory. A dictatorship was also impossible, he was told by the British Ambassador. When reporting this conversation, the Ambassador went on to make a comment on the Shah's character. The Shah, he said, was most inclined toward "running away morally, if not even physically"[61] from any problem.

❦

Eventually, helped by his twin sister, Princess Ashraf, and encouraged by words and deeds of support from the American government, the Shah succeeded in helping Qavam overcome the Azerbaijan crisis and then ridding himself of the "meddlesome" Prime Minister. After Qavam's trip to Moscow—a trip he hailed as a great success—he began to negotiate not only with the Russian Embassy in Tehran, but with a delegation from the Azerbaijan province led by Jafar Pishevari. A few weeks after Qavam's return, Soviet troops began to leave Iran, easily a key development in the resolution of the crisis. By then, Pishevari had a full-fledged cabinet and increasingly acted as a head of state. His official title was prime minister, while other provinces in Iran had governors. His government was also acting more and more like an independent state. Units of the Iranian army had been disarmed and dismissed. Iranian postage stamps "were over-printed with the words 'Azerbaijan National Government, 21 Azar 1234," and before long "a new flag appeared over government buildings in Tabriz." Finally, in a gesture that captured poetically and politically where the heart of the new Azerbaijan government was, it "adopted Moscow time, half an hour behind Tehran."[62]

The Shah began his plans for dismissing Qavam first by opposing Qavam's attempt at appeasing the Soviets and reaching a rapprochement with Pishevari. But he waited for the Soviet army's departure from Iran before making his move against Qavam. The fact that Qavam had chosen his vice-premier and propaganda and labor minister, Mozzafar Firuz, as his chief negotiator with Pishevari made it politically easier and more emotionally appealing for the Shah to fight the agreement. Firuz had long openly ridiculed and criticized the Shah, and in return the Shah developed a lifelong visceral hatred of the man. Even long after the end of the Azerbaijan crisis, when the Shah was at the height of his power and figures like Firuz were altogether marginalized, his obsessive hatred of Firuz did not dissipate.[63] Moreover, in 1946, the Shah's ability to oppose any agreement reached by Qavam was augmented by the fact that, by then, Firuz was considered "a spokesman of the pro-Soviet element in Iran, outdoing the Tudeh party itself."[64]

On June 13, 1946, with much fanfare, Qavam announced that Firuz had finally succeeded in resolving all outstanding issues between the central government and Pishevari. The claim was far from the truth. Many apparently intractable issues, including the nature and limits of the "autonomous region's" power, were left unresolved. But by then, with the Soviet troops gone, Pishevari felt more vulnerable and had softened some of his views and his rhetoric. In his own words, Western pressure on the Soviet Union—what he called his "big friend"—had changed the landscape.[65] In reality, while in Tehran, Pishevari received a long, surprisingly harsh letter from Stalin, reprimanding him for his overzealous revolutionary rhetoric. Iran and Azerbaijan are not in a revolutionary situation, Stalin said, adding that "we could no longer keep [Soviet troops] in Iran, mainly because the presence of Soviet troops in Iran undercut the foundations of our liberationist policies in Europe and Asia. The British and Americans said to us that if Soviet troops could stay in Iran, then why could not the British troops stay in Egypt, Syria, Indonesia, Greece and also the American troops in China... therefore we decided to withdraw troops from Iran and China, in order... to unleash the liberation movements in the colonies."[66]

In spite of the remaining intractable issues between the two sides, both Pishevari and Qavam had to pretend progress was being made in the negotiations: Pishevari because Stalin had ordered him to soften his position and Qavam for two different reasons. He had promised Stalin he would soon resolve differences with Pishevari and, moreover, some Western diplomats at the time believed that Qavam had calculated that his position as prime minister was guaranteed only so long as the negotiations continued. The Shah, he knew, was trying to get rid of him, and prolonging the negotiations with the Soviets and Pishevari while showing some progress was one way to stay in power and block the Shah's moves.

The Shah was equally resolved to derail the agreement and depose Qavam. Was it likely that the proposed agreement with Pishevari would, as Qavam and his supporters suggest, pave the way for a more democratic, federal Iranian government, or would it set the nation on the slippery slope that would end in secession? While it is impossible to answer this question with certainty, the fate of the People's Republics of Eastern Europe makes it far more likely that Iranian Azerbaijan would have soon followed a similar fate and disappeared behind the Iron Curtain.

The Shah focused his opposition to the agreement by adamantly opposing the part stipulating that "the Azerbaijan army will be incorporated into the Iranian army."[67] As the Shah never tired of repeating in future years, he had told Qavam that he "would prefer to have [his] hand cut off than to sign such a decree."[68] For several reasons, the Shah's opposition key amongst them, Qavam's negotiations with the Pishevari government collapsed. By then, Qavam had seen the writing on the wall. His plans for some kind of oil concession to the Soviets and an autonomy agreement with the Pishevari government were no longer a possibility, and he declared himself fully in agreement with the proposed operation by the Iranian military to retake Azerbaijan. On December 11, 1946, the Iranian military, commanded by the Shah and General Hajj Ali Razmara, entered and reoccupied the province of Azerbaijan. Before Iranian forces began to move, the Soviet Embassy in Tehran, the Tudeh Party, and Pishevari's propaganda department—one threatening war, another promising "resistance to death," and the Tudeh Party offering full support to the Pishevari government—tried to deter Qavam and the Shah from going through with the planned military operation. But both men, albeit for different reasons, held firm. In spite of the revolutionary bombast of Pishevari and his comrades—"there is death, but no retreat," they had famously announced—once Iran's military began to move into Azerbaijan, there was little serious resistance. The radical zeal of some of Pishevari's policies, the heavy-handed approach of the Soviet "advisors" and of the exiles who had returned home with the Red Army—the Muhajirs—combined to create "the terror that gripped Azerbaijan at the time."[69] This terror had by then sapped what early enthusiasm there was amongst the people and had made the ruling party weak and isolated. Before the military operation, more than once, the Shah had made "reconnaissance flights over enemy-held territory, often in old planes, sometimes in small, twin-engined Beechcraft, and always without a radio."[70]

With no Soviet army to prop them up and no people to support them, the Democratic Party of Azerbaijan collapsed sooner than anyone had imagined. Less than twenty-four hours after the invasion, the Party conceded defeat. In the morning, the Democratic Party's official organs had called on people to resist the attackers, and around eight o'clock in the evening, the same organs asked people not to fight the Iranian army. It has been estimated that during the first stage of the operation 500 people were killed on both sides. On the second day of the military operation, the Soviet Ambassador requested an emergency meeting with the Shah. He marched into the room and angrily demanded an immediate end to all hostilities. Unbeknownst to him, by then the Shah had already received reports that the Azerbaijan government had collapsed and surrendered. With glee in his eyes, the Shah showed the incredulous Ambassador copies of the reports from the region, indicating that the hostilities had ended.[71] Reports from citizens of Tabriz at the time, written on the day the military operations began, indicate that from early morning, as soon as people heard the Iranian army was on its way, they began to attack, disarm, and at times execute members of the Azerbaijan government, particularly the much-despised Muhajirs who had invariably been the most brutal in suppressing the people.[72] Even earlier, people had shown their disgruntlement with the more radical policies of Pishervari's comrades by celebrating, with more than usual fanfare, the birth dates of Shiite Imams.

In solving the Azerbaijan crisis of 1946, the Shah was helped by a number of factors. On the one hand, he had come to believe that his decisions were "really inspired and decided by that mystical power" to which he felt he owed his career. Ironically, even Qavam is reported to have occasionally engaged in the religious ritual called *estekhareh* in which the devout use either the Qu'ran or their worry beads to consult God about the wisdom or the likelihood of an action. More secular Iranians use the *Hafez Divan* for the same purpose, opening it to a random page, reading the *ghazal* (sonnet) on that page, and finding from it a guide to Heaven's designs. In Qavam's case, when faced with a dire decision like Azerbaijan, he used the worry beads he invariably carried in his pocket to find out what God wanted him to do.[73] It was, the Shah told one of his authorized biographers, "divine intelligence that" directed his actions and even determined their timing.[74] His policies in the Azerbaijan crisis, no less than any other of his decisions, were, in his mind, "part of [his] mystical life . . . and the mission ordained for [him] by higher powers."[75]

In less spiritual moments, the Shah attributed Iran's ability to get the Soviet Red Army out of the country—incidentally, the only time the Soviets were forced to give up a territory they had occupied—at least partially to Truman's "frank" and "stiff" notes to Stalin, demanding Soviet evacuation of its forces from Iran. Years later, in a press conference on April 24, 1952, Truman himself claimed that he "had to send an ultimatum" to Stalin to get its forces out of Iran. Later the same day, a White House spokesman clarified Truman's declaration by saying that "the President was using the term [ultimatum] ultimately in a non-technical sense." Truman further claimed that the U.S. message sent to the Soviet Union "was the major factor in bringing about Soviet withdrawal from Iran."[76] Recent material from the Soviet archives seems to indicate that in deciding to take his troops out of Iran, Stalin took into consideration a large number of factors, and not just pressures from the United States or promises from Qavam.[77] Without access to all the deliberations of the Soviet leadership in the days this decision was made, it is impossible to measure the relative value and power of each of these factors in shaping Soviet policy.[78] If we believe Stalin's letter to Pishevari, the major reason for his decision to withdraw Soviet forces was that Iran was not ready for a revolution.

The Shah believed that American intervention brought about a new stage in U.S.–Soviet relations, writing in his *Answer to History* that "it is fair to say that the Cold War began in Iran."[79] Others, like the American Consul in Tabriz have gone even further, suggesting that the "Cold War began on March 4, 1946. On that day fifteen Soviet armored brigades began to pour into the Northern Provinces in Iran."[80] Not accidentally, on March 5, Churchill delivered his famous speech warning of the rise of a new "Iron Curtain" around parts of the world. Truman had seen a draft of the address before it was delivered and showed his support for its content when he accepted the job of "introducing Churchill to the Fulton, Missouri audience."[81]

Not long after the end of the Azerbaijan crisis, the Shah decided to finally rid himself of *Hazrat-e Ashraf* (His Eminence), a title he himself had bestowed on Qavam in the heat of the Azerbaijan crisis, long after Reza Shah had banned the use of all such titles. The Shah knew he still lacked the independent power base to dismiss Qavam without the support, or at least the tacit approval, of the American, if not the British, Embassy. As early as March 27, 1947, he told the American Embassy about charges of corruption against Qavam that "were brought to him daily" and wondered whether he should dismiss the Prime Minister for this reason. The Shah's claim about allegations of corruption was not baseless. Qavam's greed and penchant for bribes and kickbacks was by then widely rumored in Iran, and on occasion reported by foreign governments.[82] But in 1947, the Shah's real goal was not fighting corruption but soliciting the American Embassy's support for removing Qavam. The American ambassador, George Allen, clearly understood what the Shah meant, but the United States still did not want Qavam removed, and thus Allen responded that "the responsibility for removing or sustaining the government should be placed on the *Majlis*."[83]

The Shah too understood what the Ambassador's response implied, but he was not deterred and continued his effort to dismiss Qavam. In this endeavor, the uprising of southern tribes against Qavam inadvertently helped the Shah. Tribal leaders objected to the membership of Communists in Qavam's cabinet. Qavam had no choice but to comply with their wishes, but dismissing the Communist members of his government would dissipate any remaining support he had on the Left. With the Right already against him and solidly in the Shah's camp, Qavam was now clearly vulnerable, and the Shah knew this. By mid-October, the American Embassy had also changed its mind on Qavam. The State Department instructed its embassy in Tehran to "give all appropriate" support to any government the Shah appointed to replace Qavam.[84]

By October 16, there was a rumor in Tehran that the Shah had ordered the arrest of Qavam. The once all-powerful Prime Minister who had dismissed the Shah as a novice was now worried enough to visit some of the generals close to the Shah that day "to find out what the true situation was." The generals were not very helpful, claiming ignorance of the Shah's plans. Yet they added to Qavam's anxieties by saying that what they did know was that "the Shah was disgusted with the cabinet's pro-Soviet orientation." Even before the encounter, Qavam had confided to some of his supporters that "he was primarily afraid of Iranian army."[85] The army, Qavam knew, was fully in the Shah's camp.

Anxious about his fate, a now-chastened Qavam asked to meet with the Shah on October 17. By then, the Shah had, in his own words, "spent three sleepless nights" trying to decide whether the time to fire Qavam had finally arrived.[86] According to the Shah, Qavam was "trembling with fright" when he arrived at the Court. With anger in his voice and agitation in his movements, the Shah demanded that members of the Tudeh Party and Mozzafar Firuz "must be dismissed." Left with few options, Qavam agreed to reshuffle the cabinet and rid it of Communist members, but on Firuz he offered a compromise. Instead of firing him, he would send him to Russia as Iran's ambassador. The Shah agreed but later confided to a friend that he had accepted the idea of sending Firuz to Moscow only "because Iranian ambassadors were always treated like dogs by the Kremlin."[87]

By the end of the meeting, Qavam and the Shah "drew up a new cabinet list," but the Shah had one last demand: he wanted Qavam to keep the decision to fire the Communist ministers a secret for twenty-four hours and announce it to the media as a fait accompli. This way, the Tudeh Party would have no chance to try and preempt the reshuffle by organizing demonstrations, and the Soviets would have no opportunity to make new threats. Qavam agreed to the Shah's demand, but no sooner had he left the Court than he "promptly told Firuz who told Soviet ambassador."

As expected, Russia immediately reacted angrily to the plan, making new threats. Qavam tried to use the threat to frighten the Shah into accepting another delay in their planed reshuffle, "lest the Soviet troops might enter the country."[88] The Shah did not relent. Moreover, the American Embassy had by then already assured the Shah that, in the case of a Soviet attack, the United States would be there to help. More crucially, the Shah knew that getting rid of the Communists in the cabinet would both endear him to the Truman administration and become the necessary first step in getting rid of Qavam.

A few weeks later, the Shah was ready to make his final move. His twin sister, Princess Ashraf, was an active partner in this effort. It had taken the Shah a few months to line up the votes in the Majlis and convince Qavam's once-powerful allies, and even members of his cabinet, to move against him. To solicit the crucial help of the parliament and its powerful speaker, Sardar Fakher Hekmat, the Shah had, according to the British Embassy, helped pay off the Speaker's hefty gambling debts.[89]

On December 4, 1947, to Qavam's utter surprise, all but one member of his cabinet suddenly resigned. He had become particularly vulnerable a few weeks earlier when his proposed bill to offer concessions to the Soviet Union was defeated in the parliament. Even then, he had tried in vain to delay the vote on the proposed concessions. The Shah and the Speaker, showing what the American Embassy called "statesman-like behavior" and patriotism, had worked behind the scenes and away from the watchful eyes of Qavam and his allies to defeat the bill and reject the proposed delay. The American Embassy helped the process by promising protection to Iran in case of a Soviet attack. The fact that Qavam had used his powers as prime minister to ensure that a majority of the Majlis were from his newly established Democratic Party of Iran—a party much in the tradition of populist organizations, with their uniforms, party songs, and mass demonstrations as a sign of their invincible power—turned out to be of no help. Many of Qavam's acolytes had changed their minds by the time of the vote, particularly after the insistent intervention of Princess Ashraf.[90]

The oil concession bill's defeat could have led to a crisis, particularly between Iran and the Soviet Union, making it impossible to dismiss Qavam. Much to the Shah's relief, the Russians were not keen on creating such a crisis. He believed that Stalin showed no reaction to this major setback because "the Berlin question needed all of his attention" and victories by Mao Zedong's forces offered the hope of even bigger Soviet gains in China.[91]

Qavam had a hard time accepting defeat. In a gesture that bordered between defiance and quixotic delusions of grandeur, even after the massive resignation of his cabinet, he showed up in the Majlis the next day, to be met with the further humiliation of a vote of no confidence. In his farewell speech, he declared that history would absolve him and reveal his many patriotic services to the country. Before long, fearing for his safety, he left Iran for Paris, where he waited for the next round in his shadowboxing match with the Shah. It took something of a miracle that there even was such a next round.

Qavam and Azerbaijan, Soviet encroachments, and Queen Fawzia must have all seemed paltry to the Shah as he sat bleeding, very slowly, in the back of his limousine, around 1:30 in the afternoon of a cold, rainy day on February 4, 1949. Dr. Manouchehr Egbal, once a protégé of Qavam's and a key player in the Shah's successfully orchestrated mass resignation of Qavam's ministers, was in the car, attending to the wound. Dr. Egbal had been at Tehran University as the minister of health and as a part of the Shah's official welcoming committee.

The Shah had arrived at the university around one o'clock in the afternoon. Earlier that day he had gone skiing—a lifelong passion he had developed while studying in Switzerland—and he was now visiting Tehran University's Faculty of Law and Political Science. The establishment of this school had been, according to Ayatollah Khomeini, a near-mortal blow to the power and prestige of the clergy in Iran. It deprived them of their lucrative monopoly control of the judiciary and of the courts. "We should have opposed the school's establishment," Ayatollah Khomeini would say more than once in his life. The Shah was in fact coming to the university to celebrate the anniversary of the law school's foundation. But that February afternoon, as the Shah, dressed in his military uniform and wearing a heavy overcoat, stepped out of his car—"a black Rolls Royce"[92] that day—a man whose thoughts and ideas were not dissimilar to those of Ayatollah Khomeini was waiting in the area set aside for journalists and photographers. His name was Nasser Fakhrarai, and the camera case he carried gave him the appearance of a photographer. But what he had come to shoot that day was not a photograph.

As the Shah neared the steps leading to the law school building, Fakhrarai, standing near the steps, pulled out a revolver he had hidden inside the camera case and began to shoot at the Shah, point-blank. He was nervous. His hands shook. He had been planning for this moment for at least three years. The fact that the Shah was left with no protection after the first shot afforded Fakhrarai no help. Upon hearing the first shot, the head of the Shah's security detail hit the pavement and crawled to safety under the Rolls-Royce. Members of the welcoming team all took refuge inside the building. The assassin's first three bullets only grazed the Shah's hat. The fourth bullet entered his cheek and exited from his upper lip. Several of his front teeth were knocked out. A set of false teeth to replace the damaged ones was quickly made for him. The fact that he used them became henceforth something of a state secret.[93] Only a few trusted members of his immediate family knew of their existence. An occasional, slightly audible hiss was the only hint of the false teeth's existence.

By the time the fourth bullet pierced the Shah's lip, the assassin had only two left in his revolver's chamber. There is something cinematic in the Shah's description of what happened next. "There we stood, facing each other," he writes, "with no one between us. I knew there was no reason why the next bullet won't hit me. I fully remember my reaction in those split seconds. I thought maybe I should jump him, but then realized that such a move will make me an easier target, and if I tried to escape, I figured, he will shoot me in the back."

Left with no good alternatives, the Shah decided on what he called "a series of acrobatic moves, employing a military tactic to confound the shooter." He describes how he moved to the right and then to the left, and how he swayed forward and backward, all in a few split seconds. His description is like watching a film where the bullet's motion has been slowed to a crawl. "The next bullet," the Shah writes, "wounded my shoulders." There was now only one bullet left. So far the assassin's failure of marksmanship, or the Shah's agility of movement, had saved him. What would save him now? "The last bullet jammed in the chamber," the Shah writes.[94]

The assassin angrily threw his revolver at the Shah and ran toward the grassy knoll a few steps away. There is a photo of the Shah moments after the failed assassination attempt. He is still on his feet and has pulled out a handkerchief and is using it to stop and wipe away the blood. A few feet from the grass were the campus walls, a gate, and a throng of curious, frightened observers. Fakhrarai was headed in that direction. But before he could reach the gate, soldiers jumped on him. Some say he had fallen, allowing the soldiers to catch up with him easily. "Kill the son of bitch," cried General Murteza Khan Yazdanpanah, a trusted military aide to the Shah. By then, the assassin was no longer armed, save for a small knife, shown in published pictures with a caption indicating it was hidden inside his sock. Within minutes of the failed attempt on the Shah's life, rifle butts and bullets fired point-blank had killed Fakhrarai. In his pocket the guards found his identity card showing he had gained access to the area as a staff photographer for a paper called *Parcham-e Islam* (Flag of Islam).

In the paranoid world of Iranian politics, the questionable decision of the Shah's guards to kill the assassin led to a plethora of conspiracy theories, including one that implicated those at the scene. They were complicit in the act, people whispered, and lest the assassin talk and reveal their secrets, they killed him. Another theory pointed an accusing finger at General Razmara. Like a ghost haunting the halls of power, his hand was seen behind every major event in the country in those days, and few things were as "major" as an attempt on the life of the Shah. Razmara was by then one of the most powerful generals in the Iranian military. His political ambition was an open secret. His ties to the Soviet Union and to the Tudeh Party were grist to many rumor mills. His romantic ties to Princess Ashraf afforded him special access to the Court and the Shah.[95] These factors, and the fact that he was conspicuously absent from the ranks of dignitaries gathered at the university to welcome the Shah, combined to make him a suspect.

The Shah's own description of the assassin's connections exemplifies his proclivity for conspiracy theories. "It became clear later," he wrote, "that he had connections to some religious zealots, and also there was some evidence of his connection to the dissolved Tudeh Party. It is also interesting that the assassin's girlfriend was the daughter of the gardener at the British Embassy."[96] As it turned out, the assassin had, some months earlier, taken up with a woman called Mahin Eslami, and her father did indeed work at the embassy. But Fakhrarai had also been trying to kill the Shah long before the romance began.

A few hours after the assassination attempt, the royal Court and the government both issued communiqués describing the incident. As expected, keen on using the occasion to the Shah's political benefit, the Court communiqué quoted what it suggested were the Shah's first words after surgery: "To serve the country and the beloved nation, a few bullets count for naught, and my resolve in reaching our goals remains intact."[97]

The government communiqué talked of a widening conspiracy of "traitors" keen on "undermining the foundations of the nation's security." In recent months, it said, these traitors had been emboldened in their treachery; they commenced by spreading vicious rumors against the Shah, that most "sacred official of the country," and finally their audacity reached a level wherein one of the traitors took aim "at the most sacred of all sacred authorities in the country," a person who "embodies Iran's national identity and is the foundation of the country's independence."[98]

Around seven in the evening, the Shah delivered a short message on the radio. His picture, in a checkered hospital gown, with a bandage around his mouth, became iconic, and the Shah's supporters praised it for capturing his stoic heroism. In his radio message, the Shah first thanked the "infinite grace and goodness of the Good Lord," who saved him from the assassination attempt, and then went on to thank the people for their profuse show of support. He ended by promising to "give life and limb" in the service of safeguarding the nation and securing the welfare of the people.[99]

Though the assassin had been a religious zealot, active with Islamic radicals opposed to the Shah, the Tudeh Party was blamed for masterminding the assassination attempt. In reality, Fakhrarai, a confused young man, angry at the world and at the Shah, had been a childhood friend of a member of the party—a nondescript young man called Abdullah Arghani. For several years, Fakhrarai had been talking to Arghani about his plans to kill the Shah. In 1946, three years before the day he nearly succeeded, he had forged for himself an identity card that showed him to be a photojournalist for *Parcham-e Islam*.

Fakhrarai had made his first attempt to kill the Shah in 1946 when the latter had traveled to the city of Isfahan. Fakhrarai apparently never came close enough to take a shot. On that trip, the Shah was accompanied by Parvin Ghafari, in those days rumored to be his favorite paramour.[100] The affair was hardly a well-kept secret. A few years later, one of Iran's most prolific writers of popular romance novels serialized a story he called "Our Town's Blonde." It was something of a roman à clef, particularly in its early parts, chronicling the blonde's affair with a character who bore an unmistakable resemblance to the Shah.[101] During Fawzia's absence from the country, the Shah was often seen with her—including the 1946 journey to Isfahan.

Fakhrarai's second failed attempt was made a few months later when the Shah was watching a tennis match in Amjadiye—the city's only stadium at the time. Once again, the assailant did not get close enough to shoot. From his days in Switzerland, tennis had been one of the Shah's favorite pastimes, and he had built a tennis court in one of his palaces. Tehran papers at the time marveled at the fact that the tennis court was sufficiently lit that it allowed the Shah to play a game at night if he wanted to. They wrote of his regular matches with some of the country's top players.[102]

On each of these two failed assassination attempts, Fakhrarai had shared his plans with his childhood friend Abdullah Arghani, who was by then a member of the Tudeh Party. Arghani had shared his information with Noural-din Kianouri, one of the Tudeh Party's top leaders. As soon as Kianouri learned of Fakhrarai's plans, he discussed the matter with the party *politburo*. The committee summarily dismissed the idea as "adventurism" and "terrorism" and ordered Kianuouri to cease all contacts with the assassin. But Kianouri considered himself one of the true revolutionaries in a party otherwise dominated by reformists, and thus he refused to follow the party leaders' decision, continuing the contacts with Fakhrarai, even going so far as helping to provide him with a revolver.[103] As a result, when the assassination attempt at Tehran University took place, the Shah and the police, keen on blaming the Communists, and planning to use the charge of complicity in the attack to declare the party illegal, had just enough threads to connect the Communists to the assassination attempt.

Not long after the two official communiqués following the shooting at the university, the government declared martial law; a special session of the Majlis was convened that night, and the Tudeh Party was declared illegal—a decision the government proved unable or unwilling to implement. Before midnight on the day of the failed assassination attempt, twenty-eight of the party's top leaders were arrested. But, for the next four years, in spite of the government decrees banning and dissolving the party, it continued to operate, even thrive, through its many front organizations.

❧

While "divine intervention" and acrobatic military tactics were, in the Shah's mind, what had saved him from the assassin's bullets, a few months earlier he had almost lost his life in a flying accident. In those years, his political and emotional life was fraught with bleak realities, but a bright spot had come in September of 1946 when he officially received his pilot's license. Ever since Wendell Willkie, the Republican candidate in the 1940 U.S. presidential election, had come to Tehran in 1942 and given the Shah a ride over the capital in his private jet, flying had become a passion in the Shah's life.[104] Going up in the air with Willkie gave the Shah such pleasure that he "wanted to stay up indefinitely." Only when Willkie "insisted that landing at night might be difficult did he agree to land."[105]

In a strange twist of fate, the Shah almost decided to avoid the meeting. Willkie, who suffered from athlete's foot, had, in his earlier meeting with Qavam, taken off his shoes to scratch his toes. Qavam also suspected that Willkie had allowed himself the luxury and liberty of freeing himself, noisily, of superfluous bodily gases while discussing urgent matters of state with the Prime Minister.[106] Lest he repeat his audacity of noisy shoelessness in a formal royal audience, Qavam had suggested, rather cryptically, that the Shah must cancel his meeting with Willkie. The Shah ignored the warning as he distrusted Qavam's motives. The meeting took place with no incident, and one result was the Shah's exposure to piloting and planes. In spite of his demure and invariably cautious public demeanor, the Shah had a lifelong passion for the reckless abandon of a speeding car, a fast motorcycle, or an airplane.

After the flyover with Wendell Willkie, the Shah hired an American TWA captain by the name of Dick Collbarn to teach him how to fly. The American State Department had only one piece of advice for Collbarn as he set out for his new duties: "The Shah was not to get killed."[107] Arriving at the Court, the Captain was particularly surprised by the fact that "the shah must have twenty-five custom-built cars... Buicks, Cadillacs, six Rolls-Royces, a Mercedes."[108] The Shah, the Captain concluded, was "an apt flying student." He taught the Shah how to fly British model planes, like the Anson and Hurricane, and American models like Beechcraft. Eventually the Shah fell in love with a B-17 plane he had seen in Tehran. He "started to bicker for it" and eventually bought it sometime in early 1947. The price is not known.[109]

The Shah's passion for flying and for speed almost cost him his life many times. In 1944, for example, he was flying his "small single-engine plane to a place called Kuhrang, near Isfahan." A general was the only passenger. Hardly ten minutes into the flight, "without any rhyme or reason, the engine went dead," forcing the Shah to make an emergency landing "in a narrow zigzag ravine full of rocks and cliffs."[110] The maneuvers forced the plane into a somersault, and it came to a halt upside down, with both the Shah and his passenger "hanging upside down from their seats."[111]

While the plane accident had no impact on the nation's public mood toward the Shah, the failed assassination attempt afforded him a flood of sympathy and became a useful tool for realizing one of his main goals in the first decade of his rule. From his first days in office, he was, in the words of the British Embassy, "hankering after more power," telling anyone who would listen, particularly the British and American ambassadors more than once that "the only solution [to Iran's problems] was for him to have more power." More specifically, he wanted the power to dissolve "an unsatisfactory parliament."[112] But these attempts were repeatedly met with either the stiff resistance of Iranian political forces, or push-back from the British and American Embassies. Both embassies believed an increase in the Shah's constitutional power would lead to a system of "one man rule," and they had both concluded that the Shah's past behavior did not "inspire confidence" in such a rule.[113] In explaining their opposition to the Shah's proposal, they told him that, "no European monarch has constitutional power to initiate dissolution of parliament, except Sweden where such power has not been used in past twenty five years."[114]

From early 1948, the question of changing the constitution and increasing his power became something of an "obsession" for the Shah. Even in the eyes of George Allen, the American ambassador, who was usually sympathetic to the Shah, he had begun to "show almost alarming preoccupation" with the question of constitutional change.[115]

Throughout 1948, the Shah used every occasion to convince the British and American Embassies about the wisdom, indeed the dire necessity, of his proposed constitutional change. By then he had found more than a few Iranian politicians willing to support his plans. During the month of October of that year, he threatened that "he would abdicate"[116] if he did not receive the extra powers he demanded. At about the same time, he offered to give the Majlis "a four months ultimatum" to approve his proposal, otherwise he would resign. The American Embassy still tried to dissuade the Shah from his plans, telling him that "foreign policy and national defense were already firmly in his hands" and that seeking more power was unwise. Moreover, the embassy advised the Shah strongly against the idea of using "the threat of abdication."[117]

When the Shah decided he could not convince the American and British Embassies about the wisdom of his plans, he decided to proceed and "not to heed American and British advice" against the idea.[118] Faced with the Shah's intractable position, both embassies changed their minds and decided to support the idea. Ironically, Tehran was in those days rife with rumors that the Shah's decision to increase his power was an order issued by the British.[119] Their only suggestion was that, concurrently with the revision of the constitution, the Shah should also demand the establishment of a Senate. The 1905 constitution had called for the creation of such an institution, but it had never been established.

By April 1949, the Shah finally succeeded in convening an amenable Constituent Assembly for the specific purpose of changing the constitution, augmenting his own power and diluting the power and independence of the Majlis. In his speech to the opening session of the Assembly, after conjuring the "sacred and unchanging principles of the Beneficent faith of Islam," the Shah told the members that after contemplating the problems of the country over the last few years, he had concluded that the "most elemental cause of the country's problems has been an imbalance between the powers of the three branches of government." A new constitutional amendment augmenting the power of his office would, he said, allow the country to find its place amongst the genuine democracies of the world and allow the government to work for a more just and equitable distribution of wealth in the country.[120] But the argument was specious at best. Constitutional experts have long argued that in a democracy, where checks and balances between the three branches diminish the possibility of despotism, the power of the executive to dissolve the parliament can be "democratic" only if, in the process of dissolution, the fate of the executive is put to a new vote. In the absence of such provision, the right to dissolve the parliament leads to despotism.[121]

In the case of Iran, the carefully "picked" Constituent Assembly not only gave the Shah the power to dissolve the Majlis at will, but also called for the creation of a Senate—a body composed of sixty senators, thirty of whom were appointed by the Shah, thus affording him yet another mechanism with which to influence the legislative process and dilute the power of the popularly elected Majlis.

Opposition to the Shah's plans to increase his power was not limited to Western embassies. Many in Iran, particularly amongst the opposition, also spoke against the proposed change. None, however, spoke as frankly and as prophetically as Qavam. From Paris, he wrote a missive, in the form of an open letter to the Shah, accusing him of breaching the constitution and usurping powers that even a despot like Mohammad Ali Shah—notorious for trying to roll back every democratic component of the Constitutional Revolution—had not dared claim for himself.[122] Such a power grab, Qavam predicted, would have dire consequences for the Shah.

The Shah did not deign to respond but had his Court minister, Ebrahim Hakimi, write a biting letter accusing Qavam of treason and of conspiring with the Soviets in the Azerbaijan crisis. Moreover, Qavam was stripped of his title of *Hazrat-e Ashraf*. Qavam wrote back in a no-less-defiant tone, reminding the Shah of the letter he had written commending Qavam for his work in solving the Azerbaijan crisis. True to form, Qavam went on to claim that "he, and no one else" was responsible for the solution of that crisis. Iranian papers at the time were ordered to publish only the Shah's response, not either of Qavam's angry epistles.

❧

Parallel to the tumult in his public life, the Shah's private life too was undergoing profound changes. On the one hand, Queen Fawzia still refused to return home. The Shah had made numerous gestures of reconciliation. In those days, he confided to the British Embassy, in his mind, the Queen Mother is "probably the main obstacle to [the] return of the Queen."[123] So disturbed was the Shah about his mother's interferences that he compared her to Qavam, complaining that his "position is becoming increasingly delicate between an experienced and ambitious Prime Minister on the one hand and a vindictive and domineering mother on the other." Together, he said, they have "reduced [me] to an insignificant role."[124]

According to sources in Cairo, the real reason for Fawzia's refusal to return "was not only the Queen Mother but also a Persian lady with whom the Shah had an affair."[125] Tehran was in those days a small town and was awash in rumors of the Shah's flings, of sightings of the Shah cavorting around town in one of his several fancy convertibles with a young Persian lady at his side. Of these, the most infamous was Parvin Ghafari, whose infinite appetite for gossip and self-adulation is evident in the salacious memoir she was allowed—some say forced—to publish after the Islamic Revolution.[126]

Ultimately, the British decided not to burn "their fingers" in trying to mediate between the Shah and his estranged queen. Aside from the blonde paramour, there was talk of wild parties and high-stakes poker games at the Court. None of these rumors were likely to encourage the British to intercede or the Queen to return to Tehran. With their customary caution, British officials knew what every wise man or woman knows: trying to mediate between estranged couples can only earn one "the dislike of both parties."[127]

Learning of the British reluctance to mediate, the Shah decided to send his own emissary to Cairo. It was known that King Farouk was against the idea of his sister's return. The reason for the opposition was not known, of course. The Shah's twin sister claims that Farouk's unrequited love for her was one of the main reasons. No sooner had Ashraf met Farouk, who was by then already married, than "he started talking about love and marriage." When she turned him down, Ashraf claims, he took up with another woman and was bent on divorcing his wife; and wanting to avoid being the first Muslim king to divorce his wife, Farouk, in this rather fantastic story, ordered his sister to divorce her husband. In reality, by then many Muslim kings—including Princess Ashraf's own father—had divorced their wives many a time. But regardless of the reason, Fawzia refused to come back, and the Shah wanted to at least appear to have made a serious effort to bring her back and therefore sent a special emissary.

He chose Dr. Gassem Ghani for the job; he was a respected physician and scholar who had been part of the party sent in 1939 to bring the newly betrothed Fawzia to Iran. According to Dr. Ghani, he had all but convinced Fawzia to return when suddenly she received a letter from Iran. No sooner had she read the letter than she announced her categorical decision not to return to Iran. By then she had been estranged from her daughter for several months, and even the idea of seeing her child again was not enough of an enticement. Many have suggested that the Shah's mother was the author of the letter, while others point to one of the Shah's sisters who had earlier, in a fit of anger, broken a vase over Fawzia's head.[128] The content of the letter is not known, but it is rumored to include a lurid account of the Shah's continued philandering. In those days, the British Embassy in Cairo was told that the reason for the divorce was that "the Shah besides being much preoccupied with a Persian lady wishes to marry a Persian woman and get a son wholly Persian."[129]

One reason the Shah was keen on having Fawzia back was to stop the spread of damaging rumors in Tehran about "the real" reason for the Queen's departure. While Fawzia was in Tehran, the Shah, ever busy with his own philandering, had asked a close friend, a member of his inner circle, to keep the Queen company. Whispers in Tehran had it that an unexpected emotional attachment had developed between the "keeper," a handsome, athletic young man, and his ward. Many who know Fawzia best dismiss these allegations as nothing short of vicious rumors. "She is a lady," her son-in-law, Ardeshir Zahedi, said, "and never veered from the path of purity and fidelity."

Finally, on November 17, 1947, what had been till then an open secret in Tehran took on the authority of fact when an official communiqué announced the dissolution of the Shah's marriage to Queen Fawzia. The weather, it turned out, was the real culprit! The Queen, it said, had left Iran three years ago after a long ailment, and on the orders of her physician, who believed a change of climate would help her heal faster. Now the same doctors had, according to the communiqué, decided that Tehran's "weather is damaging to her health" and forbade her to return. Never was "weather" imbued with such a rich array of metaphorical meanings. Because of this climatic exigency, "His Royal Majesty has decided that she should forgo returning to Tehran. The marriage, by mutual accord was dissolved."[130]

With the luxury of hindsight, writing in his 1961 memoirs, the Shah offers an altogether different reason for his divorce. It was, the Shah writes, her inability to produce a son that caused the breakup. He writes of the birth of a beloved daughter, Princess Shahnaz, as "the only happy light moment" of his marriage to Fawzia, adding that "for reasons that are still not clear, Princess Fawzia could not produce a male child . . . in spite of the doctor's concentrated effort," and thus, "pressured by my advisors" when Fawzia "returned to Egypt, we decided to divorce."[131] In a strange twist of fate, a few years later when Fawzia did remarry, that time to an Egyptian man, their first and only child was a boy.

Whatever the reason for the divorce in 1947, the daily grind of his ongoing political battles was making the Shah often look tired and spent, someone who needed "a complete change to cut himself off for a while from the intrigues" that surrounded him.[132] To those who saw him in those days, he seemed like a "pathetic figure but sympathetic, if one could feel that there was anything solid there." Events since the end of the Second World War had certainly tested the "solidity" of his character. The next few years would test it even further.

Chapter 9

PALACE OF SOLITUDE

Fear not, my Lord. That power that made you king
Hath power to keep you king in spite of all.
Shakespeare, King Richard II, *3.2.27–28*

In 1950, the Shah's political and private life experienced drastic changes. His wandering bachelor days came to an end, and his political life became dominated by oil. Iranian politics in the second half of the forties had become increasingly overshadowed by the question of oil and the country's attempt to wrest its increasingly valuable oil industry away from British monopoly control. The intransigence of the British and their inability to see the depth of the sentiment for this cause only made the Shah's life more complicated. The wave of nationalism that swept the countries of the Third World in the aftermath of World War II helped Iranian nationalists. By 1950, in spite of the role many different individuals had played in the oil saga, Mohammad Mossadeq was the undoubted leader and symbol of Iran's quest to nationalize its oil.

At the same time, the Shah, having just pushed through an amendment to the constitution increasing his own power, riding a wave of pro-royalist sentiments after surviving an assassination attempt, and thinking that he had finally rid himself of the troublesome Qavam, was working fast behind the scenes to increase his hold on power. He had by then launched the Senate, mandated in the 1905 constitution but not materialized until 1949. His parliamentary power increased as the law allowed him to name thirty of the sixty senators. In his first years on the throne, Britain and the United States had advised him to remain a constitutional monarch, but now, with the rise of nationalist and communist sentiments in Iran, both countries wanted and encouraged the Shah to be more forceful. In the ebb and flow of the time's unstable political situation—five prime ministers in a two-year parliamentary term—the Shah tried to carve out for himself an indispensable, unique role. The Cold War was in full force, and the Shah tried to position himself as the last bastion against the Communist threat in Iran. By August 1953, the increasing power of the Tudeh Party, the death of Stalin, the Soviet Union's muscular policy in Eastern Europe, the victory of Mao Zedong in China, the Korean War, and the beginning of anti-colonial wars in Southeast Asia all inadvertently helped the Shah.

As documents from the U.S. and British archives show, both countries concluded as early as March 1951 that the Shah was the West's best hope in fighting the Communist threat in Iran. In a directive to the U.S. Embassy in Tehran at the time, for example, Secretary of State Dean Acheson stated that "the only person who could provide the requisite leadership under the current circumstances is the Shah and we believe that the US and Britain should support him in every feasible way."[1] It was in this spirit that Acheson noted that it was "of vital importance to make clear that any aid by the United States was given to the Shah and the Iranian people . . . not Mossadeq."[2]

At the same time, at least in the State Department, there was also a small faction insisting that the best way to stop the Communists in Iran was not to support the Shah, but to go all out in support of Mossadeq. Early in 1953, this faction was still arguing against an attempt to topple Mossadeq. Instead, they suggested that the United States should give him sufficient assistance to stand up to the Tudeh Party. That group lost the argument, at least partially as a result of Mossadeq's occasional efforts to frighten the United States by flirting with the Tudeh or even the Soviet Union. The rise of John Foster Dulles and his brother Allen to the top of the American foreign policy establishment and their distrust of nationalists as bulwarks against Communism also played a key role in defeating the strategy of the pro-Mossadeq faction in the State Department. But the most important reason for the group's failure was the success of the British government in portraying them as naïve and their ideas as "silly."[3] The more Mossadeq lost his viability as a bastion against Communism, the more the Shah benefited.

In domestic politics too, the Shah was looking for an alliance with all opponents of Communism. He even tried to find some allies amongst some of Mossadeq's supporters—social democrats who had initially joined the Tudeh Party in the mistaken assumption that it was an independent voice for change and justice, and democrats who had joined the National Front in the belief that it was the voice of Iranian democracy. These two disgruntled groups had joined forces to form what they called the "Toilers' Party." Mozzafar Baghai, a powerful orator, a professor of political philosophy at Tehran University, and one of the most influential leaders of the oil nationalization movement, and Khalil Maleki, an estranged leader of the Tudeh Party and one of Iran's most dedicated and erudite social democrats, were the most eminent leaders of this party. Before the party split in two—with Baghai leading one faction and Maleki the other—the Toilers' Party was the most formidable adversary and challenger of the Tudeh Party. Another key element of the Toilers' Party's political platform was support for Mossadeq and the effort to nationalize Iran's oil. In the months before August 1953, Baghai broke with Mossadeq and became one of his chief critics, while Maleki, though critical of some of Mossadeq's tactics, remained loyal to him.[4]

During this period the Shah tried to monitor closely the work of leftist groups through the military's intelligence unit (Rokne do). Pakravan was in charge of that unit and a close ally of the Shah. He was also a member of a highly covert network of officers loyal to the Shah and opposed to the Communists. Membership was by invitation only and was solemnized during secret rituals reminiscent of Masonic rites. This network became increasingly important in the Shah's effort to maintain control of the army during the heady days of confrontation with Mossadeq.[5]

While fighting Communism was high on the Shah's mind, Iran was bedazzled by Mossadeq's nationalization movement and his battle with the British. The American government, aware of Mossadeq's rising appeal and the tide of nationalism sweeping the world, tried to convince the British to make some grand gesture of conciliation, some indication that they recognized the legitimacy and power of the movement. After much intransigence, the British finally agreed to start negotiations for a new oil agreement with Iran. But as British archival documents clearly show, their strategy from the onset was to pay lip service to the nationalist movement while maintaining their control of Iran's oil.

A note by Dean Acheson, written in November 1951, offers a remarkably clear-eyed view of the British government's vision of Iran. He writes of Churchill roaring like "a wounded lion," and of the British government's "truculent braggadocio." He argues that the "cardinal point" of British policy is "not to prevent Iran from going commie . . . [but] to preserve what they believe to be the last remaining bulwark of British solvency." He writes of the decline of the British Empire and of Britain's unwillingness to accept anything but Mossadeq's defeat.[6] The British even refused to allow Iran to examine the oil company's books—claiming such examination would threaten their national security.

Nevertheless, the British needed to appear willing to negotiate. Thus, beginning in 1948, and again in 1949, the Anglo-Iranian Oil Company (AIOC, later renamed British Petroleum, or BP) sent a representative named Neville Gass to renegotiate the terms of the company's agreement with Iran. By then AIOC was principally owned by the British government because the Admiralty bought 85 percent of its energy from the company at discount prices. Gass's interlocutor in Iran was a career politician named Abbasgoli Golshai'yan, who never survived the taint of what came to be known as the Gass-Golshai'yan or Supplemental Oil Agreement.[7]

According to the Supplemental Oil Agreement, signed on July 27, 1949, Iran's actual revenue for each barrel of oil would have gone from 22 cents per barrel to 33 cents per barrel. Britain heralded it as a new beginning for Iran—a fairer agreement than any oil-producing nation of the world had ever been offered before. This was hardly the case. By then Mexico had nationalized its oil, and the United States had offered Venezuela a 50-50 profit-sharing agreement and was about to do the same with Saudi Arabia.

Mossadeq, by then in charge of a key Majlis committee with oversight over all oil negotiations, took up the mantle of defeating the Supplemental Agreement, calling it a betrayal of Iran's sovereign rights. The Shah's position on the Supplemental Agreement was at best inconsistent. In fact there were clear discrepancies between his public pronouncements and what he told the British Embassy in private.

The British were pressuring the Shah to use his influence to help ratify the Agreement. The Shah was in those days planning his first visit to the United States and to Europe, and the British Embassy in Tehran tried to convince him to cancel his trip in order to attend to the task of getting the Agreement ratified. On more than one occasion, the Shah assured the British privately that he was in favor of the Supplemental Agreement and was doing everything in his power to help get it ratified. But he also warned that, given Mossadeq's opposition and the national mood, its passage was unlikely.

As the pressure to cancel his trip increased, the Shah told British officials that he had asked Mohammad Saed, then the prime minister, to remain in office "until he had secured the ratification of the supplemental oil agreement."[8] But neither Saed nor anyone else could muster the votes in the Majlis for the passage of such an agreement. Few politicians, and certainly not the Shah, dared offer public support for it. When the Supplemental Oil Agreement was submitted to the Majlis on December 19, 1949, the oil commission, chaired by Mossadeq, unanimously rejected it. The British Embassy, angry at the outcome, complained bitterly of the Shah's inability to deliver on his promise to help pass the bill: "It is generally felt he must be either a knave or a fool, or both."[9]

The Shah was neither. He was a pragmatic politician, keen on retaining his power and keeping his options open. He knew public support for the Supplemental Agreement was the kiss of political death. He knew that Mossadeq was the man of the hour and that nationalization of oil was the most popular and dominant demand of the moment. More than once, he publicly declared his undivided support for the nationalization movement. Anyone who opposed the movement or its leader, the Shah knew, did so at great peril. He also knew what the British might do to him should he part policy with them, and he knew that Mossadeq was no friend of the Pahlavi dynasty.

The political horizon looked bleak for the Shah. He could seize absolute power, dissolve the Majlis, and arrive at some kind of agreement that paid lip service to nationalization, but in fact perpetuated British control of Iranian oil by agreeing to some disguised form of the Supplemental Agreement. He had neither the temperament nor the public support for such an aggressive move. He also knew the United States would be opposed to this idea.

During his November 1950 trip to the United States, the Shah met with President Truman and addressed a joint session of Congress. In the course of his negotiations with Truman administration officials, including the President, the Shah learned that the United States favored a more equitable deal for Iran in its negotiations with AIOC. By the end of his trip, he was convinced that the Truman administration had concluded that nationalization of Iran's oil was a foregone conclusion and that Britain should learn to live with it. The American government had further concluded that "it was not in the interest of the West as a whole for the United States to be identified with any plan put forth by the British which did not recognize the principle of nationalization."[10] More than once during those months, the Truman administration nearly resolved to publicly break with Britain and side with the Iranian nationalists. But late in 1951 Churchill came back into power and made Truman understand in no uncertain terms that Britain's continued support in the Korean War was predicated on America's help in Iran.[11]

The Shah's second alternative was to accept Mossadeq and nationalization and resign himself to a merely ceremonial role. As he had repeatedly said, he never took this option seriously as he was unwilling to accept the role of a ceremonial leader. He also knew cooperating with Mossadeq meant a direct confrontation with Britain. By the end of 1952, the Shah had learned that even the Truman administration had lost patience with Mossadeq, making this second option even less appealing.

His third alternative was to accept as prime minister a charismatic politician who could stand up to Mossadeq and solve the oil crisis. He disliked that option, knowing full well that it was precisely as a charismatic prime minister that his father had ascended the throne and overthrown the old Qajar dynasty.

As the British waited anxiously for the Shah to find a solution to the oil question, a number of Iranian politicians contacted the British Embassy or government and suggested that they were ready and able to solve the oil problem in a manner favorable to the British. On December 10, 1950, Seyyed Zia had met with officials of the British Embassy and complained about the interference of the royal family, "particularly princess Ashraf," in public affairs. He went on to say that "activities of the Shah" had reached a stage where they threatened the dynasty. He even claimed that "there was now a good deal of talk about a republic" and that Qavam was soon going to announce his plans to create such a republic.[12] On December 17, 1950, Zia had lunch with the British Ambassador again and this time told him that the Shah was an utter failure and had failed in "everything he had undertaken." He also made it clear that he himself was "ready to take office whenever the moment was convenient and then went so far as to say that if [the British] government were interested in hearing details of a plan, he would be very glad to impart them."[13]

Almost a year later, it was Qavam's turn to contact the British and indicate that he, too, was "ready to take office" and to "dissolve the Majlis and arrange an election of a new one sympathetic to the British interests" and press for a "modified agreement with the Anglo-Iranian oil company."[14] In November 1951, he threw all caution to the wind, and met directly with the British Ambassador, saying that he hoped that, "sincerely assisted" by the British, he could come to power. Three months later, on February 7, 1952, in a meeting with Julian Amery, a high-ranking British diplomat, he laid out his detailed plans. The meeting took place in Paris, where Qavam was visiting; and much to Amery's surprise, Qavam had also invited Captain David Drummond—aka Prince Hamid Qajar, the man who in 1941 had been rejected as a candidate to replace the Shah only because he spoke no Persian. Qavam made no effort to hide his disdain for the Shah and the fact that he preferred Drummond/Qajar as a king.[15] Qavam's plans to come back to power faced two obstacles: the Shah was adamantly opposed to his appointment, and the British were still not ready to abandon the Shah in favor of a man they considered "the master of the double-cross."

In a later meeting, Qavam informed the British Embassy that the time to act was now and that he was made "anxious by report . . . that there were frequent contacts between Mossadeq and the Russian embassy."[16] During these months, Qavam, according to a British Embassy report, was receiving financial aid and support from none other than the Shah's mother, who was also worried about what she considered her son's weakness and indecision.[17]

Even the Shah's siblings were not free of the temptation to enter the fray. As early as February 1950, Ali Reza, the Shah's only full brother, met with British officials to register his approval of the Supplemental Agreement and his dismay at the Shah's handling of the matter. A few months later, he became even more critical and ambitious. On December 13, 1951, Ali Reza called the British Ambassador to his palace, and bitterly complained that "he was allowed to take no part in the affairs of the state whatsoever by his brother."[18] The fact that he was the Shah's only full brother, and the fact that the powerful Queen Mother "was very anxious for him to be made crown prince" made these comments even more significant.[19] British officials were "struck by the bitterness, mixed with contempt, with which Ali Reza spoke of his brother."[20] A few months later, the Prince again asked to see the British Ambassador and he went even further in criticizing the Shah. He made it "quite clear that in his opinion the Shah did not have the necessary strength of character" to uproot the corrupt ruling class and bring about necessary "fundamental reforms." Instead of deposing the Shah at the time—"to make a change at this critical moment" would be dangerous, Ali Reza said—he recommended that he be named commander in chief.[21]

About the same time, one of the Shah's half-brothers, Abdul Reza, had met with the American Ambassador and suggested that he be put in charge of the country's economic situation.[22] Even Sardar Fakher Hekmat, for many years speaker of the Majlis, and an ally of the Shah, complained to the British Embassy in 1951 about the Shah's inaction and indecision, and how Hekmat's words of warning "seemed merely to bounce off the thick head of the king—as he himself put it."[23] Hekmat wanted the British government to make it clear to the Shah that "unless he behaves in a more manly and decisive manner," there would be no chance to save his throne.

❧

As the Shah contended with these forces, Britain and the United States preferred the appointment of a powerful prime minister to take on Mossadeq. For both countries, Iran was too important to allow the Shah's private trepidations to become an insurmountable obstacle to that option. The Shah tried to buy himself some time by appointing loyal "caretaker" prime ministers. On each occasion he would assure the British Embassy that he had instructed the Prime Minister to get the Supplemental Agreement passed. It was no surprise that none of his chosen prime ministers succeeded in passing the Agreement, and thus, on June 26, 1950, the Shah had no choice but to agree to the appointment of General Hajj Ali Razmara as the new prime minister. By then Razmara was in his third term as chairman of the Joint Chiefs. Only weeks earlier, the Shah had declared that "he [would] never agree to General Razmara becoming Prime Minister."[24] He knew that the British had earlier had serious reservations about Razmara. In 1949, for example, they had described him as "probably the most feared and disliked man in Persia today." They called him a corrupt, ambitious intriguer "who trims his sail to any wind." They also reported on rumors of his "pro-Soviet inclination."[25]

But by June 1950, Razmara realized his hour had arrived. In a series of meetings with British and American officials, he promised to bring about both political reforms in the country and the resolution of the oil crisis by helping pass "a revised agreement" that was within the existing formula. He demanded that both embassies pressure the Shah to come out publicly in support of him. He also wanted the British Embassy to tell Ayatollah Abol-Qasem Kashani—a powerful Shiite cleric and a leader of the nationalization movement—that the cleric "would not have [British] support in opposing him."[26] Finally, the British were convinced that Razmara was the Jason who could deliver to them their golden fleece.

Razmara was easily one of the most erudite officers in the Iranian military. He had by 1950 published dozens of books on matters relating to geography, cartography, and military strategy. He was also an avid memoirist, leaving behind detailed accounts of his travels and encounters. He was a man of infinite political ambition—and considerable guile.

But it proved hard to convince the Shah to offer full support to the ambitious general. The Shah was not alone in worrying about Razmara's ambitions. The British government, arguably his most ardent advocate, worried that he might "be tempted to act across constitutional processes" and move against the Shah. But the situation was "so serious that the risk," according to the British, "was deemed well worth taking."[27]

The Shah was certainly less sanguine about such risks as they threatened his throne. For a while, he had resisted the Razmara appointment by claiming "he had not been certain" about the British attitude toward such a move. When on June 19, 1950, the British reiterated their full support for the Razmara appointment, the Shah said disingenuously that "he was relieved to hear this."[28] Ultimately, he even had to accede to British and American demands that "he should go out of his way to demonstrate he was supporting Razmara."[29] Before taking the final leap, the Shah sent Ernest Perron to the British Embassy to tell them categorically that once Razmara was appointed prime minister, "he would not be allowed to have any say in military affairs."[30]

While the Shah worried about Razmara's ambition, the new prime minister had oil on his mind. He knew he had a formidable enemy in Mossadeq, and he also knew his survival depended on his ability to solve the oil crisis. He wanted to forge an agreement that was acceptable to Britain and palatable to the people of Iran, whose nationalist sentiments had been aroused by Mossadeq. Razmara tried to convince the nation that nationalization was not in Iran's best interest. He hired an American advisor to argue that nationalization was not a wise decision for Iran. He even argued that Iran was simply incapable of managing its oil industry. "We can't even build the handle of an ewer," he infamously said in a speech before the parliament. He had envisioned a series of grandiose reforms—from decentralization of the government to dismissing corrupt government officials—and hoped to use them to win the hearts and minds of the people. He tried to pressure the Shah to decrease the military budget and allow the use of those sums for social reforms. He had also asked the U.S. and British governments for loans and aid for implementing these badly needed changes. More than once, Razmara told the British that, should they desire to provide Iran with any foreign assistance, they should make it clear that it could not be used for "unnecessary things such as airplanes."[31] Clearly, he and the Shah did not see eye to eye on budgetary matters.

As arguments between the two men ensued, the Shah complained to the British Embassy that "activity against the Shah was being carried out by Razmara or [at] any rate the people in his confidence."[32] The British dismissed these complaints and considered them the result of the Shah's jealousy and mistrust. At the same time, they believed that "the Shah had begun to oppose Razmara through the Majlis a week after his ministry began."[33] The plot thickened considerably when, in the heat of Razmara's battles with the Majlis, the Shah agreed to allow Ayatollah Kashani to return to Iran after a brief period of exile. Whisper had it that the Shah's primary intention was to have the cantankerous Ayatollah weaken the ambitious General. If indeed that was his intent, the ploy worked. Almost immediately, Kashani became one of Razmara's most forceful enemies. He declared it the duty of every Iranian to "oppose the government." Mossadeq and his allies used even stronger language in their attacks on the General. Some went so far as to compare him with Hitler.[34]

The Shah's relationship with his prime minister was further complicated by the fact that his twin sister, Princess Ashraf, was having an affair with the dashing officer. Both were married at the time, yet their letters, published in recent years, clearly indicate an intimate, intensely amorous relationship. He calls her "my kind beloved" *(Aziz-e Mehrabanam)* and addresses her using the informal singular "you" in Persian *(to)* while she calls him "my dear general" *(General-e Azizam)*. When she complains of his fickle ways, saying that he had forgotten her during one of his trips, he defends himself by saying that he had sent "everyday a telegram. Every day I have written you a note." The letters also show Ashraf's fervent attempt to keep her general in her brother's camp. It might, she says, be "God's will that my brother will have his commands and ideals materialized by you."[35]

Razmara believed he had trumped all of the Shah's machinations against him when he convinced the British government to agree to what was close to a 50-50 profit-sharing agreement. He told the Majlis that he wanted to deliver an important speech and intimated that the final resolution of the oil crisis was now at hand.

On March 7, 1951, however, as he tried to enter a mosque in the center of Tehran, an Islamist terrorist, a devotee of Kashani's, met him with three bullets. Not long after he was taken to the hospital, he was declared dead. Rumors of the Shah's hand in the assassination began to spread immediately. Razmara had been reluctant to go to the mosque that day, but Assadollah Alam, the Shah's closest confidante, had repeatedly urged him to go. Alam was, in fact, questioned by the police after the assassination. All these facts added poignancy to the rumors. The assassin, as it turned out, was a member of the Feda'yan-e Islam. The General's assassination paved the way for the passage of the Oil Nationalization Act and for Mossadeq's rise to the pinnacle of power.

The Shah's murky attitude toward nationalization was evident when he appointed Hussein Ala to replace Razmara. Soon after the appointment, Alam met with British officials, who told him to ask the Shah to "use all his influence to persuade deputies under his control [to stay] away from the Majlis," and thus render a quorum impossible. This had become the last British weapon to abort the nationalization bill. Alam told them that "43 of the Majlis's 131 deputies," known to be allied with the Shah, "would stay away."[36] At the same time, Ala, the new prime minister, told British officials that "all Persians regard nationalization as a desirable principle."[37]

In early February 1951, as the movement to nationalize oil was gathering steam, the Shah told officials of the British Embassy that he was in a "rather melancholy mood." He was worried that the Majlis might pass the nationalization bill, and he would be left with no choice but to dissolve the parliament.[38] The Shah listened to the historic March 15 proceedings of the Majlis discussing the nationalization bill on the radio and then told British officials that "he regretted that it had not been possible to arrest the movement which the National Front had inaugurated towards nationalization."[39] He wanted the British government to know that "by regularly intervening" on their behalf on such issues as oil, the purchase of locomotives, and the contract to fix Tehran's water supply, he had risked "being regarded as unpatriotic by his somewhat Byzantine-minded officials."[40] The British suspected the Shah of double-talk, if not double-cross, when nearly every member of the Majlis deemed close to him showed up for the historic March 15 vote to ratify the nationalization bill.

The Nationalization Act had been shepherded through the Majlis by Mossadeq. It was by then clear that his hour of glory was near. A month later, on April 26, he accepted the nomination to become prime minister—on the condition that the bill to implement the Nationalization Act should be simultaneously ratified. The nomination was made by Jalal Imami, a member of the Majlis known for his close ties with the Shah. Some have surmised that Imami made the nomination on the assumption that Mossadeq would not accept it. The

Tudeh Party saw it as yet another troubling sign of the increasing influence of "American imperialism" in Iran.

The Shah in 1951 was walking a very dangerous tightrope. The British were pressuring him to dissolve the Majlis, declare martial law, and nullify the Nationalization Act.[41] They insisted that he must appoint Seyyed Zia as prime minister, and they implicitly threatened that unless he followed their demands, they would not discourage "a campaign against certain of the Shah's prerogatives" by some of the non-Communist opponents of Mossadeq.[42] The meaning of the threat was not lost on the Shah. He knew well that it meant that unless he agreed to the British demand, Seyyed Zia would once again go on the attack against him. To his credit, the Shah resisted these pressures, while at the same time revealing himself in private, particularly with the British, to be an opponent of the nationalization movement.

But in those heady days, the Shah's views, along with his mood, had violent swings. The more Mossadeq gained power and popularity and the more he succeeded in marginalizing the Shah from the daily political life of the country, the more the Shah became determined to get rid of him. Yet he was at the same time increasingly beset with indecision and inaction, what a Western diplomat called his "Hamlet-like" doubts and paralysis. He wanted senators and members of the Majlis to take responsibility for Mossadeq's dismissal. He believed that he should bide his time and wait for the moment at which Mossadeq would further isolate himself. He also believed that the only way that he could be involved in getting rid of Mossadeq was through legal channels. As early as May 1950, he had concluded that "there were two enemies of the country: one was the Tudeh and the other was the National Front. Perhaps the latter was more dangerous," he said, "because it was vague and negative."[43]

When the British ploy to pressure the Shah into fast action on the dismissal of Mossadeq did not work, officials from Whitehall consulted Ann Lambton, by then a professor of Persian Studies in London and a sage on British foreign policy in Iran. Her advice was clear, categorical, and drastic: find a way to remove Mossadeq from power forcefully. He is a demagogue, she said, and the only way Britain would retain its influence in Iran would be through his removal. She also believed that the British government must ultimately handle this matter alone, as in her mind the United States had "neither the experience, nor the psychological" depth to understand Iran—a sentiment much shared in those days by British officials.[44] She introduced government officials to Robin Zaehner, a professor-spy, who could help plan and implement her proposed coup against Mossadeq. If Zaehner was one of the British masters of conspiracy against Mossadeq, then the three Rashidian brothers were Zaehner's chief instruments of mischief. No sooner had Mossadeq come to power than the brothers began to receive large funds from the British to "maintain their agents."[45]

In June 1951, when British efforts to convince the Shah to fire Mossadeq failed, they threatened to attack Iran and take over the oil region of the country: in the words of the Foreign Secretary, "to cow the insolent natives."[46] The operation, aptly called "Buccaneer," entailed sending a number of British warships to the waters off the coast of the oil-rich region of Khuzestan and authorized "the use of force, if necessary."[47] Encouraged by the Truman administration's strong opposition to the idea of a military solution, the Shah told the British Ambassador that "I will personally lead my soldiers into battle against you if you attack Iran."[48]

The Shah also had another worry. In the July 2, 1951, meeting, the Shah asked about a recent debate on Iran in the House of Commons and the suggestion by Churchill's son-in-law that "there should be a partition of Persia between Russia and Britain." The Shah noted that he could not see how in such a case "the Persians could refrain from resisting," adding moreover that in his view, "Russia would install a communist government for the whole of Persia."[49] The British even considered the idea of bringing back the Khaz'al family, who had virtually ruled Khuzestan in the early twentieth century, and again making that region an "independent" area under the family's ostensible rule.

Once the United States was "officially" briefed on the possibility of a British military attack—when the State Department was given a summary of the cabinet meeting authorizing it—the administration went all out to convince Britain to give up its Operation Buccaneer. Truman sent a note to Prime Minister Clement Atlee telling him not to use force but to try to find a negotiated solution to the problem. Secretary of State Dean Acheson and Assistant Secretary George McGhee also tried to dissuade the British. The temptation to engage in what Churchill had churlishly called "the sputter of musketry" was at least partially based on the facile assumption that a "decadent," "servile" nation like Persia was inherently incapable of launching, much less sustaining, a serious, sustained anti-colonial nationalist movement.[50] Mossadeq and his movement, in this jaundiced vision, were nothing but a passing aberration. Mossadeq was a madman, the British believed, and the Iranians as a people too fickle and selfish to remain loyal to him. Britain even toyed with the idea of getting NATO involved in its plan to find a military solution to the conflict.[51] At the same time, while the Truman administration was holding the line against a military strike on Iran, it was also beginning to worry about Mossadeq's future, the possibility that under Tudeh Party pressure, he might push Iran away from the West and either toward neutrality or, worst yet, into the Soviet camp. As early as May 10, 1951, these fears were evident in Acheson's telegram to the U.S. embassy in Tehran.[52]

Both Mossadeq and the Shah were playing the same card with the Truman and (later) the Eisenhower administrations, each presenting himself as the last line of defense against the Tudeh and Soviet influence. Mossadeq went so far as to ask for $10 million a month in "financial assistance" from the United States. He threatened that, unless he received the aid, "Iran would collapse" within thirty days and the Tudeh would take over.[53] He even tried to blackmail the United States by saying that "if US will not give him the aid," then he would be forced to "ask for Soviet assistance."[54]

The Shah, on the other hand, repeatedly argued that Mossadeq did not have the power, or even the desire, to resist the Tudeh. During the early days of Mossadeq's tenure, the Shah even suspected Ayatollah Kashani—in these days Mossadeq's most important ally—of complicity with the Tudeh and the Soviet Union. On August 30, 1951, for example, the Shah told the American Ambassador that "his government had intercepted communications between Kashani and the Russians... [Kashani] might be looking in the direction of collaboration with the Soviets."[55] The fact that, as Mossadeq became more isolated from the clergy, he was reluctantly forced to depend more and more on the Tudeh Party helped the Shah make his case.

As the two leaders played out their strategies, their relations grew tenser by the day. On July 16, 1952, in a heated meeting with the Shah, Mossadeq demanded full control of the armed forces, threatening to resign and to tell the nation the reason for his resignation, should the Shah refuse to grant him his demand. If I cede the control of the army, the Shah said, I might as well pack my bags and leave the country. The threat, in Mossadeq's mind, was only a tactical move, as he did not believe the Shah had the courage to bear full responsibility for the resignation of the popular prime minister. He was wrong. Late that night, the Shah accepted Mossadeq's resignation.

The next day, after the Majlis's vote of inclination in favor of Qavam, the Shah had no choice but to once again appoint his septuagenarian foe to the post of prime minister. For months, he had resisted such an appointment. Now, under pressure from the British and American Embassies, and from some of his own supporters, he had no choice but to give in. Qavam made two demands of the Shah before he would accept the job. The first was for the Shah to dissolve the Majlis, and the second was to allow the arrest of Kashani. The Shah refused both demands, but Qavam nonetheless accepted the task of forming a new government. It is clear that the Shah neither trusted Qavam nor was willing to sever ties with Kashani. In the words of the British Embassy, these ideas led to the Shah's decision "not to fully support Qavam." The fact that Qavam then filled his cabinet with figures known to oppose the Shah further clouded his already tenuous relations with the Shah. On the night of the appointment, the Shah let it be known, particularly to the leaders of the National Front, that he had appointed Qavam under duress.

What further weakened Qavam's position and chance of survival was his notoriously hard-nosed first manifesto. There is a new sheriff in town, he said, and he would tolerate no dissent. A powerful coalition of Kashani and Mossadeq supporters, as well as members of the Tudeh Party, was formed against Qavam. On the morning of July 21, Qavam again tried to persuade the Shah "to take the measures to establish" law and order. Once again the Shah refused. On that same day, the British Ambassador had tried to not only "play on the Shah's fears," but "make him realize that it is by letting Qavam down that he is most likely to bring his own downfall." Lest the Shah still worry about Qavam's designs on the throne, the British Ambassador tried to reassure him that no such efforts would be forthcoming.[56] But it was all to no avail. By five o'clock in the afternoon of that day, massive demonstrations in Tehran and other provinces, leaving dozens dead and hundreds injured, forced Qavam's resignation and the reappointment of Mossadeq. The Shah had defeated one foe only to face a far more powerful adversary yet again.[57]

Though Ayatollah Kashani had played a key role in restoring Mossadeq to power on that day, he also wanted to keep his options open. A few months earlier, he had sent out feelers to both the American Embassy and the Shah. For example, on January 8, 1952, Zaehner, who was working in Tehran at the time, reported rumors that the Shah has achieved "a clear understanding with Kashani."[58] A few months later, Kashani in fact met directly with Court Minister Ala, and after "offering faint praise for Mossadeq," discussed candidates to succeed him.[59]

Convinced that he had restored Mossadeq to power, in the months after July 21, Kashani became even more brazen in dictating policy to the government. He wanted women to be forced to wear Islamic covering when entering government offices; he demanded the right to name certain ministers and veto others; finally, he wanted the government to increase pressure on the Baha'i—a nineteenth-century faith that emerged from Iran and whose followers became the bane of Shiite clergy.

Mossadeq resisted nearly every one of Kashani's demands. The only issue he relented on was women's suffrage. When in 1952 he was drafting a new election law, women's groups from around the country had written to him, objecting to the omission of women's right to vote in the new law. Soon a rumor spread around the country that Mossadeq was contemplating including women's suffrage in the new law. A number of top clergy wrote to Mossadeq or issued *fatwas*, suggesting that women's participation in politics was against Islam and "sure to beget corruption."[60]

Moreover, Mossadeq's increased ties with the Tudeh and the rising star of National Front radicals like Hossein Fatemi, by then the foreign minister, made the clergy in general, and Kashani in particular, more concerned. These tensions all worked to the benefit of the Shah. In fact, in meeting with the British Embassy, the Shah's close aide, Ernest Perron, tried to claim that the advent and evolution of these rifts were the work of the Shah and the result of his astute politics. In the meantime, lest he appear to be conspiring with the British, on March 4, 1952, the Shah informed the embassy that, henceforth, any meetings between him and embassy officials should go through the Foreign Ministry.[61]

During these crucial months, the Shah's most constant companion and, in her own reckoning, the person who repeatedly brought him out of his torpor and urged him to screw his "courage to the sticking point," was a sixteen-year-old half-Persian, half-German girl whose ignorance of Iranian politics and history was matched only by her beauty and her love of Hollywood glamour.

Soraya, many believe, was the true love of the Shah's life. The trajectory of his love objects, his "elective affinities," and the character and qualities of each of his three wives, are in fact telling signposts of his evolving personality and his core values and preferences. If his first wife was chosen by his father's royal fiat, his second, Soraya, was chosen by his mother and sister, Shams. They had picked her from a picture, and Princess Shams was then dispatched to Europe to get a closer look at this exotic beauty. As Soraya makes amply clear in her refreshingly candid memoir, by the time of her betrothal, intense competition among the female members of the Shah's family—his sisters and his domineering mother—was at a fever pitch. The privilege of picking a new queen was a coveted prize they all fought over.

After Shams met and approved Soraya, her picture was shown to the Shah, who was immediately smitten. She was half-Persian by blood but profoundly European in sentiment and values. Her mother was German, and her father was a member of the Bakhtiyari tribe. As a child in Isfahan, she had been tutored by a German woman referred to as Frau Mantel, and then moved to the Behesht Ayin School. Even as a child, she showed interest in playing the role of queen—in the school's production of Cinderella.[62] According to the British Consulate in Isfahan, her departure from that city was the result of the unrequited love and unrelenting pursuit of a man—a son of Sarem al-Dowleh, one of the most powerful aristocrats in the city—leading to her parents' decision to take refuge to Switzerland.

Her stay in Europe might account partly for her shocking disdain for Iran, her remarkable ignorance of its history and culture, and her infatuation with the noble Europe of her imagination. In her personal memoir, she writes, "I was a dunce. I knew next to nothing of the geography, the legends of my country; nothing of its history, nothing of Muslim religion."[63] Her upbringing at the hand of Frau Mantel was entirely Christian and German. That was why when the news of a royal wedding spread, "some mullahs are said to have criticized the marriage to a half-European girl, mainly brought up in Europe." According to British officials, this feeling "may be quite widespread."[64]

Her description of her own identity is revealing enough. "The feeling of being both Christian and Muslim but at the same time of being neither the one nor the other has engraved in my flesh two divergent poles between which my existence has unfolded. The one is *methodically* European, the other *savagely* Persian."[65] She describes her daily life in Tehran by referring to visits "to hospitals, orphanages, charities, the people's quarters with their *djoubs* open to the sky, with the streams of dirt water which supplied their dwellings, having first served washerwomen, tramps and dogs. Poverty and squalor. Children with rickets, ravaged women and starving old men, the filth of the alleyways where the houses are no longer like houses, where poverty, real poverty prevailed."[66] On the other hand, Paris "dazzled"[67] her, and anywhere in Europe, "everyday, my heart was filled with sunshine. Life was light."[68] When she went to school in Europe, it was "wonderful to be able to go to Cinema, to drink a glass of lemonade on the terrace of a *brasserie*... a paradise hitherto forbidden."[69] In Persian schools, she found "grey uniform, the stove which smoked and poisoned the classroom, lessons, homework, work to the point of exhaustion."[70] Even caviar, a delicacy she clearly loved and tried to add to the Court's regular culinary menu, was, in her mind, one of the "fragrances of the West."[71]

Yet when the Shah saw and approved the picture, and after Soraya went on a shopping spree with Shams, the two returned to Tehran on October 7, 1950. For Soraya this was a homecoming after a five-year absence. Before long, at the Shah's insistence, arrangements began for a second royal wedding, and the official announcement was made on October 9.

The news was most jubilantly received by her Bakhtiyari family in Isfahan, and to British officials, this was a cause of concern as, in their view, "most, though not all [of the family] are an idle opium-smoking lot," and the Court may soon be "infested with a swarm" of them.[72]

The announcement of Soraya's engagement included a lie. She was in fact sixteen years old at the time, but in the official announcement she was "credited with eighteen. The difference in age might have appeared excessive."[73] The Shah was nearly thirty-one years old. In reality, for traditional men of Iran at the time, such a difference would hardly seem excessive, but it bothered the Shah.

Initially, the wedding had been planned to take place just after Christmas, and "elaborate preparations for nearly a week of festivities had been made." But Soraya fell ill on October 26. She was examined by some of the best physicians in the country but only one, the Shah's private physician, Dr. Ayadi, correctly diagnosed her as suffering from a case of salmonella poisoning. There had been at the time an epidemic of this disease in Tehran.[74] Eventually, based on the feeling that "expensive entertainments were not in accord with the spirit of the times," plans for an elaborate wedding were scuttled in favor of more simple arrangements.[75]

Even the simple wedding was badly botched. Someone had printed and distributed a large number of fraudulent invitations, and many more guests than anticipated showed up for the ceremonies. There were rumors of sabotage. Soraya herself was so weak by the time of the ceremonies that she virtually passed out halfway through the wedding. But by February 13, she was the queen of Iran.

A few weeks after the wedding, the Shah planned a trip to Jordan where, in the words of the British Embassy officials, the "young air-minded monarch" was planning to pilot a plane put at his disposal by the British air force.[76] But on April 1, 1951, during a lunch meeting with the British Ambassador, the Shah confided that he was "suffering from appendicitis and [had] been advised that he should be operated on soon." He said he was on a "strict diet," that he had been in bed for the last few days, and that he was thinking of going to France or Switzerland for the operation.[77] In those days, Hussein Ala was in charge of what was clearly a caretaker government following the assassination of General Razmara. The British Embassy wanted to know whether the Shah thought Ala could successfully resolve the oil issue; the Shah refused to give a definitive answer but said he had asked "Ala for a definitive statement whether he could solve the oil question or not."[78]

As he waited for a clear indication of Ala's position, the Shah's health deteriorated. On April 10, he sent Assadollah Alam to see the British Ambassador and say that the Shah sought the British Embassy's advice on whether he should go to Europe for the operation or have it in Iran. The Ambassador, after saying that "the Shah's health was the first consideration," suggested that a specialist be brought in. In an eerie foreshadowing of events in 1978, one Dr. Forkner, who had visited the Shah when he was visiting America, was brought in under the strictest secrecy. He performed an appendectomy on the Shah on July 5, 1951, and decided that no other operation was necessary.[79] While the operation forced the Shah to cancel his Jordan trip, he had decided even before his illness to reject the offer of flying the British plane lest it "might be embarrassing in view of the present propaganda against British influence here."[80] Nevertheless, the Shah did give a Rolls-Royce to Soraya as a wedding gift, a Rolls-Royce with special accessories provided by H. J. Mulliner.[81] He had first ordered the car two years earlier, but various problems had delayed delivery. It was a "special model of which only one has so far been built."[82]

On a smaller scale, the country's political turmoil was replicated in the Shah's private life. Soraya describes, in a bitter tone, how the Shah banned from Court Forough Zafar, the woman she most trusted and called "aunt." The charge was "seditious activities." In her view, the entire episode was nothing but a conspiracy "hatched entirely" by the Shah's mother and his sister Shams.[83] Those were the days of the Shah's confrontation with Mossadeq, the days of anxiety about bugged rooms and spies, double agents and unreliable allies.

At the same time, descriptions of the royal couple's favorite pastimes are fascinating. Aside from poker, where Soraya was a mere observer, they played parlor games like charades and telephone. Masked balls were also a favorite activity. In one held in late 1953, "Mohammad Reza decided—royalty demanded it—to disguise himself as a lion"; she describes how she was, as a result of a conspiracy, thwarted in her effort to appear as Madame de Pompadour—instead she was forced to wear "a Joan of Arc breastplate."[84]

Her description of the Shah in this period is mostly positive. She often praises him when she finds European characteristics in his behavior. "Oriental" traits are invariably cause for disparagement. She appreciated his timid tenderness in his relations with women. Despite a first marriage, she writes, and "in spite of countless mistresses he had had before me, Mohammad Reza was extremely shy with women . . . he did not like to show his feelings." His eyes, however, "were expressive. Dark brown, almost black, shining, at times hard, at times sad or gentle, they exuded charm and reflected his soul."[85] At the same time, she found that he "could not bear the smallest rebuke."

Aside from the Shah's mother and siblings, there was another source of tension between Soraya and the Shah, and that was Ernest Perron. "How can I," she writes with bitterness, "describe this *shetun* [piece of shit], this limping devil who dragged his leg and spread his poison around the palace as well as in our own quarters?" He was, she says, "a homosexual," who "detested women, all women." She found him to be "cunning, perfidious and Machiavellian, he roused hatred, stirred up gossip, reveled in every intrigue." She writes of the Shah's fascination with this "diabolical Swiss," who claimed to be a "philosopher, a poet, and a prophet"; she writes of how every morning, the Shah "would shut himself up in his room with [Perron] and talk about affairs of state or gather some piece of information which the *shetun* had been able to glean in the bazaar."[86] She had to throw him out of the room, when "one day he lewdly set about asking questions concerning my life with Mohammad Reza."[87]

In these trying times, Soraya attempted to bring some joy to life on Court evenings by having the Shah listen to Louis Armstrong, Duke Ellington, Sidney Bechet, Count Basie, and Sarah Vaughan. But it was all to no avail—the Shah looked "somber and distressed," and he remained taciturn. He even stopped playing poker with friends at night. Rumor had it that the Shah oftentimes played high-stakes games at Court, sometimes with a couple of hundred thousand *tooman* (about $70,000) changing hands. The Shah was said to be reticent about receiving or writing checks at the end of the game.[88] Though he enjoyed these poker games immensely, he quit playing. He believed his phones and his rooms were bugged. He no longer "laughed at their jests" or played parlor games organized to divert him.[89] With her characteristic candor, Soraya even writes of their embrace in the "nuptial bed" and how it was invariably "to console him."[90] About the same time, the British Foreign Office concluded that "the Shah appeared on the verge of a nervous breakdown."[91]

As Mossadeq's confrontation with the British continued, and as his relations with the Shah grew more and more strained, the Shah's mood deteriorated even further. He was "becoming increasingly tense and worried. He continued to go to his office every day but it was merely a formality. Nobody asked for his advice."[92] More than once he complained to Western diplomats that the current state of affairs was untenable for him. By April 1953, he succumbed to Mossadeq's demand and dismissed his loyal Court Minister Hussein Ala and allowed the Prime Minister to name Abolgassem Amini in his place. By then visits to the Shah by politicians were deemed by Mossadeq to be an unfriendly gesture. Ministers were banned altogether from making any such visits. The Shah's nadir was reached when even the commanders of the military were barred, on the orders of Mossadeq, from giving him reports. As Mossadeq had demonstrated in the aftermath of his July 21, 1952, confrontation with the Shah, in his mind the Shah's constitutional title of commander in chief was no more than a perfunctory formality; the Shah, on the other hand, saw his constitutional role as commander in chief as a pillar of his power and a license to micromanage the military. Even after he had succumbed to Mossadeq's demand and allowed him to take over the command of the military, the Shah tried to continue his control of the armed forces through the secret officers group that had come to exist in the aftermath of the Second World War.

As his power dissipated, the Shah began to pay ever more attention to every gesture of those he met lest they show any sign of disrespect. In Soraya's view, he began "to distort every remark," to see an affront or an assault behind every word and gesture. He felt, in her words, "like a hunted animal." At night, "he would sleep with a revolver under his pillow and repeatedly changed his room."[93]

In one meeting with the American Ambassador, late in 1951, he made no effort to "hide his great anxiety"; he declared "again and again in seeming despair... 'But what can I do; I am helpless.'"[94] He went on to say "no matter how strong and resolute I may wish to be, I cannot take unconstitutional moves against strong current nationalist feelings." He asserted that "Mossadeq's policies are leading Iran towards ruin," but then asked, "What slogans have I to change this time? Can I appeal to balanced budgets?"[95]

A few months later, the Shah sent Alam to see the British Ambassador, to reassure him that the Shah was "fully aware of the danger of keeping Mossadeq in power" and that he was determined to get rid of him. The problem was that he felt "completely alone and thought if he took action against Mossadeq no one would support him." More importantly still, he believed that "a secret hand was supporting" Mossadeq and that this secret hand, in the King's mind, was the American government.[96]

To give a sense of the country's mood, the Shah recounted to one British official how on the same day of their meeting, he had "received emissary with a message from [Ayatollah] Boroujerdi . . . stating that all Iran must stand together in face of British threat."[97] He concluded the meeting by saying, "at present, he did not know where to turn." The reference to Boroujerdi was particularly poignant. As a matter of principle, Boroujerdi rarely entered the political arena directly. Just as his clear support for Mossadeq at this time was, for the Shah, a sobering indication of his foe's power, so too, when Boroujerdi and others in the clerical establishment ended their support for Mossadeq and aligned themselves with the Shah and his supporters in early 1953, that change of heart was a harbinger of the Shah's rising star and a sign that Mossadeq's base of power was weakening.

More than once in those days, British and American officials complained that the Shah "is lacking in courage and in resolution." Loy Henderson, the American ambassador, for example, said that while the Shah "[was] conscious of his weakness," he was nevertheless inclined to "conceal his true character by finding excuses for inaction, and even laying blame for past mistakes on those around him."[98] For this reason, as early as July 31, 1952, Henderson concluded that if a coup against Mossadeq was to be successful, it had to be "carried [out] and executed by Iranian army in name of the Shah without knowledge of Shah since Shah would probably not have stamina to see it through and might at certain stage weaken and denounce leaders."[99]

During those months, the Shah's behavior at times bordered on the fatalistic. He often engaged in his passion for speed. He sometimes drove one of his many fast cars to Kalardasht—his favorite vacation spot near the Caspian coast. A British Embassy official described one such trip. The Shah drove "eighty miles an hour" in his Packard convertible. The narrow, curvy two-lane road to Kalardasht—the Chalus Road—was in those days a notorious death trap.[100]

Even the venue in which he would hold sensitive conversations reflected his "haunted" mood. When discussing plans to topple Mossadeq or choosing who should replace him, "to obtain maximum privacy," the meetings "took place in palace gardens."[101] Kermit "Kim" Roosevelt, the CIA operative who went to Iran to arrange for the fall of Mossadeq, offers startling accounts of his crucial early August 1953 meetings with the Shah—a strange brew reminiscent of a Le Carré novel made into a bad Hollywood movie. Around midnight on Saturday, August 1, Roosevelt describes crawling into the backseat of a "suitably unroyal" car, a blanket covering him as he "huddled down on the floor" as they entered the royal palace gates. Security was lax. By then, Mossadeq had substantially reduced the Court's budget, closed the special offices of the Shah's siblings, exiled the more active members of the royal family (particularly the Shah's twin sister and his mother), and demanded that the King give up his annual revenue from the Imam Reza Endowment—the richest religious endowment in the country at the time. Before long, the Shah's security detail and even the number of tanks that protected the palace were reduced as well. No sooner had the car neared the palace itself than "the finely drawn, distinctively regal features" of the Shah appeared.

Roosevelt was there to convince the Shah that the United States and Britain were both behind him and supported the idea of toppling the Mossadeq government. A few weeks earlier, the Shah had demanded to know whether the British government still supported him, and on May 28, Churchill had asked the U.S. government to convey to the Shah his personal message—that is, that Britain "should be very sorry to see the Shah lose his powers or leave his post or be driven out."[102]

The United States too declared its support for a move against Mossadeq. Now Roosevelt was there to talk tactics and strategy. They walked in the garden in the dark of night, and Roosevelt promised that the United States would confirm its earnest support of the project by having "President Eisenhower... confirm this himself by a phrase in a speech he is about to deliver in San Francisco." Britain would reassert its commitment through "a specific change made in the announcement on the BBC broadcast" the next night.[103]

With tensions between the Shah and Mossadeq mounting, on February 19, 1953, Hussein Ala, the minister of Court, received a call from Mossadeq, asking him to send a "responsible" representative from the Court to take a personal message from the Prime Minister to the Shah. Mossadeq was increasingly using health excuses not to go to meet with the Shah. The same reason, as well as his fear of assassination, was given for moving the Prime Minister's office to his private home, where he conducted many of his official meetings in bed, in his pajamas.

In the meeting with the Court representative, Mossadeq, in the presence of three of his closest aides and allies, "briskly requested emissary to tell the Shah that he could no longer tolerate unfriendly attitude of Shah and Court" and that on February 24, he would submit his resignation. He accused the Shah of "intriguing against him" and maintained that the Court was engaged in all manner of conspiracy, all intended to bring about his fall.[104] It was a dangerous gambit by Mossadeq, intended to force the Shah to either totally submit to him or leave the country. This was a move sure to alarm the American government as well as Mossadeq's more moderate supporters, since both were opposed to the idea of regime change. Keeping the U.S. government on his side remained, up until the night of August 18, 1953, high on Mossadeq's agenda. But he was banking on the idea that, under the prevailing circumstances, the Shah could not afford to be seen as playing any role in the demise of the Prime Minister. Ever since his victory in the showdown with the Shah in July 1952, Mossadeq had acted as if he was impervious to any action from the Shah, as if he knew that the King would never dare dismiss him. The emissary, as well as Mossadeq's allies, all asked the Prime Minister to "reconsider... [he was] however adamant."

The Shah was deeply distraught when he heard the message and "asked Ala to intervene." The Court Minister too found the Prime Minister "intractable." Amongst Mossadeq's charges against the Shah, the strangest was that the Shah had supported "Qavam against him." In reality, the Shah had been much against the idea of Qavam's appointment. Moreover, the appointment had come only after the parliament had shown its inclination toward Qavam. By law, after such a vote, the Shah had no choice but to appoint Qavam. Implicit in Mossadeq's complaint was that any move to support another candidate for prime minister was itself treason; many of his aides and closest advisors made this claim much more openly. Mossadeq also criticized the Shah's decision to divide some of the Crown lands "among tenants. He had said the Shah should turn lands [over] to Government and allow" it to determine their disposition. He seemed to believe that the Shah's move was a publicity stunt meant to undermine the government. In reality, belief in the necessity of a land reform had been part of the Shah's vision as soon as he ascended the throne. In fact as early as April 1950, the Shah had told the British Ambassador that land reform was a "must" in Iran and that he would begin with the Crown lands. He went on to say that landlords were terrified at the prospect of land reform and were "even in some cases working up the mullahs into a counterattack, on the ground that such a movement would be against the religion of Islam."[105] The Shah's words proved prescient: in about a decade, when he did in fact launch land reform, precisely such an alliance between the clergy and the landlords was formed to fight the Shah.

In that February 19, 1953, meeting Mossadeq also accused the Shah of encouraging the uprising amongst the Bakhtiyari tribes against the government. Ala defended the Shah, arguing that he was firm in his belief that Mossadeq should remain as prime minister, as he was "better qualified than anyone to effect a solution" to the oil crisis.[106]

When the Shah was told of Mossadeq's intractable position, he asked Ala to inform the American Embassy of the problem and to continue negotiating with Mossadeq. He also relayed a message to Mossadeq that he was "prepared to leave the country and to stay abroad until Mossadeq requested his return."[107] The Prime Minister responded that in his view, the "Shah should not leave the country."

Neither Ala nor the Shah believed him on this point. They both believed that the ultimate goal of Mossadeq's most recent threat of resignation was in fact to force the Shah's exit from the country. The American Embassy, too, concurred, believing that Mossadeq intended to use the feeling of euphoria in the country about an imminent solution to the oil problem to "crush his political enemies" and settle his score with the Shah.

Concurrent with his offer to Mossadeq to leave the country, the Shah also began to think about a possible replacement for Mossadeq, should he indeed carry out his threat and resign. For some time, his favorite candidate had been Alahyar Saleh, an eminent leader of the National Front. In May 1951, the Shah in fact had had a long talk with Saleh and had been "more favorably impressed than ever." Saleh, at least according to the Shah, had been "quite critical" of Mossadeq and "had expressed complete devotion to Shah."[108] Ultimately, the Shah's efforts to create a fissure between leaders of the National Front—particularly between Mossadeq and Saleh—failed. He had more success when it came to increasing the rifts within the nationalization movement in general. Within twenty hours of the meeting between Mossadeq and his emissary, the Shah was searching for a "means of getting message" to Saleh, while at the same time reemphasizing his opposition to General Fazlollah Zahedi.[109] Aside from Saleh's own attitude, the other obstacle to such an appointment was that the American State Department had "pronounced themselves as totally unfavorable to any idea that Alahyar Saleh should be successor to Mossadeq."[110] A showdown between Mossadeq and the Shah now seemed inevitable.

On the morning of February 24, Mossadeq went to the Court and met with the Shah. Less then twelve hours earlier, "shortly before midnight," Ala had met with Henderson at the American ambassador's residence and indicated that Mossadeq had "promised not to press his grievances against the Shah at least for the time being." The Shah had met with a delegation of deputies allied with Mossadeq and promised them that he would "make it clear once and for all that officers [in the] armed forces must look to Mossadeq not Shah for instructions." He also agreed not to meet with "persons known to be critical of Mossadeq." On the issue of land distribution, he refused to agree to Mossadeq's demand.[111] What made the Shah's position more complicated was that, later in the same day, he received a message from some leading members of the Majlis, including some erstwhile supporters of Mossadeq, asking him "not to seek reconciliation with Mossadeq." They assured the Shah that should Mossadeq attack him, the "majority of Majlis and country would be outraged and support Shah."[112]

In those days, a group of eight Majlis deputies, divided more or less equally between supporters of the Shah and supporters of Mossadeq, had been busy meeting with the two sides, hoping to heal the rift between the two men and to find a modus operandi wherein realities of the time and mandates of the constitution were both considered and implemented. Ultimately, the group of eight's efforts came to naught. Not only did Mossadeq and the Shah have starkly different understandings of the constitution, but there was also a powerful external actor, namely Great Britain, who did not favor an amicable resolution to the standoff. Moreover, by the time the group had arrived at a preliminary resolution, Mozzafar Baghai, one of the leaders responsible for creating the group, indicated that he was opposed to its implementation, as it would afford Mossadeq too much power.

On the night of February 27, a distraught Ala told Loy Henderson that the Shah was planning to leave the country and had insisted on keeping his travel plans a secret, lest there be attempts to "prevent his departure." Ala talked of the Shah's "almost hysterical state," adding that he "feared complete nervous breakdown and irrational action."[113] Ala also detailed the Shah's plans to leave in a car the next day around five o'clock in the afternoon, accompanied by the Queen, two servants, and some guards. He had asked Mossadeq for $40,000 for two months' living expenses, an additional $10,000 for the initial costs of travel, and his help in securing "an official invitation" for the royal couple from some foreign government.[114] He meant to go first to Iraq, and from there, travel to Spain or Switzerland. Mossadeq had, according to Ala, given "his word of honor" to the Shah that during his absence, he would do nothing to undermine the Shah, and "the Shah [believed] Mossadeq." Ala was sure this was just a ruse by Mossadeq and that there would be no return should the Shah leave the country. He wanted the United States to use all of its influence to deter the Shah from such a trip.[115] But, as Ala repeated more than once, the Shah himself was anxious to leave.

❧

It was in this labyrinthine context that the February 24 meeting between Mossadeq and the Shah took place. Not surprisingly, it was anything but conciliatory. Mossadeq had apparently changed his mind about the wisdom of the Shah's continued stay in the country. He was now convinced that "it might be good idea after all for Shah to leave country as soon as possible and to remain abroad until situation of the country [became] more stable."[116] The Shah knew, all too well, that precisely such a "temporary trip abroad" had ended the reign of not just Ahmad Shah but of the Qajar dynasty. The Shah's suspicion about Mossadeq's motives and plans was only increased when, in earlier discussions about the composition of the regency council (which would nominally head the government during the King's absence), Mossadeq had insisted on "passing over" the Shah's only full brother, Ali Reza, in favor of another half-brother, Gholam Reza. By law, the latter was forbidden from ascending the throne after the Shah, and thus

Mossadeq was clearly forcing out of the regency the only brother who could succeed the Shah in case his foreign sojourn turned into permanent exile.[117]

On the morning of February 28, according to the U.S. Embassy, whispers of the Shah's imminent departure swept the city. There is much evidence to indicate that not only the Court, through Ala, but Qavam, Ayatollah Behbahani, an influential cleric in Tehran, and Ayatollah Kashani had all become active in mustering forces that would converge on the Court and try to pressure the Shah to reconsider. It was rumored that Mossadeq had threatened the Shah and that unless he left of his own volition, Mossadeq would have no choice but to ask the "people to choose between the Shah and himself."[118]

The night before the Shah's rumored departure, at a dinner hosted by an American Embassy official, the guests included a number of bazaar merchants and a few political personalities; "all guests, with the exception of Khosrow Khan Ghashghai," believed the Shah's departure "would be detrimental to the interests of the country."[119] By the morning of the twenty-eighth, the embassy, along with a whole litany of de facto allies including Kashani were openly trying to "effect the cancellation or least postponement of the Shah's plans to leave."[120]

The most serious obstacle to the success of this coalition's effort came from the Shah himself. When the American Ambassador tried to engage the Shah in a conversation about the wisdom of his staying in the country, he "received an evasive answer." The Shah, in Henderson's view, was "now a nervous wreck," "had jumped at the chance of escaping," and thus "could not be dissuaded from leaving."[121] But events of that day surprised the Shah.

At eleven o'clock on the morning of February 28, not long before Mossadeq's arrival for what they both thought would be a farewell lunch, Ala met with the Shah to try for the last time to persuade him not to leave. But the Shah was not deterred. If I don't go, he said, Mossadeq "would issue a proclamation attacking [me] and members of [my] family." He did not, he said, want to engage in a squabble with Mossadeq. In the course of the meeting, news reached Ala and the Shah that Ayatollah Kashani was convening an emergency meeting of the Majlis—"with fifty-seven members present"—to discuss ways to convince the Shah not to leave the country. When the Shah received this news "he had become excited," not because it was a sign of popular support for him or because it indicated a crucial breach between Mossadeq and his key ally, Kashani, but because such developments might stop his departure. He insisted on leaving at once, "before lunch."[122] In fact, the day before, a car carrying some of the royal couple's personal belongings had already left the capital. Heavy snow impeded the car's progress.

Before long, another messenger arrived from the Majlis, reporting that a secret session of the parliament had passed a resolution indicating that the Shah's departure "at this time would not be advisable." Moreover, General

Baharmast, from the Joint Chiefs of Staff, was said to be "en route to the Court to inform the Shah that whole general staff had decided to resign in case Shah should leave the country."[123] Even that was not enough to deter the Shah. Only when a large crowd of "people demonstrated for the Shah" near the Court during the Shah's meeting with Mossadeq did he change his mind about leaving the country.

In that crowd, standing nervously atop the high wall that separated the Court compound from the outside world, was an agitated young man named Ardeshir Zahedi. "I hate heights," he said, "but somehow I found myself on the wall, leading the crowds in their chants and slogans."[124]

The meeting between Mossadeq and the Shah was tense to begin with. But when the gathered crowd began to chant increasingly violent slogans, including the demand for Mossadeq's death, the meeting came to an abrupt end. Soraya claims that she tried to calm a clearly agitated, perspiring, and "deathly pale" Mossadeq, and showed him how to leave the Court through the back door, thus avoiding the belligerent crowd. But at home too, an angry crowd awaited Mossadeq; when, according to the American Embassy, he appeared on the balcony in his famous pajamas in an "effort to quiet the throng," he was booed down. Throughout the day, "loudspeakers were calling on people if they are for Shah now is time to demonstrate the fact."[125]

After the show of popular support, a buoyed Shah was once again resolved to stay and fight on. The American Embassy assessed that "the institution of the Crown may have more popular backing than expected."[126] They also noted that Kashani "has shown more power than expected both in influencing the Majlis and in quickly marshalling for mob action his fanatical followers."[127]

The British, on the other hand, saw the Shah as "a pawn" in the power struggle between Kashani and Mossadeq. That was why British officials did not take much comfort in the show of support for the Shah that day, as it was, in their view, "certainly organized by Kashani and was not a spontaneous expression of loyalty deep-seated or significant enough to stiffen the Shah."[128]

Nevertheless, at nine o'clock on the night of February 28, the Shah broadcast a message over the radio that embodied his new spirit. He said, "As I informed [the] public by communiqué issued by Court, on advice [of] my physician, it [was] necessary for me to go abroad for [a] pilgrimage and medical treatment for [a] short time. As all day today and in fact at this very moment, while I am speaking to you, I have witnessed [the] sincere feelings of [the] people, I gave up the idea of going on this trip and I expect [the] patriotic and valiant people of Iran in all parts of the country to maintain order so that by [the] help of [the] Almighty, Iran may continue along [the] path of honor."[129] Lest there be any doubt about who had managed to bring the crowds out into the streets, Ayatollah Kashani also issued a statement, "appealing to all to collaborate" with the clergy to "prevent" the Shah from going on a trip that would have "led to agitation in [the] country."

Mossadeq was particularly unhappy about the role he believed the United States had played in stopping the Shah from leaving the country. Shortly after his ill-fated meeting with the Shah, Mossadeq met with Henderson. He was in a bad mood, "apparently suffering from severe headache." Henderson tried to convince Mossadeq to cease his attempts to get rid of the Shah, but Mossadeq contemptuously referred to those at the Court demonstrating against him, and those in the parliament passing a resolution in favor of the Shah as "British agents." On other occasions, he called the demonstrators hoodlums, criminals, agitators, and foreign agents. To Henderson, he confirmed that he had gone to the Court to bid "the Shah farewell." He was convinced that he could not "constitute necessary reform and obtain resolution of oil problem so long as Court served as basis of operation of British agents."[130]

On March 2, Mossadeq met Henderson again and asked him to "order all American citizens to keep off the streets." When Henderson retorted that the safety of American citizens was the responsibility of the government, Mossadeq responded by accusing the United States of interfering in Iran's domestic affairs and suggested that the Americans had played a key role in dissuading the Shah from leaving the country.[131] The Shah, on the other hand, remained calm and resolute in his decision to stay in Iran. He met a delegation of Majlis deputies and told them "he had done nothing reprehensible" and that the people had already spoken in his favor.[132] At the same time, a few days later, Mossadeq and a couple of his supporters confronted the Shah about the events of February 28, accusing him of laying a trap for Mossadeq. They claimed that the Shah had supposedly suggested he wanted to leave the country but organized demonstrations in his own support and against Mossadeq. The Shah, at least according to Mossadeq's supporters, responded rather meekly, "We do not want to do anything above and beyond the constitution, and we do not wish to interfere in matters that are not within the purview of the King, and if some people have used [the occasion of my trip] to unsavory ends, the government must prosecute them fully."[133]

For Mossadeq, events of that February were a fiasco; for the Shah, they were a watershed event. Clearly the balance of forces, hitherto in favor of Mossadeq, was beginning to change in the Shah's favor. Mossadeq had not only made his move against the Shah and failed, but, more crucially, his failure emboldened his foes, augmented the Shah's power, revived the King's sagging resolve, and increased tensions between Mossadeq and the American government. The once-despondent Shah, who had been tormented by an increasingly somber and defeatist attitude, was now in a much better, more self-assured, fighting spirit.

Though he was an astute politician, Mossadeq still failed to realize the importance of his failed February move. On March 3, representatives of the Prime Minister and the Shah were both summoned to Qom by Ayatollah Boroujerdi, where they were given identical letters. The epistle ended with what must have been for Mossadeq an ominous hint and for the Shah a promising sign. The Ayatollah, until then a clear supporter of Mossadeq, this time asked him and the Shah to "preserve your unity and collaboration as before and thus prevent disorder and insecurity in the country."[134] In the tumultuous meeting in the Majlis in the days after the February 28 meeting, royalists criticized Mossadeq in sharp terms for not telling the parliament about "the Shah's projected trip." Mossadeq refused to accept any blame, instead referring to "certain provocative activities" against the government "emanating from Shah's entourage"; he complained that "people broke into my house and I [was] compelled [to] climb [a] ladder in my pajamas and run away to [the American assistance organization] Point Four Office."[135]

Mossadeq ended his evasive retort by divulging his plans to hold a referendum. Almost a week before this public announcement, Mossadeq had told Henderson, the American ambassador, that he "might have a plebiscite throughout the country, Mossadeq supporters congregating in one mosque and his opponents in another."[136] During the same conversation, Mossadeq also articulated his theory of power—wherein lay the roots of his defiance toward the Shah, and toward the Majlis—a theory that came into direct conflict with the fundamentals of representative democracy. He was not, he told Henderson, the "Prime Minister of the Shah, or the Prime Minister of the Majlis, but the Prime Minister of the people."[137] He repeated much the same idea when he spoke to a jubilant crowd of supporters outside the Majlis. My real Majlis, he said, is here with you. Supporters have often praised these pronouncements as a laudable sign of Mossadeq's democratic beliefs. In fact, they are the naked pronouncements of a populist, exhibiting a clear disregard for the checks and balances that define representative democracy and differentiate it from the rule of the mob.

The idea of a referendum turned out to be surprisingly controversial. Abol Hassan Haerizadeh, once a key ally of the National Front, accused Mossadeq of "being [a] worse dictator than Reza Shah" and lambasted the idea of a referendum as the work of a "rebel government."[138] Other critics used the media to attack the idea of the referendum. By then a propaganda war against Mossadeq, some of it funded by the CIA's BADAMN operation, was in full force.[139] A dubious idea like the referendum and an even more dubious exercise of forcing government opponents to cast their ballots in separate voting stations became perfect ammunition for this campaign. Another favorite weapon was Mossadeq's continued insistence that he must be given special powers to govern—he demanded, and received from a pliant Majlis, the power to legislate. Even some of his allies began to see these powers as excessive and despotic.

By early March, Tehran was preparing to hold the referendum, and the city was awash with rumors about a new clash between the Shah and his increasingly embittered yet still ambitious Prime Minister. The ultimate goal of the referendum was also not clear. The apparent purpose was to decide whether the parliament should be dissolved. In 1949 the Constituent Assembly had given this power to the Shah. He had refused to use it against Mossadeq—particularly when the British pressured him to dissolve the Majlis, dismiss the Prime Minister, and nullify the Nationalization of Oil Act. Now Mossadeq was keen on using a referendum to dissolve a parliament elected during his own government's tenure.

The Shah and the American Embassy saw the referendum as yet another sign of Mossadeq's steady move "in [an] authoritarian direction" and in using the "technique of mobocracy."[140] The Shah and some of his supporters, as well as nearly all of Mossadeq's more radical allies and supporters, also saw it as the first necessary step in ending monarchy in Iran. The referendum further split the ranks of the movement to nationalize oil. Ayatollah Kashani was openly and belligerently against the idea of a referendum and of Mossadeq himself. Other critics and foes of Mossadeq—from Mozzafar Baghai and General Fazlollah Zahedi to Ayatollah Boroujerdi and Ayatollah Behbahani—were now openly working to topple the government. The more isolated Mossadeq became, the more he had to rely on the Tudeh Party and the most radical members of the National Front; the more radical his camp became, the more united his foes became, and the more they came to enjoy the support of the British and American governments. As he admitted in later years, Ayatollah Khomeini had told his mentor, Kashani, in 1953 that Mossadeq was an infidel and did not deserve the support of the clergy or of the Muslim nation of Iran.

By the time of the referendum, officers deemed more "loyal to the Shah than to Mussadeq" were increasingly forced to retire and were at times even arrested. This resulted in what the American Embassy called the continuous surreptitious discussion of a military coup d'état by Shah loyalists. The brutal execution of General Mahmoud Afshartus, the chief of police and a staunch Mossadeq supporter, whose badly tortured body was found outside Tehran on April 14, only added to the air of menace and confrontation in the country. Sensational allegations that many of the royalists were complicit in the murder—from Baghai and General Zahedi to the Shah himself—only added to the tension. The Shah sent "secret messages to the [Mossadeq] opposition in the Majlis and other groups loyal to him, asking for their continued support," and explaining that "if he has so far been passive . . . it is only because of his belief that he is not yet in a position openly to resist Mossadeq." The embassy officer reporting this message was incredulous, adding that "it is difficult to believe that the Shah would really have the necessary courage or resolution."[141] At the same time, it was increasingly clear that General Zahedi was emerging as the only man capable of standing up to the popular and populist Mossadeq. The fact that the General had been given a surprisingly "sympathetic reception by [the] Majlis" when he sought asylum there against Mossadeq's attempt to arrest him further convinced both the British and American governments that he was the man to replace Mossadeq. The main obstacle to the General was the fact he was not "able to obtain support of Shah."[142]

Gradually, the Shah's options for finding a moderate leader to take the place of Mossadeq dwindled. After he lost hope in Alahyar Saleh, for a few days he tried to convince the new speaker of the Majlis, Abdollah Moazzami to accept the post. He too was unwilling to move against Mossadeq. When the referendum did take place on March 3, according to government sources, in Tehran alone 1.5 million people voted in favor and only 20 against the resolution to dissolve the parliament.[143] The Shah believed that in the absence of the Majlis, he had the constitutional authority to dismiss Mossadeq.

Although Mossadeq had bet that the Shah would never dare use this power, and although Mossadeq and most of his supporters have argued since 1953 that the Shah in fact had no legal authority to dismiss Mossadeq even during parliamentary recess, both historical precedence and Mossadeq's own writings indicate otherwise.[144] First of all, there had been at least fourteen recess appointments of prime ministers when there was no parliament in session. Mossadeq not only knew this well but had often spoken favorably of Ahmad Shah, the King who had made these appointments.[145] More crucially yet, in a hitherto surprisingly overlooked letter, Mossadeq himself, as late as October 1948, confirmed that the Shah had the right to make such appointments. At that time, he and a group of opposition figures—what in fact became the embryo of the future National Front—had organized a sit-in at the Court to object to what they considered a clumsily stolen election. Mossadeq wrote a letter to Court Minister Abdol-Hussein Hajir—soon to be assassinated by Islamist terrorists close to Kashani—in which he wrote, "His Majesty is of course the source of all reforms, and the main reason for our sit-in is that in this period of parliamentary recess (*fetrat*) when the appointment of a Prime Minister does not require a vote of inclination by the *Majlis,* we hope His Majesty can appoint a government whose goal is to preserve the interests of the monarchy and the nation."[146] In other words, absent a parliament, the Shah does have the right to dismiss a prime minister. The referendum thus put into place the last piece of the puzzle that has since come to be known as Operation Ajax.

Chapter 10

AJAX OR BOOT

What must the king do now? Must he submit?
The king shall do it . . .
Shakespeare, King Richard II, *3.3.143–144*

In history, Ajax was a buffoon. In Sophocles' play, while under a spell, Ajax slaughters a whole flock of sheep, imagining them to be enemy warriors. Realizing his folly, he commits self-slaughter.[1] In Shakespeare's *Troilus and Cressida*, Ajax is a man into whom "nature hath so crowded humors that his valor is crush'd into folly, his folly sauc'd with discretion. . . . He is melancholy without cause . . . many hands and no use . . . all eyes and no sight."[2] Strange as it may seem, Ajax was also the CIA's cryptonym for an intelligence operation intended to overthrow the Mossadeq government. The British chose a more appropriate name for their part of the same operation. They called it Boot.

On the afternoon of June 23, 1953, eleven men—including Secretary of State John Foster Dulles, his brother Allen Dulles, and Kermit "Kim" Roosevelt, a CIA operative with some experience in the Middle East—gathered in Foster Dulles's roomy offices. It was raining outside, while inside the room there was the bubbly buoyancy of the Dulles brothers' optimism about U. S. power in "the American century." On the agenda was a twenty-two-page document, initially proposed by the British and worked over in days of intense planning in Cyprus by American and British intelligence operatives. Allen Dulles summarized the goal of the meeting and the gist of the document: "So that is how we get rid of that madman

Mossadeq."[3] There was little or no discussion of the morality of the operation. The dominant theme of the meeting was the possibility of Mossadeq's forming an alliance with the Tudeh Party. Ambassador Loy Henderson chimed in, saying that while he did not like "this kind of business," the "madman would ally himself with the Russians."[4] Finally John Foster Dulles got up and brought the meeting to an end, saying, "Then let's get going." And thus began Operation Ajax.

∞

Until early August 1953, the Shah had resisted the idea of a coup against Mossadeq. Yet behind the scenes, he had often worked, particularly with British officials, to weaken Mossadeq and to find a constitutional way to get rid of him. Even after Mossadeq ordered the British Embassy closed in Iran, the State Department not only shared dispatches from the American Embassy with the British government, but, more crucially, British intelligence succeeded in having its top man in Iran, Shapour Reporter, hired by the U.S. Embassy as a consultant and accredited by Western magazines as a journalist. His regular trips to the Court were easily camouflaged by the fact that he was tutoring the new Queen in English. She spoke perfect German, had a fair command of French; now MI6's top man in Iran was helping her learn the language of Shakespeare. Moreover, during this period, Ernest Perron had "regular contacts with Robin Zaehner,"[5] the British professor-spy.

Regardless of the overwhelming evidence that a series of events planned by the British–American Ajax operatives did take place in Tehran, there is still some ambiguity about what actually sealed Mossadeq's fate on August 19. A CIA memorandum for President Dwight Eisenhower, written in the immediate aftermath of August 19, says that "an unexpected strong upsurge of popular and military reaction to Prime Minister Mossadeq's Government has resulted according to late dispatches from Tehran in the virtual occupation of that city by forces proclaiming their loyalty to the Shah and to his appointed Prime Minister, Zahedi."[6] But Mossadeq and his supporters have long rejected this claim, suggesting that the "strong upsurge" of support was paid for and procured by the CIA and British operatives. In the last two decades, Ardeshir Zahedi has offered yet a third narrative, wherein the clumsy efforts of the CIA and the British worked in parallel with the efforts of his father, General Fazlollah Zahedi, and his supporters to resist Mossadeq. The two forces intersected occasionally, but were not identical. In fact, the support of thousands of patriotic Iranians and politicians like Ayatollah Kashani and Mozzafar Baghai, and not the Ajax operation, was, in Ardeshir's view, the determining factor in his father's victory.[7]

For the last quarter century of the Shah's rule, his life was to a considerable degree plagued by the question of what had happened in Tehran on August 19, 1953.

Was it a coup, or a countercoup? A proud day of national resurrection (Ghiam-e Melli) in support of an abused Shah, or a day of foreign infamy and intrigue against a democratic Mossadeq? Or, are such attempts at certainty about labyrinthine realities of history the result of a proclivity for Manichaeism, the desire to see the world as an arena wherein forces of good and evil are in constant cosmic conflict? Before the 1979 revolution, throughout the Shah's thirty-seven years on the throne—making him the fifth-longest serving monarch in the recorded history of monarchy in Iran[8]—no set of events was more crucial than that of August 1953.

The Shah and Mossadeq have both written with passion about what happened on those fateful days. Mossadeq's version declares that he was a strict constitutionalist whose only "crime" was challenging the colonial power of Britain. The Shah claims that Mossadeq was a demagogue, a sworn enemy of the Pahlavi dynasty, who used the issue of the nationalization of Iranian oil to seize despotic power and risked inadvertently turning the country over to the Communists.

There is no doubt that events of that August left an indelible mark on the Shah and the nature of his regime. There is also overwhelming evidence that the United States did in fact belatedly and at times begrudgingly join the British effort to overthrow Mossadeq. What is less clear is the precise role of these two countries' operatives in actually determining the outcome of the formative events of August 19. An answer to this question can only be given when the whole episode is sufficiently "historicized"—viewed through Cleo's cold, calculating, impartial eyes. The generation of Iranians who participated in or witnessed the events of those fateful days, as well as some of the American and British intelligence officers involved in Ajax, continue to see the day in epic terms, not as a simple moment of history. Moreover, many of the most important documents—archival material from the CIA, British MI6, the Iranian military, the Tudeh Party, the Soviet intelligence and embassy in Tehran, the offices of the Shah, and Ayatollahs Kashani and Boroujerdi, to name only the most important—are still not available for scrutiny.

Even if all of these documents were declassified and made available for careful study, it might still be impossible to answer the question of whether it was better to go down in flames of defeat while insisting on the complete fulfillment of lofty ideals and principles—as Mossadeq claimed to have done—or to accept the "best possible" offer made by the West in terms of an oil agreement—as the Shah favored—and spare the country the gaping wound that was August 1953. At one point, Mossadeq told Vernon Walters, a member of the team of Americans negotiating with him, that he did not "really want an oil agreement." Any agreement, he said, might taint his reputation with the Iranian people, as they would invariably assume foul play, even bribery. Returning to Iran empty-handed, Mossadeq said, "I return in a much better position."[9]

No less pertinent is the question of what would have happened in Iran had the events of August 19, 1953, not occurred. How long could Mossadeq have lasted in the face of the increasingly powerful Tudeh Party? Mossadeq's mystique and the Shah's constant harping against him created a romance of a "democratic utopia" that awaited Iran had the dark forces of the "Other" not intervened and overthrown Mossadeq. A reminder of the power of this mystique came in the immediate aftermath of the 1979 revolution, when at the first chance the Iranian people had to commemorate Mossadeq, more than a million of them converged on his estate a few kilometers outside Tehran and paid their tribute to an icon of their anti-colonial and democratic longings.

For the Shah, August 1953 was both the cruelest and the most triumphant month. After that August, Mossadeq became the Shah's lifelong nemesis. The Shah also became more successful in the effort to concentrate power in his office; he grew far more ambitious in his goals, and more insistent on the need for his authoritarian leadership. Moreover, in spite of the Shah's assertion that he fully supported the nationalization efforts between 1951 and 1953, his actual views and his behind-the-scenes moves and stated preferences on this issue were more complicated.[10]

Though the Shah had personally only a marginal role in the events of that August 1953 day, he nevertheless considered it the beginning of his elected monarchy. "I knew they loved me," he told his wife, "before I was merely a hereditary monarch but today I really have been elected by my people."[11] For the last twenty-five years of his rule, he ignored the tormented national psyche about events of that August day and insisted on having the nation celebrate it as a triumphant moment of National Resurrection *(Ghiam-e Melli)*.

Mossadeq and his supporters, on the other hand, have called August 19 a day of infamy, when a dastardly coup, masterminded by the CIA and British Intelligence, overthrew his democratically elected nationalist government. In this narrative, a "rented crowd," and a motley crew of pimps and prostitutes, all bought and paid for by the CIA and MI6, overthrew the government of Mossadeq. Advocates of the Mossadeq narrative received a boost when, in March 2000, U.S. Secretary of State Madeleine Albright offered an apology for the U.S. role in the August events. She offered carefully worded regrets for the fact that the United States had "played a significant role in orchestrating the overthrow of Iran's popular Prime Minister" in 1953.[12]

Memoirs by CIA and British intelligence officers involved in planning or implementing Operation Ajax, as well as the "leaked" CIA "official history" of its role in the affair, have boosted the advocates of this theory.[13] As some scholars have pointed out, even a careful reading of the CIA's self-laudatory "official history" raises as many questions as it answers.[14] Ardeshir Zahedi, himself a key player in the events of those days, has been the most relentless critic of this "secret history," often asking sardonically how a vodka-drinking American named Roosevelt who spoke no Persian, along with a motley crew of paid agents, overthrew a popular government.

In retrospect, there seems little doubt that while the Shah won the battle on August 19, he might well have lost the war. Much anecdotal evidence indicates that, in the collective memory of the nation, after that August the Shah never shook off the tainted reputation of being a puppet—a ruler forcefully restored to the throne by foreign powers. Martin Herz, a seasoned American diplomat working in Iran in the mid-sixties, observed that even though by then the Shah and his regime had achieved impressive accomplishments, in private, even regime stalwarts were unwilling to defend him.[15]

Mossadeq was a masterful politician and parliamentarian, as adept in bending the most arcane bylaws of parliamentary rule to his expedient political ends as he was at brushing the big strokes of symbolic politics. Everything about him, including his date of birth, has become a subject of contention.[16] He was given to wild swings of emotion, easily going from melancholic stupor and tears to joyous exuberance and hyperactivity. Friend and foe concur that he was deeply distrustful of others, his behavior sometimes bordering on paranoid. When traveling overseas for important negotiations, he kept sensitive documents in a briefcase he personally carried at all times. In the words of George McGhee, the American assistant secretary of state who spent "approximately 80 hours of conversation" with Mossadeq and who was considered so sympathetic to the cause of Iranian nationalization that the British government tried to remove him from his post,[17] Mossadeq was "not only a patriotic Iranian nationalist," but was "absolutely obdurate in his views . . . displayed a startling naivety about economics and business in general, not just the oil business." McGhee also emphasized that, in his view, the British too acted stubbornly and instead of negotiating in goodwill "preferred to wait for Mossadeq's expected fall."[18] Much the same image of Mossadeq is offered by Loy Henderson in several of his dispatches from Tehran.[19] The British, of course, never tired of repeating that Mossadeq was a madman, a demagogue, and utterly unreliable as a negotiating partner. Their goal from the outset was to remove him.

But Mossadeq was an intractable but powerful adversary for the Shah and the British, as much a masterful thespian as a clever populist politician, always aware of the mise-en-scène of his actions. He feigned weakness and fragility when it served his purpose and resolute defiance when the occasion called for it. More than anything, he was also aware of his own iconic reputation, thus avoiding any decision that might jeopardize this stature.

After the February confrontation between the Shah and Mossadeq, the relationship between the two deteriorated considerably. Mossadeq was then at the center of Iranian politics—domestic and international, economic and military—with the Shah playing at best a symbolic role. The retirement of many top generals in the military was ordered without even the knowledge, let alone the approval, of the Shah. The fact that the army had not come to Mossadeq's help in February 1953 had only increased his distrust of the military. He had created a commission and made General Mahmoud Afshartus, his most reliable ally in the army, its secretary; it was this commission that forced the retirement "of some two hundred senior officers."[20] From that February, there was essentially a race against time between Mossadeq and the Shah. The army was obviously the Shah's trump card. Could Mossadeq purge it before it could be used to remove him from power? The retirement of the officers was part of Mossadeq's strategy to win this race.

But a number of factors worked in favor of the Shah. Further complicating the situation for Mossadeq, and rendering it favorable to the Shah, was the fact that Mossadeq refused every offer made by the British and American governments, and even from international organizations like the International Bank of Reconstruction and Development (IRBD). With every refusal, he lost some part of his social base. When on February 20, 1953, he decided to reject the final Anglo–American offer, he used what one Western observer called surprisingly "intemperate" language, decrying the "plunder" of Iran and advocating the eradication of all foreign influence.[21] By then, the Eisenhower administration had given up its effort to find a negotiated resolution to the crisis. With every passing day, the Tudeh Party became more assertive in its ambitions. In an effort to frighten the Americans, Mossadeq increased his public contacts with the Soviet government. As early as November 1952, the American Embassy in Tehran was reporting that the "spirit of extremism in the National Front" was on the rise, and there was more and more evidence of Tudeh Party influence in the cabinet. Mossadeq was said to be "receiving [a] considerable amount of Tudeh slanted advice," and several of his ministers and undersecretaries were "not above suspicion as Tudeh tools."[22] All of these developments were inadvertently benefiting the Shah and increasing the rift between Mossadeq and the clergy. The United States finally succumbed to the two-year-old British campaign and decided to join the effort to topple Mossadeq in Operation Ajax/Boot. Even then, the Shah was hesitant to move.

Some sources have suggested that for the Eisenhower administration the die was cast on the first anniversary of July 21, 1952, when Mossadeq had been returned to power. On that day in 1953, his followers organized a demonstration in the morning while the Tudeh had a rally in the afternoon. *New York Times* journalist Kennett Love was in Tehran at the time. In his words, the pro-Mossadeq forces "mustered up a straggling assembly of a few thousand demonstrators," while the Tudeh "turned out a vibrantly-disciplined throng of at least 100,000."[23] At the end of the mammoth rally, a resolution was passed calling for, "among other things, the liquidation of American spy-nests."* This was more than enough to convince the Eisenhower administration that the Shah and the British had been right and that Mossadeq would be no match for Tudeh Party militancy. Eisenhower thus finally signed off on the plans developed in Cyprus for the overthrow of Mossadeq.

The "field commanders" of the joint American–British operation to overthrow Mossadeq were American Kim Roosevelt and a British intelligence officer named C. M. Woodhouse. In later years, some sources claimed that Shapour Reporter was the real master of British mischief. He claimed as much himself in a remarkable note he prepared on behalf of MI6 for President-Elect John F. Kennedy. He called himself "the permanently accredited liaison officer of my service to his person,"[24] the Shah, and claimed that he was in fact chief of Operation Boot.

While Reporter had by then served in Tehran for many years, Roosevelt and Woodhouse were in comparison relative novices on Iran. Woodhouse had spent most of his time in places like Greece; Roosevelt had had his first experience in intelligence when he worked with "Wild Bill" Donovan during World War II. The world of cloaks and daggers, spies and covert operations, had for him the air of romance—part Hollywood, part Rudyard Kipling, with a pinch of "Bond, James Bond." In his memoirs, with obvious relish, Roosevelt noted that for some, he conjured Graham Greene's "Quiet American."[25] For security reasons, he had given everyone involved in the operation an alias. His was "Rainmaker," while the Shah was called "the Boy Scout."[26]

Aside from Roosevelt's tendency toward self-adulating exaggeration—evident in his memoir when, amongst other things, he claims that he had picked Kim Philby as a double agent when he first saw him[27]—in life he had a knack for turning his political connections to the Shah into substantial personal financial gain. In the sixties and seventies, he was, on the order of the Shah, one of the preferred "middlemen" in some of the big deals between the Iranian government and American corporations. Wheat purchases, for example, were in his monopoly.[28] He was also reported to have acted as a middleman for Northrop's controversial sale of military hardware to Iran. Finally, even the time and the manner in which he chose to publish his memoir revealed his pragmatism. He waited until the Shah was in his political death throes; only then did he publish what he knew would be a bonanza to the Shah's critics, validating their claims about events in August 1953. But even then, he did not burn all his bridges—he asked

* Twenty-seven years later, when Islamist students took over the American Embassy, Khomeini incredibly referred to the American Embassy as a "den of spies."

Assadollah Alam, the Court minister, whether His Majesty would object to the publication of his memoir.

The tumultuous events leading to August 19 began early in the month as talk of Mossadeq's planned referendum to dissolve the Majlis became reality. He had by then also dissolved the Senate, using a legal technicality. For months, he had been ruling with the "special powers" he had demanded and received from the Majlis. Amongst these rights was the power to make legislation. He even dissolved the equivalent of Iran's Supreme Court, retiring a large number of judges. The economic situation grew more dire by the day; the government was at times even unable to make its payroll, and its efforts to print more money were blocked by Mossadeq's opponents in the Majlis. The government began to develop plans for an oil-less economy. Some have suggested that Mossadeq's initial impulse to dissolve the Majlis developed directly in response to his opponents' success in taking over the committee with oversight over money matters. Eisenhower's rejection of Mossadeq's latest request for financial aid made the economic horizon even more ominous. The referendum was simply the straw that broke the camel's back.

For weeks, the Shah had been under pressure from the American Embassy and his Court minister, Hussein Ala, to at least meet with General Zahedi,[29] who had emerged as the clear candidate to replace Mossadeq. The Shah's reluctance to meet the General had several roots. Zahedi had been minister of the interior when a large number of National Front candidates were elected to the parliament. He had served in a Mossadeq cabinet and, finally, he was a charismatic officer with a history of independence. The combination did not bode well for the Shah. As late as April 15, 1953, the Shah had "taken definite position he would not take any steps to replace Mossadeq unless the parliament gave the Prime Minister a vote of no confidence." The Shah's hesitance to move against Mossadeq was at least partially rooted in his suspicion that the British government was responsible for much of the existing tension between himself and Mossadeq; he believed they were hoping to create "a civil war so that they would have a pretext to divide Iran between themselves and the Russians."[30] The Shah even refused to accept Ala's proposal to use the occasion of large demonstrations by the Tudeh Party, coupled with a letter of concern from Kashani, then still speaker of the Majlis, to dismiss Mossadeq and appoint a "Director of Public Security" to take over the government until the Majlis could give a "vote of inclination to a new Prime Minister."[31]

But by early August the Shah's attitude, as well as his options, began to shift. The sea change might well have begun on July 27, when his twin sister, Ashraf, exiled earlier on the order of Mossadeq, traveled to Tehran incognito. She was there at the behest of the British and American governments and had been sent to encourage the Shah to go along with plans for an attempt to topple Mossadeq.

Only hours after she conveyed the message, Mossadeq learned of her return. He angrily forced not only her speedy departure, but demanded—and received—a public statement from the Shah distancing himself from his sister's return to Iran.

A few days after his twin sister's controversial trip, on August 1, the Shah met with U.S. General Norman Schwarzkopf Sr. The Shah had first met the General when he was an advisor to Iran's Gendarmerie. He was now back in Iran to encourage the Shah to join the plan against Mossadeq.[32] If all of this was not enough, Kim Roosevelt made it clear to the Shah that plans to topple Mossadeq would go ahead even without his approval. Even in his August 3 meeting with Roosevelt, the Shah still resisted the proposed operation by saying he was "not an adventurer." But Roosevelt was stern in his warnings. Failure to act, he said, would turn Iran into another Korea and lead to the Communist takeover of the country.[33]

At the same time, the Shah agreed to meet not with General Zahedi but with his son, Ardeshir. Father and son were both in hiding in those days, with a price on their heads. These meetings were conducted in great secrecy, with Ardeshir entering the Court through the backdoor, hidden in the trunk of a car.[34] On August 3, when Mossadeq held his controversial referendum in Tehran, the Shah told a confidante "that great changes would take place shortly" in the country.[35] Meeting with Zahedi was preparation for these "great changes"; not only were future plans discussed, but the Shah was also briefed on what the Zahedi camp was hearing from their secret allies within the Mossadeq government. These included the military governor of Tehran and the head of the police intelligence unit.[36]

The Shah's key meeting with General Zahedi took place on August 10, when the referendum to dissolve the Majlis was also taking place in the rest of the country. No sooner had the referendum ended than Mossadeq sent a formal appeal to the Shah for a *firman* (royal mandate) to hold new elections. But instead of giving such an order, the Shah summoned General Zahedi to the Court and informed him that he would shortly be appointed prime minister. In his own mind, the Shah could finally abide by his own rule not to take part in a coup against Mossadeq, but to remove him legally. With the dissolution of the Majlis, he believed, he had the constitutional right to issue two *firmans*—one dismissing Mossadeq and the other appointing General Zahedi as his replacement.

To give himself plausible deniability or, in his own words, "in order to put Mossadeq off,"[37] on August 11, the day after the meeting with Zahedi, the Shah and his wife, along with a small entourage, went to his favorite summer resort, Kalardasht. The official announcement declared it to be the royal couple's routine summer vacation. The decision to go to Kalardasht, at least according to Roosevelt, was made in consultation with him, and only after he and the Shah had rejected Shiraz, Meshed, Isfahan, and Tabriz as other possible destinations for the ostensible vacation. Each city was rejected for a different reason. Shiraz, for example, was deemed unfit because of its proximity to Qashgai tribes, in those days no friends of the Shah.[38]

At Kalardasht, the Shah apparently signed the two orders and asked Colonel Nematollah Nasiri, the commander of the Imperial Guard, to deliver them to Zahedi and Mossadeq. Despite considerable controversy on whether and exactly when the Shah signed the orders, it remains incontestable that the Shah more than once affirmed in those days his intention to issue the two orders.

For reasons that have never been fully explained, there was a three-day delay before the letter of dismissal was delivered. Some attribute it to sheer incompetence, others to the fact that two of the three missed days were in fact Thursday and Friday—normal weekends in Iran—and some, like the Shah, suspected conspiracy. Whatever the cause, the delay allowed Mossadeq to learn of the plans. Interestingly, Nasiri delivered the Shah's letter of appointment to Zahedi on Friday, August 14; he immediately accepted and understood himself to be the country's constitutional prime minister. Until Mossadeq's letter was delivered the next day, there were two men who each claimed to be the lawful prime minister of the country.

The letter dismissing Mossadeq was delivered the next evening around midnight. Mossadeq was waiting for the belated arrival of Nasiri; after receiving and signing the letter from the Shah, he had the messenger arrested. According to Ardeshir Zahedi, aside from the tardy delivery, Nasiri made another error by tarrying at the Prime Minister's home. "He had not gone there to arrest Mossadeq," Zahedi says, so "he should not have waited around."[39]

As these events were unfolding in Tehran, in Kalardasht, the Shah spent anxious days waiting. He was, in his wife's words, too nervous to even play cards. Their "only link to the capital," Soraya says, was a "private transmitter/receiver which connected [them] to the headquarters of Colonel Nasiri." They drank coffee all day and spent often-sleepless nights in nervous anticipation. On the night of the fifteenth, the Shah warned his wife to prepare for the possibility of a speedy departure. "At any moment," he said, Mossadeq's supporters might attack the chalet, and we "would have to leave without delay."[40]

A few hours later, the Shah's fears became reality. At four o'clock in the morning of August 16, he woke Soraya to tell her, "Nasiri has been arrested by Mossadeq's supporters. We have to flee from here as soon as possible." As the Shah wrote in *Mission for My Country*, when Nasiri was arrested, all contact between him and the Shah ceased. But at four that morning, Nasiri's driver found his way to the two-way transmitter and informed the Shah what had transpired.[41] The Shah was traumatized, believing that the entire operation had failed, and that his life and his throne were now in jeopardy. Without telling their guests, he and his wife, along with an aide, Abolfath Atabi, and a pilot, Mohammad Khatam, took a small four-seat plane to Ramsar, where the Shah's twin-engine Beechcraft awaited them in the royal hangar. They speedily boarded, worried that guards loyal to Mossadeq might arrive at any moment. Only when they had boarded did Soraya remember that she had left her dog behind, "a Skye terrier [she] adored."[42] But there was no question of retrieving the dog now. The Shah reassured his distressed wife that the servants and the friends they had left behind at the chalet would take care of the dog. The Shah piloted the plane.

Before long, their small aircraft approached the control tower in Baghdad. The Shah thought it unsafe to identify himself. Instead he told Baghdad tower that he was the pilot of a plane of tourists, that they had developed engine trouble and needed permission to land. After some confusion and delay, the Shah's plane was allowed to land. Fortuitously, King Faisal, the Iraqi monarch, was returning from a trip, and his plane landed at the airport shortly after the Shah's. The plume-plucked Shah waited for about half an hour in the 104-degree heat before King Faisal learned of his arrival and decided to grant him and his entourage asylum. On the other hand, the Iranian ambassador—Mozaffar A'lam—refused to meet with the Shah and, on instructions from the Mossadeq government, tried to have the royal couple arrested.[43] The Iranian Foreign Ministry had sent a directive to its embassies around the world that the Shah no longer held a position of authority in Iran.

News of the Shah's flight created quite a stir in Tehran. The many papers belonging to the Tudeh Party and its numerous front organizations began to attack the Shah, the monarchy, and U.S. influence, calling for the immediate establishment of a republic. Kennett Love, the American journalist in Tehran, reported that in one Tudeh Party rally, angry demonstrators shouting anti-American slogans attacked him, and only the kind protection of a wiser member of the party saved him from the wrath of the roused crowd.

The Tudeh Party's use of such concepts as "people's democracy" and a "united front" conjured the fate of Eastern European democracies that had by then all fallen into the hands of the Communists. Members of the Iranian middle class, merchants of the *bazaars* (called *bazaaris*) and industrialists, were all particularly wary of the Tudeh Party's increasingly militant and assertive discourse. Certainly, the efforts of the British agents and the CIA's own operations—like using agents provocateurs and publishing anti-Communist articles and books—worked to augment these fears and anxieties. At the same time, the new swagger in the demeanor of the Tudeh Party leadership was probably in itself enough to foment these middle-class fears.

Even more controversial than the Tudeh Party reaction was what appeared on the pages of *Bakhtar,* the paper founded and edited by Hossein Fatemi. Even during his tenure as foreign minister and spokesperson for the government, Fatemi continued to edit the paper. Beginning on August 16, the paper published increasingly incendiary reports about the Shah's departure. The most critical were written by Fatemi himself. One of Fatemi's articles was titled, "The Traitor Who Wanted to Shed the Nation's Blood Fled."[44] In it Fatemi wrote, "Go, you traitor, because even the foreigners now find you so worthless and useless that they will not pay you any wages for your most recent criminal act.... You must now pay your bills in European cabarets from the dollars and pounds you and your father have plundered.... Go you traitor who completed the thirty year history of the Pahlavi dynasty's criminal record."[45] The language of these editorials was particularly remarkable for a paper edited by a member of the cabinet that still claimed allegiance to the constitution. The underlying assumption of the articles was the idea that the end of the monarchy and the Pahlavi dynasty was a cherished and foregone conclusion.[46] Yet, as the spokesperson for the Mossadeq government, the same Fatemi declared that the cabinet did not plan "regime change."

In *Bakhtar's* rendition of what happened on August 15, and in the government's official announcement broadcast at seven in the morning on August 16, there was no mention of the Shah's *firman* dismissing Mossadeq. There are some reports that Mossadeq initially planned to broadcast a radio message to the nation, informing them that he had been dismissed by the Shah. But Fatemi and other more radical members of the National Front changed his mind.[47] Instead, the official broadcast only said that a military coup against the government had been successfully thwarted. Fatemi's editorial only referred to Nasiri's coming to the Prime Minister's home "for confidential business and giving a letter," and said that "the Prime Minister wrote the time and date of the letter's receipt on its back."[48] Yet another interesting aspect of the Fatemi editorial is that it refers to the coup attempt as solely the work of Britain, with no mention of the United States. It is a remarkable fact of historical transubstantiation that eventually the events of August became known as the "CIA coup," with all but no mention of the British role in the affair.

By the evening of August 18, all seemed lost for the Shah. Both the CIA and the British and American governments had concluded that the attempt to overthrow Mossadeq had failed. Concurrent with the CIA's report to Eisenhower on August 18 about the failure of "the move," some in the small coterie of aides working with General Zahedi had arrived at the same conclusion. They decided that they should declare the creation of "a free Iran" and send personal emissaries to the three units of the military that were still loyal to the Shah and were stationed in the provinces—one in Rasht, led by Colonel Gharani, the second a cavalry unit commanded by Colonel Bakhtiyar in Kermanshah, and the third in Isfahan, commanded by Colonel Zargami—and ask them to move toward Tehran and, if necessary, overthrow Mossadeq through what was beginning to look like a civil war.[49]

The CIA's memo for President Eisenhower claims that the failure to topple Mossadeq was caused by "three days of delay and vacillation by the Iranian generals concerned." The memo goes on to say that the United States should now "take a whole new look at the Iranian situation and probably have to snuggle up to Mossadeq if we are going to save anything there."[50]

Maybe as a part of this "snuggling up," on the evening of August 18, Henderson returned to Tehran. He had left Iran earlier to give the United States "plausible deniability" about its role in the August events. His return was so urgent that he traveled "in a special United States Air Force plane."[51] He was met at the airport by Mossadeq's son and taken directly to meet the Prime Minister. Mossadeq appeared to be in a jubilant mood, speaking with a "sarcastic smile," although exhibiting an underlying "smoldering sense of resentment." He was "fully dressed" and not in his usual pajamas.[52]

Henderson began by complaining about attacks on U.S. citizens. It is not clear whether he was, as Roosevelt claims, trying to ensure that Mossadeq supporters would be off the street the next day, thus facilitating a last-ditch effort to overthrow the government, or whether he was truly resigned to Mossadeq's victory, accepted the failure of "the move," and was simply trying to protect the lives of American citizens. The incredible fact that the CIA claims that it lost all the relevant files about the August events in Iran—thus avoiding congressional mandates to declassify and release them—and the fact that no Iranian record of the meeting has survived has made the work of understanding Henderson's motives and Mossadeq's intentions more difficult. Finally, Soviet and Tudeh Party archives, still not made available for scrutiny, could shed light on the party's remarkable passivity on August 19. Was it, as some scholars have suggested, the result of the Soviet Union's post-Stalin realization that it had fallen strategically behind the United States in the arms race?[53]

To Henderson's complaints about reports of attacks on American citizens, Mossadeq replied that Iran was, in his words, "in [the] throes [of] a revolution," and people thought that the United States was in "disagreement with them."[54]

Henderson was coyly tough, responding that if the people of Iran did not want the Americans, they were ready to "leave en masse." Mossadeq was quick to respond that the "Iranian government did not want Americans to leave."[55] Henderson then asked Mossadeq to tell him "confidentially . . . just what had happened during recent days."

Mossadeq first outlined his reasons for dissolving what he called "[a] British-purchased Majlis." Mossadeq then surprised Henderson by asking him if he had "any comments to make regarding his dissolution [of the] Majlis." Henderson had none.

Mossadeq's arguments, as he must have known, were hard to fathom for several reasons. With commendable clarity and honesty, Interior Minister Gholam Hussein Sadighi had told Mossadeq that "you have made your name as a parliamentarian," and that these "current [Majlis] elections were held during your tenure." He reminded Mossadeq of the long, albeit unhappy, history of recess appointments in twentieth-century Iran. He reminded Mossadeq that in the "first thirteen years, five months and two days of a constitutional monarchy, there was no parliament in session for ten years and two months and twenty eight days"—and thus the Shah had made the necessary recess appointments. He asked Mossadeq, "[W]hat guarantee is there that the Shah will not choose another Prime Minister after you dissolve the Majlis?" Mossadeq replied that the Shah "does not have the guts to do that."[56]

The Shah had developed the guts, and Mossadeq's referendum had been decisive in that development. Henderson refused to make any direct comment about the dissolution of the Majlis; he wanted to know about the events of recent days and specifically about the effort of General Zahedi to replace Mossadeq. Mossadeq said, "On [the] evening of 15th Col. Nasiri had approached his house apparently to arrest him. Col. Nasiri himself however had been arrested. . . . He had taken oath not to try to oust Shah and would have lived up to his oath if the Shah had not engaged in venture of this kind."[57] Henderson then asked whether it was in fact true that the Shah "had issued [a] *firman* removing him as Prime Minister and appointing Zahedi in his place." Mossadeq denied having seen such a *firman,* and went on to say that even if he had, "it would have made no difference. His position for some time had been that Shah's powers were only ceremonial in character."

Henderson knew this was the crux of the matter. I am "particularly interested in this point," he said, and then asked, "Was I to understand a) he had no official knowledge that the Shah had issued [a] *firman* removing him as Prime Minister, and b) even [if] he should find that Shah issued such [a] *firman* in present circumstances he would consider it to be invalid?" Mossadeq's reply was clear and categorical: "Precisely."[58]

In his memoir, too, Mossadeq repeats at greater length his view that the Shah did not have the authority to dismiss him. He writes that the dismissal "order was not only against the constitution, but there was no reason for it. . . . My government had never done anything against the interests of the country or of His Majesty."[59] But as he himself had confirmed in an earlier letter to the Shah—when he and other National Front leaders organized a sit-in at the Court—and as many of his advisors had warned him before he decided to dissolve the parliament, there was ample evidence that the Shah had the power of making recess appointments.

One concrete consequence of Mossadeq's discussions with Henderson was the Prime Minister's decision to ban all demonstrations on August 19, and to ask his supporters, including members of the Tudeh Party, to stay off the streets on that day. Kennett Love seemed to offer another reason for the order when he claimed that he had in fact witnessed "the first resurgence of royalist sentiments in the evening of August 18th." During much of that day, Tehran was the scene of bloody street battles between Tudeh Party activists, who had gone on an offensive "ransacking the headquarters of right-wing parties."[60] The Pan-Iranist and Sumka Parties were the two most important of these right-wing groups. American and British sources as well as some Iranian memoirs have reported that the Shah had offered financial and political support to these two parties. That support was now paying off. If in the morning royalist demonstrations seemed small, by "evening the tide began to turn." Soldiers dispatched to stop the fighting between the right- and left-wing activists began to club "both factions impartially while shouting 'Long Live the Shah.'"[61]

There are completely conflicting reports on what actually happened on August 19. Each narrative is shaped either by the real or perceived interests and values of the narrator or by the historically and linguistically determined prism through which they perceive and articulate the event. In retrospect, only a number of facts seem incontrovertible about what took place in Tehran on August 19, 1953.

By the early hours of that day, as Sadighi, Mossadeq's minister of the interior, makes clear in his remarkably honest and revealing account of that day's events, small crowds, some chanting pro-Shah slogans, some wielding clubs, began to gather around the city. Sadighi had been asked to come to Mossadeq's home early in the morning to receive instructions for yet another referendum—this time to decide whether a regency council should be formed. As he prepared to send out the necessary guidelines to governors, he noticed larger crowds gathering around the ministry, shouting slogans in favor of the Shah. When he called the military governor and ordered him to send soldiers to disperse the crowd, he was told soldiers were no longer obeying orders to attack pro-Shah demonstrators.

Early in the afternoon, Sadighi returned to Mossadeq's home and dutifully informed the angst-ridden prime minister that soldiers and officers "are siding with the people" against the government. By early afternoon, the radio headquarters fell to forces loyal to General Zahedi, and Mossadeq knew the day was lost. Till then, the radio had been broadcasting military marches all day. No effort was made by Mossadeq or anyone in the government to solicit public support for him. When the radio fell into the hands of royalists, they immediately began to broadcast fiery speeches in favor of the Shah. Mossadeq wept as he listened to these broadcasts, including General Zahedi's victory speech around four o'clock. Mossadeq had refused the request made by Tudeh Party leaders earlier in the day for 10,000 rifles. Ostensibly, they had wanted them to "fight the coup conspirators," but Mossadeq obviously did not trust them. He had also refused to accept the bitter fact that his relative, General Daftary, handpicked by Mossadeq to be the chief of police, was working with the forces trying to topple Mossadeq. More than once, he told those gathered in his house that there was nobody trustworthy left for him to rely on. In fact, when his house was finally attacked by some in the military and an angry mob, the troops assigned to protect the house fought valiantly. Up to 200 people are reported to have died in the battle for the house.

To what extent was the "unexpected strong upsurge" of popular demonstrations that day the result of the people's spontaneous action, and their decision to choose "the Shah and the Western world" over "Mossadeq and [the] Soviet Union"—as the American Embassy claimed at the time—and to what extent were they a rented crowd, paid for in Roosevelt's last-ditch attempt to revive the failed Operation Ajax? How consequential was Ardeshir Zahedi's decision to meet with foreign and domestic journalists and give them copies of the Shah's two *firmans?* Those loyal to the Shah immediately set out to publish copies of the order. This way, people learned for the first time of the existence of the two *firmans.*

Kennett Love, in an account of his experience in Iran written seven years after the events of that August 1953, reported that so many dollars had been spent in Tehran that in the days after August 19 that there was an actual "glut of dollars" in the currency black market, and the price of the dollar dropped sharply.[62] In fact, the price of a dollar did go from about twenty-five *tooman* for a dollar to about three—the official rate of exchange. But the sudden sharp and immediate drop could have been the result of the market's anticipation of an influx of U.S. aid and dollars after the fall of Mossadeq. Moreover, after Mossadeq's fall, there was far less demand for dollars because fewer rich royalist Iranians were arranging for a speedy exit from Iran.[63]

While there seems to be overwhelming evidence that some funds were disbursed amongst some street toughs and gang leaders, it is not clear to what extent the appearance of these gangs was the result of that money, or of Kashani's decision to mobilize opposition to Mossadeq that day. It is a fact that in the postwar years, Kashani and his Feda'yan-e Islam made inroads in mobilizing and organizing some of these street toughs. Long before Franz Fanon and Herbert Marcuse, two influential thinkers of the 1960s New Left, articulated their theory that the *lumpenproletariat*—déclassé parasitical social elements like pimps and prostitutes—were the liberators Marx had promised, Kashani and Navvab Safavi had organized and mobilized elements of this stratum.

Regardless of what actually happened, as early as August 21, the U.S. embassy in Tehran was reporting that, "unfortunately [the] impression [is] becoming rather widespread that in some way or other this Embassy or at least [the] US government has contributed with funds and technical assistance to overthrow Mossadeq and establish Zahedi." The embassy attributed this to the Iranians' living up "to their old traditions" of crediting "foreigners with financing [whatever] side . . . they [were] supposed to be favoring."[64] On the same day, the embassy also reported that Tehran was calm and that people throughout the country were "apparently taking it for granted [that the] issue between Shah and Mossadeq [was] finally settled and in general pleased with the outcome."[65] This was a far cry from what had happened a year earlier, during Mossadeq's July confrontation with the Shah. At that time, with every passing day after Mossadeq's resignation, Tehran had grown more tense, the population more angry, more agitated, and less willing to accept Mossadeq's replacement as the prime minister. This time there was an eerie complacency in the air.

The Shah, unaware of any of these developments, gave his version of what happened as soon as he settled in the palace in Baghdad on August 16. He asked to meet with the American Ambassador, who called on him at 9:30 that evening. Neither the British nor the American government was eager to be too identified with the Shah; both countries assumed he was a lost cause and took caution in meeting with him. Many in the British government had concluded by August 18 that their country's best policy "would be to write off the Shah and proceed on the unpalatable assumption that Mossadeq is the indisputable ruler of Persia." They were worried that "the Shah, by running away with so little dignity" had forfeited all authority in Iran. Ultimately, however, the British government decided to follow the American lead and comply with the "Shah's request for advice." The American Ambassador found the Shah "worn from the sleepless nights, puzzled by [the] turn of events but with no bitterness towards Americans." He said in "recent weeks he had felt increasingly that he would have to take action against Mossadeq." In the Shah's words, after "being assured that everything [was] arranged and that there was no possibility of failure, he left Tehran for his Caspian Palace in order to put Mossadeq off guard." In his iteration, the Shah had signed the two *firmans* when he was in Kalardasht. He complained about the three unexplained days of delay in implementing his orders and about the fact that "by some means" Mossadeq had been alerted. We now know that one of those means was the report of officers belonging to the Tudeh Party's military network.

The Shah also discussed his future plans with the American Ambassador. He felt he needed to issue a statement giving his version of events, indicating that once he realized that "his orders were not being followed, he left the country to prevent further bloodshed and further damage." The Shah went on to say that he "will hold off giving any statement until he gets advice."[66] He called Mossadeq "absolutely mad and insanely jealous...[he] thinks he can form a partnership with the Tudeh party and then outwit them, but in so doing, [he] will become the Dr Benes of Iran,"[67] alluding to the Czechoslovakian nationalist leader overthrown by the Communist Party in 1948.

While in Iraq, aside from Western diplomats and Iraqi royalty, the Shah also met with Ayatollah Shahrestani, "one of the most eminent Shia divines in Iraq" who was "strongly opposed to Mussadiq."[68] The meeting was not an isolated event but an indication of the clergy's change of heart in Iran. Shahrestani advised the Shah to go somewhere where "he would be free," where he could seek American and British advice, and make weekly broadcasts "answering Mussadiq's insults with dignity." He even suggested that the best place for the Shah to go to would be Hamburg, since his wife was half-German, or "failing that, Switzerland."[69]

In recollecting his short Iraqi stopover, the Shah also mentioned that, in recognition of the fact that Iran "was facing grave dangers," he decided to visit the shrine of Imam Ali, Shiism's revered first Imam, buried in Najaf. "I stretched my beseeching hands towards His Holiness and I have no doubt that it was by his grace that shortly thereafter, the country was saved."[70]

His stay in Iraq was short-lived. On August 18, the Shah and the Queen along with the two men in their entourage boarded a commercial flight bound for Ciampino Airport in Rome. There a "flock of journalists and photographers" awaited them and "harassed" them with questions about unfolding events in Iran and about the Shah's plans for the future. Here too, the Iranian Ambassador had "not condescended to come and greet" the royal couple, and when they did finally talk with him on the phone, he refused to return to them the key to a car they had left at the embassy during the Shah's last visit to Europe. According to Soraya, someone at the embassy finally "succeeded in stealing" the keys away from the rebel ambassador.

The Shah and his wife settled on the fourth floor of the Hotel Excelsior, "a small suite which a Persian industrialist vacated to give to us."[71] The industrialist's name was Morad Eriye—an Iranian Jew who in later years benefited much from his gesture of support. Apocryphal stories about how he had given the Shah a blank check, or had given the royal couple the use of his Cadillac, afforded him a special cachet.[72]

Having left Iran with little clothing, on their first day in Rome the Shah and his wife stole away through the "rear entrance" of the hotel to escape the paparazzi and bought a new gray suit for the Shah and a white polka-dot dress for Soraya. At the same time, the Shah warned Soraya that they "have to be very careful" with money. "We do not have much money," he said, but reassured her by adding that they "will possibly have just enough to buy a [piece of] land where we can settle down." She even claims that, so worried was the Shah about their financial situation that before departing for Kalardasht, he had asked her permission to sell some of their wedding gifts.[73] He also worried about his responsibility in supporting the other exiled members of the royal family. The news they received from Tehran on the radio on August 18, their first night in Rome, was hardly promising. Tehran was in chaos; anti-Shah forces had won the day and were demanding the end of the monarchy.

While in Rome, the Shah also met with the American ambassador, the legendary Clare Boothe Luce—journalist, playwright, diplomat, and wife to Henry Luce, the founder of *Life, Time,* and *Sports Illustrated*—who told the Shah that the U.S. government "advised" him "to issue a statement on recent events," emphasize that he had lawfully dismissed Mossadeq, that "he [had] left the country to avoid bloodshed, and that in fact he was the victim of a coup by Mossadeq."[74]

All of that changed the next day, Wednesday, August 19. Around noon, the Shah and Soraya came down from their hotel suite to have lunch. They had barely begun eating when an Associated Press reporter brought the Shah a telegram bearing the news of Mossadeq's fall. He "went pale and his hands shook so violently that he was hardly able to read. 'Can it be true?'" he asked incredulously. Early that day he had talked to Soraya of the need to find a job and of moving to the United States. Now he might be king again. He repeated several times, "this is not an insurrection. This is my government coming to power," adding that "everyone who is not a communist is favorable to my stand." It was not long before he received another telegram, this one from General Zahedi, the new prime minister, inviting the Shah to return to the country as expeditiously as possible.[75]

Zahedi decided to send the telegram to the Shah shortly after delivering his victory speech on the radio around four in the afternoon of August 19. Some of his advisors and aides suggested that he should wait a day or two before sending the telegram. Let him sweat, they said, and he will be more manageable when he returns.[76] But the General vetoed them all. As future events showed, his loyalty to the Shah was not fully requited.

To expedite the Shah's return home, a plane was chartered from KLM at the cost of $12,000. The Shah decided to leave Soraya in Rome for a few more days, arguing that Tehran still might not be safe enough for her. Aside from the Shah and his closest aides, aboard were "twenty newspaper men whom the Shah insisted on taking with him without the preliminary diplomatic red-tape concerning entry and travel visas."[77] When the airline hesitated to allow the journalists to board without proper papers and visas, the Shah, according to some journalists, "threatened to end the airline's concession to fly over Iran unless the newsmen were authorized to board."[78] This was the first obvious hint of a newly self-assertive Shah who increasingly saw the law as a malleable tool of his modernizing authoritarian designs for Iran.

The Shah seemed to have sensed how much the country had changed under Mossadeq. As the American Embassy in Tehran already understood, a "revolution . . . with deep-rooted origins in the wave of nationalism" had swept Iran. The old patterns of power had been "irrevocably shattered" and anyone who wanted to succeed in the new Iran, the embassy believed, "must shape his program on the basis of nationalist operations."[79] Maybe that was why, before leaving Rome, the Shah had sent the British government a message through the U.S. embassy, saying that in Tehran, "he may have to say some harsh things against the British, but that he will not reflect his true feelings."[80]

On his way back, the Shah stopped in Baghdad to thank the Iraqi King for his hospitality. In conversations with the journalists, he called Mossadeq "an evil man" who must be tried. He also refused to meet with the Iranian ambassador, Mozaffar A'lam. Eventually the Shah did forgive A'lam and allowed him to return to government work; but that day, his anger was too raw to agree to a meeting.

He arrived back in Tehran in the early afternoon of August 22 under tight security conditions. The new cabinet, some members of the royal family, and the diplomatic corps were all at the airport, waiting to give the Shah an official welcome. No sooner had the plane landed than General Zahedi climbed rapidly up the stairs of the plane, and a few minutes later, emerged with the Shah. It was whispered that he did not wish to kiss the Shah's hand, and that his fast move to board the plane before the Shah left it was in order to obviate a potentially embarrassing scene for the Shah.[81]

As the Shah passed the line of eagerly waiting military commanders, he noticed that Colonel Nasiri was now a general. The Shah was not happy, and he immediately let it be known that he considered military promotions his sole monopoly power. This was the beginning of tensions between the Shah and the General who had saved his throne.

A few hours after his arrival, at nine in the evening of August 22, the Shah delivered a short radio message to the "God-loving, patriotic and honorable people of Iran." He thanked them for their "sincere sentiments" and reassured them that their action had, "from [a] thousand miles way," removed all his fatigue and anxiety. With no sense of irony, he said, "As you know, on numerous occasions, I was ready to sacrifice my life for you, and in future too, I will not refuse if the occasion arises."[82] He talked of his own "unforgettable support for the national movement" and promised that "as in the past" he would work to move Iran "toward a democratic life, one fortunately mandated in Islam's esteemed teachings." As with all he said and wrote in those years, there was a heavy dose of religiosity in his words—part of his strategy of alliance with the clergy against Mossadeq and the Left. And then, in a thinly disguised reference to Mossadeq, the Shah said that the full weight of the law would be laid upon "those who violated the constitution, in spite of the oath they took, and who dissolved the Majlis, dissolved the army."[83] By the time the Shah made this announcement, Mossadeq had already decided to turn himself in. He was taken to the Officers' Club where General Zahedi had set up his headquarters. He met Mossadeq upon his arrival. After polite words of greeting, Mossadeq was taken to a room that would henceforth serve as his prison.

The Shah's real mood and lingering anxieties, as well as his newfound confidence, were all evident in his first meeting with Loy Henderson, the American ambassador. The meeting took place at six o'clock in the early evening of August 23, and, at the Shah's request, it was a private affair. Henderson began the meeting by conveying an oral message from President Eisenhower, congratulating the Shah on his return. Earlier that day, the Iranian Chief of Protocol had let foreign embassies know that "it would be appropriate for heads of state to send public congratulatory messages to the Shah of Iran."[84]

Henderson in fact took some liberties with the text of the message, adding an introductory paragraph to the message that the President had approved. He began by praising the Shah's "great moral courage." The Shah, according to Henderson, "wept as [he] read this message," and then asked the Ambassador to tell the President how grateful he was for the "interest the US had shown in Iran." He called what had happened in Iran in those crucial August days "a miracle," and said he believed it was "wrought . . . due to [the] friendship of the West, to [the] patriotism of the Iranian people and to [the] intermediation [*sic*] of God."[85] He added that in his mind, if he had failed, Iran would have had no "alternative but communism." He emphasized that it was "his intention to completely root out subversive press . . . and completely wreck Tudeh organization." At the same time, he wanted to know "how soon can [U.S. aid] come in and in what quantities and form?"[86] He and Zahedi both knew that their political success, even their survival, might well depend on the quick resolution of the oil issue and a fast revival of the troubled economy. Millions of dollars were almost immediately given to the Zahedi government. Even the Russians, who had prevaricated and procrastinated in giving the Mossadeq government the gold and currency they owed Iran at the end of World War II, were now willing to pay their debt expeditiously.

The Shah surprised Henderson when he offered his own analysis of why the plans for the night of August 15 failed. Someone, the Shah said, "must have betrayed them," and then ventured to ask, "Could it have been British agents?" Henderson's answer was categorical, delivered in a tone of stern admonishment.

He "expressed surprise" at the Shah's proposition, saying he "knew for [a] fact that [the] British were dealing honestly with him and he should get out of his head once and for all [the] idea they [were] engaging in double-dealing." And then, in a surprisingly stern tone, he told the Shah he "hoped he would never again make, either to British or Americans, remarks which might tend" to undermine the mutual confidence that existed between the United States and Britain.[87]

The Shah also talked at some length about why he was not happy with the Zahedi cabinet. He was, he said, happy with Zahedi himself and had "complete confidence in him." Nor did he believe the General had "ambitions other than [to] serve Iran and its Shah." Members of his cabinet, however, were a different story. They are, the Shah said, the "same old faces which had been rotating in office for years. He had hoped for [a] Cabinet which would stimulate the country particularly youth." He was more than ever convinced of the urgent need for rapid economic change—from land reform to new laws facilitating and encouraging foreign investment. He was also convinced "that Mossadeq's popularity was partially founded on his reputation for honesty," persuading the Shah that he should pick up the banner of fighting corruption.[88]

The Shah also told Henderson that he had been informed that "Americans [had] insisted Amini be included as Minister of Finance and that Cabinet be selected before his arrival and presented [to] him as fait accompli." The Ambassador denied the allegation, but every indication is that the Shah did not accept Henderson's denial and never came to trust Amini. Within weeks of this conversation, the Shah also changed his attitude about Zahedi. He had resolved upon his return to concentrate in his own hands much of the power that had been invested in the prime minister's office, by law and post–World War II practice. But as the American Embassy noted, General Zahedi's "past experience," his "resistance to British and Soviet policies . . . his close identification with the National Front from 1949–1952," made it unlikely that he would easily give in to the Shah's effort to weaken the role of the prime minister.[89] The Shah thus knew that the first necessary step for achieving his goal was the removal of Zahedi as prime minister. The task proved harder than he had imagined.

The United States was not the only big power to send the Shah a letter of congratulation. Winston Churchill also sent a brief oral message saluting and congratulating the Shah. As diplomatic ties between Iran and Britain had been cut by Mossadeq, Churchill's message had to be conveyed through the American Embassy. Churchill congratulated the Shah, "on [his] safe return . . .," and added, "May I express the sincere hope that success will now attend your efforts to guide Persia toward those better things which you have always so ardently desired for her."[90] The Shah responded by saying that he "deeply appreciated" Britain's good wishes, which, he said, "fortified him in meeting the difficult tasks ahead." The

Shah also "asked that this exchange of messages be held completely secret."[91] In drafting the message to the Shah, Churchill had decided against mentioning the question of oil. At the same time, he kept in mind the Shah's "almost pathological distrust of the British"—a distrust that was again confirmed when Loy Henderson delivered Eisenhower's message of congratulation.

ര

Late at night on August 23, the Shah also met with Kermit Roosevelt. No sooner had Roosevelt entered the room than a "frock-coated attendant appeared with tiny glasses of vodka and caviar canapés." If Roosevelt is to be believed, the Shah's first words were, "I owe my throne to God, my people, my army—and to you!" The Shah also talked of his plans to put Mossadeq on trial and give him "three years of house arrest in his village," and then allow him to be "free," but confined to "move about in but not outside" his village. The Shah also indicated, according to Roosevelt, that when Fatemi was arrested—"and he will be" found and arrested, he said—"he will be executed." In those days, Fatemi had taken refuge with the Tudeh Party, who were hiding him in their safe houses. By way of a gift, the Shah gave Roosevelt a "large, flat, golden cigarette case."[92]

As the Shah tried to concentrate more and more power in his own hands, and as he now faced Zahedi's resistance in this effort, both men knew the country was in desperate need of money; there was also considerable pressure on the two to resolve the oil issue rapidly. The question of when to resume the severed diplomatic ties with Britain also needed a resolution. Messages from political figures like Kashani warning against the resumption of diplomatic ties confirmed the depth of anti-British resentment in the country. The British government, on the other hand, was eager to regain its foothold in Iran and its control of at least part of the country's oil industry; they were thus exerting pressure for a speedy resumption of diplomatic ties.

The issue of relations with Britain and the resolution of the oil crisis were, of course, inseparable. By December 1953, it was decided that the time to resume diplomatic ties with Britain had arrived. The Shah and Zahedi both had some reservations about the early resumption of ties, but Loy Henderson and Alfred Escher, the Swiss ambassador to Iran who also represented the British government's interests during their embassy's closure, worked hard behind the scenes to convince them to allow the resumption of full diplomatic ties. When in December of 1953, Iran finally agreed to resume ties, Britain announced that it had named Denis Wright as its chargé d'affaires in Tehran.

Wright was surprised at the appointment as he knew nothing about Iran—he was a man more experienced in the world of oil politics. But oil was Britain's biggest concern and thus sending an "oil man" as the first diplomat made sense.

Wright eventually learned that Iran had also predicated the resumption of ties with Britain on the condition that no one who had served in Iran during the tumultuous days of Mossadeq would return to the embassy—hence Wright's appointment.[93]

At the Foreign Ministry, Wright was given his marching orders: he was to strive to resume full diplomatic ties, and if possible, "bring back AIOC alone"—that is, as the sole oil monopoly in Iran. Failing that, Wright was to strive for the best achievable form of shared control of Iran's oil with primarily American companies. Finally, he was to insist on receiving "fair compensation . . . for the loss of enterprise in Iran."[94] For the British, as future negotiations showed, the question of compensation was as much an issue of pride and revenge as a financial matter—forcing the insolent natives to submit to the will of imperial Britain.

As Wright soon realized after arriving in Tehran, he had been given a tall order. He had been in Tehran only two weeks when he wrote in his singular, wry fashion, "with the single exception of the Pakistani chargé d'affaires, who is not particularly bright," no one in Tehran believes it remotely possible to bring AIOC back. Even then, the British failed to understand the depth of nationalist sentiments against them in Iran.[95]

Ironically, Denis Wright arrived in Tehran on the last day of Mossadeq's military tribunal; just as the Shah had told Roosevelt a few months earlier, Mossadeq was sentenced to three years in prison, and the coincidence of the British envoy's arrival on the day the sentence was handed down "did not pass unnoticed in the Tehran Press."[96] As he was driving from the airport to the expansive British Embassy compound, Wright was told that a dinner appointment had already been made for him for the next night. He was to meet with special emissaries of the Shah—Ernest Perron and Bahram Shahrokh, who had made his name for being the booming voice of strident Nazi broadcasts to Iran.

The next evening, as planned, Wright met with Perron and Shahrokh. The two men reiterated the claim that they were representing the Shah and probed Wright about the terms of the oil settlement he envisioned. They then went on to "criticize General Zahedi . . . and inquired whether the British government would object if the Shah dismissed Hussein Ala as Court Minister." Wright told them "in London General Zahedi was held in high regard, while what the Shah did with Hussein Ala was his affair and no concern of the British government."[97] Wright also refused to engage the two men in any substantive discussion of oil. Moreover, the next day, Wright informed a Zahedi confidante about his unusual meeting with the two royal emissaries.

Two days later, during a small Christmas party at the embassy, the two men came back unannounced to meet with Wright. They produced a paper that they claimed contained the verbatim views of the Shah as he had articulated them just that morning. The note said that "all matters of high policy, i.e., matters above or outside the diplomatic routine should be presented to His Majesty" through either Perron or Shahrokh. It also specified that "once you have received suggestions on the oil matter... you inform His Majesty through" the same channel "in advance, and [that] before you present them to the Minister of Foreign Affairs you await His Majesty's approval or counter-proposal." The note further indicated that "His Majesty accepts the principles" proposed by Britain on how to resolve the oil issue, but also said that the agreement "must be face-saving for the Persian government."[98]

Wright found the note and its mode of delivery unacceptable. He told the emissaries that he disliked the idea of dealing with the Shah without the knowledge of the cabinet; in fact, after seeking the permission of the Foreign Office, Wright informed a member of the Zahedi government of the "full story." When Zahedi learned of the incident, he was reportedly so angry that he took a plane to Ramsar, where the Shah was vacationing, and confronted—in Wright's words "berated"—the Shah about his attempt to bypass the Prime Minister and the members of the cabinet on sensitive foreign policy and oil issues.[99] The Shah was not happy about Wright's maneuvers. He was also not willing to take the blame for Perron and Shahrokh's clumsy handling of the matter, telling Zahedi and the British that the two had acted on their own.

This was hardly a favorable beginning for the Shah's relationship with Denis Wright. At the same time, the inauspicious beginning marked the Shah's first step in his eventually successful effort to concentrate in his own hands all sensitive oil negotiations and issues of foreign policy. More than a decade later, when Wright returned to Iran as an ambassador, what had been in 1954 the Shah's unacceptable mode of handling sensitive state matters became in 1964 precisely how Wright and other important ambassadors conducted their business. The only difference was that the contact person was no longer Perron but the Court Minister. By then, Perron had died in a hospital, alone and bereft.

In spite of this initial tense encounter with Wright in 1953, the Shah did not relent in his effort to find a way to dismiss Zahedi. But the Shah's "feelers" were still met with stiff resistance by the American and British Embassies. In May 1954, when the Shah dropped hints about Zahedi's imminent dismissal, Secretary of State John Foster Dulles instructed the American Embassy in Tehran that it was "essential Shah have no doubt regarding firmness of United States support for Zahedi and our deep concern at indications Shah may be considering change of government."[100] The reason for this categorical support was clear: both Britain and the United States believed that Zahedi had the gravitas and power to resolve the oil issue.

It was not only the British and American governments that resisted the Shah's "feelers" about the idea of replacing Zahedi; the General had a powerful faction in the Majlis itself. According to the British Embassy, for example, the Majlis was divided among three groups—"the Shah's men, who are in the majority, Zahedi's supporters, and still a small 'nationalist intellectual' opposition."[101]

Aside from Zahedi's insistence on keeping all the constitutional powers of a prime minister in his own hands—he in fact demanded that the Shah must reign and not rule—there were a number of other issues that created friction between the Shah and his prime minister. Arguably the most intractable problem was the Shah's insistence on appointing Abolhassan Ebtehaj to the crucial post of director of Plan Organization, where he would have control of much of the government's purse. Zahedi was adamantly opposed to the appointment. The Shah won the battle, but Zahedi continued to complain about Ebtehaj, and the issue became a major cause of tension between the Shah and the Prime Minister.

When his initial efforts to replace Zahedi failed, the Shah decided to wait until his return from a trip he and Soraya wanted to take to Europe and the United States. Many of his advisors opposed the idea of such a trip.[102] It was too soon after the traumas of August, and the intended three-month journey was deemed unduly long. The Shah was not convinced. He kept repeating that the Queen was tired and needed some rest.

The Shah's desire to make the trip also met with some resistance from the British and American Embassies. On July 3, 1954, the Shah first told the U.S. Embassy of his plans "for an informal and unofficial visit to the US," emphasizing that he hoped to make the trip only after "an agreement is reached on the oil dispute." When consulted about plans for the trip, President Eisenhower's response was clear: the Shah should make the trip only "after there is an oil settlement."[103]

By then, the outline of the oil agreement was clearly emerging. All evidence indicates that the Shah and the Iranian regime generally had little role in the agreement, save the decision to sign it. On February 24, 1954, a message from Secretary of State Dulles to the U.S. Embassy in Tehran offered the outline of what Britain and the United States had agreed to in their February 19 aide-mémoire. Dulles declared that the "US government is prepared to support participation by AIOC to the extent of 40 percent.... American companies will participate to the extent of 40 percent. As to the remaining 20 percent, US would hope that most of it could be taken by Shell, thus increasing British shares." Whatever remained would be given to smaller oil companies, including one in France. A remaining unresolved issue was the thorny question of compensation. Britain insisted on receiving it, and the Iranian government knew that public opinion in the country would make such a payment difficult if not impossible.[104]

Not surprisingly, the basic structure of the eventual agreement that came to be known as the "Consortium Agreement" followed closely what Dulles had indicated in his note to the American Embassy in Tehran. Even the otherwise pliant Majlis was critical of the agreement. Rumors of kickbacks spread immediately. It was, for example, alleged that Ali Amini, Iran's chief negotiator, had received $5 million for his role in ratifying the agreement—an allegation he and his son have strenuously rejected. His son argues in a well-researched but sympathetic biography of his father that the check was in fact for $5.4 million and that it was given to Amini not as a bribe, but as the first installment of a $45 million package of aid promised to Iran by the Eisenhower administration.[105]

According to the British government, while the "common sense and courage of Ali Amini" deserved "full credit" for the passage of the controversial oil agreement, "ultimately [the] success of negotiations was determined by the Shah." According to the embassy, "due in part to dishonest advice from interested Persian politicians and hangers-on at the Court," the Shah had initially tried to "get a better arrangement by dealing directly with Britain." The reference to the "hangers-on" at the Court was apparently a thinly disguised allusion to the episode with Perron and Shahrokh.[106]

On September 21, 1954, Amini, in his capacity as Iran's chief negotiator, presented the details of the agreement to the parliament. He admitted that the agreement was not "what the people had desired." An ideal agreement, he said, would only be possible when Iran could compete with the major economic powers of the world.[107] A consortium of predominantly American and British companies was granted control over the sale and production of oil in a big part of Iran. A separate agreement called for Iran to pay AIOC £21 million of compensation for lost revenues during the Mossadeq era. The company in fact claimed its real losses to have been double that amount; as a gesture of goodwill, it would accept less than half the total amount. The Shah was insistent that he would only sign the agreement if the consortium fully accepted Iran's sovereign rights over its oil and acknowledged its function to be the agent of the Iranian government.[108] Nevertheless, the Shah and Amini both insisted that the Consortium Agreement was not an ideal deal but simply the best deal Iran could get at that time. They tried to lay the blame for any flaws in the agreement on Mossadeq—his government had left the country so weakened, the Shah argued, that the new government had its back to the wall and had no choice but to agree to a flawed deal.

As the complicated details of the consortium deal were being worked out, the April 19, 1954, issue of *Life* magazine displayed a picture of a notorious figure known as Sha'ban "the brainless one," suggesting that he was one of the many street toughs who had played a key role in ensuring Zahedi's victory on August 19, 1953.[109] The Shah tried to use the article as an excuse to dismiss Zahedi. He sent

Court Minister Hussein Ala to see Loy Henderson and suggest that Zahedi must be replaced "by someone... more acceptable to the West." Ala intimated that, in the Shah's view, the delay in realizing an agreement between Iran and the oil companies was caused by the reluctance of the companies to deal with Zahedi. Henderson emphatically rejected the idea and indicated his utter surprise at the Shah's most recent ploy to get rid of the Prime Minister. Moreover, Henderson said, it was "the Shah rather than [the] Prime Minister" who was likely to play the decisive role in "achieving a settlement."[110]

In confirming his role in the passage of the consortium deal, the Shah wrote that at the time, "President Eisenhower sent me a letter expressing his personal appreciation for my efforts in resolving the oil problems caused by Mossadeq's government."[111]

After four weeks of sometimes rancorous debate in the Majlis, the Consortium Agreement was finally ratified in late October and signed into law by the Shah on October 24, 1954. With the oil issue behind him, and with the failure of his latest ploy to be rid of Zahedi, the Shah decided to go to America before the end of the year and leave the resolution of his problem with the Prime Minister until after his return.

All obstacles to the trip the Shah and Soraya so anxiously wished to make seemed to have disappeared. But then, on November 2, the Shah's only full brother, Ali Reza—and thus the only sibling who could by law succeed him on the throne—died in a plane crash. He had been traveling from the Caspian coast to Tehran. The weather was stormy, and airport officials had tried to dissuade the Prince from taking off, but he did not heed their warnings. That night, the royal family was gathering at the home of the Queen Mother to celebrate the Shah's birthday. When Ali Reza, known for his punctuality, was late in arriving, everyone feared the worst. It took some time before the body and the wreckage could be located in the rugged mountains and dense forests that lie between Tehran and the Caspian Sea. Amongst the wild rumors that circulated before the discovery of the wreckage was that "the prince had flown to the Soviet Union."[112] Moreover, the Shah too was considered complicit in the alleged conspiracy to kill the dashing and ambitious Prince. Ironically, the death of his brother only made the trip to the United States more necessary; the need for an heir was now redoubled. The question of Soraya's ability to bear a child was fresh on the Shah's mind and was one of the reasons for his urgent desire to visit the United States. Not long after their return to Tehran from Rome, at the end of a masked ball, the Shah had asked Soraya, "Isn't it time we think of producing an heir to the throne?"[113]

The Shah and Soraya finally commenced their long-anticipated journey on December 5, 1954. Only a handful of days of their three-month-long journey were given to official visits in the United States, Britain, and Germany. The remaining days were given to a star-studded trek across America. The list of celebrities that met with the royal couple included Bob Hope, Esther Williams, Humphrey Bogart, Grace Kelly, Lauren Bacall, and William Randolph Hearst Jr.—including a visit to his Xanadu. A crucial part of the trip for the Shah and Soraya was their visit to New York Hospital—twenty-five years later, on his deathbed, the Shah would not only visit the same hospital but would use the same suite of rooms.[114] According to Soraya, after many examinations, the doctors assured the royal couple that there was nothing wrong with Soraya and that "everything will return to normal" once the Queen had recovered from the "shocks, upsets and vexations of the last two years."[115] She makes no reference to their visit to Boston where she was told that she could never have a child.

The fact that the Shah was taking a surprisingly long vacation was the subject of some criticism even in the American press. *Newsweek* wrote sarcastically that "even the *Shahanshah* (King of Kings), Vice Regent of God, Shadow of the Almighty, and Center of the Universe deserves a vacation. [The royal couple have spent] this winter in a private visit to the US . . . physical check-ups in New York hospitals, sight-seeing in San Francisco, dancing the mambo in Hollywood, skiing in Sun Valley, waterskiing in Miami Beach."[116]

These trips were not without some problems. In one town, a woman claimed to have the Shah's child. She was convinced to keep quiet about her claim.[117] The Miami trip turned out to be far more adventurous than the royal couple had bargained for. Someone took a picture of the Queen waterskiing in a swimming suit. Some in the Shah's entourage tried to buy the negative of the pictures from the photographer, but their effort came to naught. The political price of the photos became clear a few months after the return of the royal couple. At that time, when the Shah sanctioned a vicious attack on the Baha'i and as the international community, including the British and American governments and the United Nations, condemned the savagery, the Shah's confidante, Alam, tried to explain the reason for the assault. He met with Denis Wright and "went over to a large refrigerator in [his] sitting room. . . . He extricated from it two American weeklies . . . he showed in one of them a photograph of Queen Soraya in the scantiest of bathing costumes; in the other, a photograph claiming that the Shah had fathered a child by a well-known American socialite." Those stories found their way to Ayatollah Boroujerdi and a fiery cleric named Falsifi. The articles were used by the mullahs to blackmail the Shah into attacking Baha'i centers in Tehran and around the country.[118]

During the Shah's less pregnant negotiations with the Eisenhower administration, one of the key issues that soon emerged was the size of Iran's military and the amount of aid the United States was willing to pay to strengthen and modernize it. The Shah sought bigger and bigger packages of aid, and a stronger military; the United States advised caution. It was U.S. policy to warn the Shah "against seeking to develop a military establishment which would become an undue burden on Iran's economy."[119] At the same time, Eisenhower assured the Shah that the United States was committed to Iran's security and saw the Zagros Mountains in Iran as the "first line of defense in the Middle East" against Soviet aggression.[120] For the rest of his reign—with the sole exception of the Nixon era—the issue of Iran's military budget and its relative size in comparison to expenditures on social programs remained a thorny issue between the Shah and the Americans. From the time of his 1954 trip, the Shah also canvassed the United States for a bilateral security agreement with Iran. Instead of such an agreement, the Americans agreed to join as an observer in what became known as the 1955 Baghdad Pact. As a result, not long after the Shah's return to Iran, the country forfeited its century-old tradition of neutrality and officially joined the pact, causing the ire of the Soviet Union and many in Iran's opposition.

On February 12, 1955, the Shah left the United States for England aboard the *Queen Mary*. He and his entourage arrived there on the February 16 and stayed for no more than a week. The highlight of the trip was a dinner at Buckingham Palace, where Winston Churchill and Anthony Eden were amongst the guests. After Britain, it was Germany's turn, with the royal couple arriving there on February 23. They stayed there for two weeks. It was something of a homecoming for Soraya. The trip included an emotional reunion between the Shah and his daughter, Shahnaz, who had been studying in Belgium. Soraya, jealous of the Shah's divided attentions, threw an embarrassing tantrum on the night of the father–daughter reunion. Even after Shahnaz's return to Iran, the Shah had a continuously hard time reconciling his fatherly duties with Soraya's jealousies.

The Shah returned to Tehran on March 12, 1955. It was raining, and he and his wife were afforded a warm welcome by thousands of people who had weathered the rain. General Zahedi was at the airport but was suffering from an attack of gout and was forced to rest in the royal pavilion as he awaited the arrival of the royal plane. A few weeks after his return, the Shah began his earnest move to force Zahedi's resignation. Even before leaving on his trip, he had created a de facto committee whose composition was a surprising combination of his most trusted aides—like Ala and Alam—and a key minister of the General's cabinet, Ali Amini. They called themselves the "polit-bureau," and their job was to work with the media and members of the Majlis to prepare the ground for Zahedi's dismissal. The Shah repeatedly complained to the British and American Embassies that the Zahedi government was incapable of bringing about the changes and the radical reforms the country needed. The Shah also complained about Zahedi's "devotion to certain cronies among ministers"[121] and the corruption of some of these cronies. The Americans took seriously the Shah's complaint that Zahedi had surrounded himself with corrupt officials.[122] The British, on the other hand, believed the issue of "corrupt cronies" was just an excuse for the Shah. The Shah, the embassy wrote, has himself more than his share of such "corrupt cronies."[123]

The Shah found another excuse to get rid of Zahedi when he learned at the ariport of Zahedi's gout.[124] A third convenient excuse was a letter the Shah received from General Zahedi upon his return, "saying that either Mr. Ebtehaj must go or he [Zahedi] would resign."[125] In fact, the Shah soon learned that the rift between the two men had grown so bad that "the business of government had been brought to a standstill." While British and American sources both confirm that the General did in fact send this ultimatum to the Shah, Ardeshir Zahedi rejects the idea, saying that he never saw such a letter and that writing such an ultimatum was "not in [his father's] style."[126] What the General told Colonel Teymour Bakhtiyar about this time confirms Ardeshir's story. On March 23, the Prime Minister told Bakhtiyar that much of the tension in his relations with the Shah was the fault of Ebtehaj. Zahedi added that he could not understand why, "after all he had done for this country," the Shah was so keen "to get rid of him." He ended by saying that "if forced to resign, he would go not to Europe, but to South America, where he would be able to speak his mind about the present rulers of Persia."[127]

Less than a month after his return home, on April 6, the Shah made his final move to dismiss Zahehdi. The plan initially called for some of the Shah's trusted men to ask Zahedi to resign, but none of these indirect pressures bore any fruit. Finally, the Shah decided to intervene directly and sent Alam to convince Zahedi to go gently into the sunset. After a couple of days of negotiations, drafts of the resignation letter and other details were worked out with the Shah's indirect but full participation. Finally, on April 7, Zahedi resigned and, in circumstances strangely parallel to Mossadeq's end, the Shah used his power during a parliamentary recess to accept Zahedi's resignation and appoint Hussein Ala as prime minister.[128] In the words of the British Embassy, Ala was "the almost perfect" pliant tool—one who would allow the Shah to take "a direct and major part in governing the country." By then, Ala was "well over seventy years old and had to immediately leave the country for medical treatment in Europe." Even when back in Tehran, he "could not work for more than one or two hours a day."[129] The British Embassy tartly noted that following Zahedi's departure, "the business of government . . . has in practice been carried out by the Shah with Alam . . . as his errand-boy. The Prime Minister has little or no responsibility or authority."[130]

With the Tudeh Party in retreat and most of its leaders fled to Eastern Europe, and with the National Front more or less defeated, the Shah used the occasion of a failed attempt on the life of Ala to order a crackdown on the radical Islamists in Feday'an-e Islam who were responsible for the botched plot. Their top activists and leaders were arrested; included on the list were Ayatollah Kashani; Navvab Safavi, the founder of the group; and Khalil Tahmasebi, General Razmara's assassin. In those days, the Shah had his suspicions that "Saudi Arabian money" was being funneled to the Islamist group.[131] The Iranian government could never find any proof of this allegation. However, it was true that Safavi had in fact traveled to Egypt, where he had met with Gamal Abdel Nasser and Seyyed Qotb, one of radical Islam's most influential theorists and the leader of the Muslim Brotherhood (akhvan-al Muslemin). The British Embassy knew about these contacts and reported at the time that the Iranian group was "linked to the Moslem Brotherhood, receiving orders from them."[132] It is an interesting sign of Safavi's influence that in a recent memorial to his legacy, Ayatollah Ali Khamenei wrote that his foray into politics began when he heard a young cleric named Safavi give a rousing sermon in Mashad.

In a meeting with the British Ambassador shortly after the crackdown on Islamists, the Shah, in a "confident and cheerful mood," declared, with what the British official called a "lyrical note," that spring was on its way in Iran, and "a new page in the history of Iran" was about to be turned. The most remarkable aspect of the recent suppression of Islamists, according to the Shah, "was the absence of any popular protest against the arrest of Kashani, except for a routine one from a few mullahs." It just shows, the Shah said triumphantly, "what an exploded myth these nationalists were. Their importance in the past has been greatly overstated. He knew better now. They had nothing to offer the country. He had."[133] Maybe, unbeknownst to the Shah, the British did not share his optimism.

"Persia is drifting" declared Ann Lambton at this time. The Shah, she said, cannot govern but "will not let anyone else do it" either. In her words, he was "a dictator who cannot dictate." A number of Iranians, all known as Britain's most reliable "friends"—from the Rashidian brothers to Mohammad Saed and Seyyed Zia—had complained to either Lambton or to the Foreign Office, "begging us to do something." They complained about corrupt sycophants surrounding the Shah and leading him astray. Eventually, the British government reached the bleak conclusion that with the Shah at the helm, "good intentions coupled with weak execution has resulted in [an] intermittent and hesitant dictatorship."[134] Only the future would tell whether the Shah's eager optimism or Britain's critical skepticism was justified.

Chapter 11

CAT ON A HOT TIN ROOF

In the remembrance of a weeping Queen.
Shakespeare, King Richard II, *3.4.106*

Nineteen fifty-eight was not a very good year for the Shah. A number of serious, sometimes contentious issues that had been quietly boiling beneath the surface began to turn tempestuous. From his constant wrangling and haggling with the American government over the size of Iran's military to his desperate desire for a son with his infertile queen, the Shah's private and political life became, even more than it had been, a subject of controversy.

From early that year, those like the British ambassador, Sir Roger Stevens, who regularly saw the Shah with Queen Soraya, noticed that "the Queen was not at her ease," and that the Shah "seemed to treat her conversation with marked impatience."[1] The once playful, even passionate relationship was beginning to look frayed. It would take no more than a few weeks before the world would learn the reasons for his impatience and her distress.

Events on the international level were no less traumatic for the Shah. The "swift and brutal overthrow of the monarch in Iraq shocked and frightened" him, convincing him to "reappraise the future of his personal position."[2] He grew "nervous and disconcerted," while members of his family were "obviously jumpy." As a precaution, the Shah reinforced the protection for his residential palaces by the "transfer of tanks which [were] now in evidence in the palace grounds."[3] Soviet sources, in those days ever eager to embarrass the Shah, even reported that he "had prepared a plane to escape if an Iraqi style revolution should happen in Iran."[4]

The Iraqi coup was, for a variety of reasons, something of a personal warning for the Shah. The deposed young Iraqi monarch had been a rebuffed suitor to the Shah's daughter, Shahnaz. Moreover, it was the second time in about five years that a friendly monarchy in a Muslim country had been forcefully supplanted by a nationalist military junta. The first was the overthrow of the Shah's erstwhile brother-in-law, King Farouk of Egypt.* But by 1958 the Shah had succeeded in consolidating all power in his own hands. Ministers were now expected to report to him directly, often circumventing Prime Minister Manouchehr Egbal. It was around this time that the Shah told a meeting of the cabinet that "he was the fountainhead of all authority" in the country and that "he expected to be told in detail what was happening in every department of the government."[5]

A few of the Shah's advisors, as well as the British and American Embassies, tried to convince him at the time that such a concentration of power in his hands was impractical in the short run and was likely to threaten the survival of the monarchy in the long run. The British Embassy, for example, concluded that the Shah "is not capable of discharging" all the responsibilities he had taken into his hands. Iran will be "a naked autocracy tempered only by intrigue, greed, good manners, and inefficiency."[6]

Many observers, domestic and international, believed that the Shah had to allow a clear distinction and separation between the regime, with him as its symbol, and the government, with the prime minister as its embodiment. Such a distinction was clearly stipulated in the constitution. In the absence of such a distinction, the Shah was told, any disgruntlement with the government would have no consequence other than regime change. If the Shah took responsibility and credit for everything that happened in the country, then he would also be blamed for every failure.

The Shah, however, more than once rejected or ignored, even ridiculed, these warnings. Realizing that such a concentration of power was not only against the letter and spirit of the Iranian constitution but contrary to the historic pattern indicating the decline of actual power for nearly all other existing monarchies,

---

* It is an interesting fact of history that although both were coups by young officers against monarchies in Muslim countries, that was where the similarities ended. Iraq's coup was bloody and brutal and was, in subsequent years, followed by other equally bloody coups. In Egypt, the royal family was allowed safe passage out of the country. Even the Shah's first wife, Fawzia, who was the King's sister, was allowed to live, with her second husband and her son, in one of the royal family's homes in Alexandria. There has been no other coup in Egypt since that time.

particularly in Western modern societies with whom the Shah clearly liked to identify, the Shah often reassured himself (and anyone who cared to listen) that when it came to governance, there was something exceptional about Iran. What was true of other monarchies—other than their inexorable turn into mere symbols of national unity—was not, he believed, relevant in Iran. The Iranian people, he often said, loved their monarchy because it is "the natural order." On another occasion he said, "My father's dictatorship was necessary. My authoritarianism (*egtedar*) is also necessary today."[7] But he must have known, not so much by theoretical reason but by personal experience, that monarchy as an institution had become an endangered species, a quirky oddity in the age of modernity. Even in Iran, since the mid-nineteenth century, every monarch save one—Mozzafar al-Din Shah, who accepted the role of a mere symbol—had had a tragic end, either exile or assassination. Furthermore, the rise of a group of nationalist officers in Iraq, buoyed by Gamal Abdel Nasser of Egypt's Pan-Arabism, made the Shah wary that a group of young nationalist officers might be tempted to try something similar in Iran. As it turned out, his anxiety was not altogether baseless.

Around this time, there had in fact been alarming signs of discontent in the ranks of the Iranian military. The Communist Tudeh Party's military network, discovered not long after the fall of Mossadeq in 1953, had been successful in recruiting more than 600 officers, many of them in key command posts. The party's other covert military network, this time consisting of sergeants, was never uncovered. As late as 1958, the American National Security Council reported that "reliable estimates state that perhaps 20% of the Iranian army was disaffected."[8] In fact, in August of that year, "between 4 and 18 Iranian Army and Gendarmerie officers, most of them of field grade were arrested [for] anti-regime political activity."[9]

The rising power of Pan-Arabism in the Muslim world and of Arab nationalism in Iraq, combined with the success of the Soviet Union in ingratiating itself to Iraq and Egypt, brought about a profound change in the Shah's strategic thinking. Beginning in 1958, and for at least the next fifteen years, he grew concerned—or "obsessive," in the words of American and British diplomats at the time—about the might and machinations of Nasser, the charismatic new Egyptian strongman. Fear of Nasser and his radicalism also led to a new kind of cooperation between Iran and Israel, which in 1958 began a joint covert propaganda operation based in the city of Ahwaz, in the oil-rich Khuzestan province of Iran. The goal of the new operation was to broadcast to the Muslim world Arabic programs critical of Nasser.[10]

As a result of all of these changes, the Shah came to the conclusion that the future threat to the security of Iran would come not from the Soviet Union, but from Iraq and Egypt. Until then, Iranian military strategy had been single-mindedly focused on the fear of Soviet expansionism. As a result of the Shah's new thinking, new air bases and radar stations were built in the southern parts of the country near the border with Iraq. In a discussion with President Eisenhower in late 1959, the Shah suggested building fifty new such fields.[11]

The combination of these domestic and international challenges convinced the American and British governments that the "present political situation in Iran is unlikely to last very long." American officials predicted that the most likely outcome of the looming crisis was an "attempt by certain military elements, possibly in collaboration with civilian elements, desiring liberal reforms, to force the Shah back into the role of a constitutional monarch."[12]

There was, according to a National Security Council analysis at the time, a "growing educated middle class" in Iran, and they formed "the basic opposition to the Shah. Increasing numbers in these groups find Iran's antiquated feudal structures and the privileges of the ruling classes anachronistic in a modern world." Moreover, the "business activities, general irresponsibility and in some cases outright corruption of some members of the royal family" and others in the elite were contributing to the "growing popular discontent."[13] Though written in 1958, more or less the same words could be, and were, used twenty years later to describe the root causes of the 1979 Islamic Revolution. Ironically, while the 1958 analysis is remarkable for its precision, parsimony, and impressive grasp of reality in Iran, less than two decades later, on the eve of the revolution, the CIA not only missed the gathering storm of discontent, but only months before the fall of the Shah, concluded infamously that Iran was not even in a "pre-revolutionary stage."[14] Events of 1958 and the next few years can go a long way in explaining this historic intelligence failure and the surprising decline in the grasp of the Iranian reality by the American government and its intelligence agencies.

But in 1958, so worried were the American policy makers about the consequences of discontent amongst the Iranian middle classes that they began to ponder whether the United States "should continue to support the Shah and his regime." In fact, the September 9, 1958 meeting of the National Security Council was devoted to just this question. Ultimately, it was decided that the United States "should continue to support the Shah, but at the same time exert every effort to encourage him to undertake necessary reforms."[15] Amongst the reforms "being pushed" were "land reform and tax reform."[16] At the same time, American officials were warned not to be too "pushy" about the necessity of such reforms, lest the tone offend the Shah.

For the Shah, the troubles of 1958 began with the publication of an embarrassing "personal and secret" letter from John Foster Dulles, then secretary of state, to Selden Chapin, the U.S. ambassador to Iran at the time. Chapin had asked for a new assignment away from Iran. In response, Dulles, using surprisingly candid terms, reassured Chapin by saying, "you know of course that we have never cherished any illusions about the Iranian sovereign's qualifications as a statesman. The man tries to pose as the Cyrus of modern times. . . . He has no grounds whatsoever for doing so. The Shah should long ago have reconciled himself to the idea that he is there to reign, not to rule. His talk about the need for some purely national policy as well as his nebulous hints regarding the possibility of his revising his present policy show that he is about as successful as a politician as he is as a husband."[17]

The letter took on more significance when its content was echoed by the Turkish Prime Minister's published declaration that the Iranian regime was "in a shaky position." The Shah was "reliably reported to be 'furious' over the wire service" account of this impolitic declaration.[18] As it turned out, the Shah's fury and anxiety were, at least partially, based on a forgery. While the vote of no confidence by the Turkish Prime Minister was true, the more serious Dulles letter turned out to be a forgery. In the Shah's own mind, the KGB topped the list of "usual suspects."[19] In fact, the mastermind of the forgery has yet to be definitively identified. But what makes the enigma of the forged letter still fascinating is the fact that not long after its publication, the Shah faced a coup whose stated goal was almost verbatim the same as what Dulles purportedly demanded of the Shah—namely that he must reconcile himself to the "idea that he should reign not rule." Even the letter's reference to the Shah's marital failure was eerily prescient. The attempted coup has come to be called the "Gharani Affair" after its mastermind, Valiollah Gharani.

Gharani's career is a symptom of the cancer that was gnawing away at the core of the Shah's pillars of power. It also offers a clue to the riddle of the Islamic Revolution in Iran. Even in the late fifties, it turned out, Islamists had powerful "sleeper cells," some in the belly of the regime. There is a scholarly and diplomatic consensus that throughout the Shah's reign, the army and the intelligence agencies were the two key pillars of his power. Of the seven top military intelligence officers who served under the Shah (Bakhtiyar, Pakravan, Nasiri, and Nasser Moghadam, all four of whom were heads of SAVAK; Fardust and Alavi-Kia, who were deputy directors of SAVAK; and Gharani, head of army intelligence), at least five (Bakhtiyar, Alavi-Kia, Moghadam, Fardust, and Gharani) have been, at one time or another, accused of conspiring against the Shah. Pakravan, who was easily the most intelligent and erudite of the group and who also proved to be unfailingly reliable, served only for four years as the head of SAVAK. But Nasiri, an officer whose only apparent qualification was his fealty to the Shah, and who was never accused of brilliance, had the longest tenure (1965–1978). He was renowned for his reluctance to tell the Shah "unpleasant" truths or to take him bad news. Of the seven top intelligence officers, only one, General Alavi-Kia, went on to live a normal life. The others met violent ends: three were executed by the "revolutionary courts," one was assassinated by the Shah's secret police, and one was assassinated by a terrorist group shortly after the revolution; the fate of the seventh, Fardust, is still mired in mystery.

Of the seven officers, at least two tried to organize coups against the Shah. In 1958, it was Gharani's turn, and it was a measure of the entangled web of intrigue in his case that, in spite of the seriousness of the charge against him, he served less than three years in prison.

After his release, Gharani was put under constant surveillance, his phone bugged, his house and his every move monitored and reported. From these sources, we learn the extent of public support for him. For example, we know from police reports that in the first few days after his release, no fewer than 300 bouquets of flowers were sent to his house.[20] The number is particularly striking in light of the fact that, in those days, everyone who sent the flowers would have assumed that Gharani's house was under surveillance. From the same sources, we learn that before long, Gharani was in open collaboration with anti-Shah clerics who played a key role in the 1979 Islamic Revolution.

In fact, there is evidence that even at the time of his attempted coup, he was working with religious clerics. The British Embassy in Tehran, for example, reported that "Imam Jomeh, although appointed by the Shah is the leader of a group with which General Gharani is known to have contacts."[21] When the Shah tried to force into exile one of the clerics who had allegedly cooperated with Gharani, Ayatollah Boroujerdi, Shiism's top cleric was reported to be "furious about this development" and in protest threatened "to leave the country."[22] The Gharani accomplice was not exiled, and the Ayatollah did not go on his journey of protest.

❧

Valiollah Gharani was born in 1913 in Tehran. His family was solidly middle class and religious. He was seventeen when he joined the military, and he was one of the top three students of his class in the Officer's Academy. Special courses he took on intelligence shaped the contours of his career. Though Islamic panegyrists have tried to make of "Martyr Gharani" a devout and pious man of religion who never veered off the path of piety,[23] his peers remember him as a jolly young man, given to all the normal, sometimes-bawdy frivolities of a young officer.[24]

His early career is remarkable only for his steady but altogether routine rise through the ranks. As for many in the military, events of August 1953 were pivotal in determining the future of his career. He had by then become the commander of the Rasht brigade, one of the more important command posts of the time. During the fateful days between August 15 and 19, he remained loyal to the Shah, and his reward was his subsequent rapid rise to the position of vice chairman of Iran's Joint Chiefs of Staff. It was a measure of the Shah's trust in Gharani that he was also named the head of the Joint Chiefs' Second Division—*Rokne do*—in those days the most important intelligence post in the country. It was in that capacity that he often traveled to the United States, and it was during one of these trips that he began to plan a coup in Iran. On that trip he apparently met with Ali Amini, Iran's ambassador to the United States who was to be named prime minister after Gharani's planned coup. A list of other designated ministers for the coup cabinet was also discovered, with Gharani himself picked to be the interior minister. Ultimately the coup might have had as much to do with Gharani's wounded ego as with intrigues of politics. Like Iago, he believed that he had suffered "the curse of service," where preferment goes "by letter and affection / And not by old gradation."[25]

When SAVAK was first created in 1957 from a blueprint provided by the United States and with the help of American intelligence officers,[26] Gharani, as the chief of the army counterintelligence unit, was one of the leading candidates to become the first head of the new security organization. He had many friends and supporters, particularly in the ranks of the country's intelligence officers. Moreover, the Shah liked and trusted him, as he had shown his dependability during the events of August 1953—for the Shah the litmus test of reliability. But, ultimately, he lost his bid for the job, reportedly because British advisors convinced the Shah that a "strongman" like Bakhtiyar would be more suitable.[27] Gharani blamed his failure to get the job on Shapour Reporter, the storied representative of MI6 in Iran. And wounded pride begot a fierce desire for revenge.

Gharani began to look for any degrading information about Reporter. When he heard allegations of minor financial irregularities, he took a senior Iranian intelligence officer to the British Embassy to chronicle these alleged infractions. Reporter apparently heard about this visit and began to bide his time for a chance to return the favor.[28] The events of February 1958 offered him the chance. What made his job easier was the relentless competition between Britain and the United States over turf, power, and proximity to the Shah.

Early in January 1958, the American secretary of state, John Foster Dulles, and his assistant secretary, William Rountree, were on their way to Iran. Gharani decided that this was the time to move. On January 22, at his request, three members of the U.S. Embassy in Tehran—Fraser Wilkins, minister counselor of the embassy, Colonel Baska, and Lieutenant Colonel Braun—met the General at the house of Esfandiyar Bozorgmehr. The full memorandum of that conversation is still classified as "Sensitive; special handling required; not releasable to Foreign Nations."[29] A redacted "Memorandum for the Record" of the discussion offers the following synopsis of what transpired:

> [Gharani and Bozorgmehr said], a) The present government has no popular support and is despised by the mass of Iranian people and particularly by the professional and intellectual groups. The Soviets are quite openly engaging in penetrating and

> wooing the Iranian people.... Therefore Gharani stated that [it] is urgent that a change in government be brought about.... b) Bozorgmehr stated for Gharani that they have an intellectual group of 2000 Iranians, 1200 of whom were educated in the US and the balance attended the American university of Tehran; c) The approach to the Shah that he should reign and not rule should be made by someone outside of Iran with the inference that Secretary Dulles should make such a demand to the Shah.[30]

Nowhere in the report of the meeting is it made clear why the embassy officials decided to meet with such a high-ranking Iranian official under circumstances that clearly smacked of conspiracy, nor do they explain why they chose not to report the coup plans to the Shah.

Nine days after the meeting, Bozorgmehr, Gharani's chief accomplice in the affair, flew to Athens, where he met with Assistant Secretary Rountree. During the meeting, Bozorgmehr complained about the fact that there was now "considerably less freedom in Iran than under Mossadeq; that present government was completely without power." Bozorgmehr also talked about what he knew would be of most interest to the American officials, claiming that the "Shah and government have softened considerably toward [the] Soviet Union, with [a] constant danger Iran will accept large-scale Soviet aid."[31] Events in subsequent months showed surprisingly that the report of the Shah going "soft" on the Soviet Union was not altogether without foundation.

Back in Tehran, conscious of the internecine turf wars between different intelligence and police agencies, and of the rancor and personal jealousies amongst leaders of the regime, Gharani's next step was to concoct a clever camouflage for safeguarding his conspiracy. He told the Shah that he planned to lay a trap for disgruntled officers, politicians, and intellectuals by inviting them to participate in a conspiracy against the government.[32] But in spite of his Machiavellian guile, he had failed to take into account the continued power of British Intelligence and the personal power of his nemesis, Shapour Reporter.

The plotters were only in the early stages of their plans when they were all arrested. On February 27, in an angry communiqué the Iranian government announced that thirty-nine Iranians, including General Gharani, had been arrested for attempting to overthrow the government and that an "unnamed foreign power was involved."[33] The reference to the "foreign" power was, according to the British Embassy in Tehran, "intended to give the Americans a fright."[34] In later versions of the communiqué, the reference to foreign powers was deleted. On that same day, the Shah asked to see Selden Chapin, the American ambassador, and "with a great show of indignation" told him that "US Embassy personnel had encouraged the Gharani plot by talking to the plotters."[35] Chapin tried his best to convince the Shah that America had no role in the affair. Fearing that the Ambassador's words of reassurance might not work, the American government also combined them with a threat, indicating to the Shah that "there will be difficulties with aid appropriations if requests are made for the withdrawal of any Embassy personnel."[36]

The efforts worked, albeit temporarily. The next day, the "government modified its statement, ostensibly to quell public speculation, by stating that only five Iranians tried to seek help from foreigners to bring about a new government pledged to safeguard foreign interests. The declaration stated that the foreigners 'ignored the pleas' of the plotters."[37]

But the Shah's calm was short-lived. After a couple of days, much to his consternation, he heard about the meeting between the conspirators and the U.S. Assistant Secretary in Athens. It is not clear how he found out, but British intelligence and Shapour Reporter remain the key suspects. Once again, the Shah was incensed. The American Ambassador was called to the Court. Before setting out for what he knew might be a contentious meeting, Chapin asked the State Department for instructions on how to deal with the fulminating King. This time, Dulles ordered the embassy to stand firm. "The Shah should understand [the] nature of contacts in Athens," Dulles wrote back. "Rountree had no previous knowledge that Bozorgmehr was in Athens when [he] received telephone call asking for few minutes meeting. This lasted 20 minutes in course of which Bozorgmehr mentioned no plans for organizations, and requested nothing. He merely discussed in general terms situation in Iran. Rountree had no knowledge of Bozorgmehr's present activities or associations and was under impression Bozorgmehr was still official of GOI [government of Iran]."[38] In other words, hard as it may be to fathom, the American government again claimed that it had nothing to do with the conspiracy and that the meeting had not been previously planned but was essentially imposed on Rountree.[39]

The Shah tried to use the occasion and the embarrassment faced by the American government to begin pushing for an end to any contact between American intelligence or diplomatic officials and Iranian opposition figures. In fact, "on several occasions, high officials close to the Court as well as in the government . . . suggested that the American embassy should avoid any contacts with dissident or even opposition elements of the Majlis."[40] The United States vigorously rejected the idea at the time. "What would the Iranians say," Chapin asked officials in the Foreign Ministry, "if their embassy in Washington were told to have no contacts with the Democrats?"[41] The British were also pressured about this time on the same issue, and their response was even more categorical. "We are not prepared," said British Ambassador Roger Stevens, "to shut ourselves up in a kind of ivory tower . . . it would not be in anybody's interest that we should do so."[42] Faced with these stern rejections of his requests, the

Shah eventually changed his mind, telling Chapin that all he was asking for was that the U.S. military not discuss "intelligence and political matters with his military."[43] Seven years later, when the Shah was in a stronger position, he changed his mind again, and once more pushed for an end to all American contacts with the Iranian opposition. Concerned with the war in Vietnam, the Johnson administration succumbed to these pressures, and the result was one of the great intelligence failures in postwar American history. It is a fascinating facet of the Gharani saga that less than three years after his failed coup attempt, most of his stated goals became reality. Amini became prime minister in spite of the Shah's opposition, and many in his cabinet were the same officials Gharani had picked for ministerial portfolios in his coup cabinet. There is, then, more than one way to skin a cat, or to convince a king.

During the days and months when the Shah was preoccupied with the Gharani Affair, another long-simmering crisis, this time in his personal life, began to surface. The "impatience" the British Ambassador had detected in the Shah's usually playful relations with Queen Soraya was rooted in the fact that by early 1958, the couple had, after repeated efforts and examinations, accepted the fact that they were incapable of having any children together. The decision had come at the end of a long saga that had begun only seven months after their marriage in early 1951. When at that time the Court announced that she would be traveling to Europe "for medical treatment," rumors about her infertility began to circulate. But as Soraya clearly admits, at that time and for the first couple of years of their marriage, "so long as the Shah had to fight [with Mossadeq] for his throne, the absence of an heir scarcely counted as a problem of state."[44]

But then in October 1954, when the Shah was well ensconced in power, as the royal couple began to plan for their upcoming trip to the United States, the Shah surprised his wife by telling her "of his serious concern about the succession to the throne" and suggesting that in their upcoming trip to the United States, she should have herself examined by fertility specialists.[45] Pressure on the Shah to produce an heir had begun long before. Early in 1954, when it was rumored that the Shah was considering "nominating his only daughter as heir presumptive," newspapers in Tehran pointed out that such an appointment "could not be done without a constitutional amendment." Moreover, there were indications that one of the Shah's "aspiring" brothers had "inspired" these press reports. Ali Reza and Abdul Reza were the main suspects.[46]

With Ali Reza's death, the issue of succession found new urgency. Tensions were particularly intensified after the Shah's daughter, Shahnaz, married to Ardeshir Zahedi, announced that she was pregnant and, much to the consternation of the Court, claimed that should she have a son, her "baby would be heir to the throne."[47] The Shah was particularly upset by his daughter's claim, saying in private, that "a Zahedi could not continue the dynasty of the Pahlavis."[48]

Sensing that her days as queen might now be numbered, in July 1957 Soraya complained to the Shah that "we can't go on like this" and suggested that the Shah should change the constitution and make it possible for him to appoint one of his half-brothers as heir to the throne. Such a change, the Shah told her, "requires the approval of the Council of Wise Men." But in the articles of the constitution dealing with legal ways of amending it, there was no provision for such a council, and the Shah must have known that. He had already changed the constitution once. The Shah's concocted allusion to such a provision in the constitution, and her gullible acceptance of it, says as much about his mode of operation and his unwillingness to face up to difficult questions as it does about her limited grasp of the realities of the country of which she was queen.

Initially, according to Soraya, the Shah was opposed to her proposal. Eventually he "grew used to the alternative." He agreed to convene the "Council of Wise Men" for that purpose. It was also decided that she should leave the country and await the vote of the council and the eventual change of the constitution. There is no evidence that the Shah ever seriously considered the idea of such a change. Moreover, such a move would have been sure to raise the ire of his family, particularly his dominating mother, whose open rift with Soraya was by then a matter of public knowledge. Some have even suggested that for the last three years of her tenure as the queen, Soraya never visited the Queen Mother's home.[49]

On February 13, 1958, "almost to the day, the seventh anniversary" of her royal wedding, Soraya left Iran for Europe. Ostensibly, it was for a vacation; in reality, she had known for some time that she might never return. In the months before her departure, she "systematically put her house in order," collecting in a "suitable place those things which belonged" to her.[50]

After her departure, the Shah did convene a council of elder statesmen—past and current prime ministers and ministers as well as some generals—and entrusted them with the task not of changing the constitution, but of finding a solution to the problem of the Queen's failure to produce an heir. According to Soraya, after a few days, the council sent three emissaries to Europe to win her support for the idea that she should remain the queen but that the Shah would take a second wife, whose purpose would be to produce a male heir. She rejected the offer, even after she was reminded that the Shah's own mother had accepted the idea. She blames the Shah for the unacceptable offer, calling him, "fundamentally an Oriental." It was, she believed, because of this Oriental blood that the Shah did not model his conduct after that of the Duke of Windsor, "who sacrificed his throne to love."[51]

The Shah telephoned his estranged queen on several occasions and gave her an often-hopeful progress report of the council's deliberation. He even told her that he had suggested the change in the constitution and that they had rejected it. On March 5, the Shah called again, this time "in a cool and factual tone" and asked her to reconsider the two-wives option. She rejected the idea once again. On March 14, 1958, the Court issued a statement indicating that after three meetings of the Royal Council, and in light of the fact that the Crown Prince must be of Pahlavi descent, the Shah, "taking into consideration the interests of the nation," has decided to divorce his wife, and that she had been informed of the decision and had, in the interest of the nation, decided to accept the decision.[52]

Soraya offers a starkly different narrative. She claims that after their "cool and factual" conversation of March 5, the Shah never called back, and then on "March 14, he announced our divorce without having spoken to me again."[53]

Financial settlements, including "sums of money, as well as lands and security" that the Shah had given her during their days of marriage left her a comfortably rich woman. Though she makes no mention of alimony, it is reported that for years, she was paid a monthly allowance of about $7,000.[54] The estate auction, conducted in June 2002, shortly after her death, showed the range of valuables she had taken with her to Europe. While her Paris apartment was sold for almost $3 million, the auction netted more than $6 million. The sale included a Harry Winston platinum ring, featuring a 22.37 carat diamond, sold for $838,350; a Bulgari ruby; a Van Cleef & Arpels brooch; a 1958 Rolls-Royce; and a Gullwing Mercedes-Benz.[55] By the time of her death, she had come to be called the "sad queen," and it was a poignant sign of this sadness that her only heir was her brother and that, a week after the auction, he too died, leaving the fortune to the legal vagaries of a "next of kin." But as it turned out, the 1958 divorce did not end her romantic, or even financial, entanglements with the Shah.

Reports of the Shah's response to the divorce range from those claiming he was crassly indifferent to those who claim that "Soraya was the Shah's only true love" and that the divorce left him despondent. The British Ambassador, for example, described the Shah at the time as a "man at an emotional cross-roads," in some ways relieved by the prospects of divorce, and at the same time unable to easily "bring himself to face it."[56] Others close to the Court told the American Embassy that "the Shah is relieved to be rid of the Queen and that his first despondency was more feigned than real."[57] In one of the Shah's biographies it is even claimed that on the night the announcement of the divorce was made public, the Shah went to Hotel Darband, a fashionable Tehran nightspot at the time, "and invited a ravishing European blonde to dance."[58] At the same time, the Shah wanted to know what the British government thought about such a divorce, and he "was relieved to feel that the divorce" would not be "a stumbling block" to his upcoming trip to England and to his relationship with the British government.[59] As it soon turned out, his concern for the British view of his divorce was more than just political.

Not long after the public announcement of the divorce, the Shah began looking for a new queen, while rumors of his philandering also spread. There was talk of his affair with an Iranian girl as well as with international celebrities.[60] But he was also thinking about marriage, and "he put out feelers for the hand of Princess Alexandra,"[61] a granddaughter of King George V. Three years earlier, on a visit to England, the Shah had made it known, through various means, that he coveted the Order of the Garter,[62] or "The Most Noble Order of the Garter."* But the feelers he sent out for the Garter and for Alexandra were both met with a cold shoulder. In fact his "feeler" about Princess Alexandra was, according to Sir Denis Wright, "dead on arrival."[63]

The Shah's search for a fertile European queen next took him to Italy, where he tried to marry Maria Gabriella, the daughter of Umberto II, the last king of the country and of the House of Savoy. He had met her in Europe and on more than one occasion, spent time with her, including a week in Switzerland, where he stayed at the lakeside villa of his son-in-law, Ardeshir Zahedi. The problem in this case was more theological than political—Shiite clerics in Iran and the Pope in Italy posed serious problems for such a marriage.

Gabriella was a Catholic, and her father was particularly devoted to the demands of the faith. A marriage with the Shah would pose at least two problems. On the one hand, there was the question of religion for the couple's future children: would they be baptized and raised Catholic, as her faith demanded, or would they be raised Muslims, as required by Islamic law? Some courtiers suggested a compromise alternative: the question of the children's religion would be deferred to the time when they reached maturity.[64]

The second problem had to do with the fact that the Shah had already been twice married and divorced, and as a Catholic girl, Gabriella could only marry him after a special papal dispensation. That might well explain the unusual circumstances of the Shah's trip to the Vatican in late 1958. The Shah was scheduled to visit Italy that year, but then when Pope Pius XII died, he postponed his journey, waiting for the time when he could meet the new pontiff. In Rome,

* The order of the Garter was the oldest order of chivalry in Europe, going back to the time of Edward II, around 1348 to 1351. According to at least one myth, the Garter first came into vogue during the Crusades. Richard I, then fighting the Muslim infidels, tied garters around the legs of his knights. Membership in the Order has always been limited, often to no more than twenty-five, consisting of the sovereign and a few more blue bloods. On rare occasions, foreign monarchs, called "Supernumerary Knights" were also invited to join. Worried for much of his life about the approbation of the British, this was, one can surmise, the Shah's way of ensuring, in his own mind, that he had finally been accepted by the British.

the Shah stayed at the Hotel Excelsior, where he had stayed during the anxious days of August 1953. He met Pope John XXIII on December 1, exchanged gifts, and discussed matters of "mutual interest." Vatican documents are kept confidential for seventy-five years, and thus accessing the minutes of the meeting is still impossible.[65] All we know about the meeting is the gifts the two leaders exchanged. The Pope gave the Shah "a photograph of himself, a gold medal commemorating his coronation, a book on the Raphael apartments of the Vatican and a catalogue, in three volumes of various Islamic and Turkish manuscripts in the possession of the Vatican Library." The Shah, in return, gave the Pope "a carpet of silk and wool, woven in the workshops of Nain."[66]

The Pope, however, was not the only obstacle on the way of a marriage between the Shah and Gabriella. Shiite clerics at home were no less unhappy with such a union. Hussein Ala, the minister of Court at the time, offered a refreshingly honest assessment of the political costs and benefits of such a marriage. Mixed in is a caustic and critical account of Court life in the latter part of the fifties. Ala writes of "different responses" in the diplomatic community to the news of the Shah's possible marriage to Gabriella. According to Ala, some diplomats are surprised and ask how a Muslim king can marry a Catholic Princess. They worry that no sooner has the Shah married the Italian Princess than "a horde of Italians will converge on Iran" seeking work and contracts. Moreover, many believe that neither the Pope nor Shiite clerics will tolerate such a union. Ala goes on to report that some diplomatic circles in Tehran believe such a marriage will bring about "the overthrow of monarchy" while others will welcome it as an occasion to reform the Court and "improve its image."

Ala then offers a bleak view of the influence that the Shah's family and friends have had on the reality and image of Court life. He warns against Princess Ashraf's "meddling and mischief" and her attempt to "dominate the future queen." According to Ala, even Iranian intellectuals who are in favor of the Shah's marriage to Gabriella, and see it as a sign of progress, worry about Ashraf and the Queen Mother's interference "in the private life of the Shah." Ala ends his epistle by asking the Shah to cleanse "his private parties of unsavory characters," and to replace "parties of gambling and silly games and striptease" with "intellectual endeavors" like lectures, bridge games, films, and musical concerts.[67]

The note combines political candor with a kind of paternal concern. Its bitter tone might have had also a personal reason. Every time the Shah was looking for a bride, a number of prominent Iranian families had begun to jockey for a chance to have their own daughter become the future queen. At least according to Soraya, these self-serving calculations and machinations might well have influenced the decision of the "Council of Wise Men." One of the most storied efforts came from the Ala family itself. Not only had Ala himself been at the center of Iranian politics for half a century, but his wife, too, came from an aristocratic family of great wealth and erudition. She was known for her unabashed pride in her blood and lineage. Her daughter, Iran, was, she thought, the natural next queen. When it turned out that the Shah did not share her view, she grew so angry and embittered that, henceforth, she refused to meet the Shah or to attend the parties at the Court.

Of the families hoping to have their daughters chosen as the next queen, the Diba family of mid-level officials was an unlikely candidate for success. Farah Diba was at the time a student of architecture in Paris. Once when the Shah had visited France, she had been in the line of students received by the King. Her father had died when she was young, and she and her mother lived with her uncle and his son, Reza Qotbi, who became her surrogate brother when she was young and her closest confidante when she was queen. It was, in her telling, an idyllic childhood, save for the death of her father. Though Iran was in those years in the throes of a most vibrant political atmosphere, Farah and her family were decidedly non-political, and she was a royalist because, in her own words, "[she] was immersed in Ferdowsi's ideas: Only the kings were legitimate rulers in our country."[68] In reality, Ferdowsi's *Shahnameh*, the grand epic of Iranian history is filled with stories of kings killing their sons—at least eighteen cases of filicide by Dick Davis's count in his masterful *Epic and Sedition.*[69] It is also the story of royal hubris, of arrogance of power, and it ends with a lament on how the weakness of a king allowed the country to fall into the dangerous hands of Arab Muslims who were overrunning the once-great empire.

But regardless of the sources of Farah's royalist sentiments, no sooner was she the queen than a stream of rumors about her politics began to spread. She was accused of being everything from a Communist to a Pan-Iranist, a member of an extremist nationalist group in Iran. Even the KGB claimed that it had some influence on the Shah's selection! In reality, it was Ardeshir Zahedi and his wife, Shahnaz, who introduced Farah to the Shah. At the time, Zahedi was married to the Shah's daughter; though every female member of the royal family was apparently busy trying to find a suitable match for the King, Zahedi and Shahnaz participated in the process rather reluctantly.

At Zahedi's house, the Shah met Farah for the first time, and after a couple more meetings in the same place, where they danced and listened to music and played parlor games, the young lady was, at the behest of the Shah, taken to meet the Queen Mother. Without her approval, everyone knew, no marriage would be possible. Farah passed that test as well. Before long, the Shah asked her to take a ride with him in a new plane he had just bought. As they were flying over Tehran, on October 14, 1959, the Shah proposed, and she "said yes to his love and to the special destiny that love entailed."[70] In what, in retrospect, seems like a potent metaphor, at the end of the flight, the plane had technical difficulties.

The wheels would not open, and the plane had to fly over Tehran for some time to consume as much of the gasoline as possible. Eventually they had a choppy but safe landing.

Hers was indeed something of a Cinderella story. Overnight Farah went from the simple solemnities of middle-class life to the starchy rituals of a Court where her wedding dress was designed by Yves Saint Laurent and the tiara by the American jeweler Harry Winston.[71] In spite of all the planning, on the night of the wedding, somehow everyone forgot to bring the ring. As the cleric was about to recite the Qu'ranic verses that would sanctify the bond and declare them husband and wife, the royal couple was desperately searching for a ring. Ardeshir Zahedi came to the rescue and offered, albeit temporarily, his ring as a surrogate wedding band.[72]

The Shah, Farah tells us, chose her because she was "so natural." She was, in her own words, seen as "an unaffected girl who knew nothing of the world of courtiers and diplomats."[73] In fact, diplomats then and for many years afterwards talked about her as bringing a touch of "humanity and humility" to an otherwise distant and diffident Shah. In her memoir of exile, there is beneath the jovial façade a constant touch of melancholy. In her eyes, too, there is always a hint of sadness, of resignation to the Cinderella story fate had hurled her into. Words, particularly in memoirs, invariably tell us more than their authors intended, or at least more than they consciously wanted to convey. While still in power and in Iran, she called her life story *My Thousand and One Days*[74] and conjured both the ostentatious affluence of a *Thousand and One Nights* court as well as the sad tale of Scheherazade, the ultimate master of yarns, who concocted stories only to keep alive. In exile, long after the many travails and tribulations of her marriage to the Shah had become public knowledge, after Alam's *Daily Journals* had chronicled in painful detail the Shah's excessive philandering and the litany of "guests" flown in from Europe for the Shah's "entertainment," she called her memoir *An Enduring Love* and chose to remain stoically silent about all of those stories. But as she explains in both memoirs, not long after she accepted his marriage proposal, the wedding ceremonies took place at the Court, and then the waiting game began. Her husband, his family, her mother, and much of the nation waited to see whether she would bear a son and produce an heir to what was in those years a shaky throne.

As the Shah's *annus horribilis* had begun with a nasty, albeit forged letter, it ended with an even nastier, more threatening letter, this one from President Eisenhower. And this time, the letter was no forgery. Not long after the Gharani Affair, the Shah, maybe in partial retaliation for America's role in the incident, threatened the American Embassy that "if he is not given satisfaction by US on such matters as budgetary assistance," he would "reconsider Iran's position vis-à-vis USSR." He wanted not only more budgetary assistance, but also a bilateral treaty that would commit the United States "to come to the aid of Iran if there is indirect aggression against Iran from any source whatsoever, communist or non-communist."[75] Making such broad commitments, Dulles informed the Shah, was "beyond the commitments authorized by the US Congress."[76] In response to this rejection, the Shah took the extraordinary step of engaging in secret negotiations with the Soviet Union for a long-term non-aggression and economic cooperation pact. The United States and Britain were angered by the move and considered it at best an act of "blackmail,"[77] if not betrayal. The way the British and American government learned of the arrival of the secret Soviet delegation, and the tactics they used to dissuade the Shah from going ahead with the proposed agreement, precipitated the first major crisis of 1959.

Chapter 12

RUSSIAN HOUSE

Foolish curs, that run winking into the mouth of a Russian bear and have their heads crushed like rotten apples.
Shakespeare, King Henry V, *3.7.103–104*

In 1956, a week before the Persian No-Ruz—the Persian New Year, the first day of spring, celebrated at the moment of the vernal equinox—the British Embassy in Tehran received an offer it could not refuse. General Teymour Bakhtiyar asked Mr. Sajjadi, an Iranian member of the embassy staff, to lunch. The General was named the military governor of Tehran in the aftermath of events of August 19, 1953, and by the time of his lunch invitation had already developed an infamous reputation.

That day the General had torture on his mind. He "wished to inform the Embassy... about the question of treatment of political prisoners." He began by suggesting that he knew the embassy had by then "heard the stories widely current in Tehran about the tortures practiced by the Military Government."[1] Tehran was in fact abuzz with stories of torture and beatings, mock executions and nail pulling, solitary confinement and forced confessions. There was even talk of rape. The brunt of these brutalities was said to be reserved for arrested members of the Tudeh Party, particularly their clandestine military network.

By the time the Military Governor considered the party defeated and its military network abolished, 4,121 party members had been arrested.[2] It was a measure of the party's long tentacles that amongst the officers in charge of Richard Nixon's security detail when he traveled to Iran as vice president in 1953 was a member of the party. The head of the security detail for General Fazlollah Zahedi when he was the prime minister was also a party member.[3] The hub of the torture rumors was an infamous bathhouse—*hammam*—in one of the prisons where many of the arrested officers were first incarcerated. Whisper had it that the *hammam* was in fact changed into a torture chamber. One of the most popular heroically tragic songs of modern Iran—"Mara Bebous" ("Kiss Me"), inviting his beloved to kiss him "for the last time"—was, perhaps apocryphally, said to have been composed by one of these Communist officers on the night before his execution. Of all the Tudeh Party military network members arrested, thirty-six were sent to the firing squad, including its mastermind, Khosrow Roozbeh.[4] It has been reported that the arrest of the entire military network was the result of a fluke arrest of an officer named Abbasi in whose possession were the encrypted names of all members of the military network. Roozbeh was something of a math and chess prodigy and had used a sophisticated equation to encrypt the names. After much effort, it was ultimately the encryption officers of the CIA who broke the code. Whisper at the time, however, had it that the code was broken only after Abbasi was tortured.

General Bakhtiyar began by insisting that stories in the rumor mill were "greatly exaggerated, thanks at least in part to the Tudeh Party." The first story Bakhtiyar wanted to confirm but correct was what had been until his confession arguably one of the most serious charges made by the opposition. It was said that a bear had been used to rape recalcitrant political dissidents. The General indicated that a bear had been used, but only "once. . . . Even then the bear had not been allowed to molest the person concerned. This had been a man who in the time of the *Murdad* [August] troubles of 1953, had sent a telegram to Mussadeq . . . attacking the Shah, and suggesting that the grounds of the royal palaces should be turned into a zoological garden." The General and his interrogators had assumed that using the bear "would be an appropriate punishment for such sentiments and the man had been put in the cage much to his terror, but taken out after he expressed rapid repentance before the bear actually got its claws on him."[5]

The General went on to say that "a number of other methods of torture" ascribed to them were highly exaggerated. Their main "weapon had been flogging with a whip," and he went on to say that as their reputation worsened, as more and more people heard these whispers, often the only thing that was needed to get prisoners to confess and or give information "was to tell them that they would be transferred" to the *hammam*.[6]

As to the Shah's role in the decision to use these brutal methods, Bakhtiyar went "to some pains to explain that the Shah had only given general orders on this matter." He had told the Military Governor that he and his staff should use any method necessary "to gain information, depending on the importance and the recalcitrance" of the prisoners."[7] It is difficult to know precisely what motivated Bakhtiyar to make these revelations. Was he trying to implicate the Shah or exonerate himself? It was hard not to assume that he was campaigning for the job of the head of the new organization (SAVAK) he knew was in the planning stages. The British Embassy in fact surmised that he was trying to counter the "dirt" that his rival, the chief of the police, "had been spreading" about him.[8] While we might never know his real motive, we know what the British government decided to do with this potentially volatile information.

The first person who received a report of what Bakhtiyar had revealed was rather astounded and believed that the British government, at least on humanitarian grounds, should ask the Shah to order an end to such practices. But as the report made its way up the diplomatic and bureaucratic ladder, prudent silence was the chosen path. Someone suggested that he "does not believe that the Shah is unaware of these tortures.... [He] is determined to wipe out the Tudeh... [and he has been] just as ruthless...in allowing full military operations against the [nomadic] tribes."[9] Some surmised that the Shah had a "personal score to settle with the Tudeh party for the attack on his life."[10] Another official claimed that "torture of one kind or another has been common in Iran for a long time," though he immediately went on to add that "the majority of Iranians do not like this sort of thing," and that "nothing of this sort went on under Dr. Mussadeq's government." Finally it was resolved that "rooting out communism in Iran is a major interest and objective for [Britain] as well as Iran," and thus the British government must certainly "not appear to be undermining" the Shah's efforts in achieving this common goal. Moreover, it was decided that if the Shah should ever give the British Ambassador an opening, the Ambassador should register his government's displeasure about the torture of Communists. Before long, Britain and the United States both found themselves showing strong displeasure to the Shah not about the torture of Communists, but about his big gamble on establishing new ties with the Soviet Union.

In a character study of the Shah prepared in 1957, U.S. officials pointed to some important changes in his behavior. One of the key indications of "his growing maturity" had been his symbolic "break with his old tutor and personal secretary, Ernest Perron. Probably not even his own brothers had been more closely and continuously associated with the Shah." By all indications, Perron was sacrificed when, a few months after the fall of Mossadeq in 1953, the Shah's attempt to bypass the cabinet and the Prime Minister and establish direct ties with Britain backfired. Though they had met daily for almost two decades, the Shah would never see Perron again. His older sister, Shams, who shared Perron's deep devotion to Catholicism, took him in and allowed him to stay in her palace until the end of his life.

In a meeting with embassy officials not long after his dismissal, Perron himself offered a reason for the break, calling it "necessary for the full development of the Shah's personality." In the words of the embassy, Perron now envisaged "himself as a sort of father image with whom his majesty had to break in order to assert his own influence."[11] Though Perron was no Falstaff and the Shah no Henry, the embassy report, in the words of the writer and filmmaker Ebrahim Golestan, certainly conjures memories of this bitter break.[12]

The 1957 profile of the Shah noted another crucial change in him. While in 1951 the embassy had stressed the Shah's "lack of confidence" and his incessant need "to seek advice at every turn," he now felt less and less in need of any advice. This newfound self-confidence had both domestic and international roots. It was partially the result of his belief that his return to Iran after 1953 was a reaffirmation of his monarchy. It was also founded in his budding belief that he was not just a national but an international leader. At least in the eyes of some foreign diplomats, his sense of global mission began in November 1956, in response to the Suez Crisis. At that time, the Shah chaired a four-power Muslim heads-of-state meeting in Tehran. The meeting brought together leaders from Iran, Iraq, Turkey, and Pakistan and "provided Iran with an active role in an international crisis which [had] no parallel in modern times."[13] By the early 1970s, this sense of international import was in full bloom.

But even in 1957, when this confidence and the undemocratic elements incumbent in his authoritarian modernization were only in their earliest formative stages, some observers saw potential trouble on the horizon. Some surmised that, given his innate tendency to be "indecisive," he did not have "all the firmness necessary for a man" who wanted to rule, not reign.[14]

The 1957 profile also hinted at what soon enough became one of the biggest challenges the American and British governments faced in their dealings with the Shah. Though the report emphasized the Shah's "fear of communism," it went on to say that he had been "reportedly impressed by economic advances he observed in the Soviet Union."[15] Moreover, after much trepidation about the wisdom of accepting the Soviet government's invitation to visit the country in 1956, and after some consultation with British and American officials, he decided to go. The Soviets had by then already begun something of a charm offensive. They informed him that they had decided to lodge him at the Kremlin itself—at "Ivan Veliky tower . . . somewhere near [where] Stalin used to sleep." It was the first time a reigning monarch "was ever accommodated in the Kremlin itself . . . except Napoleon who hardly counted as a guest."[16]

After returning from Moscow, the Shah took some pride in telling British and American diplomats about the uncompromising positions he had taken while in the Soviet Union. He said the Soviet leaders had "frankly admitted past mistakes (attributed to Stalin) in their policy towards Iran. They appeared genuinely anxious to turn over a new leaf." The Shah said he even criticized his hosts for their continued support of the "subversive activities" of the Tudeh Party. British sources confirmed the story that the Shah had "stood up" to Soviet leaders, but they also reported that in private conversations, Soviet leaders "expressed considerable admiration for the Shah's abilities and personality."[17] Aside from these small diplomatic gains, little of substance was changed in Iran's relation with the USSR. The Shah's "natural inclination" was to mistrust "everybody, and when in doubt the Russians most of all."[18] Was this about to change?

As early as 1957 the Shah had grown increasingly weary of rumors that the United States was "playing with" the Iranian opposition and "working with urban middle class leaders" against him. He consistently complained that Turkey and Pakistan were receiving more aid from America than Iran did. America's continued resistance against a bigger military for Iran continued to frustrate him. He finally recognized that he and his regime were increasingly seen as wards of the United States. Flirting with the Soviets, the American Embassy believed, would become appealing to the Shah because it "[would] frighten the US into more aid" and divert public criticism away from the regime. It was, however, the common wisdom in the West that regardless of his frustrations, the Shah was sufficiently pro-Western in his core values that he would never make anything more than "surface gestures towards Soviets."[19] By January 1959, this common wisdom was suddenly challenged.

There were a number of added reasons why the Shah was tempted to flirt with the Soviets. His repeated attempts to have the United States and Britain join the Baghdad Pact (later known as the Central Treaty Organization, or CENTO) as full members had failed. He found the Eisenhower Doctrine—the promise to help any country that chose to challenge and defy Soviet subversion—less than satisfactory. In his mind, it did not go far enough to guarantee Iran's security in case of an attack by the Soviets. A sufficiently strong Iranian military that could hold the Soviets behind "the Alborz mountain line" long enough for U.S. forces to come to the rescue, a clear and categorical mutual defense pact between Iran and America, or America's full membership in the Baghdad Pact would be, in his mind, the only sufficient guarantee against the possibility of Soviet aggression.

The United States gave a variety of reasons for its refusal to join the Pact, including the claim that such a security arrangement with Iran must then be "accompanied by a security arrangement with Israel." The Eisenhower administration made it clear that it was, at that time, unwilling to make such an arrangement with Israel.[20] It was a measure of U.S.–Israeli relations in 1957, particularly after the United States had sided with Egypt and against Israel in the Suez Canal Crisis, that the United States told Turkey that if it could "get [the] Israeli government to agree not to press for a security arrangement with the US . . . then [the Eisenhower administration]"[21] would make a new assessment of the Pact and the wisdom of the United States joining it as full members.

The combination of all these factors contributed to the commencement of one of the strangest, and still enigmatic, episodes in the Shah's thirty-seven-year reign. The Shah's frustrations "came to a head in early 1959 when [he], without any word to his allies, embarked on secret negotiations with the USSR for [a] non-aggression pact."[22] So profound was the impact of this gambit that, at least according to Sir Denis Wright, who played a key role in the whole affair and in the Shah's subsequent political life, "after this episode, [Britain] never trusted him again. Never."[23]

In the first week of January 1959, Iranian Prime Minister Manouchehr Egbal met with Denis Wright in London. They met in a friend's home, away from the glare of the media and had a "mid-night session." Egbal "spoke in convoluted terms about the serious situation in Tehran." The next day, General Arfa—at the time Iran's ambassador to Turkey—"also spoke anxiously" to Wright "much along the lines taken by Egbal."[24] Both men "expressed concern about the Shah's reluctance" to sign a bilateral treaty the United States had offered in lieu of full membership in the Baghdad Pact. Neither man spoke about any other plans the Shah might be entertaining.

Back in October 1958, the Soviet Union learned of a proposed bilateral security pact between Iran and the United States. They immediately sent a strong threatening note to Iran, claiming that the new agreement was in conflict with Iran's past obligations to the Soviets and "grants the US military forces broad opportunities to subordinate Iran even further." In the Soviet view, the new pact would give the United States the right to establish a new military base on Iranian soil, and such an agreement would be against the letter of the 1921 agreement between Iran and the Soviet Union. The formal threat was followed by another, even more brazen, note declaring that the "might and capability" of the Soviet Union is far superior to Iran and that if the Soviets are made to "feel uneasiness about elements of Soviet-Iran relations" then they will use their superior might to make Iran feel equal "inconvenience."[25]

The Shah's response to this threat and to his continued tension with the United States was a surprise to everyone. According to the official Soviet history of the episode, "after a number of prominent Iranian generals" came out against the bilateral pact with the United States, the Shah "proposed to the Soviet government that the two countries sign a treaty of friendship and non-aggression." On January 19, 1959, according to the Soviet narrative, "the text, a draft of the treaty was handed to the Soviet ambassador in Tehran. Moreover, Iran demanded that the Soviet government reply to the Iranian proposal as early as possible."[26]

The Soviets, eager to make the deal, immediately sent a high-ranking diplomatic delegation to Tehran. "They met with the Shah, the Prime Minister and the Foreign Minister."[27]

While the Soviet team was in Tehran on its highly secret mission, Denis Wright arrived in Iran, apparently for a vacation. He met with his "old friend Hussein Ala . . . the Court Minister." Ala talked at length and anxiously "hinted that the Shah was flirting with the Russians." Wright, who had earlier heard vague warnings about these moves from Egbal in London, was no longer surprised by what Ala apparently thought were shocking new revelations. Wright had already heard "from an unimpeachable secret source that a high-powered Russian delegation had arrived that very day in Tehran in the greatest secrecy to negotiate a non-aggression pact with the Shah."[28] When asked about this "unimpeachable secret source" Wright clearly implied it might have been "monitored conversations" at the Court, and in the Shah's office.

Later that same day, at a luncheon, Ala informed British diplomats in Tehran what they already knew: that a high-level Soviet delegation was in Tehran, had met with the Shah, and was about to sign a non-aggression treaty with Iran. Denis Wright calls Ala's action "a courageous thing to do." What is not clear is whether Ala was acting at the behest of the Shah. Was he leaking highly sensitive state secrets to a foreign power about what he perceived was a wrong policy by the Shah? Or was the Shah engaged in a game of brinkmanship in which Ala was simply playing his assigned role when he "anxiously" informed the British about the Shah's supposed Russian "flirtation"? Did the Shah really intend to secretly sign the deal or was he, all along, hoping to "frighten the West" and engage them in a game of brinkmanship? The British Foreign Office, by then fully informed of these developments, instructed Denis Wright "to do all [he] could to stop the Shah; he was also instructed in exactly what arguments he was to use to dissuade the Shah from his perilous path."[29] Ala, too, had beseeched Wright to "speak 'very frankly'" with the Shah, informing the British diplomat that he "himself had been unable to make much impression on the Shah."[30]

For Denis Wright, the mystery was at least partially solved when, on January 29, 1959, at ten o'clock in the morning, he was "ushered into the Shah's study." The Shah began by complaining about the Baghdad Pact and the fact that he had not received enough aid. "You treat me more like a kept woman than a wife," he reportedly complained. According to Denis Wright's memoirs, he answered "that kept women sometimes earned fur coats if they behaved themselves."[31] The Shah then surprised his visitor by volunteering "that he had started negotiating with the Russians." Wright "begged the Shah not to sign with the Russians," and with tears rolling down his cheeks, he "prophesied that if he did so, he would eventually lose his throne."[32]

Much to Wright's surprise, when the Shah learned of the extent of the British government's displeasure, he feigned astonishment and sought "a scapegoat." According to the Shah, it was Seyyed Zia who was responsible for the policy.[33] Denis Wright does not mince words, concluding, "I thought then, as I do now, that the Shah was entirely to blame."[34] In meetings with Seyyed Zia, Wright confirmed his own hunch that the decision to engage in the negotiation was made by the Shah. The only other person who favored these negotiations and could have advised the Shah was the foreign minister, Aliasghar Hekmat.[35] A couple of days after Wright's visit, Britain's defense minister and the British Ambassador to Tehran also had lunch with the Shah, and they too "were able to bring home to His Majesty the full implication of his proposed action."[36]

A couple of days after the British first found out about the Shah's Russian gambit, the American government too had heard about the Soviet Union's "secret negotiating team" and wanted to have its own "very frank" discussion with the Shah. Allen Dulles, director of the CIA, assured a meeting of the National Security Council that in the CIA's view, the Shah was just trying to blackmail the West. The Eisenhower administration, Dulles declared, was bent on "holding the line" against this tactic, and a policy of carrot and stick was clearly their chosen strategy. Part of the stick came in the form of the threat of troubles amongst nomadic tribes of Iran. American officials at the meeting were informed that two of the Qashgai brothers, living in the United States at the time, had "informed [the United States] that they are proposing to go back to Iran... to weaken the Shah."[37]

Aware of the Shah's special rapport and almost filial relationship with Eisenhower, it was decided that the ultimate carrot and stick would be a letter from the President to the Shah. The day after his meeting with Denis Wright, the Shah received a surprisingly tart letter from Eisenhower. It began by reaffirming that "the direct contacts" the President and the Shah have "maintained over the past years... have always been a source of gratification to me." He then immediately referred to reports the United States had received "to the effect that your government is considering the conclusion of a new treaty with the Soviet Union." Eisenhower declared categorically and candidly that "it is my profound conviction that the principal objective of the Soviet Union in Iran remains unchanged and that that objective is inconstant with Iran's independence and integrity and with the security and stability of Your Majesty's regime." Eisenhower once again referred to their "many past contacts" adding that, "I know you are aware that a Soviet objective is to separate Iran from its friend and allies." He admitted that the United States did not know the details of the new "proposed treaty" but added menacingly that, "regardless of the actual terms of any new treaty with the Soviet Union, the impact on your friends would be unhappy."[38] He affirmed past differences "over our respective estimates of the size of the military program that should be maintained and supported" in Iran, but offered reassurances that the United States would never abandon its support of Iran's "independence and integrity."[39]

The last paragraph of the letter included a surprisingly unveiled threat. "I am confident," Eisenhower wrote, "that you would not knowingly take a step that would imperil your country's security and possibly weaken Iran's relations with its proven friends."[40] Within days after the receipt of the letter, and the meeting with British officials, the Shah decided to back out of the non-aggression pact, which, according to Soviet sources, he had proposed himself. Iran found an easy way to bring the negotiations to a dead end by demanding that articles in the 1921 and the 1927 agreements, often used by the Soviets as a pretext to threaten Iran, should be abrogated. On February 14, 1959, the Shah sent Eisenhower a letter "explaining his reasons" for initiating the negotiations for the pact with the Russians and more importantly stating "that the discussions had failed."[41]

No sooner had the negotiations ended in failure than the Soviet propaganda machine began a prolonged campaign against the Shah and his "reactionary policies." Foreign diplomats in Tehran concluded that it was "unlikely that Khrushchev will ever forgive the Shah," and that from then on, "a primary objective of Soviet policy toward this country can only be the overthrow of the Shah's regime."[42] If the KGB chief in Tehran is to be believed, Khrushchev was so angry at the Shah that he ordered him assassinated. The only reason the attempt failed, according to the KGB station chief, was the utter incompetence of the man the Russians hired to carry out the assassination. A bomb was to go off in a small Volkswagen when the Shah was on his way to a session of the Majlis. But the trigger failed to work, and the Shah was spared. Nevertheless, diplomatic relations between Iran and its northern neighbor were tense and fraught with danger. The American Embassy reported rumors—later declared "baseless"—that the Soviet Ambassador "was passing a story around Tehran" that the Soviet Union was planning to take over Azerbaijan.[43] Within months of the collapsed negotiations, the Shah was invited to visit Britain. In London, Prime Minister Harold Macmillan's goal was to place "emphasis on Anglo-American solidarity" with Iran and point out the "relative dangers of Soviet Communism."[44]

In Washington, the United States tried to use its own power of persuasion as well as the good offices of the UN Secretary-General, Dag Hammarskjöld, to "bring about a cessation of Soviet propaganda broadcast."[45] Iran even considered filing a complaint with the UN. In a letter to the Shah in August 1959, Eisenhower reassured the King that the United States "would use any opportunity" to pressure Khrushchev to cease the "vicious campaign" against the Shah.

But the Shah was not sufficiently comforted by these promises. It is reasonable to assume that his sudden decision on July 24, 1959, to declare that Iran had "extended Israel de facto recognition," as well as his decision to approve granting the Rothschild Group a contract to build an oil pipeline connecting Iran's oil fields to Eilat in Israel, were all part of his effort to consolidate his ties to his Western allies in the face of this surprisingly harsh onslaught. In early 1955, Israel's supply of "cheaper oil from Kuwait [had been] cut off on the advice" of the British government. Britain was worried that should these sales become a matter of public knowledge, its allies in Kuwait wouldn't be able to sustain the political fallout amongst other Arab states. To the British, "the obvious solution was to supply" Israel's oil needs from Iran. It was further suggested that, as in the case of Kuwait, "shipments should . . . be made to 'Cape Tours' and not directly to Haifa."[46] By the end of the fifties, the Shah was resolved to increase Iran's economic ties with Israel. Not long after the July 24 announcement, Israel's Prime Minister David Ben-Gurion emphatically asked American officials to redouble the effort to support the Shah and build up his military.[47]

Before the end of the year, on December 14, 1959, Eisenhower made a goodwill trip to Iran. He arrived in Tehran at 8:40 in the morning and left for Athens six hours later, at 2:30 in the afternoon. Though some of his conversation with the Shah was about the Soviet threat, the Shah's preoccupation was the increased military threat coming from Iraq. He wanted five new fighter-jet air fields, all geared toward defending the country against the possible Iraqi threat. Eisenhower, in his own words, was "much impressed with the extent to which the Shah's thinking had matured."[48]

The Shah also decided to strengthen his government's ability to fight back against Soviet as well as Arab Nationalist propaganda. The traumas of 1958, American suggestions that he should improve his "public image" and that the anti-Communist discourse in Iran needed to become more subtle and sophisticated, and finally the relentless nightly attacks on Radio Moscow against the Shah combined to convince him that he should find a more experienced hand to help fight these ideological battles. He dispatched one of his trusted lieutenants, General Hassan Alavi-Kia, deputy director of SAVAK, to Germany and entrusted him with the task of finding just such a propaganda advisor.

In Bonn, General Alavi-Kia met with his counterpart in the West German security police. "We need someone," Alavi-Kia said, "who can help with the ideological fight against the communists."[49] The German secret police, the General was told, had the perfect candidate. He was known as "Dr. Anti," for his relentless fight against the Bolsheviks,[50] and was considered one of Germany's most experienced polemicists against Soviet Communism. What was not mentioned in that day's discussion was that the candidate had first made a name for himself during the Nazi era but had also been active in the years after the Second World War. His name was Dr. Eberhard Taubert and, though a master propagandist, he was averse to publicity; it was said that the first picture of him was taken in October 1950.[51]

Taubert, as it turned out, was not just "an expert for anti-Bolshevik" propaganda, but also a virulent anti-Semite. He had been "Goebbels's screen writer," having been involved in making one of the Nazis' most infamous anti-Jewish films and described by one critic as "an X-ray of the legitimization of the Holocaust."[52] In fact, he had joined the Nazi Party in 1931, when he was twenty-four years old. From his first days in the party, he was involved in both its anti-Communist and anti-Semitic propaganda. After the fall of Hitler, Taubert began to work for "three thousand dollars a month" for the German Christian Democratic Party in its polemics against more radical Marxists. It was rumored that the KGB had put a million-dollar prize on his head.[53] One of the most famous anti-Communist posters in postwar Germany, portraying Soviet spies lurking in every corner, was said to be Taubert's work.

In August 1950, along with three others, Taubert established a group whose sole mandate was fighting Communist influence in Germany. It was said that the group received some 600,000 deutschmarks annually from the German government. His past, the fact that Goebbels had called him a "sympathetic fanatic," and the story that he had somehow contributed to the deaths of more than 200,000 Jews made him an increasingly controversial character. Nevertheless, before his past caught up with him, Taubert moved freely and successfully in the corridors of West German power. For a few months, he had worked closely with Franz Strauss, the conservative Bavarian politician. He was both a liability and a rich source of experience for conservative postwar governments in Germany. Intermittent reports by German investigative journalists made it difficult for conservative parties to easily use him. It was then a pleasant surprise for his friends when the Iranian government asked for an anti-Soviet advisor, and the profile of the person they sought by and large fit Taubert's expertise. In February 1959, with a salary of 3,500 deutschmarks per month, he was hired by SAVAK.[54] His work with the organization was kept a secret, and few people, including the Shah, knew of his role.

In Iran, as in postwar Germany, Taubert tried to live a semi-clandestine life. He moved in with a colonel who worked in the Iranian SAVAK. He had no friends and no hobbies. Hiking around Tehran's towering mountains was his only occasional indulgence. In Tehran, his work was concentrated on offering advice on how to fight Bolshevik influence and counter Moscow's propaganda war.

He was not the only brain behind Iran's surprisingly spry, clever, informed, and acerbic responses to the attacks by Comrade Khrushchev. Some of the most appealing broadcasts were prepared by Nasrollah Moinian, then a young journalist and aspiring bureaucrat. Before long he rose to become the Shah's chief of staff—a position he held with distinction. Amongst his innovations was the broadcast instruction on Islam on radio programs heard by Muslims of the Soviet Union.

Aside from working on the anti-Communist polemics, Taubert offered advice on a variety of political domains. For example, it is a question of some lingering interest whether Taubert had initially given the Shah the idea that soon became one of the pillars of the 1963 "White Revolution." The idea was to use army conscripts to fight illiteracy. It was called *Sepah-e Danesh* or "army of knowledge." It was one of the most successful elements of the White Revolution. Like most good ideas, this one too had many fathers, and Taubert was easily the most controversial. The idea, according to General Alavi-Kia, was first articulated in a policy paper that Taubert had prepared. It was a replica of the idea of Hitlerjugend going to the countryside to educate illiterate peasants.[55] And Hitler himself might have picked up the idea from the populist movement in nineteenth-century Russia where intellectuals flocked to the countryside to educate the masses.

But after quietly working for five years in Iran, in 1963, as the Shah was trying to normalize relations with the Soviet Union, and as the propaganda war with the Russians was about to end, firing Taubert became one of the conditions for normalized relations. Taubert was forced to leave Iran, and went to Egypt, Lebanon, and South Africa. The Russian gamble of 1959 had failed to produce for the Shah the results he anticipated. But his desire to use the Russian card did not dissipate or disappear. Only two years after Taubert left Iran, the Shah was once again trying to use Russia against the West, and, that time, he had higher cards.

A hint of what was on the Shah's political horizon came in a memorandum of a conversation between him and the British Ambassador. The Shah, the British envoy reported, "is moving toward the position of a liberal autocrat, relying largely on bourgeois support, not unlike Louis Philippe. His antipathy to the great landed aristocracy is increasingly plain."[56]

Chapter 13

THE DARK SIDE OF CAMELOT

The means that heaven yields must be embraced.
Shakespeare, King Richard II, *3.2.29*

For the Shah, there was nothing numinous about the Kennedy Camelot. The Iranian monarch was no King Arthur, and every aspect of the original medieval story—from the cuckold king to his novel democratic idea of deferring power to a roundtable of knights—was anathema to the Shah's disposition. It is far from hyperbole to suggest that the first four years of the sixties were for the Shah the most trying period after the Mossadeq ordeal. Conspiracies real and imagined, bloody rebellions in the cities, combined with his effort to lead a "White Revolution"—what the Kennedy White House had earlier called a "controlled revolution"—while trying to consolidate his hold on power made those four years for him at once tragic and triumphant. The four-year period was also singularly significant in shaping the dynamic forces that changed the fabric of Iranian society, brought the Shah to the height of his power, and the country to unprecedented prosperity. The Islamic Revolution of 1979 was in no small measure the unintended consequence of the confluence of forces unleashed in the first years of the 1960s. The country's domestic realities, as much as the changing international situation and the new policy ushered in by the Kennedy administration, shaped the Shah's policies and politics.

In February 1956, in a now-historic secret report to the twentieth Soviet Communist Party conference, Khrushchev criticized the once-deified Stalin and called him a "sadistic . . . and egotistical" leader, and something of a bumbling fool when it came to military matters.[1] Until the Khrushchev speech, the Soviet Union had followed a policy promulgated by Stalin that was in appearance and trappings ideologically austere and indebted to Marxian internationalism but was in fact fiercely nationalist and expansionist. It was predicated on the idea that there would be an inevitable Armageddon, wherein the "Socialist camp," the camp of labor led by the Soviet Union, would defeat the "imperialist camp," the camp of capital led by the United States. Instead of a global cataclysm and a nuclear war, Khrushchev now posited what he called the era of "peaceful coexistence" and "wars of national liberation." The USSR, he promised, would support these movements throughout the Third World and through them defeat the United States and bring capitalism to its inevitable end. The fact that in the early 1970s, there were at any time more than forty armed conflicts around the world that were in fact proxy wars between the two superpowers was the direct result of this theory.

In the case of Iran, soon after the bitter breakdown of negotiations over the non-aggression treaty between the two countries in 1959, Khrushchev not only launched an all-out propaganda campaign against the Shah, but also suggested provocatively that Iran was like a rotten apple, that all the Soviet Union had to do was wait and the apple would fall into its lap.

In September 1961, there was also evidence of Soviet military buildup—including troop movements near the Iranian border—that indicated "the Soviets may seek to put pressure on Iran in connection with the Berlin crisis."[2] The United States began to develop contingency plans to respond to such a Soviet move.

Another consequence of Khrushchev's secret Twentieth Party Congress report was an increasingly open ideological, political, and even territorial rift between Mao Zedong and the Chinese Communists on the one hand and Khrushchev and the Soviet Communist Party on the other. The Chinese Communist Party would soon begin supporting Maoist groups around the world, including Iran, and encourage them to fight the twin evils of political imperialism and social imperialism. By the early 1970s, several small and ineffective Maoist groups existed in Iran.

The Cuban revolution of 1959 was afforded the same romantic aura of heroism and struggle that had, a quarter century earlier, been reserved for the Spanish Civil War. Che Guevara became not only the darling of radical chic in the West, but also the universally appealing symbol of a peculiar theory of revolution. According to this theory, embodied in Iran in the life and death of figures like Hamid Ashraf,[3] a small cadre of dedicated armed revolutionaries must begin to fight oppressive regimes, allowing their own heroism and, if necessary, their martyrdom to became the catalyst that incites a hitherto intimidated, oppressed, and dormant mass into an assertive revolutionary action. About the same time, a similar model of revolutionary action was put into action in an Islamic context in Algeria, and many of the leaders of that revolution became models for the Iranian youth.

Even before the rise of this new theory, radical Islamist forces had been, since 1941, organized in a remarkably successful terrorist organization called Feda'yan-e Islam. The Shah and his regime, particularly in the first years of the sixties, had to contend with the power and fury of this group.

The easy spread of this theory amongst Iranian secular and religious youth can be at least partially explained by its structural and emotional similarity to the story of Imam Hussein, a narrative central to Shiite iconography. In that story too, a band of seventy-two dedicated revolutionaries, led by Hussein, the Prophet Mohammad's grandson, rose up and fought against the superior army of the "usurping" caliph. Their foredoomed death created the enduring myth of martyrdom in Shiism.

A corollary, or even an epistemological precondition of this Shiite theory of martyrdom, is the postulate that the genuinely pious are invariably in the minority. Che and Lenin's theory of revolution, no less than Feda'yan-e Islam's vision, demanded a similar belief that genuine revolutionaries are invariably a minority. In Iran, as in many other countries of the Third World, armed "guerrilla movements"—called in the parlance of our time "terrorist groups"—mushroomed into action. What made the Iranian experience peculiarly interesting was that the theory appeared both in an overtly religious guise and in one with a Marxist veneer. Both incarnations had similar religious roots and structural affinities. A Marxist group even called itself Feda'yan-e Khalq—the Martyrs of the People. One of the leaders of this group, Hamid Ashraf, developed by the early 1970s an almost mythical reputation for his Houdini-like ability to escape from any trap laid by the security forces. For months, the Shah became intensely anxious, even obsessive, about Ashraf's fate and pressured the security forces to use any and all means to arrest or kill the mythical fugitive.[4]

September 1960 was also the time when some of the oil-producing countries in the world—Iran, Iraq, Kuwait, Saudi Arabia, and Venezuela—decided to form a cartel and called it the Organization of Petroleum Exporting Countries, known since then by its acronym of OPEC. After the trauma of trying to sign a separate deal with Enrico Mattei, the Italian maverick oilman, joining the new organization was for the Shah both a relief and a challenge. The Shah believed Mattei's death in a plane crash, said to be an accident caused by "lack of visibility," was in fact the result of a conspiracy. "I have never believed that Mattei's death was an accident," the Shah said. He went on to add that in his view, Mattei "was amongst the first casualties" of the Shah's attempt to steer an independent course in oil negotiations.[5] The United States and Britain both tried to dissuade the Shah from signing the controversial deal with Mattei, as it would have given Iran 75 percent of the profits. Both countries moved gingerly to muscle Mattei out and, until his death, their effort failed.[6] Maybe that explains the Shah's initial reluctance to make a serious commitment to OPEC.

But gradually he changed his mind. He appointed Fuad Rouhani as Iran's representative to the new organization. Rouhani was one of Iran's most respected oil economists and jurists, known for his intimate knowledge of the complicated calculus of oil pricing and of the arcane world of oil contracts and agreements. Rouhani was selected as the first secretary-general of OPEC. Before long, the Shah himself took a leading role in pushing OPEC to demand higher prices for oil. In fact, if the Shah is to be believed, not only the troubles in the early 1960s, but the revolution of 1979, were the direct result of his role in OPEC and his becoming known as a "price hawk." In a bitter passage of his memoirs, the Shah wrote, "[F]rom the moment that Iran became the master of its own underground wealth, a systematic campaign of denigration was begun concerning my government and my person.... It was at this time that I became a despot, an oppressor, a tyrant. Suddenly malicious propaganda became apparent; professional agitators operating under the guise of 'student' organizations appeared. This campaign begun in 1958 reached a peak in 1961. Our White Revolution halted it temporarily. But it was begun anew with greater vigor in 1975 and increased until my departure."[7]

It was in the context of these changing circumstances that the Shah also had to face a new administration in Washington. He had clearly favored Richard Nixon; in his campaign, John Kennedy had openly criticized the Shah, suggesting the necessity of an overhaul of U.S. policy not just in Iran but around the world. The Cold War's Manichaean view of the world reduced everything to a simplistic dualism between "us" and "them," and "good" and "evil;" the view was shared by both the United States and the Soviet Union, but the Kennedy administration favored a more nuanced approach.

In Iran, this change of U.S. policy took place against a backdrop of the constant threat of the Soviet Union and of the character of the Shah and the danger that the "US might push him" into the temptation to leave the Western camp and join the growing ranks of nonaligned countries.[8] U.S. intelligence agencies claim that America even entertained the idea of removing the Shah, so urgent was the need for change in Iran at that time.[9] But contrary to the perception shared by many scholars and students of modern Iran, and countering the view shared by many Iranian royalists that Republican presidents were friends of the Shah and Democratic presidents his foes, pressure on the Shah to reform had begun in the last three years of the Eisenhower presidency—the Republican president with whom the Shah had developed particularly close relations.

Throughout much of the late fifties, a point of constant contention between the Shah and the United States was what John Foster Dulles, writing to President Eisenhower, called "the Shah's military obsession."[10] In the same note, Dulles, using a tone that reeked of sarcasm, brought up the fact that "the Shah consider[ed] himself a military genius" and was determined to build his military to the point where Iran became the dominant power in the region.

But in the 1950s, when much of Iran's military buildup was funded by the U.S. government, American policy makers exercised considerable control over the size and structure of the Iranian army. At the same time, the United States occasionally chose to cater to the Shah's "military obsession" as a kind of inducement, even an emotional bribe. American officials believed that "the Shah's interest in military forces is in part emotional rather than logical. . . . [This] psychological bias," they concluded, "renders him immune to logical persuasion in this field."[11] When reason was wanting, American officials tried to appeal to the Shah's emotions. In 1958, for example, when the Shah was planning a private visit to the United States, Secretary of State Dulles wrote to Eisenhower, first apologizing for getting the President "in this" and then suggesting he should "flatter the Shah with the prospects of an exchange of view with [Eisenhower] on modern military problems."[12]

During this period, American officials tried to convince the Shah, directly in private conversations and indirectly when he was visiting other places like Japan, that "domestic political and economical health [were] highest values to the defense of Iran."[13] This was America's way of resolving a paradigmatic difference of vision with the Shah. For him, the main threat to Iran was external, while U.S. analysts believed the threat to have domestic roots. As early as August 1958, CIA Director Allen Dulles told a meeting of the National Security Council, "we take a gloomy view of the Shah's future unless he can be persuaded to undertake some dramatic actions."[14] The 1958 coup in Iraq, followed by another in Turkey in 1960—two of Iran's allies in the Baghdad Pact—frightened the Shah and exacerbated American anxieties. In fact, after the Turkish coup, the National Security Council concluded that the Shah was now in more trouble "than anytime since Mossadeq"[15] and that the main danger came from the possibility of a military coup, much like what had happened in Turkey. The British were equally alarmed about the internal situation in Iran, but as a rule they concerned themselves more with trade than with democracy promotion. In fact, according to Selden Chapin, the U.S. ambassador in Iran, the British were not "completely helpful" on this score. British officials, Chapin believed, "regret to some degree their past power and prestige," and not only did they not help the American government but "from time to time" gave the Shah the idea that "Iran was not getting from US the degree of military assistance it deserved."[16]

The failed coup attempt by General Gharani in 1958 was, not surprisingly, an early warning to the Shah about the domestic threats to his rule. Lest he fail to get the right lesson from that attempted coup, on September 8, 1958, the new U.S. ambassador, Edward Wailes, met the Shah and told him about the domestic dangers that he still faced. He told the Shah about the "embassy's views on underground movement and unrest in Iran." The Shah, according to Wailes, was "impressed" with the work of U.S. intelligence and became receptive to American suggestions of "preventive measures such as anti-corruption campaign and 'fireside chats' to the people."[17] What the Shah probably did not know at the time was that in the late fifties and early sixties, "the CIA maintained roughly half a dozen paid agents in the [Communist] Tudeh Party and somewhat fewer in the National Front, among them several well-known leaders of the two organizations."[18]

Not long after the Shah's meeting with Wailes, the pliant Majlis passed the law infamously known as "Whence Your Fortune Law?" inquiring into the fortunes of the military and political elite of the country. Although by 1960 the government had announced that it had "fired, suspended, jailed, or brought before the court 4247 officials," the common perception was that "they were small fry" and that no effort was made to punish "the real sources of corruption . . . reaching into the royal family."[19]

Less than a month after Wailes's suggestion of "fireside chats," the Shah gave his first press conference. He also asked his trusted advisor and friend Assadollah Alam to try and open a dialogue with some of the moderate members of the opposition. Khalil Maleki, the well-known social democrat was amongst opposition leaders who participated in these meetings. Alam and Maleki met secretly for several months, and in the course of one of these meetings, Maleki gave Alam a draft of a party program he had prepared. Upon reading it, Alam suggested that Maleki should meet with the Shah. "His Imperial Majesty is deep-down a social democrat himself," Alam told Maleki.[20]

Maleki agreed to have such a discussion, and before long, he met with the Shah. They had met once before, in the weeks before August 1953. At that time, during a three-hour meeting, the Shah had tried to convince Maleki that Mossadeq's continued rule would only lead to a victory for the Tudeh Party. Maleki was not convinced. Now, six years later, they were meeting under different circumstances. In 1953, the Shah had felt besieged; in 1959, he had, he believed, been vindicated. The Shah wanted Maleki to act as a go-between with the opposition, but nothing came of the two men's meeting or of Maleki's proposed mediating efforts.

The Shah also began to crack down on the increasingly brazen financial activities of his family. By mid-1958, the American and British Embassies in Tehran had become concerned not only about the financial activities of the Shah's siblings, but about those of the Shah himself. The family of Queen Soraya had also become a source of occasional embarrassment. The two embassies joined forces and tried to come up with an estimate of the Shah's fortune and a profile of his economic activities. The picture they drew was not pretty. According to the British Embassy, the "royal appetite for business and for intervention in development schemes" had grown so much that there were "few branches of economic activity into which the long arms of the Shah and his friends and family" did not reach. The Shah's direct and "personal interests alone now extend publicly into the fields of banking, publishing, wholesale and retail trading, shipping, construction work, new industries, hotels, agricultural development and even housing. The Bank Omran which is 100 percent owned by the Shah . . . has recently taken a forty nine percent participation in two new companies for irrigation works and for boatbuilding and repairing on the Caspian Sea."[21]

By then it was estimated that the Shah also owned thirteen hotels; four more were under construction. Moreover, the Shah was said to be a partner in a fertilizer plant, a cement factory, a grain silo, and a beet sugar refinery.[22] His interest in the cement factory, for example grew out of a bridge game during which the Shah's childhood friend and bridge partner Majid A'lam talked of his attempt to launch a cement factory and said that he and his partners were short of capital. The Shah asked how much they needed, and when he was told that they needed about a million *tooman* ($150,000 in the rate of exchange at the time), the Shah immediately offered the needed capital and joined as a silent partner.[23] When occasions like this arise in the future, he told A'lam, let me know. Needless to say, partnership with the Shah, in fact, with any member of the royal family, opened many bureaucratic doors, and thus was much coveted by many industrialists, investors, and trading companies.

The Shah, according to the joint British and American Embassy report, was also active in commerce. He owned the Mah Trading Company, which imported "primarily from the UK and is currently involved in municipal electrification schemes in competition with the Plan Organization." The same company acted as the middleman in "such diverse schemes as the construction of a one million pound bridge over the River Karun (by a British firm) and a preliminary survey of the possibilities of uranium extraction (also by a British firm.)"[24] Another deal had the Shah involved in the production of pharmaceuticals in conjunction with a Japanese firm while "in the world of shipping, the National Iranian Shipping company is controlled by the Shah through his nominee and principal agent Maybod [Mehbod]."[25]

It was in the same years that Mehbod (sometimes rendered as Maybod) often acted as a middleman in major oil deals and openly asked for a commission, letting it be known that he was in fact working in conjunction with the Shah. The American Embassy complained to the Shah that U.S. companies were "puzzled as to Mehbod's status," particularly since they considered him "ignorant of oil business, irresponsible, opportunistic and corrupt to the extent that he openly asks for bribes to be passed on to higher levels." The Shah responded that Mehbod had denied all these allegations and that "in the absence of proof the Shah is reluctant to take any action." The Shah then added that Mehbod was a good businessman "with energy, industry, imagination and commercial contacts," emphasizing at the same time that no one should feel compelled to pay any bribe to him.[26]

As can be expected, the embassy's conclusion was not favorable to the Shah. An example of Mehbod's mode of operation was seen in the AGIP Mineraria oil concession deal in which the British Embassy was "given the plainest of evidence . . . that [Mehbod expected] a very large bribe . . . from the British firm," leading the embassy to conclude that "the Royal hands are most probably not clean."[27]

All in all, the total value of the companies owned by the Shah at the time was estimated to be worth close to $157 million.[28] The figure did not include any cash or securities the Shah might have had outside Iran. A few years later, in 1965, Mehdi Samii, a trusted advisor to the Shah, by chance heard from one of the Shah's American bankers that "your monarch has more than one hundred twenty million dollars in his different accounts."[29] The issue of his wealth had dogged the Shah from the day he ascended the throne in 1941. Though at the time he had promised to return to the nation all illicit fortunes gathered by his father, he made only token gestures of philanthropy and kept much of the inherited fortune. Now, with increasingly damaging rumors about royal family corruption, the Shah decided to place all of his companies, including the Omran Bank, in the nonprofit Pahlavi Foundation.

In a document signed on October 4, 1961, the Shah laid out in some detail the goals of the endowment. One of the first glaring aspects of the text is its many overt religious allusions. It begins with a Qu'ranic verse, and the first reason given for creating the foundation is "our total and deep faith and strong belief in God's good graces." The endowment document stipulates five overall goals for its funds and one of them is "religious matters." The other four stipulated goals, too, are strewn with either religious expenditures or religious justifications for the stipulated goals.[30] More than 2,000 villages the Shah had inherited from his father were also gradually either given gratis or sold at greatly discounted prices to the peasants who had worked on them.

Before long, the Pahlavi Foundation grew into a global empire, and although it was ostensibly an independent nonprofit foundation, the Shah used it as his personal fief. Even after the 1979 revolution, his family believed it should be given control of the Pahlavi Foundation's properties in the United States—a high-rise on New York's Fifth Avenue bought for $30 million in the mid-1960s with a small down payment and a loan guaranteed by the National Bank of Iran, and a big property in New Orleans[31]—arguing that they were never more than a trust set up by the Shah for his and his family's use. The royal family was particularly dismayed by the decision of Ja'far Sharif-Emami, one of the executors of the foundation, to turn over the rights to the Pahlavi Foundation to the Islamic government in Iran (which immediately renamed it the Alavi Foundation, after Ali, the first Imam of Shiism). In early 2009, the work of the foundation in the United States caused considerable alarm amongst American officials implementing the financial embargo against Iran. Eventually, as economic pressures on Iran increased, the assets and headquarters of the Alavi Foundation were taken over by the FBI.

In fact, even at the time of its creation, the Shah's attempt to channel his economic activities through the work of the Pahlavi Foundation was met with skepticism, particularly when it was learned that some of the Shah's most trusted officials were placed at its head. As a result, not only did the Shah's financial activities continue to be "the subject of rumor and gossip," but more crucially, as the British Embassy observed, his example was "followed throughout the hierarchy of power" in Iran.

The problem was, of course, not limited to the Shah. As the 1958 report makes clear, other members of the royal family and some friends of the Shah found ingenious, sometimes-illicit, ways to enrich themselves. The Shah's sister Ashraf and his then–brothers-in-law, Chafig, an Egyptian married to Ashraf, and Vincent Hillyer, an American married to his sister Fateme, "profited singularly" from their positions. Even the Shah's older sister, Shams, who enjoyed a far better reputation at the time, was not only said to be a silent partner of big industrial conglomerates, but had been busy constructing her own Xanadu on the outskirts of Tehran. The palace soon became known for its many eccentricities—like gold-thread bedcovers and amenities for Shams's burgeoning menagerie—dozens of dogs, cats, birds, and even a monkey.[32] Her husband claims she paid for the palace by selling some lands that had been given to her by her mother. In reality, one way she and the other members of the royal family—with the exception of the Queen Mother—defrayed the cost of their buildings was by simply refusing to pay the contractors for their work. The Shah himself was inclined to pay for the services rendered by his contractors, but the man who managed his personal accounts, Ja'far Behbahaniyan, was rather reticent about paying the Shah's debts.[33]

On the eve of the Islamic Revolution, for example, Shams owed one contractor, Hamid Ghadimi, millions of *toomans* for work his company had done for her. The only compensation for the unpaid work of the royal family contractors was the promise of help in securing other lucrative contracts, or simply the aura that came with being the royal family's contractor or architect.[34]

According to foreign diplomats working in Tehran, the Shah's promise to limit the activities of his family did little to dispel the popular notion of corruption at the highest level of the government. Moreover, although he made token gestures to limit his family's activities in times of extreme political pressure, the Shah in fact considered these activities altogether legitimate. Even after the revolution, when David Frost pushed him in his final interview on the allegations of his own and his family's massive corruption—"20 billion dollars diverted" in Frost's words—the Shah coyly dismissed the question of his own wealth by offering to sell it all to a legitimate offer for a billion dollars, adding that those who claimed he had taken $20 billon obviously didn't "know what figures represent." As for his family, he denied any wrongdoing on their behalf and repeated the claim that they had a legitimate right to enter into business. And when he was asked about specific allegations of corruption on the part of General Mohammad Khatam, his brother-in-law, who had been investigated by congressional committees in Washington, the Shah claimed he was unaware of what these supposedly wayward relatives were doing.

In reality, the Shah knew full well the stories about these allegations. When Khatam died in 1975, the Shah ordered the creation of a secret commission to inquire into the General's fortune, which, even before the investigation, the Shah had estimated to exceed $100 million. Assadolah Alam, who has written about this episode in his *Daily Journals,* adds that though in his own mind the $100 million figure seemed exaggerated, "His Imperial Majesty never says anything without deep contemplation and ample information."[35]

In ordering the investigation, the Shah also made it clear that should it turn out that the fortune had been accumulated illicitly, "it must be all confiscated and turned over to the government."[36] What is ironic is the fact that the Shah put Alam, hardly a man known for his financial probity, in charge of the investigation.

But in 1958, the British government had a direct, frustrating experience with the Shah's financial meddling. A big British company had won a multimillion-dollar contract for the extension of Iran's telephone system, only to have it given at the last minute to a German company. In his memoirs, Sir Denis Wright writes of "expressing Her Majesty Government's dissatisfaction over the award of the big telephone contract to the German, knowing that but for the Shah's intervention, it would have come to us." The Shah, according to Wright, "simulated surprise, saying that he had been definitely told that we favored the Germans getting it and he had therefore instructed the Minister of Post, Telegraph and Telephone accordingly."[37]

The British knew that the Shah's sudden diversion of the contract to the Germans was in fact the result of "his current interest in . . . the wife of the local Siemens agent." But in those days, the Shah, according to Denis Wright, still "feared to run foul of the British." He sent Wright a message through Shapour Reporter, the alleged head of MI6 in Iran, "that he was very worried about what I had said about the telephone contract," and that he will "use his influence to put future business our way," and "hoped that I would ease his mind when I next saw him by letting him know 'that little misunderstanding is over'." A few days later, in the course of a reception for the visiting Turkish President, Wright "whispered the comforting words" to the Shah.[38] No wonder then that the British Embassy in Iran at the time concluded, "Iran would be the country of the future in the Middle East, if it were not for the Iranian ruling class."[39]

The Shah's efforts to ameliorate American concerns about the future of his regime were not limited to his role in the passage of the law about illicit fortunes and his decree limiting the business activities of the royal family. The Shah's most important step was to ask the Majlis to pass "a controversial land reform bill."[40] Though pressure for such a policy was at the time clearly coming from the Eisenhower administration, the fact was that the Shah himself had been talking about the necessity of land reform ever since ascending the throne. He was also responding to the reality that in the years after the war, several groups in the opposition, particularly the Tudeh Party, had made land reform an essential part of their party platform. It was a sign of the Shah's damaged image, and of the opposition's power to shape public opinion, that in spite of the fact that the Shah had a long history of his own words and deeds in favor of land reform, the lingering notion that found currency in the public imagination at the time was that he had been "ordered" by the Americans to undertake land reform.

From the first weeks of his rule, the Shah had talked about the necessity of a "revolution from above" as the only way to abort the otherwise inevitable "revolution from below." As early as 1943, he had told a new session of the Majlis that "we must make every effort to ensure that every citizen of the country, particularly those from the working and farming classes, and the poor in general, have as much free housing, free food, education and health as is common around the modern world."[41]

But the 1959 land reform bill met with fierce resistance from two groups. The landlords—whose tentacles reached deep into every institution of power in Iran and who had been one of the Shah's pillars of support—organized "stiff opposition" to any program that would deprive them of their properties. They formed a union, the Agricultural Union of Iran, to join forces in fighting the proposed land reform.[42] Any time talk of land reform became serious, the landowners' resistance also stiffened.

In their effort to block these reforms, the landowners were joined by the bulk of the Shiite clergy. Ayatollah Boroujerdi issued a stern warning to the Shah, threatening to issue a *fatwa* declaring land received through a land reform as *haram*, or unclean. Private property, the Ayatollah declared, is protected in Islam and is not to be taken away under any pretense. For the religiously conservative peasantry it would have been unfathomable to live, work, and pray on land declared *haram* by a cleric of Boroujerdi's stature.

During the same period, Boroujerdi issued another *fatwa* banning pious families from purchasing radios, arguing that such families courted the danger of "moral turpitude."[43] He also issued *fatwas* against television and Pepsi-Cola. In both cases, he was driven as much by the fact that Pepsi and television had both been brought to Iran by the Baha'i Sabet family as by any intrinsic Islamic opposition to them. He also tried to block the launch of the first private university in Iran, which was a pet project of the Shah. The temptations of radio and television, and the novelty of Pepsi proved more powerful to the people than even Boroujerdi's *fatwas,* and the Shah was too enamored of the idea of a private university to succumb to the Ayatollah's pressure. But the Shah did not want to challenge the clergy on the land reform issue as well—at least not yet.

Another issue that roused the ire of the clergy, as well as that of many of the radical leaders of the Arab world, was the Shah's July 24, 1959, announcement that Iran had extended de facto recognition to the state of Israel. The surprising announcement was made in the course of a press conference when the Shah was visiting India, with no advance warning. Even the Iranian Foreign Ministry had received no early warning. The announcement was made only after some Arab papers "exposed" Iran's close ties to Israel, but as the Shah pointed out, Iran had recognized Israel virtually from the moment the Jewish state was created. Iran and Turkey were the only Muslim states that had afforded Israel de facto diplomatic recognition. Iran and Israel had by then established close and elaborate intelligence, military, propaganda, and economic ties. SAVAK and Mossad worked closely on a wide range of issues.[44]

From the moment the Shah made Iran's de facto relations with Israel public, he came under pressure from opposite sides of the political spectrum. On the one hand, Israel and its allies inside Iran pressured the Shah to elevate the level of diplomatic ties to de jure recognition allowing the two countries to officially exchange ambassadors. The Israeli Ambassador in Iran was treated as a fully accredited ambassador, but in strict diplomatic terms he was called not an ambassador but a "trade officer." At the same time, some in the Shah's regime, like Ardeshir Zahedi, were in favor of a more discreet relationship with Israel and friendlier relations with Arab states such as Egypt.[45]

The Shiite clergy too began an orchestrated campaign against the Shah and Israel. Nasser of Egypt spared no effort to criticize the Shah for "stabbing" the Muslims in the back in their fight against Israel. For the next decade, a proxy war of attrition using propaganda and disinformation raged on between Iran and Egypt, and the Shah became all but obsessed with Nasser. He saw Nasser's hands in everything from the 1958 coup in Iraq to disturbances in Lebanon and Saudi Arabia. In particular, the Shah was convinced that the "Arab separatist" movement that had appeared in the Khuzestan province of Iran was Nasser's first ploy for eventually claiming "Southwest Iran as an Arab land."[46] By 1966, a group called "the Arabistan Liberation Front," established in Cairo, issued a statement claiming that, "Arabistan was determined to recover its lands."[47] In the next few years, in nearly every meeting with Western leaders, the Shah would raise the specter of Nasser. Every hint of rapprochement between a Western country and Egypt worried the Shah and usually led him to raise the issue with the leaders of that country.

The aborted land reform, the establishment of the Pahlavi Foundation, the "Whence Your Fortune Law?" and limits on the royal family's financial activities were part of economic changes the Shah brought about under pressure from a concerned Eisenhower administration. But the Shah also promised American officials that he would "limit his participation in government" and that the next election would "be free."[48]

In spite of this promise, repeated more than once in private and in public, the next election to the twentieth session of the Majlis "was a fiasco," even more openly corrupt than usual. The Shah was forced to "take steps to void it" even before it was complete. But after announcing his intention on August 25, 1960, he found himself in a double bind. On the one hand, he wanted to show his democratic authenticity by canceling a flawed election; on the other hand, canceling elections by royal fiat would not be perceived as a democratic gesture. His solution was politically clever but constitutionally untenable. In his August 27 press conference, the Shah declared that, though he was not constitutionally "entitled to cancel elections, but could only dissolve" the Majlis, in this instance, "if the people, but genuinely the people and not a few agitators... should give me to understand that they sincerely desire" the annulment of the current election, "I will take action, in accordance with their demand, even if it is outside the law."[49]

Political groups in the country like the loyal "opposition" Mardom Party, as well as governors and government officials began, on cue, an orchestrated show of disgust by sending telegrams to the Shah requesting the annulment of the election. Genuine opposition groups, as well as "independent" figures like Ali Amini, who had run in the election, were also loudly complaining about the rigged election. On September 1, 1960, the last act of the carefully choreographed drama took place. By then the Shah had come up with a clever new way of annulling the election without going "outside the law." He issued a statement pointing "to the unsatisfactory nature" of the election and asked for "the collective resignation of deputies"[50] elected in the contested election, thus paving the way for a new election.

But the Shah also needed someone to blame for the flawed election. On August 28, 1960, he forced Prime Minister Manouchehr Egbal to resign. Many in Iran, including foreign diplomats, believed that by "operating constantly in the name of the Shah," Egbal had done him a disservice, creating a situation where disgruntled citizens blamed "the government and the sovereign together."[51] But now that a scapegoat was needed, Egbal obliged by resigning and quietly bearing the occasionally vicious attacks. Though he was the subject of constant attacks for rigging the election, it was clear that Egbal was by no means the "only agent of electoral fraud"—everyone from the Shah to General Bakhtiyar, Alam, and Egbal had participated. But Egbal was picked to take the fall. The choice was particularly ironic, some would say poetic justice. Egbal had turned sycophancy into an art and became infamous for signing his letters to the Shah as "Your House-born Slave"—*Golame Khane Zad.* According to one seasoned British diplomat, Egbal had become a "laughing stock because of his vanity, coupled with sycophancy and determination to be photographed as often as possible with the Shah."[52] He had even managed to have one of his two daughters married off to Mahmoud, one of the Shah's half-brothers.

Egbal's tenure as prime minister had lasted over three years. He did more than any other prime minister before him to ease, indeed invite, the Shah's domination of every facet of the Iranian government, and in return, all he seemed to expect was to be retained as prime minister. But he was first forced to resign and then flee the country, fearing for his life.

A few months before his forced resignation, Egbal had complained about the Shah to the British and American ambassadors in Tehran, who found him "profoundly depressed." The Shah, Egbal lamented, "has no confidence in him" and cavorted with what he called "louche characters." What had particularly hurt Egbal was that the Shah had "summoned a meeting of ministers . . . and told them that he was the fountain head of all authority." To the surprise of both the British and the American ambassadors, Egbal ended by saying he had no intention of resigning. Now he was forced to resign[53] and faced the real possibility of going to prison. The Shah valued loyalty, and Egbal's readiness to play his assigned role was amply rewarded as soon as the political climate allowed it.

The Shah's first choice as Egbal's replacement was his trusted minister of Court, Hussein Ala. But Ala was nothing if not cautious and aware of his own limits. The ongoing crisis, he sensed, was more than he could manage, and thus he "excused himself."[54] The Shah then decided to appoint Ja'far Sharif-Emami as prime minister.

Sharif-Emami had already served as a minister in several cabinets. During World War II, he had been amongst the group of about 200 Iranians arrested by the British on the charge of being Nazi sympathizers. By 1960 he was known as the Grand Master of Masonic Lodges in Iran; in the dominant political discourse of the time, membership in the Freemasonic Lodges was tantamount to treason and to subservience to the interests of the British Empire. He was also one of only three men who refused to kiss the Shah's hands in official ceremonies, a mandatory gesture for Iranian politicians at the time. Sharif-Emami also had a badly tarnished reputation for financial corruption, but he did have one thing in his favor. He was the son of a mullah and was by marriage related to the Moazzami family, faithful allies of Mossadeq and close friends of important figures in the National Front. However, the family connection failed to provide any tangible political advantages. No one from the National Front agreed to join the Sharif-Emami cabinet. Moreover, Sharif-Emami's response to the socioeconomic crisis was to simply offer higher wages to everyone—something neither the government nor the recession-enfeebled private sector employers could afford.

Sharif-Emami was also adamantly opposed to the "stabilization program" developed by the United States to solve Iran's economic ills. He placed his brother-in-law Ahmad Aramesh in charge of the Plan Organization—the heart and soul of the "stabilization program" and of Iran's development plans. In short order, Aramesh dismantled nearly all that Abolhassan Ebtehaj had put in place at the Plan Organization.[55] Why the Shah imagined that someone with Sharif-Emami's background, reputation, and qualifications could solve the country's chronic and serious problems in those heady days is a mystery. One may wonder if the appointment of a Freemason was the Shah's way to use Britain to counter American pressures on his regime. But the short-lived Sharif-Emami tenure only exacerbated the crisis he was supposed to resolve.

In order to mollify the increasingly vocal opposition, the Shah repeated his promise of a free and fair election in a radio address. A handful of opposition figures, including Alahyar Saleh, the revered leader of the National Front, were allowed to run. In private, however, the Shah told the British and American ambassadors that his intention was something less than an actual "free election." He told these officials that he would "select the candidates himself, at least two for each"[56] seat, and then allow the people of each district to actually choose between the two. This was in fact the way Reza Shah had held "free elections" during his time. After August 1953, the Shah insisted on "electing" all the representatives himself. Only during the two-year tenure of General Zahedi (1953– 1955) did the Shah agree to "allow the Prime Minister [to] 'select' half of the members [of the Majlis]."

Though the Shah's new proposed style of "election" was far from democratic, it was a big step forward for him. Only a few months earlier he had told the American Ambassador that it was "too early to have free elections, even from pre-chosen candidates."[57] Now he was planning to have just such pre-chosen candidates and then wanted to order local officials "not to stuff ballots." But as he soon learned, old habits die hard, and entrenched interest in each district, particularly the "rotten boroughs" of the landed gentry, were all but impossible to peacefully dislodge.

Adding to these mounting domestic problems was the election of John Kennedy in America. More than once in his *Daily Journals,* Alam claims that the Shah made illegal contributions to the Nixon presidential campaign in 1960 and did so again in 1968. Other sources have claimed that through an emissary, the Shah informed the newly elected President Kennedy that "[a] mistake had been made" and that he had been acting "on the advice of ill-meaning individuals."[58]

In fact, Nixon's 1953 visit to Iran as vice president had begun what would become a close lifelong friendship between him and the Shah, often laced with gifts of caviar and rugs from the Shah, notes of profuse gratitude, and on at least one occasion a book from Nixon. On January 27, 1955, Nixon wrote to the Shah, "it was most thoughtful of you to remember Mrs. Nixon and me, as you did, during the holiday season with the caviar. This delicacy happens to be a particular favorite of Mrs. Nixon."[59]

In 1956, one of these gifts almost derailed Nixon's political career when allegations of financial malfeasance almost led to his removal from the Republican ticket. One of the charges against Nixon at the time was that he had accepted a rug as a gift from the Shah. Nixon had neither reported the expensive gift nor turned it over to the government, as the law required. Nixon claimed that the gift had been not for him but for his wife, who was not required by law to report any gift she received. As Nixon was giving a speech to exonerate himself, the rug his chair was sitting on was in fact the one given to him by the Shah.

The Shah's trepidations about what the Kennedy administration had in store for him were evident in a one-hundred-line letter he wrote to the new president on January 26, 1961, just six days after the inauguration. On February 6, the Shah received a six-line response.

The Shah's letter, as much a plea for instant American aid as a lesson in his version of Iranian history, began by his declaration of joy "at the prospects of a young and vigorous personality taking into his hands the reins of government."

He then waxed eloquent about Iran's "ancient Zoroastrian creed" that "teaches us that in the eternal struggle between the power of good and the genius of evil," the good wins. He praised Kennedy's inaugural address for its positive disposition and its willingness to emphasize the promises of the future instead of doggedly dwelling on the problems of the past. Iran, too, he said, "can look forward to a brilliant future."[60]

His optimism grew out of his relentless desire to make Iran a modern nation, comparable to the West; such a desire had been an essential part of his vision from his earliest days on the throne. Knowing full well that Kennedy had criticized his authoritarian rule during the presidential campaign, and hoping to preempt any pressure on him to democratize, the Shah wrote in his January letter that "in all humility, it can be safely asserted that within the compass of the several hundred million people who struggle for existence in our neighborhood...Iran is the one country that enjoys a democratic regime with all the freedoms except the freedom to commit treason."[61]

Finally, lest the Kennedy administration be tempted to increase pressure on him to bring the National Front back to power, the Shah, in a thinly disguised attack on Mossadeq, criticized those who "tried to govern by instituting martial law throughout its tenure of power, by intimidation, by blackmail, by mob rule, and finally by surrender to the domination of communism."

Iran, the Shah told Kennedy, is "the key to a vast region in which actually 260 million tons of oil are extracted annually, all of which flows to the Western or non-communist countries." Iran was, according to the Shah, also the key "to Asia; it will also be the key to Africa in near future."[62] The Shah ended the surprisingly long letter by declaring that "to maintain stability and security," Iran is "in need of assistance which only America can furnish."[63] Kennedy's response to the Shah's impassioned letter was a terse, formal note, bereft of any promise of help.

The response expectedly added to the Shah's anxiety. Less than a month later, he took the unusual step of sending yet another personal letter to Kennedy, this time using General Bakhtiyar as his personal emissary. The American Embassy in Tehran tried to dissuade the Shah from sending the second note, but their effort was for naught. Long before Bakhtiyar arrived in Washington, the contents of the confidential letter he was carrying "had fortuitously come into" the possession of the United States! On February 28, days before his meeting with Bakhtiyar, President Kennedy received a memo divulging the contents of the letter and offering some "talking points" he might use in his meeting with the General.

In the letter, the Shah articulated several key concerns. He was, he said, concerned that "in the case of a détente with the USSR," the United States would "abandon Iran to the Soviets." He also feared that because of the perceived undemocratic nature of his own rule, "the US may encourage the activities of the opposition." Kennedy was advised to emphasize "his admiration for recent progress" in Iran and reassure the Shah that the United States would never abandon "free nations to Soviet Imperialism."[64] The letter also included an urgent plea for more U.S. assistance. Here too Kennedy was advised to make a vague but encouraging promise.

The actual meeting between Kennedy and Bakhtiyar took place on March 1, 1961. The issue of aid, according to the memorandum of that conversation, was the central issue of the discussion. Kennedy promised to consider the Shah's request for more aid and, as further "evidence of [America's] continuing deep interest in Iran, he was," he said, sending Ambassador-at-Large Averell Harriman to visit the Shah. Kennedy later said that he would send his reply to the Shah's letter through the American Embassy and then ended the meeting by asking the General whether he had already met with Allen Dulles, the director of the CIA.[65] The apparently innocuous question turned out to refer to an event that changed Bakhtiyar's life.

Upon his return home, Bakhtiyar complained to the Shah about the way he had been treated in Washington. "I was kept waiting for almost three weeks," he told the Shah, "before I was given an appointment with Kennedy." In fact, Bakhtiyar had arrived on February 16, and on the same day, Ardeshir Zahedi, the Iranian ambassador, informed the State Department of the General's arrival and of his desire to personally deliver the Shah's confidential letter to the President.[66] Almost exactly two weeks later, at ten in the morning of March 1, Bakhtiyar, accompanied by a translator, walked in the Oval Office.

But even before Bakhtiyar arrived back in Tehran the Shah had learned that he had secretly met with Allen Dulles, the director of the CIA, and Kermit Roosevelt, the head of the Middle East section of the CIA. The Shah also knew that, in the course of that meeting, Bakhtiyar had attacked the Shah and had solicited America's help or approval for his plan to overthrow him. As soon as the meeting ended, Roosevelt, who had developed a close relationship with the Shah since August 1953, called to tell him about Bakhtiyar's betrayal. Roosevelt himself admitted to not only meeting with Bakhtiyar but also reporting its content to the Shah.[67] In the next decade, the Shah rewarded Roosevelt generously for his services. As for Bakhtiyar, the Shah decided to wait for the right opportunity to get rid of him.

By then Bakhtiyar had built for himself a conspicuously majestic mansion near the Shah's palace and had made a habit of giving infamously loud and lavish parties there. In spite of his marriage, he cavorted around town with his lover in one of his many expensive cars. He had also developed a reputation for brazen financial corruption and for the exorbitant gifts that he gave and received;

amongst the diplomatic corps he was increasingly referred to as the second-most powerful man in Iran. These facts all worked to make Bakhtiyar the Shah's most dangerous and despised enemy.

As the Shah pondered his Bakhtiyar problem, the Kennedy administration was finishing the arduous task of transition, and the question of Iran loomed large on the horizon. Philips Talbot, a seasoned diplomat with considerable experience in the Middle East, was named to head the interagency task force on Iran. The urgency of the issue was made more apparent in early May with the start of the teachers' strike in Tehran. In later years, the Shah became convinced, particularly after repeated suggestions by Alam and by Sharif-Emami, that the United States had instigated even the teachers' strike. Sharif-Emami, for example, claims that a sudden big infusion of cash was added to the bank account set aside to support striking teachers. He also claims that on the day of the big strike, "a foreign officer" was seen riding a motorcycle and guiding the demonstrators.[68]

The teachers' strike left an indelible mark on the Shah's political psyche, as well as on the Kennedy administration's perception of the internal situation in Iran. Sharif-Emami too was undone by the strike. On May 2, 1961, up to 50,000 people, mostly teachers and students, demonstrated for higher pay. The government had brought out the army to face the demonstrators. One person—Dr. Khan'ali—was killed, and the death only radicalized the movement and helped swell its ranks. The Shah was particularly distraught because, according to reliable sources, it was estimated that "there is slightly better than fifty percent chance" that in the next few days, the army, if called up, would fire on demonstrating teachers. The American Embassy concluded that if another major disturbance should take place on May 4 or 5, "and should security forces refuse to fire in the event of need," the Shah's regime "may be gravely threatened."[69]

The telegram reporting the May 3 disturbance, and the possibility of the army's refusal to fire on the next day's planned demonstrators, was deemed urgent enough that when it arrived at the White House at five in the morning, there was some discussion among the President's staff about whether he should be awakened and informed about its content. Ultimately, they decided to wait and Kennedy saw the report at nine o'clock that morning. The report only confirmed his belief in the necessity of rethinking U.S. policy in Iran. Kennedy gave the Talbot Task Force a far-reaching mandate. He told them to consider all options and assume that nothing in U.S. policy in Iran was sacrosanct. In other words, the idea of removing the Shah from the throne was very much on the table, and minutes of the Task Force deliberations showed clearly that the option was indeed discussed at some length.

Before long, in a memorandum prepared for the President, the Task Force informed Kennedy that "despite its much lower visibility, the continued slide toward chaos in Iran could result in as grave a set-back as in South Vietnam."[70] Iran's "half-Westernized and strategically placed forces in Iranian politics," the Task Force informed the President, were hostile to the Shah and anything connected to him. At the same time, the Task Force was consistently tempered in its thinking by the reality of the Cold War, by Iran's long borders with the Soviet Union and by the Soviet Union's constant machinations in Iran. There was a possibility that disturbing the status quo in Iran would invariably pave the way for increased influence by the Soviet Union. Eventually, the Kennedy administration was advised that it would have to help create a bridge between the Shah and the middle classes and more importantly, that it would have to help foster a "controlled revolution."[71]

Meanwhile, in Tehran, demonstrations planned for May 4 and 5 promised to be even larger and looked every bit like the beginning of the "uncontrolled" revolution the Shah had feared. "Workers, and National Front groups were scheduled to join the demonstrations on the fifth." On the night of May 3, around midnight, a distraught Shah called Prime Minister Sharif-Emami to the Court. General Nasiri, the head of the National Police, and General Alavi-Kia, deputy director of SAVAK, were also summoned. The government, the Shah told the gathered officials, had received intelligence that on the following day, the striking teachers planned to use the body of Dr. Khan'ali to incite the demonstrators to a frenzied pitch and to violence. The Shah wanted the security forces to move in the dark of the night and use their assets and connections to make sure the next day's demonstrators did not have access to Khan'ali's body. General Nasiri reassured the Shah that his police forces had everything under control and that arrangements had already been made to make the body unavailable for use by demonstrators.[72]

But Nasiri failed to deliver. Early the next morning, long before the police arrived on the scene, the demonstrators were already in possession of the body. Sharif-Emami was by then convinced that there was "a conspiracy afoot" and that secret hands were at work to depose him and his government. He had apparently concluded that the Shah himself might have been one of those working behind the scenes to topple the Sharif-Emami cabinet. There is, in fact, in Sharif-Emami's Harvard Oral History interview an unmistakable pattern of serious criticism of the Shah. The irony is the fact that Sharif-Emami was considered to be one of the Shah's most trusted advisors and allies. The Shah even chose him to head the Pahlavi Foundation—a post he kept for nearly the entire period of the foundation's existence.

Early on that night of May 4, when the Shah heard about the situation, he grew anxious and agitated and was "reportedly extremely upset and ready to flee the country."[73] The gradual grind of disturbing news had by then clearly taken its toll on him. Late on the night of May 4, he finally accepted the resignation of an angry, even belligerent Sharif-Emami. Earlier that morning, in an appearance before the parliament, Sharif-Emami had been berated and attacked by members of the parliament and asked to account for the death of Dr. Khan'ali. Sharif-Emami felt, not unreasonably, that such attacks could not have taken place without at least the Shah's tacit consent. He felt betrayed, but at the same time, he felt beleaguered and bereft of options.[74] In submitting his resignation that night, he shouted at the Shah, asking why he had allowed him to be publicly humiliated in the parliament. "Why couldn't you simply ask for my resignation?" he asked angrily.[75] Sharif-Emami also believed firmly that his opposition to the American stabilization program was the real reason for the demonstrations against his cabinet. He now had no choice but to resign. When he met the Shah to tender his resignation, the Shah looked tired and listless, anxious and angry. Faced with Sharif-Emami's angry outburst, the Shah made a perfunctory attempt to convince him to stay on for a few more days, but Sharif-Emami obviously knew that his turn at the helm had ended, and the Shah accepted his resignation. Before long, he reluctantly offered the job to Ali Amini.

Amini had been anticipating the call from the Court. He consulted with some of his trusted friends, amongst them Abolhassan Ebtehaj, about what he should do when the formal call came. They all counseled that he should stand firm and demand concessions from the clearly weakened Shah. At the Court, Amini told an exhausted Shah that he would accept the job "on the condition he be given broad powers."[76] The Shah agreed but insisted on keeping for himself the right to appoint the three crucial ministries of Interior (in charge of the police), Foreign Affairs, and War (in charge of the military). With SAVAK, the police, and the military at his disposal, and with these three ministries under his control, the Shah still had more power than the constitution allowed and far less than he himself desired. While he planned his strategy in coping with a new ambitious and assertive prime minister, the Shah was still anxiously awaiting a chance to meet the new American president.

Chapter 14

GARRULOUS PREMIER

My Lord, wise men ne'er wail their present woes,
But presently prevent the ways to wail.
Shakespeare, King Richard II, *3.2.173–174*

Ali Amini had something of Polonius in him. Beginning with his first acceptance speech as the prime minister, through his many, many, many subsequent radio chats and public lectures, he came to be known for his long, sometimes meandering speeches. His garrulous nature came to be a favorite subject for satirists who made fun of his volubility and of his attempt to use words and verbiage as a balm and a substitute for jobs and real change. For the Shah, a phrase in one of Amini's talks where he declared the Iranian economy bankrupt was a convincing sign of either his unsavory intentions or his dangerously irresponsible discourse. It mattered little to the Shah that the Iranian economy had indeed been practically bankrupt for years and had survived only thanks to the infusion of millions of dollars of aid from the United States or that, at the time Amini made the announcement, the Iranian government did not have enough money to pay its most rudimentary expenses.[1] The Shah did have a point, however, in arguing that even if the economic realities were dire, the Amini announcement made them worse and frightened away millions of dollars of potential investments. In reality, the Shah's dislike of Amini was rooted as much in blood as in politics.

Amini had "Qajar blood" in him. He was a grandson of a Qajar king. His mother, Fakhr al-Dowleh, was considered by Reza Shah to be one of the most powerful and assertive members of the Qajar dynasty. She is "the only man the Qajar family has produced," Reza Shah reportedly said. In politics and in business, she was assertive, ambitious, and willing to go where few other women of her generation and class dared to tread. In business, for example, she launched the first modern taxi service in the country, something aristocratic women deemed "beneath their dignity." In politics, she was widely connected to different centers of power and unabashedly used her network of friends and family to promote her favorite son's career. She considered the premier's office something of a family heirloom and wanted her Ali to return the family to its days of glory.

If a dangerous and despised bloodline was not enough to poison the Shah's relations with Amini, there was also the question of politics. The Shah never trusted Ali Amini, considering him dangerously ambitious, incorrigibly opportunistic, and shamelessly "America's boy." From 1950 to 1955, when the Shah was in the fight of his life with the three most powerful politicians of his tenure—Qavam, Mossadeq, and General Zahedi—Amini was a member of all three men's cabinets. He was a protégé of Qavam and a blood relative of Mossadeq; General Zahedi too was a distant relative, but with him Amini had more a marriage of convenience than of shared political passions. It was a measure of Amini's character—his opportunism or knack for survival—that he eventually turned against all three prime ministers. The pinnacle of power was what Amini coveted, and neither he nor his mother would be satisfied with anything less.

No sooner had General Zahedi established his headquarters at the Officer's Club on the afternoon of August 19, 1953, than Fakhr al-Dowleh called, asking the General "not to forget my Ali."[2] There was at that time still no ministerial portfolio designated for Amini, but luck intervened. The first two candidates for the post of finance minister could not be located in the chaos of that bloody day. By late on August 18, many of the royalists had gone into hiding, fearing the end of the monarchy. Some were late in returning to their homes. Desperate to form a full cabinet before the end of the day, General Zahedi, according to his son Ardeshir Zahedi, named Amini to the vacant post of finance minister.[3]

A few months later, while Amini was still the finance minister, the Shah asked him "whether he did not look forward to being a Prime Minister." Amini's cautiously affirmative response only begot a more ominous question from the Shah. Was he not looking forward "to something more than Prime Minister"?[4] the Shah asked. The implication of the question was hard to miss. Just like his father, the Shah believed that the politically ambitious members of the Qajar family had designs on the Pahlavi throne. And Amini was nothing if not ambitious.

Even in exile, after having witnessed Amini's willingness to help save the Pahlavi throne in 1979, the Shah still disparaged him as America's "own man." At the same time, in the early days of the Kennedy administration, Amini was for the Shah the lesser of two evils. The Shah was under pressure from the United States to reconcile with the National Front and bring them into a coalition government. Even after the Amini appointment, U.S. pressure for such a reconciliation continued. The majority of the National Front leadership ultimately decided against making peace with the Shah. The memory of August 19, 1953, and the fall of Dr. Mossadeq were fresh on their minds. Mossadeq was still under virtual house arrest and barred from taking part in politics. Though they were ostensibly representative of Iran's moderate middle class, the leaders of the National Front preferred puritan but quixotic militancy over pragmatic realism. In the famous words of Khalil Maleki—himself a supporter of Mossadeq, a onetime leader of the National Front, and the lone voice advocating the wisdom of a pragmatic reconciliation with the Shah, particularly against what he considered the patently more reactionary clergy—"these [National Front] leaders are not even demagogues but merely followers of the demos."[5]

But the Shah, too, was adamantly against the idea of reconciliation. He used thinly disguised language to attack the National Front leaders for making peace with separatists in Azerbaijan in 1946. He chastised them for using the cover of night to meet with representatives of foreign governments and to "benefit financially from these contacts, and then poison the atmosphere."[6] A National Front government, he told the American Ambassador in a private luncheon at Asadollah Alam's home, "would be a precursor of communist takeover." The leaders of the National Front, the Shah went on to say, have "no purpose except to come to power." Moreover, their organization has been "badly infiltrated by communists."[7]

Aside from the age-old argument that the National Front would pave the way for Communism—the argument used by the British in 1952 when they were trying to convince the Truman administration to join in the effort to topple Mossadeq—the Shah in 1961 also offered a different argument against the idea of such a coalition. On numerous occasions he told American and British officials that in Iran, the Shah has "always been the center of power." Without a powerful king, the center could not hold. This time, cognizant of the Kennedy administration's keen interest in introducing reforms in Iran, the Shah told the American Ambassador that if there were to be any meaningful reform in Iran, it had to come under the aegis of the Shah and no one else. He also made it clear on numerous occasions that "he would abdicate rather than accept [the] position of a figurehead."[8] That was why appointing Amini was, compared to sharing power with the National Front, for the Shah the lesser of two evils—but an evil nevertheless.

That might also explain why the Amini appointment in May 1961 was a surprise to nearly everyone, including Amini himself. Though he had coveted this post all his adult life, when he was summoned to the Court and asked by the Shah to form a government, he was, according to the U.S. Embassy, surprisingly "unprepared for the job both in regard [to] having a program and a nucleus of capable individuals to help him discharge the heavy task he assumed."[9]

Before accepting the job, Amini insisted on having more power and independence than had previous prime ministers, but he still did not have complete freedom to form his cabinet. The Shah insisted on keeping his "right" to name the ministers to the three key ministries of War, Foreign Affairs, and Interior. The rest of the cabinet, hastily put together, was a coalition of lapsed Communists, Socialists, and independent critics and opponents of the Shah. There was also one leader of the National Front—Gholam Ali Farivar—who had joined the cabinet as an individual and not as a member of the organization; even so, he resigned before long under pressure from his comrades.

Another controversial appointment was Nouraldin Alamouti, named by Amini to the key Ministry of Justice. Alamouti had been a member of the famous Group of Fifty-Three, Communist intellectuals led by Taghi Arani who had been arrested during the reign of Reza Shah. It was believed that Alamouti would vigorously go after those accused of graft and would not even spare members of the royal family.

But the most controversial member of the Amini cabinet was easily Hassan Arsanjani, the minister of agriculture. Like Amini, Arsanjani was an old hand in Iranian politics, but unlike Amini, he had been unrestrained in his criticism of the Shah. He was a charismatic orator, a muckraking journalist, a self-styled Socialist by avocation, and a lawyer by vocation. What made his career particularly fit the appointment was that he advocated the necessity of land reform in Iran. Like Amini, he had once been a protégé of Qavam, and a friend and accomplice of General Gharani, the mastermind of the failed 1958 coup. In the very days when he was negotiating with the Shah's regime over his plans to establish a social democratic party, Arsanjani was secretly conspiring with Gharani to organize a coup.

The Arsanjani appointment became even more important when it emerged that implementing a land reform would be the centerpiece of Amini's plans for the "controlled revolution" he had come to lead. There is something of a consensus amongst scholars and politicians that Arsanjani's radicalism and charisma, his ambitions and his political acumen, made the Amini plan for land reform far more radical than initially intended. When the American Embassy expressed concern about Arsanjani's increasing radicalism, Amini reassured them by suggesting that such rhetoric was initially needed for "taking the wind out of the sails of the National Front."[10] At an appropriate time, Amini assured the American Ambassador, "he would accept [Arsanjani's] offer to resign."[11]

The Shah, too, began to worry about Arsanjani as he watched him give more and more rousing speeches against feudalism and landowners. Larger and larger audiences of peasants were bused into the cities and used as props for demonstrations that had more and more the discomforting aura of despotic populism. In a meeting with Israel's ambassador to Iran, Meir Ezry, the Shah asked the ambassador what he thought of Arsanjani. The Shah must have known that Arsanjani had developed close ties with Israel, whose advisors were at the time helping Iran develop large industrial agribusinesses. The Shah was himself an avid fan and advocate of these large-scale industrial farms. In response to the Shah's loaded question, Ezry gave an equally loaded response: Arsanjani was "not a minister of agriculture but minister of peasants." As Ezry himself observes, this "was a warning to the Shah,"[12] who began following Arsanjani's populism more closely.

Amini's reforms also included education, government services, election laws, and fighting corruption amongst government officials. Lest he be seen as a mere observer of the ongoing "controlled revolution," on November 14, 1961, the Shah issued a *firman*, decreeing that the Amini government was to continue full force with its reforms, particularly in education, improving the living standards of the poor, eliminating corruption, land reform, and eradicating corruption in the government. Though the royal decree was more a symbolic gesture than a serious policy statement, Amini played along, and the next day convened an emergency meeting of his ministers at which he informed them of the Shah's decree and asked them to redouble their efforts in implementing His Royal Majesty's command.

About this time, Amini also sent a trusted advisor and a member of his inner circle, Khodadad Farmanfarmaian, on a secret mission to Germany. Ostensibly, the purpose of the trip was to negotiate a German loan. In fact, Farmanfarmaian was also there to secretly meet with Robert Kennedy, the U.S. attorney general. Farmanfarmaian asked him, on behalf of Amini himself, that the United States show more public support for the Shah. An insecure Shah, Amini knew, was a ticking bomb.[13]

On the afternoon of November 15, 1961, the day Amini convened an emergency meeting of his cabinet to discuss the royal decree, in another corner of the city, the Shah was on hand to open the country's first bowling alley. Azar Ebtehaj, the assertive, ambitious, and beautiful wife of Abolhassan Ebtehaj, the onetime head of the Plan Organization, was one of the two partners who had introduced bowling to the country. The club, known simply as "The Bowling," became an overnight sensation in the capital. Its restaurant was the city's hot spot where the "jet setters" gathered. Since Soraya's days, the Shah had become an avid bowler and had a private lane constructed at the palace where he played regularly. After the launch of "The Bowling" the Shah sometimes played there. Though the royal presence added a certain cachet to "The Bowling," it was a financial drain since, on the Shah's nights for security reasons, the establishment would be ordered to keep all other customers out.[14] But there was another connection between the bowling alley and the cabinet meeting discussing the Shah's order.

Aside from the land reform, the most controversial new policy of the Amini government was the fight against corruption. A number of high-ranking officials of the regime were arrested and charged with embezzlement and misuse of public funds. Easily the most controversial act of the Amini government's anti-corruption campaign was the arrest of Abolhassan Ebtehaj. The arrest was particularly startling because Ebtehaj was known for his financial probity and considered Amini a close friend.

Since his appointment as the director of the Plan Organization in 1955, Ebtehaj had survived in power simply because of the Shah's support. His stern style of management, his no-nonsense attitude, his willingness to take on entrenched interests, his relentless attempt to streamline the country's economic planning decisions on his own, his distrust of Iranian contractors, and his belief that in those years only Western companies could be entrusted with big contracts and big projects had all worked to make him many enemies among the elite.

For years, the increasingly swollen ranks of his foes had constantly conspired against him. Their efforts failed in no small measure because of the Shah's support of Ebtehaj. Manouchehr Egbal and General Fazlollah Zahedi, two of the prime ministers during Ebtehaj's tenure at the Plan Organization, were his unabashed enemies, but neither could dislodge him from his perch of power. The fact that Western banks and lending institutions trusted and supported Ebtehaj further contributed to his ability to survive his enemies' machinations.

The Shah tended to divide key Iranian politicians between those "connected" to the United States and those with ties to Britain. However, he was confused about Ebtehaj. More than once, he asked the British and American ambassadors whether they thought Ebtehaj was "connected" to either power. In September 1955, for example, he told the British Ambassador that "the Americans thought Ebtehaj was pro-British." The Ambassador answered that in his embassy, some thought Ebtehaj "was pro-American."[15] The truth seems to be that both embassies thought Ebtehaj an unusually competent and reliable financier and an honest public servant but a bit of an eccentric genius. But by 1959 Ebtehaj's luck was running out.

On January 24, 1959, on a cold day when the Shah was bedridden with the flu, after numerous ignored requests, Ebtehaj was finally given an audience. One of the Shah's well-known ways to punish or show dismay with an official was to refuse to see him. Even if he ran into someone in an official ceremony, he would avoid exchanging even a glance with them. In his *Daily Journals*, Alam describes many such episodes. Ebtehaj, who had for years been able to get a meeting with the Shah almost at will, was now getting the cold shoulder. After a few rebuffed attempts, he finally threatened to quit going to work unless the Shah agreed to meet with him. January 24 was set for the meeting.

A few days earlier, Ebtehaj had submitted his resignation to the Shah but had heard nothing back. But now, as Ebtehaj talked, the weak and sniffling Shah simply listened without uttering a word. Ebtehaj talked of his increasing tensions with many of the country's political leaders. He also tried to make the case that the Iranian economy could not sustain the level of military expenditures the Shah consistently pressed for. The Shah said nothing; silence was another of his known discursive tools for displaying displeasure and dismay.

Though the Shah was angry with Ebtehaj and accepted his resignation, he still rejected the calls for his arrest. Knowing full well that the danger of arrest hung over his head, Ebtehaj put on the pretense of enjoying his unexpected retirement. He started work on launching a private bank, and before long, he and his wife had established the Iranian Bank—with much of the capital provided by Western banks. Azar was chosen to sit on the board of the bank, becoming the first woman to attain such a high status in the world of Iranian finance.

At the same time, Ebtehaj spent some of his time playing golf, a favorite pastime. One of his eccentricities was that, even before golf became the game of the rich and powerful in Tehran, he would occasionally appear at meetings dressed in his golf attire. He had played a role in helping a man named Khaybar Khan build Tehran's first golf course. Khaybar Khan was a flamboyant Iranian-born businessman who had returned to Iran in 1958 and set up a flashy office, hired a bevy of beautiful young women who were as much escorts as secretaries and receptionists, gave lavish parties and expensive gifts, and drove around in a Cadillac. Before long, through his friendship with Ebtehaj, Khaybar Khan had established close ties among the Iranian elite, including some members of the royal family. But by the time of Ebtehaj's resignation, Khaybar Khan had returned to the United States, and by 1962, he was talking to the American media and testifying before Congress about what he alleged was massive corruption and misuse of American foreign aid by the Shah and a few other members of the royal family. For the next five years, Khaybar Khan became nothing less than a nightmare for the Shah. The saga continued until well into 1965, at which time a federal court did in fact order all of the Shah's U.S. accounts frozen. The banks where the accounts were held immediately informed Mehdi Samii, a trusted confidante of the Shah, that unless they moved the assets before the banks opened the next day, the accounts of the Shah and, in fact, of all the royal family, would be frozen. Samii contacted the Shah and received the requisite instructions to move the accounts, but before any action was necessary, another court overturned the lower court's order and the danger passed. Within months of the episode, Khaybar Khan was discovered to have forged the most incriminating documents against the Shah.[16]

Some of his allegations were similar to the charges made by Ebtehaj when he participated in a conference held at Stanford University in the fall of 1960. Ebtehaj talked about the failure of U.S. policy in Iran, and how, in spite of having given a billion dollars to the country over a few years, the United States was "neither loved nor respected." The reason, he suggested, was that "where the recipient government is corrupt, the donor government very understandably appears in the judgment of the public to support corruption."[17]

When the Shah heard about the lecture, he was livid. Friends and family advised Ebtehaj not to return, telling him that the Shah would have him arrested at the airport. A few months before his departure for the United States, the Shah had been angered by Ebtehaj's heated argument with American generals against the idea of expanding the Iranian army.[18] The Shah also took umbrage at Ebtehaj's opposition to the construction of a chemical fertilizer near the city of Shiraz, a pet project of the Shah. Ebtehaj was opposed to the project not just because he felt it was economically unsound but because he suspected that Iranian officials had made illicit gains from the deal.[19]

Each of these transgressions had not been enough individually to turn the Shah against Ebtehaj, but now their collective weight was more than he could tolerate. When he least expected it, during the tenure of his friend Amini, Ebtehaj was arrested and charged with financial malfeasance and with signing sweetheart no-bid contracts with the Development Resources Corporations of David Lilienthal, the architect of the famed Tennessee Valley Authority. Lest Ebtehaj find a way to leave prison, the largest bail in Iranian history to that time was set for him.

But even in prison, Ebtehaj never shied away from expressing his often unique, sometimes contrarian views. Though he was an autodidact with little formal education, he was a brilliant banker and economist. His views on the land reform that was undertaken by the Amini government and that would eventually become the centerpiece of the White Revolution were an example of both his brilliance and his readiness to challenge received or popular opinion.

When Ebtehaj learned about the Shah's upcoming trip to the United States, he decided to write a pithy "personal and confidential" letter from prison to his "friends in America" hoping to convince them to stop the Iranian government's plans for land reform. Contrary to the landowners and the clergy, who were against the land reform as interested advocates of the status quo ante, Ebtehaj opposed the current plan because he thought it undermined the future long-term capitalist development of Iran.

In his letter, Ebtehaj offered ten reasons why the land reform as proposed was detrimental to Iran's national interest and capitalist development. Under a "capitalist system of free enterprise," he wrote in his letter from prison, "it is not right and just that a person may own any number of factories . . . but [be] denied the right to own more than a certain amount of farm land." He agreed that absentee landlordism was a curse and a problem for Iranian agriculture and the economy, but he suggested searching for ways to overcome "the drawbacks . . . without resorting to sequestration." Instead of confiscating property, he offered a "land reform brought about through a system of taxation, where farms would be taxed based on not 'actual but optimum yields.'" He proposed a simple but sophisticated system of taxation that would ultimately bring about the desired changes in the country's agricultural system without undermining the idea of private property.[20]

Ebtehaj's critique is particularly important in its contrast with the Shah's willingness, indeed eagerness, to use the discourse of revolution and the practice of forced sequestration to promote his own political ends. Before long, the Shah would begin to talk incessantly of the "White Revolution," and all manner of "sequestration" became part and parcel of the different principles of his revolution. The Shah had a pseudo-Socialist, statist vision of the economy where the state could and should become an economic leviathan. As Ebtehaj had predicted, not long after the land reform, the Shah proved willing to forcefully expropriate the country's only private television network, the first private university, and the country's richest private mine. How much did the Shah's constant conjuring of revolutionary rhetoric help make the idea and concept of revolution part and parcel of the Iranian political discourse? In other societies, the word "revolution" often brings to mind cataclysmic changes. By 1978, the word had been a constant part of Iran's political vocabulary for almost two decades, and the idea of expropriating successful businessmen had also become "normal." In 1962, neither the Shah nor Amini were willing to heed Ebtehaj's advice.

Amini tried to use the promise of land reform to convince the leaders of the National Front to temper their criticism of his government and avoid confrontations with the police and security forces. A temporary political cease-fire would afford him the chance to consolidate the shaky foundations of his power. But a new generation of activists had joined the ranks of the Front, and inspired by the revolutionary experiences in Cuba and Algeria, they kept pushing for more confrontational and radical policies. Incremental change of the kind promised by Amini was for them nothing but "repressive tolerance"—change intended to maintain the status quo.

And when the leaders of the National Front announced plans to hold a mass rally in the Jalaliye racetrack, Amini used his many connections to these leaders to ask them to forgo their planned rally. He asked for a respite of stability, a few months of peace during which he could establish his authority and fend off increasing attacks from members of the military. But the National Front would not relent. While younger leaders of the group increased their agitation at the university, leading to numerous confrontations between the government and the opposition, the elder leaders continued with plans for the Jalaliye mass rally.

The Jalaliye event was at once a tour de force and a coup de grâce for the National Front. The large field that had previously been used as a racetrack was filled with supporters. There was a prolonged—some say a fifteen-minute—exuberant show of support when the name of Dr. Mossadeq was first mentioned. For the Shah, the spectacle was nothing short of a nightmare, reminding him of his own darkest hours. Even more dangerous for the Shah was the idea that the large number of people at the rally would only convince the Kennedy administration to redouble their effort to bring the National Front into the government. But then the Shah received an unexpected bonanza from the mass rally.

When it was Shapour Bakhtiyar's turn to speak, he parted from the prepared text that had been approved by the collective leadership. Instead, he talked at great length and with frenzied fervor about the virtues of Iran's joining the ranks of nonaligned nations. By then, the nonalignment movement, launched by Indonesia's Sukarno in 1955, had become a formidable force around the world. The fact that Communist China had joined the movement made it even more suspect to American policy makers. In the Cold War vision, nonaligned nations were simply on a slippery slope, a short step from falling into the hands of the Communists. Even the State Department, till then a reliable supporter of the National Front, was not amused by the group's sudden advocacy of nonalignment. From then on, to the Shah's relief, support for the idea of offering the National Front a share of power in Iran began to wane amongst American foreign policy experts.

Moreover, the Shah made sure the embassy knew where he stood on the issue of nonalignment. In 1955, he had been one of the chief advocates of Iran's forfeiting its century-old declared neutrality and joining what was then called the Baghdad Pact (later renamed CENTO). In a meeting with the American Ambassador in 1961, the Shah emphasized that he was still adamantly opposed to "views on a neutral Iran" and considered such ideas absolutely indefensible. He indicated that in his view, Iran "must stay tied to the West, and if and when those ties should be broken, he would cease being Shah."[21] Though Amini was in many ways anathema to the Shah, he had at least the virtue that, like the Shah, he was a firm believer in the idea that Iran must not only stay in the Western orbit, but also become ever closer to the United States. Amini, too, had been a fervent advocate of Iran's joining the Baghdad Pact.

As these events unfolded in Iran, the United States was seriously studying its options with the Shah. On May 24, 1961, in a meeting of the National Security Council, President Kennedy, based on the recommendation of the Talbot Task Force, approved a new U.S. policy for Iran. For the immediate future, the new policy advocated that the United States "make a major effort to back" Amini as the "best instrument in sight for promoting orderly political and economic, and social revolution" in Iran, and ensure that there were no military coups against him. Moreover, to give Amini more room to maneuver, it was decided "the US should be prepared to tolerate certain seemingly anti-American actions by Amini which do not really damage any major American interest."[22]

Not only did continued American support for Amini not bode well for the Shah, but the long-term elements of the new American strategy did not favor him either. It was decided that while the United States supported "monarchy as the symbol of unity and a stabilizing influence in Iran," it should "more actively encourage the Shah to move toward a more constitutional role."

It was a measure of the Shah's resilience as a politician that, in spite of the great chasm that separated his own vision from the new policy prescribed by the Americans, the Shah not only stayed a close ally of the United States for the next seventeen years, but also gradually forced a reconsideration of that policy. The irony is that, ultimately, his success in defying the American push for democracy and finding his own independent path proved to be his undoing. Had the Shah remained a constitutional monarch, as the American policy proposed in 1961, instead of becoming a modernizing, albeit authoritarian monarch as the Shah wished, he might have been able to save his throne and the monarchy.

But in 1961, the Shah also had to contend with the fact that the new American policy suggested that "the US should encourage the formation and growth of broadly based political parties in Iran." Up until that time, the Shah had willed into existence a semi-official two-party system modeled on that of the United States. In the Iranian incarnation of this system, the Shah directly controlled the affairs of both parties by appointing reliable politicians to head the two listless organizations. In due course, the Shah found a solution for this problem as well.

Finally, lest the Shah be tempted to again blackmail the United States by using the Soviet Union as a bargaining chip, the new American strategy called for the United States to impress upon Iranian officials "the risk which may be involved in Iran rapprochement with the USSR."[23]

Not only the opposition, but also elements within the regime itself sensed the changing political climate. While traditional opposition parties suddenly became more active and aggressive, new groups also began to emerge. The most successful such new group was launched by Dr. Mostafa Mesbahzadeh, publisher of Tehran's most popular daily, *Keyhan.* He called his group the Rastakhiz, or "the resurgence."

Mesbahzadeh was a man of tact and had many connections amongst Iran's political cognoscenti and the intelligentsia. He was also close to such powerful political figures as Alam, and even to the Shah himself—particularly given the fact that in 1941 the Shah had provided some of the initial capital for launching *Keyhan* itself. Most important of all, as he had shown throughout his adult life, Mesbahzadeh had an unfailingly sharp nose for detecting changing political winds.

His Rastakhiz movement prompted people to converge on rented rooms, offices, and storefronts to talk about the situation in the country—discussions that often had a subtext critical of the regime. The organization rapidly spread throughout the country, and there was a clear sense of spontaneity about the movement's burst of energy and expansion. What afforded the meetings an even more unusual political air was the absence of the Shah's portrait in the halls where the group met. By then, having a portrait of the Shah in each office and store was virtually mandatory. Every movie began by showing a portrait of the Shah while the royal anthem was played, and audiences were expected to stand at attention while the portrait was on the big screen.

If the absence of royal portraits was, in the minds of the people, a sign of the movement's authentic spontaneity, it was also the cause of Rastakhiz's demise. As soon as the Shah was told about the meetings in halls with no royal portrait, he found a way of showing his displeasure to Mesbahzadeh, who was nothing if not cautious. Before long, he pulled the plug on his movement.

The Shah's relationship with Amini was far more complicated. He had to make sure that Amini did not amass too much power, but he also had to at least appear to still be supporting the cabinet. The Shah had still not met with Kennedy but was fully aware of his firm support for Amini.

For his part, Amini also knew that so long as he enjoyed the support of the United States, he would be safe in his seat of power. Early in June 1961, he dispatched his trusted advisor Khodadad Farmanfarmaian on an exploratory journey. Tehran was in those days awash with rumors that the Shah "intended to replace Amini by [Teymour] Bakhtiyar."[24] Farmanfarmaian met with a State Department official and pointedly asked whether in fact the "United States was cooling off in its support of Amini." The State Department "categorically denied" the allegation. The National Front refused to support Amini while using the freedoms he had provided to organize increasingly militant demonstrations against him and the regime. The Shah's support for Amini was at best tentative and temporary. In addition, the military and SAVAK, both staunchly royalist and worried about what Amini might do to their budgets, were also no friend of his cabinet. These factors made the Americans virtually Amini's sole source of support.

In early May 1961, the United States received intelligence that General Teymour Bakhtiyar was planning a coup against the Amini government. The General was brazen about his coup plans. He had even decided on the composition of his cabinet and began meeting with each of them separately in a garden near Tehran. To each he described his plans, offered them a portfolio, and sought their support.[25] The list of his designated ministers was eventually published in *Bakhtar Emrooz*—an opposition paper that belonged to the National Front. Many of those who remained powerful ministers in the next fifteen years, including Jamshid Amuzegar, were on the list.[26]

There were also rumors about General Bakhtiyar's attempt to form an alliance not only with the National Front, but with the Marxist Tudeh Party, as well as with the landowners opposed to the land reform and finally with the clergy. On May 17, the United States "took all steps necessary to discourage General Bakhtiyar against initiating any action against Amini."[27] With no support from the United States, with the Shah waiting for the right moment to rid himself of the dangerously meddlesome General, and with Amini keen on getting rid of this overambitious foe, Bakhtiyar's days were now clearly numbered.

But Bakhtiyar was not the only general conspiring against Amini. On May 15, around the same time that Bakhtiyar was planning his coup, General Hajj Ali Kia, who had been jailed on charges of financial corruption, sent a trusted emissary to the U.S. government with a message that suggested they should either plan a coup, "in which case General Kia promised the full support of his assets," or at least support a coup, "which he planned to initiate on his own." The United States responded that the "US government completely supports the current government," and has "no desire to encourage activities directed" against Amini, and would in fact "strongly discourage such activities."[28] It is not known whether the Shah knew about, or was later informed about these attempted military coups.

But at the same time, while the United States deterred ambitious generals from attempting a coup against Amini, they also decided that a "public declaration of support" for him would be the "crystallization of the Shah's fear and suspicion of Amini"[29] as "America's boy." Eventually, they decided to send Edward Mason to Tehran. He had been the head of the Harvard Advisory Group that had in 1958 helped develop a stabilization program for Iran.[30] Mason's mandate was to appraise the situation and estimate Amini's chances of survival.

The Shah, on the other hand, was still trying to arrange for a speedy meeting with President Kennedy. In addition to his two long personal notes—the first on January 26 and the second through General Bakhtiyar on March 1, 1961—he pressured the American Embassy in Tehran for an early invitation for a state visit to the United States.

The Kennedy White House was less than enthusiastic about proffering such an invitation to the Shah. They did not want the Shah to erroneously assume that the United States was now content with the situation in Iran. In other words, they wanted to keep the Shah both anxious and guessing about America's intentions. Robert Kennedy was particularly opposed to the idea of inviting the Shah anytime soon. The Shah, he said, was "not a beloved figure" in his country and there was little "advantage in having him here." According to Kennedy, there was even a chance that the Shah "may be ousted."[31]

The embassy in Tehran, sensing White House reluctance, tried to change the administration's mind by pointing to the Shah's dangerously fragile state of mind. The embassy reminded the White House that the Shah was now in one of his "periodic moods of depression."[32] Finally, the White House relented and offered to invite the Shah to visit Washington in November 1962.

But the Shah simply could not wait that long. When he heard about the November date, he demurred, arguing that in light of the country's dire situation, the proposed date was too far in the future. The American Embassy in Tehran once again supported the Shah's claim, suggesting that he was in no psychological state to wait that long. Ultimately, the White House gave in once more, and it was decided to invite the Shah for an official visit to the United States on April 10, 1962.

Then there was the question of how best to convey the invitation to the Shah. Some in the White House argued that since Robert Kennedy was planning a tour of Asia, he should make a stop in Tehran and personally deliver the invitation. The purpose of inviting the Shah, according to these officials, "was to build [the Shah] up," and thus a visit from the Attorney General would certainly help boost the Shah's shaken confidence.

But the State Department and Robert Kennedy himself were, for different reasons, against the idea. The Attorney General personally disliked, even despised, the Shah and insisted that should he be asked to visit him, he would insist on also "meeting with some of the [opposition] student groups there." The Iranian Embassy in Washington was by then already entangled in something of a conflict with the Justice Department over the fate of some of the Iranian students living in the United States who actively opposed the Shah.

In the late 1950s, thousands of Iranian students had begun to converge on European and American universities. Until then, educational sojourns in the West had been a privilege limited to the children of the elite. Indispensable to the Shah's modernization plans was a large, trained technocratic class. But Iran lacked the educational infrastructure to train such a class. A sociologist has called the late fifties the age of the technocrats. American policy in Iran also advocated that new young technocrats gradually take the place of traditional politicians. Starting in the late 1950s, cheap bus and train service from Iran to Europe became available and, before long, students from all social classes began to arrive in the West. Some of the more radical new students used their newfound freedom in Western democracies to create the Confederation of Iranian Students[33]—an international organization that became a formidable foe of the Shah throughout the rest of his tenure.

One of the first signs of the coming troubles took place in March 1960 during the party celebrating the Persian New Year. Till then, the Iranian Embassies in Western capitals had hosted these parties. Even before becoming Iran's ambassador to the United States, while he still lived in Iran, Ardeshir Zahedi had been put in charge of making sure Iranian students studying abroad received adequate help and assistance. When he was named Iran's ambassador to the United States, he showed particular interest in forging friendships and alliances with as many of these students as he could. He went out of his way to make the 1960 New Year celebration a success. But as he and his wife, Shahnaz, the Shah's daughter, arrived at the party, radical students began anti-Shah chants, and one of them threw a plate that hit Shahnaz. She was not hurt, but her already-strong aversion to appearing in official ceremonies only increased, becoming a point of tension between her and her husband. One of the students who turned the Persian New Year party into a political demonstration was Sadeq Qotbzadeh. In 1979 he was for a while the country's foreign minister, and in that capacity he was to figure prominently in the Shah's life during his pariah days of exile. In the early 1960s, Qotbzadeh was a peculiar problem for the Kennedy administration.

On February 20, 1961, the White House received a memorandum that registered one official's perplexing encounter with Qotbzadeh. For advocates of conspiracy theories, particularly those who claim that the Islamic Revolution was the work of the United States, the contents of the memo would be nothing short of a "smoking gun." The official had met at Georgetown University

> a flashy young Iranian student named Qotbzadeh... [who] says he is a Mosadeqist but... looks like a communist, and acts like a communist... even smells like a communist. He is failing his courses, will not work at his studies, and has a new girl in tow every few days.... This man sees people like Senator Humphires [*sic*], Justice Douglas, and even the Attorney General regularly. He tells everybody about how the smart men in the highest levels of the American government are all against the shah and sympathetic with Qotbzadeh and his friend, and how it will be only a little while before there will be an American-sponsored revolution in Iran and the Shah will be killed or exiled.... He says he will then be a cabinet minister.... He said long before the announcement of the cancellation of the Attorney-General's visit to Iran that the Attorney-General had promised him personally that he would not go to Tehran.[34]

The Shah's regime attempted to have Qotbzadeh extradited to Iran. Robert Kennedy was instrumental in making sure this never happened. Nearly three decades later, Qotbzadeh was a key player in the saga of the new Islamic regime's attempt to force Panama to send the Shah back to Iran. Eventually, Qotbzadeh's flamboyant, grandiose, and ambitious ideas put him on a collision course with Ayatollah Khomeini, who ordered his once-docile aide and de facto spokesperson executed.

Before the Shah's hopes for a journey to the United States became reality, as political tensions and economic difficulties continued to plague Iran, and as the political impasse between Amini and the Shah over the size of the military budget and the extent of the Shah's power continued, as Amini rebuffed the Shah's offer to "change his cabinet," getting rid of some of the more controversial ministers but staying on as prime minister, the Shah toyed with the idea of firing Amini and "acting as his own prime minister."[35]

The American Embassy was quick to disabuse the Shah of the wisdom of the idea of doing that. The message from the United States was clear: "The Shah should continue [to] support Amini and not assume direct responsibility."[36] In the same note, the embassy was instructed to tell the Shah that any additional U.S. economic assistance would be predicated on "the continuation of [the Amini] program," and that he should be kept on the job for "at least six months."[37] For the Shah, this must have been at once a blessing and a blight. He had to live with Amini for a few more months. But now there was at least light at the end of the tunnel, a conceivable date for getting rid of Amini, and as it happened, he kept Amini in his post until July 1962, exactly six months from the date of that American "advice."

The Shah did offer Amini an olive branch when he agreed to his wish to get rid of General Bakhtiyar. Early in his tenure, Amini had insisted on arresting Bakhtiyar for conspiring against the government. The Shah was happy to oblige, but only partially. After his dismissal as the head of SAVAK in 1961, Bakhtiyar had set up offices, ostensibly for business, but actually as a de facto headquarters for forces working against Amini. Generals and landlords, dismayed at the government reforms, gathered there and openly conspired against Amini. But then on January 21, 1962, students demonstrated at Tehran University, and the army entered the campus without even consulting the chancellor of the university and left behind one dead and 200 injured students—including three American young men studying in Iran at the time. Amini saw Bakhtiyar's hand behind the incident. Some sources have claimed that in fact no one, including Bakhtiyar, could have used the military without the direct consent of the Shah. They point to the Shah's apparent use of the military in 1942 to rid himself of Qavam, another of the Shah's foes.[38]

Amini, too, seemed to harbor such ideas, but when he met with the Shah, he blamed it all on Bakhtiyar and sought permission to arrest him. The Shah demurred, reminding Amini of Bakhtiyar's role in "fighting [the Communist] Tudeh Party members" and suggesting that instead of arresting the General, he should be allowed to leave the country. The next day, the Shah called Bakhtiyar to the Court and ordered him to leave the country immediately.[39] If the Shah assumed that in this way he would use one enemy to rid himself of another, he was badly mistaken.

General Hassan Pakravan had been named as Bakhtiyar's replacement as head of SAVAK in 1961, and the change was profound in terms of SAVAK's culture and image. Pakravan was known as the intellectual of the Iranian security organizations. He was a man of considerable erudition and refinement himself, and some of Iran's well-known intellectuals, including famed writer Sadeq Chubak, acclaimed poet Mohammad Zohari, and Mozzafar Baghai were amongst his friends. Immediately after taking over, he ordered an end to all torture in SAVAK prisons. In 1958, when he was still deputy director of SAVAK, he concluded that not Communists but "radical nationalists," who represented the "frustrated nationalism and reformist aspiration of the urban Middle classes," had become "the greatest danger to the future stability of Iran."[40] Now that he was named the new head of SAVAK, he had a chance to make his ideas into policy. His views were a radical departure from the dominant paradigm of the Shah and of the intelligence agencies, who believed that Communism was the main threat faced by the regime and that, in the fight against the infidel Marxists, the pious mullahs were the monarchy's natural allies and nationalist democrats a secondary foe. But Pakravan's turn at the helm was short-lived.

As the Shah gingerly maneuvered the fine line of appearing to support Amini while maintaining as much of his own power as possible, other issues also complicated his agenda. On March 30, 1961, the eighty-nine-year-old Grand Ayatollah Boroujerdi died in the city of Qom. In terms of its effect on the development of Shiism in Iran, his death had an enormous impact. A book published only weeks after the Ayatollah's death by a group that called itself the National Central Committee of Islamic Societies in Iran discusses, in detail, the perils and promises entailed in the death of the Grand Ayatollah for the Shiite world. Several of the authors of the compilation were virtual unknowns at that time, but they would become in less than two decades the leaders of the Islamic Revolution of 1979.

The book offers fascinating clues to the sophisticated network of Islamic groups that operated in Iran, even during the period when the Shah's authoritarianism was at its height. The Left was self-indulgent, believing that the inevitable laws of history would eliminate religion—"the opium of the masses"—and place them as the revolutionary vanguard on history's pedestal. The Shah and his secret police, on the other hand, were focused on fighting Communists and the National Front and believed the forces of faith to be the best antidote to the spread of the Communist disease. In the meantime, the Islamists were creating a vast, nimble, multi-layered network of groups and institutions—everything from armed organizations to the most apparently benign classes in how to read the Qu'ran.

Almost concurrent with the mid-1961 publication of the book on Shiism and the death of the Ayatollah, two of the contributors to the book, Mehdi Bazorgan and Mohammad Taleghani, both hitherto little-known members of the National Front, wrote a letter to Mossadeq, asking his permission to split from the National Front. The note caught all but no attention at the time. It heralded the birth of the Freedom Movement. The group might have remained a small footnote to Iranian history had it not, in 1979, been chosen by Ayatollah Khomeini—better yet, used by him as his democratic camouflage—to form the first provincial revolutionary government of Iran. In that capacity, the group also played a crucial role in the last months of the Shah's life.

Ayatollah Boroujerdi's death also raised for the Shah the thorny question of sending a note of condolence. It was a custom that upon the death of an ayatollah of Boroujerdi's stature, the Iranian king, as the only ruler of a Shiite-dominated state, would send a note of condolence to the presumptive successor of the dead cleric. There were at the time several ayatollahs who lived in the two Iranian cities of Qom and Meshed and in the Iraqi city of Najaf. Each of the men could easily be considered the legitimate successor to Ayatollah Boroujerdi. Moreover, since the early twentieth century there had been a constant competition between the Iraqi city of Najaf and the Iranian city of Qom to become the center of Shiite learning and authority. The Shah, worried about the emergence of a contending center of power in his domain, was keen on strengthening Najaf's claim to supremacy, and thus chose to send his telegram of condolence to Ayatollah Hakim,* in Najaf. Hakim had the added advantage of also being from the "Quietist" school of Shiism, wherein the task of the clergy is not to seize political power and create the Islamic state—as Ayatollah Khomeini later advocated—but to focus on the spiritual health of the flock and on blocking laws and values inimical to Islam.

Ayatollah Boroujerdi's death even put the U.S. government in an awkward position. On the one hand, the White House knew that the Soviet Union and Great Britain were sure to have one of their most prominent leaders send the

* In a strange twist of fate, the son of the same Ayatollah would, thirty years later, become the chief ally of the Iranian regime in its attempt to gain influence in Iraq.

Shah a note to "offer their condolences." On the other hand, the White House was also fully aware of Ayatollah Boroujerdi's role in the persecution of the Baha'i minority in 1955. The White House worried that "the Bahai's of the US, centered in the Chicago area might react unfavorably" to a formal communication from the President. Eventually it was decided that in his next meeting with the Shah, the U.S. Ambassador to Iran should offer him the President's sympathy verbally.[41]

Amini, ever sensitive to the clergy's power and hoping to garner their support for his government, not only sent notes of condolence to all the ayatollahs, but decided before long to go to the city of Qom and visit with the top clerics there. There was considerable behind-the-scenes bickering about the list of ayatollahs Amini should visit, and for reasons that have been never made clear, he chose to include Ayatollah Khomeini in that list. While certainly an influential teacher of the seminary and popular with the young generation of clerics, Khomeini was certainly not on par with other established ayatollahs of the city. The decision dismayed other ayatollahs, particularly the moderate Ayatollah Shariat-Madari, who later became Khomeini's chief clerical opponent and a secret ally of the Shah.

Though by then Amini had developed a reputation for his love of long, meandering speeches, in the meeting with Ayatollah Khomeini, it was the Ayatollah who did almost all the talking. In a tone that was surprisingly conciliatory, the Ayatollah talked of two kinds of prime ministers in the past: those who served the people and became popular, and those who worked against the people and begot only the people's hatred. He invited Amini to try and join the rank of the first group and offered an alliance with the clergy as the surest way for him to achieve that goal. Amongst the clergy's concerns, Ayatollah Khomeini said, was the fact that universities around the country were spreading the seeds of faithlessness, and he wanted Amini to unite with the mullahs—"five or six thousand of them studying in Qom's *Howze* [seminary] alone"—and rid the universities of the curse of secularism. Ayatollah Khomeini wanted the clergy consulted on the question of university curriculum. The demands seemed outlandish at the time. Less than two decades later, they became the official government policy of the new clerical regime in Iran. Even in 2010, after thirty years of clerical rule and with one "cultural revolution" behind them already, Khamenei, the leader of the Islamic regime, still defiantly railed against what he called the rampant materialism, rationalism, and skepticism of Iranian universities, particularly those teaching social sciences. He ordered an "Islamization" of the curriculum—just as Khomeini had done in 1961. Amini ended his controversial meeting with Khomeini by admitting that the Iranian government in the last twenty years had indeed "misled the people into moral and spiritual morass" and promised,

"With God's help, all of these problems will be solved."[42] The implicit criticism of the Shah was hard to miss. Amini's remarks also captured the disharmony that defined the nature of power in Iran. Though the country was in a state of crisis, the Shah and the Prime Minister were both engaged in a dance of deception—both pretended unity in public, and each worked hard against the other in private.

❧

The first few years of the sixties were also times of triumph and turmoil in the Shah's private life. First there was the birth of a much-anticipated son and an heir to the throne. On October 31, 1960, the Court issued a statement announcing the birth of a son to the royal couple. Six months earlier, on the eve of the Persian New Year, in a similar announcement, the Court had announced that the Queen was pregnant. In those days there was no ultrasound technology, and thus the gender of the fetus remained a mystery to the parents. Traditional families resorted to varieties of rituals and prayers as well as exotic herbs and strange animal parts to ensure that the child was a boy. The Queen was already feeling pressure from the royal family and was even told that she should visit a doctor to increase her "chances of bearing a son."[43] An old seamstress who had worked for the Queen's family in earlier years told her that writing a prayer on her belly with mud that had been blessed by a saint would guarantee a son while another believed that a diet of mandarins and oranges would also get her a son.[44] The future of her marriage, she knew, depended on the gender of her fetus. In her memoir, she writes of bursting into tears when she heard she had given birth to a boy. "I thought to myself," she writes in refreshing honesty, "if I had had a daughter, what would have happened?"[45]

Before the day of delivery, the attending gynecologist predicted "that the child would be a boy." The Shah, on the other hand, told a press conference that while for a "father it makes no difference whether his child is boy or girl, but as I notice that the press and people very much hoped that I have a male heir, I am glad to associate with their point of view."[46]

Her delivery had not been free from anguish. She had chosen as her gynecologist Dr. Jahanshah Saleh, a famous professor of medicine and brother to one of the Shah's favored but intractable foes, Alahyar Saleh. Her long labor had necessitated the use of pain medication, and the anesthesiologist chosen to help Dr. Saleh had, in excitement, given her a higher than normal dose, causing her a late recovery of consciousness. At 11:15 on the morning of October 31, the birth of a new imperial prince was announced with a forty-one-gun salute. While the royal family rejoiced in the hall, the Queen lay unconscious in her bed. As she writes in a querulous tone in her memoir, "in the rejoicings, I think I was almost forgotten, and only my mother thought to ask: and my daughter, how is she?"[47] On November 4, the Court announced that, "on the orders of His Majesty, the Shah, the newborn Prince has been called Reza." And then, the next day, only hours after the Queen and the newborn left the hospital, the Shah issued a new order, using article 37 of the constitution and appointing Reza as the crown prince.

The inherent tensions and contradictions in the Shah's theory of kingship—at once modern and traditional—can be seen in his *firman.* He writes, "By the Grace of Almighty God, We, Mohammad Reza Pahlavi, Shahanshah of Iran, hereby proclaim that we now offer thanks to Almighty God for his blessings, and as one of the foremost pillars of constitutional monarchy is an heir and Crown Prince, and since the Almighty God has bestowed upon us a son, by virtue of our authority, and in accordance with provisions of article 37 of the constitution, and in consideration of his natural abilities and merits, we hereby decree our beloved son Prince Shapour Reza Crown Prince." In other words, it is not clear whether the appointment is by royal fiat, dependent on the will of the people as manifest in the constitution, or based on the son's "natural abilities and merits."

It is a remarkable fact of the Shah's political life that during his entire thirty-seven-year rule, he never commissioned or made an effort to offer a serious theory of why monarchy was suited to Iran's modern situation. When the American Constitution was drafted, some of the Founding Fathers felt compelled to write the *Federalist Papers* and offer a reasoned argument explaining why the new federalism was optimal. When, in the sixteenth and seventeenth centuries, the English monarchy was experiencing a crisis, King James I wrote dozens of treatises arguing that monarchy was the best system possible for England. Though the Shah and his Court commissioned a dozen biographies of himself and the Queen, though they sponsored hundreds of books chronicling the accomplishments of the Pahlavi dynasty, the Shah's only articulated thought on the monarchy's legitimacy was repeating the claim that monarchy is a "natural system" and deeply rooted in the Persian *Geist.*

Equally revealing about the *firman* appointing the Crown Prince was the order of appearance of different social strata. The Shah ordered "that all members of our family, highest ranking clerics of Islam, members of government, elected members of the Majlis and Senate, governors, city managers, all commanders of the military and the national police" must follow the new Crown Prince; only after mentioning all of these groups did he go on to mention "everyone in the great nation of Iran." In other words, the legitimacy of the new Crown Prince was assured first and foremost by royal fiat, and of all of those who must afford the future ruler due deference, the royal family came first, followed by clerics of Islam; the people came last. This was a reversal of the order stipulated in the Iranian Constitution, where kingship was a divine gift entrusted by the people. Such kingship was not so much an anointment as a gift—thus one that could be taken back by the same people who had bestowed it. In the Shah's *firman*, his anointment played the most crucial role, and the people's consent was of least importance.[†]

Roughly four months after the announcement about the Crown Prince, in March 1961, the royal Court issued another statement, announcing that "in the royal titles of ancient Persia" the original Persian term of *shahbanou* was used in place of *malekeh* (Queen) and thus in accordance to the new decree by the Shah, "the word Shahbanou will henceforth replace the word Malekeh." Foreign embassies were also informed that henceforth, in referring to the Queen, the correct title would be "either the Empress Farah, or Her Imperial Majesty, the Empress Farah."[48]

The news of the birth of a successor to the throne was celebrated around the country, as much by spontaneous bursts of enthusiasm as by government "encouragement." There was soon also a cacophony of destructive rumors spread by the opposition. Some claimed that the Shah was in fact impotent and that the Queen had feigned pregnancy by hiding a pillow under her dress. Others suggested that the infant had in fact been a girl and that she was changed with someone else's boy at the hospital. Even the choice of a clinic in the poorer sections of Tehran became the subject of conspiracies.[49] The Queen used a hospital in the poor section of town, some whispered, only to facilitate the swap of her infant girl with a boy. The health of the newborn also became the subject of these rumors. Some said the infant was a mute while others claimed that his demeanor showed him to be less than brilliant.[50] Many of these rumors were first broadcast over radio stations based in Eastern Europe that were funded by the Soviet Union and run by the Tudeh Party.

In the decade after the birth of the Crown Prince, the Shah's older daughter, Shahnaz, also suffered more than her fair share of rumors, gossip, and emotional travails. In a few months, there were rumors that Ardeshir Zahedi and Shahnaz had "apparently decided to get divorced. Strong pressure is being brought to bear on them to wait at least until" the end of the Shah's American trip.[51] When eventually in the mid-sixties divorce did become a reality, as Alam's *Daily Journals* make clear, her life was complicated by increased tensions with her father over

† In those days in Iran, the didactic trinity written on walls everywhere—from barracks and bazaars to classrooms—was God, Shah, country. In Morocco, another Muslim monarchy at the African end of the Islamic world, the trinity, no less prevalent, is God, country, and king. In Iran, then, the country exists for the king while in Morocco, the king exists for the country.

her chosen new husband, her lifestyle, and allegations of her attempt to live a "hippie life" along with all of its accoutrements.

The weight of events, the constant tension with Amini, and his anxiety about the Kennedy administration took their toll on the Shah. Their impact could be seen around the time of his scheduled state visit to Norway in May 1961. Amini, afraid that the military might attempt a coup in the Shah's absence, tried to get the royal couple to delay their trip. The Shah rejected the idea, saying that such a cancellation would give the world the idea that there was a crisis in Iran.

On May 18 the Shah, accompanied by his wife, now officially bearing the title of *shahbanou*, arrived in Norway for what was to be an eight-day visit. To his hosts and to diplomats who saw the Shah in Oslo, he seemed clearly distraught. On the night of May 20, the Shah and his wife gave a dinner in honor of their hosts at Oslo's Grand Hotel. The Shah had brought with him a "large supply of special caviar," and according to all accounts, "the dinner was one of the finest remembered in Oslo."[52]

But during the evening, to everyone's surprise, neither the Shah nor the Queen gave a talk, nor did either "make any attempt to talk" to their guests. The Shah was, by nature, a shy and timid man, invariably polite and attentive to the decorum of hospitality and diplomacy. Aside from being visibly angry with the Iranian Ambassador, the Shah, according to diplomats who met him there, was also worried about developments in Iran. By the evening of May 25, the Shah cut his journey short and left Norway. Again it was "widely believed that political developments in Iran necessitated [the royal family's] premature departure."[53] In reality, the Shah and the Queen did not immediately return to Iran but spent a few days in Italy before returning to a tumultuous Tehran—a city made politically more volatile by the public knowledge of rifts between the Shah and the new administration in the United States.

A few months later, when the Shah and his queen visited French President Charles De Gaulle, his mood had clearly improved. The worst of the political crisis seemed to be behind him, and his visit to France might have been the most pleasant experience of the year for the Shah.

The Shah and the Queen left for France on October 10, 1961. Not only did he love France, as did his wife, but he perceived De Gaulle as something of an alterego. Those who knew him well—like Alam—knew that one of the highest compliments they could give him was to compare him to De Gaulle. Aside from all the many political qualities he admired in the General, there was also the question of his height—for the Shah one of the most important measures for judging beauty and gravitas. In men, tallness conjured memories of his father, Reza Shah. In women, lanky and lean were two of his favorite aesthetic measures. Such was the Shah's adulation of De Gaulle that some observers have claimed that the referendum of January 26, 1961, when the six principles of the White Revolution were put to a popular vote, "was inspired by De Gaulle's referendum."[54]

On the night of October 11, in his speech at the state dinner in Paris, the Shah began by talking about his own "special affinity for France, and the lofty place the French language has held in Iran's educational curriculum." The Shah praised the long history of friendship between Iran and France, "going back to the age of 'Philip le Bel'[‡] who was the recipient of the first letter from an Iranian king." Iran, the Shah said, "owes the first translation of our classics to your countrymen. Teaching Persian in Europe first began in Paris in [the] late 18th century. The first relics of our antiquity were discovered by French anthropologists."[55] The next day, André Malraux, De Gaulle's revered minister of culture, who had traveled to Iran before and had a keen interest in the history of Iranian art, hosted a gala in honor of the Shah and the Queen and invited many of the French intellectual royalty to the party. More importantly, he developed a close relationship with the Queen. In an inscription in a book he had earlier given the Queen, he had written of his delight that Iran's enchantments are now "associated with your destiny."[56] This time, he took her "through the great museums of Paris."[57]

When the royal family returned to Tehran after what had been a personally and politically successful trip, the Shah found the country awash with rumors of increasing tensions between him and his obviously frustrated prime minister. The British Embassy captured the Shah's precarious position, and the double bind he found himself in when it wrote, "if the Shah gets rid of Dr. Amini on his return [from America], this will be an indication that he will henceforth take his orders direct from his American masters. If on the other hand he retains Dr. Amini, this will be because his American masters have told him to do so."[58] Not just the Shah and Amini, but the nation, awaited the meeting between the young Prince of Camelot and the tired Peacock Prince in April 1962.

‡ Philip le Bel, or Philip the Fair (or the Handsome) ruled France from 1268 to 1314. In spite of his apparent good looks, his critics said of him, "he is neither man nor beast. He is a thing."

Chapter 15

THE BRIGHT SIDE OF CAMELOT

Thou art the midwife of my woe.
Shakespeare, King Richard II, *2.2.63*

The idea of a modernizing monarch is almost an oxymoron. Monarchy, one of the oldest forms of governance and often seen as ancient Persia's contribution to the political legacy of humanity, is, by definition, a traditional form of rule. Its legitimizing narrative is invariably based on the traditional idea of divine right—whether it was the ancient Persian and Zoroastrian notion of "Farrah Izadi" (divine aura) or the Islamic concept of "Zellollah" (shadow of Allah). Modernity, on the other hand, is founded on the idea of popular sovereignty and natural rights. People of the modern polity are citizens instead of subjects; they have inalienable natural rights; in a traditional feudal society, the rights of the subjects are only those the king deigns to give them. The constitution of 1905, in an effort to make Iran into a democratic polity, combined these two incongruent concepts by making monarchy both a divine gift and an institution predicated on the support of the people.

Machiavelli is regarded as the first political theorist of the modern age. He was the first philosopher to understand that the age of inherited legitimacy had ended. A modern prince, Machiavelli said, must develop his own language of legitimacy wherein the rights of self-assertive citizens are recognized and respected. The Shah, in this sense, was a historical anomaly, if not an anachronism—a man of contradictory affinities, a prince who had inherited his power but did little to develop a theory to legitimize it, a ruler who promoted social and economic policies that hurled Iran into the modern age, yet was insistent on ruling the country like a nineteenth-century Oriental despot. Events in the life of the Shah during the first years of the 1960s captured this contradiction.

The Shah's rule also coincided with what scholars call the "third wave" of democratization when, in less than fifty years, more than fifty countries chose the path of democracy. Maintaining and consolidating an authoritarian regime in the age of democracy was doubly difficult, and the Shah's response to a student demonstration in January 1962, a few months before he left Iran for his visit to the United States, captures his many ironic inconsistencies.

On the afternoon of a day when student demonstrations at Tehran University were brutally suppressed, when one student was killed and an estimated two hundred injured and arrested, the Shah was chairing, as was his wont, a meeting of the Supreme Economic Council. Before the meeting began, the Shah paced the large room with his hands clasped behind his back—a sure sign of anguish to those who knew him. Then he angrily said, "What do these students want?" After a brief pause, invoking the royal "we," he continued, "We have given them everything. What else do they want?"

His was a rhetorical question, intended only to register dismay. One man in the room took the road less traveled, and instead of the safe silence of acquiescence, he chose to talk—even dared to disagree. His name was Mehdi Samii. By then, he had established an impeccable reputation as an honest banker, a diligent manager of men and policies, a close confidante of the Shah, a man always willing to speak the truth.

That day, Samii was already anxious because he intended to raise with the Shah the case of Fereydoon Mahdavi, a distant relative, and a young leader from the ranks of the National Front who had been arrested along with other student demonstrators. Samii asked for permission to speak and then said, "Your Majesty, the problem is that the things you say you have 'given' them they simply consider parts of their inalienable rights. What they object to is being told they are 'given' these rights and being deprived of other rights they also think they have."[1]

When the Shah was still the crown prince and had just returned to Iran from his years in Switzerland, he tried to surround himself with men of intelligence and erudition. When, for example, he heard from Dr. Ghasem Ghani, himself a physician, scholar, and diplomat, of a weekly meeting of some of the country's leading literary lions—people like Mohammad Gazvini and Zoka al-Mulk Foroughi—he asked them to hold their meetings in his presence at the Court.[2] Anxious to learn, he quietly listened to their erudite discussions. Even as a king, many of his early advisors and courtiers were seasoned, thoughtful men of politics. But by the time he was on his way to America in 1962, the Shah had less and less interest in the company of the types of men who attended those literary gatherings. The preparations for the trip to the Kennedy White House were, in a sense, the harbinger of a crucial change in the quality of the men the Shah picked as aides and as office holders. He was beginning to lose patience with men of Amini's generation—men who had seen him in his dark and defeated hours, men like Court Minister Hussein Ala, who had a paternal sort of regard for him. Not long after his American journey, the Shah began the process of changing not just the fabric of Iranian society but the quality of the people who surrounded him. He called it a "house cleaning." Gradually and inexorably, he brought to the center of power a new class of technocrats.

Before long, even the advice of men like Samii would no longer be welcomed by the Shah. He never shunned Samii, and though he eventually stripped him of political posts, he made sure he did not suffer economically. Moreover, the ascendance of technocrats had for the Shah the added advantage of matching at least one element of the new U.S. strategy on Iran. At the same time, the men who surrounded the Shah in his private life were a combination of his childhood friends and a coterie of unsavory characters who used their proximity to the King to illicitly enrich themselves. With a few exceptions, when picking friends the Shah was a poor judge of character.

In fact, even before going to the April 1962 meeting with Kennedy, the Shah had made a major move in expediting the rise of an aggressively ambitious young man who took pride in his plans to arrive at the pinnacle of power with the help of his "American friends." His name was Hassan-Ali Mansur, and he came from a family with a long, controversial, political pedigree. Mansur's father, Ali Mansur, had been a prime minister with a badly tarnished reputation as an Anglophile and a crook. Now his son took pride in having Gratian Yatsevich, the CIA station chief in Tehran, as a tenant and as an enthusiastic ally and supporter.

Mansur had worked in Iran's Foreign Ministry since graduating from Tehran University's Faculty of Law and Political Science. In his first assignment in Europe in the months after the end of World War II, he met a colleague named Amir Abbas Hoveyda, and the two became lifelong friends. By 1957, Hoveyda had left the Foreign Ministry and accepted a job with the UN's High Commissioner for Refugees, and Mansur had decided that the slow pace of rise in the stultified hierarchy of the Foreign Ministry was ill-suited to his ambitions. He returned to Iran and also convinced Hoveyda to come back, telling him of the promise of his "American friends" to help him become prime minister. Together Mansur and Hoveyda worked to create what they called the "Progressive Circle."[3] With the Shah's support, Mansur soon had membership in the High Economic Council and a ministerial portfolio.

The late 1950s have been called the era of *dowrehs* in Iran—informal but regular gatherings of like-minded men (and a few women) who met to talk about the political situation in the country and plan for the future. The *dowrehs* would have been de facto embryos of political parties had they ever been allowed to simply follow the "natural" progression of their ambitions. The Progressive Circle was just such a *dowreh,* and with the Shah's blessing, it did eventually grow into the Iran Novin (New Iran) Party that was to dominate Iranian party politics for much of the 1960s and the first half of the 1970s. Mansur's meteoric rise to power in Iran, no doubt spurred on by the Shah's public support, was nothing if not a subtle nod to the Eisenhower and Kennedy administrations about the Shah's own intent to bring about reforms in Iran. As dispatches from the American Embassy in Tehran show, diplomats stationed there clearly understood the meaning of the Shah's gestures.

There was one last detail the White House wanted to take care of before the Shah left Iran for his visit to the United States. Aware of the problem of the Iranian students and of the Shah's intense sensitivity to critical comments in the American press, the White House took a preemptive step to lessen the likelihood of bad press for the Shah. The American Embassy in Tehran was instructed to convey to the Shah "the following list of things which should be avoided in order to maximize favorable public impression of visit. 1) Wearing of uniforms by Shah—except at Washington arrival, departure and wreath laying ceremonies; 2) Purchasing or ordering of expensive clothing, jewels, or automobiles, 3) Lavish distribution of gifts."[4]

On Tuesday, April 10, the Shah, accompanied by the Queen and an entourage of ten, arrived at New York's Idlewild Airport aboard Pan Am Flight 115. On some occasions, even before he had his own jet, if the Shah flew on the Iranian airline, Homa, he would go to the cockpit and pilot the plane part of the way, particularly during takeoff and landing. But this time the Shah was not at the controls. The royal couple arrived in New York at around five o'clock in the afternoon and was taken directly to the Waldorf-Astoria Hotel, where the Presidential Suite, the famous suite 35A, was set aside for them.

The Presidential Suite at the Waldorf is a three-bedroom apartment with a big living room and a dining room that can seat more than forty guests. In one corner is the desk used by General MacArthur; Kennedy's rocking chair is in another. A beautiful Cartier clock adorns one of the walls. The East River and the Hudson as well as the UN buildings are all visible from the windows of the suite. Outside the entrance, today there hangs a silver plaque with elegantly engraved names of the heads of state who have stayed in the apartment. Since 1931, every U.S. president has stayed there at least once; other heads of state mentioned as past residents include Queen Elizabeth, King Hassan, Emperor Hirohito, Nikita Khrushchev, and even Nicolae Ceauşecsu, the Romanian despot.[5]

In 1962, and every other time the Shah stayed at the hotel, particularly after Iran's oil revenues suddenly jumped and the Shah's entourage grew bigger and more extravagant, he was afforded an even more ostentatious royal treatment—but today, for reasons that are not clear, the name of the Shah is missing from the silver royal register.

At ten o'clock on the morning of April 11, the royal entourage left New York for National Airport in Washington, where they were met by President Kennedy and his wife, Jacqueline. The Shah, dressed in a dark suit, had recently had a haircut and looked more like a military cadet than a head of state. Kennedy stood behind the podium, with the Shah, the Queen, and Mrs. Kennedy standing behind him, and, looking into the cameras, he welcomed the Shah and the Queen to the United States, suggesting that the two leaders shared much, as they both wanted freedom, peace, and a better life for their people.

When it was the Shah's turn to speak, he read from a prepared text and seemed nervous. His English was correct but had something of a novice in its locution. Instead of looking at the cameras and the microphones, he stood at an angle and had his eyes fixed on President Kennedy and his wife. He talked of the "magic meaning" that the word "America" had come to have around the world. After the brief welcoming comments, the Shah and the President rode in the presidential limousine while Mrs. Kennedy and Queen Farah followed in the next car. They drove to Blair House, the official state guest house used by foreign dignitaries. The Shah gave the President the gift he had brought him, "a tenth century ceramic bowl, eight and a half inch in diameter," in "off-white glaze, decorated with bird and scroll designs."[6] After a private lunch and a visit to an Islamic center, and after placing a wreath at the Tomb of the Unknown Soldier in Arlington National Cemetery, at eight o'clock that night, the King and Queen of Iran, both dressed in formal attire, attended the state dinner given in their honor by President and Mrs. Kennedy. The Shah wore a blue royal sash across a white shirt and a tuxedo jacket. The Queen wore a long yellow gown, a white fur cape, and a matching bejeweled tiara and necklace. Mrs. Kennedy was dressed in a long pink and white gown, with long white gloves that extended well above her elbows.

Aside from the meetings with President Kennedy and others in his administration, the Shah had three big speeches to give on that trip—the first was the night of the state dinner. The second was his talk before a joint session of Congress, and the third was his appearance before the National Press Club. He seems to have followed a common strategy in all three. He wanted to point to Iran's rich history and its shared values with the West. He wanted to argue for more military assistance and a bigger Iranian army. Most important of all, the Shah wanted to highlight his own legitimacy as a reformer. It was a measure of the value he placed on this trip that, before leaving for America, he had hired a tutor to improve his English. His impeccable command of French had always been a great asset, and from then on, his ease with English would also become part of his international identity and a subject of repeated praise by the Western media.

By then, Shojaedeen Shafa had been the Shah's speechwriter for about four years, and two of the Shah's American speeches, with their repeated references to Iran's past poets and thinkers and their influence on the West, were evidence of his influence. During the White House state dinner, Kennedy began his brief welcoming remarks by observing, "[I]t has never been easy to be a Persian, from the oldest times in history till today." Were the words meant to conjure echoes of Montesquieu and his treatise on the difficulties of being a Persian in the modern age? Kennedy then talked about how "the Shah has carried the burden" of ruling his country for twenty years already "and might carry it for another twenty years." As it happened, he was wrong by only three years. In an effort to show his support for Amini, Kennedy praised the Shah "for surrounding himself with able, and dedicated Ministers." Yet the President avoided, as much as possible, mentioning Amini's name. Finally, reflecting the many references in his briefing papers to the Soviet threat, Kennedy ended his talk by referring to the fact that Iran lived "in the belly of the bear" and then commended the Shah for keeping his country safe from the Soviet threat. When it was the Shah's turn to speak, he began by referring to the history of the strong and amicable relationship between Iran and the United States. He talked of the first American missionaries who came to Iran, and he praised the work of men like Dr. Samuel Jordan, who gave "his life and youth to promoting culture and education in Iran." He conjured the memory of Ralph Waldo Emerson, the quintessential American intellectual and poet, citing his lyrical eulogy of the Persian poet Sa'di and his virtues of honesty. The Shah then quoted Kennedy's own *Profiles in Courage,* concluding from it that he had hitherto been able to stand up to the malicious attacks on him only because justice was on his side. The pomp and ceremony of the state dinner and the Shah's attempts to underscore his pedigree as a genuine reformer were all a prelude to his much-anticipated discussions with Kennedy scheduled to begin the next day.

At 9:30 the next morning, the Shah walked into the Cabinet Room of the White House for the first round of his meetings with Kennedy. The American and Iranian delegations were already seated around an oval table. They had been informally discussing Soviet machinations in the Middle East—an issue on which both sides were in complete agreement. On each side of the table, the center seats were left empty, designated for the Shah and the President. But before being seated, Kennedy led the Shah into a small private room off the Oval Office where the two talked alone for fifteen minutes. No notes of this meeting were taken.

Once the Shah and Kennedy emerged from their private meeting, the President began by offering a brief account of their private discussion. Even the short summary he provided makes it amply clear that theirs had been a heated and contentious meeting, what diplomats call "a frank and serious" discussion. According to Kennedy, "the Shah had discussed Iran's requirement for greater military assistance and the President had said that no build-up of the Iranian armed forces would enable it to withstand a Soviet attack alone and that the greatest present danger to Iran was internal and that [the] current government program in Iran [namely Amini] appeared to be aimed at reducing this danger."[7]

Here then was the crux of the problem: the Shah was worried about the Soviet and Iraqi threat and wanted a bigger army and more military expenditure, while Kennedy believed the biggest threat facing the Shah was the domestic situation and wanted to push for more reforms and a bigger slice of the budget for social expenditures. Since it was the U.S. government that had to pay for much of any expansion of the Iranian military, Kennedy's views carried particular weight. He wanted to convince the Shah that the Iranian army was "essentially for maintenance of internal security," and for that purpose, Iran needed "a modern, albeit significantly smaller force." To sweeten the deal, the United States proposed a new program that provided the Iranian army with sophisticated equipment.[8] Moreover, Kennedy had ordered his staff to prepare a "list of all commitments and semi-commitments of any importance made by the United States for defense of Iran." In other words, Kennedy wanted to reassure the Shah that, in the event of a Soviet attack, the United States would be there to help. The list of such commitments included twelve items—"from the tri-partite declaration of Tehran, December 1, 1943," to the famous August 26, 1959, letter from Eisenhower reassuring the Shah that "Iran does not stand alone in the face of these [Soviet] pressures."[9] The Shah was not convinced. I can't tell my military, he said, that they shoulder no responsibility in the defense of their country against Soviet aggression.

Before his next meeting with Kennedy, the Shah was to appear before a joint session of Congress—an honor bestowed only on important visiting dignitaries. Though the Shah had already appeared twice before such a joint session, the third appearance was controversial and nearly canceled. A few members of Congress had objected to the invitation and threatened to walk out when the Shah was introduced. It was a sign of the Shah's precarious position in the new era of American politics that only after considerable cajoling by the American Embassy in Iran were congressional leaders persuaded not to cancel the invitation. Julius Holmes, the American ambassador to Iran at the time, was an unabashed supporter of the Shah and in Washington was sometimes jokingly called the Shah's envoy.

The Shah's speech to Congress, delivered on Thursday, April 12, around one o'clock in the afternoon, was the longest of his trip. It expanded some of the ideas he had first articulated during his remarks at the White House dinner. The big difference was that in the congressional speech he put more emphasis on the reforms that had begun in Iran. He made sure the Congress knew that it was he who "had given the government of [Amini] some authority to carry out these changes."[10] Like Kennedy, the Shah had no desire to use the dread Amini name.

The Shah's last major speech was to the National Press Club. He was more at ease on this occasion and even engaged in some light banter with the journalists. He offered an optimistic image of Iran's future, but also tried to convey a sense of nonchalance about power. "Let me tell you bluntly," he told the journalists gathered there, "that this king business has given me nothing but headaches. Over the last twenty years since the beginning of my rule, I have not had even one day of peace and comfort, something every human being is entitled to."[11] The intended audience for his blunt message was not so much the journalists gathered there but officials of the Kennedy administration. One of the ironic paradoxes of the Shah's character was that while he certainly clung to power tenaciously and fought vigorously to increase his personal hold on levers of authority, he was also from the beginning a reluctant monarch, ready to give up the throne whenever a serious threat appeared on the horizon. The Shah also tried to reassert his dedication to reforms and underscored the fact that long before the Kennedy administration came to power, he was a reformer. He talked of the days when the world and Iran were both caught in the throes of the Second World War, and how even then he had advocated social justice and demanded that every Iranian must have a guaranteed minimum of "free education, free health care, decent housing, adequate clothing and adequate food." The Shah went on to add, with clear hints of pride in his choice of words, that "the next day, some of the people present in that meeting began to say the Shah of Iran has become a communist."[12]

The Shah bedazzled the journalists with what the British Ambassador to the United States called his "diplomatic adroitness" when, in response to a question about whether Iran was still selling oil to Israel, he said with a smile, "we know nothing about that."[13]

In July 1962, about three months after he returned home from America, the Shah accepted Amini's resignation. Many in Iran, as the Shah himself knew, believed that the sole purpose of his American trip had been to convince Kennedy that Amini was expendable. If there is any evidence for such an alleged agreement between the Shah and Kennedy, it must be the aide-mémoire covering the Shah's second discussion with Kennedy on April 13. The President "said that it was true that there were special situations in different countries which required special solutions. The Shah, however, is the keystone of Iranian security and progress and, the President continued, must keep pushing toward further development."[14] Beneath the thin veneer of diplomatic formalities, the message seems clear: the United States wanted reforms and thought Amini was fit for the job, but if the Shah could undertake the same reforms, the United States would be just as happy. This clearly seemed to be the Shah's interpretation. The lead editorial of *Etela'at,* the Tehran daily that reliably reflected the Shah's views on pending issues, offered the same interpretation.[15] As diplomats who met the Shah after his return noticed, his depressed, even despondent, mood had turned to a jovial, self-assured confidence.

Pleasant as many aspects of his American trip were, the Shah also had to face the embarrassing fact that Iranian students in the United States had organized angry demonstrations against him. The Shah, according to a CIA report, was "particularly bitter" about the demonstrations. This was the beginning of the Confederation of Iranian Students' relentless activities against the Shah. For the rest of his tenure, he would never again travel to a Western European or American city without the specter of student demonstrations haunting him. Ironically, by the late 1960s, Communist countries were the only places the Shah felt safe from the harassment of demonstrations by leftist Iranian students!

After the official trip, the royal couple stayed on for a few more days in the United States. The Queen had never been to America before, and this, the Shah told the American Ambassador, would be a good chance for her to see some of the continent. He also wanted to spend one night in London.

The London trip was declared by the Shah to be private. In spite of the fact that because of other visiting dignitaries, it was a particularly "inconvenient time" for the British government to host the Shah, they went out of their way to roll out the royal red carpet for him and his entourage—including a meeting with Queen Elizabeth.[16] The issue of this meeting almost created something of a diplomatic rift between the Shah and his British hosts. The Shah was initially asked to join a dinner the Queen had already planned to give in someone else's honor, but he took umbrage at the idea. He felt "that his position demands that he should be invited in his own right and not as a guest at a dinner given on another occasion."[17] The British government changed plans to fit the Shah's wishes; their efforts were a revealing sign of the incipient competition between Britain and the United States over influence in Iran and amity with the Shah.

The Shah's private London visit in fact had a purpose other than a mere stopover for rest or for catching a performance of *My Fair Lady.* "The sole purpose," as the Foreign Office soon learned, "was to collect his personal aircraft"—a small private jet he had bought. Moreover, he did not want the British government to make this part of his trip known to the press.[18] Maybe he had the American warning against expensive purchases in mind when he made the request to keep his purchase of the plane quiet.

The Shah and his wife made one more stop before returning home, going to Montreux to visit the Shah's daughter, Shahnaz; her husband, Ardeshir; and his father, General Zahedi. The General was by then in frail health, and the Shah was keen on trying to reconcile with the man who had saved his throne in 1953 but had lived in virtual forced exile since 1955 and bore some resentment against him. Whether the General ever forgave the Shah for what he considered was his royal ingratitude is not clear.

Back in Iran, the Shah received help from two sources in his attempt to get rid of Amini. On the one hand, dissension within the Amini cabinet had all but paralyzed it. Amini's relationship with his ambitious minister of agriculture Arsanjani was at a breaking point. Arsanjani had begun avoiding not just cabinet meetings, but other important committees and functions. He had become "openly contemptuous of Amini" and had said more than once "that he will brook no interference from him or anyone else in the land reform or agricultural affairs."[19]

Arsanjani was not the only minister in defiant revolt. Safi Asfia and Khodadad Farmanfarmaian, two of the cabinet's key economic technocrats, were also resigning, each for different reasons. Many of the younger technocrats were turned off by the fact that in the midst of a serious national crisis, Amini had taken time off to go on a pilgrimage to Mecca—a two-week ordeal at the end of which the pious sojourner returns carrying the coveted title of "Hadji" (one who has gone on a pilgrimage to Mecca). Amini's picture in the traditional garb of a pilgrim—a long piece of white cloth, with no stitches made on it anywhere, as required by Islamic law, wrapped around the pilgrim's body like a shroud—appeared on the front page of some newspapers and became for weeks the subject of satirical comments. Adding to Amini's problems was the ballooning budget shortfall, estimated to reach more than $200 million for the next fiscal year.[20]

The Shah also received unexpected help from Edward Mason, who was sent by the White House to get a firsthand look at the situation in Iran. He arrived in Tehran on a fact-finding mission in June 1962 and found the Iranian situation "most discouraging," with the operational budget swollen and the deficit increasing. The relentless demands for increased pay for teachers by the cantankerous minister of education, Mohammad Darakhshesh—the leader of the striking teachers who had been given a ministerial portfolio to appease the strikers—and the Shah's unwillingness to accept a decrease in the military budget combined to make a balanced budget a pipe dream. Moreover, Mason found that Amini was "ill, exhausted, unable or unwilling to assert his will [and] restore fiscal order." All of these facts convinced Mason that the "Shah alone possesses sufficient power and authority to take necessary action."[21] Mason further concluded that "under prevailing circumstances US should not attempt bail out operational budget by any kind of support." Mason must have learned what everybody else seemed to have known for some time: without America's support and the constant infusion of U.S. aid for the operational budget, Amini could not survive.

A few days after Mason delivered his assessment to the White House, Kennedy sent a "personal message to the Shah" conveying his "personal concern over the apparent serious deterioration" in the economic situation, reminding the Shah that when they had "our most cordial talks here in Washington, we agreed that accelerated economic development was the best road toward a bright future for Iran."[22] What Mason had found out in a few days the Shah had known for a few months. The Shah knew that his "Amini problem" would be resolved only if he kept the military budget at least constant. Kennedy's letter was a subtle, albeit not forceful, request for a reduced military budget, but the Shah simply chose to ignore the request. He must have sensed that the new U.S. policy was to live with the Shah "and attempt to mold [him], i.e. support the Shah's reform program and work through him rather than attempting to circumscribe his role."[23]

On the afternoon of July 17, Ali Amini and his minister of finance, Jahanguir Amuzegar, met to discuss the new budget. After going over the numbers a few times, they realized they had a substantial shortfall of at least $35 million—even after a 10 percent across-the-board reduction of expenditures. They decided that, unless they could balance the budget, the cabinet should resign; before informing the Shah of their decision, they decided to meet with the American Ambassador and ask for an emergency loan.

Around eleven o'clock in the evening on the same day, Amuzegar arrived at the U.S. Embassy and asked for an emergency meeting with a very surprised Ambassador Julius Holmes. Unless the United States was willing to give the government an emergency $35 million loan, Holmes was told, the Amini cabinet would resign. Holmes believed that Amini was simply bluffing, and he therefore unceremoniously said no to the loan request. The next morning, Amini convened an emergency meeting of his cabinet and informed them of his decision to resign. Amini had assumed that the United States would somehow find a way to solve his budgetary crisis, but after Mason's report, the Kennedy administration was no longer willing to bankroll the Amini experiment.

According to the British Embassy, the Shah "accepted the [Amini] resignation with a marked degree of personal satisfaction."[24] He then appointed Assadollah Alam as prime minister. By then Alam had become at once the Shah's master of mirth and his enforcer, his reliable aide in the most sensitive political and even family issues. Alam's mandate was clear. He was to continue the reforms started by Amini but accept the fact that they would henceforth all be under the direct aegis of the Shah. Even the name used to describe these reforms was to change. On the day of Amini's appointment, *Etela'at,* Tehran's conservative daily, considered a mouthpiece of the Court, wrote an editorial called "White Coup or Red Revolution." Change in Iran was inevitable, the paper opined, and there were two paradigms for this change. One was promoted by the Soviet Union and was a "Red Revolution"; the other was supported by Kennedy and was a "White Coup."[25] The Shah, the paper said, had wisely chosen the "White Coup." A few months later, Amini, in the course of answering a journalist's question, said, "there is nothing unusual going on in Iran. . . . This government has simply decided to pursue a White Revolution that it deems necessary and in the nation's best interest."[26] It has been the consensus of historians that this was how the term "White Revolution" was coined. Some of the Shah's critics, hoping to underscore their claim that the entire project of reforms was masterminded by the United States, claim that even the term "White Revolution" was coined by Chester Bowles, the American official sent to Tehran by Kennedy in 1962.

But in a fascinating report, the British Embassy in Tehran claims that in 1958, Alam went to the embassy and offered a "program of reform which he said he wanted the Shah to adopt. He used the now much quoted phrase 'White Revolution'. It is possible that in voicing these views Mr. Alam was acting as a 'sounding board' for some of the Shah's own ideas."[27] However, before long, not only did the White Revolution itself metamorphose into "The Shah and People Revolution," but, in the Shah's narrative of this revolution, there was no place for Amini.

There was something surprising about the Alam tenure. When the appointment was first announced, foreign diplomats in Tehran observed that Alam would be nothing but "an instrument and the mouthpiece" for the Shah. In the view of the American Embassy, "the Alam appointment was the closest thing to direct rule of Shah. Alam completely devoted servant . . . from outset there will not [be a] question in anyone's mind of independence on part of PM."[28] The embassy made another revealing observation about Alam: they had come to believe that many members of the new cabinet, "including Alam have or have had British connections and may have been under British influence."[29] Was the Shah trying to assure Britain of its continued relevance in Iran by the appointment of an Anglophile prime minister to carry out a program supported by the United States? Whatever the Shah's intentions and whatever the embassy's estimation, in reality, Alam went on to play a crucial role in July 1963, saving the monarchy in its first major confrontation with the clergy.

The Shah's clash with the clergy was the culmination of a few years of planning on both sides. In 1955, when, under pressure from the clergy, the Shah had approved the attacks on members of the Baha'i faith, the British Ambassador went to talk with the Shah "about the bad influence of reactionary mullahs." The Shah, in response, said "he agreed that the mullahs must be kept in their place, and out of politics" but he thought it would be about two years before he could take them on and avoid any serious problem. The Shah missed it by a few years, and the confrontation took place not in two but in eight years; even then, trouble was not altogether avoided.[30]

The first stage of the big confrontation with radical clerics took place over an apparently insignificant proposed change in the election bylaws for local councils. Until then the law had called for everyone to take the oath of office using the Qu'ran. In recognition of the fact that there were large numbers of religious minorities in Iran—Zoroastrians, Jews, Christians, and Baha'i—the new language simply suggested that the oath must be taken with a book. Mullahs began a concentrated campaign using their elaborate networks to agitate against the new law. Their main line of attack was that the law was part of an assault on Islam and paved the way for Jews and Baha'i to use their own holy books to take their oaths.[31] The mullahs opposed the new proposed law from a reactionary perspective. Nevertheless, nobody in the opposition came to the support of the new proposed legislature.

Ayatollah Khomeini took the unusual step of writing a letter to the Shah. The letters exchanged were notable both for their decorous language and their firm, unbending positions. Ayatollah Khomeini had heard "reports that in the new election law . . . Islam is not indicated as a precondition for standing for office and women are being granted the right to vote. . . . As you know, national interests and spiritual comfort are both predicated on following Islamic laws. Please order all laws inimical to the sacred and official faith of the country to be eliminated from government policies."[32]

A couple of days later, the Shah responded. The first noticeable part of the retort is the way he chose to address Khomeini. In an obvious dig, the Shah did not use the title of ayatollah but instead called him "Hojat-al Islam," a much lower rank. The Shah said that the "new laws proposed by the government contain nothing new, and I want to remind you that I am more than anyone keen on respecting our religious rules. . . . At the same time, I want to remind you of the conditions of the time, and the situation in other countries of the world."[33] The Shah ended his note by telling the cleric that he would forward his letter to the Prime Minister.

A few days after receiving the Shah's terse note, Khomeini wrote back, this time threatening the monarch with the wrath of the Muslims. At the same time, he offered him some words of advice. "Don't allow sycophants to attribute their anti-Islamic acts to your Majesty." If ever there was a chance for a compromise between the Shah and Khomeini, it was in the course of these rare epistolary contacts. But compromise was not on either man's mind.

The clergy finally brought enough pressure on the government that Alam, in a press conference, announced that the proposed bill had been withdrawn. Ayatollah Khomeini, till then a little-known figure outside religious circles, took the lead in writing a letter to all religious leaders around the country congratulating them on their first major victory. He wrote less like just another cleric but like the leader of an unfolding revolution. The tone was messianic and self-assured, and the goals set for the movement were ambiguous but tantalizing. This was 1962.

For the Shah, however, the decision to withdraw the law was only a tactical retreat. Before long, on January 6, 1963, he announced a six-part program, the first volley of the renamed "Shah and People Revolution." It included, amongst other things, two articles the clergy adamantly opposed. Article one called for land reform. This was, according to the British Embassy, "one of the most revolutionary measures in 3000[-year] history of Iran."[34] The second article called for the right of women to vote and stand for office. The other four points covered nationalization of forests, sale of state-owned enterprises, profit-sharing by workers in 20 percent of corporate profits, and finally the creation of a Literacy Corps—the idea of using army conscripts as teachers in the Iranian countryside where illiteracy was sometimes estimated to be near 90 percent. While the major controversy of the Literacy Corps was simply the question of pride of authorship (three different sources claimed to have initially come up with the idea), the land reform and women's right to vote became the most contested issues of the White Revolution. The entire clerical hierarchy went into high gear to oppose these two elements. Moreover, on January 9 the Shah announced his decision to hold a referendum on January 26. The date was picked "in order to complete operations before the beginning of the *Ramdam* [*sic*]"—the month of fasting for Muslims.[35]

To counter the argument that the Iranian constitution did not allow for a referendum—an argument made against Mossadeq—the Shah argued that addenda 26 and 27 to the constitution "stipulate that the powers of the country are derived from the nation," thus allowing him to go directly to the people and ask for a legal mandate for his White Revolution.[36] The White House was not pleased with the decision for an entirely different reason. The Shah, they concluded, had decided "to wrap himself firmly in mantle of 'revolutionary monarch.'" In their opinion, the Shah had "bought Arsanjani's idea of building political bases among the peasantry and decided to have his own revolution without US advice."[37] Moreover, in what in retrospect turned out to be an almost prophetic prediction of the 1979 revolution, the White House was worried that land redistribution without extensive social reform would result in chaos and turn the "newly activated peasantry against the Shah."[38] What they failed to predict was that with the rise of Iran's oil revenues, cities would become magnets for these disgruntled peasants and that in the cities they would turn against the Shah and be absorbed by the clergy's wide network of organizations, becoming foot soldiers of the Islamic Revolution. The life of Iran's controversial twenty-first-century president, Mahmoud Ahmadinejad, follows this trajectory rather closely.[39]

The Shah and his regime did all they could to turn the referendum into a tour de force. Some of the leaders of the opposition, with the exception of the clergy, were arrested. On January 23, for example, according to the CIA, the government "brought 3000 peasants from Varamin" and "twelve buses from Karaj" to march in the streets of Tehran and shout pro-Shah slogans. Flexing his military muscle, the Shah also ordered a battalion of paratroopers to parade through Tehran that day. A tank company was ordered onto the Jalaliye racetrack—earlier the site of the big National Front rally.[40] The symbolism was hard to miss. On the same day, in the city of Qom, about 300 seminarians led about 3,000 demonstrators on a march against the referendum in the morning, while in the afternoon the government brought 5,000 peasants into the city to show support for the Shah. The peasants allegedly attacked the mullahs who had been against the regime, shouting slogans and wielding sticks.[41]

The referendum was at once unusually democratic and expectedly undemocratic. It was democratic in that women were for the first time allowed to vote, but their votes were not going to be counted. This was partially to put women on a collision course with the clergy who had opposed women's suffrage. Khomeini's views at the time, for example, were clear and categorical. Using a thinly disguised allusion to the Shah, Khomeini said, "the Court of the illegitimate Usurper has decided to offer men and women equal rights and trample on the edicts of the *Qor'an* and *Sharia'* and they want to take eighteen year old girls to serve in the army." Other ayatollahs were even more vituperative in their opposition to women's right to vote and their equality before the law. In many areas—from laws of inheritance and divorce to laws on custody of children in a case of divorce to testimonies in the court of law—Islamic *sharia* is decidedly against women. Some critics have pointed to the composite of these laws as the legal foundation for gender apartheid in Iran.[42] The early signs of this gender apartheid were evident in the clergy's opposition to the Shah's intended reforms in favor of women. Ironically, the Iranian opposition, even amongst the feminists, also never supported these reforms, dismissing them as "cosmetic" and superficial. But in 1963, the participation of women in the referendum was intended to show them who their foes were and also to give them a taste of power. "Women were unlikely to leave the political world," the American Embassy reported, "without a fight."[43]

While the participation of women, albeit merely symbolic, added to the democratic value of the referendum, the fact that voters were required to vote in open ballot boxes, under the watchful eyes of the police and security forces stationed in every voting place, made the results highly suspect. Not surprisingly, 99.5 percent of those who voted cast a ballot in favor of the White Revolution, with a little more than 4,000 people out of an electorate of nearly 6 million daring to ask for a "No" ballot.

The success of the referendum was a cause of tempered joy in the Kennedy White House. Robert Komer, President Kennedy's point man on Iran, who was refreshingly frank in his views and notes, decided that "it has been a long time since we last massaged the Shah." The referendum and the proposed reforms, he said, "provide a first-class occasion for JFK to do it (and to remind him that Big Brother is watching)."[44]

Kennedy did write the note of congratulation; no sooner had the Shah received it than he decided that it offered him an opening to further consolidate his relations with the American President. He immediately sent a message inviting President and Mrs. Kennedy to visit Iran at their earliest convenience. The response was not satisfactory to the Shah. Kennedy, after "expressing deepest gratitude" and reiterating his "interest in the Shah's progressive reform movement," informed him that he must nevertheless decline the invitation.[45]

But the Shah had other, more immediate problems to face after the referendum. He was aware of the clergy's opposition to his reforms and their boycott of the referendum, and he was angry at what he felt was a de facto alliance between them and disgruntled landowners; he went on a carefully calibrated offensive. The regime had also received reports that the clergy were planning to turn the roused passions common in this month of Muharram into political demonstrations against the Shah and his reforms. It is during the first ten days of the month that Shiites mourn the martyrdom of their Third Imam, Hussein, in the Battle of Karbala in A.D. 642, and processions of flagellating men and weeping women crowd city streets. The Shah and his trusted prime minister, Alam, set out a multifaceted strategy. They began marshalling military and security forces for the possible day of reckoning, and the Shah also commenced a public relations campaign against the mullahs.

On the one hand, he needed to label his clerical opponents not just as reactionaries but as lackeys of foreign powers, particularly of Gamal Abdel Nasser in Egypt. Even with the luxury of hindsight, the Shah, in his *Answer to History*, suggested that in "1963 Tehran riots were inspired by an obscure individual who claimed to be a religious leader, Ruhollah Khomeini. It was certain, however, that he had secret dealing with foreign agents. Later the radio stations run by atheist émigrés, belonging to the Tudeh Party, accorded him the title of Ayatollah."[46]

Virtually every claim in these three sentences is at best inaccurate, if not altogether wrong. Sadly, with many passages like this, *Answer to History* has become yet another example of what François Dumouriez famously said of the courtiers surrounding the King after the French Revolution—"they have forgotten nothing, and learned nothing."

Moreover, as the Shah confided to Ambassador Holmes in 1963, he knew that in attacking the mullahs, he must not seem "anti-religious." As a result, concurrently with his surprisingly blistering attacks on the clergy who dared oppose him, he also gave many speeches "reemphasizing his own Muslim faith and that religion is essential for any nation." More than once he referred to his three spiritual experiences as a child, when he was saved by Shiite imams. He tried to offer himself as at once a defender of the faith and a crusader against reactionary clerics. In Qom, he told the assembled peasants, "I can tell you today that in practice and in past experiences, no one can claim to be closer to God and to saints than me."[47]

His attacks on the clergy were surprisingly uncompromising. On April 2, 1963, taking a page out of his father's playbook, the Shah traveled to the city of Qom, the heartland of Shiite power in Iran, and not only delivered deeds to farmers from eighty-seven different villages but delivered a detailed and stinging attack on the clergy. Never a great speaker, in this and other similarly belligerent talks, he soared to new heights of oratory. Often he talked without notes, and in the excitement of the moment, with the adulation of a crowd that both had a financial stake in the reforms and had been coached to exhibit monarchist exuberance, he eloquently criticized the clergy. Evidence shows clearly that in some of these meetings, uniformed members of the military were spread throughout the crowd, acting both as coaches of exuberance and guards of safety.

On that April day, the Shah spoke of the clergy's "little, empty and antique" brains that wished to turn back society to the days of the Middle Ages. Making an unmistakable reference to the practice common in some villages whereby every peasant girl was required to be deflowered by the landlord before her nuptial night, the Shah, knowing full well Iranian men's obsession with questions of "honor" and "virginity," asked, rhetorically, why these obscurantist mullahs were insistent on keeping alive the feudal system in which "before the first night of nuptial, some shameful acts were required." And, then, he made a clear threat against his opponents by saying, "if necessary we will even shed the blood of some innocent people to eliminate this group of miserable ignorant elements. There is no alternative and it shall be done."[48]

Four days later, in the city of Kashan, he made an even more blistering attack on the clergy. He called them "black reaction"—his unmistakable code name for the clergy opposed to him. By then "red reaction" had also become his favorite code for Communists. He defiantly declared, "the days of black reaction have ended. Theirs were the days when they used to get a free ride off the people's shoulders. Today is the time of logic and reason, and they, like madmen, are trying to lie."[49]

As the Shah was preparing for a confrontation with the clergy who opposed him, the mullahs, increasingly under the leadership of Ayatollah Khomeini, also began to prepare for their fight with the Shah. Until the death of Ayatollah Boroujerdi, Khomeini had been forced to remain in the shadows. Nevertheless, he had, in spite of Ayatollah Boroujerdi's injunction, decided to support and align with a young, fiery, rabble-rousing cleric turned terrorist called Navvab Safavi, the founder of Feda'yan-e Islam (Martyrs of Islam), the most powerful Islamic terrorist group in modern Iranian history.[50] Safavi had been executed by the Shah's regime in 1955. Now, with Boroujerdi's death, Khomeini was stepping into the limelight and appealing not only to the more radical, younger elements of the clergy but to the remnants of Safavi's followers.

In those days, the network of Islamic forces was as nebulous and nimble as it was invisible to the untrained eye, which, incidentally, included SAVAK. The network included classes in the Qu'ran, religious camps for different ages, mourning groups in charge of organizing processions and mourning ceremonies, women's groups, and a number of publishing houses, many located in the city of Qom, which published large-circulation magazines and books. There were also a large number of political groups. Aside from the Freedom Movement—the more religious wing of the National Front—there were at least three other underground organizations active against the regime.

In March 1963, Ayatollah Khomeini called the leaders of the three underground groups to his house and asked them to unite their forces in anticipation of the coming battles with the regime. After some cajoling, the groups agreed and created one organization. Khomeini even suggested a name for the new group—Mo'talefe—the Coalition—a name that would be "neutral" and acceptable to all groups. Under Khomeini's advice the new group created a military wing to be used in terrorist acts, as well as a political wing. They immediately set out to create a national network that used public phones, often around mosques, to organize united actions. It was a measure of the power of the new group in 1963 that they could distribute 250,000 copies of some of Khomeini's proclamations. Even then, when tape recorders were a novelty in Iran, tapes of some of his talks were also distributed widely through this clandestine network.[51] SAVAK learned of this group's existence only a year after its creation.[52] In 1978, the network of Khomeini's seminarians became the main vehicle for establishing clerical hegemony over the burgeoning but deeply disunited democratic movement.

Khomeini put only two constraints on the group's activities. Before killing anyone, they must have the *fatwa* of a cleric, and they should not "receive arms from anyone but should buy it." But considering the group's extensive influence inside the bazaars of the country, finding money to support the group was not a difficult task. Before long, the terrorist tentacles of the group would reach not just deep inside the Shah's regime, but within the walls of his palaces. The 1965 assassination of a prime minister and the failed attempt on the Shah's life that same year were both the works of religious zealots.

Once formed, the group, helped by a number of other ad hoc groups and personalities, began advertising for Ayatollah Khomeini as a new *marja-e taglid,* or "source of emulation." Shiism divides the community of believers into two groups: the handful of emulated ayatollahs and the rest of the flock. Each Shiite must choose an ayatollah to emulate. What makes an educated cleric into a *marja-e* is the publication of a treatise called *Towzih-al Masael* (Answers to Questions)—a catechism-like narrative that consists of that cleric's answers (*fatwas*) to questions. Khomeini, by then a popular teacher at the seminary, decided to publish his *Towzih-al Masael* at this time. Many of his students claim that they pressured Khomeini into publishing the text. With the death of Boroujerdi, those who "emulated" him would bus people from around the country "in groups of twenty" to Qom, ostensibly to meet with Khomeini and appraise him as a potential ayatollah to follow. In reality, the purpose of these "meetings was to exchange views and information which could then be passed to other groups."[53] A telephone network and a "special fund" to defray the cost of the movement were also established.

The two armies, one composed of the military and security forces and belonging to the Shah, and the other consisting of the supporters of Khomeini, clashed on June 5, the tenth day of Moharram, when passions were aroused. In the early hours of that day, commandos attacked Ayatollah Khomeini's house in Qom, put him under arrest, and brought him to Tehran in an unmarked car. News of his arrest arrived in Tehran before he and his captors did. His network of supporters took to the streets, shouting slogans, burning banks and cinemas, attacking governmental offices, even attempting to take over the radio station. Alam also estimated that "approximately 2000 of the demonstrators were fanatical and pro-mullah" and the rest were "the South Tehran mob which responds to any opportunity to destroy and loot."[54] Other sources have put the figure of demonstrators in the tens of thousands. It is also true that other bigger cities were participating in this mass uprising.

Even before the uprising begun, Alam had asked and surprisingly received the Shah's consent to command the military and security forces for the duration of the uprising. His idea was simple: he would use the full force of the military to put down the uprising, and if he succeeded, the Shah could take the credit and suffer no blame. If Alam failed, the Shah could fire him and accuse him of mismanagement.

Lest the Shah prove indecisive in the middle of the confrontation, Alam made sure his contacts with him that day were minimal. The armed forces were ordered to shoot to kill. Alam told the generals, "[T]he guns you were given are not toys. Use them." The morning of June 5, the Shah called Alam and asked, "[N]ow that we have a revolution on our hands, what will you do?" Alam said, "[G]uns and canons are in my hand. . . . I will tear their mothers apart." The Shah "laughed from the bottom of his heart and said I agree and I am fully behind you."[55]

By that night, Tehran was awash with rumors about rivers of blood and of an imminent court-martial for Ayatollah Khomeini with a death sentence to be handed down for treason. The organizations and networks he had used, with leaders like Ali Khamenei, Hussein Ali Montazeri, and Ali Akbar Hashemi Rafsanjani—all future leaders of the Republi—got busy encouraging ayatollahs from around the world to write to the Shah and confirm that Khomeini was a full-fledged ayatollah—and was thus protected by a provision of the Iranian constitution prohibiting the death penalty for ayatollahs. In fact, no such provision exists, and the constitutional movement proved the power of their popular base when they executed Sheikh Fazlollah Nuri, an ayatollah at the time, a foe of the constitutional movement, and later a hero of Khomeini. Yet if Alam is to be believed, the possibility of the death penalty was for Khomeini was simply a false rumor. On the afternoon of June 6, Alam told U.S. Ambassador Holmes that "Khomeini [would] be tried by [a] military court for inciting against public order and resistance to enforcement of law. He expected the court would not give more than a prison sentence."[56] More crucially, Alam even claims that while religious leaders had formally sent notes supporting Khomeini, "they had sent word to the Prime Minister that their appeals should be disregarded." Alam was counting on "jealousy of Khomeini" and "individual rivalries" amongst the mullahs for preventing Khomeini from ever emerging as the leader of the Shiite community.[57] Incredible as Alam's claim about private communications against Khomeini from ayatollahs might seem, it fits what is now known about the bad blood between the unyielding mullah and other more moderate clergy—particularly Shariat-Madari. In fact, Ayatollah Shariat-Madari believed that on June 5, Khomeini, in cooperation with a supposed army of nomadic tribes led by the Qashgai brothers, was actually planning to seize power.

On the afternoon of June 8, when the Shah and Ambassador Holmes were in a meeting, Hussein Ala and Abdollah Entezam—an elder statesman and for many years the head of Iran's oil company—went to the Court and, according to the Shah, "they shouted at me, and said enough is enough, enough bloodshed, dismiss the government of Alam, and make your peace with the mullahs." The Shah heard their arguments but then, in his own words, "threw [Ala and Entezam] out of [his] office," summoned Alam to the Court, and ordered him to arrest the two men. Alam also makes clear that the Shah had ordered out not just Ala and Entezam but the other three elder statesmen who had met at Ala's home and complained about the government's approach to the crisis; Alam claims he did not follow the Shah's orders, however, asking him for forgiveness.

Reports and rumors about the number of people killed on June 5 ranged from the opposition's claim of "thousands" to the regime's official figure of about 120. The American Embassy gave the number of dead as 200. When the Shah was in exile, and free from the immediate incentive to fudge or fidget, a curious Denis Wright—sent to the Bahamas by Margaret Thatcher to meet the Shah—asked him about the "real number of those killed" that June, and the Shah declared that the same number announced by the government at the time had been correct.[58] Moreover, contrary to the fear that the army would not fire on their fellow citizens—something that had frightened the Shah two years earlier—the army proved willing and killed "no small number" of protestors.[59] The White House, on the other hand, was not happy with the events of June 5. Two weeks after the event, Ambassador Holmes was instructed to protest to the Shah "about the incompetence of his government."[60]

By June 9 the city began to return to normalcy. For the rest of his political life, Alam never ceased reminding the Shah that he saved the throne and deracinated the power of the clergy. A few days after the bloodshed, when Denis Wright met Alam, he found him "like a cheerful schoolboy, and [he seemed] quite unworried by last week's rioting. Rather like an ostrich, I fear."[61] Wright concluded, however, that "nothing is quite the same." Serious trouble, he wrote, "has been nipped in the bud for [the] time being but this won't be the end."[62] A couple of weeks after the June riots, a dispatch from the British Embassy in Tehran concluded that "the weakness of character and judgment" the Shah had shown in the past had not been "exorcized.... The country is waiting for leadership which somehow despite all the brave words, the Shah never quite provides."[63]

At the same time, taking his cues from the Shah, Alam continued trying to convince leaders of the National Front, many of them then in prison, to join a coalition government. If before the bloody suppression such a coalition was hard to imagine, after that June it was virtually impossible to fathom. The U.S. Embassy kept asking about the time when the imprisoned National Front leaders would be released, and the Shah clearly felt he must make at least one more gesture of readiness for reconciliation. As he told the American Ambassador on July 18, 1963, he had agreed to the broad outlines of a deal with the National

Front. In fact, while they were in prison, the leaders met with an Iranian who introduced himself as a "well-wisher" who had close ties to representatives of the U.S. government and tried to hammer out the terms of this deal. The deal called for the release of the leaders and a meeting with the Shah "when they would give him oral assurances that they accept his leadership and realize that during this revolutionary period, the Shah must play more active role than of constitutional monarch." The only hitch, as the U.S. Embassy observed, was that the National Front leaders wanted to first be set free and then work out the finer elements of the agreement, but the Shah did not trust them. Eventually, the Shah agreed to have the men put "on parole for a stated period to see whether or not they would comply with the understanding tentatively reached."[64] The deal ultimately fell through, as the younger, more radical elements of the National Front agitated against it.

What is not clear is whether the Shah really intended to seek reconciliation with the National Front or whether he made the offer in the hope of sowing dissension amongst the ranks of the Front and in this way separating the more moderate elements from the rest. In reality, the reverse happened. Some of the more radical members of the National Front became convinced after the bloody suppression of the June uprising that there was no room for reconciliation with the Shah. They took up arms against the regime. The religious elements created the Mujahedin-e Khalq (MEK) and the Marxists founded the Feda'yan-e Khalq Iran (Martyrs of the People). In less than six years, in what came to be known as the Siahkal Incident—taking its name from the village nearby—a small group of these radicals fought against the small military post stationed there. The battle would shock the Shah and the intelligence agencies and lead to the use of increasingly harsher methods by SAVAK and numerous reports of torture.

The leaders of the National Front were not the only ones surprised by developments after June 5. Alam clearly felt he was owed a long tenure in appreciation of his role in saving the Crown. He had at least one other major accomplishment. Again, under the direct command of the Shah, Iran normalized its tense relations with the Soviet Union. This was the first step in a major shift in the Shah's foreign policy. If, in 1963, he promised the Soviets that Iran would never allow a foreign military base on its soil,* two years later, after an important trip by the Shah to the Soviet Union, a new leaf was turned in the relations between the two countries. Iran agreed to sell gas to the Soviet government in return for help in establishing a steel mill—something the Shah and his father had coveted for

* The Shah kept his promise only in the most literal sense of the agreement. Iran in fact allowed the U.S. and British intelligence agencies to establish highly sensitive listening stations in Iran's northern provinces that monitored Soviet nuclear activities.

more than three decades. In many private conversations, Alam tried to take at least some of the credit for this normalization.

But none of these real or claimed services could save him. In fact, he had a big surprise in store. A little more than two weeks after the June 5 uprising, the Shah shared his intentions to dismiss Alam and appoint Hassan-Ali Mansur with an American Embassy official. Furthermore, the Shah felt the need to engage in the "ruthless dismissal" of some of the "people surrounding him," a "house cleaning." Amongst those the Shah wanted to dismiss were Ja'far Sharif-Emami and Abdollah Entezam. He also planned to create "a single political party . . . to become the main political force in the future."[65] Before long, the Shah put his support behind the Progressive Circle and ordered the creation of the Iran Novin Party. At this time, the Shah confided to the British Embassy that he was now "convinced of the need of a one-party system in order to reach the people."[66] These pronouncements are particularly interesting in light of the fact that only three years earlier, in *Mission for My Country,* the Shah had condemned one-party systems as befitting only totalitarian Communist societies.

In the meantime, one of the accusations against Ayatollah Khomeini was that he had accepted money from Nasser of Egypt. Khomeini was also accused of creating an unholy alliance with General Bakhtiyar, and it was this alliance, the regime claimed, that had played a role in fanning the flames of discontent. Many in Iran and some of the diplomats stationed in Tehran at the time doubted the veracity of the charge that Khomeini had taken money from Nasser. Denis Wright, for example, wrote in his journal, "a tense day . . . marshal law . . . Persian government is claiming Nasser's hand behind it. I doubt this very much."[67] Using the safety of exile, Bakhtiyar had in fact begun to actively work against the Shah. He had no qualms about his potential allies. Whoever was against the Shah—from Nasser in Egypt to Ayatollah Khomeini, Communist members of the Tudeh Party, or members of the newly established Confederation of Iranian Students, and after 1968, the Ba'ath party in Iraq—he saw as a potential ally and went out of his way to form an alliance with them.[68]

In fact, Bakhtiyar's actions against the Shah had begun in the days when he was still the head of SAVAK. In the fall of 1959, he had let American officials know that "he was sympathetic to the idea of action which would place him at the head of Iranian government."[69] On March 10, 1959, the CIA reported that "Bakhtiyar has been making contingency plans" for the time "the Shah lost control."[70] A month later, the same source reported to a meeting of the National Security Council that Bakhtiyar was "continuing to formulate plans" in the event "the Shah disappears." Bakhtiyar even tried to frighten the American government into supporting him. In August of that year, Bakhtiyar told American officials that "present policies of Shah and government are leading Iran towards revolution" and that "he expects the Shah will flee to Europe in near future."[71] Proof of this prediction, Bakhtiyar told American officials, was that the Shah was converting "royal property into hard currency" and no longer showed any "interest in domestic investments."[72] Ironically, Bakhtiyar who had by then come to symbolize all the brutalities of SAVAK, whose name conjured terrifying tales of torture against the opposition and rampant financial corruption in the regime, claimed that the chief source of his discontent was the fact that the Shah forced him to use SAVAK to rig elections. In recent elections, American officials were told, the Shah had personally picked "every one" of the Majlis deputies.[73] These efforts to woo American support for the idea of a coup had all failed. Interestingly, there is no evidence that the CIA reported any of these machinations to the Shah. Only in 1961 when Bakhtiyar tried to convince the Kennedy administration to support his plans, did Kim Roosevelt inform the Shah.

What Bakhtiyar had failed to accomplish with the Eisenhower and Kennedy administrations in the years between 1959 and 1962, he tried to achieve in exile. He first tried to solicit the help of the British. On October 12, 1962, he met with Denis Wright, who had served in Iran for many years and was soon to return as ambassador. The meeting took place in the Ritz Hotel in Cannes, where Bakhtiyar was spending some of his time. Bakhtiyar was known as a bon vivant and an incorrigible womanizer, and the French Riviera had always been one of his favorite spots. He talked of "growing discontent among all classes in Iran" and of increasing Russian influence in the country. He blamed "the Shah exclusively" for the country's serious troubles. Iran's sole salvation, Bakhtiyar said, was "for a strong man and an equally strong team" to rule in the name of the Crown Prince. There was, of course, no doubt that the strong man he had in mind was none other than Bakhtiyar himself. Denis Wright was less than supportive. He first gave the standard British claim when they wanted to refuse help to someone, saying, "Britain did not get involved in the domestic political situation" of Iran. Bakhtiyar knew as well as anyone how influential the British were in Iran's domestic politics—Bakhtiyar himself owed his job as the head of SAVAK at least partially to their support. But the crucial part of Wright's response came when he said it was the policy of Her Majesty's government "to support the Shah."[74]

After that October 1962 meeting, the British government faced a dilemma. Should they keep silent and hope that the Shah never found out about the meeting, or should they tell him about the meeting and risk his wrath but also stoke the fires of his paranoia about what he considered the constant British machinations against him? Denis Wright argued that they should tell the Shah exactly what had happened—emphasizing that as far as they were concerned, Bakhtiyar had virtually ambushed him—and assure him that no other contacts with the General were planned.[75] The British government chose the Wright approach, but the Shah was not convinced that they were telling the truth. In fact, a few years later, one of the biggest public confrontations between Iran and Britain took place over Bakhtiyar's alleged ties to the British.

The Shah's troubles on the days of the June uprising were not limited to Khomeini, Bakhtiyar, angry landlords keen on keeping their villages from expropriation, and a disgruntled urban population. On the night of June 6, 1963, the royal family and a handful of their friends were gathered for what was beginning to have the regularity of ritual—an evening at the house of one of the members of the Shah's family, dinner, a card game for some, a film for all, and early retirement to their individual homes. That night it was Princess Ashraf's turn. The Shah and the Queen were, as was customary, the last to arrive. That night, with occasional sounds of gunfire in the air, the Shah arrived in his Royal Air Force uniform. He still smoked in those days and after sipping some Scotch (Black Label was his favorite) and smoking half a cigarette with his long holder, he began to go around to meet with the guests. Everyone was nervous. Groups of three and four had gathered around the large hall and chatted in hushed voices. When the Shah finally came to the group that included Dr. Yahya Adle, his friend of many years and a member of the loyal opposition Party of Martyrdom, he was shocked by the sudden verbal volley of angry words coming from Adle. "Do you know what is happening around the city?" Dr. Adle asked. In a voice trembling with anger, he said, "[Y]ou can't keep your throne afloat on a river of blood." The hall suddenly came to a complete silence. "Yahya, you don't know what you are talking about," replied the Shah. Those like Adle who knew the Shah well were aware that when he was particularly angry at a friend, he would call him by his first name. But to everyone's surprise, Adle's outburst cost him nothing other than this one sentence.

Dr. Adle's surprising burst of anger that night was simply the tip of the iceberg. Scholars like Ann Lambton considered June 5, 1963, "a turning point" in the history of Iran in that it was on that day that the Shah "showed unexpected resolution in dealing with trouble-makers."[76] This was a far cry from the judgment passed by Sir Roger Stevens in 1958 as he was leaving his post as British ambassador to Iran. "He is, I fear," he wrote of the Shah, "incapable of formulating, let alone executing a really constructive policy of any kind. . . . So long as he is on the throne of Persia, it is hard to imagine that there will be a decent government, let alone social justice."[77]

The radical clergy claimed that the day was proof positive that reform within the Shah's regime was untenable and the only solution was a revolution. For forces loyal to Ayatollah Khomeini, June 5, 1963, was nothing short of the birth of the "Khomeini Movement." For Alam, on the other hand, June 5 was the end of the Shah's Khomeini problem. From that day on, he never ceased reminding the Shah that thanks to his efforts, the mullahs were no longer a viable political force. For the Shah, the day was also historic in that it once and for all exposed the reactionary nature of his opposition.

But reports of the army's opening fire on defenseless demonstrators and of "thousands of dead"—as the opposition claimed—did little to improve the Shah's image or to endear him to the Kennedy administration. In May 1963, in a brief prepared at the White House, the opinions and suggestions of different factions in the administration were clearly articulated. What is incredible is the stark reality that virtually no one supported the Shah and his increasingly personal rule outright. According to the brief, "Attorney General, Justice Douglas, and some legislators and academic figures believe US should force the Shah to turn power to pro-Mossadeq urban white collar groups around the National Front."[78] Associate Supreme Court Justice William Douglas in fact went one step further himself, writing that "I talked to Jack [Kennedy] frequently about conditions in Iran and the corruption that was rampant. Then when he entertained the Shah at the White House, when he was here on an official visit, Jack concluded that the Shah was corrupt and not a person we could trust. . . . The idea was to withdraw American support for the Shah causing his abdication," and bring to power a regency that "had already been selected."[79] Other sources suggest that, aside from Ali Amini and the Qashgai brothers, a couple of other National Front leaders were considered for the Regency Council. The State Department opposed this alternative and concluded that it would only lead to a "replay of Mossadeq era chaos with Communists having learned not to miss their cues."[80]

But Robert Kennedy and Justice Douglas were not the Shah's only critics in the Kennedy administration. Another group, particularly popular in the Department of Defense and the CIA, believed that the Shah was "weak, inefficient and confused and has needlessly raised [a] hornets nest." They advocated that the United States force the Shah to "halt reforms and turn over power to military based traditional groups." A third group wanted the United States to force the Shah to turn over power to "a young Western trained economist."[81]

Kennedy's assassination on November 22, 1963, put an end to these speculations. There was a new president and a new policy. What is invariably surprising about the liberal-minded administration is the ease with which they talked of "regime change" in Iran and about deciding in Washington what the structure of power should be in Tehran.

Kennedy's last correspondence with the Shah was about the same issue that had preoccupied the two men from the beginning and that had become a point of contention between them. It related to the size of the Iranian military and the nature of the threat to Iran. In the letter, Kennedy used a new argument, telling the Shah that since the Cuban Missile Crisis in October 1962, it had become obvious that the United States had strategic superiority over the Soviet Union, and thus the Shah did not need to worry about the Soviet threat.[82]

The Shah was sensitive to the attitude of the U.S. and British governments towards him and was affected by the tensions with the Kennedy brothers. On November 22, hours after Kennedy was assassinated, the State Department concluded that "the Shah needs fresh assurances."[83] On the other hand, on hearing the news of the Kennedy assassination, the Shah personally dictated to Foreign Minister Abbas Aram an angry diatribe against Kennedy addressed to President Lyndon Johnson. In the letter, the Shah accused Kennedy of a failure to understand the intricacies of Iranian politics and of unduly interfering in the affairs of the country. The Shah had specifically ordered Aram to send the letter without showing it to anyone. But Aram shared the letter with Alam, and both decided against sending it.

After a few days, Alam informed the Shah of his decision not to send the letter. The Shah, visibly shaken and angry, threw the letter to the ground, leaving the room in a rage. For the next two weeks, he refused to talk to Alam or to grant him the regular audiences set aside for the Prime Minister. Even at parties and official ceremonies, the Shah pointedly shunned Alam and made no attempt to hide his dismay. Finally, of course, they reconciled,[84] but the Shah's bitter feelings toward the Kennedys lingered and, as Alam's *Daily Journals* show, reared their head regularly, particularly in biting remarks the Shah made about the Kennedys in private. Even the long, meandering letter that was eventually sent to Johnson offered both condolences for the assassination and confidence and hope that U.S.–Iranian relations would thrive in the coming years, free from any misunderstanding.

The psychological impact of those trying years on the Shah's political persona can be seen in the two profiles of him prepared during the height of these tensions. One was written by officials of the British government, the other by an American journalist.

On the day after the fall of the Amini government in July 1962, an American journalist named C. D. Jackson visited the Shah in Tehran in preparation of a profile he was writing for *Time* magazine. Editors of the magazine, on a "confidential basis," sent a copy of the essay to Press Secretary Pierre Salinger for President Kennedy's information. Jackson met the Shah on August 7. He described the Sa'ad Abad Palace as a "disappointment . . . some kind of European hodge-podge, a mixture of Italian, French and, as far as I was concerned, North German Lloyd."[85] About the same time, in a visit to the Court for an official ceremony, the British Ambassador noticed "the extent to which Westernization had affected the essentially Persian style . . . a string orchestra played Western music . . . nothing Persian at all except the pillaw [rice pilaf] at the end of a European dinner."[86] Jackson found the room where he met the Shah even less appealing. "The furniture was atrocious, the decorations were ghastly."[87] As to the Shah himself, he appeared to be "in good shape, lean, good condition, dark soulful eyes, tremendous busy dark eyebrows and hair beginning to go a little [gray] at the temples. His tailor is not very good and the guy from whom he gets his neckties should be subjected [to] some sort of ancient Persian punishment."[88]

The Shah began the interview by offering a thinly disguised critique of the Kennedy policy in Iran, relying on the standard cultural relativist argument that the "countries were totally different. They were different racially. They were different to their customs and mores." He opined that "as far as Persian history was concerned, where there had been a really strong leader, Persia had almost conquered the world."[89] He also made what was by then one of his standard complaints, criticizing the administration for "continuing military aid to" his nemesis, Nasser in Egypt.

The interview ended with another question that would, in later years, become a far more urgent issue for the Shah. Jackson asked the Shah whether "he ever got depressed" and whether he had any friends. The Shah "replied yes, that [he] got depressed, not very often" and that he had no friends, "anywhere. I have companions for jokes, but no friend to whom I can look up to as wiser than I am, who can give me the right kind of advice."[90] For Jackson, the responses indicated that he was talking to a "modern Hamlet . . . a man with all the right instincts, intelligent, capable of understanding what the game is but with a fundamental, temperamental reluctance to play the game to the fullest."[91]

Another profile, this time prepared by the British Embassy, captures the early stages of the Shah's authoritarian power, as well as the vulnerability of such absolute power. The author of the report writes that already, "No public situation, civil or military, domestic or external, economic, political or social, no senior appointment, no promotion, transfer, reward, or punishment takes place" without the Shah's approval. But the report points to the reality that the "complexities of the modern state are inevitably beyond the control of a single individual." Because of "exorbitant panegyrics of sycophants" who the Shah had gathered around him, he was, according to the profile, being "increasingly convinced that only he is capable of governing this country." Even more dangerous, according to the report, was the fact that though "he is genuinely patriotic, he is also egotistical and not incorruptible. He is inclined to lose his nerves, and some accuse him of cowardice. If he is autocratic, he can also be indecisive and irresolute, readily changing his mind according to the latest advice." Worst of all, according to the report, as the result of recent developments, "he has become acutely unpopular."[92]

If the ambitions of Amini, the anger of teachers, and the new paradigm of politics promoted by the Kennedy administration were not enough to make the early 1960s interesting for the Shah, there was also the problem of the indomitable Khaybar Khan—onetime ally turned indefatigable foe, who used the American media and the Congress to make serious allegations of fraud against the Shah, his family, and courtiers. He fabricated checks showing large deposits in the Shah's accounts from funds set aside by the United States for social causes in Iran. It took the Shah many years and the help of many lawyers to finally convince the U.S. government that Khaybar Khan was not a reliable source.

In this period, another issue that occupied the Shah's mind was the question of a Status of Forces Agreement (SOFA) with the United States. The Shah wanted American advisors to train Iran's military, particularly the air force. The U.S. Department of Defense, on the other hand, preconditioned the arrival of these advisors on the passage of a SOFA–something the United States has with every country where it has stationed forces. The SOFA being suggested in Iran, however, was more extensive, as it completely exempted not only the servicemen but their families from prosecution in Iranian courts. The State Department was against the idea of insisting on such a SOFA, predicting that it would give rise to nationalist sentiments and would be considered a revival of the old colonial habit of Capitulation Rights. Many in Iran, including some in the government, also opposed the proposed SOFA for the same reasons. The Shah shepherded through the Iranian parliament the proposed agreement and, cognizant of rising public sentiments against the bill, even encouraged some members of the Majlis to oppose it. Eventually the law was passed after Prime Minister Hassan-Ali Mansur knowingly lied to the parliament about its actual content. The most forceful opposition to the bill came from Ayatollah Khomeini who was eventually exiled for his virulent anti-Shah, anti-Israel, and anti-American rhetoric.[93] The Prime Minister soon paid with his life for his role in the affair, and Khomeini was catapulted into the center of Iranian politics.

The events of 1963 had clearly affected the Shah's physical and psychological condition. In February of 1964, accompanied by the Queen, he took a trip to Europe. They were supposed to be gone for only two weeks; they stayed for five. As always, rumors began to spread. People whispered: why is he gone for so long? An explanation was required. *Etala'at* offered the official explanation in an editorial. The trip, it said, was primarily motivated by the Shah's "need for rest" and for "treatment for abdominal trouble, which usually stems from over-work and particularly tense intellectual activities and thought." In other words, so worried was the Shah about the country and so hard had he been working that he had developed something of an ulcer.

The American Embassy was not convinced. They said they were not sure that he in fact "had [an] ulcer. He has chronic liver trouble but not clear whether this flared up." What they learned from a "fairly reliable report from Vienna medical source described his condition as 'anxiety complex.'"[94] This turned out to be the first hint of the Shah's anxiety.

Maybe his anxiety, as much psychological as political, was rooted in the fact that he knew, more by his unarticulated instinct than by reasoned insights, that the socioeconomic forces he had put into motion would sooner or later clash with his increasingly authoritarian style of rule. For the Shah, character was destiny. He was neither an efficient dictator, nor a man willing to accept the constraints on his power set in place by the constitution and made necessary by the increasingly modern characteristics of Iranian society—characteristics he himself had played a key role in creating.

Chapter 16

THE DESERT BASH

His rash fierce blaze of riot cannot last.
For violent fires soon burn out themselves;
. . . .
Light vanity, insatiate cormorant.
Shakespeare, King Richard II, *2.1.33–38*

During the last week of April 1972, Kermit ("Kim") Roosevelt visited Tehran on behalf of "one of his American business associates." Given "his close personal relationship" with the Shah, he was invariably granted a private meeting with the King. And in those days, as Iran's oil revenues increased and the number of supplicant heads of state and company executives visiting Tehran increased exponentially, getting a private audience with the Shah was no easy matter. As recorded in his *Daily Journals*, Assadollah Alam repeatedly urged the Shah to refrain from meeting with this head of state or that executive, saying that such meetings were no longer befitting His Majesty's exalted international stature. Roosevelt was an exception.

In the course of the meeting, the Shah talked solely about the international situation. He complained about King Faisal of Saudi Arabia and President Anwar al-Sadat of Egypt. Nasser was no longer on the Shah's list of worries, but Soviet gains in the region—particularly in places like Iraq, Syria, and Afghanistan—were of constant concern. He ended his meeting with Roosevelt by declaring that "in spite of the difficulties involved, he felt he must play a more active role as a regional leader in organizing anticommunist forces."[1]

Domestic matters were not mentioned that day. By them, the Shah increasingly viewed himself as a regional and global leader, not just a head of state. His leadership in OPEC, Iran's emergence as the most powerful nation in the Persian Gulf, the prominent place he occupied in the Nixon administration's strategic vision for the Middle East, as well as the endless procession of Iranian and foreign sycophants, affirmed his growing sense of grandeur. When someone suggested that Iran launch a campaign to give the Shah the Nobel Peace Prize, the Shah wrote in the margin of the report, "If they beg us, we might accept. They give the Nobel to anybody these days *[kaka siah*]*. Why should we belittle ourselves with this?"[2]

Though the Shah was not interested in discussing domestic matters with Roosevelt, the old CIA hand met with a number of "well-informed senior Iranians" and from them he heard that the country faced "pressing domestic problems." The Shah's global preoccupations were causing him to pay these problems not "enough attention." Roosevelt was told of a "growing gap between 'the government' and 'the people,'" of serious inflationary pressures on the economy, and, most important of all, of the serious erosion of "the credibility of the government."[3]

In the same period, both the American Embassy in Tehran and the CIA began to notice hints of trouble. The embassy, for example, found that "over the past several months, a number of more or less chronic causes of popular dissatisfaction" had "taken on consistently sharper edge." It even reported that Amir Abbas Hoveyda, by then in his seventh year as prime minister, might be replaced, "if only as a sop [to] the public discontent," and suggested that "it would be a good bet" to assume that Jamshid Amuzegar would be the successor.[4] Corruption in high places, the disproportionate size of the military budget, and the mistreatment of the clergy—most specifically the arrest of a famous cleric (apparently Falsifi) and the publication of his picture in highly compromising congress with a young girl—were declared to be the direct causes of the discontent. Concurrently, in one of its intelligence estimates, the CIA first praised the Shah's work ethic and the improvements he had successfully brought about in the people's livelihood. It noted that "most people have been too busy doing well in other spheres to fuss about politics." Nevertheless, the report called the Shah "an isolated figure, living in a formal court atmosphere" with a "regrettable lack of communication upward to him." It reported that not only would no Iranian official dare tell the Shah "he is wrong about something," but even foreign ambassadors "cringe before the Shah's responses to official presentations which displease him."[5] The Queen, by then amongst the handful of people who still dared confront the Shah with

---

* *Kaka siah* literally means "any black face"; there is a hint of racism in the everyday use of the term.

unpleasant truths, captured this atmosphere when, much to the King's consternation, she disciplined the Shah's dog, adding, "everyone is obsequious, even to your dog. I won't do it."[6]

The Shah's blithe disposition toward matters domestic, and his obliviousness of the credibility gap between the government and the people, is particularly remarkable in light of what had been happening to him, and to his family, in the few years before the 1972 meeting with Roosevelt. On the morning of April 10, 1965, he had decided to drive himself the short distance between his residential palace and his office in the Marble Palace. As he neared the steps of his office, a conscript named Reza Shamsabadi who was on guard duty that day shot at the Shah with his service machine gun. With remarkable agility and some luck, the Shah managed to climb the stairs and make it into his office, closing the door and taking cover behind his desk. Shamsabadi was able to enter the building before the other guards shot him dead. Bullet holes in the door to the Shah's office indicated how close the assailant had come.

To avoid panic and maintain an air of normalcy, the Shah decided to keep his full day's schedule. In fact, in the early afternoon, he drove alone and without any escort or guard to the house of his son-in-law, Ardeshir Zahedi. When the Shah was asked why he had ventured out only a few hours after a failed assassination attempt, he repeated an old Persian adage, "the same house won't be hit by thieves twice in the same night."[7]

That day, the Court issued a brief statement about the failed assassination attempt. Behind the scenes, SAVAK and the Imperial Guard each tried to blame the other for what had clearly been a gross lapse of security.[8] Someone should have identified the assailant long before he had the opportunity to assassinate the Shah. The assailant in fact had a record of both assaulting a prime minister (Ali Amini) and consorting with radical Islamist circles. Nevertheless, he had been picked to be part of the elite unit carrying loaded machine guns and entrusted with protecting the royal palaces.

This period coincided with the rise of two men to the pinnacles of power, both of whom remained in their crucial posts for almost fourteen years. The first was Amir Abbas Hoveyda, appointed by the Shah to the post of prime minister when Islamist terrorists assassinated Ali Mansur in 1965. Hoveyda was a newcomer to the center stage of Iranian politics, and it was commonly assumed that his would be a caretaker appointment and that he would be replaced with a more seasoned politician as soon as the crisis of the Prime Minister's assassination had passed. But Hoveyda proved everyone wrong. With a deft combination of efficiency, sycophancy, and hardball politics against his adversaries and his competitors, as well as a strong strategic alliance with Parviz Sabeti, the rising star of SAVAK, Hoveyda stayed in power for more than thirteen years. His dismissal in 1977 was seen as a sea change by the opposition, while his arrest, on November 7, 1978, was for many the beginning of the end for the Shah.[9]

The second person whose career experienced a meteoric rise in that decade was General Nematollah Nasiri, who had replaced the educated, soft-spoken General Hassan Pakravan as the head of SAVAK in 1965. In the weeks after the June 1963 uprising, the Shah had confided to an American official that he meant to remove Pakravan. Had he done his job, the Shah believed, the June uprising could have been avoided.

During his brief tenure, Pakravan had revamped SAVAK: torture was forbidden and a group of scholars acted as a de facto think tank. Pakravan himself started negotiating with some of the regime's most stalwart enemies. In 1964 he unsuccessfully tried to convince Khomeini to give up "the dirty world" of politics. He also met with the political dissident Bijan Jazani when the latter was in prison. Returning to his cell after one of these meetings, Jazani told one of his trusted comrades, "this guy is different and really wants to create a dialogue."[10] Before this foray into reconciliation could bear any fruit, however, the Shah dismissed Pakravan and replaced him with Nasiri, whose only recommendation for the job was his absolute fealty to the Shah. Under his command, SAVAK became increasingly known for its brutality and use of torture and for its controversial influence on every facet of Iranian political life.

In his *Answer to History*, the Shah surprisingly claims that it was in fact the Prime Minister who was "directly responsible for the day-to-day operation of SAVAK" and that, as head of state, he only intervened to "exercise the right of pardon." The fact that the head of SAVAK was nominally a vice premier gave the Shah's claim its bureaucratic veneer. In reality, there is overwhelming evidence that from its inception, SAVAK was controlled directly by the Shah and that the Prime Minister had little to do with the actual running of the agency. Moreover, in spite of overwhelming evidence of torture by SAVAK—far less than the opposition claimed in those years, but a reality nevertheless—the Shah always insisted that there was no torture or execution of political prisoners during his reign: "[As for] those who were arrested for political reasons—I cannot include arsonists and saboteurs in this category—I affirm that they were properly treated and that they were never molested in any way. No one can tell me the name of a single politician who has been liquidated by SAVAK."[11] While his caveat about "arsonists and saboteurs" seemed to imply that they were tortured, even the claim that no one was liquidated by SAVAK was not true. The famous case that belies the Shah's claim involved Jazani, the political prisoner with whom Pakravan had engaged in a dialogue.

In the course of its ongoing and bloody war with Marxist urban guerrillas, SAVAK was surprised to learn that Jazani had been one of the founding leaders of the group. When the group assassinated a high-ranking member of SAVAK, Jazani, along with eight other leading political dissidents, all serving time on earlier charges, were taken outside Tehran's Evin Prison by a group of SAVAK interrogators and summarily executed. The official story was that the group had been shot "while attempting to escape." This turned out to be the only case of known extrajudicial murder of its kind committed during the Shah's thirty-seven-year rule. There is no evidence that the Shah knew about or ordered the killing, but in thinking about Jazani's tragic life trajectory, one can't help but wonder what might have happened to him, and to Iran, had Pakravan's attempt at reconciliation with opposition figures like Jazani borne some fruit. If ever such a reconciliation might have been possible, it was in 1965, when the Shah was at the height of his power and when his personality was undergoing a "steady metamorphosis." He was increasingly self-sufficient and making "remarkable strides" toward bringing Iran into the modern world.[12]

By then, a brilliant group of economists and technocrats—from Mehdi Samii and Alinaghi Alikhani to Reza Moghadam and Khodadad Farmanfarmaian—had taken over the crucial ministries and banks in charge of the country's economic policy. They were, in the words of a report prepared for Senator Robert Kennedy, representatives of Iran's "new men." They were fierce nationalists but no longer enamored of Mossadeq and the National Front.[13]

Many of these "new men" had trained in universities in the West and had left secure positions at top Western institutions to come back to Iran and change the society they loved. A kind of "reverse brain drain" had begun. This new technocratic elite began to map out for Iran an impressive plan of industrial development. The Khayami brothers of Iran National embodied the new spirit of entrepreneurship propagated by the Shah and the elite. What had begun as a small garage in the city of Meshed was by 1978 the Iran National industrial conglomerate and was considered one of the most successful automotive industries in all of the Middle East. The company was by then employing more than 12,000 workers and producing 136,000 cars annually. In the beginning, about 80 percent of each car produced by Iran National was imported from England and simply assembled in Iran; by 1978, the figure of imported parts had been reduced to about 20 percent. More than 120 different companies were by then producing components for Iran National. Had the revolution not happened, one of the Khayami brothers said wistfully, "Iran National would be where [the] South Korean car industry is today."[14]

In spite of the Shah's vigorous support for the private sector and entrepreneurship, he also had a "statist" tendency. This was rooted in his belief that he was actually a Socialist, "more socialist and revolutionary than anyone," he once said. Not only was the private university he helped to establish forcefully nationalized, but the first private television station, also created with his help, was bought by the government in less than a decade. While the Shah tolerated no independent labor unions, he supported labor laws that were surprisingly fair to the workers. Moreover, he forced all big industries to give half of their stock to their workers—yet another gesture of "socialism" that was incongruent with his support for the private sector.

In a sense then, for the Shah the decade between 1965 and 1975 was a pivotal period. In retrospect, a more tragic rise and fall, a more remarkable example of the economic accomplishments of a modernizing authoritarian monarch and the inevitable result of the hubris of such absolute power is hard to imagine. Just as Iran was entering what the American sociologist Walt Rostow has called its "take-off period"—a necessary time of concentrated change in preparing for a leap out of the vicious cycle of feudalism and poverty—and just as the Shah felt he was on top of the world, dark clouds appeared on the horizon. In his mind, the assassin's bullets he had dodged in 1965 were no more dangerous than what he had firmly believed in 1963 were the Kennedy administration's plans to turn Iran into a republic.[15] Interlaced through the many reports from the American and British Embassies praising the glories of the Shah's accomplishments were early warnings of a storm on the horizon. What in retrospect is remarkable is how many such warnings there were and how not just the Shah but the big powers and their intelligence ministries and bureaucracies failed to notice or take action.

These warnings were invariably overshadowed by the Shah's increasingly euphoric and assertive confidence and by the impressive improvements in Iran's economy. Even the American Embassy was reluctant to send Washington reports that might be critical of the Shah. One diplomat posted in Tehran in the early 1970s says he was told that reports critical of the Shah were not welcome in the White House or the State Department.[16] He had, for example, heard stories of the Shah's dalliance with a young woman and that he might indeed be planning to marry her.

The rumor, Alam makes clear in his *Daily Journals*, was true. On June 12, 1973, Alam told the Shah of a "girl named G. [Gilda was her name] who had been spreading strange rumors in the city, claiming His Majesty had fallen madly in love with her." Alam ventures to add, "But of course the king never falls in love with anyone." Two weeks later, Alam again reported that there was a rumor that "Your Majesty has taken a second wife."[17] The Shah's response was no less incredible than Alam's flippant comments. "I have been with this bitch [*pedar sukhteh*]. I too have heard the rumors. They have even reached the ears of Shahbanu. Call the woman to your office and tell her that she will be arrested if she continues with these shenanigans."[18]

The rumors continued. In those years, as Alam's journals make amply clear, the Shah's "only recreation," his only "respite " from what he called the burdens of his office and "the constant grumblings at home," was the company of increasingly larger numbers of women, "guests" in Alam's parlance, who were flown in, often from Europe, for an "outing" with the Shah. "If I don't have this recreation a couple of times a week," the Shah told Alam once, "there is no way I could bear the burden of my office."[19] Occasionally, "local material" was used. A special house was furnished by an Alam aide to facilitate these "outings." So numerous were the men eager to act as royal procurers that the Shah eventually ordered them all to stop and entrusted only a handful of aides with the infamous job. The Queen, though obviously distraught at these infidelities, never felt threatened by them. But this time, the rumors about "G." were different. Even the Queen's mother grew concerned and told Alam, "fortunately my daughter is not attached to this luxury" (meaning she could easily ask for divorce). When Alam reported the conversation to the Shah, he flippantly dismissed the implied threat ("*zeki*" [contextually Persian for "bullshit"] he reportedly said!) but after some discussion with Alam, the two decided "we should find a husband for the girl (G.)."[20] Nevertheless, during the very same meeting, Alam gave the Shah "a letter from a very nice girl," and reported that "His Majesty was happy."

As always, Alam's instinct was to blame Hoveyda for spreading rumors about the Shah's indiscretions. He told the Shah that Hoveyda "wants to turn the Queen into an angel and create a negative image of His Majesty."[21] The Shah's instinct, on the other hand, was to blame the KGB for the rumors. Neither man blamed the rumor on the Shah's crass infidelities. Moreover, the Shah's suspicion of KGB complicity and many pages in Alam's journals are stark reminders of the political and economic costs and consequences of these "outings." The same pages show that on the rare occasions when the Shah questioned the wisdom of his own sexual indiscretions, Alam, in his most destructive moments of sycophancy, reassured the Shah—or his "master" as he calls him—that the country was prosperous, and no one begrudged the King a bit of fun.[22]

By 1975, these rumors spread to Western papers and American officials. Even Henry Kissinger had an opinion on the subject, telling Ardeshir Zahedi that a divorce would be detrimental to the image of the Shah in the United States. Eventually, the plan of action devised by the Shah and Alam was put in place. G. was married off, and magazines in Tehran published images of the wedding. The Shah asked Alam to ensure that the Queen saw the article.

But this was not the end of the story. After being parted from the Shah, G. started a heated affair with General Mohammad Khatam—the commander of Iran's air force and the husband of the Shah's sister Fateme. By the time this affair began, Khatam had developed the reputation of being one of the most corrupt officers in the country. Even the Shah suspected him of financial malfeasance. On June 7, 1975, for example, the *New York Times* wrote about close ties between Khatam and the "swashbuckling Central Intelligence Agency operative" Kermit Roosevelt. As a result of this friendship, the *Times* wrote, U.S. manufacturer Northrop (Roosevelt's alleged client) had become a major contractor for Iran's air force. In yet another article, the *Times* claimed that Khatam and a partner had received a $28 million kickback for a $2.2 billion contract with Grumman.[23] The U.S. Senate held hearings about these allegations, and the U.S. Embassy called Khatam the head of the "Iranian Air Mafia," claiming that he and his accomplices received a percentage on every contract relating to air travel and the air force in Iran.[24] At the same time, earlier reports by the same embassy had praised Khatam for his favorable disposition toward American military hardware and for his ability "to curb some of the Shah's extreme decisions."[25] A report prepared by the U.S. government even concluded that should something happen to the Shah, Khatam was the only officer who had the charisma, gravitas, and popularity to seize and maintain power.[26]

When, on September 12, 1975, Khatam died in a hang-gliding accident, rumors of foul play pointed to the Shah as a likely culprit. Some royalists insisted that Khatam was killed by Western powers in preparation for the 1979 revolution. "All capable officers, capable of saving the Shah, had to be eliminated," they claim.[27] Extensive investigations into the accident by experts from the Iranian army and by Bob Moise, the American engineer who had built the kite, discovered no indication of foul play. The Shah had told Alam a month before the accident that the General was no longer of "sound mind" and that he had asked for his resignation as commander of the air force. He had been told that he would be sent as an ambassador to a capital of his choice. During the period leading up to his death, Khatam's friends also reported that he was depressed.

In his journal, Alam is unusually coy about the events surrounding the death of the General and the Shah's comments about it. The Shah speculated that Khatam "might have planned to kill himself and thus intentionally did not open his hang glider." Alam goes on to say that the Shah shared with him certain facts about Khatam "so sensitive" that he "must take them to [his] grave."[28]

Khatam was not the only general who was a source of concern to the Shah in those years. In the 1960s, Teymour Bakhtiyar was also often on the Shah's mind. After the Shah had ordered him to leave Iran in 1962, Bakhtiyar settled in Europe, "a very hated but extremely rich man." There, the old anti-Communist warrior suddenly "changed color and became 'non-aligned.'" All his attempts to ingratiate himself with either the United States or Britain had failed. He was now desperate to find allies amongst the countries of the Third World and even in the ranks of the Iranian opposition, and he began to repackage himself as a revolutionary. The Shah, on the other hand, ordered SAVAK to closely monitor

Bakhtiyar's every move. A maid in one hotel and eavesdropping equipment in another allowed SAVAK to know much of what the General did.[29]

But the Shah's relationship with Bakhtiyar changed after his tumultuous 1967 state visit to Germany. The Shah was informed that he needed extra security this time. German police had arrested some men from a team of terrorists who had been hired by Bakhtiyar to assassinate the Shah.[30] In the course of the Shah's visit to West Berlin, an Iranian student failed in his effort to have a car filled with bombs and, "directed by remote control," hit and destroy the Shah's limousine.[31] At the same time, in Berlin, the Shah faced one of the largest demonstrations ever organized against him; one student was killed in clashes with the police. The whole trip was a public relations fiasco for the Shah, and he was informed that Bakhtiyar had been at least partially responsible for the massive demonstrations and the failed assassination attempt.

Even before returning to Tehran, the Shah ordered the Majlis to pass a law confiscating all of Bakhtiyar's properties in Iran. A court tried him in absentia and condemned him to death. Moreover, the Shah was led to believe that Bakhtiyar still had a network of allies within SAVAK, so a purge of his purported supporters took place.

The Shah's "Bakhtiyar problem" became even more serious when the Ba'ath Party seized power in Iraq in 1968. In the new party, Bakhtiyar finally found his most reliable ally. He was invited to settle in Baghdad and eventually given an Iraqi diplomatic passport, allowing him to travel freely around the world. Moreover, the Ba'ath Party pressured different members of the Iranian opposition to meet with Bakhtiyar. Leaders of the Tudeh Party, activists from the ranks of the Confederation of Iranian Students, and "a large number of Iranians domiciled in Iraq" met with Bakhtiyar and listened to his proposal for a united front against the Shah. The Iraqi government made it clear to these Iranians that unless they cooperated with Bakhtiyar, they would be expelled and their properties confiscated. Some sources have even claimed that Ayatollah Khomeini was amongst those who not only met with but agreed to cooperate with Bakhtiyar.[32]

The most controversial contact was between Bakhtiyar and the Tudeh Party. A man named Abbas Shahriyari, eventually nicknamed "a man of a thousand faces," who was the head of the reactivated Tudeh Party cells in Tehran, had initiated the contacts between the General and the party. About the time that the first secretary of the Tudeh, Reza Radmanesh, was scheduled to meet with Bakhtiyar, the KGB informed the Tudeh Party central committee that Shahriyari was in fact an agent of SAVAK. But Radmanesh refused to believe the charge,[33] and the meeting took place. Thanks to Shahriyari, Bakhtiyar's contacts in Iran were all put under surveillance.

In April 1968, on his way to Baghdad from his home in Switzerland, Bakhtiyar stopped in Beirut, where he was arrested and convicted on a charge of "illegal [arms] smuggling." The Iranian government used all of its power and connections in Lebanon to have Bakhtiyar extradited to Iran, where a court had already passed a death sentence against him.

But the Iraqi government was pressuring Lebanon to allow Bakhtiyar to continue on to Baghdad. Eventually, after nine months, Iraq won Bakhtiyar's release and arranged for his travel to Baghdad. It is reported that "an estimated one million dollars in bribes" was given to the Lebanese President to ensure that he did not sign Bakhtiyar's extradition papers for Iran.

In Baghdad, Bakhtiyar redoubled his campaign against the Shah, but unbeknownst to him and his Ba'athist patrons, the circle of his aides and supporters was filled with SAVAK agents. According to one estimate, sixteen of Bakhtiyar's closest aides, including his cook and his typist, were agents of SAVAK. Their order was to kill Bakhtiyar, for the Shah was becomingly increasingly impatient with the General's continued activities.

Aware that the Shah was tightening the noose around him, in early 1970 Bakhtiyar tried to convince the Ba'ath Party to help him kill the Shah. Saddam Hussein, by then already the party's second in command, rejected Bakhtiyar's request.[34] Finally, on August, 7, 1970, Bakhtiyar was shot by one of the double agents who had wormed his way into the General's inner circle. Five days later, Bakhtiyar died; the Shah, according to Alam, rejoiced at the news.

The successful assassination had come on the heels of some bad news from Iraq, where SAVAK had been behind a failed coup attempt. The man SAVAK had entrusted with the job of leading the coup had informed Ba'ath Party officials of the Iranian overture and had been instructed by Iraqi officials to become a double agent. The Iraqi security forces waited till the last minute and then arrested everyone involved with the coup attempt. All forty-one of those arrested were executed.[35]

During this period, the Shah demanded and often received concessions from both the British and American governments. One of his earliest demands was for both countries to end their contacts with opposition forces inside Iran. Six years earlier, he had made the same demand, only to have both countries roundly reject the request. This time, however, the Shah was in a different, more powerful position. The United States not only ceased its contacts with opposition figures but began to reduce the number of intelligence officers assigned to work in Iran. By the mid-1970s, their total number in Iran had reached pre–World War II levels. Even embassy contacts with Ali Amini—by then an ex-prime minister with no political role and a judicial case pending against his wife—had become problematic for the Shah. He threw the equivalent of a diplomatic tantrum when, in

1968, Armin Meyer, the American ambassador in Iran, invited Ali Amini to dinner.[36] Though the embassy calls the Shah's reaction "byzantine," something that "only a Persian mind can fathom,"[37] it did decide to henceforth contact Amini only through an intermediary.[38]

Worried that its relationship with the Shah might be endangered, Great Britain also chose "not to deploy any of its own intelligence service in Iran," feeling they had "little option other than to rely on SAVAK."[39]

With virtually no contacts with the opposition, both Britain and America relied on reports they received from the Shah and from SAVAK, or on claims made by the opposition outside the country. If the Shah was overly optimistic and blind to his regime's weakness, the opposition demonized the Shah and could not even entertain the possibility that he was making any positive changes in Iran. They even found a way to dismiss the Shah's role in OPEC as yet another proof of his role as "a lackey of U.S. imperialism." Higher oil prices, advocates of this theory proposed, were more of a burden on Europe and Japan, and thus the Shah's insistence on higher prices was simply benefiting the United States.

A good example of how the Shah and the opposition approached political questions can be found in the issue of political prisoners. The opposition outlandishly claimed that Iran had "hundreds of thousands of political prisoners," whereas the actual number was closer to 4,000. No less exaggerated was their claim that thousands had been killed and tortured to death by SAVAK. The actual number of people executed for political crimes during the Shah's thirty-seven-year reign was about 1,500—still a high number but less than the figure offered by the opposition.[40] On the other hand, for years, when the Western media asked the Shah about the plight of political prisoners and torture in Iran, the Shah invariably dismissed the question by saying Iran had no political prisoners, only criminals.

In Alam's *Daily Journals*, there are numerous references to episodes, some involving shouts and tears, in which the Queen tried to convince the Shah that more must be done to reach a compromise with the opposition, particularly those in the intellectual class. The government agencies run by her friends or family, particularly Iranian National Radio and Television, managed by her cousin Reza Qotbi, and the Organization for the Intellectual Development of Children, managed by her childhood friend Lili Amir-Arjomand, were often the only place opposition intellectuals could find employment. Pressure on Qotbi to purge his staff increased substantially when SAVAK discovered and stopped a plot by a few television employees and camera crew to abduct the Queen and the Crown Prince.[41] Even before this plot, Alam had been ordered more than once by the Shah to work with SAVAK and investigate the allegation that Iranian National Radio and Television was "infiltrated" and "dominated" by Communists.

More than once in this period, the Queen asked the Shah to control the excesses of the police and SAVAK. For example, when the police raided a night club known as a hangout of Tehran's jet set—what the British Embassy called the "jeunesse dorée of Tehran"—the Queen complained about police behavior. Not only had they shut down the nightclub, but they had physically abused the customers and forcefully "shaved a number of influential scions of hippy appearance." That same day, Hossein Zenderudi, an acclaimed painter and a favorite of the Queen, was "seized by the police while traveling in a car and had his artistic locks chopped off in an insulting manner."[42] When the details of the story recounted by the Queen were confirmed, the Shah immediately ordered the dismissal of the chief of police. The gesture, according to Alam, "had a positive impact on the people."[43] The moral of the story, according to the British Embassy, was that "the permissive society with court backing seems to have won this round against the police." The incident also was an example of the Queen's increasing "interference in political matters on the side of liberalization."[44]

These events were all taking place during the Shah's dramatic decade of rising power and independence between 1965 and 1975. One of the first signs of this new independence was his decision to sign a major economic and military deal with the Soviet Union. In return for the purchase of Iran's gas, in 1965 the Soviets agreed to build a steel mill for Iran—something that had come to represent for both the Shah and his father a "dramatic symbol of Iran's movement into the modern world."[45] No sooner had Britain and the United States learned the details of the deal than they tried to pressure the Shah to change his mind. The United States was particularly worried that such an agreement would be a first step in the Shah's eastward tilt. The American Ambassador pleaded with the Shah to reconsider, pointing out that "Americans are human and there is not slightest doubt they would be deeply hurt that valued and admired friend like Shah has decided to trade in arms with our adversaries . . . particularly at the time when whole American nation is gripped by anxiety over Vietnam."[46] But the Shah refused to change his mind.

In November 1965, the Shah had informed U.S. Ambassador Armin Meyer that he was uneasy about what he called a "growing estrangement between the US and Iran." In addition to his grievance against John Kennedy for having forced Amini on him, the Shah described how, under pressure from the United States and its promise of aid, he had walked away from the 1959 agreement with the Soviet Union. Yet in the six years since, the United States had failed to live up to its promises. When, on March 16, 1966, Meyer raised some of Washington's concerns about the new Russian deal, the Shah, "in a dark mood," recalled how Eisenhower had rejected his pleas for help in constructing a steel mill.

If the agreement with the Soviet Union was the most telling sign of the Shah's newfound independence, the two big events he organized in that period—his coronation in 1967 and the celebration of 2,500 years of monarchy in 1971—signaled his emergence as a more self-assured figure of domestic dominance and international significance. The decline of the British Empire, the falling star of Nasser of Egypt, the U.S. entanglement in Vietnam, China's growing tensions with Russia, and finally the rise in the price of oil all combined to encourage the Shah to become increasingly assertive. A belated decision to have his coronation was one sign of this new confidence. For a variety of reasons, his coronation had been delayed. In the forties, he was fighting to remain relevant and royal; in the fifties, early plans called for him to have a coronation concurrent with a party to celebrate twenty-five hundred years of monarchy.

The coronation was an elegantly simple event, modeled after Reza Shah's. The big difference was that this time the Queen was also being crowned as the regent. Indeed, on September 11, 1967, the leadership committee of the Constituent Assembly, convened especially for the purpose of revising the constitution, informed the Shah and the Queen that the requisite amendments to articles of the constitution had passed the assembly. One new article stipulated that the Crown Prince must be twenty before he could ascend the throne. Another article made the Queen regent in the event that the Shah died before the Crown Prince was of age. It was decided that the coronation would take place on the Shah's forty-eighth birthday, October 26, 1967. The Crown Prince was to have a key role in the ceremonies and, perhaps not coincidentally, he was exactly the same age at the time as the Shah had been when his father crowned himself king and expected the young Crown Prince to play his role.

The Shah had decided to make the coronation "a major but essentially domestic affair," after "informal soundings in London, Copenhagen, and elsewhere showed that Her Majesty the Queen and other sovereigns" wouldn't be able to attend with "such relatively short notice." Moreover, he had insisted on avoiding any "waste and extravagance."[47] It has been estimated that the total cost of the event was £1,250,000.

The most complicated elements of the event itself were the design of a new crown for the Queen and the construction of two royal horse-drawn carriages, which would carry the royal couple and the Crown Prince from their residential palaces to Golestan Palace, where the ceremonies were to be held. Finding someone capable of constructing the carriages was no easy task. The world's most reputable builder of such carriages lived in Vienna and had to be coaxed out of retirement to build two carriages that would be at once traditional and royal and also comply with modern security requirements.[48] Horses for the carriage were bought in Hungary.

Making the Queen's crown was less difficult. Under strict security, the Crown Jewels were given to one of the most famous jewelers in the world, Van Cleef & Arpels, who were asked to weave the invaluable gems into a design that was traditionally Persian as well as modern. While the Shah crowned himself, the Queen knelt before the Shah and received her crown from his hands.[49] The event itself lasted no more than thirty-five minutes and went smoothly. All past prime ministers, with the exception of Ali Amini, had been invited.

On October 28, the heads of diplomatic missions in Tehran met with the Shah to offer the gifts they had chosen to commemorate the coronation. They had earlier agreed to find something "personal from the head of the state for the Shah's personal use." While the British gave him a "silver-gilt fruit basket," the Italians offered a "lapis lazuli and gold trinket box," the Russians offered "a huge china umbrella stand, and the US gave a Tiffany-made silver-gilt bowl." The oddest gifts were the King of Nepal's "mounted rhinoceros horn" and Japan's fresh apples. The Argentinean gift was lost in transit at Heathrow.[50]

More flamboyant, expensive, and controversial than the coronation was the 1971 celebration of 2,500 years of monarchy in Iran. The idea, first conceptualized in 1959, had initially been rather limited in scope. A small number of the country's elder statesmen, as well as the top officers of the government, were appointed by the Shah to the Committee to Celebrate 2,500 Years of Monarchy. Their task, in the Shah's words, was to "celebrate our culture's proud heritage" and show the world that "Iran's continued existence and its national sovereignty is possible through the continuation of monarchy."[51] In the beginning, it was assumed that the Shah's coronation would take place during the same celebration. But by 1966, the Shah had changed his mind.

A decade after the formation of the committee, virtually nothing had been done to plan the celebration. The Shah lost patience, and with little forethought or consultation, ordered the celebration to take place in 1971. Suddenly, planners were faced with the reality that in some eighteen months, hundreds of dignitaries, many of them heads of state, and hundreds more journalists, were going to converge on Persepolis, the ancient capital of the Persian Empire. Nothing could be a more majestic reminder of Iran's past imperial grandeur than the ruins of Persepolis. Yet, the nearest city, Shiraz, had no airport capable of handling the requisite large planes. There was only one luxury hotel, with no more than a couple dozen rooms, and even they did not measure up to the grand celebration the Shah had envisioned.

According to the CIA, "tens of millions of dollars [were] spent on an airfield suitable for 707s"; new roads to and from the airport to Persepolis had to be expeditiously built.[52] Contractors demanded and received extra money to work virtually around the clock to finish the projects on time. Then there was the question of security. Most of the heads of state would arrive in Shiraz late at night, and the road to their accommodations in the desert would be dark, and therefore dangerous; specialists from the oil company were brought in to line the road with temporary gaslight fixtures.

The idea of building luxury hotels to house the hundreds of dignitaries was easily dismissed as impossible. Thus emerged the controversial notion of building a city of tents near Persepolis. The most expensive tentmaker in the world, Jansen AG of Switzerland, was asked to design not only small tents to house the guests, but a gigantic tent to host the gala dinner. The tents had to be fireproof and air-conditioned. They were designed to withstand winds of up to a hundred kilometers per hour.[†, 53] Two hundred and fifty Mercedes-Benz bulletproof limousines were bought to ferry about the heads of state. While Limoges was ordered to design special serving plates, Haviland supplied china cups for coffee. Fancy linen and towels were ordered from Porthault, and "several thousand glasses were ordered from Baccarat."[54] It had been the Queen's order that the guests must all "feel they are staying in a palace." A French designer was commissioned to make two sets of thirty dresses "for the ladies in waiting," one for lunch and one for dinner. Elizabeth Arden was hired to set up a beauty salon with forty stylists ready to service the ladies at a moment's notice.

After the site for the tent city had been picked, a new problem reared its head. The organizing committee found that the patch of wilderness they had designated was a notorious den of venomous snakes. According to one member of the committee, the area was treated with a special spray, developed for the occasion, and then "a five ton truck was used" to carry away the snakes, lizards, tarantulas and other dangerous denizens of the desert.[55]

The extravagant expenditure of millions of dollars turned what had begun as an attempt to assert Iran's imperial past, educate the world and Iranians themselves about Iranian history, and herald the arrival of a new and greater Iran, into an embarrassment for the Shah and a bonanza for his opposition. The 2,500 schools and clinics that were to be built, the 2,500 books that were commissioned on every conceivable facet of Iranian society and history, and the launch of *Acta-Iranica*—a truly remarkable encyclopedia of Iran—were overshadowed by the rumor and reality of corruption and the embarrassment of nouveau riche extravaganza.

It has been a common adage of Iranian history that the soul of the nation was riven between a Zoroastrian first millennium and an Islamic second millennium. A

† It has been suggested that the idea for the tent city's design came from a sumptuous 1520 summit between England's Henry VIII and France's Francis I that was called the Field of the Cloth of Gold because of the extravagance of the costumes and the tents.

key goal of the 2,500 celebration, in the words of one of its originators, Shojaedeen Shafa, was to accentuate the pre-Islamic imperial grandeur of Persia to the detriment of its Islamic component. It was hoped that this celebration would mark and buttress the notion of a third millennium of imperial Persian grandeur based on the Pahlavi dynasty's modern and secular narrative of identity. But, ultimately, the celebration ended up having the opposite effect—it played right into the hands of the opposition. Indeed, less than a decade later, when the new clerical regime came to power, it set out to banish from Iranian history any allusion to the imperial Zoroastrian past and instead accentuate the role of Islam in shaping Iranian identity.

Both the Shah and the opposition waged an elaborate public relations war about the ceremony. Ayatollah Khomeini issued a statement asking heads of state to boycott what he called "the devil's festival." The Confederation of Iranian Students tried to mobilize the Iranian diaspora and Western public opinion to pressure Western countries not to attend. The Iranian regime used hard-knuckle politics to convince heads of state to take part. The British and French governments were warned that "the future of the important copper deposits at Kerman in which British and French firms were struggling for the contract" was inexorably linked to Queen Elizabeth's and "President Pompidou's [presence] at the celebration." The Dutch Ambassador was told to "produce Queen Juliana" or else, while the German government, ever eager to hold its position in the Iranian economy, was told that it must ensure the attendance of the German President.[56]

Ironically, the only country that was more than eager to send its head of state to the celebration was not welcome. Israel made it clear that it would be happy to participate at the highest level, but the Shah demurred. Not only would an Israeli presence have caused virtually every Muslim head of state to stay away, but ever since Ardeshir Zahedi's appointment as foreign minister, Iran had been trying to "balance" its regional policy by improving its ties with Arab states. So Israel was not invited.

But in spite of the pressures exerted by the Shah's regime, some of the most important heads of state failed to show up. For the Shah, one of the biggest blows was the news that Queen Elizabeth would not attend. According to the British Ambassador, the Shah was "rather grumpy" when he heard the news. He then demanded that instead of the Queen, he "would like the Prince of Wales" to come. Even that, he was told, was impossible. This time the excuse was that he was "doing his service in the royal navy." Reluctantly, he settled for Prince Philip and Princess Anne. They offered to help with the nightmarish questions of protocol that would arise—so many heads of state, each with different seniority and standing in the diplomatic rules of etiquette. The Shah was appreciative of this help, and of Prince Philip's and Princess Anne's participation. He gave the Princess Royal a stallion as a token of his appreciation for her presence.[57]

Even President Nixon chose not to attend, sending in his place Vice President Spiro Agnew. The Russians sent President Podgorny, while Tito of Yugoslavia, Emperor Haile Selassie of Ethiopia, and Prince Rainier III of Monaco and his wife, Princess Grace, were the other important invitees who agreed to come. In spite of the heavy French accent of the festivities—from food and wine to tents and towels—French President Georges Pompidou refused to attend. "If I did go," he said in biting sarcasm, "they [would] probably make me head-waiter."[58] The Shah was told that the reason for Pompidou's decision to skip the celebration was his unhappiness with the seating arrangements. "Who the hell does he think he is?" the Shah reportedly asked.

The British Embassy described the event itself as "a sumptuous celebration . . . of daring enterprise," a "good idea but marred by the element of excess."[59] It shared the fate of "so many other good projects in Iran," derailed by a touch of the "megalomania from which the Shah," according to the embassy, now suffered. The municipality of Tehran alone, according to the British Embassy, had spent $81 million on the celebrations. A member of the organizing committee has challenged these estimates, claiming that only $22 million was spent. Documents published by the Islamic Republic, based on the ancien régime's archives, provide even larger numbers than those suggested by the British Embassy.

Waiters and sommeliers were imported from Europe, some of them from the hotel in St. Moritz, where the Shah and his family owned a chalet. They served only the "Bacchic best": magnums of Chateau Lafite (1945), bottles of Blanc de Blancs, Moët Chandon (1911), and Dom Perignon Rosé (1959). Twenty-five thousand bottles were shipped from Paris for the six hundred guests. The servers were reportedly paid $2,500 for their weeklong trip. Dinner was a six-course, five-hour extravaganza, created by the famed Max Blouet; much of it was flown in from Maxim's of Paris. It included fifty roast peacocks, "quail's eggs stuffed with golden caviar, crayfish mousse, saddles of lamb." The only thing Persian on the menu was the caviar. The Shah, allergic to caviar, was served a vegetable instead. In 1980, the *Guinness Book of Records* chose the ceremony as the most extravagant party on record.

Iran's radical groups, particularly the new urban guerrilla organizations, which had emerged only a few years earlier, had vowed to disrupt the celebration and negate the claim that the Shah's regime was an "island of stability." Amongst the efforts to disrupt the event was the failed attempt to kidnap Shahram, the Shah's nephew, and the successful though inconsequential destruction of an electric power line near Tehran. The regime's success in containing damage was made possible by the arrest of a large number of dissidents and careful watch on another

1,500 individuals deemed potentially disruptive. As Ardeshir Zahedi wrote in a letter to the Shah, rumor had it that prisons were so overfilled that SAVAK had rented special houses and used them as temporary prisons. Zahedi also criticized the fact that only French food was served. If we have twenty-five hundred years of glorious civilization, he asked rhetorically, why then can we not serve them "Persian dishes like *kabab kubideh* or even *ab-gusht?*"[60]

Some of the costs for the celebration were paid for by contributions from businessmen. How many of these contributions were made voluntarily, and how many were made under direct or implicit duress is not clear. The Armenians of Iran, for example, were "told to cough up one million dollars."[61]

The controversial celebration was taking place just as the Shah was finally realizing his dream of becoming the dominant force in the Persian Gulf. In 1965, he had learned that Britain intended to leave its bases in the Gulf, and he had indicated his determination to have Iran replace Britain as the dominant military power in the region. The British were keen on "disabusing" the Shah of any such notion. Denis Wright recommended that, in meetings with the Shah that year, the British government "should not pull our punches in explaining that it is illusory to think that there is any chance of Iran inheriting our role."[62] More than once, British officials made it clear that the reason for their opposition to the Shah's plans was their close ties with the Arab sheiks ruling in the lateral states of the Persian Gulf. The British resistance to the Shah's plans created a period of considerable tension in the relations between the two countries. At one time, Zahedi, in a moment of anger, threatened a military confrontation with the British. On another occasion, he declared the British Ambassador persona non grata; "the air was cleared"[63] only after the Shah got involved. In fact, according to Denis Wright, the decision not to have Queen Elizabeth attend the 2,500-year celebrations was more than anything "because of the difficulties we were having with the Iranians over our withdrawal from the Persian Gulf."[64] The Shah was unhappy with the British, too. In May 1968, the British Embassy reported hearing from "too many unimpeachable sources . . . that the Shah and most of his advisors (not just the wild men such as Ardeshir Zahedi) are fed up with the British."[65]

For the Shah, one problem on his way to becoming the hegemonic force in the region was Iran's lingering claim of sovereignty over Bahrain. He had come to believe that those claims were impossible to actualize, but he was unwilling to give up Iran's claim with no gains. No less strategically indispensable for Iran's regional hegemony were the three islands of Big Tomb, Small Tomb, and Abu-Musa—small but located at the heart of the Strait of Hormuz, where the Persian

Gulf meets the Indian Ocean. Dominate the islands, the Shah knew, and you dominate the most important waterway in the world.

In order to establish the legal foundations of Iran's claims to the three islands, the Shah ordered the Foreign Ministry to dispatch a seasoned diplomat, with some experience in archival research, to be posted to London, where his responsibility would be to trace Public Record Office records for any documents asserting Iran's legitimate claim to the islands.[66] The Shah also appointed a seasoned diplomat as his personal emissary to negotiate with Denis Wright about the fate of both Bahrain and the three islands. The British were relieved that the Shah had not left these sensitive negotiations in the hands of Foreign Minister Ardeshir Zahedi, who was known for what the British viewed as his extreme nationalism, his anti-British sentiments, and his insistence on Iran's claim of sovereignty over Bahrain. Eventually, the Shah agreed to a face-saving solution: Iran agreed to have the UN hold a referendum in Bahrain and promised to abide by the wishes of the citizens, should they opt for independence. For the Shah, the more crucial part of this agreement was the de facto recognition of Iran's rights to the three strategic islands.

During this period, the Shah was also constantly reminding the Americans of his desire to become the dominant force in the region. When Richard Nixon visited Tehran in 1967 in preparation for his new presidential campaign, he had an unusually long meeting with the Shah. Nixon recounted the key elements of this discussion to the American ambassador, Armin Meyer. The Shah, he said, had interesting ideas about the future security of the region: the defense of the Persian Gulf must be left to Iran, thus sparing the United States the need to spread its forces across every corner of the world. A year later, after the Shah met with Dean Rusk while visiting the United States, the Secretary of State's "net impression" was that the Shah was "rather hoping that the US will pick Iran as its 'chosen instrument' in the Middle East."[67] When Nixon became president, the Shah's dream became a reality—Iran was picked in the grand scheme of the Nixon Doctrine to be the dominant force, the policeman of the Persian Gulf. In Henry Kissinger's words, the Shah was willing to fill the vacuum left in the region "by British withdrawal, now menaced by Soviet intrusion and radical momentum." In the midst of the Vietnam War, Kissinger wrote, there was no way the United States could take on this added role.[68]

As the Shah set out on an ambitious military expansion, he also decided to take out another piece of insurance against domestic or international guerilla activities. Though Yasser Arafat and his PLO were the most crucial source of training for Iranian guerillas in those days and though the Palestinian leadership went out of its way in public pronouncements to attack the Shah and his regime, particularly for their close ties to Israel, the Shah paid Arafat $500,000 by way of support on September 14, 1969.[69] It was understood that both sides would try to keep this unusual transaction away from the eyes of American and Israeli officials. In his letter confirming the receipt of the check and thanking the Shah for his generous assistance, Arafat called the Shah his *akhi,* brother or comrade.[70]

Becoming the dominant force in the Persian Gulf had several immediate consequences. The Shah's decision in 1974 to send Iranian forces to Dhofar in the strategically important kingdom of Oman to fight Communist insurgents was one direct result of this new role. Instead of American or British forces fighting the Chinese- and Soviet-supported fighters, it was the Iranian special forces and air force that successfully pushed back the Dhofari guerillas. There were some 2,500 Iranian troops operating as "an independent brigade but formally taking their orders from the British commander of the Sultan's armed forces."[71] As the Shah informed an American military delegation, the Dhofaris were by themselves "not a serious problem." However, they were being furnished with sophisticated equipment by the Soviets. . . . There were over 100 Cubans and several East Germans supporting the rebels."[72] According to the British, the South Yemen government, a Soviet satellite, was also offering the guerrillas help at that time.

In this period, the Shah grew particularly concerned about Soviet influence in Iran's neighboring countries. Not only was Russia gaining more of a foothold in Iraq with the rise of the Ba'ath Party, but the Shah's fear of Soviet expansion was only redoubled when the prime minister of Afghanistan, Daoud Khan, organized a coup and declared the country a republic. The Shah immediately wrote to the British government, indicating his belief that the Soviets were behind the coup. While visiting Washington, D.C. on July 24, 1973, a week after the coup in Afghanistan, the Shah told Kissinger of his plans to have the deposed king "flown secretly to some point in Afghanistan . . . and he [would] appeal for help."[73] SAVAK apparently had fresh intelligence on the issue of Russian complicity in the coup. The British Foreign Secretary wrote back to the Shah, saying that while Britain shared his concern and believed that Russia "almost certainly had foreknowledge of the coup," the British did not believe "[the Russians had] instigated it."[74] More crucially, the Afghan king, Zahir Shah, rejected the offer of help, preferring a life of exile in Rome—partially underwritten by the stipend the Shah arranged for him.

But the Soviet role in Afghanistan was not the only source of disagreement between the Shah and his Western allies. The price of oil was easily one of the most constant sources of tension, even acrimony. As the Shah pushed for higher oil prices, the global economy faced not only a serious energy crisis but a recession. Late in 1967, Ambassador Meyer had reported a "most unpleasant" visit with the Shah, when the latter used "terms such as 'robbery,' 'thieves,' and some unprintable epithets. Shah professed to be completely disgusted with consortium's behavior." At one point the Shah even declared that "if the companies wanted war they could have it," adding that this time the war would not be "with a Mossadeq but with a united Iran behind the Shah himself."[75]

In January 1971, Nixon wrote to the Shah asking for help in finding a solution to the growing conflict between OPEC and consumer nations. Oil supply, Nixon wrote, "is vital to the free world. Therefore, your interests in oil and ours are bound intimately together. The consuming countries need a secure source of oil available on reasonable terms." The Shah's response was categorical. Without mentioning Mossadeq by name, he referred to the fact that Iran "already owns our resources according to the Oil Nationalization Act of 1951." He added that Iran was different from other countries in the region in that it was the only one in a position to "becom[e] a developed country." Finally, he blamed the oil companies for the current state of negotiations between the oil-producing nations and Western companies. A similar message was sent to British Prime Minister Edward Heath.[76]

The Nixon administration discussed how to respond to the Shah's intransigence; the idea of trying to remove him from power was bounced around. Kissinger and Nixon ultimately won by arguing that removing the Shah might well lead to the coming to power of a regime that would be even more troublesome for the United States.

On Vietnam, too, the Shah supported Nixon—but increasingly on his own terms. For years, the Shah had been one of the staunchest defenders of the U.S. position in Vietnam. In October 1967, he had even offered to try to act as a mediator and find a solution and had tried to use Fereydoon Hoveyda as his special envoy on Vietnam. Hoveyda was at the time the head of a division in Iran's Foreign Ministry that dealt with international organizations. He had lived in France for many years and had developed close relationships with some of the West's most acclaimed intellectuals. Goddard, Truffaut, Warhol (who did a portrait of him), and Pasolini were amongst his friends. His surprising appointment to the post of Iran's ambassador to the United Nations was in part the result of the Shah's troubled infatuation with intellectuals: he despised their disposition yet desired their approval. In private, he invariably referred to them as Antellectual, "*an*" being a Persian vernacular term for excrement. That someone like Hoveyda would accept the UN post also indicated that moderate members of the Iranian technocratic class had by then decided that only by allying themselves with the Shah, even accepting his authoritarian leadership, could they hope to push Iran toward modernization, and eventually democracy.

Nevertheless, there was still a measure of mutual distrust between the Shah and members of the intelligentsia who had joined his regime. Thus it was with some trepidation that Fereydoon Hoveyda rushed back to Tehran in October

1967 after he was pulled out of a meeting at the UN and given a note that read: "Top Secret: To Fereydoon: Board immediately Iran Air's direct flight to Tehran. Necessary orders have been issued to the captain and to Mehrabad airport. Signed MRP (the Shah's initials)."[77]

His worries began to gnaw at him when a police car was waiting for him on the tarmac at the Tehran airport, and he was told that they were "not at liberty to tell" him where they were taking him. By ten o'clock they arrived at Niavaran Palace, where there was a party, and he was taken to the library. Almost immediately the Shah appeared and told Hoveyda in a voice that "was solemn. 'What I am about to tell you is an absolute secret between me and the President of the United States. It should remain so because the slightest leak might provoke an international crisis.'"[78]

His "top secret" mission, according to Hoveyda, was to go to France and, through contacts amongst his "leftist friends," get in touch with representatives of the North Vietnamese government. President Johnson, the Shah said, was tired of the war and wanted an honorable peace, but circumstances did not allow him to make a peace gesture. He had thus asked the Shah to act on behalf of the United States and attempt to broker a deal. It took Hoveyda only four days to receive his negative answer from the North Vietnamese government.

Documents from the American archives offer a slightly different version of these events. It was in fact the Shah who first offered his help in finding a "new initiative regarding Vietnam."[79] President Johnson was advised to tell the Shah that the United States "deeply appreciated his interest and concern" but added that they would offer no explicit approval of his efforts, as it "would be a kiss of death."[80] About the same time, the Shah also offered to act as a mediator in the Arab–Israeli conflict, but the United States politely demurred and asked the Shah to postpone, for the time being, the idea of sending a special emissary to launch such a peace initiative.[81]

A few years later, however, the United States did need the Shah's help in earnest. On October 21, 1972, a special Nixon envoy met with the Shah just as he had returned from the Soviet Union. Nixon wanted the Shah to immediately agree to send to South Vietnam Iran's entire fleet of ninety F-5 airplanes. Such a transfer, the Shah was told, was essential if honorable peace was to be achieved in Vietnam. The United States of course offered to expeditiously and appropriately compensate Iran for the planes. Much to the envoy's surprise, the Shah offered full support for the U.S. effort in Vietnam but agreed to send only a "total of 32 aircraft," arguing that sending any more would jeopardize Iran's national interests.[82]

The Watergate scandal and Nixon's resignation were not happy news for the Shah. As soon as the story broke, the Shah asked Zahedi to keep close watch and report on any major developments. In the beginning, the Shah and Zahedi both believed the Nixon line that it was much ado about nothing. It was Senator Barry Goldwater—a close friend of Zahedi's and a big supporter of the Shah—who delivered the sobering news that a majority of the Senate was now in favor of Nixon's impeachment. The Shah kept up his ties with Nixon even after his fall. He continued to send him gifts of caviar, and, more than once, he arranged for Nixon to find employment representing American companies wishing to do business with Iran.[83]

During the Ford and Carter administrations, in addition to the problem of oil, two new issues became irritants to the Shah's relationship with the United States. The first was the perennial problem of the Shah's desire to buy more military hardware, including some of the most sophisticated planes and radar. The second issue was Iran's nuclear program. The issue of military purchases was complicated by the Shah's desire to buy AWACS—new planes equipped with the most sophisticated radar—and F-14 and F-16 planes equipped with Phoenix air-to-air computer-guided missiles. It is estimated that close to a third of total U.S. arms sales went to Iran during the decade between 1965 and 1975.[84] America's resistance on some of these sales angered the Shah.

President Ford was particularly worried about tensions in the Iranian–American relationship. At a private dinner on October 21, 1975, he asked Ardeshir Zahedi, "Please tell me candidly: What is wrong? Is there any trouble or misunderstanding between us?"[85] Zahedi complained about the American inability to understand the Shah and his motives. Attacks in the media, he said, were a good example of this "failure to communicate." So frustrated was the Shah with these attacks that in September 1977, while in a "very somber mood," he told William Sullivan, Carter's choice as the American ambassador in Iran, that he thought he had arrived at "a turning point in his future relations with the US. The issues at stake," he said, "were far greater than AWACS." He said he had been amazed "by the things he had read" in the American media and "by the comments made by some of the senators." The Shah ended his complaints by saying he was seriously considering forgoing the idea of AWACS and instead buying a similar plane produced by the British called the Nimrod.

Eventually, after the Shah agreed with the administration's request for "special security" arrangements for AWACS in Iran, the United States agreed to the controversial sale. Yet, before they could be delivered, the revolution came. As the domestic situation deteriorated in Iran, the United States worried about the safety of its highly secret and sophisticated Phoenix missiles, which had been sold to Iran earlier. Lest they fall into Soviet hands, the United States, with the help of Israel, flew all Iranian air force planes armed with Phoenix missiles out of the country for "safety checks"; the aircraft were returned only after the missiles had been dismounted from the planes.[86]

Aside from modern weapon technologies, the question of Iran's nuclear program was also a subject of considerable tension between the Shah and the United States. Iran's nuclear program had begun with a small reactor given by the United States to Tehran University in 1959. It was part of the American Atoms for Peace program announced by President Eisenhower in December 1953. With Iran's increased oil revenues, and with the Shah's new vision of Iran as the hegemonic force in the region—even reaching as far as Africa, where the Shah was spending millions of dollars helping King Hassan of Morocco, and where Britain was "keen to persuade [the Shah] to use his oil power on South Africa"[87] to convince it to become more democratic—a nuclear program became for him the symbol of progress and power. He summoned Akbar Etemad, a trained nuclear physicist, to the Court in 1973, told him of his desire to launch a nuclear program, and asked Etemad to develop a master plan.

Two weeks later, the Shah met with Etemad again. Prime Minister Hoveyda was also present. The Shah quickly read the thirteen-page draft document Etemad had prepared, went over it a second time, and then turned to the Prime Minister and ordered him to fund what turned out be one of the most expensive projects undertaken by his regime. There was no prior discussion in the Majlis, where the constitutional power of the purse lay, or in any other governmental body or council. Like every major policy decision in those days, it was a one-man act. Thus was launched Iran's nuclear program.

Plans called for a "full-fledged nuclear power industry" with the capacity to produce 23,000 megawatts of electricity. By 1977, the Atomic Energy Organization of Iran (AEOI) had more than 1,500 employees (who were, on the order of the Shah, allowed to become the highest-paid government employees). The Shah had arranged for the training of Iranian nuclear experts around the world (including a $20 million endowment at MIT), had engaged in an intensive search for uranium mines in Iran and around the world, and had launched several nuclear research centers around the country.[88] The AEOI was in those days one of the most heavily funded programs in the country.

One of the firms working with AEOI at the time was called URIRAN; it was headed by Reza Niazmand, a career technocrat. URIRAN's job was to "prospect for uranium" and to sign contracts "with foreign aerial survey firms for a complete radiometric survey of Iran."[89] It was rumored that URIRAN was also working with companies in South Africa and Israel on nuclear-related activities. In 1976, $171.7 million was set aside for "additional purchase of uranium" while AEOI's budget for the year was $1.3 billion.

While Germany and France showed immediate eagerness to sell Iran its desired reactors, the United States was initially reluctant to sell any, "without conditions limiting [the Shah's] freedom of action." The German company Kraftwerk signed the first agreement to build the now-famous Bushehr reactor with an initial completion date of 1981 and an estimated cost of $3 billion. As Bushehr was located in a dangerous zone that was prone to frequent and strong seismic activity, extra funds were set aside to protect the site against the dangers of an earthquake. It was said at the time that the German government was so eager to find a foothold in the Iranian market that it guaranteed the investment of Kraftwerk against any loss.[90] The American companies, on the other hand, were barred from these contracts until the federal government's concerns about the Shah's intentions were mitigated.

The Shah was adamant that Iran should enjoy its "full rights" within the Treaty on the Non-Proliferation of Nuclear Weapons (NPT)—an agreement Iran had immediately signed upon its formulation and that called for non-nuclear states to forfeit the search for a nuclear bomb in return for easy access to the peaceful uses of nuclear energy. But Iran not only insisted on the right to have the "full fuel cycle," it also was interested in processing plutonium—a faster way to a nuclear bomb than enriched uranium.

Concerns were further aroused shortly after the February 1974 Franco–Iranian agreement on nuclear cooperation, when the Shah told *Le Monde* that one day "sooner than is believed," Iran would be "in possession of a nuclear bomb."[91] The Shah's surprising comment was at least partially in response to the 1974 Indian test of a nuclear weapon.

Realizing the repercussions of his comment, the Shah ordered the Iranian Embassy in France to issue a statement declaring that stories about the Shah's plan to develop a bomb are "totally invented and without any basis whatsoever." The U.S. Embassy in Tehran too, after talking with the Shah, reassured the American government that he is "certainly not yet" thinking about leaving NPT or joining the nuclear club. The Shah told Ambassador Helms that he believed "this nuclear armaments race is ridiculous. What would one do with them?" But even as he was trying to reassure the American government about his intentions, the Shah did indicate that, should any country in the region develop the nuclear bomb, then "perhaps the national interests of any country at all would demand that it would do the same."[92] The embassy ended its report by indicating that it believed the Shah's statements denying any plans to develop a bomb to "accurately reflect Shah's current intentions."[93] Assadollah Alam, the Shah's Court minister, claimed more than once in his *Daily Journals* that in his view, the Shah "wanted the bomb" but found it expedient to adamantly deny any intent at the moment.

The United States was particularly worried that "the annual plutonium production from the planned 23,000 MW Iranian nuclear power program will be equivalent to 600-700 warheads."[94] Nonetheless, by June 1974, the United States was finally willing to sell Iran nuclear reactors but only after "incorporating special bilateral controls in addition to the usual" international safeguards.[95] These safeguards were, in the mind of U.S. officials, necessary not just because of concerns about the Shah's intentions but because "in a situation of instability, domestic dissidents or foreign terrorists might easily be able to seize any special nuclear materials stored in Iran for use in a bomb."[96]

While the Shah was willing to consider some of these safeguards, he was insistent that Iran could not be treated "differently from countries with which [America] had previously signed power reactor agreements." By then Iran had already signed "letters of intent" with German and French companies for a "total of four nuclear power plants," and the Shah had signaled his plan to procure eight more from the United States. The State Department not only favored the sale of these reactors, but even encouraged the Bechtel corporation to solicit the "Shah's investment (on the order of 300 million dollars)" in a "private uranium enrichment facility to be built in the United States."[97] These proposals were all predicated on the Shah's willingness to accept more rigorous controls "over plutonium than [the United States] had heretofore included in our other agreements." Although eager to offer assurances to the United States, the Shah flatly rejected the idea of affording the Americans a veto on "reprocessing of US-supplied fuel."[98]

Both the Ford and the Carter administrations were under a complicated array of pressures and opportunities regarding Iran's nuclear program. Some in Congress were increasingly worried about the Shah's military expenditures and ambitions, and thus averse to the idea of giving him easy access to nuclear technology, but American companies were keen on getting a share of Iran's increasingly large market for such technology. Finally, both administrations knew that negotiations with the Shah on the nuclear issue could "prove to be extremely important to [America's] relations" with Iran. The Shah, the U.S. administrations knew, saw these negotiations as "a fundamental test to whether" Iran will continue to have a special relationship with the United States.[99] At the same time, the United States was convinced that the Shah might be tempted to acquire a nuclear bomb under certain circumstances, amongst them, "dismemberment of the Pakistani buffer state . . . [a] quest to be recognized as 'the fifth great power' . . . [and] Iranian desire for political-military hegemony within the Persian Gulf."[100]

As negotiations on these issues lingered, and seemed to have reached an impasse, and the Shah held firm to his rejection of any U.S. veto right, the Department of Defense recommended that the United States reconsider its hard-line approach and accept the Shah's demands.[101] American defense officials were worried that the Shah's unhappiness over this issue carried the threat "of poisoning other aspects of US-Iran relations." The fact that France and Germany were more than happy to sell to the Shah what the United States was withholding, and the fact that the Shah, through Etemad, had made clear gestures of possible cooperation with India on Iran's nuclear program, made the case for a U.S. "reconsideration" of its position more urgent.[102] President Ford, and later President Carter, agreed to accommodate the Shah, but still only to the extent that U.S. interests in non-proliferation were met.[103] Only after the Shah indicated his willingness to "pursue bilateral safeguard agreements," and signaled that he was no longer pursuing "a reprocessing plant" in Iran, was the Carter administration willing to allow American companies to sell reactors to Iran. But by then, the first hints of internal political trouble had already appeared on the horizon. Within months of this crucial agreement, the Shah was too preoccupied with the evolving domestic crisis to pay much attention to the nuclear negotiations. No sooner had Ayatollah Khomeini come to power than he ordered all work on Iran's nuclear program stopped, criticizing the Shah for ever pursuing such a program. Within a few years Khomeini changed his mind, but by then the West was much more distrustful of Iran's intentions.

The Shah's crucial decade from 1965 to 1975 was also critical for the regime's cultural politics. Iran in this period was a discordant combination of cultural freedoms and political despotism—of increasing censorship against the opposition but increasing freedoms for everyone else. It is far from hyperbole to claim that during the sixties and seventies, Iran was one of the most liberal societies in the Muslim world in terms of cultural and religious tolerance, and in the state's aversion to interfere in the private lives of its citizens—so long as they did not politically oppose the Shah. Indications of this tolerance were many: from the quality of life of Iran's Baha'i and Jews to the artistic innovations and aesthetic avant-gardism of the Shiraz Art Festival. The famous Italian filmmaker Pier Paolo Pasolini traveled to Iran often and shot parts of his controversial *Decameron*—an erotic romp about the sexual shenanigans in medieval monasteries—in Isfahan. He was not alone in making these trips. Some of the world's foremost artists and playwrights—from Andre Grotovski to Peter Brooks—converged on Shiraz to perform or on Tehran to look for funding for films. By the early 1970s, Princess Ashraf and her husband, Mehdi Bushehri, had become interested in producing films.

Much to the consternation of the Shiite clergy in this period, the Baha'i enjoyed freedom and virtual equality with other citizens. The same was true about Iranian Jews—some 100,000 of them, who had lived in Iran for over 3,000 years. In the words of David Menasheri, it was the Jews' "golden age," wherein they enjoyed equality with Muslims and in terms of their per capita incomes "they might have been the richest Jewish community in the world."[104] Some of

Iran's most innovative and successful industrialists, engineers, architects, and artists were either Jewish or Baha'i. The Arj family, dominant in the production of home appliances in Iran; the Sabet family, who brought television and Pepsi to the country; and finally Habib Elghanian, who introduced the nation to the magic of "plastic," were all members of the Baha'i and Jewish faiths. The Shah's private physician, Dr. Ayadi, was an active member of the Baha'i faith and was instrumental in facilitating Baha'i security and prosperity in Iran.

The Shah had a surprisingly blithe attitude toward the sexual life of those around him. Though he occasionally received reports from SAVAK about the private lives of courtiers—a mistress here, a ménage à trois there, and an openly homosexual lifestyle in a third—he was, especially for a leader of a Muslim society, remarkably tolerant, even indifferent to the erotic and other private activities of those around him. It was, for example, a sign of his respect for the private lives of his sisters that he never made an issue of his older sister Shams's decision to become a Catholic. Nor did he publicly take issue with the storied private life of his twin sister, Ashraf. Though more than once he commented on and chided her behavior in private, particularly to Court Minister Alam, and though he refused her entreaty to have the Iranian government underwrite her rather quixotic dream of either herself or one of her protégés becoming the secretary-general of the UN,[105] he made no effort to interfere in her private life. His reticence in pressuring his sisters on these private issues was a sign of both his timidity and his liberal disposition; his aversion to confronting them about their brazen economic activities was a further indication of his timidity, as well as of the arrogance of his power.

❧

Power is most insolent when it is most insular. It was a measure of the Shah's isolation that he ignored one of the most telling warnings about the effects of the regime's economic and social policy, made by Qassem Lajevardi, a senator and a scion of one of Iran's most successful industrial conglomerates.

In a fascinating speech on the floor of the Senate, he offered a de facto manifesto for Iran's nascent industrialist class.[106] In spite of its dire warnings, no one in the government—from the Shah and the Court to the cabinet and SAVAK—deigned to ask Lajevardi to further clarify his position.[107]

Lajevardi began his remarks by pointing out the startling fact that 103 of the 104 government-run companies were losing money—the only one that showed any profit was the oil company.[108] He also talked of the dangers of price control, knowing well the Shah's proclivity to use force to control prices, going so far as deputizing an army of students to identify and, if necessary, arrest businessmen accused of price gouging. The policy angered not just modern industrialists like

Lajevardi but also members of the bazaar, long a bastion of support for the moderate opposition and for the clergy. Nowhere in the world, Lajevardi said, had the effort to forcefully control prices led to success. He went on to also criticize the government policy of arbitrarily deciding workers' wages. Wages, he said, must correlate with productivity and cannot, as was the case in Iran, be treated as a political bonus. Industrialists will invest, he said pointedly, only if they are allowed to make a fair profit. By then, a massive flight of capital from Iran had already started—a flight that would be redoubled when the political situation deteriorated.

In spite of the disparate nature of his complaints, there was a common theme to them: capitalism needs security, rule of law, and the force of the market to develop, and it cannot grow if it is held hostage to the vagaries of a single person, even if he is a sagacious leader like the Shah.

In Lajevardi's cautious criticism lay the essence of the contradiction that threatened the Shah's modernizing authoritarianism: the more he won his battles with oil companies and increased Iran's revenue, the more these petrodollars helped create and train a larger and larger technocratic middle class, the more he promised the people standards of living higher than those of Japan or Germany, the more these impressive accomplishments convinced him of his global importance—the more he inadvertently prepared the conditions of his own downfall. The middle classes he helped create wanted democracy, and the hubris of his increasing authoritarianism made them increasingly uneasy. The statistical portrait of the Shah's accomplishments was indeed impressive. In 1941 there were only 351 high schools and 8 universities in the country; in 1974, on the eve of the Shah's creation of the one-party system, there were 2,314 high schools and 148 universities. In 1941 there were only 482 large industrial institutions in Iran, whereas in 1974 the number had increased to 5,651.[109] The annual growth of industry went from 5 percent per year in 1962 to 20 percent in 1974. The share of industrial production in the gross national product increased from 11.7 percent to about 17 percent, while employment in the private sector went from 1.3 million workers in 1962 to more than 2 million in 1974.[110]

Even more impressive changes had been made in the number of women in schools. While the percentage of illiteracy amongst women was in 1972 still higher than amongst men, between 1961 and 1972 the number of female students at different educational levels increased 13 percent for primary schools, 30 percent for high schools, 88 percent for technical schools, and 65 percent for institutions of higher education.[111] Yet, in spite of these accomplishments, even someone like Lajevardi was by 1975 disgruntled.

The ultimate measure of a wise ruler, Edmund Burke argued after observing revolutions in France and England, is not just the ability to change society, but also the ability and disposition to preserve those changes—everything else, he said, is "vulgar in conception and perilous in execution." There is no doubt that from 1965 to 1975, the Shah guided Iran through remarkable changes. Some of them even survived the fall of his regime. Iranian women refused to give up their rights and return to their "sacred motherly duties" just because Khomeini and his cohorts seized power. It is equally true that the totality of those changes, their tempo and texture, as well as the Shah's style and substance of leadership, ultimately begot the Islamic Revolution of 1979. If, in that decisive decade, the celebration of 2,500 years of monarchy was the most lavish and controversial event organized by the Shah, then what happened during the Shah's speech at the tomb of Cyrus at Pasargad, billed as the official launch of the ceremonies, was a potent metaphor of what lay ahead. As the Shah began to speak—telling Cyrus that he "could repose in peace for we are awake"—his unusually tremulous voice proved no match for the sandstorm and heavy winds that were suddenly unleashed. If the speech at the Cyrus tomb became the subject of much ridicule, one of the Shah's most enduring legacies is the Shahyad Monument built to commemorate the 2,500 celebrations—a monument that powerfully captured his aborted vision for Iran.

Chapter 17

ARCHITECTURE AND POWER

This earth shall have a feeling.
Shakespeare, King Richard II, *3.2.24*

Architecture is the poetry of power. In modern despotic societies, when the aesthetics of politics and the mise-en-scène of marches and meetings become an inexorable part of the calculus of power, this strange synergy of politics and architecture is even more pronounced. Two buildings, one private and the place of his residence, the other public and the symbol of his era, capture the complexities of the Shah's character and the nature of his power in the last two decades of his rule.

Architecture has always been part of the lexicon of power in Iran. Kings and clerics used monuments to symbolize, legitimize, or consolidate their political or spiritual power. In pre-Islamic Persia, the palaces of Persepolis, and no less than Taq-e Kasra—the tallest free-standing arch in the world—were designed for the purpose of impressing and intimidating friends and foes, subjects and enemies. With the seventh-century Arab invasion and the advent of Islam, not only did Iran as a unified power begin to dwindle, but the erstwhile imperial grandeur was overshadowed by a new, austere aesthetic sensibility of Islam. The bas-reliefs of Persepolis and the paintings in Sassanian Iran underscored the prevalence of human representational art in ancient Persia. In the Islamic aesthetic regimen, however, with its ban on making an image or statue of a human (such creation,

Islam believes, is an usurpation of God's monopoly on creation), calligraphy and tile-work took the place of the representational arts. The genius of Persian architecture was, more than anywhere, channeled into the construction of mosques and, on a few occasions, palaces.

Some 700 years after the Arab invasion, Isfahan, a city with an almost 3,000-year history as a human habitat and the first abode of Jews fleeing to Persia from Babylonian captivity, was picked as the new capital of a newly unified, centralized, and invigorated Iran. The city's majestic Naghsh-e Jahan (map of the world), a large square designed by Shah Abbas, reflected his vision of power. He ruled Iran from 1581 to 1629 and fought against the Muslim Ottoman Turks, allying Iran with Christian Europe. In traditional Iran, the court, the mosque, and the bazaar had been the three pillars of power. The balance of power among the three elements at any one time shaped the nature of authority. If Isfahan captured the self-assurance of Iran during the apex of the Safavid dynasty, and if the design for Naghsh-e Jahan exhibited Shah Abbas's image of the ideal balance of court, mosque, and bazaar, Tehran became and remained the capital under the next two dynasties. The sleepy village first became a monument to the rise of Agha Mohammad Khan, who founded the new Qajar dynasty in 1781. But the city's radical transformation to a modern metropolis took place during the Pahlavi era, when it became a metaphor for the modernizing, authoritarian ethos of those fifty-four years.

As a human habitat, Tehran and its environs are said to be 8,000 years old. Until it became a capital some 200 years ago, it was a half-derelict village caught between marauding tribes. Scholars have traced the etymology of the word "Tehran" to the habit of the medieval inhabitants of this small village who built their homes underground, thus the name of "Tahran," or literally "Undergrounders." The village lived in the shadow of its prosperous neighbor, the city of Rey. When Mongolian armies attacked and destroyed that grand and prosperous city in 1220, the troglodytes of Tehran "took refuge in their subterranean homes, and came out only when they felt safe."[1]

During the reign of the Qajar dynasty, new buildings and palaces were constructed in and around Tehran. Amongst them was a new royal summer residence, nestled in the slopes of the picturesque mountains that dominate the city's northern skyline. Tehran is an anomaly amongst metropolises of the world for its lack of proximity to rivers or seas. Instead, it enjoys the majestic beauty of mountains on its northern borders. The cool breezes on those mountains made their slopes the favorite summer resort for the rich inhabitants of the city. Fath-Ali Shah (r. 1797–1843), whose long reign epitomized the Qajar dynasty's corrupt anachronism, was the first king to build a house in the cool climes of those mountain slopes. It was near a village called Kardebeh, and it was surrounded by gardens that included some reed, or *ney* in Persian. Niavaran, or "the place of reeds," became the name of the more than 130,000-square-yard (eleven-hectare) compound of palaces and office and utility buildings.

In 1888, Nasir al-Din Shah ordered a new palace built on the compound. It was called Sahebgraniyeh, a derivative of *sahebgeran*, "Possessor of Good Grace," one of a long litany of the Qajar king's grandiose royal titles. His other titles included the "Pivot of the Universe" and "Shadow of God." Although the Shah's use of the title "Aryamehr"—"Light of the Aryans"—was derided as grandiose and bombastic by his critics, in comparison to the Qajar king's quixotic grandiosity, it was decidedly humble. Another telling contrast is the Shah's use of the Sahebgraniyeh Palace, compared to the way his predecessor had used the place. Though the small palace had itself no more than a dozen rooms, it was surrounded by about fifty small, four-room apartments, each set aside for one of the wives from the lusty Nasir al-Din Shah's infamously large harem.

During the early years of the Pahlavi era, the palaces in the Niavaran complex were left unused, becoming all but derelict. In 1938, in anticipation of the Crown Prince's imminent marriage to Fawzia, the Sahebgraniyeh Palace was renovated for the wedding ceremony. But eventually the ceremonies were held at the Golestan Palace, and Sahebgraniyeh was once again left to the ravages of time. By the late 1950s, as the number of foreign dignitaries visiting Iran increased, the government decided it needed a new guesthouse. The Niavaran complex was chosen as the site, and Aziz Farmanfarmaian was picked to design the building.

He was one of the early harbingers of a crucial new turn in Iranian modernity and its incumbent sense of aesthetics. It was a turn that permeated nearly every facet of the society. Iranian modernist artists, once enamored of the West and dedicated to imitation of the Western masters, began to experiment with a new modernity that was at once local and global, informed by Iranian tradition yet infused with values and visions from around the world. This new modernity affected prose and poetry, where artists like Ebrahim Golestan, Houshang Golshiri, and Mehdi Akhavan-Sales mined the tropes and lexicon of classical Persian literature to fashion modern works of fiction and poetry. In music, Abolhasan Saba fused the classical structures of Persian music *(dastgahs)* with formative ideas of Western classical music like counterpoint. In architecture and painting, the days of emulating the buildings of Frank Lloyd Wright and Le Corbusier or the paintings of Picasso and Pollack gave way to new styles that were at once Persian and Western, traditional and modern.

The marriage of the Shah to Queen Farah, whose aspirations as a student of architecture were aborted by the offer of marriage to the Shah but who remained an architectural aficionado all her life, helped strengthen the emergence of this new sensibility. She saved some of the country's most beautiful and bustling old neighborhoods and bazaars from the razing bulldozers of greedy developers and corrupt, ambitious officials. Her one big failure was her inability to save the old neighborhoods around the shrine of the Eighth Imam of Shiism, located in the city of Meshed. In that case, the Shah was convinced by the arguments of the advocates of urban renewal. Some have argued that the decision to raze the traditional markets and neighborhoods around the shrine was intended as a challenge to the power of the clergy whose stronghold included just such bazaars.

The Queen also helped renovate several beautifully ornate classical buildings that had previously been left derelict. An example was her decision to hire Italian experts to wash off the thin layer of plaster that had been used by prudish men of power in the Qajar period to cover the erotica drawn on the walls and ceiling of Shah Abbas's bedroom at Aligapu, his palace in Isfahan. Shortly after February 1979, with the victory of the Islamic Revolution, a new form of pious prudery led to the decision to once again cover the erotic fresco with a white layer of plaster.

Even the design of buildings set aside for tourists reflected this new modern sensibility. The Tehran Hilton, the first foreign luxury hotel in Tehran, was yet another replica of the homogenized designs of the "familiar" Western hotel—long rows of rooms placed in a placid linear grid. On the other hand, the Shah Abbas Hotel, in Isfahan, built just a few years later, modified the traditional Persian designs for a caravansary and turned it into a modern hotel with all the amenities of a luxury hotel but unmistakably Persian. At the Queen's insistence, the same sensibility shaped the design of the new Niavaran Palace.

Farmanfarmaian had graduated from France's most acclaimed school, the École des Beaux-Arts. In Iran, his early buildings were nothing but renditions of the modern style of European or American masters. But beginning with Niavaran, he found a way to combine traditional Persian motifs with the functionalism and individualism of modern architecture.

In Western modern architecture the house is viewed as a "living machine" designed for the comfort of the individual. In traditional Iran, a complicated set of rules about the private and the public dictate essential elements of design. In that tradition, the inner sanctum was to be protected from the intruding gaze of strangers. Moreover, the most luxurious parts of the house were set aside for guests. Climatic exigencies were another factor dictating the kind of raw material used in traditional buildings. Farmanfarmaian's goal and achievement was to combine the most functional and graceful elements of Persian and Western styles of architecture and arrive at what he called "a genuine modernity" and a "true connection to the Persian source."[2] His philosophy of architecture and aesthetics, rooted in his populist political disposition and acquired in pre–World War II Socialist France, all worked to make the Niavaran design unusually simple and bereft of grandiosity, yet graceful and efficient, unmistakably Persian and elegantly modern. When the building finally became the royal family's main residence, the Queen's own sensibilities shaped the final design of the building and also its uniquely cosmopolitan interior design. At the same time, the big reception hall on the second floor of the Sahebgraniyeh Palace adjacent to the Niavaran Palace became the Shah's main office, and it too reflected the Shah's taste and character.

Before moving to Niavaran, the Shah's main residence had been the Sa'ad Abad Palace. While living and working at Sa'ad Abad, the Shah held the most important official ceremonies at Golestan Palace, where the Peacock Throne was kept. By the late 1960s, as the city expanded more and more into the cooler northern climes of the slopes of the mountains and the upper and middle classes moved to those slopes, the increasingly congested and soot-covered southern parts of the city and the bazaar were left to the traditional and poor classes. Tehran became the oil El Dorado, millions converged on the city, creating shanty towns and poorer neighborhoods, virtually all located in the southern part of the city. As events in June 5, 1963, had shown, the combination of poverty, religious fervor, and rising expectations, along with the regime's inattention to the urgent task of socializing new urbanites in the rules of urban living, turned these areas into a political powder keg. By then, the Golestan Palace, near the heart of the bazaar, was hard for the Shah to reach and even harder for his security detail to protect. In the Shah's last years, it was rarely used.

In contrast to Golestan, Sa'ad Abad sat on the slopes of Towchal Mountain, overlooking Tehran. The compound with its eighteen palaces and eight ornate and graceful gates had been built by Reza Shah on a property covering a 1.1 million square meters of wooded land. A river flowed through it. Reza Shah had bought the property for 400,000 *tooman* from a Qajar prince—a small fortune at the time, equal to about $200,000. He ultimately built eighteen palaces for himself, his wives, his children, and his brothers and sisters and their children. In the last years of the Shah's rule, one of the buildings was also set aside for the use of Farideh Diba, the Queen's mother. A couple of the palaces in the compound were sold by the Shah's sisters to the government, one for use as the administrative headquarters of the court ministry, the other as the official residence of the court minister. There were allegations that the government of Hoveyda paid an exaggerated price for these palaces to placate some of the Shah's siblings and turn them into his allies.[3]

For years, the Shah's residence in Sa'ad Abad was called the White House. It was there, in a separate room on the second floor, that he had set up his elaborate miniature electrical trains—with locomotives, cargo and passenger cars, stations, trees, and houses near the tracks. In the late 1950s, in deference to Soraya's passion for bowling, the Shah had also ordered a bowling alley built in the basement of the White House. The eighteen buildings of Sa'ad Abad reflected Reza Shah's taste, simple in design, Persian in motif, and green in their surroundings. By the time the Shah moved to Niavaran, over 400 people worked in the old palace compound. Moving to Niavaran physically separated the Shah from the rest of his family, but the ritual of spending virtually every night with them continued.

The Shah's two previous wives—Fawzia, accustomed to the storied opulence of Egyptian royalty, and Soraya, who craved and emulated the lavish living of the international jet set—complained about the paucity of space and the inelegance of Sa'ad Abad, as well as that of the Marble Palace (where the Shah lived soon after his return from Switzerland). Soraya thought the place had "a detestable atmosphere" with "ill-sorted furniture" and "kitchens [that] were ancient." She lamented the lack of "Parisian decoration," and in her own words, like Snow White in the cottage of the seven dwarfs, she "tried to remake" it into a more livable and more European home. Now, Queen Farah was keen on making Niavaran in her own image.[4]

As it turned out, the palace also became a perfect metaphor for the Shah's paradigm of Westernized modernization. The Marble and Golestan palaces had the virtues and the weaknesses of traditional Persian architecture, and they both reflected Reza Shah's naturalism. In contrast, Niavaran was, in both design and function, eclectically cosmopolitan. A number of Iranian and Western architects, designers, and aesthetes helped the Queen in designing and decorating the palace and collecting an impressive array of masterpieces of modern art and ancient artifacts. These aides and designers included such famous figures as Charles Savigny, Keyvan Khosravani, and Bijan Saffari, and the Queen's relative Kamran Diba.[5] It was a measure of the Shah's and the Queen's sensibilities that, although Khosravani and Saffari were openly gay, they nevertheless remained favorite fixtures of the royal family's entourage. The Shah in particular enjoyed Khosravani's quick sense of humor and his ability to make fun of courtiers and politicians alike. The food service at the court, he wrote, was "something even worse than the room service in a third rate hotel. I could never get a hot tea there."[6] In a tone of brilliant satire he describes the difficulties of getting a simple meal, or a glass of whiskey with ice, at the royal Court. He also acted as something of a fashion advisor to the Queen, helping her find rare Persian fabrics and designing them into gowns and dresses with Persian motifs. For more than a decade, he was considered the top designer and an aesthetic advisor for the Queen. The Queen's decision to wear these dresses went a long way in revitalizing the disappearing craft of handwoven fabrics in Iran. Khosravani's descriptions of the Queen's habits and proclivities, even her relationship with her small gray

Cornish poodle—"a particularly neurotic and noisy dog"[7]—are brilliant and searing in their honesty. At the same time, Khosravani also offered occasional advice on new developments on the art scene.

Before long, the Queen's collection of more than 350 artifacts and masterpieces required a space of their own. A wing of the Shah's Sahebgraniyeh Palace was turned into a private Jahan-Nama (Window to the World). It had all the trappings of a museum, but it was simply for the viewing pleasure of the royal family. Twenty-three million *tooman* ($7.5 million) was spent transforming the onetime residential palace into a museum.[8] What is clear from Alam's *Daily Journals* is that neither the Queen nor the Shah spent money according to a predetermined budget. The Shah and the Court were, according to the constitution, ostensibly provided a yearly budget by the government. But in the case of the Shah, and even the Queen, they spent money as they saw fit, decided on allocating contracts, and then ordered the Court Minister to pay for it. More often than not, the government was ordered to shoulder the bill. The use of government facilities and military planes for the personal use of the royal family was so common and taken for granted that it was rarely commented upon.

For the Shah, in particular, the entire country was his virtual private fiefdom. On September 30, 1975, John Oakes of the *New York Times* wrote after visiting Iran that "in no country of the world can Louis XIV's famous aphorism—'L'état c'est moi'—be applied with more accuracy than Iran."[9] The next day, the Shah read the article and angrily told Alam, "the bastard [pedar soukhteh*] has said that I am Louis XIV. He was the essence of reaction and I am a revolutionary leader."[10] A few days later, the same Court Minister submitted the "central thesis" of an upcoming speech he was to give for the Shah's approval, and said, "I am going to say that [Your Majesty and your father] embody Iran and that Louis XIV's phrase, 'L'état c'est moi,' aptly applies to you." The Shah was not angry this time, but instead said, "When I look at myself, it is true that I see or want nothing other than Iran. Thus your suggestion is not wrong."[11]

Even Western embassies had begun to notice the blurring of the lines between the Shah's personal assets and expenses and those of the government. On one occasion, this conception helped absolve the Shah of the allegation of bribery. In June 1968, Iran placed an order for forty helicopters with the American company Augusta Bell. Britain's air attaché reported that, in return for the order, the Shah had already received two helicopters and was expected to receive another "two large helicopters in de luxe VIP trim, also free." Another British official at the embassy opined that while it was impossible to decide whether the allegations

---

* *Pedar soukhteh* is a common phrase in the vernacular. "Father-burned" is its literal meaning; its actual meaning is determined contextually. Here "bastard" seems like the right translation.

were true, even if they were true, it should not be "categorized as bribery" since whatever use the Shah found for the helicopters would invariably "be . . . for state and governmental purposes" and thus the gift of the helicopters means Iran will be "getting a few more helicopters."[12]

With an apparently infinite supply of money at her disposal, the Queen began to buy art, and before long her art collection included, amongst other things, five Picassos, four Braques, a Gauguin, and a Chagall. Giacometti's *Standing Man* stood next to a lulled cat from Peru. An Egyptian bird sat next to exquisite pottery and statues from ancient Persia. Masters of abstract expressionism were also amply represented, testifying to the Queen's wide-ranging aesthetic sensibilities. Tehran became a mecca for art dealers and big-name American and European architects, who converged on the city to sell a design or an artifact and claim a share of the oil revenue. What the Queen could not find in Tehran, she either found in her travels in Europe or America or had her aides or agents find for her. Some of the regime's opponents at the time criticized these purchases as extravagant.

Easily the most controversial of this collection was a De Kooning painting (*Lady No. 3*). The Islamic regime in Iran refused to display this and many other modern masterpieces on "moral" grounds and eventually decided to exchange it for a few pages of an old illuminated *Shahnameh*—often thought to be the most beautiful illuminated text in Iran. A large number of middlemen and dealers were involved in the negotiations, and some have suggested that, in return for bribes and kickbacks, the Iranian officials fraudulently undervalued the price of the rare De Kooning masterpiece.[13]

The Queen's eclectic taste was evident not just in the collection but even more in the interior of the palace. The prevalence of French motifs made the atmosphere equally comfortable for the Shah, who was in his cultural taste a dedicated Francophile. French was, after all, the language the Shah and the Queen preferred to use when conversing with the Crown Prince. His nurse, too, was a Frenchwoman. The palace was two and one-half floors, with 9,000 square meters of living space. The building was "entirely hidden behind a mass of trees." There was a helicopter pad allowing the Shah to get around the city by air. In the 1970s, congestion and the fear of terrorism made travel by car almost impossible for the Shah. When using the helicopter, he often took over the controls. There was also a large reflective pool and a carefully manicured landscape that separated the Niavaran Palace from the Shah's office. Though the distance was short, the Shah occasionally drove one of his many fast cars from home to office, but more often he simply walked. His love of speed, a constant passion of his life, was now an option available only when he was on vacation in places where security was not an issue.

Niavaran Palace's interior appointments were at once Iranian and European. The tile- and mirror-work as well as the elaborate decorative plaster were the creation of some of the most acclaimed Iranian masters—names like Master Abdollah and Master Kazempour. A few years earlier, such masters would have had no role in a "modern" building in Tehran. But in a city where the Shah and the Queen set the fashion for much of the elite, having traditional appointments in new buildings soon became a fad.

The entrance hall to Niavaran was a palatial grand salon, with a gallery of rooms above it. In the words of *Architectural Digest*, which featured the Niavaran Palace in an issue in 1977, it was "an Eastern version of the Roman atrium."[14] The big room was "intentionally flavored" with paneling that was "French in conception" next to tile-work and plaster curlicues that were unmistakably Persian. Lighted display cases exhibiting "Persian papier-mâché" and gold artifacts stood next to masterpieces of French painting and rare French tapestry. On one wall hung a painting by Marie Laurencin, while next to the fireplace was a small work by Utrillo. Grand Empire chandeliers of Russian origin gave the room an air of majesty, while other parts of the salon were chock full of a wide assortment of artifacts.

The reception room as well as the dining hall were both "richly furnished in a conventional French manner." Exquisite Persian rugs, antiques, and mirror-works provided the Persian flavor of the rooms. Here and there, works of Persian masters, from Sohrab Sepehri and Abolghassem Saidi to Parviz Tanavoli[†] were also displayed on the walls.

Between the public part of the palace and the private residence where the Shah and the Queen had their bedrooms was a small private cinema with a green rug, a sculpture by Parviz Tanavoli, and a painting by Abolghassem Saidi. Watching a film after dinner was by then a permanent part of the Shah's nightly program. He preferred light comedies—French comedians were amongst his favorites—and preferred Hollywood productions over somber and serious art films. Sometimes controversial films that had befuddled the censors but were deemed important were sent to the Court for the Shah and the Queen's final verdict.

Occasionally the Queen tried to get the Shah to watch more serious films, particularly those made by Persian directors. One such film was Dariush Mehrjui's *Dayereh Mina*, an unsparing look at the profitable traffic in the blood of Tehran's poor and addicted masses. The film had become controversial because Dr. Manouchehr Egbal, the one-time prime minister and the perennial head of Iran's Medical Association, wanted the film banned because it offered a negative

† In recent months, some of the masterpieces of these artists have been sold for hundreds of thousands of dollars each. A couple have sold for more than $1 million.

image of medicine in Iran. The Queen insisted that the Shah should see the film, and finally, on the night when it was brought to the Court, halfway through it the Shah angrily got up and marched out of the screening, arguing that these so-called intellectuals were only happy when they looked at the dark side of life. On another occasion, talking about a film that had been produced by the Organization for the Intellectual Development of Children, headed by Lili Amir-Arjomand, a close friend of the Queen, the Shah again dismissed the film saying, "What the hell is a lyric film? What use does it have for an ill-intentioned man to make a film?"[15] The organization had become one of the most successful, yet controversial, institutions in the last years of the Shah's rule. It had begun the practice of using mobile libraries, affording children of even the most remote villages and towns access to books. The organization also produced films, including the first shorts made by Abbas Kiarostami.

The Shah's taste in films was complicated. On the one hand, when he heard that Ebrahim Golestan's documentary about the oil industry in Iran had won several international prizes, he asked to see the film and the director. Golestan took the film to the Court with some trepidation, for the last line of the film was consciously ambiguous. It talked of the West taking Iran's oil and leaving the country with nothing but the foam left on the beach in the wake of a big wave. The Shah not only clearly understood the implied message in the phrase but as he talked with Golestan after the end of the private showing, he said, "so long as I am here I will not allow them to leave us only the foam."[16]

On the other hand, in the late 1960s, as the Shah was trying to improve Iran's image around the world, the acclaimed filmmaker Albert Lamorisse, whose *Red Balloon* had won many awards, was commissioned to make a short documentary on Iran. He made what some have called a "poetic praise" of the best in Iran's tradition and history. The film had emphasized older buildings and ancient monuments, and when the Shah saw it, he summarily dismissed it as having missed its mission. There are no dams and new buildings, he complained. Much to his consternation, Lamorisse was forced to re-edit the film and include footage of new buildings and Iran's modernizing military.[17]

If the royal couple's cinematic taste was occasionally at odds, there was no controversy when she turned part of a loft into a private library. The space was designed by Aziz Farmanfarmaian and Charles Sevigny, an American designer living in Paris in the seventies. Halfway through the construction of the small space, Alam, then the minister of Court, complained to the Shah that already 12 million *tooman* ($1.5 million) had "been spent [on the library] and nothing is done. . . . The Shah simply laughed" and instructed Alam to pay the expenses.[18] The Shah took no part in these decorative decisions but occasionally complained about cost overruns. Such complaints were invariably prompted by Alam, who was by then clearly despised by the Queen for his role in arranging the Shah's trysts.

Alam retaliated by constantly whispering in the Shah's ear about the cost of these renovations, or about the fact that the contracts were invariably given to relatives and friends of the Queen. The renovation of the royal couple's Swiss ski chalet, Suvreta, in fashionable St. Moritz was, on the orders of the Queen, given to Parviz Bushehri, who, again according to Alam, "charged ten times the fair price, and no one, including the Shah said anything."[19] When Alam tried to solicit the Shah's support in questioning the estimated price, the Shah ordered his Court Minister to "just sign it."[20] On more than one occasion, Alam complained to the Shah about "the lady Her Majesty has picked to help decorate Niavaran, Sa'adabad and Nowshahr [on the Caspian]. I must, according to my duty inform Your Majesty," he told the Shah one day "that everything is costing fifty percent more than what they should. And it is not clear what is the cargo of all of these planes we have put at her disposal, and fly back and forth to Europe." Again the Shah simply smiled, ordered Alam to keep quiet and pay the bill, and said, "You know I have to live a little too." Alam clearly understood the Shah's implied message. "Her Majesty must be allowed to do anything [the Queen] wants and her entourage engage in any shitty work, so that the Shah hears less grumbling."[21] Here then was the political price the Shah was paying for his philandering. More importantly, stories and rumors about these allegations of corruption were fast becoming a potent political issue.

Numerous reports from the British and American embassies in late 1978 make it clear that the issue of corruption was one of the chief grievances of the opposition. In an October 5, 1978, report, the British Embassy wrote about claims based on information from "someone in a position to know and whose information is invariably reliable that during the recent period of crisis Princesses Shams and Ashraf and their families moved about 1.8 billion dollars out of Iran. This amount is almost exactly... the amount which the Swiss banking representatives here reckon surfaced during the period in foreign money havens."[22] By the time the Shah decided to make a public pronouncement on his family's activities, it was far too little, far too late.

In 1975, as the Queen was creating her library, the regime seemed in complete command of the situation, and as reports from the American and British Embassies clearly testify, they all believed the regime safe and secure for the foreseeable future. The cost of the Queen's library was small change compared to the government's multibillion-dollar annual oil revenue. When it was finally finished, the library had more than 23,000 books, and included old and new, Persian and Western texts. The oldest manuscript was a French book published in 1609. In the 1977 *Architectural Digest* essay about the palace, there is a photo of the library that shows a Paul Jenkins painting sitting on an easel. On the wall of the library hangs a large assortment of embroidered benevolent talismans; on the window ledge sits a long array of family pictures. The unusual combination of religious relics and modern paintings, accompanied by an assortment of antiques and art deco furniture, captured the Queen's peculiar cosmopolitanism.

The Shah's office in Sahebgraniyeh was a contrast in sense and sensibilities. It was simple in design and dominated by the glitter of the beautiful nineteenth-century mosaic mirror-work on its walls and rare Persian rugs on its floors. Nasir al-Din Shah had used the palace as a pleasure dome, with his harem spread around his perch of patriarchy. For the sick and weakened Mozzafar al-Din Shah, it was a place of rest. It was in the yard of this palace that, in 1905, he finally signed the *firman* that declared Iran a constitutional monarchy. The Shah, on the other hand, who probably worked more in one month than his Qajar predecessors did in a year, had turned the hall on the second floor of the building into his office. His desk, a handcrafted work of exquisite Persian artistry *(monabatkari)* sat in a corner, always impeccably tidy. On the walls, there were no paintings. Their only adornments were two large mirrors and two old swords, a shield with arrows sticking out of it like rays of the sun, and a bow. On the ceiling and parts of the wall, decorative plaster with beautiful Qajar fresco paintings drawn between elaborate frames of plaster gave the room a nineteenth-century Persian aura.

Not long after moving to Niavaran, the Queen began plans to build a new, bigger palace in Farahabad, a royal hunting ground near Tehran used by the Shah and the royal family at the time for riding. The Shah initially agreed, but when a government financial crisis required a budget cut, and Mehdi Samii, then director of the Plan Organization, told the Shah of the existing financial crunch, the Shah immediately scuttled plans for the construction of the palace.[23] On at least one other occasion, the Shah rejected suggestions to build a palace for the royal family. It was to be in the city of Meshed. "What do we need a palace for?" the Shah asked Alam.

While the Shah was averse to conspicuous architectural construction and consumption, his willingness to spend money for his life-long passion for expensive fast cars, fast boats, and planes was a notable exception. By the mid-1970s, he had a fleet of expensive cars that was legendary amongst speed aficionados. In an exhibit commenced in Tehran a few years after the revolution, it was claimed that the royal family collection of expensive cars included at least "140 vintage and classic" cars.[24] Amongst the Shah's prized possessions were one of the only six Mercedes-Benz 500 coups (another one was used by Hitler to review troops); a Panther Lazer; a specially designed Maserati 500GT, ordered by the Shah in 1959; a 1939 Bugatti 57 C, a gift of the French government to the Shah at the time of his first marriage (that mysteriously landed in Romania after the revolution and sold for a million dollars); a Lamborghini Countach; a Rolls-Royce Phantom (one of 17 ever produced); a Ferrari 500; and finally a bronze C-30 Chrysler coupe prototype, with "pure gold dashboard, refrigerator, record player," bought by the Shah for his second wife, Soraya.

❧

If Niavaran and the design of his office captured the Shah's aesthetic sensibilities about private spaces, the Shahyad Monument was no less eloquent in articulating his vision of Iran. It heralded a Tehran transformed by changing times and conflicting identities and creatively bridged the city's tormented past with its triumphant mood about its future. The Shah's new, grand, sometimes grandiose, vision of Iran; his constant promise to build a "Great Civilization," better than anything produced in the West while at the same time showing an openness to all things Western; and his increasing interest in conjuring the history of Iran's ancient grandeur to consolidate his claim to power are all captured in the monument's design. In retrospect, the Shah tried to use majestic monuments and imposing ceremonies like the celebration of 2,500 years of monarchy in lieu of offering a theory that legitimized his rule.

His decision to hold his "desert bash" at a location where Persepolis provided the backdrop and his choice of the tomb of Cyrus for the delivery of his big speech only confirm his use of monuments as political props. The implied message in the use of these ancient monuments was that longevity affords legitimacy, and both buildings symbolized Iran's pre-Islamic imperial grandeur. The new monument, called Shahyad—Persian for "memorial to the Shah"—was to capture, celebrate, and embody this tradition of monarchical grandeur and the Shah's place in this pantheon. A young architect, barely out of college, came up with a design that encapsulated all the key elements of the Shah's political paradigm.

Hussein Amanat was the wunderkind of modern Iranian architecture. He was still living at his parents' home and planning to depart for the United States and graduate work in architecture when, in June 1966, he saw an advertisement in *Etela'at* announcing a national competition for a new monument. The only guideline provided was that "it could not be taller than forty five meters." The monument was to be built near the capital's airport, and anything taller would have been dangerous. A few months earlier, the committee to celebrate the 2,500 years of monarchy had commissioned the firm of Bonyan, whose partners included some of Iran's top architects, to come up with a design for the monument. The director of the firm, Nosrat Moghanah, was known to be a friend of the Shah and of many members of the committee, but the Shah was not happy with the

6 million *tooman* ($900,000) plans submitted by Bonyan and ordered a national competition for a new design.

By the time Amanat decided to participate in the competition, there was little time left before the deadline. He solicited the help of some of his college peers, turned his bedroom into a studio, and began to work on his envisioned design. For three days, he and his friends worked incessantly to complete his plan. His concept called for a tower that would conjure Taq-e Kasra but symbolically represent the reign of the Pahlavi dynasty. Around the central building, in the vast surrounding space, each of the great dynasties of the past would be represented by a small yard. Only after going through the past dynasties would a visitor arrive at the monument that stood at the center of the edifice and symbolized the rule of the Shah and his father. The grand curved marble pillars of the monument made of white stone (Joshagad) from Isfahan afforded it the air of a majestic curtain flowing in the wind—and wind invariably conjures the anticipation and the anxieties of change. On one side, the curtain opened to the mystery and vistas of Iran, while from the opposite vantage point, it opened a wide window to the world waiting outside. The outer face of the monument also resembled the plumage of a peacock.[25] After submitting his proposed design, Amanat continued his plans to leave for Illinois. Then, much to his surprise, he was told he had won the competition. But the jury's choice was not in itself sufficient. The final choice would have to be made by the Shah and the Queen. On the designated day, Amanat and twenty other finalists were called to the Court, where they were each given a chance to explain their architectural ideas to the royal couple. To Amanat's great joy, the Shah and the Queen confirmed the jury's choice. But his joy was soon tempered by the realities of bureaucratic and professional corruption and jealousies. It took about a year before Amanat was actually given the contract.

Amanat's victory in the competition had a symbolic significance unrelated to architecture. His victory was an apt metaphor for a new decade in Iranian politics when Iranians of talent and merit, regardless of their faith and family, could find a job or an income commensurate with their talent. The only exceptions were those opposed to the regime. Even in their case, the regime invariably tried to "co-opt" them by affording them lucrative jobs or contracts. Previously, a "thousand families" had, according to the lore of Iranian politics, ruled Iran—or 40 national families and 150 to 200 "provincial families" according to the CIA[26]—and thus blood and connection had guaranteed a ticket to power and position. The power of the 40 families did not disappear, but there were now, with the expansion of the economy, more seats at the table of power and economic opportunity, and many more talented men, and slowly and gradually women, could join the table. More crucially still, in that decade, people of talent and dedication could also rise on the social, political, and economic ladder even if they were not Muslims. The fact that Amanat was a devout member of the Baha'i faith in no way hampered his victory. The Shah's religious critics, of course, claimed that membership in the faith was, in fact, an added advantage.

But by 1971, when the construction of Shahyad was completed, Tehran was fired by the power of petrodollars. The Shah's new and vigorous "open-door" policy was meant to encourage The world to visit and invest in Iran. Tehran was a city enamored of the West, particularly America, and obsessed with its past. More than 50,000 Americans lived in Tehran alone. Shahyad became the perfect metaphor for the many cultural paradoxes that were the rapidly changing Tehran.

Shahyad's simple pre-Islamic arches, reminiscent of Taq-e Kasra, along with ornate Islamic domes, inspired by the Sheikh Lotfollah mosque,[27] and decorated with sophisticated arabesque designs, were concurrently Persian and Islamic. The effect of the dualism and clash of Persian pre-Islamic grandeur and Islamic influences was redoubled when the challenge of modernity was added to the problem—creating what one critic has called the "cultural schizophrenia"[28] of modern Iran—and the genius of Shahyad was that somehow it captured these complicated crosscurrents. Shahyad was a gateway to the future and a celebration of the past. As the Shah spoke of the coming "Great Civilization" and offered his own rule as the "gateway" to this utopia, Shahyad became that symbolic gate. In Shahyad, as in other artifacts of the modernist age, form was content, and the building's form cleverly drew inspiration from its symbolic function.

As an iconic structure, Shahyad became the object not only of adoration and emulation, but also of satire and criticism. Rumors about its allegedly exorbitant cost and about massive financial malfeasance among those involved in its construction made it one of the favorite subjects of the opposition's campaign of whispers and gossip. The total cost of the monument, according to sources in the Islamic Republic, was about 40 million *tooman* ($5.5 million). The complicated concrete work of the monument was entrusted to the same company that had completed the famous Sydney Opera House.

But even those who did not subscribe to sundry financial allegations used Shahyad to poke fun at the Shah and his regime. In Ebrahim Golestan's subversive *Mysteries of the Ghost Valley*, the nouveau riche man with an unmistakable resemblance to the Shah builds a phallic monument to his own grandeur after inadvertently finding "underground" riches. The monument built in the film mischievously but unmistakably conjured Shahyad.[29] The Islamic Republic's attempt to erect a new tower—an incongruent mix of the Seattle Space Needle and the minaret of a mosque—and make it the symbol of the new Islamic Tehran has failed so far.

When Amanat, along with other finalists for the Shahyad competition, met with the Shah and the Queen, it was not the first time the young architect had met the King. Architecture students were required to submit as their final thesis a project of their choice. Amanat had submitted a design for a resort on the coast of the Persian Gulf. In preparation, he had traveled widely in the area, and his design integrated the natural contours of the territory with its potential political economy. The project stipulated that the Persian Gulf area, until then seen only as a rich reservoir of oil, offered great untapped possibilities for tourism and trade. The Plan for the United Development of the Natural Resources of Khuzestan region, developed during Ebtehaj's tenure as the director of the Plan Organization and modeled after the Tennessee Valley Authority, called for the agricultural development of the region after the construction of a major new dam.[30] But the new proposal called for a new attitude toward the region. A jury of faculty chose Amanat's design as the best for that academic year. The Shah, too, on his visit to give prizes to the top graduating students, was keenly interested in both the idea and the design of the resort. The Kish project, nearly finished before the fall of the Shah, was akin to the Amanat proposal. The Kish idea called for creating on that beautiful but sparsely populated island a "free city" that would be the Paris and Hong Kong of the Persian Gulf—a place of epicurean license and commercial delight, an open city of pleasure and profit. When the revolution aborted the project, the rulers of the United Arab Emirates realized the need for such a city and created in their kingdom the unfulfilled dream of the Shah. Today's Dubai is the child of yesterday's aborted Kish project.

Ironically, the year Amanat won the prize for the best project, the runner-up design was for a new seminary in the city of Qom. Once again the Janus face of Iranian culture was evident in the two disparate designs and the two conflicting paradigms of identity—one that sought to integrate Iran into the global march of modernity, and the other opting instead for a return to the comfort of an "authentic self" molded by tradition and laced with Islam. Before Iran's plans for turning the Persian Gulf into a tourist haven could become reality, seminarians, led by the exiled Ayatollah Khomeini, helped foment the revolution of 1979. Amanat had won not just the competition for Shahyad, but the competition for the best graduating project of the year. At the same time, his competitor's plan for a seminary had, maybe unwittingly, tapped into alternate forces of Iranian history.

Chapter 18

THE PERFECT SPY

> *. . . little joy have I*
> *To breathe this news, yet what I say is true.*
> *Shakespeare,* King Richard II, *3.4.85–86*

The Cold War began in Iran, and the fall of the Shah was the beginning of its end. The Shah was, amongst other things, both a victim of the Cold War and one of its most fervent advocates. When historians try to tally the costs and benefits, the victors and the vanquished of the Cold War, they might well conclude that the fall of the Shah and the rise of radical Islam—and with it, the tectonic shifts in the political landscape of the Middle East—were some of the most profound unintended consequences of the Cold War. Long before the CIA tried to use Islam and Islamists to fight the Soviet Union in Afghanistan, the Shah and SAVAK had been trying to use religion to contain and combat Communism. The CIA and the Shah both seemed initially to have succeeded in their efforts, but the price for the miscalculation in Iran was the throne itself, while in Afghanistan the result was the tragic domino effect of terror and the terrorist attacks on September 11, 2001.

Compounding this strategic miscalculation was the false sense of security the Shah felt after the violent suppression of the pro-Khomeini riots in June 1963. Assadollah Alam had been the prime minister in those turbulent times, and in later years, when he was the Court minister, with more daily access to the Shah than anybody else had, he often whispered in the Shah's ear that the clergy were no longer a relevant political force in Iran. The mullahs, Alam declaimed with self-serving bravura, were politically destroyed, ideologically disarmed, and socially marginalized and no longer constituted a viable threat.[1] Even in exile, a few months after the Islamic Revolution in Iran, the Shah still believed that it was in fact the Communists who had masterminded his fall.

All through his political life, the Shah was preoccupied with fear of the Soviet menace. Even the coup of 1921, the first step in his father's meteoric rise in politics, was, according to the Shah, more than anything else an attempt to abort an imminent Bolshevik revolution in Iran.[2] Twenty-five hundred kilometers of common border with the Soviet Union and the relentless history of Russian expansionist mischief in Iran—rooted in the alleged "Peter the Great's Last Will," exhorting his progeny to capture Iran and thus find access to the "warm waters of the Persian Gulf and beyond"—were the historical backdrop of the Shah's fear of the Soviet Union. This apprehension was exacerbated by the Manichaean view of the world promulgated by theorists of the Cold War on both sides of the Iron Curtain.

But by 1975, Iran's relations with its giant Communist neighbor to the north were the best they had ever been. The only years that were in this sense comparable to the seventies were the first few years of Reza Shah's rule when, thanks to Court Minister Teymourtash's "friendly"[3] attitude toward the Russians, the Soviet Union accounted for close to 40 percent of Iran's foreign trade.[4] By 1972, the USSR had emerged "as Iran's third largest arms supplier."[5] The rise of trade with Russia began in 1966, when, in spite of some pressure from the United States, Iran signed a major economic agreement with the Soviet Union. In a July 7, 1966, meeting with the Shah, when Armin Meyer, the American ambassador, pointed out the dangers of flirting with the Soviet Union, the Shah said he did not need the United States to "lecture him re inequities of dealing with the Soviets." He assured Meyer that he had no illusions about Soviet intentions but that his aim was improving relations with Russia while not falling prey to their temptations.[6] In the same meeting, the Shah "warned that when he turns to Soviets, USG should not set in motion political movement in Iran." The Ambassador answered that the "very thought . . . is ridiculous."[7] A few days later, in another meeting on the same topic, the Shah railed against those who were "puppets" of the United States and against "taking orders" from the Americans, declaring that "he did not care to emulate" them.[8] Some of the Shah's brothers told Vice President Hubert Humphrey that the Shah would go through with the Russian deal unless President Johnson invited him to Washington and told the Shah "how much you love him."[9] None of these pressures or inducements worked. The Shah went ahead with the deal and by the mid-seventies more than 8,000 Soviet technicians were working in Iran. Their areas of expertise ranged from metallurgy and mining to agriculture and steel production. So heavy was the traffic of these experts in and out of Iran that the Moscow–Tehran train was usually booked several months in advance.[10] Iranian industrialists had also begun exporting huge quantities of Iranian products to the Soviet Union. Everything from soap and shoes to cars and air conditioners was being exported to the vast Soviet empire.[11]

But deep tensions, rooted in ideological differences and bred from fifty years of distrust, lurked beneath the surface solemnities of "peaceful coexistence." As an "Intelligence Estimate" by the U.S. government at the time made clear, "While pursuing their policy of reconciliation with the Shah during the 1960s and 1970's, the Soviets retained all of the various tools available for use against him. These include critical public and private statements, support for a clandestine radio station broadcasting into Iran, continuing ties to the Tudeh Communist party which has its own history of subversion in Iran; a continuing espionage network within Iran, implicit approval for the training of Iranian dissidents by other forces hostile to the Shah; the capacity to conduct cross-border infiltration and arms deliveries; support of anti-Shah movement; and of course a military capability on the Iranian border."[12]

Of these "tools of subversion," the KGB was for the Shah the most feared nemesis. Much to his consternation, in the early 1970s, he realized that some of the activities of Soviet spies had reached inside the royal household. There was, for example, the discovery that a member of the staff at the Court had ties to Soviet agents; she was, according to Alam, quietly dismissed. More important was the case of the Saberi family.

Around 1972, SAVAK's counterespionage units put Roshanak Saberi, an employee of Iran's Foreign Ministry, under surveillance. After she went to a meeting with a Romanian "diplomat" who in fact worked for the KGB she was arrested. Before long, she confessed to passing information to the Soviets and indicated that her brother, Abbas Saberi, had recruited her for the work. Ostensibly a rich and generous rug merchant in Paris, Saberi turned out to be a key KGB operative.

Abbas Saberi himself had been, early in his espionage career, part of what the KGB called the "ideological recruits"—believers in the cause of socialism who, like Kim Philby and his gang of Cambridge spies, offered their services to the "Bastion of Revolution" gratis and out of a sense of ideological camaraderie. Gradually, most of these ideological recruits became simple spies for hire. Saberi and his wife owned a famous store in Paris where they specialized in expensive Persian rugs. The KGB had successfully diverted attention from the true nature of Saberi's activities by spreading the rumor that he was in fact an apostate who had stolen funds from the Tudeh Communist Party in Iran and escaped to France.

Saberi and his wife lived a life of bourgeois affluence and comfort in France—a large apartment in Paris and an expensive vacation home in one of the most exclusive suburbs of the city. From the early 1940s, the couple had been the patron saints of distressed Iranian exiles in Paris. Their apartment was also a veritable salon for émigré intellectuals and political activists. Even high-ranking officials of the Shah's regime, including Abdollah Entezam, Iran's ambassador to France for several years, and General Hassanali Alavi-Kia, one of the founders of SAVAK and from 1961 to 1967 the head of SAVAK operations in Europe, frequented the Saberi house.[13]

Two of the people closest to the Shah had also been one-time visitors to the Saberi residence and had borrowed money from Saberi. Both had been exiled to Paris during the Mossadeq era. The first was Princess Ashraf, who was staying at the Hôtel de Crillon, the most expensive hotel in Paris, at the time. Though she was about to purchase a late-model Cadillac, she nevertheless felt poor and strapped. She wrote letters to her family and to trusted officials at the Court, asking for financial help.[14] She also, according to general Alavi-Kia, borrowed some money from Saberi in return for a handwritten promissory note. The note was never cashed in or publicly used against the princess. Saberi kept it, apparently as a badge of honor.

The other person who had benefited from Saberi's largesse was Hussein Fardust, the Shah's close friend and confidante. He too had been exiled to France during the Mossadeq era and was indeed in a desperate financial situation. He borrowed money from Saberi, and this debt adds a new layer of enigma to his already storied life. In 1954, not long after the Shah's return to power, he received a report from General Zahedi, then the prime minister, suggesting that Fardust might be working for a foreign intelligence agency. Ardeshir Zahedi was the messenger and witnessed how the Shah grew visibly angry and threw away the report, saying in anger, "can't they see me even have one friend." No more reports were sent to the Shah about the matter and soon Fardust continued to be one of the Shah's most trusted aides. After the 1979 revolution, allegations about Fardust's ties to intelligence agencies surfaced again.[15] In 1953, he was in Paris, contemplating a new career in medicine, and it was then that he borrowed money from Abbas Saberi. By the time SAVAK discovered Saberi's role in recruiting spies for the KGB, the French authorities had also raided his house and concluded that he had been one of the key KGB operatives in Europe.

For the Shah, compounding the anxieties caused by the Saberi case was his suspicion that an Iraqi mole had penetrated the ranks of the Iranian army.[16] He ordered SAVAK to look for the spy. By the early seventies, Iraq was developing closer ties with the Soviet Union, and the Shah's worst nightmare was about to become reality. Soviet actions in Iraq, he confided to Kermit ("Kim") Roosevelt, who was visiting Iran as a businessman on April 26, 1972, were part of Soviet aspirations in the Persian Gulf.[17]

As early as November 1971, SAVAK had informed the Shah and the United States that, should the Soviets succeed in bringing about the coalition they had planned in Iraq between the Ba'ath Party, the Communist Party of Iraq, and the Iraqi Kurds, they would in effect give the country "a status similar to that of Eastern Europe."[18]

The Soviets, for their part, went out of their way to convince the Shah "that the Soviet rapprochement with Iraq is not aimed against Iran." They informed him that in spite of demands by Iraq, they had refused to "protest Iran's seizure of Islands in the Persian Gulf."[19] But the Shah was neither convinced nor comforted. In a May 7, 1972, meeting with President Nixon and Henry Kissinger, the Shah reiterated his position that, as the Soviet Union had closer ties with Iraq, they might soon succeed in establishing a "coalition of the Kurds, the Ba'athists, and the [Iraqi] Communists," and as a result, "the Kurdish problem, instead of being a thorn in the side, could become an asset to communists."[20] And when Kissinger asked what the Shah thought "should be done" to divert this danger, the Shah said, "Iran can help with the Kurds."[21] Both the State Department and the CIA "were inclined to continue to avoid involvement in Iraq." They were both worried that the Soviets would construe any help to the Kurds of Iraq as "a move against them."[22] On June 23, 1972, the National Security Council concluded that the "major view in town is that the US should stay out of direct support for the Kurds."[23] But the Shah continued to insist on his own vision of dangers in Iraq, and eventually Nixon reluctantly agreed with him and with the idea of funneling funds to Kurdish insurgents in Iraq. Israel too came on board with little resistance. Of course, for the United States and Israel, support for Iraqi Kurds was nothing new. For example, unbeknownst to the Shah, as early as August 1969, U.S. agents had flown to the Kurdish regions of Iraq and given one of the Kurdish leaders, Mullah Mustafa Barazani, $14 million in aid.[24] Moreover, Israel had had close ties to Iraqi Kurds for some time.

Beginning on August 1, 1972, a covert tripartite operation by Iran, Israel, and the United States was launched to destabilize the increasingly belligerent and unabashedly pro-Soviet Iraqi government. The idea was to help Iraqi Kurds in their struggle against the central government. The Shah initially agreed to contribute $30 million (which he soon boosted to $75 million) per year to the project.[25] It was in this period that the Shah's fear and frustration over Iraq led him to order SAVAK to organize a coup to topple the Ba'ath regime.

Iran had had a Kurdish problem of its own in the late 1960s, spearheaded by Iranian Maoists inspired by the Chinese revolution. That movement had been easily suppressed by the Shah's army. Nevertheless, the Shah knew full well that an independent Kurdistan in Iraq was sure to become a magnet for Iranian Kurds. Kissinger, cognizant of the Shah's concerns, aware of Turkey's similar Kurdish angst, and keen on destabilizing the Ba'athist regime in Iraq, famously declared that the strategy of the covert operation by the triangle of the United States, Iran, and Israel was to help the Iraqi Kurds enough so that they would become a nuisance for the Ba'athist regime but not so much that they would become an independent state. It is a revealing twist of fate that the man sometimes acting as the intermediary between the Iraqi Kurds and their outside supporters was none other than Ahmed Chalabi.[26]

The Shah was serious about carrying out this destabilizing policy. In 1973, when it became clear that Iraq's new offensive might strangle the Kurdish movement in the country, the Shah went so far as to order units of the Iranian army stationed in the Kurdistan province of Iran to enter Iraq disguised as Kurdish fighters, or *pishmargah,* and join the fight against the Ba'ath regime. The commanders of the Iranian forces were ordered to avoid, at all costs, the possibility of one of their soldiers falling into Iraqi hands.[27]

The Iraqis were not the only ones kept in the dark about the Iranian army's covert cross-border operations. Surprisingly, the army's deployment, the nature of its engagement, and reports of the clashes were strictly confidential and kept not only from the Iranian people, but from much of the cabinet and from all of the parliament, which ostensibly had the power of the purse. Iran's engagement in Oman, where Iranian Special Forces and the air force were used to suppress and turn back a Communist insurgency, was similarly kept secret from the cabinet, the parliament, and the people of Iran. Even today, four decades after those fateful years, there is little reliable detail and documentation about Iran's foray into playing the role of the gendarme of the region. But in those days, the Shah's will was the law of the land, and no one in the government dared question him about the legality or the wisdom of these decisions, or about the size of the Iranian military budget. Every year, one lump sum that included the military, the intelligence agencies, and all the auxiliary expenses was rushed through the parliament. The Prime Minister's multimillion-dollar "secret discretionary" fund was one of the camouflage funds through which some of these "incidental" costs were defrayed.[28]

In the meantime, the Iranian army was engaged in its covert activities in Iraq, and tensions between Iran and Iraq over a variety of issues—from navigation rights over the river that separates the two countries to the fate of thousands of Iranian Shiites who had been living in Iraq—were on the rise. More than once, Iraq had forced thousands of these Iranians living in Iraq to leave the country, leaving their homes and wealth behind. Iraq offered safe haven and facilities to a whole range of Iranian opposition groups. Radio Iraq was managed by some of these opponents and was increasingly acerbic in its criticism of the Shah.

As willing as the Shah was to lead the effort to help the Iraqi Kurds, he was no less willing to suddenly end his support when, in 1975, he surprised much of the world by signing an agreement with the Iraqi government. Even the American government was taken aback when, shortly before the agreement, the Shah decided to inform them of his impending decision. According to an assessment by the U.S. Embassy, there were at least five reasons why the Shah decided to reach an "accord with Iraq." In their view, "Iraqi concessions of Thalweg Principle,* probability of Kurdish defeat in absence of increased Iranian assistance, threat to Iran's OPEC leadership, internal problems and Government of Iran's perception of change in the Middle East" contributed to the Shah's decision.

According to the CIA, the accord between the Shah and Saddam Hussein that was signed in Algiers in 1975 had a secret codicil that stipulated that Iran must end its support of Iraqi Kurds and close its borders to fleeing Kurdish activists. While some Kurdish leaders, like Barazani and his family, were flown first to Tehran and then to the United States, the rest of the movement were left at the mercy of Saddam. At the same time, in Tehran SAVAK was looking for the Iraqi mole and in the process learned a surprising piece of intelligence from its own mole in the Soviet Embassy.

The mole was a man called Aliov, and he worked in the Soviet Embassy as a cultural attaché. He reported that KGB agents in Iran had been regularly meeting someone in the Iranian army on Naft (Oil) Avenue in Tehran. When SAVAK finally established the identity of the spy on Oil Avenue, it scored its biggest coup against Soviet espionage in postwar Iran. At the same time, the mystery of the Iraqi mole that had been of concern to the Shah was solved. The case also underscores the extent of the Shah's involvement with SAVAK's sensitive counterespionage operation. In the effort to find the Iraqi mole and the Soviet spy, the Shah was not only informed at every step but was the one who made all the crucial decisions.

With the hint they had received from their embassy mole in 1975, SAVAK checked the identity of every household on Oil Avenue and its neighboring streets. It turned out that three army officers lived in the area. All three were put under twenty-four-hour surveillance. Their phones were tapped. A lieutenant

* One of the main precipitating causes of tension between Iran and Iraq was the sudden claim by the new Ba'ath regime that Shatt al Arab, the river that has long been part of the border between the two countries, was an Iraqi waterway. Iran refused to accept the claim, and the Shah ordered Iranian ships to travel up the river, flying Iranian flags. Fighter planes from the Iranian air force provided cover for these ships. The thalweg line is the standard internationally accepted way to demarcate the middle of the navigable channel in waterways that are shared by states.

colonel was the first who came under suspicion. He was arrested and after some "rough interrogation," SAVAK authorities were convinced that he was not the spy they sought.

After a while, SAVAK agents assigned to the case saw a man with a dog pass by a known KGB agent who worked at the Soviet Embassy; neither man slowed their pace as they discreetly exchanged a small envelope. It did not take long to figure out that the man with the dog was General Ahmad Mogharebi. The Shah was immediately informed of this surprising development and was asked for permission to arrest the General. The army had its own intelligence and counter-espionage division, and SAVAK asked the Shah to decide whether the army unit should be brought into the investigation. The Shah's response was categorical—and characteristic of his style of managing the military and intelligence forces. Keeping the military, SAVAK, the city police, and other security organizations in a state of constant competition and contention was part of his "divide and rule" strategy. In fact, by the late 1960s, when the regime was first faced with a rising tide of urban guerrilla activities, these tensions were bad enough that they hampered the ability of the government to fight the foes, leading to the creation of the "Committee to Fight Terrorism" that brought together all these different agencies under a unified command and immediately developed an infamous reputation.

It was no surprise then, that in the Mogharebi case, the Shah did not want the army involved or even informed about the ongoing investigation. More importantly, he emphasized that he did not want Mogharebi arrested yet. Instead, he wanted him, "caught in the act, with no room for denial or guesswork."[29]

By then, the KGB had a new man in Iran. His name was Vladimir Kuzichkin, and his candid, albeit long-winded, memoir, *Inside the KGB*, provides a fascinating account of the workings of the much-feared Soviet Embassy in Tehran.[30] Embassies often reflect the societies they represent. In the mid-seventies, the Soviet Embassy in Iran, according to Kuzichkin, was a den of corruption and inertia. He describes an embassy gripped by a culture of gossip, backbiting, dangerous leaks of sensitive information, and petty jealousies. Amongst the staff, he says, there was "an air of permanent holiday."[31] The embassy personnel despised the Ambassador for having a mistress and for lining his pockets. In his turn, the Ambassador was wary of rocking the boat lest he be recalled from his plum posting. In the consular office, where Kuzichkin worked, four of the five alleged diplomats were in fact KGB agents.[32] They were there not just to spy on Iranians, but to keep a close watch on the 8,000 Soviet citizens working in Iran.

The two expansive compounds of the embassy were as much about espionage as about diplomacy. One was located in the center of the city, and the other in Golhak, an affluent suburb of Tehran in the early part of the twentieth century, and traditionally used as the embassy's summer residence. The intelligence heart of the embassy consisted of two rooms, located on the sixth floor, and forbidden to all except a handful of KGB agents. The rooms housed all the electronic equipment used for surveillance and eavesdropping. In one room they "intercepted and recorded the radio conversations of SAVAK's external surveillance teams, and...Iran's military counter-intelligence....'Mars' was located in a separate room...intercepting encoded Iranian communications involving such targets as various ministries, the SAVAK headquarters and the American embassy."[33]

While the KGB was busy eavesdropping on the Iranian government, SAVAK and the American and British intelligence agencies were no less busy eavesdropping on the Soviet Union and its embassy in Tehran. In the two suburbs of Noshahr and Babolsar, two small cities in Iran's northern province of Mazandaran, the U.S. government operated two highly classified and critical listening stations that monitored crucial parts of the Soviet Union where nuclear test facilities were located. Both U.S. stations had been built underground to avoid detection by Soviet satellites, and both were in areas designated as "Royal Hunting Grounds" and were thus safely off limits to the public. The British operated a series of stations of their own on that border, and they too acted independently of SAVAK.[34] Iranians were not allowed to contact the personnel in these stations. Occasionally, a high-ranking British or American intelligence officer would meet with the Shah and brief him on what was going on. The Americans had also built in their own embassy in Tehran, under a structure that was ostensibly a garage, a vast secure room for gathering and transmitting intelligence.[35]

Throughout his life the Shah had an insatiable appetite for the secret world of espionage. He enjoyed his regular weekly meetings with the CIA and MI6 station chiefs in Tehran as well as the occasional briefings he received from managers of the espionage stations.[36] In addition, when the sudden increase of oil revenues allowed the Shah to satisfy his every wish and whim, he was reported to purchase intelligence reports not just from foreign agencies, but also from private security companies.[37]

Along with the American and British efforts to spy on the Soviet Union, SAVAK was busy monitoring the Soviet Embassy in Tehran. In fact, SAVAK had purchased a four-story apartment building overlooking the entrance to the embassy. While the first floor was ostensibly a doctor's office, officers of the Eighth Directorate, in charge of anti-Soviet counterespionage, used the top three floors to monitor the traffic in and out of the embassy. SAVAK agents also manned a kiosk that supposedly sold soft drinks, located right across from the embassy entrance.[38] At one time, the "surveillance of the Soviet embassy [in Tehran] was so tight" that embassy officials asked Moscow "to retaliate against the Iranian embassy in Moscow."[39]

No sooner had SAVAK begun investigating the KGB's army connection than they realized that every move of their surveillance teams was clearly known to the Soviets.[40] Kuzichkin confirms the story of the KGB eavesdropping on the radio frequencies used by SAVAK. He also indicates that the Soviets knew from the outset what was going on in the "doctor's office."[41]

Eventually, using an elaborate scheme that employed a large number of cars that never used their radio transmitters, thus remaining undetected by the Soviet agents, SAVAK learned how the Mogharebi system of espionage operated. They were baffled by what they discovered. Soviet agents would arrive in the vicinity of the General's house, park their car, wait a few moments, and then leave. On one occasion, the Soviet agent got out of the car carrying something like a briefcase, walked toward an empty lot nearby, waited for three to four minutes, then returned to his car and departed from the scene. The SAVAK agents, a safe distance away, watched every move.

Around May 1977, Mogharebi left for a holiday in the United States, where he owned a house in the state of Arizona and where his children went to school. SAVAK used his absence to search his house. What they found looked like tools of the spy trade but were unlike anything they had seen before.

The Shah was immediately informed about the potentially incriminating evidence found in Mogharebi's house and was asked for permission to arrest the General when he returned home from his American holiday. Once again, the Shah demurred, insisting instead that Mogharebi be caught in the commission of his espionage act.[42] Mindful of Iran's important and improving relations with the Soviet Union, the Shah wanted an airtight case. But Mogharebi and his KGB handlers had devised a complicated mode of operation, making it difficult for SAVAK to catch them in the act. Aside from going to work, the General left the house only to walk his dog. He made and received no suspicious phone calls, and he had no unusual visitors.

The break finally came one night late in September 1977. Two agents of the KGB arrived on Oil Avenue. The first was Boris Kabanov, an amiable man, much adored at the embassy, where he worked under the cover of a consular official. The second was his driver, Titkin. They had received a signal from "the man," the code name for Mogharebi, asking for a rendezvous in the normal place. Seconds after the arrival of the KGB car, Mogharebi emerged from the house, accompanied by his dog. Kabanov got out of the vehicle, and as he passed Mogharebi, quickly handed him an envelope and immediately went back to the car. He had barely settled in his seat when his car was surrounded by agents of SAVAK. Kabanov brandished his diplomatic passport and refused to open the door. The agents, in constant communication with SAVAK headquarters, were ordered to break the window, force the two Russians out of the car, and arrest them. Meanwhile, another team of agents arrested Mogharebi. He tried to resist and cried for help. His son and his orderly rushed out of the house to help, but their efforts were in vain. Mogharebi was arrested with the incriminating envelope in his pocket.[43]

The KGB apparently never paid much for the intelligence they received. A few hundred dollars was the common rate. Anything over $10,000 required the approval of the chairman of the KGB.[44] Mogharebi's last wage of sin was a mere 30,000 *tooman* (or about $4,500). According to Soviet archivist Vasili Mitrokhin, though initially recruited on ideological grounds, Mogharebi had, by the early 1970s, become "an increasingly mercenary agent," with a regular monthly stipend that was 200 rubles in 1972 and was increased for good service to 500 convertible rubles by 1976. He was also at that time awarded "the Order of the Red Banner."[45] With his pay in his pocket, the most effective KGB spy in postwar Iran was arrested. His KGB handler and the driver were released the morning after the arrest to the custody of the Soviet Embassy and were given forty-eight hours to leave Iran. Moments after the arrest, the Shah was informed about the case's closure. Through the head of SAVAK, he commended the Eighth Division for their work.

At the time of his arrest, Mogharebi was in charge of strategic planning for the entire Iranian military. Every "war plan," every new defensive formation, every projected new base and airfield passed over his desk. The last piece of intelligence he conveyed to his Soviet handlers was about Iran's plans to build "a new secret airstrip in the desert."[46] The secret airstrip of his report might well have been the one used some five years later by American Special Forces in their ill-fated attempt to rescue American hostages held in the embassy in Tehran.

Upon his arrest, owing to the unusual nature of his case, Mogharebi was not taken to a prison, but instead to a SAVAK safe house. In the first few hours of interrogation, he denied any guilt and claimed that he had been in contact with the agents on the assumption that they were Americans.[47] Eventually he confessed to his crime and described the nature of his long relations with the Soviets. The mystery of his longevity turned out to be simple. From the beginning of his Soviet collaboration, he had stipulated that he would never meet any agents in the streets and that he only worked from his house. For this reason, the KGB had developed an elaborate system whereby Mogharebi sent a signal to his handlers asking for a rendezvous. They would appear on his street at the designated hour. He in his house, and the handler in his car, would turn on their transmitters and receivers—what they called the "Close Information Link System"—and in moments the transfer of intelligence was complete. The machines were so sophisticated that SAVAK's technical department was unable to figure out how they worked. Eventually, with the help of MI6 in London and the CIA in Langley, the mystery of the machine was discovered.[48]

For the Soviets, the arrest of Mogharebi was a major blow. They began a desperate search for the "possible causes of the Mogharebi debacle."[49] One obvious reason, they thought, was that they had overused him in the last years. According to Kuzichkin, the Soviets had no other real agents in Iran, and as a result they overburdened Mogharebi with too many requests, thus making him vulnerable. Before his arrest in 1977, he had met with his handlers no fewer than twenty-five times.[50]

In spite of the common perception of the KGB as an omnipotent powerhouse of intelligence in Iran, aside from Mogharebi, their feared network of spies consisted of an Afghan diplomat, Homayoon Akram, code-named Ram, and a Persian, nicknamed Teymour, who essentially milked the Soviets and passed them insignificant bits of information.

"The man," Mogharebi, turned out to be the only source with any real information not only about the army, but also about "The Casket"—the code name for the Shah's Court—and "Barracks" or SAVAK.[51] Even if we add to this picture the readiness of pro-Soviet Communists to turn over intelligence, the KGB emerges as much weaker than anyone imagined.[†] Yet the Shah considered them politically omnipotent and saw their hand not only in every major political upheaval in the country, but even in some of the most mundane details of life.

Roughly two years later, when millions of people took to the streets, the Shah reiterated his belief in the KGB's omnipotence by telling the American Ambassador that only the British, the CIA, and the KGB could manage such a massive demonstration in Iran. By then, the KGB, bereft of its master spy, was scraping the bottom of the barrel, trying to activate a spy who had been inactive for more than two decades. He was a relative of Hoveyda who was code-named Zhaman. He had been initially recruited as "an ideological agent," but for much of the sixties, according to KGB sources, he had been too busy building a fortune. But in the mid-seventies, Zhaman took part in KGB active measures operations, passing disinformation prepared by the KGB for the Shah.[52] A key part of his "disinformation" was telling the Shah that "the CIA was planning to create disturbances in Tehran and other cities."[53] As an avid advocate of conspiracy theories, the Shah was more than willing to accept this "disinformation."

Another example of disinformation, this time intended not for the Shah but for the purpose of affording the KGB an air of omnipotence, was their claim that

---

† The KGB's capacity must not be confused with the Soviet Union's cultural influence in Iran at the time. For example, during much of the 1970s, the de facto day-to-day editor of *Keyhan,* the country's most popular daily, was Rahman Hatefi. He turned out to have been all along a leading member of the Tudeh Party. A cursory look at the headlines for the paper during his tenure indicates a clear but subtle tilt toward the Soviets—in spite of strict censorship by SAVAK. Some have suggested that the Shah knowingly allowed the tilt in order to keep the West on the edge about the clear and present danger of the Soviet Union in Iran.

they had "influenced the Shah's choice of his third (and last) wife," Farah Diba. The future queen was "unaware of the KGB interest" in her, but she was part of "a circle of Communist student friends." The KGB even claimed that one of her relatives was an agent of the Soviets.[54]

Even in exile, weeks before his death, the Shah reiterated the idea that the Iranian revolution was in fact the work of "international Communism" and the omnipotent KGB.[55] In reality, however, beneath this image of omnipotence was, at least in Iran, the reality of a weak, often incompetent organization. And with the loss of General Mogharebi, they had lost their only ace in Iran.

The loss of Mogharebi had another consequence that once again directly involved the Shah. There was a shakeup in the KGB residency in Tehran, and the man who was blamed for the debacle was forced into retirement. The new Station Chief had a sordid past in Iran. In 1959, eccentric Soviet Premier Nikita Khrushchev, exhibiting his colorful impetuosity, had ordered the KGB to assassinate the Shah.

The KGB had at the time sent an agent named Fadeikin to Iran to assassinate the Shah. He bought a Volkswagen for the job, filled it with explosives, and hired an "illegal" (the KGB term referring to anyone who had been smuggled into a country and could come and go without any official trace) to detonate the car when the Shah was on his way to open a new session of the Majlis. But a mechanical malfunction saved the Shah. The "illegal" hired for the job pushed the button, but the detonator failed to operate. The Soviets of course blamed their hapless minion for not pushing the button hard enough. The same man who had made a mess of the assassination attempt was appointed the head of KGB offices in Iran on what turned out to be the eve of the Islamic Revolution.

Chapter 19

THE PERFECT STORM

O God, O God, that e'er this tongue of mine,
That laid the sentence of dread banishment
On yon proud man, should take it off again.
Shakespeare, King Richard II, *3.3.134–136*

On September 22, 1973, Ardeshir Zahedi, then Iran's ambassador to the United States, sent one of his many "strictly confidential" reports for the Shah's eyes only. The content of these reports was so sensitive that Zahedi would not even trust his staff with the task of typing them, writing instead in his own almost illegible handwriting. They were then placed in a special briefcase with only two keys—one in Tehran with the Shah and the other with Zahedi in Washington. He had seen this system used for the transfer of highly sensitive materials when he was Iran's ambassador to Britain. The same firm that made the safe courier briefcase for the office of the British Prime Minister made one on order for the Shah–Zahedi correspondence.[1] Couriers would carry the briefcase to Tehran with the case handcuffed to their wrists and then bring back the response—sometimes in the margins of the notes in the Shah's polished and neat handwriting, and sometimes by letters from the Shah's chief of staff, Nasrollah Moinian, or his private physician, Dr. Ayadi. Judging by the number of reports he read and commented on from Zahedi alone, it appears that, as his confidantes claim, he did indeed sometimes work well into the night.[2] Zahedi's reports were not, of course, the only ones the Shah read carefully. Other top officials of the regime say that while the Prime Minister and other cabinet members generally ignored their reports, the Shah read them carefully and "returned them with his decisions."[3]

Early in his second turn as Iran's ambassador to the United States, Zahedi learned through the wine-induced confession of a "reliable American source" who worked at the White House that coded confidential telegrams from the Iranian Embassy to the Shah were regularly intercepted by agencies of the U.S. government.[4] As he wrote to the Shah, even before receiving this news, Zahedi had suspected as much. A few weeks earlier, Henry Kissinger had prematurely mentioned a matter that Zahedi had confidentially reported to the Shah only in an encrypted message.[5]

In the September 22 note—written on pages of a legal pad, with the Shah's marginal notes appearing in red pencil—Zahedi reported meeting with a high-ranking U.S. official. The name of the official does not appear on the document and today, more than thirty-five years later, Zahedi has no recollection of his identity. The report is remarkable for the nature of the official's inquiries and the Shah's responses.

The first question related to the Shah's "physical and mental" health. "Is the Shah well?" the American official asked Zahedi. The question is surprising for, at the time, there had been no public discussion of the Shah's health in Iran or in the West. Were some agencies in the United States already privy to some news about the Shah's health problems? Toward the end of 1973, or about the time the American official asked his surprising question, the Shah, while vacationing on the isle of Kish, noticed "a curve on his left hypochondrium [abdominal area]."[6] He had consulted first his own physician, Dr. Ayadi, whose medical acumen the Shah did not always trust, and then Dr. Abbas Safavian, Alam's friend and physician. They decided to consult with European physicians, and thus it was that on May 1, 1974, Dr. Georges Flandrin flew to Tehran and, under a great veil of secrecy, diagnosed the Shah as suffering from a "lymphocytic blood disease." Neither dispatches from the U.S. and British Embassies in Tehran in those years nor declassified National Intelligence Estimates give any indication that either of the governments had any knowledge of this diagnosis or of the Shah's health problem. It became the policy of the Shah and his three male confidantes—Alam, Ayadi, and Safavian—as well as his French physicians, to keep the story of the Shah's illness strictly confidential, not even telling the Queen, who was by law the regent in the event of the Shah's death. She learned about the sickness more than three years later. Ironically, in those days, Tehran was so rife with rumors of the Shah's illness, even of his death at the hand of an angry nephew, that at one time Zahedi arranged for Barbara

Walters to visit Tehran and interview the Shah, thus confirming his continued good health.

The Shah clearly worried that if Western powers learned about his sickness, they would use it against him. He was in those days engaged in increasingly acrimonious negotiations with Europe and the United States regarding the price of oil. So worried was he about the Western response to his demands for higher prices that he ordered the government to substantially increase Iran's supply of stored sugar, tea, wheat, and a few other necessities—"lest they try to pressure us by imposing an embargo," he told Fereydoon Mahdavi, the minister in charge of trade. The haste of these purchases eventually led to allegations of kickbacks received by officials in charge of the $250 million sugar transaction. Even Shapour Reporter, the storied MI6 man in Iran, was implicated in the embarrassing case. In court papers in Iran, he confirmed that he had accepted £300,000 for acting as a representative of the British company.[7]

The Shah's fears of an embargo turned out to be baseless, but his belief that Western powers might use his sickness against him were neither hyperbolic nor paranoid. As Roger Owen, then the British foreign secretary, made clear, "Had the US and UK governments known about the Shah's cancer, they would have acted decisively to force the Shah to admit his illness publicly, and to leave Tehran and appoint a regency."[8]

Zahedi's American interlocutor on that September 22 meeting went on to say that he had heard that all was not well in Iran, that there was mounting dissent and dissatisfaction among larger and larger swaths of the population. "Is the Shah increasingly isolated from reality," the official asked, "and surrounded by those who do not tell him the truth?" "This is all nonsense," the Shah wrote. "This kind of information is given to them by a bunch of American puppets." A few weeks after receiving this report, the Shah told the combative Italian journalist Oriana Fallaci that he not only "receive[d] messages" from God, but that he received reports from a dozen different sources about all that went on in the country.[9] When in 1971, Alam suggested to the Shah that he should occasionally invite simple people from different strata to the Court and hear from them "the people's complaints." The Shah dismissed that idea as well, repeating the mantra, "I receive reports from multiple sources."[10]

The American official also claimed that sometimes even the economic statistics given to the Shah were not accurate. Here on the margin the Shah wrote, "this stuff is probably fed to them by Mehdi Samii and [Khodadad] Farmanfarmaian." These men were two of Iran's most respected and experienced bankers and economists, known for their probity and professionalism. By the time of this discussion between Zahedi and his American source, both men were out of government jobs, working in the private sector.[11]

The American interlocutor continued his remarkable line of queries by saying that, according to his information, the numbers of militant dissidents were swelling from the ranks of the intellectuals and that signs of student discontent at the universities were hard to ignore. Why is the Shah not apprised of this dire situation? the American official asked. The Shah wrote in the margin, "these are all propaganda and old cliché [using the English words for "propaganda" and "old cliché"]; in Iran there are no true intellectuals; these are all Marxists; recently we have even found Islamic-Marxists." More than once in those days, the Shah made such dismissive public pronouncements about the opposition. More than once he accused them all of being at best inadvertent tools of foreign powers.

The 2,500 years of monarchy celebration in 1971, what *Newsweek* had called "the Bash of Bashes," was a propaganda bonanza for the opposition, particularly the Confederation of Iranian Students, which had spared no effort in tarnishing the image of the Shah and his regime. They went so far as to forge documents that showed that SAVAK was illegally active in Europe and the United States and was tracking not just Iranian students but Western opponents of the regime, even members of Western governments.[12] The documents created a public relations nightmare for the Shah and were followed by investigations by Western governments into SAVAK's alleged illegal activities in Europe and the United States.

The Confederation organized one of the biggest rallies in its history when the Shah made his last official visit to the Carter White House in November 1977. Students and activists were encouraged to travel to Washington from all over the United States. The Iranian Embassy also rallied royalists from all over the country to come to Washington and welcome the Shah; travel expenses plus a generous honorarium were used as inducements. For reasons hard to fathom, both massive groups had been issued permits by the Washington police and the FBI that allowed them to come dangerously close to each other and to the White House. When, as expected, they engaged in a pitched battle, the police tried to separate them with the use of tear gas. A picture of the Shah wiping off tears induced by this gas was broadcast all over the world and became a poignant image of his beleaguered state.

More than once the Shah and SAVAK accused not only the Soviet Union and China but the United States and Western European nations of supporting, indeed underwriting, the Confederation. The Shah's comments, written in the margins of this confidential note, strongly suggest that he did not make those pronouncements simply to score easy political points, but that he in fact firmly believed them.

When the American official asked Zahedi about increasing public resentment about corruption, again the Shah dismissed the charge, writing in the margin, "it is [the] Western sickness with money that causes some problems." He also asked Zahedi—more in a tone of sarcasm than concern—to demand specific names from his American interlocutor.

In those days, even when SAVAK's Third Division, which was in charge of internal security, submitted reports about corruption in high places and described them as an issue of national security, the Shah brushed them off. For example, one such report was prepared on Hushang Davalu Qajar; he was called the "sultan of caviar," and one of the Shah's more sympathetic biographies calls him "the most notorious of the Shah's friends."[13] He was the closest thing to the Shah's court jester, making jokes at everyone's expense, preparing culinary delicacies the Shah favored, and acting efficiently as his designated Master of Royal Mirth. Davalu was also known for his heavy addiction to opium. Alam refers to a couple of occasions when Davalu tried to interest the Shah in exploring the soothing powers of what Coleridge called the "milk of paradise." Alam claims that he strongly objected to the idea, reminding the Shah that people were executed for dealing opium. Davalu was said to be a "born courtier, a sycophant par excellence . . . and a superior pimp." Though the Queen generally despised these royal procurers of pleasure, Davalu was such a pleasant conversationalist that even she "enjoyed his company and invited [him] to the Court."[14]

Davalu's house was renowned for its day-long sessions of opium smoking and, because he was known for his influence on the Shah, became a mecca for those seeking special favors. It was reported that the special suite of rooms Davalu kept at the luxurious Georges V Hotel in Paris also became a virtual opium den when he was in town. Everyone seemed to look the other way in accommodating his addiction. However, in 1971 on his annual ski trip to Switzerland, the Shah learned that there was a Swiss warrant for Davalu's arrest. He was being sought for allegedly having passed a large quantity of opium to another Iranian citizen. Incredibly, the Shah ordered his official plane to whisk Davalu home to Iran; he then entrusted Alam with the job of solving the resulting legal, diplomatic, and public relations nightmare. According to Alam's journals and to documents that have since been made public, hundreds of thousands of dollars were spent on lawyers, doctors (who testified that Davalu needed a daily dose of 25 grams of opium for medical reasons), Swiss journalists (to ensure more friendly coverage of the episode), and even Swiss jurists (who were invited to Iran for a royal vacation as a token of gratitude). The money was spent to both contain the crisis and ensure that Davalu served no time in prison.[15]

After his inquiry about corruption, the American official asked Zahedi whether the Iranian army remained reliably loyal to the Crown. "Why should they not be satisfied and reliable?" the Shah wrote tartly on the margin, adding that they were provided with all they needed. When the reliability of the bureaucracy was questioned, the Shah wrote in English, they have "misguided paternalistic information about us." The Shah's final reactions to more statements of concern were no less angry. He accused the American official of simply repeating the claims of the Tudeh propaganda machine and the "National Front, who are their lackeys." He then asked, not necessarily rhetorically, whether "it is true that they [the United States and the Russians] have conspired together against us."[16]

The Shah's last comment on the 1973 Zahedi report reflected his attitude toward critical reports, particularly at this period. He asked Zahedi to reduce to a "minimum his contacts with this person," and then, as if in an afterthought, he wrote "in reality it is we who are concerned about their [the Americans'] future." Rapidly rising oil revenue and sharply increasing improvements in nearly every standard economic indicator further allowed the Shah to ignore these rumblings of discontent or what he once called "these gloomy prophets of doom." [17]

By the time of Zahedi's remarkable September report, the Shah was increasingly self-assured and openly critical of what he disparagingly considered the many maladies of the "blue-eyed" Western world and its democracy. Early in his reign, he had regularly praised democracy, and he fondly remembered his education in the democratic society in Switzerland. By the early 1970s, his disposition had changed dramatically. He regularly chided Western democracies for their lax moral and political ethos, prophesying their imminent demise. He was certain, he often claimed, that the singular righteousness of his own ways and values would be recognized. The Shah's new disposition, combined with the rapidly changing fabric of Iranian society and the global trend toward democracy, created a particularly incongruent and thus volatile situation in Iran.

About a year before the Zahedi note, on November 11, 1972, Joseph Farland then U.S. ambassador to Iran, had met with Alam and "voiced some anxiety about signs of disgruntlement amongst the clergy." Not only the 2,500-year celebration but the further enfranchisement of women had raised their ire. By then, Iran had in the person of Faroukh Ru Parsa, a much-acclaimed educator, its first woman minister. Princess Ashraf was increasingly active, not just in controversial economic activities, but in politics. She was spearheading a government-sponsored women's movement that championed in increasingly defiant language more rights for Iranian women. A remarkably progressive new proposed family law that went a long way in affording women equal rights in the mid-seventies was arguably one of the most enduring works of this organization. Around this time, Ashraf also asked for several million dollars from the Shah to ensure that she could become the president of a UN General Assembly meeting. The Shah was opposed to this idea and rejected the request. Nevertheless, her increasing public presence was, even for the pro-Shah clergy, the cause of considerable consternation.[18] Ironically, only a few weeks before this conversation with the

American Ambassador, Alam had reported to the Shah that he had heard a sermon on the radio by a famous cleric who had prayed for everyone except the Shah. Anyone who seeks popularity, Alam ventured to say, seems to do so by "distancing themselves from us." Yet when Alam heard Farland's concern, he repeated to him what he had often recited to the Shah as a mantra: the grumbling of the clergy is nothing but petty infighting. He added in his normal grandiose manner, "when I was Prime Minister . . . mullahs united with Communists and nomadic tribes . . . rose up against the regime. They could not do a damn thing. I destroyed them; I crushed them once and for all." Farland responded to this facile, self-deluding narrative by simply saying, "If you say so."[19] In less than seven years, Alam's "crushed" clerics deposed the Shah and created a new regime of clerical despotism.

The American Embassy was, of course, not entirely convinced by Alam's words of reassurance. A couple of years later, in 1975, the new American ambassador, Richard Helms, captured the nature of the Shah's vulnerability when he wrote that "the conflict between rapid economic growth and modernization vis-à-vis a still autocratic rule" was the greatest uncertainty about the Shah's future. Helms went on to say that "alas, history provides discouraging precedents" for a peaceful resolution of this conflict. "I can recall no example of a ruler," he said, "willingly loosening the reins of power."[20]

Helms was only partially right. Not long after his report, the Shah began a liberalization process. However, the timing for this liberalization could not have been worse. A fall in the price of oil was shrinking government revenues, and, at the same time, there were increasing inflationary pressures on the economy. The election of Jimmy Carter in November 1976 not only forced the Shah to expedite his liberalization plans, but also emboldened Iran's democratic opposition; moreover, the Shah's physical ailments and characteristic indecisiveness in times of crisis rendered him increasingly less capable of decisive action. Add to these already-momentous patterns a fact known to political theorists since Aristotle—that authoritarian societies face their biggest challenge when they seek to liberalize—and the combination had the makings of a perfect storm: as rare a phenomenon in the world of meteorology as in the realm of politics.

Some in SAVAK tried to warn the Shah about what a Carter presidency and his human rights policy might mean for the Shah and the future stability of his regime. Parviz Sabeti, in charge of domestic security, prepared a new intelligence estimate for the Shah that addressed this issue. It warned of a potentially serious crisis facing the regime and demanded a plan of action to confront and contain the crisis. It indicated that the same coalition of opponents that had challenged the Shah in 1963—the urban middle class, students, members of the bazaar, the urban poor, Marxist groups, some nomadic tribes, and the radical clergy and their Islamist allies—were waiting for an occasion to challenge the Shah again. In 1963, the report claimed, the opposition had been buoyed by the Kennedy administration's talk of democracy and reform, and in 1977, Carter's human rights policies were once again awaking in them a will to fight. The SAVAK report asserted that this time the challenge would be even more serious than in 1963: there were more people living in concentrated quarters in cities, more urban poor, more Marxists, more revolutionaries (many trained by Palestinian groups in armed struggle), more college students, and more moderate democrats willing to join the opposition. If they sensed any weakness in the regime, they would engage in confrontation, and this time, the report said, it might be more difficult to roll back their challenge. In one fascinating study prepared as a master's thesis by Parviz Nik-khah, the sudden surge in the 1960s and 1970s in the number of Talabe (singular for Taliban, Arabic for "seminarian") was found to be a serious sociological anomaly, requiring both explanation and attention. In Iran itself, from 1925 to 1941, during the reign of Reza Shah, the number of seminarians had decreased from 2,949 to 784.[21]

Generally, as societies modernize, Nik-khah rightly pointed out, and as urbanism increases, the number of seminarians tends to diminish. In Iran, the reverse had happened. Moreover, in the last decade of the Shah's rule, the increase in the number of mosques and seminaries had been even more remarkable. By 1977, there were more than 75,000 such establishments in Iran. Yet, in spite of the fact that Nik-khah was in charge of research for Iran's National Radio and Television, and in spite of the fact that, earlier in his life, he had been a theorist of the new Iranian Left, no attention was paid to his findings.[22] The conclusion of the SAVAK report was more political and indicated that any hint of weakness in the regime, of succumbing to the human rights policies of the new Carter administration, could trigger a rapid slide into a systemic crisis.[23]

The Shah was incensed by the SAVAK report. He accused Sabeti of treasonously overlooking the fruits of the Shah and People Revolution. Do they mean to say, he reportedly asked, that we have accomplished nothing in the last two decades? Are workers not with us after we made them stockholders in the factories they worked in? Will women who have been enfranchised during our reign join the opposition? The underlying premises of the report and the retort captured the Shah's illusion and SAVAK's delusion. Economic progress, the Shah believed, would mollify people's demand for democracy; his secret police continued to seek the solution with an iron fist.[24]

Parts of SAVAK's early warning were in fact strikingly similar to the analysis offered by Anthony Parsons, the British ambassador during the heat of the crisis. The Shah, Parsons said, "had kept the country under severe discipline for 15 years," while he had pursued his policy of rapid modernization. It was inevitable that when this discipline was relaxed, there would be a violent release of popular emotion.[25] Parsons noted that the "massive influx into the cities from the rural areas" had created a "rootless urban proletariat of dimensions hitherto unknown in Iran" who had nothing to look forward to, and "in this state of mind, it was natural for them to turn back to their traditional guides and leaders, the religious hierarchy."[26]

However, since the traumas of 1953, the Shah had insisted on the indispensability of his authoritarian rule. As he did deliver rapid economic progress, and as it is hard to argue with success, the paradigm of authoritarian modernization had remained unchallenged. A CIA profile of the Shah prepared in the mid-1970s concluded that he now believed that democracy "would impede economic development."[27] Sometimes he criticized the endemic frailties of democracy; other times, he merely asserted that Iranians were not yet ready for democracy. He believed that only he could and should determine when and whether the time for such a democratic transition had arrived. By the time the Shah was willing—or was pressured by Carter—to make some of these changes, he was already deemed too vulnerable and weak by his opponents. Before long, they wanted his throne, not just an offer of a democratic opening.

ꝏ

The rapidity of economic development in the 1960s and early 1970s had fueled the Shah's grandiosity. According to the CIA, the Shah had a concept of "himself as a leader with a divinely blessed mission to lead his country from years of stagnation . . . [into] a major power, supported by a large military establishment."[28] In 1977, Iran spent 10.6 percent of its GNP on the military, France spent only 3.9 percent, Turkey 5.5 percent, and Iran's local rival, Iraq, only 8.75 percent of their corresponding GNP.[29]

As Iran was undergoing rapid economic change, the Shah followed a scorched-earth policy against the country's moderate and leftist forces. He also believed that the clergy—with the exception of the Khomeini supporters, who were suppressed—were his reliable allies in the fight against Communists and secular nationalists. His policy left the clergy and their nimble network of organizations an opportunity to grow and to monopolize the public domain. When in October 1969, "moderate religious leaders" sent a message to the Shah and to the U.S. Embassy that they were worried "about the situation" in the country and "angry at Khomeini" for putting them in the difficult position of either choosing his radicalism or being branded as a "reactionary mullah of the court," the Shah chose to ignore their warnings. More than once, similar warnings from the moderate clergy—about everything from the Shah's sudden decision to date the calendar from the birth of Cyrus the Great rather than from Mohammad's hegira

(1355 suddenly became 2535) to new progressive laws about women and family protection—were dismissed. Open letters and declarations from moderate secular politicians—leaders of the National Front, independent moderate opposition figures like Khalil Maleki and Mozzafar Baghai—were ignored or, more often, punished. Instead, the Shah basked in the self-congratulating complacency of courtiers like Assadollah Alam, who was constantly "reminding" the Shah that radical clergy like Khomeini had been neutralized in 1963.[30] The more the Shah ignored the moderate clergy, the easier it became for Khomeini and his radical allies to gain and consolidate hegemony over religious forces in Iran.[31]

Aside from using all of these grievances against the Shah in traditional mosques, religious forces had by the 1970s also developed the idea of the *hosseiniye*—a lecture hall that used modern trappings to cultivate a Shiite theology that was more rational in approach and shorn of superstition. The halls usually allowed people to sit on chairs, by then a habit of the middle classes, and forgo the more traditional mosque practice of sitting on the floor. The most famous of these halls, called Hosseiniye Ershad, was built in one of Tehran's upper-class neighborhoods. The financial support came from members of the bazaar who were close to the religious members of the National Front (the Freedom Movement), and the ideological management of the center was in the hands of Khomeini supporters. Every move they made, we now know, was made after consultation with Khomeini, who was in exile in Najaf.[32] At this *hosseiniye,* more-moderate clergy like Ayatollah Mottaheri and eloquent Islamist orators like Ali Shariati, himself an active member of the National Front when he was a student in Europe,[33] offered a version of Shiism that was more amenable to modernity and democracy. Amongst those influenced by Shariati's rhetoric was Mir-Hossein Mousavi, who now leads the Green Movement, and his influential wife, Zahra Rahnavard.[34] Though Shariati was known partially for his fierce critique of the Shiite clergy—calling them symbols of a despotic and stale Islam—he usually praised Khomeini as an exception, calling him a "progressive" cleric fighting relentlessly against despotism and colonialism.

By the early seventies Khomeini had found supporters amongst secular intellectuals as well. The most important such support was initially offered by Jalal Al-Ahmad, an influential writer and essayist of the 1960s who had called the clergy leaders in the important fight against colonialism. Al-Ahmad had even argued that the clergy were an essential part of the country's intellectual class. More than any other ideology, the writings of the likes of Al-Ahmad and Shariati prepared the context for Khomeini's leadership of the democratic movement. By promoting economic changes that created a new, wealthy, more educated middle class and then denying them the political rights they sought, and by allowing only the clergy to organize and mobilize the population, the Shah inadvertently pushed these moderate forces into Khomeini's camp. As early as 1962, Khomeini advisors had written that the political future of Iran was in the hands of those who could mobilize the rising middle class. Using a modern iteration of Shiism, the clergy were virtually the only group given a chance to mobilize and organize this critical social class.

Ironically, by the early 1970s, even the Shah realized that his regime faced a serious political challenge. In October 1972 he grew disgruntled with Amir Abbas Hoveyda's Iran Novin Party.[35] The party had originally been created to organize the middle class, but by the early 1970s it was staging party congresses that smacked of Communist Party rituals. Searching for a remedy, the Shah summoned Mehdi Samii to Court. Samii was one of Iran's most respected technocrats and had extensive connections amongst middle-class moderate intellectuals and the leaders of the National Front. He had gone to England in the mid-1930s on a government scholarship and had taken courses with Harold Laski. The Shah told Samii of his worries about the future and about the "problem of transition"—particularly after his death—and asked him to launch a new political party that would successfully solicit the support of the Iranian educated middle classes for a peaceful transition.

After some initial resistance, Samii agreed to take up the challenge. His reticence was particularly understandable in light of Alinaghi Kani's fate. In 1971 Kani had been named secretary-general of the Party of Martyrdom, supposedly the loyal opposition to the Iran Novin Party. According to the U.S. Embassy, during his brief tenure, Kani invigorated the party and made it appear a more legitimate loyal opposition.[36] In a party demonstration in Isfahan, Kani had called the Hoveyda cabinet "reactionary" and declared that if free elections were held, he and his party would easily defeat Hoveyda. The Shah was livid when he heard reports of the meeting. "How dare he say that elections are not free during my reign," he fumed to Alam, with no apparent irony. Within twenty-four hours, Kani was dismissed from all his positions.[37]

Nevertheless, beginning in late 1972, Samii met regularly with the Shah for almost five months, discussing and setting out the parameters of the new party's actions. Fortunately, Samii took copious notes every time he met with the Shah. These notes indicate that the Shah wanted a new kind of loyal opposition party, a centrist party with hints of social democratic ideas in its proposed platform. Of course, the Shah could still not fathom a truly independent loyal opposition, one that could in fact attract "those elements which would not join" the existing parties. The Shah told Samii he would "be looked after salary-wise." At the same time, the Shah emphasized that "he was against a one-party system," as it would invariably entail a distasteful dictatorship.[38] The Shah insisted that the principles of "his revolution" could not of course be subjected to criticism. Samii gingerly answered that "in order to create the institution (His Imperial Majesty underlined the term institution), and to build up reliable public men, there had to be debate and criticism." The Shah agreed, but added unequivocally that such criticism could not take the form of "Kani calling my government reactionary" or doubting the legitimacy of elections.

The minutes of these meetings clearly show that the Shah knew what his regime needed, but was unwilling, or afraid, to allow it to develop. The Shah gave an example of what his envisioned loyal opposition could do. He suggested that the police, for example, had recently "found that the dynamite used by saboteurs was sold to them by people of our railroad administration. We would give the tip to [the new party] to attack the government." In other words, he envisioned himself as the master puppeteer who could determine when and where the opposition would "attack." He claimed that he wanted "democracy" but insisted it be "the real, not the fake, not the American type," adding, "I have to have some choice."

In the course of these meetings, the Shah lamented the nature of politics—"dirty, one has to tell lies and enter into all kinds of deals with all kinds of people"—and "the spiritual and moral corruption everywhere." For reasons that are not clear, the only country the Shah excluded from his harsh judgment was Austria! One can surmise that his love of the country might have been rooted in the fact that his physician for many years had been Austrian. He emphasized that his goal was "building up self-confidence and self-respect in the people, a belief in our own power and ability . . . to fight the tendency of the people, especially the youth, to deny, to denigrate, to reject."

In their third meeting, Samii indicated that if he was to build an institution that could "in crisis, when time comes for succession, be helpful in maintaining the Constitution, then he would need some concessions"; there would need to be "serious dialogue with students and youth in general," he said. The Shah curtly dismissed the idea, adding that he did not "think they had very much to say."

The most heated debate took place over the question of what to do about the clergy. Samii said, with surprising frankness, that at that time "religion seems to provide the only channel of protest" and that Shiism had "become merely a political instrument"; nonetheless, he noted that religious leaders, "even if they were stooges of Communism," must be listened to.

The Shah was "skeptical and said that to try to treat with an *akhound* [cleric] was like going to bed with a madman." He nevertheless said that he was "concerned that in modern societies, religion was necessary to provide stability." Eventually, the Shah agreed to allow Samii to establish contact with the clergy, but insisted that no concessions were to be made and added that there was no need to mention the idea of dialogue with the clergy in the party manifesto.

The Shah's approach to religion was contradictory: he encouraged the growth of mosques and other religious institutions but, particularly after 1963, was altogether opposed to the idea of "listening to the clergy, much less making concessions to them"—even if they were moderate clergy who were opposed to Khomeini. By the time he changed his mind in 1978 and tried to solicit the support of such clergy, it was far too late. Khomeini was the undoubted leader of the vast network of religious organizations and forces, and moderate clerics did not dare openly criticize or challenge him.

The Shah and Samii agreed that the party would first bring together ten of the country's most reputable technocrats, intellectuals, and politicians as its founding members. The number would then increase to sixty. One of the ten was picked by Samii not because of his credentials but for his close ties to the Shah. This way, Samii believed, "the Shah would always know exactly what we were up to, and hopefully this would alleviate his anxieties."[39] The Shah assured Samii that the proposed new party could participate in elections and even negotiate with other opposition forces. Of course, as he repeated more than once, it would be he who "would guide [the party] and give it the cue." Samii talked of endemic corruption, the need for an independent judiciary, the necessity for suspending military tribunals, civilian control of the military—on none of these issues did he receive satisfactory answers from the Shah. Four years later, under duress, the Shah accepted these changes and many other demands of the opposition. It is difficult not to wonder what might have happened to Iran if the Shah had made some of these concessions to Samii while in a position of strength, rather than to the opposition four years later when he was weak and vulnerable.

But then one day the founding member Samii had included because of his ties to the Shah suddenly resigned. Samii immediately realized that the Shah had had a change of heart, and with some trepidation, on the last day of the Persian year in 1974, he went to the Court. The Shah began the discussion by lamenting his weight loss of seven kilos in the last week—a sign of his still-secret disease. Then a tearful Samii suggested that he must resign from the task of forming this party. The Shah accepted the resignation all too readily. What had started with a private bang ended with a whimper. The Samii project might have been the Shah's last chance to create an "institution" that he knew his regime needed if there was to be a peaceful orderly transition, or if his country faced a crisis.

The fact that the price of oil had suddenly quadrupled appeared to be a key factor in the Shah's change of mind. Instead of a legitimate party led by Samii, he opted instead for the development of a one-party system. All other parties were dismantled in favor of the new Rastakhiz (Resurgence) Party. The Shah—his two hands jutting from his vest in an attempt to appear authoritative—declared in a nationally broadcast press conference that everyone must join the new party and that those who refused should leave the country.

The Resurgence Party of 1975 was a stillborn monster and an immediate source of discontent, even ridicule. The key party ideologues were mostly from the ranks of lapsed Stalinists,[40] mixing bad ideas with bad politics. Even Hoveyda, the first appointed secretary-general of the party, often ridiculed it in private while in public professing fealty to the idea and to the Shah.[41]

How the Shah came up with the idea of a one-party system for Iran is hard to pinpoint. On numerous occasions, including in his first memoir and even as late as his conversations with Samii, he had underscored his opposition to single-party systems, describing them as harbingers of totalitarianism.

Some believe the idea for the party first came to the Shah from Anwar al-Sadat in Egypt; others point the finger to a group of five mostly American-trained technocrats who were part of the Queen's "think tank" and who suggested the one-party system based on Samuel Huntington's prescription for political development in developing countries.[42] The Shah initially rejected the group's proposal, asking in anger, "Haven't they read my book?" By then, in a gesture reminiscent of leaders like Mao, the Court had produced a handsome edition of the Shah's *Collected Works*. The collection is indeed replete with statements against one-party systems. Others think the Shah took his cues on the single-party system from Mexico.

The Shah had first toyed with the idea of a single party in the early 1960s and had spoken of it intermittently in the subsequent years. In each case, he had walked away from the idea. But this time, without any consultation with anyone, including the Prime Minister, SAVAK, Alam, or the Queen, he announced the creation of the new one-party system at a press conference. A few days earlier, he had told Abdol-Majid Majidi, director of the Plan Organization, of his decision. The Shah was at the time vacationing in St. Moritz, and Majidi rushed to a public phone in the Suvretta Hotel to inform Hoveyda that the days of his Iran Novin were now numbered.

During his press conference, the Shah not only announced the creation of a single party, but appointed a clearly surprised Hoveyda as its first secretary. The idea was a disaster. It failed to increase "political participation," as the Shah and the Queen's think tank kept promising, but instead became a political albatross that created nothing but discontent. The fierce battle between Hoveyda and Alam to dominate the party led to further paralysis. Each man had by then a number of lapsed Marxists amongst his staff, and each tried to place their "theorists" in places of authority. It mattered little to the Shah or to the men and women who eagerly, albeit cynically, served in the new party that the idea of limiting political activity to one party was against the letter and spirit of the constitution. By then the Shah's words were the law, and party theorists and activists competed for a chance to develop a party platform and ideology commensurate with the Shah's desires and designs.

One of the most incredible of these party theorists was Professor Ahmad Fardid, the man who introduced Martin Heidegger to Iran and developed a sophisticated anti-Semitism narrative that nourished the paranoia of young people like Mahmoud Ahmadinejad. Soon after the fall of the Shah, the same Fardid became one of the most notorious advocates of the new regime, using Heideggerian mumbo-jumbo to legitimize the despotic rule of the clergy. The Shah had, strangely, ordered the new party ideology to be based on "dialectics," which opened the door for both lapsed Marxists and Heideggerian anti-Semites to legitimately leave their dialectical mark on the party.

Not long after the creation of the party, the Carter administration came to power and began to pressure the Shah to democratize and show more respect for human rights. Carter's choice of William Sullivan as the new ambassador to Iran in June 1977 was, for some of the Shah's aides, the first hint of trouble. Sullivan had served in South Asia, where he had developed a reputation as a "tamer of dictators." But he knew nothing about Iran, as he readily admits in his own memoirs. Ardeshir Zahedi, who was Iran's ambassador to the United States at the time, recommended that the Shah refuse to issue the required agreement for Sullivan's appointment, but the Shah rejected the idea. We should not, he told Zahedi, pick a fight with Carter so early in his presidency.[43] Ironically, so incompetent was Sullivan in the performance of his duties, and so different were his ideas from those of the White House that before two years, Jimmy Carter too wanted "to recall him"; but by then the damage had been done, and Cy Vance, the secretary of state, opposed the idea of a recall.[44]

The issue of human rights was not the only sore spot in U.S. relations with Iran. In the last years of the Nixon administration and throughout the Ford administration, the two countries had been fighting an open, often-bitter war of diplomacy on the price of oil and on Iran's nuclear program. When the Shah refused to use his influence in OPEC to reduce the price of oil, the United States made a covert pact with Saudi Arabia to bring it down. The Shah claims that this refusal—and not the democratic aspirations of the people—was the real source of his downfall. Some scholars agree that the sudden drop in oil prices indeed contributed to the fall of the Shah.[45] Just as Iran's revenues were drastically reduced with this drop in the price of oil, the Carter administration resumed pressure on the Shah to democratize and liberalize.

In one of his earliest meetings with the Shah, Sullivan told him that, according to his preliminary inquiries, Iran's current rate of rapid economic development could not be maintained. The Shah was visibly shaken and ended the meeting prematurely. For a couple of weeks, he refused to meet with Sullivan again. He saw the comment as a clear indication that the Carter administration was unhappy with Prime Minister Hoveyda. Sullivan claims that he had no such intention. Nevertheless, a few days after this embittered meeting, Hoveyda was dismissed, and Jamshid Amuzegar was appointed prime minister.

Amuzegar began his tenure with a serious handicap, for he had no choice but to implement an austerity program. He was nevertheless initially remarkably successful in the economic management of the country, reducing internal inflation from over 30 percent a year to about 10 percent. He injected a "measure of realism in the people's expectations."[46] But in the political domain, he was deemed a failure—a "loner" who "never established an easy working relationship with the Shah." He was bereft of charisma and incapable of "engendering any popularity." Finally, his "handling, or lack of handling, of the religious leadership and their followers was little short of disastrous." He either ignored them or at best made "perfunctory appearances" at religious ceremonies.[47]

In the eyes of some royalists, Amuzegar's "austerity" program included cutting the stipends the government secretly paid the clergy. It was these stipends that, according to this theory, assured the clergy's support of the regime. For many, cutting these stipends was the single most important source of the revolution. For almost fifteen years after the revolution, Amuzegar kept silent about this allegation. He finally chose to clear the air in 1994, when he claimed that money had been paid directly to the clergy by the White House since 1953, and that it was Carter, not he, who cut the stipends.[48] In reality, stipends to the clergy were minimal and were handled mostly by the Court or by SAVAK. Even more crucially, those who accepted these handouts were usually not amongst Khomeini's supporters. As Nasir Asar, the long-serving Hoveyda liaison with the clergy, made clear, radical clergy "never deigned to take our money."[49]

More crucial than clerical stipends was the country's economic reality. By 1978, Iran's "GNP growth in real terms dropped to 2.8 percent." This economic slowdown was exacerbated by unusually high inflation rates. Like much of the West, Iran faced the strange hybrid phenomenon of "stagflation." Some in the U.S. Congress began to worry about Iran's budgetary priorities (and the fact that, in line with the Shah's views, precedence was given to military matters over social needs). These anxieties led to the concept of "link[ing] Iran's human rights performance with arms transfer."[50]

Politically, too, Amuzegar was fighting an uphill battle. In 1977, the dismissal of Hoveyda as prime minister—a post he had held for almost fourteen years, longer than any other minister in Iran's constitutional period—signaled to the opposition the end of an era. Some saw it as the beginning of the end of the Shah.* As Carter's human rights policy went into effect, the opposition began to constantly test the waters with the regime and push for more and more freedom.

Even this inauspicious constellation of the stars was not enough to end the Shah's regime. In the last two years of his rule, at each critical moment, the Shah arguably made the worst possible choice. He showed weakness when he needed to show strength, and he feigned power when he had none. The reasons for this remarkable series of errors were personal and political, and they were rooted not only in the Shah's storied vacillations, but also in his view that the whole movement was a conspiracy of outside forces against him. He changed his mind about who masterminded the conspiracy, but he never wavered in his belief that conspiracy was the causal root of the democratic movement.

In his last book, *Answer to History,* written in exile long after he had been "un-kinged," the Shah still argued, with disturbing certainty, that it was a conspiracy of Western and Communist forces that overthrew him. He argued that to "understand the upheaval in Iran . . . one must understand the politics of oil." He went on to claim that as soon as he began to insist on a fair share of oil wealth for Iran, "a systematic campaign of denigration was begun concerning my government and my person . . . it was at this time that I became a despot, an oppressor, a tyrant."[51] What the Shah failed to understand was that it was in fact the democratic aspirations of the Iranian people that begot the movement against him and that, ironically, his own social and economic policies of the 1960s and 1970s helped create the very social forces—particularly the middle class and the new technocratic class—that united to overthrow him. Even if Western or Communist powers were indeed conspiring against him, their plans worked only because there was fertile domestic ground for them.

Even when the Shah looked for domestic causes of the revolution, he was under an illusion. He concluded that he should have exercised more authoritarianism, not less. "Today, I have come to realize that the events of 1978–9 [were] attributable in part to the fact that I moved too rapidly in opening the doors of the universities, without imposing more severe preliminary selection. The entrance exams were too easy."[52] He called the students "spoiled children" who helped wreak havoc on Iran. In another passage, he contemplated the idea of having agreed to the military's proposed bloodletting. The blood that had been shed since the revolution, he said, has been incomparably greater than the most egregious plans of his military.

* In those days, I was a political prisoner in Evin. Some of the future leaders of the Islamic Republic—from Rafsanjani to Montazari—were my block-mates. They refused, as a matter of principle, to watch television. The only time they broke their self-imposed taboo was the night Hoveyda's resignation was announced.

The Shah dismissed nearly every form of opposition to his rule as a tool of Western governments to bring pressure on him.[53] In 1977, as the democratic movement was picking up momentum, he ordered some of his top oil negotiators to meet with Western oil companies and "give them what they want."[54] In the months leading up to the revolution, he was desperately trying to understand what the United States and Britain "wanted of him." He called to Court political figures he knew had close ties to the two governments. He asked Ahmad Goreishi (a scion of an aristocratic family and a close friend of Richard Helms) and Homayoun Sanatizadeh (also reportedly close to the U.S. government) as much in anxiety as in anger—"What do these Americans want of us?"[55]

Aside from his belated decision to liberalize, the second root of the revolution was tied to the nature of the Shah's character. Ironically, his strength of character as a man was his weakness as a leader. In the 1960s and 1970s, he increasingly took on the persona of an absolutist leader, decisive and determined, even brash and brutal. But no sooner did the dark clouds of crisis appear on the horizon than he began to lose his resolve, and all the vacillations and weaknesses that had almost ended his rule in 1953 appeared once again. The once-defiant Shah who had hectored the president of the United States and haughtily dismissed the elder statesmen of his realm as useless reactionaries was now in desperate need of "advice," not only from these same "elders," but from the British and American Embassies. He made virtually no decision in the last year without first seeking "advice" from these divergent sources. And contradictory advice often begot either indecision, or actions that were, in retrospect, blatantly absurd and sure recipes for disaster.

ꝏ

As the crisis continued, the Shah grew more desperate for signs of support from the West, particularly from the United States. But the messages he got from America were contradictory. For example, when concerned Iranians asked Ambassador Sullivan "if he would seek a personal message of support for the Shah from President Carter," Sullivan "fobbed [the Shah] off by saying that such a message would be unusual and inappropriate [at] the present time."[56] The response depressed the Shah. A few weeks later, the Shah was told that he would in fact be "receiving a telephone call" from the President. "According to Sullivan the Shah was clearly delighted, 'his chin moved from his knees to at least his chest.'"[57]

In reality, there were profound contradictions in the directions the American Embassy was receiving from the White House, the National Security Council, and the State Department. The confusion and bitter bureaucratic infighting created a vacuum wherein Sullivan followed his own "foreign policy." While Zbigniew Brzezinski, the national security advisor, suggested using an "iron fist" to establish law and order, followed by rational concessions to the opposition, the State Department under Cyrus Vance insisted on the continuation of the liberalization policy. Henri Precht, in charge of the Iran Desk at the State Department in this period, was also an avid supporter of liberalization. The Shah considered him nothing less than a foe. In an interview, he calls Precht "that son of bitch McGovernite" and faults him for some of the confusion in U.S. foreign policy.[58] Carter himself constantly vacillated between these two starkly different paradigms. Sullivan, too, was dancing to an increasingly bizarre tune. His self-admitted ignorance of Iranian history and Islamic traditions, which was a source of wonderment when he was first appointed, now came back to haunt him. The Shah swung from one extreme to another, invariably to disastrous result. Khomeini, dangling a tactical but tantalizing democratic platform, used each of the Shah's moves to his own profit, ultimately convincing Sullivan that he would create a democratic polity in Iran. Not only were Khomeini's cohorts in direct contact with the embassy in Tehran, but Sullivan supported the idea of the United States establishing ties with Khomeini himself in Paris. According to Carter, Sullivan "lost complete control of himself" when he learned that the United States had approached Khomeini "through the French instead of directly as he had pushed."[59]

As Amuzegar proved unable to control the crisis, the Shah decided to replace him. In his *Answer to History*, he laments the fact that he moved too quickly. Following Amuzegar's dismissal, the Shah decided to create a government of "national reconciliation" and chose Jafar Sharif-Emami for the task. He had been the president of the Senate for almost two decades and had led the Shah's Pahlavi Foundation ever since its creation, overseeing the expansion of the foundation into different fields of the economy, from owning and operating every casino and most luxury hotels in the country to purchasing the Omran Bank, one of the most powerful financial institutions in the country. In 1961, during his first term as prime minister, not only had he failed miserably in dealing with the severe recession, but the U.S. Embassy considered him responsible "for some of the plunders which had gone on."[60] Since that time, he had been known for harboring anti-American sentiments. He had also acquired the moniker of "Mr. Five Percent," based on the allegation that he received 5 percent on every major government contract.[61] On top of all this, he was generally known to be the Grand Master of Masonic Lodges in Iran, a fact confirmed when Esmail Rain published his famous three-volume study of Masons in Iran. In other words, it is hard to imagine a figure worse suited to the job of forming a government of national reconciliation than Jafar Sharif-Emami.

But he had several things working in his favor. First and foremost, some of the clergy, particularly Ayatollah Shariat-Madari, had suggested him as a possible candidate to replace Amuzegar. It was a measure of the radical mood of the times that, although Shariat-Madari played a key role in bringing Sharif-Emami to office, the atmosphere created by pro-Khomeini clergy was such that he did not dare offer public support. He decided instead on "caution, deliberately refraining from allowing himself to be identified" with the new cabinet.[62] Sharif-Emami also had the support of the British Embassy. According to the British Ambassador, he was "a well-respected figure, a former prime minister and of impeccable religious credentials."[63]

By this point, the Shah was growing less and less involved in the daily affairs of government. Sharif-Emami's strategy was simple enough. He made concessions to every demand of the opposition, sometimes anticipating what those might be, and offering the concession even before the demand was made. The calendar was changed back to its Islamic origin. The casinos were shut down. Some political prisoners were freed, while dozens of ministers, generals, and key officials were arrested. The most controversial of these was the arrest of Amir Abbas Hoveyda on November 7, 1978. Ostensibly, the Shah, the Queen, and five highly placed advisors decided on his arrest on that day. However, the Shah had informed the British Ambassador a week earlier about the imminent arrest of both Hoveyda and Nematollah Nasiri, who had only recently been appointed Iran's ambassador to Pakistan. Under General Moghadam's leadership at SAVAK, censorship virtually ended, hundreds of political prisoners were freed, criticism of the government was not just allowed but encouraged—but it was all to no avail. As far as the opposition was concerned, Sharif-Emami's concessions were nothing but a sign of weakness.

Some in SAVAK had a very different view of how to handle the situation. On Saturday, May 13, 1978, all chiefs of security and police were called to Tehran for a conference. Nasiri, still SAVAK chief, "put forth the view that the way to handle the disturbances was to close the bazaars in cities such as Qom, and use all the necessary force, including killing people." But General Fardust, also present at the meeting, presented an alternative approach, more congruent with what became Sharif-Emami's mode of behavior. Fardust argued that military conscripts could not be counted on to carry out such a crackdown. He recommended instead "that the government open a dialogue with the people." As Fardust himself admitted, his views were adopted by those in the room only because they assumed he was speaking for the Shah. The meeting ended by those present asking Fardust to convey to the Shah their concurrence with the position he advocated.[64]

But these concessions only increased the opposition's appetite for more. Eventually, on September 7, 1978, faced with increasing riots and strikes, the cabinet decided to declare martial law in Tehran. For reasons that have never been fully explained, the announcement of martial law, though made in the early afternoon, was not broadcast until after midnight. By eight o'clock the next morning, some 800 people had congregated in Jaleh Square. Within an hour that number swelled to about 10,000. Soldiers tried to enforce the curfew, asking the demonstrators to disperse; then tear gas and live ammunition were used. The city was suddenly awash with rumors of "thousands killed" by soldiers. According to the foreign embassies, the actual number was anywhere from a dozen to 300.[65] The day was immediately labeled "Black Friday." The Sharif-Emami experiment in appeasement had failed.

It is hard to pinpoint the moment at which the unwieldy coalition that eventually overthrew the Shah began to coalesce. One thing is certain: Carter's human rights policies had an impact in reinvigorating the dormant democratic movement. Many consider the trigger to have been an ill-advised article that was published in *Etela'at* in January 1978. The article, titled "Iran and the Red and Black Colonialism," had grown out of the Shah's anger at Khomeini's latest, particularly nasty pronouncements against the Pahlavi dynasty. He had called the Shah a "filthy pilferer" of public coffers. Khomeini's eldest son had died, and rumors of SAVAK's involvement—though never confirmed even by Khomeini—spread throughout the country. An angry Shah ordered SAVAK and Hoveyda, then Court minister, to prepare a blistering attack. SAVAK was—rightly, as it turned out—reluctant to stir up a hornets' nest. Hoveyda, on the other hand, was more than eager to carry out the Shah's orders. He had two of his journalistic hacks prepare the article. Some claimed that Hoveyda's eagerness stemmed from his enmity toward Amuzegar and a lingering hope of a return to power.

Whatever the reason for Hoveyda's eagerness, the two journalists, both notorious for their opportunism, speedily prepared a scurrilous attack on Khomeini. It combined fact and fiction, accusing Khomeini of being of Indian origins and of being a British agent. The fact that his grandfather had moved to India was later confirmed by his brother and his biographers. But in those days, the article was seen as a sinister character assassination. Darius Homayoun, then minister of information, received a yellow envelope embossed with the seal of the royal Court. He had already been informed that it contained an article the Shah wanted published. Without reading the article, Homayoun sent it to *Etela'at* and asked them to publish it forthwith. But upon reading the text, both the editor and the publisher of the daily paper realized its incendiary potential. They called Homayoun to register their reservations. Prime Minister Amuzegar, was consulted, and he too, without bothering to read the essay, ordered it published. If His Majesty wants something published, Amuzegar reportedly said, then it shall be published. Amuzegar was, of course, not alone in this sentiment. For years, Hoveyda had ensured the implementation of his orders by insisting they "were from the Boss [*Arbab*]." The article was published on January 8, on page seven of *Etela'at,* and within hours, riots began to erupt in the city of Qom, and blood was shed.

Wiser ayatollahs like Shariat-Madari knew the dangers inherent in this hornets' nest. He immediately contacted the Court and suggested that the Shah swiftly issue an apology and bring to a speedy close the unfolding eruption. But Shariat-Madari's wise suggestion was ignored, and within days, even he had no choice but to join the increasingly loud chorus of critics of the regime, all demanding an apology.

As the movement in support of Khomeini gathered steam, Saddam Hussein offered, as a gesture of goodwill, to rid the Shah of this "meddlesome priest." The Shah refused, suggesting that killing Khomeini would only make him a martyr. Apparently, the French intelligence services made a similar offer to the Shah, and his response was the same. Also, according to Iran's Ambassador to Iraq at the time, a few months before this sudden eruption, someone in Khomeini's entourage had inquired about the possibility of the Ayatollah's returning to Iran "to die." The Shah had summarily rejected the request.[66]

Others believe the first salvo of the 1979 revolution was a 124-page open letter to the Shah that was written in 1977 by the famous journalist Ali Asghar Haj Seyyed Javadi, in which he detailed the breaches of law committed by the government, the Court, and the Shah himself. Some point to the ten nights of poetry at the Goethe Institute in Tehran as the genesis of the movement. On those nights some of the country's leading dissidents read works critical of the regime, its censorship, and its undemocratic ways. An estimated 10,000 people stood for hours in the open air, often in pouring rain, to listen to these dissident artists and intellectuals. In May 1977, fifty-three of the country's top lawyers and law professors wrote a letter to the Shah, accusing his government of interfering in the work of an independent judiciary. Less than a month later, three top leaders of the National Front (Karim Sanjabi, Darius Forouhar, and Shapour Bakhtiyar) wrote an open letter of their own to the Shah, criticizing the regime's economic policies and suggesting that the mishandled land reform and subsequent bad policies had wrecked the country's agricultural sector. They demanded an end to despotism, respect for the Iranian Constitution and for the Universal Declaration of Human Rights, an end to the one-party system, freedom of the press, and release of all political prisoners. In quick order, other groups of lawyers, professors, and political activists entered the epistolary fight for democracy.

One of the most important of these letters was signed by ninety-eight prominent writers, poets, and translators; it marked the reemergence of the Iranian Writers Association—a group that played an important role in the subsequent democratic struggle in Iran. With every passing day, as it became evident that the regime was no longer punishing those who signed these daring declarations, their numbers suddenly increased. The Iranian Committee for the Defense of Freedom and Human Rights was founded, and in its ranks were not only most leaders of the National Front, but also Mehdi Bazorgan—the future prime minister of the Islamic regime.

Ironically, what fed the appetite of these critics was the Shah's decision to establish two royal commissions to look into allegations of mismanagement and malfeasance in the Hoveyda government. Some of the journalists known for their ties to the Court also began surprisingly acerbic attacks on Hoveyda. Ali Asghar Amirani, the famous editor of *Khandaniha,* was easily the most noticeable of such newly emboldened critics. It is hard to imagine that his attacks were not sanctioned by the Shah. Whatever the reason, these attacks only fanned the flames of discontent among the people and weakened the resolve of the royalists. If "loyal servants" like Hoveyda and Nasiri could be arrested, no member of the ancien régime was safe. A massive flight of capital began as individuals and their fortunes sought safe harbor in Europe and the United States. Those who chose to stay and try to save the regime ended up paying a heavy price, sometimes with their lives, for their fidelity to the Shah or the country.

The findings of the royal commissions, some of them broadcast on radio and television, seemed to further confirm opposition claims of massive fraud and misuse of public funds. Nasrollah Moinian, the Shah's impeccably honest chief of staff for about two decades, was in charge of one of the commissions. The findings did not offer a complimentary picture of the country's economic realities.

Despite the role his own policies had in the creation of the crisis, the Shah felt betrayed not only by the West, but also by the people of Iran. Sometimes he accused his opponents of being nothing but "Marxists, terrorists, lunatics and criminals." When in October 1978 he finally took a helicopter flight to witness one of the most massive demonstrations, he came back despondent, angry, and convinced of foreign connivance. That night, he met with British and American officials and told them in no uncertain terms that he held their governments responsible for what he had seen that morning. "What have I done to you?" he asked. He believed that the West's "betrayal" of him far exceeded the "giveaway at Yalta."[67]

In 1978 the Shah and most Iranian government officials had an exaggerated view of the power of America and Great Britain to "direct events" in Iran. A few critical reports by the BBC and the American media were more than enough to convince both the people and the regime that the Shah was now vulnerable and that the West had not only abandoned him, but was now out to get him. Even Khomeini reportedly listened to nightly broadcasts of Voice of America, the BBC, and Radio Israel to get a sense of Western policy. So pervasive was the belief that the American and British media—particularly the BBC and the Voice of America—represented the official views of their governments that, after a few critical reports in both outlets, both countries' ambassadors felt compelled to try to dispel the notion. Nonetheless, more than once, Iran "semi-officially" objected to the British government about the content of BBC broadcasts, even threatening to end some contracts with British companies.

The BBC in particular was deemed to be so powerful, and its influence so pernicious, that some of the Shah's generals from the air force suggested using the cover of night "to take out the relay towers of the BBC."[68] In recent accounts offered by the BBC itself, they admit to having had a "critical" disposition toward the Shah. They write that "the image of BBC changed in the collective perception of the population. It was no longer the voice of 'British colonialism' but a trusted friend."[69] They attribute this anti-Shah tilt to the personal inclinations of their staff and not to some coordinated British government policy.

Tensions over these broadcasts reached such a level that in September 1978, Sir Anthony Parsons, the British ambassador, informed the Shah and Prime Minister Sharif-Emami of his decision to dispatch an "entirely trustworthy" emissary to meet with Ayatollah Shariat-Madari, "as leader of the most important moderate opposition," and reassure him that the BBC did not reflect official British policy and that Great Britain's "true position" was in fact full support for the Shah.[70] The U.S. government took similar steps to reassure the Shah that, in spite of what the American media reported, the American government continued to support him.

Like a traditional Oriental potentate, the Shah felt the society owed him a debt of gratitude for the progress and the freedoms he had "given them." And in fact, in the last fifteen years of his rule, there had been not only unprecedented economic growth, but unparalleled cultural and religious freedom in Iran. Double-digit growth of the GNP was not the exception but the rule. Iran ranked with Turkey, South Korea, and Taiwan as the countries that were industrializing most rapidly and were most likely to join the ranks of developed economies. But for most in Iran's opposition, these cultural and economic freedoms and accomplishments were either a form of "decadent libertinism," or a mere cosmetic to cover the more fundamental lack of democracy. On the eve of the revolution, it was political freedom that was the focus of the opposition's demands. And in one of the great ironies of modern history, this movement chose as its leader the man most likely to severely curtail the cultural and political freedom people were demanding.

Moreover, most Iranians touched by modernity—and its notions about the natural rights of citizens—considered the freedoms the Shah thought he was "giving" them their inalienable rights.[71] They held him responsible for having deprived them of these rights and resented the fact that he expected them to show gratitude for their newly bestowed freedoms. The Shah felt, in the words of a confidante, "like a man who had lavished everything on a beautiful woman for years, only to find that she had been unfaithful all along."[72] The authoritarian system he had established made him the sole "decider" for nearly every major economic, political, and military decision in the country. Whether it was the decision to allow visas for an American university marching band or the precise timing of the arrest of a known Soviet spy, he expected to have the final say. When his deteriorating health and his anxious mood and, more importantly, his failing grip on power, rendered him incapable or unwilling to make any decisions, as happened in late 1978, the weaknesses and vacillations that had been the hallmark of his character in his battle with Mossadeq reemerged, and the entire machinery of the state came to a grinding halt. The Mossadeq mystique also affected both the Shah and his supporters, who mistakenly believed that the United States must have some master plan to keep the Shah, or at least the monarchy, in power. But unbeknownst to the Shah, by early November 1978, both the British and American Embassies had concluded that doing another August 1953 to save the Shah was not in their interest. Moreover, in 1953, the Shah had had the support of the army, much of the entrepreneurial class, and the top echelon of the clergy as well as the full trust and relentless effort of a capable Minister of Court who spared no effort to save the throne. In 1978, however, everything was different. The clergy were either against him or, cowed by Khomeini's radicalism, unwilling to publicly support him. The entrepreneurial class was in utter disarray and had long ago been forced to abandon any political ambition. Even the ranks of the military had been showing, from early September 1978, signs of discontent, if not outright rebellion. By December 1978, the British and American Embassies were both detecting "signs of dissention and disarray at the top of the armed forces." Commanders complained that the Shah was bereft of purpose, suggesting that his father had been made of sterner metal and that such a crisis "would have never happened under Reza Shah."[73]

In the weeks before the collapse of the regime, American officials, cognizant of these facts, tried to establish new ties to the opposition. They wanted to avoid a civil war, which would have benefited the Soviets. They also wanted to ensure that the Communists would not use chaos as a pretext to seize power. British and U.S. policy began to shift. On October 30, 1978, British Prime Minister James Callaghan's office decided that the Shah did not have any chance of surviving and informed the Foreign Office that they should "start thinking about reinsuring."[74] Around the same time, the Carter administration also concluded that the Shah was not likely to survive.

General Robert Huyser (sent by Carter on a special mission to Iran) and "General Gast (the MAAG [Military Assistance and Advisory Group] chief in Tehran) were in close touch with the military . . . [and] were working to facilitate contact between them and Khomeini's forces."[75] The decision to work with Khomeini and his forces came after contacts were established between him and American officials in Paris. After some initial trepidation, the United States decided to learn more about Khomeini's plans. He (in Paris) and his supporters (in Tehran) were asked to answer a series of questions. The responses were, according to U.S. officials, of the "standard Third World type"—there was clearly no hint of clerical despotism. In the meantime, even the American Embassy in Tehran arrived at a new "reading" of Shiism. Sullivan not only wrote about "thinking the unthinkable" and planning for an Iran without the Shah, but also concluded that Khomeini was keen on establishing a democracy in Iran. The United States began facilitating Khomeini's rise to power.

The movement that overthrew the Shah was democratic in nature and aspirations. Some 11 percent of the 38 million people of Iran participated in the movement, compared to 7 percent in the French Revolution and 9 percent in the Russian Revolution. The slogans of the day were unmistakably democratic as well: 38 to 50 percent were directed against the Shah himself, 16 to 30 percent favored Khomeini personally. At most, 38 percent asked for an Islamic Republic—none asked for a clerical regime.[76] The most common slogan was "Independence, Freedom and an Islamic Republic."

In the months leading up to the Western decision to "reinsure," Khomeini hid his ultimate goal and true ideology and took on the guise of a democratic leader. Not only did he dissimulate when responding to the U.S. questionnaire, but in his more than one hundred interviews in Paris, there was no mention of *velayat-e faqih*. But in fact, from his first book in Persian, written in the aftermath of the fall of Reza Shah, to the collection of his sermons on an Islamic government, compiled by his students in Najaf in the late 1960s, Khomeini consistently advocated the absolute rule of jurists, enforcing sharia law.[77] Even in the annals of Shiite theology, Khomeini's view was deemed radical and was espoused by only a handful of ayatollahs.[78] Ironically, he was aided in his deception by the fact that the Shah had banned Khomeini's books for decades, making them unavailable to Iranian readers or critics.

To add further credibility to this democratic pose, Khomeini allowed a few ambitious, Western-trained aides such as Abol-Hassan Bani-Sadr, Sadeq Gotbzadeh, and Ebrahim Yazdi[†] to become the public face of his movement in Paris. The three were his de facto spokesmen and helped consolidate the democratic façade.

† Today, Bani-Sadr lives in exile after being impeached as the first president; Gotbzadeh was executed on the charge of plotting a coup; and Yazdi, the leader of the Freedom Movement, is in jail for his role in the 2009 post-election demonstrations.

At the same time, unbeknownst to the world, Khomeini had already organized a few trusted clerics in Tehran—nearly all had been his students in earlier years—into a covert "Revolutionary Committee." Some members of this committee, particularly those from the Freedom Movement, were in close contact with American Embassy officials in Tehran, and they eventually convinced the Ambassador that the "Islamic movement dominated by Ayatollah Khomeini is far better organized [and] enlightened and able to resist communism than its detractors would lead us to believe," and that it might be able to "produce something more closely approaching Westernized democratic processes than might at first be apparent."[79] A more misguided reading of what Khomeini stood for is hard to imagine.

For the Shah, the end seemed near when late in 1978 workers in the critical oil industry went on strike. In a remarkable lapse of planning, it turned out that Iran's much-vaunted military lacked the technological or organizational know-how to take over the oil industry and keep the government afloat. By then, no country was deemed as central to deciding Iran's future as the United States. A U.S. Embassy memorandum, written in 1978 on the eve of the revolution, noted "the 'secret hand' theory...deep in the Iranian grain...blames the US (among others) for Iran's many problems."[80] George Ball, head of Carter's special task force on Iran, wrote a report that captured these dynamics deftly: "All parties are looking to the United States for signals,"[81] he wrote. "We made the Shah what he has become. We nurtured his love for grandiose geopolitical schemes and supplied him the hardware to indulge his fantasies." Ball went on to say, "Now that his regime is coming apart under the pressures of imported modernization," the United States should pressure the Shah to give up much of his power and "bring about a responsible government that not only meets the needs of the Iranian people but the requirements of our own policy."[82]

After the "Black Friday" incident in September 1978, it was clear that Sharif-Emami's experiment in shaming or appeasing the opposition into accord by offering them a surfeit of concessions had failed utterly. His decision to arrest prominent past leaders backfired, becoming a source of ridicule to the opposition and of wavering support in the rapidly dwindling ranks of royalist stalwarts.

The Shah, after several meetings with British and American officials, and after accepting that his experiment with Sharif-Emami had failed, on November 5, said there was now no choice but to impose a military government. It was time to flex the military's muscle in order to intimidate the opposition. Earlier, SAVAK had submitted a list of about 1,500 people it wanted arrested. The plan was put forward to the Shah by Parviz Sabeti, with Hoveyda—still Court minister—acting as intermediary. With some trepidation, the Shah agreed to the arrest of 150 "mostly less-known characters." After a couple of weeks, even those arrested were released on the order of the Prime Minister. By November, instead of implementing SAVAK's hard-knuckle plans, the Shah agreed to a massive purge of SAVAK itself. Sabeti was amongst those "relieved of duty," and it became clear to the political cognoscenti that the Shah was ready to concede defeat.

When rumors of the Shah's plan to install a military government spread, the opposition feared that General Oveisi—nicknamed the "Butcher of Tehran"—would be the head of the new military government. According to Aslan Afshar, his chief of protocol, the Shah went so far as to tell orderlies at the Court to summon Oveisi to his office. Then, according to Afshar, the British and American ambassadors asked for an emergency meeting with the Shah. After the meeting, a dour and dejected Shah told Afshar to cancel the summons to Oveisi. Instead, he appointed General Azhari, then chairman of the Joint Chiefs of Staff, who was altogether bereft of charisma and the aura of intimidation needed in a military governor.

Azhari had a hard time finding people willing to serve in his cabinet. On more than one occasion, it was left to the Shah to call and demand that someone accept the task for the love of the country. Hussein Najafi, one of the most respected jurists of his generation, was one such candidate. He had already served in the Sharif-Emami cabinet, but was now unwilling to continue in the post, rightly arguing that he had a reputation as a jurist who followed the letter of the law. In a military cabinet, he said, "you want someone to bring fear to the hearts of the people, not someone who will reassure them of the law's full implementation." But the Shah would not relent, and at his insistence, a reluctant Najafi was named minister of justice.

Even if General Azhari's own timid behavior, and the incongruent mix of his cabinet ministers, was not enough to deprive it of its aura of authority or military menace, the Shah's notorious speech the day before his appointment was the last nail in the coffin of the "military option." The controversial speech was by all accounts prepared by two of the Queen's closest advisors, Seyyed Hussein Nasr and Reza Qotbi. By then, the Shah's speechwriter of many years, Shojaedeen Shafa, had already left Iran, and contrary to rumor, had no role in preparing the speech. "Had I been in Iran," he said, "I would have never allowed his Majesty to make such an ill-advised speech."[83]

On the morning of this infamous speech on November 5, 1978, when the Shah arrived at his office and noticed the television crew setting up, he asked his Chief of Staff what they were preparing for. He was told that a speech was on its way from the Queen's office. When the Shah finally saw a draft, he was reluctant to deliver it. Ultimately, after consultation with the Queen and her advisors, he was convinced. Dressed in civilian cloths, bereft of any mark of majesty or authority, looking tired and wan, the Shah for the first time referred to the opposition movement as a revolution. "I have heard the voice of your revolution," he said, adding that he fully realized that many errors had been committed in the past. Given a chance, he would now reign according to the letter of the constitution. Delivered only a day before the installation of the supposed military government, the repentant speech was yet another sign of the Shah's loosening grip on the reins of power. The speech also indicated the rift that existed at the Court between the Queen and her advisors, who consistently advocated reconciliation with the opposition, and those who advised the Shah to use his military to re-establish law and order. The vacillations between these two extremes only fed the opposition's appetite for power.[84]

If the repentant speech was intended to convince the opposition to join a government of national reconciliation, it was a complete failure. Most of the secular National Front leadership had decided by late 1978 against either forming a coalition with the Shah or forming a government of its own while the Shah was still in power. The National Front cannot be entirely blamed for the failure of a secular democratic coalition. The Shah had long been adamantly against reconciliation with the National Front, making "vitriolic denunciations" against them as late as June 1978 during a private meeting with British officials. He declared at the time that the National Front leaders were beyond "the lines of political acceptability."[85]

Aside from these old political wounds what made a compromise with the Shah more difficult was the tragic fire in the Rex Cinema, in the city of Abadan. On August 19, 1978, doors to the theater were locked from outside and the place was set ablaze. More than four hundred people burned to death. The regime tried to accuse the Islamists of instigating the murderous act, while the opposition claimed that it was in fact the regime that had burned the theater to tarnish the opposition's reputation. In subsequent years, it has become increasingly more evident that it was in fact radical Islamists who put the Rex Cinema ablaze.

As the tempo of anti-Shah demonstrations increased, some American businessmen working in Iran decided to "level a public relations campaign in support of the Shah."[86] More importantly, some members of the Iranian bourgeois class, finally cognizant of the imminent danger to their investments and way of life, belatedly tried to organize pro-Shah groups and demonstrations. The effort was led primarily by Ali Rezai, the head of a major industrial conglomerate. He had been in close contact with Princess Ashraf, who encouraged the group to act. In a meeting attended by some of the country's top industrialists, almost 20 million *tooman* ($3 million) was raised. But like most of what the Shah's supporters did, it was too little, too late.

In retrospect, it seems likely that the Shah's last chance for survival was the appointment of Gholam Hussein Sadighi as prime minister. He had been an interior minister during Mossadeq's time and remained unwavering in his support for the man he called "the Ultimate Leader." The Shah had been instrumental in arranging for his early release from prison in the aftermath of August 1953. He is a patriot, the Shah reportedly declared at the time. A revered professor at Tehran University, Sadighi was considered the father of modern sociology in Iran. He was renowned for his mastery of Aristotelian text and was also one of the leaders of the National Front, having played a pivotal role in revitalizing the Front in the early 1960s. He remained unbending in his opposition to the Shah—whom he considered a coup-installed illegitimate claimant to the throne. In what will go down in history as a remarkable show of courage, Sadighi decided to forgo his personal animosities when he felt the country was in danger.

In early October, as it became clear that only a genuine government of national reconciliation might save the country from Khomeini, Sadighi finally agreed to meet with the Shah. He had only two conditions: the first meeting would take place with at least two other trusted elder statesmen present, and there should be no discussion of an appointment as prime minister in that meeting. The Shah agreed, and the first meeting was spent on general discussion of both the past and the current crises. When the Shah claimed that he had the full support of President Carter in his decision to leave the country for a while, Sadighi stopped him. It was, he said, unbecoming to a king to worry about the support of an American president. Moreover, he insisted that, in his view, the idea of the Shah's leaving Iran at the time was ill-advised.[87] This surprised the Shah; all the other National Front leaders he had met wanted him to leave the country.

All in all, there were five meetings between the Shah and Sadighi. In the second meeting, on December 10, only the Shah and Sadighi were present, and it was then that the job of prime minister was offered to the prudent old Aristotelian. His most critical demand was that the Shah remain in Iran. He also demanded that the bloodshed stop. He then promised to work on forming a cabinet.

A few days earlier, the Shah had also met with Karim Sanjabi, the leader of the National Front. Sanjabi predicated his acceptance of any role in a government on Khomeini's prior approval. He had just returned from meeting with Khomeini in Paris, where he had made a statement—a statement the Ayatollah had refused to sign, lest the presumptive leader of the secular forces develop any delusions that he was on a par with Khomeini—in which he not only accepted Khomeini's leadership, but also the increasing role of Islam in shaping the ideology of the movement. Upon his return to Tehran, Sanjabi told the Shah that "no solution would work without a green light from Khomeini." He added that at present "this was impossible to obtain except on the basis of the Shah's total abdication." More incredibly still, he "suggested that the present military government should remain in office for another couple of months to see if Khomeini's influence might be on the decline and if a situation might then obtain where some kind of national government could be formed."[88] A more dangerous combination of cowardice and mendacity is hard to imagine.

Ali Amini, another credible candidate for the job of prime minister was, in the Shah's words, "on a different tack." His proposal was that the Shah should withdraw "to Bandar Abbas [in the South] and that a monarchical council should be set up which would carry out all the functions of the monarchy, except the command of the armed forces, which would remain with the Shah."[89]

In those days, Tehran had become a virtual circus, full of political lightweights with delusions of grandeur or political figures well past their prime offering themselves to the Shah or to the British and American Embassies as the sole savior, the country's messiah. Iraj Pezeshkpour, the leader of the Pan-Iranist Party whose only hour of glory had been in the late sixties, was amongst those who met secretly with the Shah and offered himself as a candidate for prime minister.[90] A few weeks earlier, when the Shah had let it be known that Majlis deputies were free to speak their minds, Pezeshkpour made what the British Embassy called "an inflammatory speech" establishing himself as a critic of the government. Clearly, however, he did not have the gravitas to tackle the crisis facing the country. Sadighi remained the most credible candidate.

National Front leaders of different hues all tried to convince Sadighi not to accept the position. But he was altogether indifferent to the petty machinations of his National Front comrades, each of whom was eager to deter Sadighi for their own often personal reasons. To those who appealed to his lifelong reputation as a foe of the Shah and a friend of Mossadeq, he responded that the reputation he had achieved was not a private asset to be taken to the grave, but something "I must use in the service of my country."

The third meeting between the Shah and Sadighi took place on December 25, when Sadighi laid out some of his plans—a final resolution of the question of the Shah's properties in Iran and a radical change in SAVAK, though not its dissolution. He proposed an end to martial law, a reduction of the military budget, the appointment of General Fereydoon Jam as minister of war, the dismissal of Zahedi as ambassador to the United States, an independent judiciary, and an end to military tribunals. The Shah agreed to nearly all of these demands, offering some resistance on the military budget. "What are you going to do with Iraq?" he asked. Sadighi insisted that his goal was not to weaken the military, but to make a temporary reduction to allow the government to survive the current economic crisis. Sadighi reiterated his insistence that the Shah must stay in the country.

He could go to the destination of his choice—for example, the Caspian coast or Kish Island—and appoint a committee that would act as liaison between the cabinet and himself. Sadighi knew that his survival depended on the support of the military and that such support was dependent on the Shah's favorable disposition and his continued presence in the country.

While the Shah waited to see whether Sadighi could succeed in forming a cabinet, he told the American and British ambassadors that he had been thinking about what would happen if Sadighi could not calm the situation. Then, he said, there would have to be a "crackdown by the armed forces. There would be at that stage no choice between that course and surrender." The Shah further added that if it came to a crackdown, he "could not personally associate himself with it . . . and would withdraw to Bandar Abbas to 'visit his navy' while the army did its stuff." Ambassadors Parsons and Sullivan were both reluctant to support this contingency plan. Parsons said that he was not sure that the army would in fact carry out orders for such a crackdown: in "certain areas they [would] refuse," and this would be disastrous. Clearly, the policy of Britain and the State Department was at that point to encourage the Shah's liberalization policy, eschew the use of the military against the people, and hope that in the end "wiser counsels among the opposition will prevail" and bring some semblance of order to the domestic scene.[91]

Three days later, Sadighi met again with the Shah and reported that he had prepared a list of potential members of his cabinet. The only thing that was now required for his appointment was a vote of confidence by the Majlis and the Shah's final word. "As far I am concerned," Sadighi said on December 28, "I can begin work today."[92] By then, in his legendary meticulous manner, Sadighi had prepared a plan of action, "down to every hour," for his first weeks as prime minister. Khomeini proved unwilling to attack Sadighi in public, and all that was needed was the Shah's final word.

But as Sadighi knew, the Shah had been meeting with other candidates during these same weeks. On January 6, 1979, in what turned out to be the last meeting between a beleaguered Shah and a defiantly nationalist Sadighi, the Shah talked of his meeting with Shapour Bakhtiyar, another National Front leader, praising the latter as "a brave nationalist man." Unlike Sadighi, Bakhtiyar had made it clear that he would accept the challenge of forming a cabinet only if the Shah agreed to *leave* the country. Clearly, for a distraught, angst-ridden Shah, who was by then taking six milligrams of chlorambucil as chemotherapy for his lymphoma, and at least ten milligrams of Valium a day to calm his jittery nerves, the idea of leaving Iran might have been music to his ears. Nevertheless, why the Shah decided to reject Sadighi's plans and opt instead for Bakhtiyar remains a mystery. Carter's *White House Diary* provides some clues when he reports that Sullivan insisted that the Shah should be forced to leave Iran, because only with such a departure would Bakhtiyar have a chance to survive.[93]

The Shah might have also changed his mind after the conversation he had with the British ambassador, Anthony Parsons. When the Shah described for Parsons the different potential candidates, the Ambassador was clearly not in favor of Sadighi. Parsons urged that Sadighi "would be well advised to consult the religious leaders in Qom," added that "unfortunately he is generally regarded as an atheist," and finally ventured that Khomeini was "bound to do his utmost to destroy a government led by Sadighi."[94]

On December 7, 1978, the White House announced that Valéry Giscard d'Estaing, the president of France, had invited President Jimmy Carter, German Chancellor Helmut Schmidt, and British Prime Minister James Callaghan to "personal and informal conversations on political matters and international developments of special interest to their mutual relations." The meetings were to be held on January 5 and 6, 1979, in the French West Indies island of Guadeloupe, one of the last vestiges of France's lapsed colonial grandeur. Each head of state would be accompanied by only one assistant.[95]

For the Shah and many of his supporters, this meeting has taken on mythic proportions. It was, they claim, the "watershed" moment when the decision to "get rid of the Shah" was finalized. Zbigniew Brzezinski was the assistant accompanying Carter; for the Shah, this should have been excellent news. He knew that Brzezinski was one of his most stalwart supporters. Just before departing for the meeting, Brzezinski told reporters that "the worsening situation in Iran was likely to figure prominently in the four leaders' discussions."[96] He added that "Carter will reiterate his support for the embattled Shah of Iran" and that he anticipated the other leaders to agree "with Carter's backing for the Shah."[97] Two days before the summit, Brzezinski suggested to Carter that he send an "emissary to Tehran after Guadeloupe, as a sign of US interest, and as the reflection of a common Western interest."[98]

There are apparently no minutes of the four leaders' meetings at the Hamak Hotel, on the southern coast of the Guadeloupe island of Grand Terre. They met "under [a] thatched roof, open-air cabana affair known locally as *ajoupa*—[the] Caribbean perhaps thirty yards away." More than 120 journalists traveled with the President, and somehow they knew that during the first three-hour meeting, Carter and Callaghan "did most of the talking."[99]

At the end of the summit, the four heads of state offered some remarks about the meeting. In none of the four brief comments was Iran even mentioned. More than once it was suggested that there were no decisions made during the meetings, but simply amicable discussion covering such topics as SALT, Cambodia, China, Russia, and Japan. The only leader who made what appears to be an allusion to Iran was Carter, who declared: "We discussed the potential trouble spots of the world, and we tried to capitalize upon the unique opportunity that one or several of us have to alleviate tension, to let the people of these regions find for themselves, with our assistance on occasion . . . a better quality of life and enhanced human rights."[100]

There are fascinating differences between "official" accounts of the meeting and what the leaders later remembered or wrote in their memoirs. Carter recalls "little support for the Shah" in the meeting with the leaders "unanimous in saying that the Shah ought to leave as soon as possible."[101] Other leaders' recollections of the meeting—particularly those of the French and German leaders—essentially repeated the same idea: the Shah was bereft of support and Khomeini was the sole, albeit less than desirable, alternative. In their recollections, however, it was in fact Carter who first suggested the idea of the Shah's departure.

The United States was monitoring Soviet reaction to the Guadeloupe Summit rather carefully; official Soviet commentary saw it as a reflection of "growing differences" within the capitalist world, and as yet another attempt by the big four to "coordinate a response to Japan and its rising might." A day before the conference, on January 5, the Soviet regime accused the United States of "political skullduggery" and of attempting "to change the course of events in Iran." From the tone of the Soviet reports, the skullduggery they expected was intended to keep the Shah in power, not undermine him.[102] Afterwards, the Soviets claimed that, from what they knew of the meeting, there had been no discussion of Iran.[103]

As noted, while Carter was in Guadeloupe, negotiations were going on in Iran for the formation of a government of national reconciliation. After his last meeting with the Shah, Sadighi declared his readiness to commence work immediately and said that he would wait for the Shah's decision. But the Shah decided he did not want Sadighi. He chose to appoint Bakhtiyar.

Carter received information about the new Bakhtiyar cabinet while still in Guadeloupe. It was clear to everyone that "the appointment of General Jam to War Ministry may be the key to gaining army support [for] the new government." Sadighi had made a Jam appointment one of his conditions for accepting the job of prime minister. The American report affirmed that Bakhtiyar and the Shah had both urged Jam—who had a "reputation for outstanding ability and integrity"[104]—to return from Europe, where he had been living since 1971.

Jam was known to have retained "significant contacts within the armed forces" and for having had several confrontations with the Shah—particularly during his tenure as chairman of the Joint Chiefs of Staff. He had complained that "no officer, in any capacity had independent authority." Jam had also lamented that all good officers had been purged. His own dismissal had come when, in response to some Iraqi provocation, he had ordered a few units of the Iranian army to the

Iraqi border. Who gave you permission to stick your nose in this? the Shah had demanded, adding menacingly, "in Iran no one is allowed to take this kind of liberty." After this humiliating encounter, Jam was relieved of his duties, forced to retire from the military, and sent to Spain as Iran's ambassador.[105]

The return of Jam proved a disaster. In his meeting with the Shah on January 3, he insisted that if he was to be effective as Minister of War, he needed to have all the constitutional powers afforded the ministry in its control of the military. The Shah "stubbornly insisted [on] not only retaining his role . . . of commander-in-chief . . . but also on controlling the military budget."[106] Disgusted, Jam left Iran; with him went the chance for the Bakhtiyar government to maintain some control of the military in the absence of the Shah. It took the military thirty-six days before it turned against the new Bakhtiyar government and tried to make its peace with the mullahs. The U.S. Embassy helped General Moghadam, the head of SAVAK, and General Abbas Garabaghi, chairman of the Joint Chiefs of Staff, to actively pursue the goal of making peace with the mullahs. In a "commanders meeting" that brought together the country's top military brass, one general, in a moment of candor, declared that the military was "melting like snow." As the Shah made last-minute plans to leave the country, he could exclaim with Shakespeare's Richard II: "O, that I were a mockery king of snow."[107]

Chapter 20

THE SHAH'S LAST RIDE

And my large kingdom for a little grave,
A little, little grave, an obscure grave...
Shakespeare, King Richard II, *3.3.154–155*

On the cold, slushy morning of January 16, 1979, Tehran awoke to a day of anxious anticipation. The city was once again awash with rumors. For years, rumor had become the tool of subversion. Censorship is not just the mother of metaphors, as Jorge Louis Borges suggests, but also begets rumors, a veritable tool in any opposition's arsenal in authoritarian regimes.

That day, the winds of change lurked in the air. For too long, the country had been suspended in the paralysis of a political stalemate. Neither the regime nor the opposition had the power to end the crisis. For a variety of reasons, a compromise was unreachable; something had to give. Historians tell us that a prolonged period of paralysis between conflicting forces usually gives rise to a Caesar, to a kind of Bonapartism. But in Iran, everyone expected the Shah to blink. A week earlier, right after the Guadeloupe meetings, U.S. Secretary of State Cyrus Vance had announced that "the Shah has said that he plans to leave Iran on vacation."[1] The announcement reflected the conclusion the British and American governments had reached about the Shah by early November 1978. The Guadeloupe conference of the top four Western powers in early January had only confirmed this decision. With both governments insisting that they would not support a military crackdown, with the opposition becoming more radical with every passing day, the Shah was politically dead.

In the past, too, the Shah had often blinked in times of crisis yet had somehow survived; but this time, his adversary, Ayatollah Khomeini, was a man of steely determination. He had emerged as the de facto leader of the amorphous democratic movement only by virtue of his unbending resolve and untarnished reputation, and he was keen to use any weakness in the Shah to overthrow the monarchy. Two days after the announcement of the Shah's intention to go "on vacation," Khomeini announced the formation of an Islamic Revolutionary Council. And as a harbinger of things to come, the composition of the council was—and remained—a secret. Eleven days after the beginning of the royal family's vacation, Ayatollah Khomeini "sent a personal message to US," that cleverly combined threats with promises of peaceful transition. He recommended "that in order to avert disaster, [the U.S.] advise the army and Bakhtiyar to stop intervening in Iranian political affairs." He concluded his message by "asserting his preference for solving the problem peacefully."[2] For several weeks before this message, he and his entourage in Paris and his allies in Tehran had been in touch with the American Embassy.

The Iranian people not only knew nothing about Khomeini's letter or about other extensive contacts between him and American officials in Paris or Tehran; they were also generally ignorant of Ayatollah Khomeini's real intentions. His fourteen years of exile had afforded him the unique luxury of having no track record of compromising with the regime. A sinecure tarnished one potential nationalist leader; a few lucrative contracts compromised the integrity of another; yet a third lost his gravitas when he was shown in a photograph prostrating himself before the King and Queen. Khomeini had lived in the relative safety of Najaf during the years when the Iraqi government, particularly under Saddam Hussein, was a fierce foe of Iran. There, Ayatollah Khomeini had issued one proclamation after another, attacking the Shah in increasingly virulent language. In the 1960s and 1970s, these radical pronouncements were often seen as the quixotic rants of an embittered, exiled foe of the regime. In 1978, however, he modulated his words about his intentions but remained steadfast in his uncompromising opposition to the Shah.

Of those who knew what those plans were, who knew the true mettle of Ayatollah Khomeini, some, like Ayatollah Shariat-Madari, were unwilling to fight him publicly. They saw him as a modern-day Savonarola whose piety was but a veneer for power-lust and who was dedicated to the idea of forcing the establishment of a new puritan Shiite society, with Khomeini as the absolute arbiter of truth. In the days before the revolution, these forces mostly chose silence. In the handful of cases in which they dared to speak, as Shapour Bakhtiyar did during his brief tenure as prime minister, their warnings were altogether lost in the cacophony of hysterical adulation for the coming revolution. Others, like Mehdi Bazorgan, kept silent in return for a place at the table of power. Like everyone else in the opposition, Bazorgan believed he could temper Ayatollah Khomeini's radicalism. Even the fact that in 1963 Khomeini had railed against women's right to vote and against land reform was conveniently forgotten. Selective public amnesia, prodded by a masterful public-relations campaign—including the audacious claim that his profile had appeared on the moon—made of him an ambiguous symbol, a tabula rasa, allowing each element of the radically disparate coalition against the Shah to see him not for what he was, but for what they dreamt he would be—for some, a pious reincarnation of Mossadeq; for others, a Kerensky who would pave the way for their planned Bolshevik revolution.

Iranian society and the American Embassy in Iran were not alone in this dangerous game of wishful self-delusion. Prominent Western intellectuals such as Michel Foucault saw Khomeini as a breath of fresh air after a century of intellectual regurgitation of the Enlightenment's "sterile" ideas. Not only was this an instance of Foucault's remarkable arrogance in making historic judgments about a society and religion he knew virtually nothing about, it also reflected the "progressive" Western intellectual's romantic weakness for any radical force that was anti-American or anti-Western.

In the absence of reasoned debate about Khomeini and his ideas, his Paris proclamations, all carefully crafted to fit the moment, became most people's only introduction to the man. Exercising remarkable discipline in Paris, he held the pose of a liberal. On that January 16, this political discipline was about to bear fruit.

At two o'clock in the afternoon in Iran, all ears turned to the radio. For that generation of Iranians, the two o'clock news had the regularity of the seasons; it was *the* anointed time for the news. In the Shah's days of power, the lead every day was invariably his deeds and words. After that came an account of the Queen's daily activities. Only then came the real news of the day. When Reza Qotbi, the Queen's closest confidante and relative, was appointed as the head of Iran National Radio and Television, one of his early innovations was to change the line-up of the news, allowing each day's real story to lead. Before long, he was forced to "reconsider," and the old anointed line-up was revived. One of the first signs that the Shah's power had genuinely declined came late in 1978 when he was no longer the lead on every day's news. But on that January day, the Shah was, not by fiat but by desert, the lead of the day.

At the Court, all that day, indeed all that week, life had taken on a frantic pace and a transient look. Furniture was covered with sheets; paintings were taken off the walls; boxes lay about. By January 14, five crates, enough to fill the second jet that was to accompany the Shah's official plane, had been packed with valuables and the personal belongings of the Shah and his family. Earlier, a small charter jet had taken Eliasi, one of the Shah's most trusted valets, to Geneva, where he reportedly deposited in banks the "most valuable papers" of the Shah. The charter flight was kept a strict secret.[3] What the valet took is not known. Every day, rumors of these and other transactions—like the alleged transfer of almost $2 billion by leading officials of the ancien régime, whose names, along with the amounts of their individual transfers, were published by a group claiming to be employees of the Central Bank of Iran—swept the city, disheartening the Shah's supporters and cementing the resolve of the opposition.

The Shah had been growing increasingly short-tempered and overtly anxious to leave Iran. What went through his mind, we may never fully learn. What we do know is that he felt "betrayed" not just by his people, but by his allies in the West. He felt he had been "misled by sycophants for years and that the people seemed to have rejected everything he had done for them."[4] In reality, twenty-five years of sycophancy in courtiers, his decided aversion to hearing the bitter truth, and his oft-repeated claim that he received reports from multiple sources had resulted in his near paralysis when faced with the reality of massive opposition to his rule. The unbreakable bond the Shah had always believed connected him to the people was torn asunder in his mind, and the sobering reality of the people's anger could no longer be ignored.

For at least sixteen years the Shah had moved closer to becoming the ultimate source for nearly all key decisions in the country. In 1965, the State Department had put together a list of the decisions that could only be made by him. The Shah, the report said,

> is not only king, he is *de facto* Prime Minister and is in operational command of the armed forces. He determines or approves all important governmental actions. No appointment to an important position in the bureaucracy is made without his approval. He personally directs the work of the internal security apparatus and controls the conduct of foreign affairs, including diplomatic assignments. No promotion in the armed forces from the rank of lieutenant up can be made without his explicit approval. Economic development proposals—whether to accept foreign credit or where to locate a particular factory—are referred to the Shah for decision. He determines how the universities are administered, who is to be prosecuted for corruption, the selection of parliamentary deputies, the degree to which opposition will be permitted, and what bill will pass the parliament.[5]

This incredible concentration of power was in place even before the 1970s, when the Shah's personal authoritarianism, and its accompanying cult of personality, reached a new height.

Amir Abbas Hoveyda has been rightly criticized for facilitating, indeed encouraging, this royal power grab. Now the Shah, the nerve center for all decisions, was beset with depression, indecision, and paralysis, and his indecision led to the immobilization of the entire system. Paralyzed by a potent combination of qualities in his character, the medications he had been taking, and the unexpected turns in his fortune, his mood grew increasingly volatile and unpredictable. One day he was full of verve and optimism, and the next day or hour he fell into a catatonic stupor.

Because of his regular meetings with the American and British ambassadors, we can map out his mood swings. One day, he was reluctant to meet with anyone, and if he gave an audience, he made it clear that he had little time or interest. The next day, he spent hours in meetings where he paid close attention to the advice offered by those he met. Hardly a day passed without some new suggestion by one of his loyal generals or one of the newly minted self-appointed royal advisors. Some saw terror and brute force as the remedy, while others saw concessions to the opposition as the solution. One group of generals offered a plan to use the air force and bomb the throngs of demonstrators in the cities of Qom and Tehran. There was the idea that the Shah should usurp the leadership of the revolution by hanging a few of his own supporters from the poles of electricity lines in city squares. As ludicrous as it might seem, the Shah, by arresting some of his most dedicated allies and generals, made a half-hearted attempt at this very idea. Finally, there were those who saw pity as a panacea, suggesting that the Shah should talk openly about his sickness and appeal to the Iranian people's sense of decency. "They would never throw out of the country a man dying of cancer," Zahedi said.

The Queen had several solutions of her own. Her plans were rooted in her desire to save the dynasty and protect her son's chance at the throne. As the Shah's mood and health deteriorated, not only did he become increasingly dependent on her presence and support, but more and more she and her coterie of advisors and friends took an active, if not determining, role in running the affairs of state. Eventually, she told the Shah that he should leave—as he seemed to be the focus of people's wrath—and allow her to stay "as a symbol of your presence." The Shah did not accept the offer, saying sardonically, "You don't have to be a Joan of Arc."[6] Hers was, of course, not the only idea the Shah did not accept. He rejected virtually all other suggestions as either infantile or incongruent with the real complexities of the world.

The Shah tended to take false comfort in conspiracy theories featuring an impotent, enfeebled "We" and an omnipotent "Other." Conspiracy theories had become the bane of Iranian politics in the nineteenth century, just at the time when opium also became the new rage. Both helped soothe souls humiliated by a sense of historic defeat—at the hands of the Russians, the West, Fate, and all the conspirators. The sort of power that conspirators are purported to have is nothing less than a secularized version of the omnipotence of a messiah or Mahdi. A people who have lost faith in their messiahs but have yet to reach genuine social mastery of their fate need conspiracy theories to assuage their anxieties and satisfy their existential human urge to have a narrative explanation—a history—of their lives and of what has befallen them. The Shah suffered from all the social sources of this malady; but his own experience, what he had witnessed during the humiliation of his father at the hands of the British in 1941, and finally, his own private demons, exacerbated the effects of this national proclivity.

During his last months in power, every major decision he made was arguably the worst possible choice. A partial explanation of his devastatingly wrong decisions was his flawed, conspiracy-laden analysis of the situation. In his attempts to "address" the purported international sources of the revolution, he consistently failed to address the real domestic sources of discontent. Often, the world made sense to him only in terms of a conspiracy. That was why his mood was in no small measure dependent on what he perceived to be the current level of support from the United States and Britain.

A few days after Black Friday, September 7, 1978, when the army had opened fire on demonstrators defying a curfew, he was in a meeting with a group of visitors from Europe. In the middle of the meeting, an aide informed him that President Carter wanted to talk with him on the phone. He left the group and went upstairs to a room where he could talk in private. The conversation lasted ten minutes, said his chief of protocol, Aslan Afshar, and "the Shah was brimming with laughter when he came out of the room. He spryly jumped down the stairs two at a time, and told me to immediately send a telegram to Carter. 'Write it in a warm tone and thank him for the call.' "[7] The sheer fact that Carter had called was for the Shah a sign of support and enough to improve his sagging morale. In retrospect, it is a remarkable fact that while Tehran was burning and Iran moved ever closer to the precipice of chaos, Carter was preoccupied with Camp David, and with convincing his guests, Begin and Sadat, to sign a peace agreement. To his credit, Sadat knew the importance of the situation in Iran and while at Camp David at least once convinced Carter to call the Shah and offer words of support.

While the Shah sought advice from both British and American governments, in reality he trusted neither. In late September 1978, during a meeting with Anthony Parsons, the British ambassador, he let it be known that he was "obviously worried that the Americans are plotting with the opposition."[8] More than once he articulated the same sentiment about the British to American and Iranian officials. Distrust of the Soviets was, of course, a constant pillar of his vision. Ultimately, when he felt that his attempts at "reconciliation" with his omnipotent foreign foes or allies had failed, he became despondent and anxious and unable to rule.

Documents from the British and American archives show that the main reason these countries began to search for an alternative to the Shah, and the reason they were so keen on getting him expeditiously out of the country, was their conclusion that he was no longer able, or willing, to lead. Until October 1978, it had been the policy of both governments to try to preserve the monarchy. At the same time, in this period, the two governments also repeatedly talked of the need to limit the Shah's power. All too often, the Shah showed signs of "complacency," "brooding," "depression." When in December of 1978 the Comte de Marenches, the head of the French secret police and an old friend of the Shah, arrived in Tehran to discuss with him whether the French government should renew Ayatollah Khomeini's visa, he came away convinced that the Shah's days were numbered. The Shah met the Comte in a dark room, wearing a pair of "dark large glasses." The Shah told the Comte that he preferred that the French government keep Ayatollah Khomeini in Paris. Otherwise, the Shah said, he would end up somewhere like Syria, closer to Iran. When the Comte de Marenches went back to Paris, he told French President Valéry Giscard d'Estaing, "C'est Louis XVI." The President responded, "alors, c'est la fin."[9] Less than four years earlier, a *New York Times* journalist had compared the Shah to the Sun King, Louis XIV. Now, he was being compared to the Louis who helped bring about the French Revolution.

Of those entrusted with the task of assessing the Shah's chances of survival, none was more important than George Ball, head of Carter's Iran task force. In early December 1978, he suggested that the United States should discreetly "open a disawoable [*sic*] channel of communication" with Khomeini and concluded in no uncertain terms that the days of the Shah as a potentate had ended, and that he could at best retain the throne as a figurehead. Iranians want, Ball concluded, "a government responsive to the people."[10]

Somehow, though the Shah never met with Ball, he knew through his contacts with Ambassador William Sullivan that the American government had for some time wanted him to leave the country. More than once while in exile the Shah complained about Sullivan's impolitic "hurry" to force him out of Iran. When Sullivan restlessly looked at his watch, the Shah understood it to mean that the hour for him to leave the country had arrived. Carter's *White House Diary* confirms Sullivan's insistence that any solution to the problem in Iran would depend on the Shah's speedy departure from the country. On the morning of January 16, the Shah met with only a handful of servants and valets. Of all who had been given a chance to accompany him on the new trip, few accepted the offer. In spite of the official pretense that he was leaving on a holiday for recuperation, everyone at the Court, and arguably most people in the country, knew that this was a one-way trip. In the past, accompanying the Shah on a royal jaunt was a privilege coveted by all in the Court. This time, those who went knew they courted the danger of permanent exile.

The Shah took a helicopter from the palace to the airport. Another helicopter took members of the entourage. As he sank into his seat, he pushed his "grief-stricken face against the window, and gazed at the city below, as if he wanted to capture for his mind every image."[11] At the airport, the Shah, ever attentive to protocol, paid careful attention to all who had taken the trouble to come for the official farewell ceremonies. At the same time, he was impatient, anxious to leave. He was agitated when he saw the gathered reporters. "Who asked them to come?" he asked his aides impatiently. As with much else that happened at the Court those days, nobody knew.

It was a tragic exercise in futility, a game where both sides knew the truth behind the public façade. Nonetheless, he told the gathered reporters that he was tired, that he was going away for a vacation and would return as soon as he had recovered. But the grimace on his pained face, the tears in his eyes, the vacuity of his gaze, ever wandering in the empty yonder, and his inability to look any of his well-wishers in the eye, all belied the official pretense of a healing holiday. One of the officers fell at the Shah's feet and asked for permission to save the throne with his life. The Shah, still looking beyond the man's anguished face, raised him to his feet, allowed him to kiss the proffered hand, and then moved past him. The Queen looked on, a fur hat on her head, anguish and compassion for her husband in her eyes. The picture capturing her look and his countenance became iconic of the moment.

General Garabaghi, by then the chairman of the Joint Chiefs, by law and custom normally entrusted with running the army in the Shah's absence, had been nervously trying to get the Shah to sign the normal constitutional decree that temporarily transferred to the general the powers of the commander in chief. In the past, such decrees had routinely been signed the night before the Shah's departure and sent to the general in charge. This time, no decree had come the night before, and even at the airport, the Shah seemed reluctant to sign the document. Eventually, after several beseeching looks and requests, the Shah finally beckoned to the nervous General, motioned to him to turn around and bend over, and on his half-bowed shoulders, haltingly went through the motions of signing the decree. When the General asked whether the Shah had any last-minute orders, he dismissed the question with a shrug of his shoulders and, in a barely audible voice said, "Do what you think is right. I have nothing to say."

Perhaps the Shah knew that the day before, on the afternoon of January 15, 1979, Garabaghi had agreed to meet with opposition leaders Ayatollah

Mohammad Beheshti and Mehdi Bazorgan.[12] He must have known that, since late December General Gast (the MAAG chief in Tehran) and Huyser had been working behind the scenes to facilitate meetings between military commanders and Khomeini allies.[13] He must have heard that General Reza Moghadam, the last head of SAVAK—traditionally the most reliable pillar of support for the monarchy—"had taken out of the American hands" the business of bringing the armed forces and Khomeini supporters to an amicable truce. Moghadam was one of the many generals and allies of the Shah who were trying to arrive at a "private pact" with the Khomeini forces. And finally the Shah knew that Garabaghi had been a protégé of General Fardust, the childhood friend who now stood accused of complicity with the Shah's enemies. In the Shah's famous interview with David Frost in January 1980, when he was asked about the allegation that Garabaghi and Hussein Fardust had betrayed him and had been secretly working with the clerics long before his fall, he responded that their fate was a "tragedy only [a] Homer and Shakespeare could describe." He added that in his "inner heart" he hoped that the stories of conspiracies hatched by the two generals were untrue. They would be "so vile, so disquieting" if they were true.[14] Of the two, only Garabaghi was at the airport. By then, Fardust spent his afternoons in a private club, playing cards with the dwindling number of patrons who still frequented the once-bustling place of power and status.

The Shah arrived at the Royal Pavilion at the airport before Bakhtiyar, the prime minister–designate, who was at the Majlis, waiting for a vote of confidence. For Bakhtiyar, these constitutional formalities were the foundation for his fragile claim to legitimacy. To everyone else, they seemed like rearranging deck chairs on the sinking *Titanic*. The Shah, anxious to leave, asked his aides to call Bakhtiyar and find out what had delayed his arrival. But striking employees had disconnected the phones at the Royal Pavilion. Eventually, the army's wireless connection was used, and to the Shah's relief, it was learned that the newly confirmed Prime Minister was on his way.[15] Although Bakhtiyar had fought against the Shah for more than three decades, when he finally arrived, the sad solemnity of the moment, or perhaps the bereft countenance of the Shah, brought tears to Bakhtiyar's eyes. The Shah shook his head, and said, "I hope you will succeed. I give Iran into your care, yours and God's."[16]

Bakhtiyar and General Badrei, the commander of the Imperial Guards, followed the Queen and the Shah onto the plane. Neither man would survive the eventual terror of the impending revolution. Inside the plane, both men displayed due deference to the King, bade him a formal farewell, and left. The Shah, teary-eyed, went to the cockpit and piloted the plane during takeoff and for the first hour of the flight. According to the chief of his security detail, the Shah's decision to pilot the plane that day was not based solely on his passion for flying: "He was worried they might conspire to take him somewhere other than the planned destination."[17] As it turned out, this time the Shah's fears were well founded: within weeks, the flight's chief pilot, Captain Moezzi, revealed that he had joined the opposition before this last trip.

Initial plans had called for the Shah to go to the United States, but a few days before departure, he received a call from President Carter, asking him to stop over in Egypt to consult with President Sadat and President Ford on the Camp David Accords and then head for the United States. Visas for him and his entourage, he was told, would be awaiting them in Egypt. In the meantime, in the United States, the State Department had asked Walter Annenberg, the former ambassador to Great Britain, to "receive the Shah and a party of up to 15 and put them up through the first week of February" at his estate in Palm Springs. The contingency plan called for the Shah to move later to another safe location, "possibly with Rockefellers."[18]

After his decision to leave the country had been made, the Shah told Aslan Afshar to call President Sadat's office and find out what the best time would be for the royal plane to arrive in Egypt. He was informed, much to his dismay, that phone connections to Egypt had also been cut by striking employees. The American Embassy in Tehran allowed the use of its special lines to contact Sadat's office. It was agreed that the Shah would leave Tehran on the afternoon of January 16.

Unbeknownst to the Shah, a number of other countries had also been contacted about offering him a visa or asylum, and virtually all had said no. Sometimes the countries offered political reasons for their refusal, and other times their answers had the crass reality of mercantilist truth. Germany, for example, replied that they could not offer the Shah asylum or support "by reason of the large German investments in Iran and the 13,000 Germans" who were working there on the eve of the revolution.[19] At that point, Egypt and America were the only two countries willing to offer the royal family a place to stay.

No sooner had the Shah's plane left Tehran than *Keyhan*, Tehran's most popular daily at the time, issued a special edition with the entire top fold of the paper covered with two words: "Shah Left." Ironically, it was the Shah's "seed money" that had launched *Keyhan* thirty-six years earlier. He had wanted a pro-monarchy publication, but by 1979, the paper's de facto editor was Rahman Hatefi, one of the top leaders of the underground Tudeh Party in Iran. Under his leadership, the paper had on its staff a whole array of writers and journalists opposed to the regime who used every opportunity to promote their ideas and ideology.

The news of the Shah's departure rapidly spread throughout the capital. There was an air of gaiety and celebration in the air. Not just in Tehran, but in many provincial capitals, there were "mass demonstrators"[20] celebrating the Shah's departure. In a surprisingly well-managed "spontaneous outpouring" of exuberance, throngs of people took to the streets, and there were celebrations well into the night. The air of revelry began to taper off early the next morning in overcast Tehran. While the city was brimming with anxious excitement, doors to the expansive U.S. Embassy compound were locked, with no sign of the American flag anywhere. The embassy reported "a few threats to foreigners," but everywhere American citizens were spared any threat or actual attack.

Revolutions invariably have an element of the carnival about them. They are a country's moment of cathartic celebration. In their early hours of jubilant celebration, fears, constraints, and the Apollonian logic of the quotidian give place to the spirit of Dionysian excess, of make-believe egalitarianism, of shared community and suspension of rancorous rifts. That day, Tehran experienced its revolutionary carnival. As people danced in the streets, cars drove around aimlessly with many of their inhabitants braving the cold and hanging out of the cars like human flags. The police and the military seemed to have suddenly melted into the air. Self-declared lords of misrule distributed free candy to passing cars and demanded that drivers turn on their lights and blow their horns. The normal sounds of the city's hustle and bustle were drowned in the collective blaring of car horns.

Bands of bearded vigilantes, which had gradually become a constant staple of every large gathering in Tehran, watched in quiet disapproval. Within a year, their mores would become the law of the land, and they would exact a heavy price on the population for their moments of "heathenish" joy. It took only days to realize that beneath the veneer of the "spontaneous" but orderly popular demonstrations, there was an embryonic force that soon came to be called the "Committee"—local militia-cum-gangs-cum-revolutionaries—based in local mosques, led by the clergy of those mosques, increasingly armed, and increasingly ideological. As the royal army and police melted away, these committees took over their functions.

There was, in contrast, little joy aboard *Shahbaz,* the Boeing that had been designed as the royal plane. After piloting the plane for over an hour, the Shah quickly moved past the dozen seats for guards and guests and headed for the royal compartment. It consisted of a sitting area, a conference table, a bedroom, and a bathroom. Dr. Lucy Pirnia, a friend of the Queen; Kiumars Jahanbini and Yazdan Navisi, respectively the Shah's and the Queen's bodyguards; Aslan Afshar, the de facto chief of protocol for the Shah; Mahmoud Eliasi, special valet for the Shah; Ali Kabiri, for many years the chef of the Court; and finally, the man responsible for minding the royal dogs—Beno, the Shah's big German Shepherd, and Catsu, the Queen's puppy—were, aside from the crew, the only people on the plane. Egypt was their destination.

By then the Shah was hungry and asked for something to eat. But the airport's catering department had refused to supply the royal plane with food. "Let them make their own sandwiches," the catering director had derisively declared. Moreover, the crystal glasses and the chinaware usually used on the plane had all been pilfered. As it happened, Kabiri, perhaps in anticipation of problems at the airport, had prepared some food. Some passengers remember a pot full of rice and *geyme,* one of the Shah's favorite dishes, while others remember *bagali polow*—rice and fawa beans.[21] Using makeshift plates and utensils, the Shah and the rest of the passengers were finally fed. A somber silence was in the air, and there was little appetite among the entourage.

After about an hour, Jahanbini was called to the back of the plane, where the Shah and the Queen had settled. As he walked through the door, he saw the Shah, his right hand cushioning his reclining head, lying down on the couch. He had taken off his jacket and tie; his red, slightly inflamed eyes betrayed the long anguished hours he had spent awake. Without moving his head, the Shah raised his eyes and asked, "What do you people think of our decision to leave?" By then Jahanbini had been serving the Shah for almost a quarter of a century and, by his own admission, this "was the first time His Majesty was asking my views on something."[22] At the same time, Jahanbini had noticed the Shah's gradual decline into a state where he distrusted everyone. He had been surprised to learn, for example, that the Shah had ordered the generals in charge of the air force base in Tehran to henceforth heed only orders coming through Eliasi, the Shah's valet, about who could leave Iran. In other words, the Shah distrusted not only the civilians serving him in the Court, but many in the military hierarchy. In the past, he had been obsessive about maintaining ranks in the military, and keeping them strictly walled off from any civilian contact. Now he was asking generals to take orders from a valet.[23] With every passing day, long-established hierarchies and habits had begun to collapse, and in the chaos that ensued, forces of change found more and more room to maneuver.

With this context in mind, Jahanbini assumed that the Shah's question was part of an attempt to see whether the members of the royal entourage were dependable. He responded, quickly and categorically, "Your Majesty, I and your other servants have total belief in the wisdom of Your Majesty's every decision. Everyone is completely convinced of the wisdom of your decision to leave." Remembering the conversation a quarter of a century later, Jahanbini added wistfully, "and I was not lying. We all thought the Shah had something up his sleeve." Here again, the August 1953 events would haunt the Shah and his supporters: as the Americans had helped bring the Shah back to power then, they must have a similar plan this time, too. The royalists assumed the Americans were not going to leave the fate of Iran in the untested hands of mullahs, or worst yet, in the hands of Communists. What they did not know was that by then, Ambassador Sullivan had concluded that doing another August 1953 was not in the interests of the United States.

Some of the generals who remained loyal to the Shah were obviously worried about the future of a country run by Khomeini, while others might well have been banking on another August 1953, when those who remained loyal to the Shah had been amply rewarded when he was restored to power. One of the generals who paid a heavy price for such loyalty to the Shah in 1979 was Ali Neshat.

Before leaving Iran, the Shah had entrusted General Neshat with a sensitive mission. By then, all the documents in the Shah's office at the Court (*Daftar-e Maksous*, or the Special Office) had been removed to a basement in the Sa'ad Abad Palace. The most sensitive documents had either been sent out separately with Eliasi on the chartered plane or went with the Shah when he left Iran.[24] More than once, in his daily journals, Assadollah Alam cryptically refers to "documents so sensitive" that he dared not even mention their topic. They were kept in a safe in the Shah's office. What happened to those documents, and what they contained, remains unknown. They could have been part of what Eliasi took to Switzerland. But there were also thousands of pages of documents dealing with the affairs of the state or of the royal family. They were all placed in the basement of the palace before the Shah left. General Neshat, commander of the Imperial Guard, was entrusted with the task of burning them the moment the Shah left the country. For the last decade of the Shah's rule, under the legendary management of Nasrollah Moinian, the office had been known for its exemplary efficiency. By the mid-1970s, much of its work was computerized. Every letter was stamped when it was received. Another stamp indicated the day and the hour the Shah read or was informed of its content. A separate box registered what the Shah had ordered. In more sensitive cases, the Shah read the reports himself, making comments or issuing orders in the margin, always brisk and brief, sometimes in a purple pencil, sometimes in red. Sometimes he even marked the file in which the document should be placed. In the days after the royal family's departure, General Neshat made a bonfire in the gardens of the palace and burnt all of the documents. Rumors continue to persist that copies of all of these documents exist somewhere outside Iran. The Islamic Republic has published so far some 600 volumes of documents from SAVAK and other governmental offices, but much of what they have published has been devoid of serious substance. Nearly nothing has been published, for example, about the Shah's fortune. Moreover, the published documents have clearly been handpicked to serve the ideological purpose of demonizing the Shah and his regime. General Neshat was executed by the Islamic Republic a few weeks after the Shah's departure and the burning of the documents.

Before the Shah left Iran, the constitutionally mandated Regency Council was created ostensibly to manage the affairs of the state during his temporary absence. The first choice for the job had been Sadighi but he refused the offer, saying that since he had been opposed to the idea of the Shah leaving the country, he couldn't head a regency that would rule in his absence. The man eventually chosen to head that council, Seyyed Jalal Tehrani, seemed ill-fitted to the sensitive task. Tehrani was famously ill-tempered and self-centered, more of a scholar than a statesman. Shortly after arriving in Paris to meet with Ayatollah Khomeini, he announced that he was resigning from the council. His letter of resignation—or, more accurately, his statement of recantation—was surprisingly redolent of Islamic jargon and Shiite piety. He wrote that, in light of "public opinion and the view of His Eminence Grand Ayatollah Khomeini, May God extend his bounty, that the said Council is illegal,"[25] he was resigning from his post. Tehrani was known as a man of much, albeit esoteric, erudition, a man fascinated by astrolabes and medieval astrologers. His support for the Shah had always been somewhat doubtful, and the fact that he was chosen for the critical job of heading the Regency Council is yet another example of the strangely inexplicable decisions made by the Shah during his last months in Iran. In his memoirs, Bakhtiyar intimates that it was the Shah who suggested making Tehrani the head of the council. The reason was apparently his known close ties to the clergy, particularly to Ayatollah Khomeini.[26] It has been rumored that Tehrani was blackmailed into tendering his resignation after Khomeini supporters showed him photos they had of him in a compromising situation.[27]

The Shah and his family stayed in Egypt briefly. The meeting with President Ford to discuss Camp David—promised by President Carter before the Shah left Iran—never took place.[28] Sadat went out of his way to make the Shah feel not just safe but royal.

After a week, the royal family set out for Morocco, but it was only a few weeks before the Shah—much to his dismay and disbelief—was told he must leave the country. King Hassan was under pressure from Moroccan religious circles to get rid of him. Some in the Moroccan royal family had been opposed to the idea of allowing the Shah to visit from the beginning. Moreover, aside from the French intelligence agency's warning that the Moroccan monarch would face serious opposition from his domestic foes and critics, and the concern that the Shah's presence would overshadow the proceedings of an upcoming Islamic conference in Morocco, there was, in early February, the effort of the new Iranian regime to file extradition papers "with the Moroccan government for the return of the Shah."[29] This was the first legal step by Ayatollah Khomeini to demand the return of the Shah to Iran. Even if there was no realistic chance or legal ground for ever convincing Morocco or other countries to send the Shah back to Iran, these pressures, along with regular threats by Islamic regime radicals to send terrorist teams to kill him, made life more and more difficult for the royal couple. Khomeini obviously believed that the more the Shah was isolated and his pariah status underscored, the more royalists in Iran would be disheartened. He used the same argument when he ordered speedy the trials and executions of members of the ancien régime. Ayatollah Khomeini was known for holding grudges and for exacting revenge on those who had crossed him. He therefore spared no effort to pressure, embarrass, frighten, threaten, and isolate the Shah in exile. These efforts, some legal, some obviously illegal, continued until the Shah's last days.

Few things underscored Khomeini's success and the Shah's pariah status as much as the fact that, until a few hours before the time he was ordered to leave Morocco, his next destination was not clear. No country was willing to provide the Shah even a visiting visa, let alone asylum.

And then, shortly before his departure from Morocco at the end of March, the government of the Bahamas agreed to give the Shah and his family a temporary tourist visa. While in the Bahamas, on May 6, the Shah met with the U.S. Ambassador, who was carrying a message from President Carter. Earlier, the Shah had offered to delay his U.S. arrival to a time when it would not "create inconveniences for the US." Moreover, he wanted to make sure that his children would be able to go to school in America. Carter wanted the Shah to know that "his understanding of the very difficult situation" that his journey to the United States would create both for the United States and for the Shah was much appreciated, and that when "conditions are more settled," they could return to the question of his journey to the United States. In Morocco the Shah had been told that, should he settle in America, both his life and his fortune would be consumed by lawsuits. As for the children, Carter wanted the Shah to know that they would of course be welcome to "pursue their education," provided that in such a case "specific security arrangements for them could be made with private security services."[30]

In the Bahamas, the Shah received another piece of disappointing news. Since mid-February, he had been using Alan Hart, a British journalist, to sound out the British government about the possibility of settling in England, where he already owned a large estate. Hart had also been chosen to write a book about the Pahlavi dynasty. Through Hart, the Shah let it be known that settling in Britain would be "his first choice." He promised not to bring a large security detail and to lead "for a year or two a completely secluded life." He stipulated that there were "no loyal military officers in Iran with whom he could communicate." He guaranteed to "abstain from all political activity." He indicated that he did not want to go to the United States; not only did he not like the American way of life, but he thought the United States "bore an especially heavy responsibility" for "the downfall of the Pahlavi regime."[31]

Although the ruling Labour Party had rejected the Shah's request on grounds that giving him safe harbor might jeopardize "UK's future relationship with Iran," Margaret Thatcher had promised that, if she were elected prime minister, she would certainly give the Shah asylum. When she did win the election in May,

British Intelligence, the Foreign Ministry, and other government offices immediately warned her against the wisdom of allowing the Shah into Great Britain. Not only would British interests be jeopardized, she was told, but British diplomats might be taken hostage if the Shah was given asylum in England. Commercial calculations or political caution cannot fully explain why big powers like the United States and Britain were so unwilling to cross the new regime, and why they were even willing to allow clerics in Tehran a de facto veto power over who received a visa to enter the United States or Britain.

In May 1979, Sir Denis Wright was sent to the Bahamas to give the Shah the bad news that he was not welcome in Britain. Wright was initially reluctant to accept the mission. He was by then on the board of Shell Oil, and he did not, in his words, want his involvement to become public knowledge, cause the wrath of the new regime, and endanger Shell Oil company interests. He did not, he said, "want the trip to jeopardize [my] position," Moreover, he had long ago planned a fishing trip and agreed to go only if the timing could be arranged so as not to disrupt his plans.

Eventually, on May 20, 1979, traveling under the assumed name of Edward, and "wearing dark glasses," Wright arrived in the Bahamas and met with the Shah. After some reminiscing about the past, the Shah, according to Wright, "received the bad news with magnanimity."[32] Moreover, the Shah indicated that he "accepts but does not understand" the British government's decision. At the same time, his pride forced him to insist that "we had not asked for asylum."[33] With Britain no longer willing to let him in, and with his visa for the Bahamas expiring, the Shah was once again in need of a country willing to give him a temporary abode. After much cajoling and pressure, particularly from the United States, Mexico finally agreed to issue him and his family a visa.

Throughout the summer, pressure on Carter to allow the Shah into the United States continued. He grew so frustrated with the ceaseless flow of letters, messages, and implied and explicit threats—like Henry Kissinger's threat that he would withhold his support of an agreement with the Soviet Union unless Carter caved on the Shah—that finally one day, he snapped, and told his National Security Advisor, "Fuck the Shah,"[34] and asked him to go on to other issues.

With every passing day, the Shah's health deteriorated. He lost thirty pounds, and he looked jaundiced and emaciated. Mexican physicians were, like almost everyone else, kept in the dark about the Shah's real illness. While the French doctors traveled from Paris and "surreptitiously administered chemotherapy," the Mexican physicians began to treat him for malaria.[35] None of the many physicians—French, Austrian, American, Mexican, Panamanian, and Egyptian amongst them—who treated the Shah "knew his entire story." From some, his diagnosis of cancer was hidden; others were denied the information that, at the age of eighty-seven, his mother had been "found to have the same type of cancer he had."[36] Not only did his health and his chances of recovery suffer from this game of stealth and deception, but ultimately the Carter administration, and the U.S. government, paid a heavy price for it. Would the Islamic regime have been as paranoid about the Shah's travel to the United States if, by the time of his travel to New York, the story of his cancer had been an established fact? As it was, the worse his health became, the more pressure there was on Carter to let the Shah in; the President was assured that the only place the Shah could receive adequate care for his cancer was in the United States.

On September 28, 1979, the State Department was informed by David Rockefeller's office that "the Shah was ill in Mexico and that Rockefeller had sent his personal physician to examine" him and that, before long, this would be followed by a request that he be admitted to the United States for health reasons and on humanitarian grounds.[37] Agencies in the U.S. government, from the CIA to the State Department, began to think about the possible ramifications of such a move. The Iran Desk at the State Department decided that "the US should make no move toward admitting the Shah until we have obtained and tested a new and substantially more effective guard force for the Embassy [in Iran]."[38]

It is not clear to what extent Rockefeller's interest in the matter was based on his extensive financial dealings with the Shah and the royal family. He had been for years the Shah's private banker and the designated executor of his will. In 1978, his Chase Manhattan Bank had decided to give Iran a loan of $500 million even though the Iranian attorneys the bank had retained to check into the legality of this transaction had advised against making the loan. After the revolution, the new Iranian regime began making substantial withdrawals from Iran's Chase Manhattan account. The combination of these facts gave rise to all kinds of conspiracy theories.[39]

According to one theory, the Rockefellers and their allies, like Kissinger, pressed for the Shah's entry into the United States, "knowing that that act would precipitate violence in Iran and make a freeze [of Iran's assets] inevitable. Such a freeze [would] make a repayment of the dubious loan possible." The Chase theory became so "prevalent in the press" that in July 1981, the Senate Committee on Banking, Finance, and Urban Affairs prepared a report "that directly and ineffectively attempted to deny the Chase Manhattan thesis."[40] It remains a fact that Chase Manhattan was indeed "near the top of the list" of American banks "who were able to turn a profit on the hostage crisis."[41] Regardless of the motivation, there is also no doubt that what precipitated the crisis was the reluctant decision by the Carter administration to allow the Shah into the United States.

A long litany of prominent Americans had by then also argued that the Shah must be allowed in, at least on humanitarian grounds. His health had deteriorated in Mexico, and he needed another operation, which, his supporters argued, could only be safely performed in the United States. But the Carter administration continued to resist these demands. Initially, the Shah had also been against the idea of going to the United States. When the Queen suggested such a trip, the Shah shouted at her and the other aide who had suggested the idea, "I am not wanted there and I am not welcome. Forget it." The State Department conducted its own examination of the Shah by dispatching its medical director to visit him. He found the Shah to have "enlarged neck glands, increasing abdominal distress, as well as [being] deeply jaundice[d]. There is no doubt that he has malignant lymphoma which is escaping standard chemotherapy." He concluded that "highly technical studies are needed" to diagnose, grade, and analyze his lymphoma. These studies, he concluded, "cannot be carried out by any of the medical facilities in Mexico."[42] Years later, Dr. Benjamin Kean, a key member of the Shah's medical team, disagreed with this assessment—an assessment, incidentally, central to the decision to allow the Shah into the United States—saying that "he [Kean] knew the sophisticated equipment needed for the Shah's diagnosis and treatment could be found in Mexico."[43]

Whether the conclusion by the State Department's medical director was political or purely medical, the pressure on the Carter administration to allow the Shah into the United States was incessant. Senator Charles Percy of Illinois, for example, long known as an ally of the Pahlavi regime,[44] wrote to Secretary of State Vance on October 2, 1979, asking why the United States "can offer haven on quick notice to members of the [Soviet Union's] Bolshoi, taking into account all the implications of this," but could not "work something out for the Shah."[45]

Indeed, as a result of this caution, the United States went out of its way to convince the new Islamic regime that there was no conspiracy involved in giving the Shah a visa. On October 21, the U.S. chargé d'affaires met with Mehdi Bazorgan, the prime minister of the Islamic regime, and told him of the Shah's serious medical condition. If the Shah is sick, Bazorgan asked, why does he not go to Europe? In a later meeting, Iranian officials demanded that their own physicians examine the Shah. The United States agreed, but the Shah would not permit regime physicians to examine him. To break the impasse, the State Department tried to arrange a meeting between the Shah's physicians and the Iranian medical team, but for reasons that are not clear, even "that arrangement never worked out."[46]

The day after the meeting with the Prime Minister, U.S. embassy staff in Tehran met again with Iranian officials—this time with Foreign Minister Ebrahim Yazdi, who repeated the regime's demand that the Shah be visited by a group of Iranian physicians. Moreover, he wanted to make sure that the United States would abide by the agreement to not only prohibit the Shah from any political activity in the United States, but to extend the ban to the Queen as well. Yazdi said the

Iranian government now regarded her "as currently more politically involved than the Shah, citing...an interview with unspecified French periodical."[47]

Not long after that meeting in Tehran, in the evening of October 22, 1979, a private Gulfstream aircraft landed at LaGuardia Airport, carrying the Shah, the Queen, and a small coterie of aides. Carter's decision to issue the Shah a visa had been a difficult one. In his own words, "I was told the Shah was desperately ill, at the point of death," and that New York was the only place where he could get the requisite medical attention. Moreover, Carter believed that "Iranian officials had promised to protect" American diplomats in the event that the Shah was allowed to visit the United States for medical reasons.[48] The Shah arrived in New York and was taken directly to New York Hospital.

The experience must have created in the Shah a "riot of emotions." He was taken to the same room he had used in 1955 when, in his salad days, he had visited the hospital with Soraya. He had been worried about fertility then; now mortality was on his mind. Both times the hospital had to keep the visit "private." This time, the White House had tried to keep the Shah's arrival secret and prevent it from becoming a media circus. Robert Armao, who had been assigned by David Rockefeller to be the Shah's special assistant in exile, "decided for security reasons, not to register the Shah in the Shah's own name," but then, for reasons hard to fathom, he decided to use the name of David Newsome, undersecretary of state for political affairs. Newsome was understandably not amused, particularly after the *New York Times* broke the story.[49] The ramifications of this eventually forced the resignation of the hospital's vice president for public affairs, who believed "the public had a right to know the entire medical story to justify the Shah's admission to the US."[50]

As the Shah was settling into his hospital room in New York, a group of young students held a meeting in a small house in one of Tehran's sprawling suburbs. They represented all the major universities in Tehran. Two delegates from each institution had come to represent their universities' most zealous Islamic students. They were meeting to plan a response to the U.S. decision to allow the Shah into the United States, and they agreed to take over the American Embassy in Tehran. Amongst those present in the first plenary meeting was a young man from a third-tier technical university called Elm-o Sanat (Science and Technology); his name was Mahmoud Ahmadinejad. He participated only in the first plenary meeting and stopped attending after he realized they were not also going to take over the Soviet Embassy. The rest of the students completed their plans and, to the shock of the Carter administration and the world, on November 4, 1979, they climbed the walls of the American Embassy and took diplomats and other staff hostage. Six American diplomats who happened to be outside the embassy compound at the time took refuge in the Canadian Embassy and were eventually whisked out of the country under assumed names in an operation masterminded by the CIA. Before long, Ayatollah Khomeini expressed his support for the occupation of the embassy, and so began the 444-day ordeal of the hostage crisis. The students' main demand was the return of the Shah.

Aside from his own medical problems and his concern about the hostage crisis, the Shah's stay at the hospital was uncomfortable for a variety of other reasons. His therapy, for example, required that on more than one occasion, he be taken from his room in New York Hospital to the Memorial Sloan-Kettering Cancer center across the street. For security reasons, the Shah, always in the dark of the early morning hours, was wheeled through the tunnel that connects the two buildings. He sat under a blanket, surrounded by a handful of hospital staff and security men, and was then carried through the chilly caverns beneath the New York streets—a scene reminiscent of Homer's Hades. Moreover, although he was given an exclusive suite of rooms on the seventh floor, he could still hear the shouts of demonstrators congregating in front of the hospital, some demanding his extradition, others his execution. He often watched the news, and there too he was more than once forced to hear criticism of his rule, of SAVAK's brutality, and of his family's corruption. He listened to Anthony Parsons—for the last years of his rule the British ambassador to Iran and now Britain's ambassador to the UN—lambaste him at a meeting of the UN. "Listen to that son of a bitch," the Shah said in a halting voice to Ardeshir Zahedi, who was in the room at the time.[51] Furthermore, he was sure his room was bugged. The most sensitive messages he would jot down on a yellow writing pad he kept by his bed. We cannot be sure if his fear was entirely justified, but we do know that, on the orders of President Carter, his phone was indeed bugged.[52]

On November 30, it was decided that the Shah could leave the hospital. He had already declared that his preferred destination would be Mexico, where he had lived before, and where the President had invited him back. But on the morning of November 30, much to his consternation, he was informed that he was no longer welcome in Mexico. The ostensible reason given was that "his presence is becoming a threat to [their] national interest." The Mexicans were worried about their diplomats being taken hostage, they said.[53] Queen Farah offers a different reason, suggesting that Fidel Castro had told the Mexican President that "Cuba would vote for his country's entry into the Security Council of the United Nations on condition that he refused to give" the Shah a refuge.[54] Either way, the Shah was cornered. Robert Armao contacted the State Department and said, "His Imperial Majesty was officially throwing himself at the administration's mercy." Until then, the Shah had tried to avoid making any official requests of the United States. He felt betrayed by them, but now he was out of options.[55]

As the Shah lay sick in bed, the Carter administration was of two minds about what to do with him. With every passing day, the hostage crisis took on more significance in Carter's re-election bid. Some in the administration favored pushing the Shah out of the United States as expeditiously as possible. Others, like Brzezinski, opposed the move, saying it would "compromise America's national honor" and amount to "giving into a student mob."

Initially, Carter sided with those opposed to pushing the Shah out. But on November 14, he changed his mind again, this time appointing Vice President Walter Mondale as the "point-man on the effort to get the Shah out of the US as soon as possible."[56]

When Lloyd Cutler, Carter's emissary, went to see the Shah in the hospital to talk about his departure, he told him that there were only three countries willing to take him—South Africa, Paraguay, and Egypt. The United States was against the idea of the Shah's going to Egypt, as it might threaten Sadat's position. The Shah was adamantly against going to either of the other two countries. He was also told that while he was in the United States, he couldn't go to his twin sister's home on Beekman Place in Manhattan. A new stalemate had developed. The Shah was told he was leaving the hospital without knowing where he might seek asylum—or even where he might stay while his visa problems were resolved.

Even something as simple as taking the Shah out of the hospital was a security nightmare—anti-Shah demonstrators and the paparazzi were on a twenty-four-hour vigil outside. On the night of the transfer, they moved the Shah "through an underground tunnel to the Sloan-Kettering Institute" to "an unwatched exit onto First Avenue."[57] From there the Shah's entourage went to LaGuardia and boarded a U.S. Air Force DC jet, which flew them to Lackland Air Force Base in Texas.

From the plane, the royal couple was taken to the base hospital and given two rooms in the psychiatric ward. The Shah was "put in a room with a walled-up window," and the Queen was "taken to an adjoining room where there was no door handle on the inside but a microphone on the ceiling."[58] Both rooms had all the trappings of a prison. Without saying a word, the Shah moved to the bed, pulled a sheet over his head, and lay down.[59] He was exhausted, too tired even to object. But his wife was not. Are we prisoners, are they trying to hand us over to the mullahs? she asked angrily. She even wondered whether "the whole incredible setup was put in place just to drive us mad."[60] Camp commanders reminded her that these were the safest rooms they could find, and they talked about the safety concerns of a place like Lackland, where students could freely come and go, and promised to move them to better facilities as soon as possible. Three hours later, the Shah and his wife were moved to a small three-room bungalow that was usually set aside for visiting officers.[61]

The Shah spent two weeks at the base. Once they put their unpleasant arrival behind them, the Shah cheered up, particularly when he could swap "aviation experiences with some of the officers." But from the beginning, it was clear that Lackland was a temporary point of transit. The Shah still needed an asylum, and only three countries were willing to give it to him. While on the base, the Shah heard the news that his nephew, Prince Shahriar, had been assassinated in Paris on December 7. He had been an officer in the Iranian navy and was the only member of the royal family who had dedicated himself to continuing the fight against the clerical regime. The death put the Shah into "a mood of silent despair." Princess Ashraf, Shahriar's mother, joined him at the base, only adding to his grief. Further increasing his anguish was the fact that, while at Lackland, the Shah was informed that South Africa had withdrawn its offer of asylum.[62]

In retrospect, although a 2008 survey by *The Times*[63] identified the Shah as one of the world's ten "most decadent dictators"—along with such exiled figures as Mobutu, Idi Amin, and Ferdinand Marcos—and in spite of the fact that, even in the harshest assessment of his critics, his decadence and crimes paled in comparison to a Mobutu or an Idi Amin, no other member of this cohort of infamy was treated with as much contempt and derision as the Shah. These others were all given safe asylums, where they lived and enjoyed the "fruits" of their decadent rule. The Shah, however, was subjected to every form of indignity and embarrassment imaginable at the time. Ayatollah Khomeini's role in this sad saga is explained by his penchant for revenge, and his enmity toward the Shah. What is more difficult to fathom is the international chorus that accompanied this bloodlust. A dying man, "un-kinged" and hounded by terrorists, was denied even the dignity of a quiet corner to die.

The stalemate was finally broken on December 12, when Hamilton Jordan, Carter's chief of staff, flew to Texas and gave the Shah the good news that Panama had agreed to offer the Shah its "hospitality." Though physicians had concluded that the Shah needed another operation, he decided to leave the United States as soon as possible and "do the operation later, in Panama."[64] More than once, he told his American interlocutors that he would abide by any decision they made about his time of departure and that he would do anything he could to expedite the release of the American hostages. He invariably added that he believed that no concessions would bring about a release of the hostages. The regime in Iran consisted, in his mind, of nothing but criminals and Communists and was not amenable to the normal logic of diplomacy.

When the American Ambassador tried to inform the Panamanians that their controversial guest was on his way, he eventually found General Omar Torrijos—the strongman who actually ran the country—drunk in bed in one of his dozens of houses. It was decided that the Shah would stay in the house of a successful businessman named Gabriel Lewis Galindo, who had made his fortune providing banana boxes for the United Fruit Company—once one of the most notorious of the Rockefeller family companies. Now he was asked to rent his house on the island of Contadora to the Shah and his entourage. The island, located at the northern end of the Pearl Archipelago, was a vacation spot of the Panamanian rich. Long after the Shah's departure, the spot gained fame by housing the popular show *Survivor* for three seasons. In 1980, the survivors were the Shah and his shrinking entourage.

In what can only be construed as a cruel joke by Torrijos, he had designated as the Shah's local host a "professor of Marxist philosophy at Panama University, a poet, a playwright, a sergeant in General Torrijos security guard."[65] He was nicknamed Chuchu and he had been a friend to Graham Greene and had hosted him every time he came to the island. On the fifteen-minute helicopter ride that took the Shah from Panama City to Contadora, the Shah looked gaunt and glum. He imagined himself sharing the fate of Napoleon and said "something about Elba" to one of his aides.[66]

From the first moment of their arrival in Panama, there was no chemistry "between the shy, arrogant monarch and the exuberant populist dictator." The General found the Shah the "saddest man [he had] ever met," yet he understood the source of his melancholy. It must be hard, he said, to fall "off the Peacock Throne onto Contadora."[67] He called the Shah a *chupon,* an orange bereft of juice and the flesh. "This is what happens to a man squeezed by the great nations," he said. "After all the juice is gone, they throw him away."[68] Even in Morocco, one of the members of the royal family who spent time with the Shah described him as "truly bereft. There was nothing left there," he said. Yet in spite of his appearance and of the increasingly grim reports from Iran, at times the Shah regained his sense of grandeur. In talking with Aristides Royo, the president of Panama, he referred to himself as "a descendent of Darius" and rejected any comparison with Napoleon, saying that when Napoleon arrived in St. Helena, he knew "his empire [was] finished. Mine is intact...my dynasty will prevail.... I won't go back but my son will."[69]

Security for the island was easy to control. About 200 National Guards were assigned to protect the royal family. The Shah worried about an attack from the sea, and "so gunmen were stationed on the beach, and frogmen in the water... and even more drastically, sonar devices were planted on the sea bed to detect either boats or divers."[70] One problem on the island was unreliable phone service to the United States and other overseas countries. Shortly after the Shah's arrival, a U.S. Army communications system was put in place, allowing "the Shah and the Empress [to place] calls to the US and Europe."[71]

The other problem, of course, was the Shah's cancer and the quality of the medical treatment he was receiving. It had become clear that he needed another operation, this time to remove his spleen. Panamanian doctors insisted on doing the operation; the Shah was "fearful... about being assassinated on the operating table."[72] In reality, the Shah had relegated the decision about who should do the surgery to Dr. Kean, who ultimately and strangely decided on Dr. Michael DeBakey—known mostly for his experience as a heart surgeon.

And finally there was the question of possible Panamanian complicity in a plan to hand over the Shah to the Islamic regime. At times the Shah and the Queen even doubted the resolve of the Carter administration to stand up to the regime and Tehran and thus feared that the United States might be tempted to exchange the Shah with the hostages. But according to Carter, the United States never seriously considered that option. At the same time, he confirms that his emissaries met in Paris with representatives of Sadeq Gotbzadeh to discuss the release of the hostages.

Even before arriving in Panama, rumors about the conditions of the Shah's stay there swirled in the media. In a press conference with President Royo of Panama, reporters wanted to know whether there were any conditions for the Shah's visit, and specifically, whether he had promised to invest large sums in the country. Would there be limits on his movements? Who would pay the cost of using the country's National Guard to protect the Shah? There were no preconditions, Royo announced, adding that the Shah would "naturally cover the expenses for his stay." The answer was only partially correct. The Shah paid for the food of the soldiers assigned to protect him. They ate at the hotel near the rented house where the Shah lived, and the monthly bill for the food came to $21,000.[73] Moreover, according to the same reports, the Shah met with a number of businessmen not long after arriving in the country—but making investments was not a precondition for his stay in the country. Before long, there were rumors that the Shah had offered to buy the island of Contadora, where he was staying, for $425 million. President Royo denied knowing anything about the offer, adding that the island was "worth a lot more."[74]

On January 15, 1980, the State Department received a message from the British Embassy in Tehran that included the text of an official extradition request from the Islamic Republic to the government of Panama. It was a letter from Iran's foreign minister, Sadeq Gotbzadeh, and was addressed to Panama's President Royo. The letter praised "the long anti-imperialistic struggle of the people and government of Panama" and "applaud[ed] the large contribution of Panama to the overthrow of the dictatorship of Somuza." It went on to declare that the Iranian regime did not doubt that "despite the pressures exercised by American imperialism," the people and government of Panama "will not tolerate any longer the presence on their soil of the deposed Shah of Iran, a tyrant and criminal." The letter also included what it called a "Warrant for the Arrest of Mohammad Reza Pahlavi," requesting the Shah's arrest and the "seizure of all the documents and effects at his disposal."[75] In what in retrospect seems like a well-orchestrated psychological war on the Shah, Iranian officials soon let the world know that an agreement had been made with Panama and that the Shah had already been put under arrest, would "be held there for sixty days," and then brought back to Iran for a trial. Another official declared that a contract with the famously efficient terrorist "Carlos the Jackal" had been put on the Shah's head. The Islamic regime had declared earlier that "whoever assassinated the deposed Shah and members of his immediate family would be carrying out the order of the Islamic Revolutionary Council."[76] This was only the first of many instances in which the regime put out contracts on the lives of its opponents or those whose art or writings it found distasteful. It has been estimated that the regime assassinated more than 200 of its opponents in Europe.[77]

A week after receiving the extradition letter, President Royo wrote a note to the "Islamic Council of the Revolution" outlining "the requirement[s] for an extradition demand" and stating that in the meantime, the Shah is "under the care of Panama's Security Authorities." He ended his letter by noting that, in considering the extradition request, Panama would make every effort to abide by international law and hoped that, in return, the government of Iran would follow Panama's "example and release the hostages."[78]

The United States was rightly worried that this kind of statement by Panamanian officials would be construed in Iran as an indication that the extradition of the Shah was a serious possibility and would thus prolong negotiations for the release of American hostages. The U.S. Ambassador in Panama was "instructed to meet with Aristides Roya [*sic*] and ask [him] to retract his statement regarding the extradition of Mohammad Reza Pahlavi."[79]

The United States was put in something of a double bind. Clearly, the release of the hostages was predicated on the arrest and extradition of the Shah. But such a step was not only opposed by many powerful Americans—David Rockefeller, Henry Kissinger, and Richard Nixon amongst them—it also would have led to a serious distrust of America by its allies. On January 30, 1980, a meeting in Secretary of State Vance's office brought together all the key decision makers to discuss the extradition request. It was resolved to send an official to Panama to meet with a Panamanian lawyer who had been a "former law partner of President Royo" to "obtain as much information as possible" about extradition laws in Panama. This official was then to travel to Contadora and meet with the Shah. It was made clear that this official's "mandate was strictly fact-finding" and nothing more. Clearly cognizant of tensions already arising between the Shah and his Panamanian hosts, the official was directed, at all costs, to avoid appearing as though he was "attempting to negotiate differences between the two sides. Rather the Panamanians must perceive his visit sympathetically."[80]

The brewing tensions with Panama and the Shah's increasing mistrust of his unpredictable host finally broke into the open when, around March 20, the Shah received word from Kissinger that he should leave Panama immediately. At the same time, the Carter administration was making every effort to keep the Shah in Panama. It is not clear what their motive was in this effort. Hamilton Jordan and Lloyd Cutler were dispatched from the White House for precisely this reason.[81] But their efforts failed. A private jet was chartered from a company suspected of having ties with the CIA. It was finally time for the Shah to accept Sadat's open invitation and return to Egypt.

The flight from Panama to Egypt was not bereft of excitement. It left Panama on March 23, 1980. Halfway to their destination, the plane landed in the Azores Islands, ostensibly to refuel. When the stopover lasted almost eight hours, the Shah and his entourage grew concerned that the Carter administration might have decided to exchange the Shah for the hostages after all. But after the painfully long delay, the charter flight was allowed to resume and took a tired, despondent Shah to his final destination. He arrived in Cairo on March 24, 1980. As he landed and saw Sadat and a full military guard awaiting him at the airport, tears welled up in his eyes. On his way to the military hospital, he told Sadat, "I've done nothing for you, yet you are the only one to accept me with dignity."[82]

There were a variety of reasons for Sadat's bold decision to offer the Shah asylum in Egypt. Aside from his own obvious sterling humanity and compassion for the once-powerful Shah, Sadat in those days was involved in a process of challenging and marginalizing the rising Islamist forces within Egypt. As the American Embassy in Cairo observed, "offering asylum to the Shah" was part of Sadat's "thinly veiled attacks on [the] Islamic right in Egypt."[83]

As news of the Shah's deteriorating health spread around the world, the torch the Shah and Soraya had carried for each other for more than three decades flared up again. Through "secure" channels, Soraya let the Shah know that she desired to meet him again. A few years after their acrimonious divorce, the two had discreetly reconnected. Many a time when the Shah traveled to Europe, he found a way to quietly slip away and meet with Soraya. Some have claimed that the meetings usually took place in Gstaad, an "elegant Swiss ski resort."[84] Moreover, in the course of these years, every time she was in financial need, the Shah was more than happy to help. In one instance, in the mid-1960s, she asked for and received $10 million. Now she knew he was on his deathbed, and they both wanted one more chance to meet. At the same time, the Shah by then felt increasingly dependent and indebted to his third wife. The meeting with Soraya must, he said, be arranged in a way that would not hurt the Queen.

Ardeshir Zahedi was the conduit of the initial Soraya letter. President Sadat had to be brought in, as his security forces were needed to ensure Soraya's discreet arrival in and departure from Egypt. But the Shah and Soraya were truly "star-crossed lovers," and before any last farewell meeting could be arranged, the Shah's health took a turn for the worse. The meeting had to be delayed to a later date, and that later date never came. A few lonely years later, Soraya died in Paris.

Shortly after arriving in Egypt, a team of physicians led by Dr. DeBakey removed the Shah's spleen—a spleen that was "full of nodules indicating localization of cell lymphoma." In other words, the cancer had spread far and wide, and the Shah's end was not far away.

After the operation, the Shah was moved to the Kubbah Palace, where he recuperated with the rest of his family around him. He occasionally received visitors or worked with two American editors—Tom Weir and Christine Godek—on the final edition of his sadly deficient memoir, *Answer to History.* Tapes of these discussions show a bitter, angry Shah, willing to lay the blame for the revolution on anyone or anything but himself. He tells the editors that "cutting my wings, cutting me to size, was surely" the wrong-headed Western policy that eventually begot the revolution. He complains of how during the crisis, "Vance never contacted me directly." And when the confused editors asked why he needed direct contact from U.S. officials about what was clearly a domestic problem, an angry Shah retorted, "I was *incredule* to believe in alliance."[85]

In the midst of these engagements, the Shah was attending to his wealth. His was a complicated network of companies, foundations, accounts and banks, landholdings on the Costa del Sol of Spain, and properties around the world. On May 28, 1979, less than six months after the Shah left Iran, his attorney, Jean Patry, informed him that, following his orders, they had withdrawn "from the Union de Banques Suisse all the assets deposited under the name of the Foundation Lutecia, and the Established Daletze after having cashed the bonds which could be cashed.... We established in Liechtenstein the Foundations Niversa, Zarima and Rukan. These Foundations... agreed to open each from accounts with respectively Union De Banques Swisse, Geneva Bank, Credit Swiss, Geneva Bank, Chase Manhattan Bank (Swisse), S.A. and Banque GutzwillerKurzzBingener, SA."[86]

A few months later, on October 17, 1979, the "Trust Company of Willeustand NY," was set up under the laws of the Netherlands Antilles; it was set up to follow the Shah's orders and, in his absence, to "take instructions from Empress Farah Diba." The assets of the foundation were to be distributed, according to the Shah's dispositions, by giving "20% to your wife; 20% to your elder son; 15% to your Farahnaz; 15% to your daughter, Leila; 20% to your younger son; 8% to your daughter Shahnaz, and 2% to your granddaughter, Mahnaz Zahedi."[87] The heirs designate "could only receive half of their share when they are twenty one," and "they may dispose freely of the 50% remaining share only at the age of 30." What these percentages are worth is a matter of wild conjecture, ranging from some $30 billion (according to the Islamic regime) to $120 million (according to some of the royal family's allies). Those most likely to know estimate the Shah's fortune to be close to a billion dollars, including the sale of the St. Moritz house (of which Italian Prime Minister Silvio Berlusconi eventually became an owner!) and its exquisite antiques and rugs. Many controversies, including the sale of the Queen Mother's jewels and the lawsuits against Ahmad Ansari—a relative of the Queen who invested some twenty million dollars of her and her oldest son's assets and was sued by the two when he declared that those investments had lost their value[88]—continued to cloud the issue of the distribution and actual size of his fortune.

The question of the Shah's wealth lingered long after his death. In a petition filed in the New York County Supreme Court (Index no, 22013/79), lawyers for the Islamic Republic claimed that the Shah, as "supreme authority" in the country, held a special "position of trust" and that he failed in his "fiduciary obligation . . . to the citizens of Iran . . . abused his position of trust and confidence to enrich himself . . . by diverting government funds and property to his own use . . . and accepting payments, bribes, interest in business ventures." The Empress is "alleged to have cooperated with the Shah in the furtherance of these acts." Based on these allegations, the Islamic regime sought a judgment for the court to put a freeze on all the assets of the royal couple and force them to pay "compensatory damages in the total amount of twenty-five billion dollars . . . and punitive damages . . . totaling one billion, five hundred million dollars, and for a judgment of thirty billion dollars for conversion by the defendants of money and property in 1979."[89] On September 14, 1981, the court dismissed all claims. A similar lawsuit was filed in the Supreme Court of New York against the Shah's twin sister, seeking "equitable relief, damages of 3.1 billion dollars and punitive damages in unspecified amount."[90] The Iranian regime claimed that in 1978 alone, more than $15 billion had left Iran, "much of it winding up in Swiss bank accounts." This claim, too, was rejected by the court.

After yet another operation, this time to attend to what physicians called his "subdiaphragmatic infection," after a "liter and a half of pus and necrosed pancreas debris was drained from his body," and after yet another period of recuperation and newfound hope for recovery, on the night of July 26, the Shah went into a coma. Heroic measures by physicians resuscitated him for one last brief visit with his family. At 9:45 on the morning of the July 27, 1980, sixty-year-old Mohammad Reza Pahlavi, not long before called the "King of Kings, the Light of the Aryans," passed away.

The next day, Ardeshir Zahedi and Aslan Afshar worked with Egyptian authorities to map out the details of the funeral. A procession began at the Abdin Palace and ended at the Al-Rifa'i Mosque, where the Shah was buried, not far from where his father had been laid to rest over three decades earlier.

In spite of his long illness, in spite of having occupied the throne for thirty-seven years, and although he repeatedly claimed in exile that his son would return to power, the Shah left no political will. The Queen decided to draft such a will on his behalf. In her own words, "As I was there and witnessed the King's deepest thoughts during his last days, I considered it my duty to put together" what was claimed to be his last will. The alleged will ended with these words: "I trust the young Crown Prince to Almighty God and to the great people of Iran."[91] Some of the Shah's confidantes, particularly Ardeshir Zahedi, objected to the posthumous drafting of the will.

A few months after the death of the Shah, Stanley Escudero, an American official who had served in Tehran for a while offered his analysis of "What Went Wrong in Iran." Why, he asked, did the United States "not see this coming"? He argued that, "rather simplistically stated, the Shah's system of rule depended upon a firm hand at the top, supported by a ruthless security mechanism, and the financial capacity to reduce dissatisfaction through development programs, outright subsidy, and the co-option of those who might have otherwise opposed the regime." He goes on to say that "years of repression, corruption, mismanagement, sycophancy, hollow promises, and just general inefficiency," made for popular discontent. Moreover, in his view, many Iranians are "cynical and distrustful of their government," and thus overlooked or doubted "the many significant accomplishments of imperial rule. Rapid modernization and burgeoning educational opportunities also helped set the stage for the Pahlavi collapse." The American diplomat concluded that the reason the United States failed to see the storm was that, from the late 1960s, "it had become the unspoken policy of the [State] Department and the Embassy . . . to curtail reports critical of the Shah."[92]

In other words, the Shah's desire for rapid modernization, combined with his increased authoritarianism, helped create the tragedy of his reign—a period of increasing, albeit unequal, prosperity, ending with the rule of a de-modernizing clerical regime.

On a personal level too, the Shah was, in the classical sense of the word, a tragic figure—a hare pretending to roar like a lion. At the end, he was both a victim and a figment of his own imagination, haunted by personal and historical demons and dreads, believing in his own anointed grandeur, yet ruling over a nation that simply refused to play the docile role he imagined for it. What Othello said of himself can well be said of the Shah: he had "done the state some service," and he had loved Iran, not wisely but too well. "Perplexed in the extreme," he indeed "threw a pearl away / Richer than all his tribe."

EPILOGUE

There is no history . . . only biography.
Ralph Waldo Emerson

Why did the Shah fall in 1979? Why would a country undergoing one of the world's fastest modernization projects, a country experiencing 20 percent annual increases in its GNP, suddenly opt for a revolution, and choose as its leader a cleric who dismissed modernity and modernization as pernicious colonial ploys? Why would a revolution, led in fact by the middle class, and taking place at the crest of what has been called the Third Wave of democratization, bring about not a democracy but clerical despotism? What role did the "resource curse"—the disruptive impact of petrodollars—play in begetting these cataclysmic tumults? Finally, are there any lessons to be learned in the rise and fall of the Shah that can guide today's policy makers in dealing with Iran's clerical regime? *The Shah* is an attempt to offer some answers to these critical questions.

During the Shah's thirty-seven-year rule, Iran experimented with everything from "guided democracy" and "authoritarian modernization" to pseudo-totalitarian and military rule. During this period, there were four competing paradigms of modernization (and modernity). Secular nationalists wanted democracy, rule of law, an empowered civil society, and a market economy; religious advocates of modernization wanted a modicum of democracy, within a reformed Shiism that would provide the society's moral fiber along with a market economy. Supporters of these two paradigms vacillated between advocating for a non-aligned Iran or for one allied with America but independent. The third paradigm was promoted by radical Marxists, who wanted modernization forced on society by the absolute power of a state controlled by their "vanguard party," a planned economy, and a Russian tilt in Iran's foreign policy. The Shah offered his own eclectic paradigm of modernization. A separate paradigm, critical of modernization and modernity and rejecting the desirability of both, came most notably in the ideas of Ayatollah Khomeini. The paradox of the fall of the Shah lies in the strange reality that nearly all advocates of modernity formed an alliance against the Shah and chose as their leader the biggest foe of modernity. The roots of this paradox, as *The Shah* argues, lie in the Shah's eclectic paradigm of modernization, combined with the inconsistencies of U.S. policy.

The Shah's vision of modernization was based on several axioms: Change in Iran required a concentration of authoritarian power in his own hands; democracy was an impediment to this change; in the battle for change, his biggest foes were the communists and the secular nationalist democrats. His most strategic ideological allies, he believed, were the moderate Shiite clergy.

The Shah believed in the urgent need to end feudalism and create a market economy, linked to Western capital markets. But he also had a pseudo-socialist vision, wherein the state would dominate key sectors of the economy and use all tools, including the military, to control prices and inflation. Even wages were, in his vision, to be decided more by his regime's political exigencies than the laws of the free market or measures of productivity.

By the mid-seventies, the unintended consequences of the Shah's vision began to appear. Not only the members of the bazaar—the traditional heart of trade in Iran and a source of support for democratic change—but even members of the modern industrialist class who had greatly benefited from the Shah's modernization plans were either too disgruntled with his regime or too politically impotent to help him. The unwritten covenant between the Shah and the modern industrialists had stipulated that they eschew engagement in politics in return for his pro-business policies. By 1977, this covenant came back to haunt them. Those who had most benefited from the Shah's modernization project were ill-organized and unable to rescue him in his hour of need.

The political economy of oil also had a complicated, even contradictory, influence on the Shah's eclectic model of modernization. As the price of oil rose, the pace of economic development also increased. A larger and more educated middle class was created, and land reform, begun in early 1961, gave millions of peasants a piece of land. But the failure of the state to provide sufficient financial and technological support to this class made it increasingly difficult for them to remain in the villages and sustain themselves economically. By the late-sixties, the rise in Iran's oil revenues turned the cities, particularly Tehran, into a magnet for these villagers. The massive internal migration that took place changed the demographic profile of Iran from a feudal, village-based economy to a rapidly industrializing, increasingly urban, capitalist system. Sharp economic inequality, the inability or refusal of the regime to provide services to the shanty towns that had mushroomed around Tehran, and finally, the traditional cultural conservatism of these peasants-turned-urbanites created a chasm at the heart of Iran's big cities. Tehran was the exemplar of the cultural and economic disharmony and tension that arose between the rich northern neighborhoods, steeped in cosmopolitan mores and manners, and the southern neighborhoods and shanty towns, over-populated by disgruntled citizens who resented both the affluence and Western cultural affectations of the rich.

Land reform and the other elements of the Shah's modernization project were intended to create for him a new and more durable coalition of support—composed of peasants freed from the shackles of feudalism, newly enfranchised women, a middle and technocratic class, and the new entrepreneurial industrialists, all enjoying the fruits of the Shah's pro-business, petro-fueled policies. The moderate clergy, according to this plan, would provide the moral cement and the much-needed anti-communist ideology of this coalition, while the security and stability of the coalition, and thus of the Shah's regime, would be provided by the might of the military and SAVAK.

In reality, the Shah's modernizing push in the sixties and seventies not only lost him his traditional base of support amongst the landed gentry and clergy, but his envisioned coalition never coalesced: the peasants who stayed in their villages played no role in politics, even during the months before the 1979 revolution; the middle and technocratic classes, unable to take an active role in politics, became increasingly dissatisfied with the Shah's authoritarianism. The two-party system the Shah launched in the late fifties during his experiment with "guided democracy" was never more than a hollow shell.

In the early seventies, however, the Shah temporarily toyed with the idea of allowing the emergence of at least one genuine political party. It would be needed, he said, to help maintain stability during the trauma of transition after his death. But then the price of oil jumped again, and the Shah not only lost interest in this party, but created instead a pseudo-totalitarian one-party system. The economic prosperity made possible by the new oil revenues, he believed, would be more than enough to satisfy the political aspirations of the people, particularly the middle classes. Long before the "China Model" (affording people affluence in lieu of their democratic rights) became of interest to political scientists, the Shah tried and failed to make such a covenant with the people of Iran. Not only did the middle class demand their democratic rights as soon as they saw a chance, but support from other parts of the Shah's imagined coalition proved no less chimerical.

Most of the newly landed peasants who converged on the cities joined the ranks of the Shah's opponents. An example of this pattern can be found in the life of the Ahmadinejad family, coming to Tehran in the early sixties and bringing with them their pieties and religious conservatism. The Shah not only made no effort to socialize this vast multitude, but—by making promises about improved standards of living—increased their expectations. Their estrangement from even the rudiments of modern culture, the Shah's virtual scorched earth policy against moderate democrats and the Left, his support for the growth of religion as an antidote to Marxism, and the glaring economic chasm yawning in the big cities pushed much of this urban population, and eventually the bulk of the working class, into the ranks of the opposition, making them perfect prey for the ideological claws of the clergy, who promised them a return to their "authentic selves" in this world and salvation in the other. When the Shah's regime went into a crisis in 1977—brought about by a sharp decline in the price of oil, his declining health, and Jimmy Carter's human rights policies—the vast, nimble network of religious organizations came to dominate the democratic movement, and that network itself was easily dominated by Ayatollah Khomeini's radical, well-organized supporters.

In those months, Khomeini pragmatically assumed the mantle of a democrat. The fact that his books had been banned by the Shah in Iran for two decades made it difficult for people to understand the true nature of his ideology. He had in his early days made no effort to hide his undemocratic ideas. But in the months before the revolution, he made no mention of his past opposition to land reform and to women's right to vote; he never once talked of *Velayat-e Faqih*, the core concept of his vision, wherein the only legitimate rule is that of a cleric *(faqih)*, whose legitimacy depends *not* on the will of the people but on divine rights.

Khomeini's studied silence, and his success in pitching his ideas in a language consanguine with "progressive anti-colonial discourse," allowed for his strange marriage of convenience with moderate democrats and radical Marxists.

In trying to explain the fall of the Shah over the last three decades, a whole array of modernization theorists have argued the mantra that the Shah fell because his Westernized economic development was too rapid. The clerical regime in Tehran has offered a slightly revised iteration of the same theory: It was, they say, the Shah's secularism, his Westernizing disposition, his departure from the ways and values of Islam, his preference for modernity's "disenchanted" world instead of the cherished enchantments of Islam that begot his fall. *The Shah* offers an alternative explanation of not just why the Shah fell but also why the clerics won. Surely there were the normal instabilities found in the transition from a traditional to a modernizing monarchy and society. But it was also the Shah's attempt to use religion as an antidote to Marxism—his decision to allow, indeed encourage, the expansion of mosques and other religious centers while forcefully disallowing all other forms of civic organization—that in fact crowned the clergy as the victors after his fall in 1978.

The inconsistencies and miscalculations in the Shah's modernization model were compounded by strategic inconsistencies in America's Iran policy. Moreover, these policy decisions were invariably made in reaction to the specter of the Cold War. More than once, proposals to pressure the Shah to democratize were tabled or tempered for fear that they might benefit the Soviets. In the last two critical decades of the Shah's rule, the United States drastically changed its policy on Iran three times, each time with far-reaching consequences.

In 1961, the Kennedy administration strongly urged the Shah to make the kind of changes in Iran that would have transformed the social demographic fabric of the society into a more modern polity. The necessary corollary of this policy would have been the gradual assumption by the Shah of the role of a constitutional monarch. The assassination of Kennedy disrupted his administration's policies on Iran. Within six years of his death, the United States drastically changed its policy. Economic success, made possible by rising oil revenues, increased the Shah's appetite for more power; in America, the realities of economic pressures and the agonies of Vietnam forced a radical rethinking of U.S. policy, not just in South East Asia but in Iran.

In the early seventies, just as the Shah's modernization plans were bearing fruit and Iran was experiencing rapid industrial growth, just as American pressure for democratic change was most needed, the Nixon Doctrine ended all pressures on the Shah to democratize. Moreover, the same surge of oil income not only allowed the Shah more independence from the United States, but encouraged him to make grandiose promises to Iranians about the country's rising standards of living—fueling the dangerous phenomenon that people's expectations were rising faster than his government's ability to satisfy them.

But in a few years, as these expectations continued to rise and as Tehran and other cities were overflowing with peasants in search of their share of petrodollars, American policy changed yet again. In 1977 the Carter administration decided to resume pressures on the Shah to democratize. By then the Iranian economy had nose-dived because of a sudden fall in the price of oil, the Shah was suffering from cancer, and the opposition was buoyed by Carter's election and renewed talk of democratization.

As the crisis deepened, the once defiant, even belligerent Shah suddenly became indecisive and desperate for signs of support from the United States. The United States' experience with the Shah in 1953 should have clearly warned them that he was likely to vacillate again in the face of a crisis—and how much in such moments he needed clear signs of support. But such support was not forthcoming.

Carter was preoccupied with negotiations between Egypt and Israel for the Camp David Accord, and there were profound differences of opinion among the White House, the National Security Council, and the State Department on what to do in Iran. National Security Advisor Brzezinski wanted the United States to support the Shah and help him establish law and order; the State Department insisted on the continuation of the liberalization policy; and for months the CIA refused to see the seriousness of the threat to the Shah. In the chaos of these discordant views and of the Shah's emotional paralysis, the American ambassador, William Sullivan, found an unusual opportunity to follow his own maverick policies. The Shah, caught between these differing forces, suffering from cancer, and undergoing chemotherapy, went from one extreme to another. The democratic concessions he made under duress during these months only fanned the flames of revolution. Had he made those concessions earlier, when he was at the height of his power; had he abdicated in 1974 when he first realized he had cancer; and finally, had Iran's democrats followed a different policy, it is possible to imagine a different trajectory for Iran.

The failure to foresee the fall of the Shah was easily one of the most important intelligence failures of the twentieth century. U.S. agencies were presciently predicting a revolution in 1965, but thirteen years later, on the eve of the revolution, they insisted that Iran was not even in a pre-revolutionary stage. In the fifties and early sixties, the United States had extensive contacts with members of the opposition, and their points of view helped America better understand the dynamics of Iranian society. From the mid-sixties, under pressure from the Shah—worried about the conspiracies his American allies might be hatching behind his back—these contacts were all but ended; the result was the colossal intelligence failure of 1978.

This intelligence failure manifested itself not just in America's inability to foresee or appreciate the seriousness of the crisis faced by the Shah, but also in its misinformed and misguided prescription for a solution. From November 1978, the American Embassy was quietly working behind the scenes to facilitate what political scientists call a "pacted transition" between some in the opposition and the Iranian military.

As newly declassified American documents show, the U.S. Embassy not only acted as a facilitator for these negotiations but also decided whom the military should negotiate with. In the months before the revolution, Khomeini and his allies initiated extensive contacts with the American government and embassy in Tehran and Paris. William Sullivan, sadly ignorant of the history of Iran and of Shiism, concluded in November 1978 that the only force capable of creating a democracy in Iran, and also standing up to the Soviets, was that of Khomeini and his supporters. *The Shah* is a new look at how these colossal errors were made.

By learning from this history, we can see how the United States and the Iranian democrats can avoid the errors of the past.

In fact, both the United States and the regime in Tehran have hitherto failed to learn the right lessons from the story of the Shah's fall. The United States, for example, could take away four crucial points from this history. If U.S. policy-makers had carefully studied the contours of the Shah's nuclear negotiations—and *The Shah* offers a brief summary of them based on new archival material—they could have better navigated the treacherous waters of Iranian nationalism. Secondly, they could have easily exposed the vacuity of one of the clerical regime's pivotal claims against the United States: that in questioning the intentions of the regime's nuclear program, the United States is engaged in a double standard; it gave the Shah whatever he wanted, the clerics claim, but now denies the Islamic regime their inalienable rights under the non-proliferation treaty. *The Shah* shows just how intense the negotiations and disagreements between the Shah and the United States really were.

Third, *The Shah* shows the nature of the coalition of forces that overthrew the Shah. Events since Iran's June 2009 contested election have shown that the same coalition is the backbone of the movement now challenging clerical despotism in Iran. Future American policy must take into consideration the continued power and relevance of this democratic coalition in determining Iran's future.

Finally, *The Shah* shows that the interests of the United States and Iran are both better served when the United States supports the democratic aspirations of the Iranian people.

Ayatollah Ali Khamenei has also drawn the wrong lessons from the fall of the Shah. He has more than once intimated that the Shah lost his throne because of the concessions he made to the opposition. Like the Shah, Khamenei also blames "outside forces" for the rise of the democratic movement. But the Shah lost his throne because he failed to make concessions at the right time and because he failed to see the domestic roots of the movement against him. Understanding the fall of the Shah helps map out the contours of a transition to democracy in the future, as well as the shape of the ongoing instability in Iranian politics over the last three decades.

At the vortex of these dynamic changes stood the character of the Shah. Every policy decision made by the Shah and his American allies landed on the hard rock of Iran's social realities and his personal idiosyncrasies. Biography, then, is an indispensable tool in assessing the chances of any policy's failure or success. *The Shah* fills a gaping hole in understanding and demonstrates that character is destiny, not just for the Shah, but for determining the fate of every policy, both American and Iranian.

NOTES

Abbreviations

CPL	Jimmy Carter Presidential Library and Museum, Atlanta, Georgia.
FDR	Franklin D. Roosevelt Presidential Library and Museum, Hyde Park, NY
FO	Foreign Office; files in Public Records Office, London
FRUS	U.S. Dept. of State, *Foreign Relations of the United States of America* (Washington, D.C.: GPO)
JFK	John F. Kennedy Presidential Library and Museum, Boston, MA
NA	National Archives, Washington, D.C.
NPL	Nixon Presidential Library and Museum, Yorba Linda, CA
NSA	National Security Archive, George Washington University, Washington, D.C.
NSF	National Security Files; files at the John F. Kennedy Presidential Library and Museum, Boston, MA
PRO	Public Records Office, London

Frequently cited sources

Assadollah Alam, *Yadasht Haye Roozaneh* [*Daily Journals*], edited by Alinaghi Alikhani, 6 volumes (Bethesda, Md., n.d.). Cited as Alam, *Daily Journals*.

Princess Soraya Esfandiary Bakhtiary, *Palace of Solitude*, translated by Herbert Gibbs (London, 1991).

Empress Farah, *My Thousand and One Days: An Autobiography*, translated by Felice Harcourt (London, 1978).

Hussein Fardust, *Zohour va Soghoute Saltanat Pahlavi, Khaterat-e General Sabeq Hussein Fardust* [The Rise and Fall of the Pahlavi Monarchy, Memoirs of Ex-General Hussein Fardust], 2 volumes (Tehran, 1370/1991). Cited as Fardust, *Memoirs*.

Mohammad Reza Shah Pahlavi, *Answer to History* (New York, 1980).

Mohammad Reza Shah Pahlavi, *The Collected Works of the Shah* (Tehran, 1975). Cited as Shah, *Collected Works*.

Mohammad Reza Pahlavi, "La Chronique Roseene," *L'Echo du Rosey*, Noel 1935.

Mohammad Reza Shah Pahlavi, *Mission for My Country* (London, 1961)

Sir Denis Wright, "The Memoirs of Sir Denis Wright: 1911–1976," 2 vols. (unpublished memoirs).

Ardeshir Zahedi, *The Memoirs of Ardeshir Zahedi*, 2 vols. (Bethesda, MA, 2006).

Zahedi Papers, Montreux, Switzerland. Zahedi private collection.

1 The Flying Dutchman

1. William Shakespeare, *Othello*, 5.4.324–325.
2. Alam, *Daily Journals*, vol. 5. On page 44 he tells the Shah he is a prophet; on the same page, he compares him with Napoleon; on page 254 he calls him the "emperor of the Shiites." Throughout the six volumes, he makes comparisons with De Gaulle.
3. Alam, *Daily Journals*, vol. 6, pp. 21–23.
4. Ibid., p. 75.
5. In 1964 Mehdi Samii was the head of Iran's Central Bank; the government was so desperate for money that he used his personal friendship with the executives of Bank of America to secure a $5 million loan. Mehdi Samii, interview with author, Los Angeles, September 3, 2006.
6. NSA, CIA, "The Shah's Lending Binge," 1977.
7. Parviz Sabeti, telephone interview with author, September 3, 2004.

8. NSA, CIA, National Intelligent Estimate, October 8, 1971, "Nothing Succeeds Like a Successful Shah," p. 5.
9. Colonel Kiumars Jahanbini, interview with author, Washington DC, November 5, 2004. The Colonel was the head of the Shah's bodyguard unit for over a quarter of a century. He kindly agreed to be interviewed. He has hitherto refrained from talking to any scholar or journalist. I am grateful for his confidence.
10. Mohammad Reza Shah Pahlavi, *Answer to History* (New York, 1980), p. 167.
11. General Azarbarzin, interview with author, Los Angeles, April 25, 2005.
12. *Keyhan*, 16 Farvardin 1358/April 1979, p. 4. General Azarbarzin, who was for many years one of the highest-ranking generals in the Iranian air force, confirms the help given to Morocco—as well as to other countries. General Azarbarzin, interview with author, April 27, 2005.
13. Ardeshir Zahedi, interview with author, New York, May 8, 2005.
14. Richard Parker, telephone interview with author, June 11, 2002.
15. Ardeshir Zahedi, interview with author, Montreux, December 6, 2004.
16. Farhad Sepahbodi, interview with author, Sedona, August 2, 2001.
17. Several people, including the bodyguards of the Shah and the Queen, told me of this strange decision.
18. Shawcross reports this episode; William Shawcross, *The Shah's Last Ride* (London, 1989); I also heard it from Jahanbini. Aslan Afshar claims he was the aide who suggested the idea to the Shah. Aslan Afshar, interview with author, Nice, March 29, 2009.
19. For an account of the behind-the-scenes discussions about what to do with the Shah, see David Rockefeller, *Memoirs* (New York, 2002), pp. 356–375.
20. The chief of his security detail, Colonel Jahanbini told me of the Shah's near-obsession with his radio in those early days; Jahanbini, interview with author, November 6, 2004.
21. Shah, *Answer to History*, p. 13.
22. Mohammad Reyshahri, *Khaterat* [Memoirs] (Tehran, 1383/2004), p. 74.
23. Farah Pahlavi, *An Enduring Love: My Life with the Shah* (New York, 2004), p. 307.
24. William Shakespeare, *The Tragedy of King Lear,* 1.2.105.
25. Shawcross, *The Shah's Last Ride*, p. 99.
26. Majid Alam, interview with author, San Diego, September 3, 2003.
27. He was banished for defying the Shah's orders. *Le Monde* published a report alleging that Princess Ashraf had been arrested at an airport in Switzerland and charged with drug trafficking. As it happened, the paper had made a mistake: a Persian princess had been arrested, but it was not Ashraf. She wanted to sue the paper, and the Shah, who was hoping in those days to mend his relations with European media, had ordered her not to pursue the lawsuit and to settle for the apology offered by the paper. She refused to obey, and as she had been helped in all of this by Sepahbodi, he was banished from the Foreign Ministry. In fact, afraid that he might be put in prison, the Princess arranged for him to fly out of Iran and stay in Europe for a while. Once the Shah's anger subsided, Princess Ashraf interceded on behalf of her friend and, after some reservations, he was offered the Moroccan Embassy.

2 A Compromised Constitution

1. For a beautiful prose rendition of the Zahhak story, and indeed of the entire *Shahnameh*, accompanied by the finest selection of exquisitely reproduced miniatures, see Dick Davis, *The Lion and the Throne: Stories from the* Shahnameh *of Ferdowsi*, vol. 1. (Washington, DC, 1998), pp. 23–33. By way of disclosure, readers should know that Mage Publishers, who published Dick Davis's three-volume masterpiece translation of *Shahnameh,* has published four of my books.
2. Mohammad Reza Shah Pahlavi, *Mission for My Country* (London, 1961), p. 51.
3. Ibid.
4. For a discussion of these trips, see Abbas Milani, "Nasir-al Din Shah in Farang: Perspectives of an Oriental Despot," in *Lost Wisdom: Rethinking Modernity in Iran* (Washington, DC, 2004), pp. 51–63.
5. Ashraf Pahlavi, *Faces in a Mirror: Memoirs from Exile* (New York, 1980), p. 1.
6. Marvin Zonis, *Majestic Failure: The Fall of the Shah* (Chicago, 1991), p. 27.
7. Ibid., p. 28
8. Shah, *Mission for My Country*, p. 45.
9. Ibid., p. 49.
10. Mohammad Reza Pahlavi, *Besouy-e Tamadon-e Bozorg* [Towards the Great Civilization], (Tehran, n.d.), p. 7.

11. Alam, *Daily Journals,* vol. 2, p. 346.
12. Amir Afkhami, "Compromised Constitutions: The Iranian Experience with the 1918 Influenza Pandemic," *Bulletin of the History of Medicine* 77, no. 2 (Summer 2003): 391.
13. For a discussion of the flu and its global impact, see John Berry, *The Great Influenza: The Epic Story of the Deadliest Plague in History* (New York, 2004).
14. Anthony R. Neligan, *The Opium Question with Special Reference to Persia* (London, 1927), p. 27; see also Afkhami, "Compromised Constitutions," pp. 384–386.
15. The Kerman figures are for 1925 and are quoted in Afkhami, "Compromised Constitutions," p. 385.
16. Some sources have gone so far as to claim that no country in the world suffered as much from the war as did Iran. See Mohammad Gholi, Majd, *Persia in World War I and Its Conquest by Great Britain* (Lanham, Md., 2003). His tendency to pick and choose the sources that confirm what he, a priori, wants to prove, makes many of his assertions doubtful.
17. For an informed account of the Agreement, its friends and foes, see Homa Katouzian, *State and Society in Iran: The Eclipse of the Qajars and the Emergence of the Pahlavis* (London, 2000), pp. 25–164.
18. PRO, "Leading Personalities in Iran, 1947," FO 371/62035. I have changed the order of some of the sentences from the original narrative.
19. Mehdi Bamdad, *Tarikh-e Rejal-e Iran* [History of Iran's Politicians], vol. 5 (Tehran, 1347/1968), p. 123.
20. Seyyed Zia Tabatabai, "Interview with Dr. Sadredin Elahi," first published in Iran and reprinted in a fuller version in an émigré paper, called *Jong*, October 1990. In the reprint, it is indicated where and how SAVAK had censored the original interview. Nothing that would deprecate the royal family or Reza Shah was allowed in print.
21. For a history of this movement, see Cosroe Chaquèri, *The Soviet Socialist Republic of Iran, 1920–1921: Birth of the Trauma* (Pittsburgh, 1995).
22. A copy of the cover of the book was provided in *Reza Shah Kabir* (Tehran, 1356/1997).
23. PRO, Cox to Norman, July 10, 1921, FO 371/6446. The mendacious role of Mohammad Ali Mirza is discussed at length in Cyrus Ghani, *Iran and the Rise of Reza Shah: From Qajar Collapse to Pahlavi Power* (London, 1998), pp. 224–249.
24. There is an entire file of fascinating reports on the lives of Bolsheviks in Iran, as reported by the British Embassy. See PRO, FO 371/10841.
25. PRO, "Internal Summary," September 5, 1925, FO 371/10842.
26. PRO, Mr. Norman to Earl Curzon, March 1, 1921, FO 379/6403, p. 3.
27. Ibid., p. 4.
28. Ibid., p. 4.
29. Ibid., p. 5.
30. PRO, Mr. Norman to Earl Curzon, February 22, 1921, FO 371/6401.
31. PRO, Mr. Norman to Earl Curzon, March 1, 1921, FO 379/6403, p. 6.
32. PRO, Mr. Norman to Earl Curzon, February 25, 1921, FO 371/6401.
33. Ibid., p. 1.
34. PRO, "Persian Political Situation," February 26, 1921, FO 371/6601.
35. Shah, *Mission for My Country*, p. 40.
36. PRO, Mr. Norman to Earl Curzon, May 26, 1921, FO 371/35077.
37. Ibid.
38. PRO, Mr. Norman to Earl Curzon, March 1, 1921, FO 371/6403. This is easily one of the lengthiest accounts of the coup provided by the British Embassy in Tehran.
39. PRO, Mr. Norman to Earl Curzon, March 1, 1921, Enclosure no. 3, FO 371/6403.
40. Seyyed Zia, Interview with Dr. Sadredin Elahi, part 2, p. 9. There he says, "Mussolini was my hero." Throughout the interview Seyyed has waxed eloquent about Lenin and his political virtues.
41. PRO, "Foreign Countries Report: Persia," No. 38, March 1921, FO 248/6402.
42. PRO, Mr. Norman to Earl Curzon, March 1, 1921, FO 379/6403, p. 8.
43. R. N. Bosten, "Baznegari be Zendegiy-e yek rooznameh nevis siy-o dosaleh Gomnan ke nagahan nakost vazire Iran shod," [Revisiting the life of an unknown thirty-three-year-old journalist who suddenly became Iran's Prime Minister], *Rahavard*, Summer 1371/1992, no. 3, p. 112.
44. PRO, Mr. Norman to Earl Curzon, May 26, 1921, FO 371/35077.
45. Bosten, "Revising the Life of an Unknown Thirty-three-year-old Journalist," p. 111.
46. PRO, Mr. Norman to Earl Curzon, May 25, 1921, FO 371/6404.
47. PRO, L. Oliphant, to Foreign Office, June 6, 1921, FO 371/6406.

48. William Shakespeare, *Richard II*, 1:1. 196.
49. A facsimile of the order is published in *Reza Shah Kabir* (Tehran, 1356/1977).
50. PRO, "Summer Intelligence Review," No. 10, March 7, 1925, FO 371/10842.
51. In an early sign of his authoritarian disposition, when Reza Khan tried to register his preferred last name, he was informed that someone else, called Mahmoud, had already picked Pahlavi. Reza Khan ordered the man to give up his last name! In protest, the man refused to pick another name and simply picked his first name as his surname, becoming Mahmoud Mahmoud. He went on to become a prominent historian of the Iranian Constitutional Revolution.
52. PRO, Tehran to Foreign Office, April 25, 1925, FO 371/10843.
53. Ibid.
54. For a discussion of the role of different strata, and particularly for a revisionist account of the clergy's role in opposing the idea of a republic, see Vanessa Martin, "Muddaris, Republicanism, and the rise to Power of Riza Khan, Sardar-I Sepah," in *The Making of Modern Iran: State and Society Under Reza Shah Pahlavi, 1921–1941,* edited by Stephani Cronin (London, 2003), pp. 65–75.
55. PRO, Tehran to Foreign Office, December 31, 1924, FO 371/10840.
56. PRO, Sir P. Loraine, to Foreign Office, January 22, 1925, FO 371/10840.
57. Quoted in Cyrus Ghani, *Iran and the Rise of Reza Shah: From Qajar Collapse to Pahlavi Power* (London, 1998), p. 361.
58. PRO, Sir P. Loraine, to Austen Chamberlain, Nov. 2, 1925, FO 371/10840.
59. For an account of these machinations, see Ghani, *Iran and the Rise of Reza Shah,* pp. 224–249.
60. PRO, Sir P. Loraine to Foreign Office, September 28, 1925, FO371/10840.
61. PRO, Sir P. Loraine to Foreign Office, October 10, 1925, FO371/10840.
62. Ibid.
63. PRO, Sir P. Loraine to Foreign Office, December 12, 1925, FO 371/10840.
64. PRO, Tehran to Foreign Office, February 2, 1926, FO 371/11489

3 The Peacock Throne

1. Vita Sackville-West, *Passenger to Teheran*, with a new introduction by Nigel Nicolson (New York, 1990), p. 131.
2. Abbas Amanat, *Pivot of the Universe: Nasir-al-Din Shah Qajar and the Iranian Monarchy, 1831–1896* (Berkeley, 1997), p. 25.
3. Ibid., p. 19.
4. A brief account of the Throne is provided in the great encyclopedia of Persian language and culture, *Dehkhoda*. The encyclopedia was eventually published under the auspices of Tehran University. Today, a new edition bereft of entries critical of the clergy is published.
5. Sackville-West, *Passenger to Teheran*, p. 77.
6. Ibid., p. 124.
7. Ibid., p. 125.
8. Ibid.
9. Ibid.
10. Ibid., p. 130.
11. Ibid., p. 126.
12. Ibid., pp. 126–127.
13. PRO, Tehran Legation to Foreign Office, December 24, 1925, FO371/10840.
14. Ibid.
15. *Reza Shah Kabir* (Tehran, 1356/1957); the book is in commemoration of the centennial of Reza Shah's birth, and included copies of historic documents and photos and no page numbers. A copy of the program that day is included in *Reza Shah Kabir.*
16. Suleiman Behboudi, *Reza Shah: Khaterat-e Suleiman Behboudi* [Reza Shah: The Memoirs of Suleiman Behboudi], edited by Gholam Hossien Mirza Saleh (Tehran, 1372/1984), pp. 281–285.
17. Ibid., p. 32.
18. Ibid., p. 297.
19. Sackville-West, *Passenger to Teheran*, p. 133.
20. Behboudi, *Reza Shah*, pp. 281–285.
21. PRO, Tehran to Foreign Office, October 15, 1925, FO/371/10840.
22. Behboudi, *Reza Shah*, p. 290.

23. Ibid., p. 133.
24. For a discussion of blue and its many connotations, see my "Modernity and Blue Logos," in *Lost Wisdom: Rethinking Modernity in Iran* (Washington, DC, 2004), pp. 139–154.
25. Hassan Arfa, *Under Five Shahs* (New York, 1965), p. 138.
26. K. K. Karanjia, *The Mind of a Monarch* (London, 1977), p. 38.
27. Margaret Laing, *The Shah* (London, 1977), p. 44.
28. Ibid., p. 46.
29. PRO, Tehran Legation to Foreign Office, February 3, 1926, FO 371/11489.
30. Ashraf Pahlavi, *Faces in a Mirror: Memoirs from Exile* (New York, 1980), p. 11.
31. Shah, *Mission for My Country,* p. 52.
32. Ibid., p. 54.
33. Laing, *The Shah,* p. 44.
34. In 1923, there were 440 primary schools with 44,205 pupils and 47 secondary schools with 9,399 students. In 1941, at the end of Reza Shah's reign, there were 2,424 primary schools with 25,383 pupils and 301 secondary schools with 24,112 students. The number of teachers' colleges had jumped from 1 in 1921 to 36 in 1941. See General Hassan Arfa, *Under the Five Shahs* (New York, 1965), p. 281.
35. Arfa, *Under Five Shahs,* p. 291.
36. Behboudi, *Reza Shah,* p. 325.
37. Ashraf Pahlavi, *Faces in the Mirror,* p. 27.
38. Majid A'lam, interview with author, San Diego, September 3, 2003.
39. Behboudi, *Reza Shah,* p. 324.
40. PRO, Tehran Legation to Foreign Office, October 20,1926, FO 371/11490.
41. Shah, *Mission for My Country,* p. 52.
42. Ibid., p. 55.
43. Ibid., p. 53; Meccano is a line of metal construction toys, first produced in 1901 in Liverpool by a man named Frank Hornby. Before long they were being sold in Europe and the United States. The company still exists.
44. Ibid., pp. 53–54.
45. Karanjia, *The Mind of a Monarch,* p. 40.
46. Shah, *Mission for My Country,* p. 54.
47. Karanjia, *The Mind of a Monarch,* p. 44.
48. Shah, *Mission for My Country,* p. 55.
49. Ibid., pp. 54–55.
50. Ibid., p. 55.

4 Jocund Juvenilia

1. PRO, "Report on Personalities in Persia," February 24, 1940, FO/371/11489.
2. Ibid. p. 59. A whole chapter of the memoir is called "Royal Tutelage."
3. General Hassan Arfa, *Under the Five Shahs* (New York, 1965), p. 226.
4. Princess Ashraf Pahlavi, *Faces in a Mirror: Memoirs from Exile* (London, 1980), p. 23.
5. R. K. Karanjia, *The Mind of a Monarch* (London, 1977), p. 66.
6. Dr. Javad Sheikhol-Eslami, *So'oud va Soghut-e Teymourtash* [The Rise and Fall of Teymourtash] (Tehran, 1379/2000), p. 183. Quoting a British Foreign Office document, from the British Embassy in Tehran to the Foreign Office, the British ambassador calls Teymourtash one of the troika of power in Iran.
7. Benedict Anderson, *Imagined Communities: Reflections on the Origins and Spread of Nationalism* (London, 1991).
8. Mohammad Reza Pahlavi, "Introduction," *Reza Shah Kabir* (1355/1976). The book is a commemorative of the centennial of Reza Shah's birth; his son, the Shah, wrote an introduction to it.
9. PRO, Berne to Foreign Ministry, November 11, 1935, FO 371/18992.
10. PRO, Berne to Foreign Office, October 17, 1931, FO 371/15356.
11. PRO, British Embassy, Tehran to Berne, August 31, 1936, FO 371/15356.
12. Fardust, *Memoirs,* vol. 1, pp. 38–40.
13. Frederick Jacobi Jr. "New Boy," *New Yorker,* February 26, 1949, p. 56.
14. Ibid.
15. Ibid.
16. Ibid.

17. Ibid.
18. Ibid.
19. Ibid.
20. Ibid.
21. Ibid., p. 57.
22. Ibid.
23. Ibid.; I have checked the school roster for that year and indeed both Charlie Childs and the author of the essay, Jacobi, were students at Le Rosey.
24. Ibid.
25. Ibid.
26. Ibid.
27. Mohammad Reza Pahlavi, "La Chronique Roseene," *L'Echo du Rosey*, Noel 1935, p. 3.
28. Ibid.
29. In the joke, one of the school's British boys, called Hannay, is lonely and melancholy; a comrade approaches, and in sympathy asks, "Are you sad my friend?"; "No," says the Brit. "Are you gay?" asks the friend. Again "No," says the Brit. "What the hell are you then?" asks the frustrated friend. "A Brit," answered Hannay. About the same time, in Iran, Reza Shah was beginning to take more overtly anti-British positions, and the British Embassy was taking more interest in the education of the Crown Prince—asking the consulate at Berne to check up on the young prince.
30. Mohammad Reza Pahlavi," La Chronique Roseene," L'*Echo du Rosey*, Juin 1933, p. 15.
31. Mohammad Reza Pahlavi, "La Chronique Roseene," *L'Echo du Rosey*, Novembre 1933, p. 9.
32. Ibid., p. 8.
33. Mohammad Reza Pahlavi, "La Chronique Roseene," *L'Echo du Rosey*, Noel 1934, p. 16.
34. Mohammad Reza Pahlavi, "La Chronique Roseene," *L'Echo du Rosey*, Printemps 1934, p. 19.
35. L. C. Roever, "La Saison de Tennis," *L'Echo du Rosey*, Juin 1935, p. 7.
36. Mohammad Reza Pahlavi, "La Chronique Roseene," *L'Echo Du Rosey*, Noel 1934, pp. 3–4.
37. Ibid., p. 5.
38. Ibid., p. 7.
39. Mohammad Reza Pahlavi, "La Chronique Roseene," *L'Echo du Rosey*, 1935, p. 3.
40. PRO, Berne to Foreign Ministry, November 11, 1935, FO 371/18992, pp. 2–3.
41. Ibid., p. 3.
42. Daniela Meier, "Between Court Jester and Spy: The Career of a Swiss Gardener at the Royal Court in Iran; A Footnote to Modern Iranian History," *Middle East Critique* 9, no. 16 (Spring 2000): 75
43. PRO, British Embassy, Tehran to Berne, August 31, 1936. FO 371/15358.
44. Meier, "Between Court Jester and Spy," p. 76.
45. Ibid., p. 2.
46. Gerard de Villier with Bernard Touchias and Annick de Villier, *The Shah,* translated by June P. Wilson and Walter B. Nichols (New York, 1976), p. 55.
47. Ibid., p. 56.
48. The title of a book by a member of the Shah's opposition tells it all. The book is called, *Ernest Perron Shohare Shahe Sabeq* [Ernest Perron, Husband of Deposed Shah] (Tehran, n.d.).
49. For an introduction to Kohut's ideas, see Heinz Kohut, *The Analysis of the Self* (Chicago, 1971).
50. Marvin Zonis, *Majestic Failure: The Fall of the Shah* (Chicago, 1991), pp. 115–119.
51. Fardust claims that the Crown Prince had an affair with a maid and that 5,000 Swiss francs were given to her to keep her quiet. See Fardust, *Memoirs,* vol. 1. pp. 38–40.
52. Ibid., p. 60.
53. Margaret Laing, *The Shah* (London, 1977), p. 60.
54. Quotes are all from *Mission for My Country* and are quoted in Zonis, *Majestic Failure: The Fall of the Shah*, pp. 48–49.
55. Zonis, *Majestic Failure: The Fall of the Shah*, p. 48.
56. Ashraf Pahlavi, *Faces in a Mirror: Memoirs from Exile*, p. 22.
57. Ibid.

5 Happy Homecoming

1. PRO, Sir P. Loraine's Private Interview with HM Shah Reza Pahlavi, February 2, 1926, FO 248/1377.

2. The details of the episode are reported in the memoirs of Seyyed Hassan Taghi-Zadeh, who was, at the time, minister of roads, and in charge of the railroad construction. See Seyyed Hassan Taghi-Zadeh, *Khaterat-e Seyyed Hassan Taghi-Zadeh* (Tehran, 1362/1983), p. 210.
3. For a discussion of these developments, see Michael Zirinsky, "Riza Shah's Abrogation of Capitulations, 1927–1928," in Stephen Cronin, ed. *The Making of Modern Iran: State and Society under Reza Shah, 1921–1941* (London, 2003), pp. 81–99.
4. Nigel Nicolson, ed. *Vita and Harold: Letters of Vita Sackville-West and Harold Nicolson* (New York, 1992), p. 150.
5. PRO, Tehran to Foreign Office, November 23, 1926, FO/371/11489. The file had been classified and closed until 2002—the longest number of years that documents of the Foreign Ministry were kept closed, indicating how sensitive the British considered the otherwise simple matter.
6. PRO, Nicolson to Chamberlain, November 23, 1926, FO/371/11489.
7. For an account of the affair, see Donald N. Wilber, *Riza Shah Pahlavi: The Resurrection and Reconstruction of Iran: 1878–1944* (New York, 1975), p. 154–155.
8. For a discussion of article ten, see Mohammad Ali Movahhed, *Khabe Ashoftey-e Naft* [The Oil Nightmare], vol. 2 (Tehran, 1378/1999), pp. 923–931. Movahhed's book is one of the most authoritative sources on the subject in Persian.
9. Ali Akbar Hakamizadeh, *Asrare Hezar Saleh* [Thousand-Year-Old Mysteries] (Tehran, n.d.).
10. Ruhollah Khomeini, *Kashfol-Asrar* [Opening of Secrets] (Tehran, n.d.).
11. It is a measure of Hakamizadeh's significance to the debate that the initial title of Ayatollah Khomeini's book included a reference to *Thousand-Year-Old Mysteries*. In later editions, reference to Hakamizadeh was excised from the title, lest it afford the heretical book undue significance. For a discussion of these developments, see Mohammad Taghi Hadj Bushehri, *Az Kashf-al Asrar ta Asrare Hezar Saleh*, a short monograph published independently.
12. For an account of clerical responses to these changes, see the short monograph published independently by Mohammad Taghi Hadj Bushehri, *Az Kashf-al Asrar a Asrare Hezar Saleh*, pp. 20–23.
13. Seyyed Mohammad Hussein Manzur-al Ajdad, ed., *Marjayeyat dar Arseye Siyasat va Ejtema* [Ayatollahs in the Political and Social Domain] (Tehran, 1379/1990), p. 228.
14. Mehrangiz Dowlatshahi, *Women, State and Society in Iran, 1941–1978*, edited by Gholam Reza Afkhami (Washington, DC, 2002), pp. 6–8.
15. For a brief discussion of the episode, see Seyyed Mohammad Hussein Manzur-al Ajdad, ed., *Marjayeyat dar Arseye Siyasat va Ejtema* [Ayatollahs in the Political and Social Domain] (Tehran, 1379/1990), p.229.
16. In his daily journals, Assadollah Alam, the Shah's Court minister, recounts many such moments. See, for example, Alam, *Daily Journals*, vol.6, p. 52.
17. Ashraf has provided an account of these events in her memoirs, *Faces in the Mirror* (New York, 1980), pp. 9–10.
18. *Iran-e Bastan*, January 14, 1933. The English text of the mission was provided by the paper itself. I owe a special debt of gratitude to Mrs. Parvin Ashraf of the Princeton University Library for her help in finding this and other magazines of the period.
19. *Iran-e Bastan*, January 21, 1933, p. 2.
20. *Iran-e Bastan*, May 4, 1933, p. 1.
21. *Iran-e Bastan*, December 9, 1933, p. 1.
22. *Iran-e Bastan*, December 20, 1933, p. 3.
23. I visited Le Rosey, talked to school officials, and inquired about the Shah's records. They asked me to write them a letter of inquiry and promised to answer it. The words are from a letter to the author by the school principal, along with the archivist.
24. Ibid.
25. The reports prepared by SAVAK about different personalities invariably include personal gossip as well as news of political views and actions. Several collections of these documents have been published, and they all show the same pattern. Moreover, several people, including General Alavi-Kia, for many years deputy director of SAVAK, as well as Ahmad Goreishi, Parviz Sabeti, Fereydoon Mahdavi, and Fereydoon Hoveyda also told me about the Shah's proclivity for gossip.
26. Shah, *Mission for My Country*, p. 62.
27. Fardust, *Memoirs*, vol. I, p. 58.
28. Mahmood Jam, "Avalin o Akharin Didar man Ba Malek Farouk" [My First and Last Meeting with Malek Farouk], *Salnameye Donya* [Donya Annual Edition], no. 18, p. 5.
29. Ibid., p. 58.

30. Ibid., p. 59.
31. Quoted in Adel Sabit and Dr. Maged Farag, *1939: The Imperial Wedding* (Cairo, 1993).
32. Jam, "Avalin o Akharin Didar man Ba Malek Farouk," p. 59.
33. Ibid., p. 60.
34. Shah, *Mission for My Country*, p. 439.
35. Ibid., p. 438.
36. Ibid., p. 438.
37. PRO, Tehran to Foreign Ministry, November 18, 1939, FO 371/23262.
38. Ibid.
39. PRO, Tehran to Foreign Office, October 21, 1939, FO 371/23262.
40. *Gahnameye Panjah Sal Shahanshahi Pahlavi*, [Chronicle of Fifty Years of Pahlavi Rule], vol. 1, pp. 163–164.

6 Crown of Thorns

1. *FRUS*, 1940, vol. 3, p. 635.
2. Miron Rezun, *The Iranian Crisis of 1941: The Actors, Britain, Germany and the Soviet Union* (Cologne, Germany, 1982), p. 28.
3. I have discussed these passports and Iran's effort to save its Jews in *The Persian Sphinx: Amir Abbas Hoveyda and the Riddle of the Iranian Revolutio*n (Washington, DC, 2000); I have also discussed it briefly in a January 5, 2005, editorial in the *International Herald Tribune*.
4. For a discussion of Madame Blavatsky's influence on Nazism, see Nicholas Goodrick-Clark, *The Occult Roots of Nazism: Secret Aryan Cults and Their Influence on Nazi Ideology* (New York, 1992).
5. FDR Library, "US Embassy in Tehran to the President, June 1, 1938."
6. FDR Library, "President Roosevelt to Reza Shah Pahlavi, August 12, 1938."
7. PRO, "The Soviet Threat to British Interests in the Middle East," December 6, 1939, FO 371/24583.
8. *FRUS*, 1940, vol. 3, p. 631.
9. Rezun, *The Iranian Crisis of 1941*, p. 37.
10. PRO, Tehran to Foreign Office, November 18, 1939, FO 371/23269.
11. PRO, Telegram from Tehran to Foreign Office, May 1, 1941, FO 371/27150.
12. PRO, "Intelligence Summary Report," August 1941, FO 371/22241.
13. For a succinct account of German espionage in Iran, see http://www.iranica.com/articles/germany-ix; see also Hamid Shokat, *Dar Tir Ras-e Havadeth* [On the Path of the Whirlwind] (Tehran, 1386/2007), pp. 151–175.
14. PRO, "Intelligence Summary Report," August 1941, FO 371/22241.
15. Shokat, *Dar Tir Ras-e Havadeth*, p. 168.
16. PRO, "The Soviet Threat to British Interests in the Middle East," December 6, 1939, FO 371/24583.
17. *FRUS*, 1941, vol. III, p. 383.
18. PRO, "The Soviet Threat to British Interests in the Middle East," December 6, 1939, FO371/24583.
19. Shah, *Mission for My Country*, p. 135.
20. PRO, "Intelligence Summary Report," June 17, 1939, FO 371/23262.
21. PRO, Tehran to Foreign Office, January 26, 1940, FO 371/24570.
22. Amin Banani, interview with author, Palo Alto, November 29, 2007. He was a young Boy Scout and had participated in the program.
23. Banani, interview with author.
24. Ibrahim Golestan has not only written about this atmosphere in his powerful stories, but also confirmed their reality to me in interviews. Interview with author, London, November 20, 2007.
25. PRO, "Annual Political Report for 1940," FO 371/27149.
26. Suleiman Behboudi, *Khaterat-e Suleiman Behboudi* [Memoirs of Suleiman Behboudi], edited by Gholam Hussein Mirza-Saleh (Tehran, 1372/1993), p. 395.
27. Ibid. Behboudi was acting as a conduit between the Court and the ministries and thus was in a perfect position to know the role of the Crown Prince.
28. PRO, "Annual Political Report for 1940," FO 371/27149.
29. Ibid.

30. PRO, "Intelligence Summary Report," November 18, 1939, FO 371/23262.
31. PRO, "Annual Political Report for 1940," FO 371/27149.
32. PRO, Tehran to Foreign Office, October 26, 1926, FO 248/1377.
33. *Gahnameye Panjah Sal Saltanat Pahlavi* [Chronology of Fifty Years of Pahlavi Rule] (Tehran, 1976), vol. 1, p. 165. The book was published by the Court on the occasion of the fiftieth anniversary of Pahlavi rule.
34. Sir Reader Bullard, *The Camels Must Go: An Autobiography* (London, 1961), p. 226.
35. PRO, Tehran to Foreign Office, July 11, 1941, FO 371/2715.
36. PRO, Churchill to Foreign Minister, June 9, 1941, CAB 120/661.
37. Churchill Papers, "Churchill to Foreign Secretary, 6/9/1941," Prime Minister's Personal Minutes. Churchill Papers are held at Churchill College; their online catalogue can be reached at http://www.chu.cam.ac.uk/archives/collections/churchill_papers/biography/.
38. *FRUS,* 1941, vol. 3, p. 408.
39. Fereydoon Jam, Iranian Oral History Project at Harvard, tape 2.
40. Shah, *Collected Works,* vol. 1, *Mission for My Country,* p. 130.
41. Ibid., p. 123.
42. *FRUS,* 1941, vol. III, p. 400.
43. Ibid.
44. Bullard, *The Camels Must Go,* p. 20.
45. PRO, Bullard to Foreign Office, 25 August 1941, FO 371/27207.
46. *FRUS,* 1940, vol. III, p. 625.
47. *FRUS,* 1941, vol. III, p. 400.
48. Ashraf Pahlavi, *Faces in the Mirror: Memoirs from Exile* (London, 1980), p. 40.
49. Sir Reader Bullard, *Letters from Tehran: A British Ambassador in World War II, Persia*, edited by E. C. Hodgkin (London, 1991), p. 69.
50. *FRUS,* 1941, vol. III, p. 419.
51. *FRUS,* 1940, p. 648.
52. Ibid., p. 642.
53. Ibid., p. 675.
54. *FRUS,* 1941, vol. III, p. 360.
55. *FRUS,* 1941, vol. III, p. 389.
56. In a number of dispatches from Iran, Bullard makes this point and complains about U.S. behavior. For a shorter account of his complaints, see his memoirs, *The Camels Must Go.*
57. Sir Alexander Cadogan, *The Diaries:1938–1945*, edited by David Dilks. 8 vols. (London, 1971); quoted in Cyrus Ghani, *Iran and the West* (London, 1987), p. 65.
58. Ghasem Ghani, and his circle of friends were amongst these liberals. I was told of his dismay by his son, Cyrus. Interview with author, Los Angeles, September 3, 1999.
59. *FRUS,* 1941, vol. III, p. 447.
60. PRO, "Intelligence Summary," July 15, 1939, FO 371/23262.
61. Suleiman Behboudi, *Reza Shah: Khaterat-e Suleiman Behboudi* [Reza Shah: Memoirs of Suleiman Behboudi], edited by Gholam Hussein Mirza Saleh (Tehran, 1372/1983), pp. 370–399.
62. General Fereydoon Jam, interview with author, London, May 21, 2001. He has repeated much the same idea in his interview with Harvard University's Oral History Project on Iran.
63. One of my uncles was an officer in the military, and my father was a conscript. Both were among those who tried to wash away any hint of military entanglements in their homes.
64. General Fereydoon Jam, interview with author, London, May 21, 2001.
65. Ibid.
66. PRO, FO to Tehran Embassy, May 20, 1941, FO 371/27149.
67. Bullard, *Letters from Tehran*, p. 70.
68. *FRUS*, 1941, vol. III, p. 455.
69. Ibid.
70. Bullard, *Letters from Tehran*, p. 77.
71. PRO, Tehran to Foreign Office, September 15, 1941, FO 371/27216.
72. PRO, "Public Opinion in Iran," January 24, 1941, FO 371/27183.
73. Bullard, *Letters from Tehran*, p. 125.
74. PRO, Letter by AC Samuel, July 18, 1955, FO 371/11481.
75. Bullard, *Letters from Tehran*, pp. 79–81.
76. Amin Banani's family was among this group. He told me of his experience in an interview in Palo Alto, November 29, 2007.

77. PRO, Tehran to Foreign Office, September 18, 1941, FO 248/1406.
78. Bagher Ageli, *Zoka-al Molk Foroughi va Shahrivar Bist* [Foroughi and the 29th of Shahrivar (Tehran, 1358/1979). These are, according to the author, the memories of Foroughi, as recounted to his son.
79. PRO, April 18, 1934, Larry Baggaltin to CFA Werner, FO 248/1392.
80. *Memoirs of Prince Hamid Kadjar*, edited by Habib Ladjevardi (Boston, 1996), p.108. The memoir is part of the Harvard Oral History Project.
81. Bullard, *Letters from Tehran*, p. 82.
82. PRO, Tehran to Foreign Office, September 17, 1941, CAB 12 T/654.
83. Behboudi, *Khaterat-e Suleiman Behboudi,* p. 399.
84. PRO, War Cabinet to Embassy in Tehran, September 15, 1941, FO 371/27216.
85. R. K. Karanjia, *The Mind of a Monarch* (London 1977), p. 56.
86. For example, see Alam, *Daily Journals,* vol. 6, pp. 62–64.
87. PRO, Cairo to Tehran, 628/12/41, FO 248/1406.
88. Ibid.
89. Karanjia, *The Mind of a Monarch*, p. 98
90. The Shah's sentence is a paraphrase of Shakespeare's famous line, "Uneasy lies the head that wears a crown" (*Henry IV, Part 2,* 3.1.31).

7 Hurley's Dreams

1. *Life*, September 21, 1942, p. 97,
2. Shah, *Collected Works*, vol. 1, *Mission for My Country*, pp. 431–43.
3. PRO, Tehran to Foreign Office, September 20, 1941, FO 248/1406.
4. The same report by Bullard indicates that "it is hoped that Ala may become Minister of Court." See PRO, Tehran to Foreign Office, September 20, 1941, FO 248/1406.
5. Ann Lambton, interview with author, Berwick-Upon-Tweed (England), August 10, 2003.
6. PRO, Tehran to Foreign Office, January 10, 1944, FO 371/40209.
7. PRO, Bullard Letter to Baxter, January 10, 1944, FO 371/40209.
8. Diplomats and Iranians who witnessed the ceremony or heard it on the radio have written about this nervous disposition.
9. PRO, Foreign Office to Tehran Legation, September 17, 1941, FO 371/27248.
10. PRO, Sir Bullard to Foreign Office, October 9, 1941, FO 248/1406.
11. Fereydoon Hoveyda, for years Iran's ambassador to the UN and himself a film connoisseur with many connections amongst the Hollywood glitterati, and Ardeshir Zahedi, also known for his connections to the jet set, particularly the beautiful women of the set, have told me about this passion of Princess Ashraf.
12. Shah, *Answer to History,* p. 69.
13. Shah, *Collected Works,* September 17, 1941/26 Shahrivar 1320 (Tehran, 1355/1976).
14. Fereydoon Jam, interview with author, London, August 3, 2009.
15. Fereydoon Jam, Harvard Oral History Project, tape 2.
16. Several sources have written about aspects of this sad episode. For a brief account of the entire issue, see Fakhradin Azimi, *The Crisis of Democracy* (London, 1989).
17. PRO, Bullard to Foreign Office, September 1, 1941, FO 371/27261.
18. Mohammad Gholi Majd, *Great Britain and Reza Shah: The Plunder of Iran, 1921–1941* (Gainesville, Fla., 2001), pp. 371–376.
19. Fereydoon Jam, interview with author, London, August 3, 2003.
20. Ibid.
21. Both quoted in Majd, *Great Britain and Reza Shah,* p. 323.
22. Ibid.
23. The translation was made by the British Embassy at the time; see Tehran to Foreign Office, November 20, 1945, FO 371/52731.
24. Fardust, *Memoirs*, vol. 1, p. 109.
25. *Ettel'at*, no. 3659, Mehre 2, 1320/September 27, 1941.
26. Ibid.
27. PRO, Tehran to Foreign Office, December 17, 1941, FO 371/35071.
28. A copy of the telegram is reproduced in Majd's *Great Britain and Reza Shah,* p. 325.
29. Majd, *Great Britain and Reza Shah*, p. 324.
30. PRO, Tehran to Foreign Office, June 11, 1947, FO 248 1478.
31. PRO, Tehran to Foreign Office, December 17, 1943, FO 371/35077.

32. Fardust, *Memoirs*, vol.1, pp. 122–123.
33. PRO, Tehran to Foreign Office, April 11, 1944, FO 371/40186.
34. Shah, *Collected Works*, 6 Khordad 1328/1949.
35. Parviz Nikkhah was his name; he studied the number of seminarians for his master's thesis. Jamshid Garachedaghi, interview with author, Berkeley, June 30, 1999.
36. PRO, Audience of the Shah, January 29, 1944, FO 371/30178.
37. *Marja'yat dar Arseye Ejtema va Siyasat* [Ayatollahs in the Realm of Society and Politics], edited by Seyeed Mohammad Hussein Manszur-alajdad (Tehran, 1379/2000), p. 267.
38. Ahmad Kasravi, *Shiigari* [Shiism] (Tehran, 1322/1942).
39. *Marja'yat dar Arseye Ejtema va Siyasat*, p. 272.
40. Hamid Shokat, *Dar Tir-rase Hadese* [On the Path of the Whirlwind] (Tehran, 1385/2006),pp.157–159.
41. Shah, *Collected Works,* Aban 2, 1320/October 24, 1941.
42. Ibid., Shahrivar 26, 1320/1941.
43. PRO, Tehran to Foreign Office, October 16, 1941, FO 248/1406.
44. Ibid.
45. PRO, Tehran to Foreign Office, October 9, 1941, FO 248/1406.
46. PRO, Tehran, "Military Attaché Intelligent Summary," No. 7, February 14–20, 1944, FO 406/82.
47. PRO, Tehran to Foreign Office, December 16, 1942, FO 371/31378.
48. PRO, Tehran to Foreign Office, December 9, 1942, FO 371/31378.
49. Ibid.
50. Ibid.
51. PRO, Tehran to Foreign Office, December 10, 1942, FO 371/31378.
52. PRO, Tehran to Foreign Office, December 9, 1942, FO 371/31378.
53. PRO, Tehran to Foreign Office, December 10, 1942, FO 371/31378.
54. PRO, Tehran to Foreign Office, December 15, 1942, FO 371/31378.
55. PRO, Tehran to Foreign Office, November 11, 1942, FO 371/31387.
56. The Hurley Report as well as the rest of his papers are housed in the University of Oklahoma Library. I have written about the report and its fate in "Hurley's Dream," *Hoover Digest,* No. 3, July 30, 2003.
57. PRO, Sir Reader Bullard to Kerman Consulate, September 22, 1941 FO 371/27247.
58. PRO, External Affair India to S/S India, October 5, 1941, FO 371/27247.
59. Ibid.
60. PRO, Sec. of State for Colonies to Governor of Mauritius, October 8, 1941, FO/371/17247.
61. PRO, Bullard to Foreign Office, October 24, 1941. FO 371/27248.
62. Ibid.
63. Ibid.
64. Ibid.
65. Gholam Hussein Mirza-Saleh, *Khaterat-e Suleiman Behboodi, Shams Pahlavi, Ali Izadi* [Memoirs of Behbudi, Shams and Isadi] (Tehran, 1372/1992), p. 434.
66. Reza Shah, "Nasayeh va Payam-e Tarikhi Ahlahazrat Reza Shah Pahlavi be Farzande Tajdar-e Khod," [The Advice and the Historic Message of His Majesty Reza Shah to his Crowned Son]. *Tehran Mosavar.*
67. Ibid., p. 1.
68. PRO, Foreign Office to Tehran, May 20, 1947, FO 248/1478.
69. PRO, Foreign Office to Tehran, March 12, 1947, FO 248/1478.
70. Ibid.
71. PRO, Tehran to Foreign Office, March 12, 1947, FO 248/1478.
72. PRO, Tehran to Foreign Office, April 29, 1947, FO 248/1478.

8 Dawn of the Cold War

1. R. K. Karanjia, *The Mind of a Monarch* (London, 1977), p. 70.
2. Ibid., p. 72.
3. Shah, *Answer to History*, p. 72.
4. Karanjia, *The Mind of a Monarch*, p. 168.
5. Ibid., p. 72.
6. PRO, Bullard to Eden, January 27, 1944, FO 371/40181.
7. PRO, Tehran to Foreign Office, January 27, 1944, FO 371/31378.
8. Ibid.

9. In many essays, Milan Kundera has made just such a charge. Central Europe was part of "Middle Europe," he says, and should have remained in the West; see for example, Milan Kundera, "The Tragedy of Central Europe," *New York Review of Books*, April 26, 1984, pp. 33–38.
10. Shah, *Answer to History*, p. 73.
11. PRO, Le Rougetel to Bevin, September 3, 1946, FO 321/52731.
12. PRO, Audience given by the Shah, September 4, 1946, FO 371/52731.
13. PRO, Tehran to Foreign Office, February 14, 1944, CAB 12T/654.
14. Ibid.
15. Fardust, *Memoirs*, vol. 1. p. 127.
16. Jamil Hasanli, *At the Dawn of the Cold War: The Soviet-American Crisis Over Iranian Azerbaijan, 1941–1946* (Lanham, Md., 2006), p. 26.
17. Simon Sebag Montefiore, *Young Stalin* (New York, 2007), p. 16.
18. Ibid., p. 196
19. Natalia I. Yegorova, " 'The Iran Crisis' of 1945–46: A View from the Russian Archives" (working paper 15, Cold War International History Project, Woodrow Wilson International Center for Scholars).
20. Tadeusz Swietochowski, *Russia and Azerbaijan: A Borderland in Transition* (New York, 1995), p. 139.
21. For a discussion of these bylaws, see Fernando Claudín, *The Communist Movement: From Comintern to Cominform*, vol. 1, *The Crisis of the Communist International* (New York, 1975).
22. Decree of the CC CPSU Politburo to Mir Bagirov CC Secretary of the Communist Party of Azerbaijan, on "Measures to Organize a Separatist Movement in Southern Azerbaijan and Other Provinces of Northern Iran," July 6, 1945. Cold War International History Project, Woodrow Wilson International Center for Scholars.
23. Mossadeq's speech in the parliament, quoted in Mostafa Elm, *Oil, Power, and Principle: Iran's Nationalization and Its Aftermath* (Syracuse, N.Y., 1992), p. 45.
24. Hasanli, *At the Dawn of the Cold War*, p. 266.
25. Elm, *Oil, Power, and Principle*, p. 45.
26. Ironically, even some on the American Left concluded that "Soviet interests necessitated influence in Northern Iran," and this influence, they wagered "could provide Azerbaijan with necessary reforms." Ibid., p. 129.
27. *FRUS*, 1944, vol. 5, p. 48.
28. Dr. Mohammad Mossadeq, *Khaterat o Ta'alomat* [Memoirs and Contemplations] (Tehran, 1357/1979), p. 359. Mossadeq first quotes the entire passage from the Shah's memoirs that is critical of Mossadeq and then offers his response.
29. PRO, Bullard to Foreign Office, January 20, 1944, FO 371/40186.
30. PRO, British Embassy in Tehran to Foreign Office, January 20, 1944, FO 371/40186.
31. Swietochowski, *Russia and Azerbaijan*, p. 137.
32. PRO, Bullard to Foreign Office, June 4, 1945, FO 248/1452.
33. PRO, British Embassy in Tehran to Foreign Office, March 8, 1944, FO 371/40186.
34. PRO, British Embassy to Foreign Office, January 28, 1945, FO 371/45449.
35. Elm, *Oil, Power, and Principle*, p. 47.
36. Karanjia, *The Mind of a Monarch*, p. 78.
37. Elm, *Oil, Power, and Principle*, p. 47.
38. *FRUS*, 1947, vol. 5, p. 892.
39. Swietochowski, *Russia and Azerbaijan*, p. 260.
40. PRO, British Embassy in Tehran to Foreign Office, September 3, 1946, FO 371/52731.
41. *FRUS*, 1945, vol. 8, p. 49.
42. Hasanli, *At the Dawn of the Cold War*, p. 51.
43. Louise L'Estrange Fawcett, *Iran and the Cold War: The Azerbaijan Crisis of 1946* (Cambridge, U.K., 1922), p. 56.
44. Ibid., p. 374
45. Ibid,. p. 374.
46. *FRUS*, 1947, vol. 5, p. 922.
47. Ibid.
48. Quoted in Gary R. Hess, "The Iranian Crisis of 1945–46 and the Cold War," *Political Science Quarterly* 89, no. 1 (March 1974): 135.
49. Ibid., p. 136.
50. *FRUS*, 1946, vol. 7, p. 362.
51. Quoted in Hess, "The Iranian Crisis," p. 134.
52. PRO, British Embassy in Tehran to Foreign Office, June 26, 1946, FO 371/2731.

53. Fardust, *Memoirs*, vol. 1, pp. 140–141.
54. Hasanli, *At the Dawn of the Cold War*, p. 152.
55. I was told the identity of the man. Though he is dead, his children are alive, and some live in Iran.
56. General Alavi-Kia, interview with author, San Diego, September 3, 2004.
57. PRO, British Embassy in Tehran to Foreign Office, April 16, 1946, FO 371/52731.
58. PRO, British Embassy in Tehran to Foreign Office, September 3, 1946, FO 371/52731.
59. *FRUS,* 1946, vol. 5, p. 356.
60. PRO, Tehran to Foreign Office, April 16, 1946, FO 371/52731.
61. PRO, Audience given by the Shah to Air Commodore W. L. Runcimen, 1946, FO 371/52731.
62. Fawcett, *Iran and the Cold War*, p. 57.
63. Ebrahim Golestan, interview with author, March 29, 2009, Nice, France.
64. Robert Rossow Jr., "The Battle of Azerbaijan, 1946" *Middle East Journal* 10, no. 1 (1956): 26.
65. Ibid., p. 25.
66. Hasanli, *At the Dawn of the Cold War*, p. 299.
67. Swietochowski, *Russia and Azerbaijan*, p. 156.
68. In his rendition, the Shah claims that the agreement called for the promotion of every rebel officer by two grades. See *Answer to History*, p. 76.
69. Rossow, "The Battle of Azerbaijan," p. 19.
70. Shah, *Answer to History*, p. 77.
71. Rossow, "The Battle of Azerbaijan," p. 31.
72. Rasul Ja'farian, ed. Bohran Azerbaijan: *Khaterat-e Mirza Abdullah Mojtahedi* [The Azerbaijan Crisis, Memoirs of Mirza Abdullah Mojtahedi] (Tehran, 1381/2002) p. 354.
73. The episode is reported in the memoirs of Ebtehaj. For an account of the episode, see Hamid Shokat, *Dar Tir Rase Havadeth: Zendegiye Siyasiye Qavam-al-Saltaneh* [A Political Life of Qavam] (Tehran, 1385/2006).
74. Karanjia, *The Mind of a Monarch*, p. 90
75. Ibid.
76. *FRUS,* 1946, vol. 7, p. 348.
77. For a discussion of these factors, see Shokat, *Dar Tir Rase Havadeth*.
78. For a detailed account of these episodes, written from the point of view of affording to Qavam his due historical respect, see Shokat, *Dar Tir Rase Havadeth*.
79. Shah, *Answer to History*, p. 79.
80. Swietochowski, *Russia and Azerbaijan*, p. 154.
81. Hess, "The Iranian Crisis," p. 135.
82. In 1945, for example, the French government claimed that Qavam had received a bribe to reappoint a diplomat to the post of ambassador in Paris. See my *Persian Sphinx: Amir Abbas Hoveyda and the Riddle of the Iranian Revolution* (Washington, DC, 2000).
83. *FRUS,* 1947, vol. 5. p. 923.
84. *FRUS,* 1946,vol. 7, p. 531.
85. *FRUS,* 1947, vol. 7, p. 979.
86. Ibid., p. 538.
87. Fawcett, *Iran and the Cold War*, p. 74.
88. *FRUS,* 1946, vol. 7, p. 538.
89. PRO, "Embassy Minute," December 6, 1947, FO 248/1462.
90. Many memoirs of the time reveal the extent of Princess Ashraf's intervention. For example, see Amir Teymour Kalali, *Khaterat-e Amir Teymour Kalali*, ed. Habib Ladjevardi (Bethesda, MD. IOHP, 1997). A copy of the memoirs was provided to me courtesy of his family, particularly his daughter and son-in-law, Laleh and Mohsen Moazzami. Palo Alto, December 5, 2005.
91. Karanjia, *The Mind of a Monarch*, p. 115.
92. Mahmoud Torbati Sanjabi, *Panj Golouleh Baraye Shah* [Five Bullets for the Shah] (Tehran, 1381/2002), p. 92.
93. Ardeshir Zahedi, interview with author, Montreux, March 26, 2009.
94. Shah, *Collected Works,* vol. I, *Mission for My Country* (Tehran, 1975), pp. 102–4.
95. For a brief account of his career, see my *Eminent Persians* (Syracuse, N.Y., 2008), vol. 1, pp. 483–490.
96. Shah, *Collected Works,* vol. 1, *Mission for My Country* (Tehran, 1975), p. 103.
97. Sanjabi, *Panj Golouleh Baraye Shah*, p. 92.
98. *Salnameye Donya*, Fifth year, p. 38.

99. Shah, *Collected Works*, "The Shah's Message to the People, 17 Bahman 1327," in vol. 1320–1340 (1941–1961), n.p.
100. Sanjabi, *Panj Golouleh Baraye Shah*, p. 93.
101. Tehran Mossavar published the novel by Sadreddin Elahi. He kindly provided me a copy of the text. He described the responses he received to the novel, including a visit from Parvin.
102. *Salnameye Donya*, Fourth year, 164.
103. Sanjabi, *Panj Golouleh Baraye Shah*, p. 85.
104. PRO, British Embassy in Tehran to Foreign Office, September 3, 1946, FO 371/2731.
105. "Talk of the Town, Willkiana," *The New Yorker*, December 26, 1942.
106. Ardeshir Zahedi, interview with author, Montreux, March 27, 2009.
107. "Talk of the Town, Progressive," *The New Yorker*, October 25, 1947, p. 25.
108. Ibid.
109. Ibid.
110. Karanjia, *The Mind of a Monarch*, p. 199.
111. Ibid.
112. PRO, British Embassy in Tehran to Foreign Office, June 26, 1946, FO 371/45496.
113. *FRUS*, 1947, vol. 5, p. 990.
114. *FRUS*, 1948, vol. 5, p. 92.
115. *FRUS*, 1948, vol. 5, p. 94.
116. *FRUS*, 1948, vol. 5, p. 189.
117. *FRUS*, 1948, vol. 5, p. 191.
118. *FRUS*, 1949, vol. 6, p. 480.
119. Iraj Pezekshzad, interview with author, Stanford, CA, May 10, 2009.
120. Shah, *Collected Works*, "Speech before the Opening Session of the Constituent Assembly," vol. 1320–1340 (1941–1961).
121. Roberto Mangabeira Unger, "The Future of Religion and the Religion of the Future," Tanner Lecture, Stanford University, April 16, 2009.
122. For a text of Qavam's letter and the Shah's response, see Mohammad Ali Safari, *Galam va Siyasat* [The Pen and Politics] (Tehran, 1371/2002), pp. 911–923.
123. PRO, British Embassy in Tehran to Foreign Office, June 19, 1946, FO 371/2731.
124. Ibid.
125. PRO, British Embassy in Cairo to Foreign Office, July 5, 1946, FO 371/2731.
126. Her memoir, published under the direct auspices of the Islamic Republic of Iran, has all the characteristics of a semi-pornographic romance novel. See Parvin Ghafari, *Ta Siyahi: Dar Dam-e Shah* [Into Darkness: In the Shah's Clutches] (Tehran, 1376/1997).
127. PRO, British Embassy in Cairo to Foreign Office, July 5, 1946, FO 371/2731.
128. Ardeshir Zahedi, interview with author, Montreux, March 27, 2009.
129. PRO, British Embassy in Cairo to Foreign Office, September 5, 1945, FO 371/45496.
130. *Salnameye Donya*, Fourth year, p. 65.
131. Shah, *Collected Works*, vol.1, *Mission for My Country*, p. 443.
132. PRO, British Embassy in Tehran to Foreign Office, May 19, 1948, FO 371/68726.

9 Palace of Solitude

1. *FRUS*, 1952–1954, vol. X, p. 8.
2. *FRUS*, 1952–1954, vol. X, p. 284.
3. C. M. Woodhouse, *Something Ventured* (London, 1992), p. 121.
4. For a brief account of these tensions, see life of Maleki in *Eminent Persians* (Syracuse, N.Y., 2008), and *Khaterat Siyasi Khalil Maleki [Political Memoirs of Maleki]*, edited and with an introduction by Homayoon Katouzian (Tehran, 1368/1999). Baghai, too, has offered his version of events. See his Harvard Oral History interview with Habiv Lajevardi, later published in a book edited by Mahmoud Toloui.
5. Abdullah Shahbazi, personal correspondence.
6. *FRUS*, 1952–1954, vol. X, p. 280.
7. See my chapter on Golshai'yan in *Eminent Persians*.
8. PRO, "Persian Political Situation," November 12, 1949, FO 371/75468.
9. PRO, British Embassy, Tehran, to Foreign Ministry, November 18, 1949, FO 371/75468.
10. *FRUS*, 1952–1954, vol. X, 1951, p. 39.
11. PRO, Churchill to Truman, August 16, 1952, FO 371/98691. For a lengthy discussion about "Churchill's Games With Truman," see Mostafa Elm, *Oil, Power, and Principle: Iran's Oil Nationalization and Its Aftermath* (Syracuse, N.Y., 1992), pp. 248–266.

12. PRO, Seyyed Zia, December 10, 1950, FO248/1513.
13. PRO, British Embassy, Tehran to Foreign Ministry, 20, December 20, 1950, FO 248/1513.
14. PRO, Foreign Office to Chancery, April 11, 1951, FO 248/1513.
15. PRO, Amery to Selwyn Lloyd, March 25, 1952, FO 371/98683. In an interview with Mustafa Elm, Drummond/Qajar confirmed the meeting.
16. PRO, British Embassy, Tehran to Foreign Office, September 25, 1951, FO 248/1513.
17. PRO, British Embassy, Tehran to Foreign Office, December 14, 1951, FO 248/1514.
18. Ibid.
19. PRO, Tehran to Foreign Office, April 3, 1950, FO 248/1493.
20. PRO, Tehran to Foreign Office, March 18, 1950, FO 248/1493.
21. PRO, British Embassy, Tehran to Foreign Office, September 21, 1952, FO 248/1541.
22. Ibid.
23. PRO, British Embassy, Tehran to Foreign Office, December 14, 1951, FO 248/1514.
24. PRO, Tehran to Foreign Office, February 1, 1950, FO 371/82310.
25. PRO, Tehran to Foreign Office, May 11, 1949, FO 371/35077.
26. PRO, Tehran to Foreign Office, June 25, 1950, FO 248/1493.
27. PRO, FO to Washington, June 7, 1950, FO 371/8231.
28. PRO, Plans for the Reform of the Persian Government, June 23, 1950, FO 371/8231.
29. PRO, Tehran to Foreign Office, August 25, 1950, FO 248/1493.
30. PRO, Tehran to Foreign Office, June 5, 1950, FO 248/1493.
31. PRO, Tehran to Foreign Office, August 17, 1950, FO 248/1493.
32. PRO, Tehran to Foreign Office, October 3, 1950, FO248/1493.
33. PRO, Tehran to Foreign Office, September 28, 1950, FO 248/1493.
34. M. Reza Ghods, "The Rise and Fall of General Razmara," *Middle Eastern Studies* 1, no. 1 (1993).
35. Kambiz Razmara and Kaveh Bayat, *Khaterat Va Asnad-e Sepahbod Hajd-Ali Razmara* [Papers and Memoirs of General Razmara] (Tehran, 1382/2003), pp. 465–473.
36. Elm, *Oil, Power, and Principle*, p. 82.
37. PRO, British Embassy, Tehran to Foreign Office, March 19, 1951, FO 371/91524.
38. PRO, British Embassy, Tehran to Foreign Office, February 8, 1951, FO 248/1514.
39. PRO, British Embassy, Tehran to Foreign Office, March 15, 1951, FO 248/1514.
40. PRO, Counselor Conversation with the Shah, August 15, 1951, FO 371/82212.
41. PRO, British Embassy, Tehran to Foreign Office, February 8, 1951, FO 248/1514.
42. PRO, British Embassy, Tehran to Foreign Office, April 21, 1952, FO 248/1514.
43. PRO, British Embassy, Tehran to Foreign Office, May 21, 1950, FO248/1493.
44. Ervand Abrahamian, "The 1953 Coup in Iran," *Science and Society* 65, no. 2 (Summer 2001): 182–215.
45. Woodhouse, *Something Ventured*, pp. 114–125.
46. These are the words of the foreign minister, quoted from a PRO document in Elm, *Oil, Power, and Principle*, p. 91.
47. *FRUS,* 1952–54, vol. X, pp. 67.
48. Shah, *Answer to History,* p. 85.
49. PRO, British Embassy, Tehran to Foreign Ministry, July 2, 1951, FO 248/1514.
50. William Roger Louis, "Musaddiq and the Dilemmas of British Imperialism," in James A. Bill and William Roger Louis, eds., *Musaddiq, Iranian Nationalism, and Oil* (London, 1988), pp. 228–261.
51. Elm, *Oil, Power, and Principle*, 163.
52. *FRUS,* 1952–1954, vol. X, p. 51.
53. *FRUS,* 1952–1954, vol. X, p. 328.
54. Ibid.
55. *FRUS,* 1952–54, vol. X, p. 153.
56. PRO, Tehran to Foreign Office, July 21, 1952, FO 248/1541.
57. PRO, Tehran to Foreign Office, July 28, 1952, FO 248/1541.
58. PRO, The Shah and Kashani, January 8, 1952, FO 248/1541.
59. *FRUS, 1952–1954*, vol.X, p. 405.
60. Seyyed Mohammad Hossein Manzar-al-Azdad, *Marjaeeyat dar Arseye Ejtema' va Siyasat* [Ayatollahs in the Realm of Society and Politics] (Tehran, 1374/1995), p. 476.
61. PRO, Tehran to Foreign Office, March 4. 1952, FO 248/1541.
62. PRO, British Consulate, October 13, 1950, FO 371/82401.
63. Princess Soraya Esfandiary Bakhtiary, *Palace of Solitude*, translated by Hubert Gibbs (London, 1992), p. 18. The first English translation of her memoirs, called *The Autobiography of Her*

Imperial Highness Princess Soraya (translated by Constantine Fitzegibbon), is even more marred by cultural indiscretions and historic errors. There she calls her wedding an "Arabic ceremony" and misnames the Shah's brothers and sisters. For a critical overview of that edition see, Cyrus Ghani, *Iran and the West: A Critical Bibliography* (London, 1987), 121–122.

64. PRO, British Consulate in Isfahan, Foreign Office, October 13, 1950, FO 371/82401.
65. Princess Soraya, *Palace of Solitude*, p. 9 (italics mine).
66. Princess Soraya, *Palace of Solitude*, p. 78.
67. Ibid., p. 29.
68. Ibid., p. 24.
69. Ibid., p. 22.
70. Ibid., p. 21.
71. Ibid., p. 28.
72. PRO, British Consulate in Isfahan, Foreign Office, October 13, 1950, FO 371/82401.
73. Princess Soraya, *Palace of Solitude*, p. 41.
74. Ibid., p. 50.
75. PRO, British Embassy, Tehran to Foreign Office, February 19, 1951, FO 371/91672.
76. PRO, Foreign Ministry to Air Ministry, February 12, 1951, FO 371/91672.
77. PRO, British Embassy to Foreign Ministry, April 4, 1951, FO 371/91672.
78. Ibid.
79. PRO, British Embassy to Foreign Ministry, June 27, 1951, and British Embassy to Foreign Embassy, July 5, 1951, FO 371/91672.
80. PRO, British Embassy, Tehran to Foreign Office, March 31, 1951, FO 371/91672.
81. For this car, a number of telegrams were exchanged between the British Embassy and the Foreign Office. All of them can be found in FO 371/91672.
82. PRO, Board of Trade to Tehran, December 5, 1950, FO 371/82401.
83. Princess Soraya, *Palace of Solitude*, p. 86.
84. Ibid., p. 114.
85. Ibid., p. 45.
86. Ibid., p. 84.
87. Ibid.
88. One of the regular poker players in those days was Manouchehr Riyahi, whose wife was a sister to the wife of one of the Shah's half-brothers and who made a fortune by running a cabaret in Tehran that used Polish women as dancers and hosts. For an account of his days at the Court, see Manouchehr Riyahi, *Sarab Zendegi* (Tehran, 1371/2001), pp. 530–581.
89. Princess Soraya, *Palace of Solitude*, p. 92.
90. Ibid., p. 93.
91. PRO, "Persia," February 27, 1953, FO 371/104562.
92. Princess Soraya, *Palace of Solitude*, p. 90.
93. Ibid., p. 91.
94. *FRUS,* 1952–1954, vol. X, p. 187.
95. Ibid.
96. PRO, L. F. Pyman to Foreign Office, January 15, 1952, FO 248/1541.
97. *FRUS*, 1952–1954, vol. X, p. 187.
98. *FRUS*, 1952–1954, vol. X, p. 406.
99. *FRUS*, 1952–1954, vol. X, p. 427.
100. PRO, Tehran to Foreign Office, September 16, 1950, FO 248/1493.
101. *FRUS*, 1952–1954, vol. X, 1953, p. 730.
102. Ibid.
103. Kermit Roosevelt, *Countercoup: The Struggle for the Control of Iran* (New York: 1979), p. 156.
104. *FRUS*, 1952–1954, vol. X, p. 674.
105. PRO, Tehran to Foreign Office, April 8, 1950, FO 248/1493.
106. *FRUS*, 1952–1954, vol. X, p. 675.
107. Ibid., p. 676.
108. *FRUS,* 1952–1954, vol. X, p. 385.
109. *FRUS,* 1952–1954, vol. X, p. 679.
110. PRO, Tehran to Foreign Office, June 1, 1952, FO 248/1535.
111. *FRUS,* 1952–1954, vol. X, p. 680.
112. Ibid., p. 681.
113. *FRUS*, 1952–1954, vol. X, p. 682.
114. Ahmad Ali Shaygan, *Zendegi-namehy-e Siyasi, Neveshteha va Sokhanraniha* [Political Life, Writings and Speeches], ed. By Ahmad Shaygan, vol. 1 (Tehran, Agah Press 1384/2005), p. 515.

115. *FRUS,* 1952–1954, vol. X, p. 683.
116. *FRUS,* 1952–1954, vol. X, p. 681.
117. *FRUS,* 1952–1954, vol. X, p. 682.
118. *FRUS,* 1952–1954, vol. X, p. 685.
119. Ibid.
120. *FRUS,* 1952–1954, vol. X, p. 685.
121. PRO, British Embassy, Washington DC, to Foreign Office, February 27, 1953, FO 371/104526.
122. *FRUS,*1952–1954, vol. X, p. 686.
123. Ibid.
124. Ardeshir Zahedi, interview with author, Montreux, March 20, 2006.
125. *FRUS,* 1952–1954, vol. X, p. 688.
126. Ibid., p. 689.
127. *FRUS,* 1952–1954, vol. X, p. 689.
128. PRO, Foreign Office to Secretary of State, March 3, 1953, FO 371/104526.
129. PRO, "Iran Report," March 4, 1953, FO 371/104563.
130. *FRUS,* 1952–1954, vol. X, p. 687.
131. PRO, "Persia," March 4, 1953, FO 371/104563.
132. Ibid.
133. Shaygan, *Zendegi-namehy-e Siyasi, Neveshteha va Sokhanraniha,* p. 517.
134. PRO, Iran Report, March 4, 1953, FO 371/104563.
135. PRO, American Embassy, London, March 1, 1953, FO 371/104563.
136. PRO, Iran Report, February 24, 1953, FO 371/104563.
137. Ibid.
138. PRO, American Embassy, London, March 1, 1953, FO 371/104563.
139. Roosevelt, in *Countercoup* (p. 126) refers to the CIA's role in this campaign. There have been other fuller accounts of the campaign.
140. *FRUS,* 1952–1954, vol. X, p. 742.
141. PRO, "Persia," March 12, 1953, FO 371/104563.
142. *FRUS,* 1952–1954, vol. X, pp. 722–723.
143. Shaygan, *Zendegi-namehy-e Siyasi, Neveshteha va Sokhanraniha,* p. 539.
144. Karim Sanjabi, a professor of law and a close advisor of Mossadeq, declares in his Harvard Oral History interview that, in his view, the Shah did have the right to dismiss the prime minister when there was no parliament.
145. Jalal Matini, *Negahi be Karnamey-e Siyasi Dr Mossadeq* [A Glance at the Political Career of Dr. Mohammad Mossadeq] (Los Angeles, 2006), p. 363. Of those receiving such recess appointments, only one, and then only after he was dismissed, questioned the King's right to make such appointments.
146. Shaygan, *Zendegi-namehy-e Siyasi, Neveshteha va Sokhanraniha,* pp. 152–154. The full text of the letter can be found on page 154.

10 Ajax or Boot

1. In his *Legacy of Ashes,* Tim Weiner does point to the strangeness of this choice for a CIA operation. See Tim Weiner, *Legacy of Ashes: A History of the CIA* (New York, 2007), p. 83.
2. Shakespeare, *Troilus and Cressida,* 1.2.22–30.
3. Weiner, *Legacy of Ashes,* p. 8.
4. Ibid., p. 18.
5. Sir Denis Wright, "The Memoirs of Sir Denis Wright (1911–1976)" (unpublished memoirs), vol. 1, p. 212. He kindly gave me access to not only the full text of his memoirs but to most of his private papers.
6. *FRUS,* 1952–1954, vol. X, p. 755. The editors say there is an indication on the note that Eisenhower saw it on 8/21/1953.
7. Ardeshir Zahedi had, in the aftermath of August 1953, offered his version of events in a series of articles called "Five Days of Crisis." *Life* magazine had offered him a large sum for the right to publish the memoirs, but General Zahedi had forbidden his son from going through with the deal. The version was published in Iran. Much the same version is retold in the first volume of his recently published memoirs. See Zahedi,

Memoirs [Persian], vol. 1. A French translation of the volume has already appeared and an English version is apparently on the way.

8. Cyrus Ghani, *Iran and the West: A Critical Bibliography* (London, 2002).
9. George C. McGhee, "Recollections of Dr. Mohammad Mussadiq," in *Musaddiq, Iranian Nationalism, and Oil,* James A. Bill and Wm Roger Louis, eds. (London, 1988), p. 300.
10. The Shah made the claim in many speeches, and in his two memoirs. For example, see *Answer to History,* pp. 79–84.
11. Princess Soraya, *Palace of Solitude,* p. 108. The book calls her Her Imperial Highness, Princess Soraya. Not long after her departure from Iran after her divorce, she tried to use this title for a book of memoirs and the Iranian court fought to stop her from using the title.
12. http://www.fas.org/news/iran/2000/000317.htm.
13. For the CIA's account, see Donald Wilbur, "Clandestine Service History: Overthrow of Premier Mossadeq of Iran, November 1952–August 1953." The actual text was written by Wilbur, a Princeton professor and a CIA operative and leaked to the *New York Times* in 2000. "Secrets of History: The CIA in Iran, Special Report.: How a Plot Convulsed Iran in '53 and in '79," By James Risen, *New York Times,* April 16, 2000, p. 1. The other two most important memoirs, discussed further in the chapter, were Kermit Roosevelt's *Countercoup: The Struggle for the Control of Iran* (New York, 1979), and Christopher Woodhouse's *Something Ventured* (London, 1992).
14. See for example, Darioush Bayandor, *Iran and the CIA: The Fall of Mossadeq Revisited* (New York, 2010).
15. "A Diplomat's View from Tehran," U.S. Embassy in Tehran, reprinted by Georgetown University, Series on History of Diplomacy, Washington, DC, 1980.
16. For some of these controversies, See Jalal Matini, *Negahi Be Karnamey-e Siasi Dr Mohammad Mossadeq* [A Glance at the Political Career of Dr. Mohammad Mossadeq] (Los Angeles, 2006).
17. For a detailed account of the effort and of McGee's tensions with the British, see the well-researched history by Mostafa Elm, *Oil, Power, and Principle: Iran's Oil Nationalization and Its Aftermath* (Syracuse, N.Y., 1992), pp. 85–89. Some in Britain even accused him of instigating the movement and encouraging Mossadeq to have American oil companies replace the AIOC.
18. McGhee, "Recollections of Dr. Mohammad Mussadiq," pp. 298–302.
19. *FRUS,* 1952–1954, vol. X, p. 417.
20. Kennett Love, "The American Role in the Pahlavi Restoration on August 19, 1953," Allen Dulles Papers, Seeley G. Mudd Manuscript Library, Princeton University, p. 28.
21. Ibid.
22. *FRUS,* 1952–1954, vol. X, p. 514.
23. Love, "The American Role," p. 25.
24. In a detailed article about Reporter's role in the 1953 events, Abdollah Shahbazi refers to this remarkable letter and promises to divulge its contents later. He has yet to publish the full text, but in personal correspondence, he described to me some of the main points in the first page of the four-page document.
25. Roosevelt, *Countercoup,* p. 110.
26. Ibid., p. 163.
27. Ibid., p. 109.
28. I was told about this aspect of Roosevelt's life by several people, including Fereydoon Mahdavi, onetime minister of trade during the Shah's reign. He was in charge of foreign purchases, and realized that for wheat he had to go through Roosevelt. Interview with author, Paris, September 4, 1999.
29. *FRUS,* 1952–1954, vol. X, p. 725.
30. Ibid., p. 723.
31. Ibid.
32. *FRUS,* 1952–1954, vol. X, p. 781. The author or British source of this fascinating eight-page document is unknown, according to the editors of the *FRUS*, 1952–1954 volume.
33. Wilbur, "Clandestine Service History," Appendix B, pp. 6–7. In his *Iran and the CIA*, Bayandor also covers these pressures and their impact on the Shah, pp. 87–98.
34. Zahedi, *Memoirs* [Persian], vol. 1, pp. 143–154.
35. *FRUS,* 1952–1954, vol. X, p. 781.
36. Zahedi, *Memoirs* [Persian], vol. 1, p. 144.
37. *FRUS,* 1952–1954, vol. X, p. 746.

38. Roosevelt, *Countercoup*, p. 160.
39. Zahedi, *Memoirs* [Persian], vol. 1, p. 153.
40. Princess Soraya, *Palace of Solitude*, p. 100.
41. Shah, *Collected Works*, vol. 1, *Mission for My Country*, p. 197.
42. Princess Soraya, *Palace of Solitude*, p. 101.
43. Ibid., p. 104.
44. Dr. Hossein Fatemi, "Khaeni Ke Mikhast Vatan ra Be Khako Khoun Bekeshad Farar Kard," [The Traitor Who Wanted to Shed the Nation's Blood] *Bakhtat-e Emrooz*, 26 Mordad 1332/ August 17, 1953.
45. Ibid.
46. Dr Hossein Fatemi, "Melat Bot-Shekan," [Iconoclast Nation] *Bakhtar Emrooz*, 27 Khordard 1332/August 18, 1953.
47. Gholam Reza Afkhami, *The Life and Times of the Shah* (Berkeley, Calif., 2009), p. 170.
48. Ibid.
49. Zahedi, *Memoirs* [Persian], vol. 1, pp. 143–169.
50. *FRUS*, 1952–1954, vol. X, p. 748.
51. Love, "The American Role," p. 33.
52. *FRUS*, 1952–1954, vol. X, p. 748.
53. For example, see Francis J. Gavin, "Politics, Power, and U.S. Policy in Iran, 1950–1953," *Journal of Cold War Studies* 1, no. 1 (Winter 1999).
54. *FRUS*, 1951–1954, vol. X, p. 749.
55. Ibid., p. 749.
56. Gholam Hussein Sadighi, "Dar Bareye Enhelal Majli" [On Dissolving the Majlis], courtesy of the Sadighi family.
57. Ibid., p. 751.
58. Ibid., p. 752.
59. Dr. Mohammad Mossadeq, *Khaterat va Taalomat*, p. 270.
60. Love, "The American Role," p. 34.
61. Ibid.
62. Ibid., p. 41.
63. Ebrahim Golestan, phone interview with author, July 30, 2010.
64. *FRUS*, 1952–1954, vol. X, p. 759
65. Ibid., p. 756.
66. Ibid., p. 746.
67. Ibid., p. 748.
68. PRO, British Embassy, Baghdad, to Foreign Ministry, August 21, 1953, FO 371/104570.
69. The British Embassy in Baghdad reported the content of the discussion. Quoted in Ruehsen Moyara de Moraes, "Operation 'Ajax' Revisited: Iran, 1953," *Middle Eastern Studies* 29, no. 3 (July 1993): footnote 49.
70. Shah, *Collected Works*, 26 Tir 1336/1957.
71. Princess Soraya, *Palace of Solitude*, p. 104.
72. For an account of his life, see his chapter in my *Eminent Persians* (Syracuse, N.Y., 2008).
73. Prince Soraya, *Palace of Solitude*, p. 106.
74. PRO, Rome to Foreign Office, August 18, 1953, FO 371/104659.
75. The text of the telegram is provided in Ardeshir Zahedi's *Memoirs* [Persian], vol. 1, p. 227.
76. Ardeshir Zahedi, interview with author, Montreux, December 22, 2006.
77. "Shah Denounces Mossadeq," *New York Times*, August 22, 1953.
78. "Shah Leaves Rome to Fly to Tehran," *New York Times*, August 21, 1953.
79. *FRUS*, 1952–1954, vol. X, pp. 760–761.
80. PRO, Message from the Persian government, August 21, 1953, FO 371/104659.
81. Ebrahim Golestan, interview with author, Hayward Heath, U.K., December 19, 2006. He was at the airport, filming the scene of the arrival.
82. Shah, *Collected Works*, vol. 1941–1961, 1 Shahrivar 1322/August 23, 1953. The collected works gives the date of the message as August 23, but in fact it was, according to numerous sources, delivered on the night of August 22.
83. PRO, American Embassy in London, Foreign Office, August 23, 1953, FO 371/104570.
84. *FRUS*, 1952–1954, vol. X, p. 765.
85. Ibid., p. 762.
86. Ibid., p. 763.
87. Ibid., p. 764.
88. PRO, Tehran to Foreign Office, April 12 1955, FO 371/114810.

89. *FRUS,* 1952–1954, vol. X, p. 761.
90. PRO, FO to Washington, August 25 1953, FO 371/104659.
91. PRO, Sir W. Strang to Tehran August 29 1953, FO 371/104659.
92. Roosevelt, *Countercoup*, pp. 199–200.
93. Wright, "Memoirs," vol. 1, pp. 187–188.
94. Appendix to chapter 10 of Wright's memoirs included the full text of his marching orders, titled "Policy of Her Majesty's Government in the Re-establishment of Diplomatic Relations with the Persian Government, December 17, 1953."
95. Wright, "Memoirs," vol. 1, p. 220.
96. Ibid., p. 207.
97. Ibid., pp. 207–208.
98. Ibid., p. 217.
99. Ibid., p. 213.
100. *FRUS,* 1952–1954, vol. X, p. 1017.
101. PRO, Tehran to Foreign Office, May 12, 1954, FO 371/109985.
102. PRO, Tehran to Foreign Office, October 20, 1954, FO 371/109985.
103. *FRUS*, 1952–1954, vol. X, p.1038.
104. *FRUS,* 1952–1954, vol. X, pp. 931–932.
105. Iraj Amini, *Barbal-e Bohran* [On the Wings of Crisis] (Tehran, 2009), p. 105.
106. PRO, "Iran Annual Political Report 1954," FO 371/114805.
107. Amini, *Barbal-e Bohran*, vol. 1, p. 8.
108. PRO, Tehran to Foreign Office, July 1 1954, FO 371/11066.
109. After the Islamic Revolution, Shaban escaped to the safety of exile, ending up in Los Angeles where he agreed to do an extensive interview with a seasoned journalist, wherein he denied playing any role in the events of August 19. He suggests that for much of that day he was in fact in prison.
110. *FRUS,* 1952–1954, vol. X, p. 012.
111. Shah, *Answer to History*, p. 95.
112. PRO, Tehran to Foreign Office, November 3, 1954, FO371/109985.
113. Princess Soraya, *Palace of Solitude*, p. 115.
114. Ardeshir Zahedi, interview with author, Montreux, March 20, 2006.
115. Princess Soraya, *Palace of Solitude*, p. 125.
116. "Young Ruler to Watch: Shah's Job in Iran: A Sturdier Economy," *Newsweek*, February 14, 1955.
117. Ardeshir Zahedi, interview with author.
118. Wright, "Memoirs," vol. 1, p. 280.
119. *FRUS,* 1955–1957, vol. XII, p. 703.
120. Ibid., p. 704.
121. *FRUS,* 1955–1957, vol. XII, p. 727.
122. *FRUS,* 1952–1954, vol. X, p. 1014.
123. PRO, Tehran to Foreign Office, January 4, 1955, FO 371/114805.
124. PRO, Tehran to Foreign Office, March 15, 1955, FO 371/114868.
125. PRO, Tehran to Foreign Office, April 5, 1955, FO 371/114808.
126. Ardeshir Zahedi, interview with author, Montreux, March 20, 2006.
127. PRO, Tehran to Foreign Office, April 5, 1955, FO 371/114810.
128. PRO, Tehran to Foreign Office, April 12, 1955, FO 371/14810.
129. PRO, Tehran to Foreign Office, April 5, 1955, FO 371/114810.
130. PRO, Tehran to Foreign Office, August 3, 1955, FO 371/114811.
131. PRO, Tehran to Foreign Office, December 20, 1955, FO 248/1562.
132. PRO, Tehran to Foreign Office, November 23, 1955, FO 248/1563.
133. PRO, Tehran to Foreign Office, January 30, 1956, FO 248/1568.
134. PRO, "Iran Annual Review 1956," FO 371/12707.

11 Cat on a Hot Tin Roof

1. PRO, British Embassy, Tehran to Foreign Office, March 4, 1958, FO 371/133065.
2. *FRUS,* 1958–1960, vol. XII, p. 586.
3. Ibid., p. 584.
4. This is part of a report on Iran given to Communist China's Foreign Ministry by the Foreign Minister of the Soviet Union. Chinese Foreign Ministry Archive, document no. 109–01347-03.
5. PRO, "The Internal Situation in Iran," July 23, 1957, FO 371/12705.

6. Ibid.
7. Shah, *Collected Works*, Azar 1337–1341 (1958–1962), p. 263.
8. *FRUS,* 1958–1960, vol. XII, p. 584.
9. Ibid.
10. Several sources have confirmed the existence of this project, including General Alavi-Kia, and Israel's ambassador to Iran, Moir Ezry. See his memoirs, *Yadnameh*, translated from the Hebrew by Ebrahim Khakhami (Jerusalem, 2000), pp. 205–210.
11. *FRUS,* 1958–1960, vol. XII, p. 659.
12. Ibid, p. 597.
13. *FRUS,* 1958–1960, vol. XII, p. 606.
14. For an insider's astute appraisal of why the CIA failed in its analysis of Iran, see Robert Jervis, *Why Intelligence Fails: Lessons from the Iranian Revolution and the Iraq War* (Ithaca, N.Y., 2010).
15. *FRUS,* 1958–1960, vol. XII, p. 589.
16. Ibid.
17. PRO, J. Foster Dulles to Chapin, October 8, 1957, FO 371/133009.
18. *FRUS,* 1958–1960, vol. XII, p. 584.
19. PRO, "Secret Minutes," March 5, 1958, FO 371/133009.
20. Ahmad Norouzi Farsangi, *Nagoftehay-e Zendegiy-e Sepahbod Gharani* [The Untold Life of General Gharni] (Tehran, 1382/2003), p. 466.
21. PRO, British Embassy, Tehran to Foreign Office, March 4, 1958, FO/371/13309.
22. Ibid.
23. Farsangi, *Nagoftehay-e Zendegiy-e Sepahbod Gharani*. Throughout the book, Gharani is referred to as "martyr," or Shahid. They make of him a devout man from childhood.
24. General Alavi-Kia, interview with author, San Diego, September 3, 2005.
25. Shakespeare, *Othello*, 1.1.35–36.
26. Numerous sources have written about this early history. For example, General Alavi-Kia, himself one of the founding deputy directors, talked at great length about the role of a handful of American colonels, particularly one who had served in Iran since late 1953. See also Mark J. Gasiorowski and Nikki R. Keddie, eds., *Neither East Nor West: Iran, the Soviet Union, and the United States* (New Haven, Conn., 1990), pp. 141–151.
27. General Alavi-Kia, interview with author, San Diego, September 3, 2005.
28. Ibid.
29. *FRUS,* 1958–1960, vol. XII, p. 539.
30. Ibid.
31. Ibid., p. 537.
32. General Hashemi, interview with author, London, August 7, 2004.
33. *FRUS,* 1958–1960, vol. XII, p. 541.
34. PRO, British Embassy, Tehran to Foreign Office, March 4, 1958, FO 371/133009.
35. *FRUS,* 1958–1960, vol. XII, pp. 539–540 .
36. PRO, British Embassy, Tehran to Foreign Office, March 4, 1958, FO 371/133009.
37. *FRUS,* 1958–1960, vol. XII, p. 541.
38. Ibid., p. 542.
39. Ibid., p. 537.
40. Ibid., p. 553.
41. PRO, British Embassy, Tehran to Foreign Office, Secret Minute, March 3, 1958, FO 371/133009.
42. Ibid.
43. *FRUS,* 1958–1960, vol. XII, p. 582.
44. Princess Soraya, *The Autobiography of Her Imperial Highness*, translated from German by Constantine Fitzgibbon (Garden City, N.Y., 1964), p. 147.
45. Ibid., p. 145.
46. PRO, British Embassy, Tehran to Foreign Office, April 14, 1954, FO 371/109985.
47. "My Baby Would Be Heir to Throne," *Daily Mail*, November 25, 1957.
48. Soraya, *Autobiography*, p. 151.
49. Fardust, *Memoirs*, vol. 1, p. 208.
50. Soraya, *Autobiography*, p. 153.
51. Ibid., p. 154.
52. *Gahnameye Panjah Sal Saltanat Pahlavi* [Chronology of Fifty Years of Pahlavi Rule], vol. 2 (Tehran, 1356/1977), p. 933.
53. Soraya, *Autobiography*, p. 158.

54. Fardust, *Memoirs*, vol. 1, p. 209.
55. *Anything Goes*, July–August 2002, vol. 11, no. 12.
56. PRO, British Embassy to Foreign Office, May 13, 1958, FO 371/133019.
57. *FRUS*, 1958–1960, vol. XII, p. 549.
58. Gérard de Villiers with Bernard Touchias and Annick de Villiers, *The Imperial Shah: An Informal Biography*, translated by Jane P. Wilson and Walter B. Nichols (Boston, 1976), p. 213.
59. PRO, British Embassy to Foreign Office, May 13, 1958, FO 371/133019.
60. Fardust, *Memoirs*, vol. 1, p. 209. In his memoir, Alam, the Shah's confidante, also refers to the fact that the Shah boasted about his affair with Grace Kelly. In a biography of Kelly, the story is confirmed.
61. Wright, "Memoirs," vol. 2, p. 389. Sir Denis Wright kindly gave me access to the entire manuscript as well as many other documents in his collection.
62. My information on the Garter comes from Answers.com, an Internet site.
63. Sir Denis Wright, interview with author, Duck Bottom, England, December 13, 2000.
64. Ardeshir Zahedi, interview with author, Montreux, March 19, 2007.
65. I wrote a letter to the Vatican Archives and asked for the minutes of the meeting. I was informed of the seventy-five-year rule.
66. PRO, British Legation to the Holy See to Foreign Office, December 2, 1958, FO 371/136803.
67. Private report, Ala to His Majesty, 19 Dey 1337/January 9, 1959, *Tarikhe Moaser-e Iran* [Journal of Contemporary History of Iran], (Summer 1376/1997): pp. 145–147.
68. Farah Pahlavi, *An Enduring Love: My Life with the Shah*, translated by Patricia Clancy (New York, 2004), p. 47.
69. Dick Davis, *Epic and Sedition: The Case of Ferdowsi's Shahnameh* (Washington, DC, 1999).
70. Ibid., p. 81.
71. Ibid., p. 97.
72. Zahedi, *Memoirs* [Persian], vol. II, 1954–1965, pp. 102–103.
73. Ibid., p. 83.
74. Empress Farah, *My Thousand and One Days: An Autobiography*, translated by Felice Harcourt (London, 1978).
75. *FRUS*, 1958–1960, vol. XII, p. 625.
76. Ibid., p. 625.
77. Ibid., p. 622.

12 Russian House

1. PRO, "Torture in Iran," March 19, 1956, FO 248/1560.
2. Ervand Abrahamian, *Tortured Confessions: Prisons and Public Recantations in Modern Iran* (Berkeley, Calif., 1999), p. 92.
3. Ardeshir Zahedi recounted the story to me in an interview. Zahedi, interview with author, Montreux, March 20, 2007.
4. For an account of his life, see my *Eminent Persians: The Men and Women Who Made Modern Iran* (Syracuse, N.Y., 2008).
5. The file that includes this report along with comments from embassy, Foreign Office, and British government officials had been closed "till 2032"—long after the normal period allotted for declassification of sensitive files. I made a special request for a reconsideration of this decision and within a few months learned that the file had indeed been opened for scrutiny. It is called "Torture in Iran, March 19, 1956," and it is in PRO, FO 248/1560.
6. PRO, "Torture in Iran," March 19, 1956, FO 248/1560.
7. Ibid.
8. Ibid.
9. Tribal troubles were for much of the Shah's time a nagging problem. From the time of Reza Shah, the central government's attempt to forcefully settle these nomadic tribes had caused considerable consternation amongst them. The tribes had shed much blood defending their way of life. Sometimes foreign powers, including Britain and the United States, would use these tribes and their anger at the central government to pressure the Shah. Not long after the report about torture, the Shah approved a plan suggested by Mohammad Bahmanbeygi, a member of one of the most rebellious of these tribes. The idea was for roving schools to move with these nomadic tribes and educate their new generation. The effort bore fruit and the last decade of the Shah's

rule was essentially free from any serious tribal challenge. The revolution of 1979 changed the political dynamics amongst the tribes again. For an account of Bahmanbeygi, see my *Eminent Persians.*

10. PRO, "Torture in Iran," March 19, 1956, FO 248/1560.
11. *FRUS,* 1955–1957, vol. XII, p. 917.
12. Ebrahim Golestan, interview with author, London, April 28, 2010. He kindly read an early draft of this chapter and offered his invariably astute and brilliant observations.
13. PRO, "Iran Annual Review, 1956," FO 371/12707.
14. *FRUS,* 1955–1957, vol. XII, p. 917.
15. Ibid., p. 919.
16. PRO, Tehran to Foreign Office, May 21, 1956, FO 371/120752.
17. PRO, From Moscow to Foreign Office, July 12, 1956, PREM/1535.
18. PRO, Tehran to Foreign Office, July 18, 1956, PREM/1535.
19. *FRUS,* 1955–1957, vol. XII, pp. 951–952.
20. Ibid., p. 675.
21. Ibid.
22. Wright, "Memoirs," vol. 2, p. 312. He kindly gave me access to his private papers as well. When his handwriting was hard to read, or when, hoping to avoid detection by possible secret police moles in his office, he had written in shorthand scribbles, he kindly and patiently read them out loud to me. Sir Denis Wright, interview with author, Hadenham, England, December 11, 2001.
23. Sir Denis Wright, interview with author, Hadenham, England, December 11, 2001.
24. Wright, "Memoirs," vol. 2, p. 312.
25. "Soviet Government Statement to the Government of Iran," *Current Digest of the Soviet Press,* XI, no. 31 (September 2, 1959).
26. "Perfidious Policy of Iranian Government, Pravda, February 14, 1959," *Current Digest of Soviet Press,* 1959, XI, no. 6–7, pp. 24–26.
27. Ibid., p. 25.
28. Wright, "Memoirs," vol. 2, p. 314.
29. Ibid., p. 315. In his memoirs, he refers to the following file as the one that contains all the correspondence on this topic: FO 371/140797.
30. Wright, "Memoirs," vol. 2, p. 314.
31. Ibid., pp. 315–316.
32. Ibid., p. 316.
33. Ibid., p. 319.
34. Ibid., p. 321.
35. In interviews with me, Ardeshir Zahedi suggested that when as ambassador designate to the United States and later as foreign minister, he reviewed the ministry confidential files and he learned of Hekmat's role. Zahedi, interview with author, Montreux, March 20, 2005.
36. PRO, "Iran Annual Review, 1959," FO 371/14954.
37. "Editorial Note," *FRUS,* 1958–1960, vol. XII, p. 626.
38. *FRUS,* 1958–1960, vol. XII, pp. 627–628.
39. Ibid., p. 629.
40. Ibid.
41. *FRUS,* 1958–1960, vol. XII, p. 638.
42. PRO, "Iran Annual Review, 1959," FO371/149754.
43. *FRUS,* 1958–1960, vol. XII, p. 641.
44. PRO, British Embassy in Tehran to Foreign Office, April 23, 1959, FO 371/140882.
45. *FRUS,* 1958–1960, vol. XII p. 645.
46. PRO, "Persian Oil for Israel," January 18, 1955, FO 371/114852.
47. *FRUS,* 1958–1960, vol. XII p. 646.
48. Ibid., pp. 658–659.
49. General Alavi-Kia, interview with author, San Diego, November 15, 2003.
50. "Taube nagt am Kohlstrunk," *Der Spiegel,* no. 42 (October 18, 1950): 15. Hamid Shokat, who for a while worked as my research assistant at Stanford and on the *Eminent Persians* project, helped find and translate the article.
51. Klaus Körner, "Erst in Goebbels', dann in Adenauers Diensten," *Die Zeit,* August 24, 1990.
52. Stig Hornshøj-Møller, "On the Nazi Propaganda Film 'Der ewige Jude,'" Paper presented at the Imperial War Museum, London, 1997.
53. "Taube nagt am Kohlstrunk," p. 15.
54. Körner, "Erst in Goebbels', dann in Adenauers Diensten."

55. General Alavi-Kia, interview with author, San Diego, November 15, 2003.
56. PRO, Conversation of Russel to Shah, May 6, 1958, FO 371/133019.

13 The Dark Side of Camelot

1. Immediately after the party Conference, the CIA heard about the existence of the report, recognized its importance, and marshaled all of its forces to get its hand on a copy. Two months later, Mossad, the Israeli intelligence agency got hold of a copy and made a gift of it to the U.S. government. After some discussion in the White House and the CIA about what to do with the document, it was eventually "leaked" to the *New York Times* through the State Department. The United States then made every effort to broadcast the content of the report to citizens living in the Soviet Union and its satellite states. The Soviet government denied the authenticity of the report, and it was only after the end of Communism that Russian citizens were finally allowed to read the full document. For an account of the CIA's role in the discovery and dissemination of the Secret Report, see Tim Weiner, *Legacy of Ashes: A History of the CIA* (New York, 2007), pp. 123–127.
2. JFK, "Contingency Planning for Possible Soviet Move or Demonstration against the Shah, September 13, 1961."
3. For his biographical sketch, see my *Eminent Persians: The Men and Women Who Made Modern Iran* (Syracuse, N.Y., 2008).
4. Parviz Sabeti, the head of SAVAK's Third Division, told me of the Shah's constant worrying and nagging about Ashraf and his freedom. Sabeti, phone interview with author, September 4, 2005.
5. Shah, *Answer to History*, p. 97.
6. "Memorandum from the Secretary of State's Special Assistant, August, 20, 1957," *FRUS,* 1955–1957, vol. XII, pp. 937–939.
7. Shah, *Answer to History*, p. 97.
8. JFK, RW Kromer, "Comments on First Iran Task Force Draft. 8 May 1961."
9. JFK, Oscar Cox to WW Rostow, "Memorandum on the National Front, 9 May 1961."
10. *FRUS,* 1958–1960, vol. XII, p. 533.
11. *FRUS,* 1955–1957, vol. XII, p. 963.
12. *FRUS,* 1958–1960, vol. XII, p. 534.
13. Ibid., p. 550.
14. Ibid., p. 585.
15. Ibid., p. 675.
16. *FRUS,* 1955–1957, vol. XII, p. 962.
17. *FRUS,* 1958–1960, vol. XII, p. 588.
18. Mark J. Gasiorowski, *U.S. Foreign Policy and the Shah: Building a Client State in Iran* (Ithaca, N.Y., 1991), p. 96.
19. NSA, 390, "An Assessment of the Internal Political Situation, May 3, 1960," p. 11.
20. Dr. Amir Pishdad, interview with author, Paris, August 22, 2002.
21. PRO, Tehran to Foreign Office, August 7, 1958, FO371/133027.
22. Ibid.
23. Majid A'lam, interview with author, San Diego, September 3, 2002,
24. PRO, Tehran to Foreign Office, August 7, 1958, FO371/133027.
25. Ibid.
26. *FRUS,* 1955–1957, vol. XII, p. 870.
27. PRO, Tehran to Foreign Office, August 7, 1958, FO371/133027.
28. Ibid.
29. Mehdi Samii, interview with the author, Los Angeles, March 18, 2002.
30. Shah, *Collected Works*, p. 2673.
31. Mehdi Samii, interview with the author, Los Angeles, March 18, 2002.
32. *Pahlaviha be Ravayate Asnad* [The Pahlavis According to Documents], 2 vols. (Tehran, 1378/1999), vol. 2, pp. 78–220.
33. Hamid Ghadimi, interview with author, London, April 2002.
34. Ibid. I asked him about a document published by the Islamic Republic, giving the figure of the total owed to his company by Shams. He confirmed the figure, "down to the penny," in his words.
35. Alam, *Daily Journals,* vol. 5, p. 377.
36. Ibid., p. 378.

37. Wright, *"Memoirs."* The story of the contract appears on page 283. He had willed the memoirs to Oxford University, where it should be available to scholars.
38. Ibid., p. 283.
39. PRO, Foreign Office to Russels, September 30, 1957, FO 371/127147.
40. *FRUS,* 1958–1960, vol. XII, p. 621.
41. Shah, *Collected Works*, p. 1020.
42. *FRUS,* Vol. XII, 1955–1957, p. 879. There is also a panegyric but informed account of this resistance from a member of one of the families that organized it. Though written in the guise of a work of scholarship, it is in fact an ideological treatise, keen on defending the rights and prerogatives of the landlords. See Mohammad Gholi Majd, *Resistance to the Shah: Landowners and the Ulama in Iran* (Gainesville, Fla., 2000).
43. Seyyed Mohammad Hussein Manzural Ajdad, ed., *Marjai'yat dar Arseye Ejtema va Siyasat* [Ayatollahs in the Social and Political Arena] (Tehran, 1379/1990), p. 422.
44. For a detailed account of Iran and Israel's intelligence relations, see Abdolrahman Ahmadi, *SAVAK va Dastgah Etela'ti Israel* [SAVAK and Intelligence Service of Israel] (Tehran, 1381/2001).
45. For an elaborate account of these matters, see the memoirs of Israel's ambassador to Iran, Moir Ezry, *Yadnameh* [Memoirs], 2 vols. (Jerusalem, 2001).
46. *FRUS,* 1955–1957, vol. XII, p. 867.
47. PRO, Tehran to Foreign Office, 12 November 1966, FO 371/186665.
48. *FRUS,* 1958–1960, vol. XII, p. 676.
49. PRO, Tehran to Foreign Office, September 6, 1960, FO 371/164228.
50. Ibid.
51. PRO, "Political Situation in Iran," March 6, 1960, FO 371/147956.
52. Wright, "Memoirs," vol. 2, p. 413.
53. PRO, Tehran to Foreign Embassy, July 23, 1957, FO 371/127075.
54. PRO, Tehran to Foreign Office, September 6, 1960, FO 371/164228.
55. For Aramesh's version of events, see *Khaterat-e Siyasiye Ahmad Aramesh* [Political Memoirs of Ahmad Aramesh], edited by Golam Hussein Mirza-Saleh (Tehran, 1369/1990). Aramesh was also a critic of the Shah and sometime after the end of his tenure at the Plan Organization, he was shot by security forces on suspicion of involvement with terrorist groups.
56. *FRUS,* 1958–1960, vol. XII, p. 712.
57. NSA, no. 390, "Assessment of Internal Political Situation, May 3, 1960."
58. Amir Taheri, *The Unknown Life of the Shah* (London, 1991), p. 136; Fereydoon Hoveyda, Iran's representative to the UN, claimed to have witnessed dollar-stuffed briefcases sent to the United States in the diplomatic pouch and given to the Nixon campaigns in 1968 and 1972. Ardeshir Zahedi, on the other hand, categorically denies all such claims. During the Watergate investigation, a few American journalists tried to verify the claim that illegal contributions had been made by the Shah but no one could find anything other than circumstantial evidence. There is no doubt about the Shah's close relations with Nixon.
59. NPL, Nixon to the Shah, January 27, 1955, PPS, 320.45.
60. JFK, NSF, Doc. 119, "Shah's Letter to President Kennedy, January 26, 1961."
61. Ibid.
62. Ibid.
63. Ibid.
64. JFK. "Dean Rusk to President Kennedy, February 28, 1961."
65. JFK, "March 1, 1961, Memorandum of Conversation between President Kennedy and Lieutenant General Bakhtiyar."
66. James A. Bill, *The Eagle and the Lion: The Tragedy of American-Iranian Relations* (New Haven, Conn., 1988), p. 138.
67. Barry Rubin, *Paved with Good Intentions: The American Experience and Iran* (Oxford, 1980), pp. 108–109; Mark Gasiorowski, in his *U.S. Foreign Policy and the Shah: Building a Client State In Iran* (Ithaca, N.Y.,1991), p. 181, also reports the meeting and Roosevelt's subsequent action.
68. Jafar Sharif-Emami, *Memoirs of Jafar Sharif-Emami*, edited by Habib Ladjevardi, Iranian Oral History Project (Boston, 1999), pp. 223–238.
69. JFK, "Tehran to White House, May 5, 1961."
70. JFK, "Memorandum for President, RW Kromer, August 4, 1961."
71. Ibid.
72. Sharif-Emami, *Memoirs*, pp. 231–236.

73. JFK, "Basic Facts in the Iranian Situation," n.d.
74. Sharif-Emami, *Memoirs*, pp. 231–236.
75. General Alavi-Kia, deputy director of SAVAK, was standing outside the door and overheard the heated discussion. General Alavi-Kia, interview with author, San Diego, April 22, 2003.
76. JFK, "Basic Facts in the Iranian Situation," n.d.

14 Garrulous Premier

1. Jahanguir Amuzegar, a respected economist who was Amini's minister of finance is convinced that by every economic measure, the Iranian economy was indeed bankrupt.
2. Ardeshir Zahedi, interview with author, Montreux, April 14, 2009.
3. Ibid.
4. JFK, "John Wiley to President, February 21, 1961."
5. Khalil Maleki, *Do Nameh* [Two Letters] (Tehran, 1357/1958). Both letters are addressed to Dr. Mossadeq; in them, Maleki describes the situation and offers biting criticism of the National Front leadership.
6. Shah, *Collected Works*, p. 2402.
7. JFK, "Tehran to State Department, May 13, 1961."
8. Ibid.
9. JFK, "Tehran to State Department, August 27, 1961."
10. JFK, "Tehran to State Department, June 28, 1961."
11. Ibid.
12. Moir Ezry, *Yadnameh* [Memoirs], 2 vols (Jerusalem, 2001), vol. 1, p. 106.
13. Khodadad Farmanfarmaian, interview with author, London, December 11, 2002.
14. Azar Ebtehaj, interview with author, London, June 20, 2003.
15. PRO, Tehran to Foreign Office, September 18, 1955, FO 248/1557.
16. In several interviews, Mehdi Samii provided me with details of these actions. Ahmad Tehrani, a lawyer working for Iran's Foreign Ministry and a trusted aide to Ardeshir Zahedi, also provided some details of the case, as he was dispatched by the Iranian government to challenge Khaybar Khan's allegations.
17. Abolhassan Ebtehaj, *Khaterate Abolhassan Ebtehaj* [Memoirs], 2 vols. (Tehran, 1375/1986), vol. 2, p. 808.
18. Khodadad Farmanfarmaian talked of Ebtehaj's vehemence in arguing against excessive military expenditures for Iran while talking to American generals.
19. Alam, *Daily Journals*, vol. 4, p. 63.
20. Ebtehaj, *Memoirs*, vol. 2, pp. 853–857.
21. JFK, "Tehran to State Department, May 14, 1961."
22. JFK, "NSC, Record of Action, May 24, 1961."
23. Ibid.
24. JFK, "Telegram, Tehran to State Department, June 22, 1961."
25. Amongst the industrialists who supported his efforts was Mahmoud Rezai. His brother Ali Rezai was informed about these developments and had been a silent observer of some of these discussions. Ali Rezai, interview with author, San José, Costa Rica, August 21, 2002.
26. I was told about some of these meetings by Ali Rezai, whose brother was a close ally of Bakhtiyar and who had participated in some of these meetings, including the one with Amuzegar.
27. JFK, "25 May 1961 Memo for Philip Talbot," *FRUS*, vol. XVIII, Microfilm Supplements.
28. Ibid.
29. JFK, "State Department to Tehran, June 28, 1961."
30. For a discussion of this group's work, see George Baldwin, *Planning and Development in Iran* (Baltimore, 1967).
31. JFK, "Ball to Attorney General, January 26, 1961."
32. JFK, "Some First Thoughts on the Shah, March 30, 1962."
33. There are now two histories of the Confederation, one in two volumes in Persian and a shorter, one-volume account in English. See Hamid Shokat, *Jonbesh Daneshjouyee Conferation Jahani* [The Internation Student Movement of the Confederation], 2 vols. (Koln, 1985); for a brief English version, initially written as a doctoral dissertation, see Afshin Matin-Asghari, *Iranian Student Opposition to the Shah* (Costa Mesa, Calif., 2002).
34. JFK. "Memorandum for the Files, John Bowling, February 20, 1961."
35. JFK, "Amini's Relations with the Shah, July 29, 1961."

36. JFK. "State to Embassy in Tehran, October 31, 1961."
37. Ibid.
38. Masud Behnoud, *Az Seyyed Zia to Bakhtiyar* [From Seyyed Zia till Bakhtiyar] (Tehran, 1369/1990), p. 463.
39. *Ali Amini be Ravayate Asnade SAVAK* [Amini According to SAVAK Documents] (Tehran, 1379/1990), p. 39.
40. PRO, "Report on 'Silent Opposition' in Iranian Politics," February 21, 1958, FO 371/133009.
41. NA, "State Department to Embassy in Tehran, March 3, 1961."
42. *Ali Amini be Ravayate Asnade SAVAK*, pp. 36–37.
43. Empress Farah, *My Thousand and One Days,* p. 51.
44. Farah Pahlavi, *An Enduring Love: My Life with the Shah*, translated by Patricia Clancy (New York, 2004), p. 107.
45. Empress Farah, *My Thousand and One Days,* p. 52.
46. PRO, Tehran to Foreign Office, November 10, 1960, FO 371/149832.
47. Empress Farah, *My Thousand and One Days*, p. 52.
48. PRO, Tehran to Foreign Office, March 27, 1961, FO 371/15658.
49. PRO, "Rumors about the Crown Prince," November 10, 1960, FO 371/149832.
50. In her two memoirs, *An Enduring Love* and *My Thousand and One Days*, the Queen chronicles some of these vicious rumors.
51. PRO, Tehran to Foreign Office, March 27, 1962, FO 371/164227.
52. PRO, Oslo Embassy to Foreign Office, June 3, 1961, FO 371/157657.
53. Ibid.
54. PRO, "Annual Report for 1963," British Embassy, FO 371/17551.
55. Shah, *Collected Works*, p. 2681.
56. Farah Pahlavi, *An Enduring Love*, p. 93.
57. Ibid., p. 117.
58. PRO, Tehran, to Foreign Office, March 27, 1962.

15 The Bright Side of Camelot

1. Mehdi Samii, interview with the author, Los Angeles, March 15, 2003.
2. Dr. Ghani kept a daily journal that included everything from the mundane to matters of state. His son, Cyrus, published the entire thirteen volumes, and then organized an English translation of a selection from the larger volumes. See Ghasem Ghani, *A Man of Many Worlds: The Diaries and Memoirs of Dr. Ghasem Ghani* (Washington, DC, 2007).
3. For a discussion of the group and their genealogy, see my *Persian Sphinx: Amir Abbas Hoveyda and the Riddle of the Iranian Revolution* (Washington, DC, 2001).
4. JFK, "State to Tehran Embassy, March 21, 1962."
5. In 2003, when I was interviewing Ardeshir Zahedi in New York, he kindly arranged with the management of the hotel for me to visit the famous suite 35A.
6. JFK, the description appears in the catalogue of gifts to the President and First Lady.
7. JFK, NSF, Box 119, "Memorandum of Conversation, April 13, 1962."
8. JFK, NSF, Box 117, "Background Paper, April 3, 1962."
9. JFK, NSF, Box 117, "Visit of the Shah of Iran, Background Paper, April 2, 1962."
10. Shah, *Collected Works*, p. 2795.
11. Ibid., p. 2790.
12. Ibid., p. 2793.
13. PRO, British Embassy in Washington to Foreign Office, April 16, 62, FO 371/164227.
14. JFK, NSC, Box 116, "Robert W Komer to Bundy, April 23, 1962."
15. *Etela'at,* Farvardin 26, 1341/April 15, 1962.
16. PRO, Visit by the Shah, April 17, 1962, FO 371/164227.
17. PRO, British Embassy in Washington to Foreign Office, April 25, 1962.
18. PRO, British Embassy in Washington to Foreign Office, April 21, 1962.
19. JFK, NSC, Box 116, "American Embassy to State Department, May 26, 1962."
20. Ibid.
21. JFK, "Telegraph from State Department, Embassy in Tehran, June 16, 1962."
22. JFK, "Personal Message from President to the Shah, June 20, 1962."
23. JFK, "Kromer to Bundy, May 16, 1963."

24. PRO, "Iran's Review for 1962," FO 371/170372.
25. *Etela'at*, 27 Ordibehesht 1340.
26. *Etela'at*, 21 Bahman 1340.
27. PRO, "The New Iran Party," February 12, 1964, FO 371/175712.
28. NA, "The New Iranian Government, 23 July 1962."
29. Ibid.
30. PRO, Wright Dispatch, September 21, 1955, FO 371/114811.
31. Considering that in 2006, when a newly elected member of the U.S. Congress asked to take the oath of office using not a Bible, but the Qu'ran—he was an African-American Muslim—there was a nasty commotion, the law proposed by the Shah and his Prime Minister in 1962 was indeed a major step forward and far ahead of its time.
32. *Tarikh-e Giyame Panzdah-e Khordad be Ravayat Asnad* [The June 5th Uprising According to Documents], edited by Javad Mansuri (Tehran, 1377/1998), pp. 252–253.
33. Ibid., p. 252.
34. PRO, "The Iranian Domestic Situation, 1962," FO 371/170372.
35. JFK, "Tehran to State Department, January 3, 1963."
36. JFK, "Tehran to State Department, February 9, 1963."
37. JFK, "Komer to Bundy, January 15, 1963."
38. Ibid.
39. For a discussion of this history, see my "Pious Populist: Understanding the Role of Iran's President," *Boston Review* 32:6 (November/December 2007), 7–14, 4.
40. JFK, "Tehran to State Department, January 23, 1963."
41. JFK, "CIA, Telegram, January 23, 1963."
42. For example, see Akbar Ganji, *The Road to Democracy In Iran*, edited by Joshua Cohen and Abbas Milani (Cambridge, Mass., 2008), pp. 43–89.
43. JFK, "Tehran to State Department, January 26, 1963."
44. JFK, "Kromer to Bundy, January 29, 1963."
45. JFK, "Talbot to Holmes, February 28, 1963."
46. Shah, *Answer to History*, p. 104.
47. Shah, *Collected Works*, p. 3308.
48. Ibid., p. 3204.
49. Ibid., p. 3208.
50. Many sources have talked of this alliance. Ayatollah Montazeri, a onetime close ally of Khomeini and chosen by him as a successor, has, in his memoirs, given a glimpse into Navvab's early days in the seminaries of Qom and Khomeini's defiant support of him. Ayatollah Motazeri's *Khaterat* was made available on the Internet.
51. In those days, I was about thirteen years old and lived in Tehran. I remember accompanying my mother to the bazaar in Tehran, where she was given a copy of one of Khomeini's tapes, which she later played for one of my uncles, Fakhraddin Shadman. He had been once a minister in the Shah's government but by then was sidelined, facing the wrath of the King. The fact that my mother and uncle would engage in such dangerous acts speaks much about the nature of the times. For an account of Shadman's life, see my *Lost Wisdom: Iran's Encounter with Modernity* (Washington, DC, 2008).
52. "Heyat Mota'lefe Islami," *Sharg*, Special Issue devoted to the Islamic Revolution, 15 Bahman/February 4, 2006.
53. Vanessa Martin, *Creating an Islamic State: Khomeini and the Making of a New Iran* (London, 2000), p. 67.
54. JFK, NSF, Box 116 A, "Tehran to State Department, June 6, 1963."
55. Alam, *Daily Journals*, vol. 5, p. 42.
56. JFK, NSF, Box 116 A, "Tehran to State Department, June 6, 1963."
57. Ibid.
58. Denis Wright took notes of this historic meeting and shared them with me when I interviewed him.
59. JFK, NSF, Box 116 A, "Tehran to State Department, July 11, 1963."
60. JFK, NSF, Kromer, Box 424, "Kromer to Carl, June 21, 1963."
61. Wright, "Memoirs," vol. 1, p. 377.
62. Ibid., p. 376.
63. Quoted in Wright's "Memoirs," p. 380.
64. JFK, "Tehran to Secretary of State, July 18, 1963."

65. JFK, "Tehran to State, June 24, 1963."
66. PRO, "The Iran Novin Party," February 12, 1964, FO 371/17512.
67. Wright, "Memoirs," vol. 2, p. 376.
68. Mehdi Khanbab Tehrani, in his conversations with Hamid Shokat (published in an important series of interviews with leaders of the Confederation) and in several conversations with the author, details these instances of cooperation.
69. *FRUS,* 1958–1960, vol. XII, p. 694.
70. Ibid., p. 670.
71. Ibid., p. 694.
72. Ibid., p. 695.
73. Ibid., p. 697.
74. PRO, Denis Wright to Foreign Office, October 12, 1962, FO 373/164186.
75. Denis Wright, interview with author, Hadenham, England, October 3, 2002.
76. Sir Denis Wright's Valedictory Dispatch, April 20, 1977, courtesy of Denis Wright who gave me access to his personal papers.
77. Quoted in Denis Wright's Valedictory Dispatch.
78. JFK, "Briefing for Governor Harriman, May 2, 1963."
79. William O. Douglas, *The Court Years: 1939–1975* (New York, 1980), pp. 303–304.
80. JFK, "Briefing for Governor Harriman, May 2, 1963."
81. JFK, "Briefing for Governor Harriman, May 2, 1963."
82. JFK, Oral Histories, R W Kromer, vol. IV, p. 11.
83. *FRUS,* 1961–1963, vol. XVIII, p. 371.
84. Alam, *Daily Journals*, vol. 1, p. 41.
85. JFK, "Iran, Overseas Report (Confidential), August 7, 1962," p. 2.
86. Wright, "Memoirs," vol. 2, p. 372.
87. JFK, "Iran, Overseas Report (Confidential), August 7, 1962," p. 2.
88. Ibid.
89. Ibid., p. 5.
90. Ibid., p. 6.
91. Ibid., p. 7.
92. PRO, Tehran to Foreign Office, October 5, 1961, FO 371/157658.
93. I have covered this episode in some detail in my *Persian Sphinx, Amir Abbas Hoveyda and the Riddle of the Iranian Revolution* (Washington, DC, 2000), pp. 160–163.
94. NA, Department of the Army, Confidential Report, Week 10, March 1964.

16 The Desert Bash

1. *FRUS,* 1969–1976, "Memorandum for Henry Kissinger, 8 May 1972, Richard Helms," vol. E-4, Electronic copy.
2. Zahedi Papers, "Letter to the Shah, 29 Dey 1355."
3. Ibid.
4. *FRUS,* 1969–1976, "Report, 28 February 1972."
5. NA, CIA, "Nothing Succeeds Like a Successful Shah, 8 October 1971."
6. Alam, *Daily Journals*, vol. 5, p. 495.
7. Ardeshir Zahedi, interview with author, Montreux, March 28, 2009.
8. For documents relating to this bureaucratic infighting, see *Majaray-e Su' Gasd be Shah dar Kakh Marmar* [Assassination Attempt on the Shah in the Memrar Palace According to SAVAK Documents] (Tehran, 1378/1999).
9. See my *Persian Sphinx: Amir Abbas Hoveyda and the Riddle of the Iranian Revolution* (Washington, DC, 2000). The book is a biography of Hoveyda.
10. Farokh Negahdar, interview with author, London, October 2, 2002.
11. Shah, *Answer to History*, p. 158.
12. JFK, "The New Men and Their Challenge to American Policy in Iran," Senator Kennedy Papers.
13. Ibid.
14. Abbas Milani, *Eminent Persians: The Men and Women Who Made Modern Iran,* vol. 2 (Syracuse, N.Y., 2008), pp. 632–637.
15. Ahmad Mirfenderasky, *Dar Hamsayegiy-e Khers* [In the Neighborhood of the Bear] (London, Ketab Center, 1997, p. 268.
16. NSA, Stanley T. Escudero, "What Went Wrong in Iran," Document No. 2629, 1980.
17. Alam, *Daily Journals*, vol. 3, p. 100.
18. Ibid., p. 87.

19. Alam, *Daily Journals*, vol. 4, p. 35.
20. Alam, *Daily Journals*, vol. 3, p. 87.
21. Ibid.
22. In my essay on Alam's *Daily Journals* (vol. 5), I have covered this and many other similar episodes. The essay is reprinted in *King of Shadows* (Los Angeles, 2006).
23. David Binder, "Northrop Cites Undercover Role," *New York Times*, June 7, 1975, and Paranay Gupte, "Grumman's 'Fees' to Iran Beg Question," *New York Times*, February 23, 1976.
24. NA, "The Iranian Air Mafia, US Embassy in Tehran."
25. *FRUS*, 1964–1968, vol. XII, p. 195.
26. Cyrus Ghani, *Iran and the West: A Critical Bibliography* (London, 1987), p. 211.
27. A book chronicling his life and edited by A. Morovati as well as a couple of officers under his command have made this claim. General Azarbarzin was amongst them.
28. Alam, *Daily Journals*, vol. 5, p. 258.
29. In a three-volume compilation of documents from SAVAK, published by the Islamic Republic, details of these surveillance modes are offered. See *Sepahbod Bakhtiyar be Ravayat Asnad SAVAK* [General Teymour Bakhtiyar According to SAVAK Documents] (Tehran, 1378/1999).
30. General Alavi-Kia was at the time the head of SAVAK in Europe. He told me about details of the trip.
31. Margaret Laing, *The Shah* (London, 1977), p. 174.
32. PRO, "Ba'ath, Tudeh and the Confederation," January 11, 1971, FCO 17/1512.
33. This information can be found in Stasi files on the Tudeh Party. See Hauptabeilung, 5, 4, Berlin Treff Mit Im "Charly" 10.51972.EGA. I am indebted to Hamid Shokat for translating the document.
34. *Sepahbod Teymour Bakhtiyar Be Ravayat Asnad SAVAK* [General Bakhtiyar According to SAVAK Documents], vol. 1 (Tehran, 1378/1999), p. 338.
35. NA, "Iraq's Coup Attempt, Jan. 1970"; see also NA, "How to Buy a Revolution, October 15, 1969."
36. *FRUS*, 1964–1968, vol. XII, p. 469.
37. Ibid., p. 473.
38. NSA, "Ali Amini, February 29, 1968."
39. David Owen, *In Sickness and in Power: Illness in Heads of Government during the Last 100 Years* (London, 2009), p. 204.
40. Emad Baghi, one of Iran's leading human rights activists and an opponent of the death penalty, told me about his study and the total number of those executed for political crimes.
41. For an account of this failed attempt, see Abbas Samakar, *Man Yek Shoureshi Hastam* [I am a Rebel] (Los Angeles, 2001).
42. PRO, "The Police and the Permissive Society in Iran," 6 October 1970, FO 248/1649.
43. Alam, *Daily Journals*, vol. 2, p. 98.
44. PRO, "The Police and the Permissive Society in Iran," 6 October 1970, FO 248/1649.
45. *FRUS*, 1964–1968, vol. XII "Tehran to State, November 25, 1965," p. 190.
46. *FRUS*, 1964–1968, vol. XII "Tehran to State, July 7, 1966," p. 271.
47. PRO, "Coronation of His Imperial Majesty the Shahanshah," 30 November 1967, FO 248/1637.
48. Mehdi Samii was in charge of these arrangements and in the course of several interviews, on the phone or in Los Angeles, he told me about his efforts to find the right experts to build the carriages and the difficulties of using the Crown Jewels for the construction of the Queen's crown.
49. For details of the celebration, I have relied on interviews with Mehdi Samii. The Queen, too, in her *An Enduring Love: My Life with the Shah*, translated by Patricia Clancy (New York, 2004), provides a brief account of the event (pp. 151–158).
50. PRO, "Coronation Gifts for the Shah," 30 October 1967, FO 248/1637.
51. *Bazm Ahriman* [Devil's Party], vol. 1 (Tehran, 1377/1998), p. 9.
52. NA, CIA, "Nothing Succeeds Like Success, 8 October 1971."
53. Houchang Nahavandi, *Akharin Roozha* [Last Days] (Los Angeles, 2004), p. 100.
54. Ibid., p. 23.
55. Abdulreza Ansari, "Interview with Keyhan," *Keyhan*, no. 1089 (January 18, 2006), p. 1.
56. PRO, "The 2500 Anniversary of the Founding of the Persian Empire by Cyrus the Great," FCO 56/323, p. 5.
57. Sir Peter Ramsbotham, Iranian Oral History Project, Harvard University, Center for Middle Eastern Studies, October 18, 1985.
58. Daniel Yergin, *The Prize: The Epic Quest for Oil, Money, and Power* (New York, 1993), p. 564.

59. Ibid., p. 5.
60. Zahedi Papers, Zahedi to Shah, n.d.
61. PRO, "The 2500 Anniversary of the Founding of the Persian Empire by Cyrus the Great," FCO 56/323, p. 7.
62. PRO, Secretary of State to Prime Minister, March 2, 1965, FO 371/180802.
63. Wright, "Memoirs," vol. 2, p. 399.
64. Ibid., p. 390.
65. PRO, Tehran to Foreign Office, 30 May 1968, FCO 8/28.
66. Ebrahim Teymouri was the diplomat entrusted with the job. He spent four years in London, collecting a four-volume collection of documents on the subject. He has referred to his assignment in an article he wrote about Abbas Aram, onetime Foreign Minister of Iran. See "Gousheyee az Khaterat Abbas Aram" [Some Moments from Aram's Memoirs]. I was provided a copy of the manuscript courtesy of Mr. Mortezai, Iran's onetime ambassador to Israel.
67. *FRUS,* 1964–1968, vol. XXII, p. 563.
68. Henry Kissinger, *The White House Years* (Boston, 1979), p. 1264.
69. The first from account number 2/85678 in Union De Banques Swiss and the other from an account in Arabiya Bank.
70. A copy of the check and copies of letter exchanged between the two sides were provided to me, courtesy of Ardeshir Zahedi.
71. PRO, "Chancellor of the Duchy of Lancaster's Visit to Iran," FC08/2270.
72. NA, "Iranian Cooperation with Oman and Sudan, March 1974."
73. Crucial segments of the memorandum of the conversation in which the Shah offers details of what he planned to do in Afghanistan have been "sanitized" and thus made unavailable. NA, "Memorandum of Conversation, White House, July 23, 1973."
74. Alam, *Daily Journals*, vol. 3, p. 180.
75. *FRUS,* 1964–1968, vol. XXII, p. 457.
76. For the text of letters, see Alam, *Daily Journals*, vol. 2, p. 385.
77. Fereydoon Hoveyda, "My Secret Mission to End the Vietnam War," *American Foreign Policy Interests* 23, no. 4 (2001): 243–252.
78. Ibid.
79. *FRUS,* 1964–1968, vol. XXII, p. 387.
80. *FRUS,* 1964–1968, vol. XXII, p. 401.
81. *FRUS,* 1964–1968, vol. XXII, p. 392.
82. *FRUS,* 1969–1976, vol. E–4, electronic copy.
83. Several letters from Zahedi to the Shah containing messages from Nixon offer details of these dealings. Zahedi Papers.
84. Barbara Zanchetta, "The United States and the Loss of Iran," Working Papers on International History and Politics, no. 4, June 2009.
85. Zahedi Papers, Letter to the Shah, October 21, 1975.
86. I initially heard about the episode from General Azarbarzin. I checked with Anthony Cordesman, the respected scholar on Iran's military, and he confirmed the story.
87. Owen, *In Sickness and in Power*, p. 204.
88. Akbar Etemad provided some of this information in interviews I did with him in Paris and on the phone. Moreover, a summary can be seen in NSA, "Department of State, the Atomic Energy Organization of Iran, April 16, 1976," Nuclear Vault.
89. Ibid., p. 4.
90. Ibid., p. 10.
91. NSA, "Department of Defense, Interview with the Shah"; some of the most important documents about nuclear negotiations are clustered in a file called the Nuclear Vault; see http://www.gwu.edu/~nsarchiv/nukevault/ebb268/index.htm.
92. Ibid., p. 2.
93. Ibid.
94. NSA, "Memorandum for Secretary of Defense, June 22, 1974," Nuclear Vault.
95. NSA, "Cooperation with Iran, Alfred L. Atherton Jr., June 20, 1974," Nuclear Vault.
96. Ibid., p. 4.
97. NSA, "Action Memorandum, December 6, 1974," Nuclear Vault.
98. NSA, "Report of the NSSM 219 Working Group," Nuclear Vault.
99. NSA, "Memorandum for the Assistant to the President for National Security Affairs, April 18, 1976," Nuclear Vault.

100. NSA, "Briefing Notes: Iran and Nuclear Weapons, 29 July 1975," Nuclear Vault.
101. NSA, "Department of Defense, Iran Nuclear Agreement," Nuclear Vault.
102. NSA, "Department of Defense, Iranian Nuclear Policy," Nuclear Vault.
103. NSA, "Brent Scowcroft, Next Steps in Our Negotiation of a Nuclear Agreement with Iran, February 4, 1976," Nuclear Vault.
104. David Menasheri," The Jews of Iran: Between the Shah and Khomeini," in *Anti-Semitism in Times of Crisis*, ed. Sander L. Gilman and T. Katz (New York, 2002), p. 356.
105. On her wish to have Mr. Rahnama in the post, and the Shah's dismissal of the idea and denigration of the candidacy as a "joke," see PRO, "Iranian Foreign Ministers," October 28, 1966, FO 371/18665.
106. Qassem Lajevardi, phone interview with author, October 14, 2003.
107. Ibid.
108. Qassem Lajevardi, Speech to the Senate, Official Transcript of Senate Proceedings, 2535/1976, p. 195.
109. Firouz Tofigh, "Development of Iran: A Statistical Note," in *Iran, Past, Present and Future*, edited by Jane W. Jacqz (Aspen, 1976), pp. 57–69.
110. F. Najmabadi, "Strategies of Industrial Development in Iran," in *Iran, Past, Present and Future*, edited by Jane W. Jacqz (Aspen, 1976), p. 105.
111. Mamideh Sedighi and Ahmad Ashraf, "The Role of Women in Iranian Development," in *Iran, Past, Present and Future*, edited by Jane W. Jacqz (Aspen, 1976), pp. 201–210.

17 Architecture and Power

1. Abbas Milani, *Lost Wisdom: Rethinking Modernity in Iran* (Washington, DC, 2004), p. 84.
2. Aziz Farmanfarmaian, interview with author, Paris, October 12, 2002.
3. Abbas Milani, *The Persian Sphinx: Amir Abbas Hoveyda and the Riddle of the Iranian Revolution* (Washington, DC, 2001). I have discussed these reports and rumors in the book at some length.
4. Princess Soraya, *Palace of Solitude*, p. 68.
5. Kamran Diba has recently published a memoir in the form of an interview with Reza Daneshvar. See *Baghi Miyan Do Khiyaban* [A Garden Between Two Streets: In Conversation with Reza Daneshvar] (Paris, 2010).
6. Keyvan Khosravani, personal correspondence with author, Paris, n.d.
7. Ibid.
8. Alam, *Daily Journals*, vol. 5, p. 207.
9. John B. Oakes, "The Persian Mind," *New York Times*, September 30, 1975.
10. Alam, *Daily Journals*, vol. 5, p. 273.
11. Ibid., vol. 5, p. 399.
12. PRO, "Bribery and Corruption," 27 June 1968, FCO 7/400. In the same report, it is claimed that one of the Shah's brothers received $200,000 as a bribe. The embassy finds that allegation hard to believe "if only because no business firm in their right minds should rate his influence as worth that much."
13. For example, Kamran Diba made just such an argument. See his *A Garden Between Two Streets*, pp. 229–231.
14. Philipe Jullian, "Architectural Digest Visits the Empress of Iran," *Architectural Digest*, December 1977, pp. 68–72.
15. Alam, *Daily Journals*, vol. 5, p. 30.
16. Ebrahim Golestan, interview with author. He has also referred to this episode in some of his interviews.
17. Khosravani, personal correspondence with author, n.d.
18. Alam, *Daily Journals*, vol. 3, p. 315.
19. Ibid., vol. 1, p. 300.
20. Ibid., vol. 1, p. 220.
21. Ibid., vol. 5, p. 164.
22. PRO, British Embassy, Tehran, to Foreign Ministry, 5 October, 1978, BT 241/3045.
23. Mehdi Samii, interview with author, Los Angeles, March 18, 2004.
24. Both the *New York Times* and the London *Telegraph* reported about this exhibit and about some of the cars in the collection. See Nazila Fathi, "Cars Seized After Iran's Revolt Find Home and Showroom," *New York Times*, September 8, 2003; "Shah's Car Collection Is Still Waiting for the Green Light," *Telegraph*, October 7, 2004.

25. Faryar Javaherian, "Shahyad: A Multi-Faceted Symbol," Irannameh, 24 year, no 4. The article is an architect and art historian's account of the building process. For the online version of the article, see http://www.fis-iran.org/fa/irannameh/volxxiv/iss4-mixed/faryar-javaherian.
26. NSA, CIA, "Iran in the 1980s," document no. 1210.
27. Javaherian, Shahyad.
28. Darius Shayegan, *Cultural Schizophrenia: Islamic Societies Confronting the West* (Syracuse, N.Y., 1992).
29. For a discussion of the film and how it was made, see the section on Golestan in my book, *Persian Sphinx,* pp. 241–263.
30. For an account of the plan and its implementation, see Ali Reza Ansari et al., *Khuzestan's Development*, edited by Gholam Reza Afkhami (Washington, DC, 1994).

18 The Perfect Spy

1. Any of the five volumes, hitherto published, are replete with such references.
2. Shah, *Collected Works,* p. 2055.
3. Some sources have argued that he was more than just friendly and was in fact an agent of the Soviet Union. For an account of his life, and the different narratives about his character, see for example, Sheikhol-Eslam, Javad, *So'ud va Sogute Teymourtash* [Rise and Fall of Teymourtash] (Tehran, 1379/1990).
4. In his Ph.D. dissertation at Stanford University, Reza Moghadam offers fascinating data on Iran's foreign trade and the surprising significance of the Soviets during the Teymourtash period. See Reza Moghadam, "Iran's Foreign Trade Policy and Economic Development in the Interwar Period," Ph.D. diss., Stanford University, 1956.
5. NSA, CIA, "Moscow and the Persian Gulf," May 1993.
6. *FRUS,* 1964–1968, vol. XXII, p. 273.
7. Ibid.
8. Ibid., p. 279.
9. Ibid., p. 283.
10. Vladimir Kuzichkin, *Inside the KGB: My Life in Soviet Espionage*, translated by Thomas B. Beattie (New York, 1990), pp. 120–122.
11. Esmail Amidhozoor, interview with author, Woodside, NY, October 23, 2004. He was an owner of Bella Shoes. I have also interviewed Siavoush Arjomand, head of Arj Industries, which sold home appliances to the Soviet Union. Arjomand, interview with author, New York, August 14, 2002.
12. NSA, National Foreign Assessment Center, "Soviet Involvement in the Iranian Crisis."
13. For an account of the Saberi operation, see General Manouchehr Hashemi, *Davari* [Judgment] (London, 1373/1994); see also General Alavi-Kia, phone interview with author, August 17, 2004; I have also talked to Ebrahim Golestan for the story of his friendship with Saberi; I also interviewed General Hashemi in London for the details of the Saberi case.
14. *Pahlaviha* [The Pahlavis], edited by Jalaledin Zaminizadeh, vol. 2 (Tehran, 1378/1999), p. 303.
15. During several interviews, Ardeshir Zahedi told me about the message he took to the Shah about Fardust. Once General Zahedi was informed of the Shah's response, he decided that "we have done our duty; nothing else must be done." Ardeshir Zahedi, interview with author, Montreux, March 20, 2006,
16. General Hashemi, interview with author, London, July 4, 2004.
17. NPL, "Memorandum for Dr. Henry Kissinger, 8 May 1972."
18. NPL, "Iranian Approaches to the US Government, ND."
19. NPL, "Intelligence Memorandum, 12 May 1972."
20. *FRUS,* 1969–1976, vol. E-4, electronic copy.
21. Ibid.
22. NPL, "Supporting the Kurdish Revolution, March 27, 1972."
23. NPL, "Memorandum for General Hague, June 23, 1972."
24. John K. Cooley, *An Alliance against Babylon: The U.S., Israel, and Iraq* (Ann Arbor, Mich., 2005), p. 85.
25. Ibid., p. 90.
26. Cooley refers to the fact that, while he was involved with the project to help the Kurds, it was Chalabi who acted as the intermediary. Cooley, *An Alliance against Babylon*, p. 87. Kanan Makiye, the Iraqi intellectual instrumental in convincing the United States that it should invade Iraq, and a close friend of Chalabi, confirms that long before the publication of Cooley's book, Chalabi "used to talk, even brag about this early episode of his life." Makiye, interview with author, Stanford University, April 16, 2007.

27. The commander of the Iranian forces in the operation was General Sanei. He kindly provided me with a copy of a written report of the operation. I also interviewed him about his activities. General Sanei, interview with author, Toronto, Canada, May 30, 2005.
28. A number of people who were in crucial political roles during the Shah's days have told me about the different aspects of these arrangements. Abdol-Majid Majid, Ahmad Qoreishi, Parviz Sabeti, and Kashefi, the man who handled the Prime Minister's secret discretionary funds, talked to me about these details.
29. General Hashemi, interview with the author, London, July 4, 2004.
30. Kuzichkin, *Inside the KGB,* p. 147.
31. Ibid.
32. Ibid., p. 135.
33. Ibid., p. 144.
34. Fardust, *Memoirs,* vol. 1, pp. 349–351.
35. I was told of the existence of this room by Armin Meyer, U.S. ambassador to Iran from 1965 to 1969. Interview with author, Washington DC, March 14, 2000.
36. I was told of these meetings and the Shah's affinity for them by Sir Denis Wright, England's ambassador to Iran from 1963 to 1971, as well as by Armin Meyer, the U.S. ambassador to Tehran, and Henry Precht, Iran Desk Officer during the Islamic Revolution. Earlier, Precht had served at the embassy in Tehran. He has recently published a fictionalized account of his diplomatic experiences. See Henry Precht, *A Diplomat's Progress* (Savannah, Ga., 2004). Two chapters (pp. 83–125) are about Iran.
37. Several sources refer to this appetite and his search for more and more sources of intelligence. For example, Ahamad Goreishi, interview with author, Walnut Creek, California, September 22, 1999. Alam's diaries and the memoirs of Israel's ambassador to Iran also refer to his fascination with espionage.
38. General Hashemi, interview with author, London, July 4, 2004.
39. Christopher Andrew and Vasili Mitrokhin, *The Mitrokhin Archive II* (New York, 2005), p. 180.
40. General Hashemi, interview with author, London, July 4, 2004.
41. Kuzichkin, *Inside the KGB,* p. 151.
42. General Hashemi, interview with author, London, July 4, 2004.
43. Kuzichkin's account of the arrest (pp. 196–198) is, by and large, corroborated by the version offered by General Hashemi.
44. Kuzichkin, *Inside the KGB,* p. 57.
45. Andrew, *The Mitrokhin Archive*, p. 178.
46. General Hashemi, interview with author, London, July 4, 2004.
47. Ibid.
48. Ibid.
49. Kuzichkin, *Inside the KGB*, p. 200.
50. Andrew, *The Mitrokhin Archive*, p. 533.
51. Kuzichkin, *Inside the KGB*, p. 115.
52. Andrew, *The Mitrokhin Archive*, p. 179.
53. Ibid., p. 182.
54. Ibid., p. 172.
55. I was provided copies of the ten hours of tapes of the interview. The source has asked to remain anonymous. I was allowed to take notes and listen to the tapes of the entire ten-hour meeting. They provide a rare window into the Shah's thinking weeks before his death.

19 The Perfect Storm

1. Ardeshir Zahedi, interview with author, Montreux, March 20, 2006.
2. Zahedi, interview with BBC, August 2009, http://www.iranian.com/main/2009/aug/ardeshir-Zahedi.
3. Bagher Mostowfi, *San'at Petroshimi dar Iran,* [The Evolution of Iran's Petrochemical Industry], edited by Gholam Reza Afkhami (Washington, DC, 2001), p. 100.
4. Zahedi Papers, Handwritten Note for the Shah, n.d.
5. Ibid.
6. Dr. Flandrin's detailed letter explaining the history of the Shah's medical condition is provided in Queen Farah's memoirs. See Farah Pahlavi, *An Enduring Love: My Life with the Shah* (New York, 2004), p. 245.

7. Hussein Alizadeh, also implicated in the deal and later exonerated of all charges, gave me detailed information as well as copies of court documents, including the deposition of Shapour Reporter.
8. Roger Owen, *In Sickness and in Power: Illness in Heads of Government during the Last 100 Years* (New York, 2010), p. 208.
9. Oriana Fellaci, interview, *New Republic*, December 1, 1973.
10. Alam, *Daily Journals,* vol. 2, p. 58.
11. For accounts of their lives, see my *Eminent Persians: The Men and Women Who Made Modern Iran, 1941–1979* (Syracuse, N.Y., 2008), vol. 1, pp. 147–149, and vol. 2, pp. 760–771.
12. Mehdi Khanbaba Tehrani, himself one of the leaders of the Confederation, provides shocking details of this forging operation in his highly informative interview with Hamid Shokat. See Hamid Shokat, *Negahi az Darun be Jonbesh Chap dar Iran* [An Insider's Look at the History of the Left in Iran] (Tehran, 2002).
13. Gholam Reza Afkhami, *The Life and Times of the Shah* (Berkeley, Calif., 2009), p. 51.
14. Ibid., p. 52.
15. For a documentary history of the episode, see Hossein Kuchekian Fard, "Rosvai-Suisse [Embarrassment]," *Tarikh-e Moaser-e,* 4 (Winter 1376/1997): 134–207.
16. Zahedi Papers, Handwritten Note for the Shah, September 22, 1973.
17. Ibid.
18. Alam, *Daily Journals*, vol. 2, p. 334.
19. Ibid., vol. 2, p. 335.
20. NSA, no. 9799, U.S. Embassy, Tehran, "End of Tour Report, August 4, 1975."
21. Shahrough Akhavi, *Religion and Politics in Contemporary Iran: Clergy-State Relations in the Pahlavi Period* (Albany, N.Y., 1980), p. 127.
22. I was given a lengthy summary of this thesis by the professor who supervised it, and who is now teaching at the University of Pennsylvania, Wharton School of Management. I am thankful to Professor Garashedaghi for his willingness to discuss both the thesis and his own acute observations about Iran. *Some scholars have pointed to the overall sharp rise in the number of mosques compared to the restrictions on the number of secular civil society institions.* See for example Ali Mirsepassi, *Negotiating Modernity in Iran: Intellectual Discourse and the Politics of Modernization* (Cambridge, 2000), 161–167.
23. Parviz Sabeti, telephone interview with author, September 3, 2005.
24. I have not seen a copy of the report. In an interview with the author, Sabeti offered details of this report and the Shah's reaction to it.
25. PRO, "Iranian Internal Situation," 12 October 1978, PREM 16/1719.
26. PRO, "Iranian Internal Situation," 16 September 1978, PREM 16/1719.
27. CIA, Mohammad Reza Pahlavi, Shah of Iran, October 23, 1978. I obtained a copy through a Freedom of Information Act request.
28. CIA, Profile of the Shah, Freedom of Information Act Request.
29. Alam, *Daily Journals*, vol. 1, p. 75.
30. Alam recounts other episodes in the fifth volume of his *Daily Journals*. I have discussed the letters, the response, and how the government's decision to ignore them strengthened Khomeini. See my "Alam and the Roots of the Iranian Revolution," in *Sayyad Sayeha* [King of Shadows] (Los Angeles, 2005), pp. 46–79.
31. NSA, no. 2048, "Religious Leaders Fear Departure of the Shah," January 9, 1969.
32. For an account of this center's management, see Ali Rahnama, *An Islamic Utopian: A Political Biography of Ali Shariati* (London, 2000).
33. For a sympathetic account of his life, see ibid.
34. For an account of their lives, see *The New Republic*, March 11, 2010, pp. 12–15.
35. Manouchehr Shahgoli, a close ally of Hoveyda, went to the American Embassy at the time and told diplomats that the Shah had dismantled the party and opted for the one-party system because he "realized how strong the party itself was getting... [T]he Shah decided it was time to crush yet another organization." NSA, no. 2177, "US Embassy, Tehran, Iran, Hoveyda Loyalist Lets off Steam, January 25, 1977."
36. *FRUS,* 1969–1976, vol. E-4, electronic copy.
37. Alam, *Daily Journals*, vol. 2, p. 243.
38. Mehdi Samii, Notes, October 6, 1972. Copy of the notes was provided to me courtesy of Mehdi Samii.
39. Mehdi Samii has kindly provided me with his notes, taken at the time of his meetings with the Shah. They are a remarkable document in the honesty of their discussion.
40. For a tragicomic narrative of these lapsed Stalinists fighting on behalf of their patrons—Hoveyda and Alam—in developing party structure and ideology, see Hamid Shokat's interview with Kourosh Lashai, in his series on the Oral History of the Iranian New Left. *Neghai az daroon Be jonbesh-e chap-e Iran* [A look from within Iran's Leftist movement] (Tehran, 1381 / 2002).

41. In my *Persian Sphinx: Amir Abbas Hoveyda and the Riddle of the Iranian Revolution* (Washington DC, 2000), I have described in some detail Hoveyda's cynical disposition toward the new party.
42. I have written at some length about the origins of the one-party idea in *The Persian Sphinx: Amir Abbas Hoveyda and the Riddle of the Iranian Revolution* (Washington, DC, 2000), pp. 275–287.
43. Zahedi papers, "Letter to the Shah," n.d.
44. Jimmy Carter, *White House Diary* (New York, 2010), p. 276
45. For a detailed account of this behind the scenes, see Andrew Scott Cooper, "Showdown at Doha: The Secret Oil Deal that Helped Sink the Shah of Iran," *Middle East Journal* 62, no. 4 (Autumn 2008), 567–591.
46. PRO, G.B. Chalmers in Tehran to Foreign Office, 6 September 1978, FCO 8/3184.
47. Ibid., p. 3.
48. Jamshid Amuzegar, "A Letter from Dr. Jamshid Amuzegar," *Rahavard*, 34 (Summer/Fall 1373/1994): 271–275.
49. In several interviews with the author, some in Washington and a few on the phone, Asar offered detailed accounts of his office's dealings with the clergy.
50. NSA, "A Brief Overview of the US–Iran Relations," p. 27. The report was prepared in the early 1980s; it has no author or other indications about who commissioned it.
51. Shah, *Answer to History*, pp. 93–97.
52. Ibid., p. 116.
53. Ibid., p. 146.
54. Movahhad Mohammad Ali, interview with author, London, September 17, 2009. He was one of the top negotiators for Iran and has written a two-volume authoritative history of the oil movement, from the time of Mossadeq until the fall of the Shah.
55. Both men kindly recounted to me accounts of their meetings with the Shah.
56. PRO, Embassy in Tehran to Foreign Office, September 8, 1978, FCO8/3184.
57. PRO, Embassy in Tehran to Foreign office, November 9, 1978, FCO8/3184.
58. I was provided a copy of the tape but asked to not identify the source.
59. Carter, *White House Diary*, p. 276
60. NA, "Tehran to State Department, August 27, 1961."
61. See the chapter on his life in my *Eminent Persians*, pp. 305–310.
62. PRO, Tehran to Foreign Office, September 7, 1978, PREM 17/1518.
63. PRO, "Iran's Change of Government," August 29, 1978, FCO/3184.
64. NA, "Memorandum of Conversation, Eslaminia with US Embassy," Tehran, May 15 1978.
65. PRO, "Internal Situation," 8 September 1978, FCO/3184.
66. Hossein Shahid-Zadeh, *Rahvard Roozgar* [Gift of Time] (Los Angeles, n.d.), pp. 350–359.
67. William Shawcross, *The Shah's Last Ride: The Fate of an Ally* (London, 1989), p. 99.
68. I interviewed some of the generals who told me about their plans. The Shah demurred. General Azar-Barzin, interview with author, Los Angeles, September 2006.
69. Dr. Massoumeh Torfeh, "The BBC Persian Service, 1941–1979," in www.open.ac.uk/socialsciences/diasporas/conference/pdf/history_bbc_persian_servie.pdf.
70. PRO, British Embassy to Foreign Office, September 29, 1978, PREM 16/1716.
71. Mehdi Samii, a prominent technocrat, describes an angry Shah telling him and a few others gathered in a meeting, "After all we have given them, why are they still opposing us?" Samii dared to declare that the problem was that they considered what the Shah thought he has given them to be their rights. Mehdi Samii, interview with author, Los Angeles, September 3, 2008.
72. PRO, British Embassy to Foreign Office, 25 September 1978, PREM 16/1719.
73. PRO, "Iranian Internal Situation," 12 December 1978, PREM/16/1719.
74. PRO, 30 October 1978, Prime Minister's office to Foreign Ministry, PREM 16/1719.
75. For Sullivan's discovery of democratic Islam, see NSA, "Understanding the Shiite Islamic Movement, February 2, 1979," document no. 1298.
76. Charles Kurzman, *The Unthinkable Revolution in Iran* (Cambridge, Mass., 2004). Also, two different studies, one by Mohammad Mokhtari and the second by Mehdi Bazorgan, the first a poet and the second the first prime minister of the IRGC, come up with slightly different percentages on the content of the slogans. For a discussion of the two studies, see Mohsen Milani, *The Making of Iran's Islamic Revolution: From Monarchy to Islamic Republic*, 2nd ed. (Boulder, Colo., 1994), p. 136.
77. For a collection of Khomeini's books, see *Islam and Revolution: Writings and Declarations of Imam Khomeini,* translated and annotated by Hamid Algar (Berkeley, Calif., 1981). For a brief biographical sketch of his life and intellectual development, see the chapter on Khomeini in my *Eminent Persians,* pp. 350–358.
78. For a brilliant exposition of this history, see Mahdi Haeri Yazdi, *Hekmat va Hokumat* (London, Shadi Press, 1995)
79. NSA, "Understanding the Shi'ite Islamic Movement, February 2, 1979," document no. 1298.

80. US Embassy in Tehran, "Alternative Views from the Province," in *Asnad-e Laneye Jasusi* [Documents from the Den of Spies], vol. 16 (Tehran, n.d.).
81. George Ball, "Issues and Implications of the Iranian Crisis," p. 16. A copy of the report can be found in Princeton University Library, Seeley G. Mudd Manuscript Library.
82. Ibid., p. 20
83. Shafa, personal correspondence with author.
84. I have been told about the circumstances surrounding this speech by several people who were present at the Court at the time. They include the Shah's chief of protocol, Afshah, and the head of his security detail, Colonel Jahanbini. Others such as Shafa, Ardeshir Zahedi, and Hushang Nahavand have provided background details. I have a copy of a handwritten note sent to me from Iran by one of my students, purporting to be a copy of the text itself. The Shah had made minor changes on the handwritten draft. Reza Kotbi refused to discuss the handwritten draft.
85. PRO, Tehran to Foreign Office, 6 July 1978, FCO 8/3184.
86. Digital National Security Archive, "Proposed American Pro-Shah Group," December 28, 1978.
87. A member of the Sadighi family kindly provided me with some details of these meetings, including critical passages from the daily notes he took in his legendary attention to details.
88. PRO, Tehran to Cabinet Office, December 19, 1979, PREM 16/1720.
89. Ibid.
90. An account of these meetings is provided in Afkhami, *The Life and Times of the Shah*, p. 491.
91. PRO, "Meeting of the Nine," Iran, 7 September 1878, PREM 16/11719.
92. Dr. Sadighi's daily notes, courtesy of the Sadighi family.
93. Carter, *White House Diary*, p. 273
94. PRO, Tehran to Cabinet Office, December 19, 1979, PREM 16/1720.
95. CPL, "White House Press Office, December 7, 1978."
96. CPL, "Carter Summer Lead, AP, January 4, 1979."
97. CPL, "AP Lead, January 4, 1979."
98. CPL, "Additional Sensitive Security Issues for Guadeloupe, January 2, 1979."
99. CPL, "Pool Report, January 5, 1979."
100. CPL, "Remarks of the Principals at the Guadeloupe Meeting, January 6, 1979."
101. Jimmy Carter, *Keeping Faith: Memoirs of a President* (New York, 1982), p. 445.
102. CPL, "Morning Summary, January 6, 1979."
103. CPL, "Morning Summary, January 9, 1979."
104. CPL, "Memorandum for Brzezinski, January 6, 1979."
105. Fereydoon Jam, "Letter to Bani Ahmad," in *Nagin* (new series), 1379/2000, p. 40.
106. Ball, "Issues and Implications," p. 3.
107. *King Richard II*, 4.1.260.

20 The Shah's Last Ride

1. NA, "Secretary of State's Press Conference, January 11, 1979."
2. NSA, "The Evolution of the US–Iranian Relationship," document no. 3556, pp. 46–47. The text of telegram no. 2949. from Paris, January 29, has never been declassified. Only the segments quoted above are used in a brief history of the U.S.–Iran relations prepared by someone who clearly had access to all the declassified documents.
3. Several people, in separate interviews, told me independently about this flight. Some suggested there was more than one flight.
4. PRO, British Embassy in Tehran to Foreign Office, 25, September 1978, PREM 16/1719, p. 2.
5. NSA, "Bureau of Intelligence and Research, Department of State: Secret Intelligence Report # 13," document no. 603.
6. Farah Pahlavi, *An Enduring Love: My Life with the Shah,* translated by Patricia Clancy (New York, 2004), p. 295.
7. Aslan Afshar, interview with author, Cannes, France, March 29, 2009.
8. PRO, British Embassy in Tehran to Foreign Office, 25, September 1978, PREM 16/1719.
9. Christine Ockrent and Comte de Marenches, *Dans les secret des princes* (Paris, 1986), p. 255.
10. George Ball, *"Issues and Implications of the Iranian Crisis,"* Seeley G. Mudd Manuscript Collection, Princeton University Library, p. 3.
11. Amir Aslan Afshar, interview with author, Nice, France, March 29, 2009.
12. NSA, "Proposed Meeting between Iran's Military and Khomeini Supporters, January 15, 1979."
13. PRO, Tehran to Foreign Office, January 20, 1979, PREM 16/2131.

14. David Frost interview with the Shah, January 1980.
15. Amir Aslan Afshar, interview with author, Nice, France, March 29, 2009.
16. Farah Pahlavi, *An Enduring Love*, p. 8.
17. Colonel Jahanbini, interview with author, Washington, DC, November 8, 2004.
18. NSA, "Secretary of State, Outgoing Telegram, January 1979," document no. 02072.
19. PRO, British Embassy, Bonn, to Foreign Office, December 28, 1978, PREM 16/1720.
20. NSA, "American Embassy to Secretary of State, June 17, 1979."
21. In conversations with Afshar and Jahanbini, I was told about the food problems aboard *Shahbaz*.
22. Colonel Kiumars Jahanbini, interview with author, Washington, DC, November 8, 2004.
23. Ibid.
24. Several people, including Ardeshir Zahedi and Colonel Jahanbini, told me about the transfer of valuables and documents by special charter plane.
25. *Etela'at*, 3 Bahman 1357/1978.
26. Shapour Bakhtiyar, *Siyo Haft Rooz Pas az Siyo Haft Sal* [Thirty-Seven Days After Thirty-Seven Years] (Los Angeles, 2002), p. 57.
27. Hossein Borujerdi, *Posht Parehaye Englab Eslami* [Secret Stories of the Islamic Revolution] (Berlin, 2002), p. 424. The author even offers the name of the young man who was in the picture with Tehrani.
28. Ford was in Cairo at the time but his presidential library has no evidence that he ever met with the Shah in that period.
29. PRO, Prime Minister to Foreign Office, 19 February 1979, PREM/16/2131.
30. NSA, "Secretary of State to Embassy in Nassa, May 2, 1979," document no. 2014.
31. Sir Denis Wright, interview with author, Duck Bottom, Hadenham, England, December 11, 2001.
32. Ibid.
33. Wright, "Memoirs," Sunday May 20, 1979. He kept these journals often in something similar to shorthand. He kindly went over every page, reading out loud the parts I could not decipher.
34. David Harris, *The Crisis: The President, the Prophet and the Shah—1979 and the Coming of Militant Islam* (New York, 2004), p. 188.
35. Ibid., p. 189.
36. "The Shah's Health: A Political Gamble," *New York Times*, May 17, 1981.
37. NSA, "State Department Memo, The Shah of Iran, 29 September 1979," document no. 2180.
38. NSA, "Precht to Saunders, 8/1/79."
39. James A. Bill, *The Eagle and the Lion: The Tragedy of American–Iranian Relations* (New Haven, Conn., 1988), p. 346.
40. Ibid., pp. 344–347.
41. Ibid., p. 344.
42. NSA, "Secretary of State to US Embassy, Tehran, October 21, 1979," document no. 3347.
43. "The Shah's Health," *New York Times*, May 17, 1981.
44. In *The Eagle and the Lion*, James Bill produces a figure portraying concentric circles of support surrounding the Shah. Senator Percy was particularly close to Ardeshir Zahedi, who was for years Iran's ambassador to the United States. I have examined Zahedi's own papers and he confirms Bill's assessment.
45. NSA, "Saunders to Secretary of State, October 16, 1978," document no. #3307.
46. "The Shah's Health," *New York Times*, May 17, 1981.
47. NSA, "US Embassy in Tehran to Secretary of State. October 22, 1979," document no. #9951.
48. Bill, *The Eagle and the Lion*, p. 347.
49. NSA, "Memorandum to Mr. Warren Christopher, November 3, 1979."
50. "The Shah's Health," *New York Times*, May 17, 1981.
51. Ardeshir Zahedi, interview with author, Montreux, March 29, 2009.
52. Harris, *The Crisis*, p. 245.
53. Ibid., p. 247.
54. Farah Pahlavi, *An Enduring Love*, p. 343.
55. Harris, *The Crisis*, p. 247.
56. Ibid., p. 232.
57. Ibid., p. 254.
58. Farah Pahlavi, *An Enduring Love*, p. 346.
59. Colonel Jahanbini, the Shah's bodyguard, provided me with the account.
60. Farah Pahlavi, *An Enduring Love*, p. 345.

61. Many sources have provided accounts of the Shah's day in Lackland; see Harris, *The Crisis*, pp. 254–256.
62. Farah Pahlavi, *An Enduring Love*, p. 347–349.
63. Times online, Money Central, "The 10 Most Decadent Dictators,"September 26, 2008.
64. Farah Pahlavi, *An Enduring Love*, p. 349.
65. William Shawcross, *The Shah's Last Ride: The Fate of an Ally* (London, 1989), p. 272.
66. Ibid., p. 274.
67. Ibid., p. 275.
68. Ibid., p. 276.
69. Ibid., p. 281.
70. Ibid., p. 278.
71. NA, "Panama to State Department, Dec 17, 1979."
72. Ibid.
73. Shawcross, *The Shah's Last Ride*, p. 282.
74. NA, Electronic Reading Room, document no. 84 DOS 2751 RSA. The text is not titled; not all of it is readable but a note indicates it to be the best available copy. It is the text of a press conference with the President of Panama in January 1980.
75. NSA, "British Embassy to State Department, January 15, 1980," document no. 03545.
76. John Kifner, "Khomeini Restricts Sentence of Death to Crime of Murder, *New York Times*, May 14, 1979.
77. Iranian human rights lawyer, Payam Akhavan of McGill University, gave the two hundred figure at a recent conference. See "Iran: What Prospects for Change?" S&D Conference, European Parliament, June 30, 2010.
78. NSA, "American Embassy in Panama to State Department, January 24 1980," document no. 03547.
79. NSA, "Request for Extradition, December 30, 1979, Secretary of State to American Embassy in Panama."
80. NSA, "Memorandum of Meeting: Shah and Panama, January 30, 1980," document no. 3571.
81. Gholam Reza Afkhami, *The Life and Times of the Shah* (Berkeley, Calif., 2009), p. 590.
82. Ibid., p. 595.
83. NSA, "US Embassy in Egypt to Secretary of State, July 1979."
84. Minou Reeves, *Behind the Peacock Throne* (London, 1986), p. 95.
85. I was given these tapes, by then in a private collection, and was allowed to take extensive notes.
86. I was given a copy of this document courtesy of Ahmed Ansari.
87. Ibid.
88. He has gone on to write a book in Persian about his court case and his acrimonious break with the royal family. The fact that he has appeared on television shows in the Islamic Republic of Iran has opened him to the charge of becoming a tool of propaganda for the regime in Tehran. The proceedings of the court are also available and partially reprinted in his book.
89. James Bill kindly provided me with a copy of the court proceedings.
90. *Islamic Republic of Iran v. Ashraf Pahlavi*, index no. 44327 [federal court document].
91. Farah Pahlavi, *An Enduring Love*, p. 391.
92. NSA, Stanley T. Escudero, "What Went Wrong in Iran," document no. 2629.

Index